Murex Shells of the World

Murex Shells of the World

An Illustrated Guide to the Muricidae

GEORGE E. RADWIN AND ANTHONY D'ATTILIO

With color photographs by David K. Mulliner

STANFORD UNIVERSITY PRESS  Stanford, California 1976

Stanford University Press
Stanford, California
© 1976 by the Board of Trustees of the
Leland Stanford Junior University
Printed in the United States of America
ISBN 0-8047-0897-5
LC 75-7485

This book is dedicated to the late Mrs. Ruth Richmond of Beverly Hills, California, whose generosity in freely lending rare and valuable specimens for our use contributed greatly to the completeness of the book, and whose death in 1972 saddened all of those who knew her.

In a sense this dedication extends beyond Mrs. Richmond to the multitude of amateur malacologists who, like Mrs. Richmond, ungrudgingly make their collections available to professional workers in the field.

Acknowledgments

We wish to express our appreciation and gratitude to the many people who have assisted us in the preparation of this book. So many individuals have aided us in various ways that we cannot mention them all here. Nevertheless, we must list the following persons who provided specimens on loan or as gifts, provided information on references, habits, or distributions, or supplied photographs of type specimens:

Mr. & Mrs. C. Ames
Mr. J. Bailey
Dr. S. S. Berry
Mr. L. J. Bibbey
Mrs. C. Boone
Dr. K. J. Boss
Mr. H. Bullis
Dr. G. B. Campbell
Mr. P. W. Clover
Mrs. C. Connolly
Dr. G. Davis
Dr. W. K. Emerson
Mrs. B. Good
Dr. T. Habe
Col. & Mrs. G. Hanselman
Mrs. G. Hansen
Mr. M. G. Harasewych
Mr. & Mrs. J. Hertz
Mr. R. Hubert
Mr. & Mrs. R. Janowsky
Dr. P. Jung
Dr. A. M. Keen
Mr. R. N. Kilburn
Mr. W. G. Lyons
Mrs. A. Marti
Messrs C. & C. Martin
Mrs. V. McClure
Dr. J. H. McLean
Mr. & Mrs. J. Michel
Mr. H. Mienis

Mrs. M. Mulliner
Mrs. J. Nijsson-Meyer
Mr. W. Old, Jr.
Mr. P. Percharde
Mr. J. Phillips
Mr. & Mrs. D. Pisor
Dr. W. F. Ponder
Mr. & Mrs. L. Poorman
Mr. & Mrs. B. Purdy
Mrs. R. Richmond
Dr. J. Rosewater
Mrs. N. Rulon
Dr. D. R. Shasky
Mrs. C. Skoglund
Mr. A. Smith
Mr. C. Snell
Dr. A. Solem
Mr. G. Sphon
Mr. R. Talmadge
Mlle. A. M. Testud
Mr. L. Thomas
Mr. and Mrs. I. Thompson
Mrs. G. Thornley
Dr. J. J. Van Mol
Dr. E. H. Vokes
Dr. B. Wilson
Dr. W. P. Woodring
Mr. W. L. Woods
Miss E. Wright

Before a project like this is undertaken it is advantageous to have access to a comprehensive collection as a foundation upon which to base the early decisions and generalizations so necessary to the development of an extensive work. We were fortunate to have had available to us the D'Attilio collection, perhaps the finest private collection of the Muricidae available today, in terms of numbers of species represented, size of species-lots, and distribution coverage. This collection was painstakingly put together over a period of more than 35 years by the junior author. The debt of gratitude owed by him and, on the part of both authors, by the book itself, to his many trading contacts all over the world can only partially be repaid by mentioning them here. Some of those who have made outstanding contributions in this regard are:

Mrs. C. Angermeyer
Mr. E. Bergeron
Mrs. M. Bowman
Mrs. R. Burch
Mr. & Mrs. A. DeRoy
Mr. A. Kalnins

Mr. S. Kinoshita
Capt. T. Nielsen
Mr. M. Pinto de Oliveira
Mr. & Mrs. C. Shy
Mr. A. Teramachi

We wish especially to thank Dr. W. K. Emerson, Dr. J. H. McLean, Dr. E. H. Vokes, and Mr. L. J. Bibbey for their very helpful advice and their encouragement during the course of the book's development.

We are grateful also to Mrs. C. Hertz, Mrs. R. Radwin, and Mrs. B. Good for their diligence and unflagging cheerfulness in typing the final draft of the book, to Mrs. B. Good for her care in compiling the Index, and to Mrs. N. Casper and Miss B. Black for additional typing assistance.

Contents

Abbreviations x

Introduction 1
Family MURICIDAE 15
Subfamily MURICINAE 19
Subfamily OCENEBRINAE 111
Subfamily MURICOPSINAE 141
Subfamily TROPHONINAE 175
Subfamily TYPHINAE 193
Incertae Sedis 215
Species of Uncertain Identity 217
Appendix: New Species 219

Glossary 241
Supplementary Data on Figures 259
Literature Cited 273
Index 285

32 pages in color follow p. 100

Abbreviations

AHF-LACM On permanent loan to the Los Angeles County Museum from the Allan Hancock Foundation (Los Angeles, Calif.)
AMNH American Museum of Natural History (New York, N.Y.)
ANSP Academy of Natural Sciences (Philadelphia, Pa.)
BM(NH) British Museum (Natural History) (London)
CAS California Academy of Sciences (San Francisco, Calif.)
LACM Los Angeles County Museum of Natural History (Los Angeles, Calif.)
MNHN Muséum National d'Histoire Naturelle, Laboratoire de Malacologie (Paris)
NSMT National Science Museum (Tokyo)
SDSNH San Diego Natural History Museum (San Diego, Calif.)
SIO Scripps Institution of Oceanography (San Diego, Calif.)
SUPTC Stanford University, Paleontological Type Collection (Stanford, Calif.)
USNM National Museum of Natural History, Smithsonian Institution (Washington, D.C.)
WAM Western Australian Museum (Perth, Western Australia)

Murex Shells of the World

Introduction

The Muricidae constitute one of the best-known and most distinctive families of mollusks and exhibit many remarkable feeding and reproductive adaptations. They are voracious predators, occupying important niches in many food webs and taking on economic importance wherever shellfisheries exist. And much that is basic to an understanding of the working of the gastropod radula, that rasping organ so vital to the success of the class, has been learned from studies of feeding in muricid snails.

But in spite of the family's size and biological importance, no comprehensive taxonomic treatment of the Muricidae has been forthcoming in the 95 years since Tryon (1880). And since the validity of biological research depends on a knowledge of the identities and limits of the species used in experiments, the lack of an up-to-date systematic treatment of the family as a whole, based primarily on the shell and radular morphology, has been a serious handicap to research in physiological, behavioral, and other biological disciplines.

Accordingly, we have seen it as our responsibility to make of the present work not simply an updated iconography, but rather a comprehensive contribution to the knowledge of the family. We have taken pains, first, for all of the species treated herein for which specimens or other illustrative sources were available, to provide reliable illustrations, in most cases full-color photographs of depository specimens. Second, we have prepared accurate, detailed descriptions, except where specimens were unobtainable, for all of the almost 400 species treated herein; some of the species have never before been accorded adequate descriptions. We have supported these descriptions with basic nomenclature and synonyms, morphological and nomenclatural notes, range data, a Glossary defining (and in some cases illustrating) all terms used in the book, References Cited for all sources in the names and synonymy, detailed data on the specimens appearing in the illustrations, and an Index to all taxa and synonyms appearing in the book. Third, we have altered the traditional classification in many respects; and in order to clarify our reasons for these changes we have prepared line illustrations of the radular dentitions of the type species of genera, as well as certain significant protoconchs, opercula, and types of surface sculptures and textures. Fourth, we have included an Appendix describing 16 new species. Finally, in the ensuing pages, we have assembled a literature review of the classification, biology, and life history of the animals that are so often ignored by collectors or students intent upon examining their shells.

The Phylum and the Family

The phylum Mollusca is generally divided into six classes: the Monoplacophora, Polyplacophora, Bivalvia (Pelecypoda), Scaphopoda, Gastropoda, and Cephalopoda. Of these, the Bivalvia (the "clams") and the Gastropoda (the "snails") are by far the largest groups in numbers of species and individuals; and the Cephalopoda (octopuses and squids) are by far the biggest and probably the most interesting animals. The largest and most diverse of the classes, the Gastropoda, are animals that have a single, generally coiled shell (a few groups lack the shell), a flat, sole-like foot, a well-developed head region, a full complement of sensory organs (most housed in an anterior or posterior mantle cavity), and, with few exceptions, a well-developed radular feeding apparatus. The life cycle is generally contracted, with the loss of the trochophore (the primitive molluscan larval stage) and the advent of the veliger (a second larval stage).

The Gastropoda are traditionally divided into three subclasses distinguished primarily on the basis of type and position of respiratory organs. The Prosobranchia are characterized by a torsion-produced anterior mantle cavity and gills, the Pulmonata by an anterior, vascularized pulmonary chamber, the gills having disappeared in the course of evolution, and the Opisthobranchia by a posterior mantle cavity brought about by a detorsional phenomenon.

The Prosobranchia, which include most marine gastropods, are generally divided into three orders: the more primitive Archaeogastropoda, including those prosobranchs with noncopulatory reproduction, all or part of the left gill and kidney persisting, and the rake- or comblike (docoglossate or rhipidoglossate) radula types; the Mesogastropoda, with copulatory reproduction, the progressive loss (from primitive to advanced forms) of the left gill and kidney as a result of shell impingement, and the moderately reduced taenioglossate radula type; and the Neogastropoda, supposedly the most advanced group, with copulatory reproduction (at times in conjunction with well-developed reproductive behavior), the uniform loss of the right gill and kidney, and the reduced stenoglossate or toxoglossate radula types. The neogastropod suborders Stenoglossa and Toxoglossa are separated on the basis of their radular distinctions: the toxoglossate forms have extremely reduced radulae consisting generally of packets of darts (in some cases, these have completely disappeared); the stenoglossate forms have a radula with one or three longitudinal rows of teeth. Three stenoglossan superfamilies are recognized, the Muricacea, the Buccinacea, and the Volutacea, the three distinguished by radular differences and salient shell characters. In our judgment the Muricacea comprise five families, distinguished from one another on the basis of radular details and shell form.

The Muricidae, in common with the other muricacean groups, are distinguished from most other neogastropods by an intricate and elaborate sculpture of spinose, frondose, or lamellose varices of the shell. In this respect, amateur collectors of muricid shells enjoy an aesthetic dimension not afforded by the cowries or cones—shells of outstanding beauty collected primarily for their remarkable color patterns and smooth forms. The shells of muricid species exhibit their own unique, subtle, fleshy hues of brown, orange, or purple and, in many cases, a finely scabrous surface texture, but it is their spectacular or bizarre sculpture that sets them apart. The degree of sculptural development is influenced by environmental as well as genetic factors, and the subtle influence of these two forces on shell morphology has produced some remarkable examples of polymorphism as well as convergence.

The genus *Murex*, as understood by Linné, was a vast assemblage to which perhaps 2,500 presently accepted species could be assigned, species presently assigned to several superfamilies and suborders. Lamarck and his contemporaries, in the first quarter of the nineteenth century, restricted "*Murex*" to what is today our concept of the family Muricidae—or even beyond, to what we would understand as several of the larger subfamilies of the Muricidae (e.g. the Muricinae and the Ocenebrinae). Röding (1798), Montfort (1810), and Perry (1811) were the first to divide the family into genera. Although the major iconographies, such as Kiener (1842), Reeve (1845–46), Küster & Kobelt (1878), Sowerby (1879), and Tryon (1880), treated virtually all muricoid forms as *Murex*, such workers as Swainson (1833, 1840), J. E. Gray (1847), H. & A. Adams (1853), Jousseaume (1880), and Bucquoy & Dautzenberg (1882) followed a trend toward generic subdivision. The subdividers were not simply following the post-Linnaean trend to generic splitting; they evidently discerned within the family many groups whose species were more closely related to each other than they were to species in other groups.

Decisions and Assumptions Affecting Classification

The biological validity of individual genera or species cannot be proved. Nor can any classification of a natural group be wholly satisfactory, and ours is no exception. There is substantial disagreement concerning the precise limits of the family Muricidae, as well as its division into subfamilies, and our determination of its proper content will be found wanting by some. Similarly, the existing classifications of some muricid groups—subfamilies or otherwise—have been chaotic, and our reconstructions will be found radical by many systematists. Finally, within the Trophoninae, relationships and even species delimitations are so poorly understood, in our opinion, that we have attempted nothing beyond describing and illustrating the type species of the more plausible genera, and listing a few of the more persistent names otherwise appearing in the literature. An adequate ordering of the Trophoninae, a primarily deep-water group only sparsely collected, will be years in the making.

In determining taxonomic validity at the generic level we have chosen to recognize a larger number of taxa than other workers have, on the assumption that by this finer generic subdivision we will have better understood the totality of this large family. Above the generic level we have narrowly limited the family Muricidae by excluding from it certain groups (e.g. the Thaididae, Rapanidae, Columbariidae, and Coralliophilidae) that are occasionally (and in our view inappropriately) included, and by dividing the family proper into the subfamilies Muricinae, Ocenebrinae, Muricopsinae, Trophoninae, and Typhinae. Like genera or species, these represent arbitrary units in a continuum that have been segregated for the purpose of more clearly understanding the parts of the whole; the limits of these groups have been set simply by our perceptions of more or less apparent breakpoints in these continua. That the distinctions between the subfamilies as we know them are neither profound nor totally consistent is evident from a comparison of their more diagnostic characters (see Table 1, pp. 4 and 5).

Practical considerations have led us to establish a cutoff date (mid-1971) for the incorporation of newly described species. Because of the many technical considerations attending the erection of a taxon, new information cannot be added up to the moment of publication. To our knowledge, however, very little work of a substantial nature has been published in the five years since that determination was made, and very few well-argued new species have been described.

We have decided, again for practical reasons, to incorporate into the manuscript an Appendix of new species that have come to our attention during the preparation of this book. These do not, by any means, constitute all of the undescribed species of Muricidae known to us.

We have given considerable thought to the virtues of employing subgenera and subspecies. In the end we have decided to avoid these categories, since there is real difficulty in determining the limits, in any typology, of these terms. Systematists are by no means in agreement on their meaning, even in groups (e.g. birds) whose members are well known to all. In the Mollusca, the second most diverse phylum of animals in terms of numbers of species, many forms inhabit relatively inaccessible regions of the world's oceans, and small samples of forms of obscure affinities have encouraged systematists to erect new taxa.

Too often the overcautiousness of a systematist inspires the erection of a taxon at a level that fails to answer three fundamental questions: How great a sampling of natural populations is necessary to establish the distinctness of a proposed new taxon? At what degree of difference do two forms remain subspecies? How much more distinct must they be to be deemed completely distinct species? There are no hard and fast answers to these questions. In keeping with our decision to favor specific lumping and generic splitting, we have opted for synonymizing supposed subspecies and recognizing (as genera) supposed subgenera. We do not suggest that these are ultimately satisfactory determinations, merely our practical solution to an immediate problem.

Anatomical Features Characterizing the Family

Aside from shell form, there are certain anatomical features* that are apparently common to many or most of the members of the Muricidae, or so, at least, it would seem if the scattered reports on a small number of species are to be considered representative of the family generally. Few if any of these features are unique to the Muricidae, but taken as a whole they seem to distinguish the family from all others.

The majority of these anatomical characteristics can be associated with the feeding activities of muricids. Several can be correlated with the mechanics of muricid feeding, a subject that has been well-treated in the literature (Blake, 1958, 1960; Carriker, 1955, 1961; Carriker & Smith, 1969; Haskin, 1958; Radwin & Wells, 1968). The anatomical features shared generally throughout the Muricidae are the following:

1. A well-developed, bipectinate osphradium, which, despite some objections, continues to be viewed as an organ of chemoreception (Hyman, 1967, p. 267). Its presence and degree of development seem to reflect the degree of "hunter" behavior exhibited in the food-seeking of carnivorous neogastropods (Hyman, 1967, p. 265).

2. A moderately long, pleurembolic proboscis much like those in other carnivorous gastropod groups (Hyman, 1967, p. 207).

3. A moderately long radula, or rasping organ, with a rachiglossate radular dentition of several hundred similar transverse rows, three teeth per row (a rachidian tooth and two lateral teeth).

---

* The terms employed herein and in the main body of the text are defined and in many cases illustrated in the Glossary (p. 241).

TABLE 1
Characteristics of the Five Subfamilies

Characteristics	MURICINAE (p. 19) 28 genera, 180 species	OCENEBRINAE (p. 111) 12 genera, 61 species
Shell characters:		
Size	Largest and smallest in the family, length 6–305 mm	Moderate for the family, length 10–150 mm
Ornamentation	Varices three or more, more or less prominent, with simple or foliated spines and intervarical nodes; spiral sculpture fine	Varices variable in number, generally three or more per whorl (sometimes none), winged, sometimes with short points or spines; very fine spiral sculpture
Surface	Finely to coarsely scabrous (except where intritacalx is present)	Finely to coarsely scabrous or imbricate
Intritacalx	Present in almost half the genera, generally simple or lamellar (in *Aspella* and *Dermomurex*, complex)	Present in scattered species in several genera, simple; no consistent pattern apparent
Shape and color pattern	Fusiform to biconic; color generally a white or brown ground, with markings or suffusions of brown, orange red, or purple	Trigonal or stoutly fusiform; ground with brown markings, color tan or brown, generally more subdued than in the Muricinae
Aperture and siphonal canal	Aperture varying in shape, size, and other features; interior of outer apertural lip denticulate or lirate; canal short to long, generally narrowly open	Aperture varying in size and shape; canal generally fused, without overlap
Protoconch	Generally short (two whorls or less); whorls simple and convex (exceptions among species of *Murex s.s.*, *Pterynotus*, and *Homalocantha*)	Generally short, in many cases with sharply angulate whorls
Operculum	Unguiculate, thickened marginally, having a depressed central area with irregular concentric rings	Thin and trapezoidal, the center not depressed; there is a weak, oblique zone along which it folds when dried
Rachidian tooth of radula:		
Central cusp	Shallow	Borne on a strong, prominent, and slender cowl
Features of base	Simple, shallow, gently curved, and rectangular	Moderately deep and rectangular, with strong double endpoints
Number of cusps and dependence	Five, all independent (except in *Homalocantha* and *Purpurellus*)	Five, the intermediates appended to the laterals
Denticle presence and position	None	Two to four between each lateral cusp and the base endpoint
Distribution	Worldwide (primarily tropical and subtropical)	Worldwide (primarily temperate)
Depth range	0–300 m	0–100 m

The moderate length occupies a middleground between the very long radulae of some groups of grazers (e.g. Littorinidae) and the short radulae of some nonboring carnivores (e.g. meat-tearers, such as the Buccinidae; Carriker, 1961).

4. An accessory boring organ (ABO) widespread in the Muricidae and clearly associated with the shell-boring habit of the group (Carriker, 1961).

5. Two pairs of buccal or salivary glands that emit a mucoid substance or other kind of lubricant. The production of proteolytic enzymes from these glands has also been reported in several muricid species (Fretter & Graham, 1962, pp. 238–39).

6. The gland of Leiblein (found throughout the Muricacea), a large, solid mass of tissue lying behind the anterior nerve ring. This gland has been

TABLE 1 (*continued*)

MURICOPSINAE (p. 141) 9 genera, 74 species	TROPHONINAE (p. 175) [29 genera, 29 species]	TYPHINAE (p. 193) 14 genera, 44 species
Moderately small for the family, length 5–85 mm	Small for the family, length 16–60 mm	Small for the family, length 5–40 mm
Varices variable in number, generally four or more per whorl, each bearing spinose or foliaceous projections; typically, with a gap in the spiral ornamentation at base of body; fine spiral sculpture	With more or less strongly developed lamellose structural elements, these perhaps corresponding to varices; spiral sculpture weak or lacking in most cases	Two groups: (1) four or five varices per whorl, each whorl bearing one or more spines, with anal tubes between varices; (2) three varices, with tubes coalescent with varical shoulder spines; spiral sculpture mostly lacking
Many fine growth lamellae, thrown into fine imbrications where they intersect spiral threads	Generally smooth under intritacalx	Smooth under intritacalx
Simple, in at least half the genera	Simple, present in virtually all of the northern genera and many austral species	Simple in most genera, very complex in trivaricate group (*Cinclidotyphis, Pterotyphis, Tripterotyphis*)
Similar in shape and color to the Muricinae, but in more subdued shades	Generally fusiform or stoutly fusiform; color almost always white, in some cases with bands of pink or brown	Roughly fusiform; color generally pale-tan or white ground suffused with translucent, fleshy brown, purple, or pink
As in the Muricinae, but with stronger denticles on interior of outer apertural lip; columellar lip may be pustulate anteriorly; anal sulcus weaker than in the Muricinae; canal of moderate length, narrowly open	Aperture variable but generally simple, ovate, and generally nondenticulate; canal short to long and narrowly open	Aperture forms an entire peristome, generally projecting, with a flaring margin and no apparent anal sulcus; canal sealed by an overlap of the left side over the right
Variable, with no clear pattern, some with strongly tabulate whorls, others with typically convex whorls	Uniformly simple and short, with convex whorls	Uniformly short, with few simple, convex whorls
Essentially indistinguishable from that of the Muricinae	Essentially of the muricine type (but not in *Trophon s.s.*)	Essentially of the muricine type
Borne on a strong, prominent, and broad cowl	Shallow	Shallow
Very deep, with strong, single endpoints	Broad but shallow, as in some muricine genera	Shallow, as in the Muricinae
Five; all independent	Five, all independent, crowded toward center of tooth	Most have five, all independent; in some aberrant forms, notably *Typhisopsis* and *Siphonochelus*, varying in number and position
In a few species as wrinkles or folds between lateral cusps and base endpoints	None	Where present, erratic in position and size
Worldwide (primarily tropical and subtropical)	Worldwide (commonest in cooler and deeper waters)	Worldwide (tropical and subtropical)
0–300 m	0–500 m, most in 100–300 m	0–1,900 m, most in 15–600 m

shown to produce powerful amylolytic enzymes (Fretter & Graham, 1962, p. 239).

7. The valve of Leiblein, consisting of two flaps projecting backward into the lumen of the pharynx, their free surfaces fringed with long cilia. This structure prevents regurgitation of food from the posterior portions of the gut when the proboscis is extended (Fretter & Graham, 1962, p. 217).

8. A true anal gland, in the form of a caecal outgrowth of the rectum in the anal region. This gland apparently functions to remove certain substances from the blood and to expel them with the solid wastes (Fretter & Graham, 1962, p. 233).

9. A hypobranchial gland having several apparent functions, one better known than the others. As in other stenoglossan groups, this gland produces a mucoid or slimy substance that ce-

ments extraneous particles together as they leave the mantle cavity. The result is a viscous conveyor belt that is moved by beating cilia (Fretter & Graham, 1962, pp. 121–22). The gland also emits a clear fluid that becomes the Tyrian purple dye of antiquity, a characteristic unique to the Muricacea (Fretter & Graham, 1962, p. 127, see p. 12, below).

10. As in other stenoglossan groups, a ventral pedal gland, which receives the eggs from the capsule gland enveloped in a soft capsule, hardens and molds the capsule, and expels it.

All but the last two of these features are involved in finding, penetrating, and assimilating prey, a fact that emphasizes the special requirements of a carnivorous diet combined with a shell-boring habit.

Detailed research on any aspect of an aquatic animal's biology or ecology inevitably produces—for air-breathing man—certain logistical problems. This has discouraged work on large numbers of diverse species. Thus we find in the literature on the family a reasonably large body of work on a very small number of species—those that are easy to collect and to maintain in captivity. Attempts to extrapolate from such a sample to the family as a whole entail obvious intellectual risks, and in what follows, the reader should bear this caveat in mind.

The Radula

The muricid radula (see the accompanying figure) has been studied extensively by Carriker (1961) and Fretter & Graham (1962), and we have already discussed its function in feeding. For the main text of the book, we have prepared drawings indicating the radular dentitions of the type species of the genera treated. (A drawing indicating the details of the radula is given in the Glossary, p. 241.) We believe that the radula is one of the more valuable taxonomic criteria in this family when used at the generic and subfamily levels (Radwin & D'Attilio, 1971). It has been suggested that the differences in radular dentition reflect simply differences in feeding habits, and are therefore too plastic to be of taxonomic value. This reasoning, though not without merit, seems inconsistent with generally accepted evolutionary principles, for a tool must be in hand before a task requiring its use can be performed. One also supposes, occasional convergence notwithstanding, that a number of animals whose ancestors conferred on them the genetic capability of evolving a common form of radular dentition are most likely derived from a common phyletic stock at not too high a taxonomic level.

Several nonmuricid but muricacean (thaidid) species have been reported to exhibit sexual dimorphism in their radular dentition. More or less striking differences are to be seen in the radulae of males and females of *Nassa sertum* and *N. francolina* (Maes, 1966) and of *Drupella fragum* and *D. cornus* (Arakawa, 1958), but no functional significance has yet been suggested. No such phenomenon has been reported in the Muricidae.

Another example of sexual dimorphism, not related to that exhibited by the radula, has been reported by Griffith and Castagna (1962): statistical treatment of shell-length data from a large sample of *Urosalpinx cinerea* and of *Eupleura caudata* has shown that the females attain a greater shell length than the males.

Feeding Methods and Cues

The manner of feeding reported for some muricid species and presumably used by most others has long been known (Orton, 1929). But on the basis of the literature available it appears that muricids actually employ three or four different feeding techniques in penetrating the shells of their prey (see Table 2). Of these, one seems to be much the most prevalent: The radula is used to bore a cylindrical hole through the shell of the prey and thus to bring the proboscis within reach of the animal within. Members of at least ten different muricid genera are known to utilize this method, although some are known to use other methods as well (Paine, 1966; Radwin & Wells, 1968). The snail mounts the bivalve, snail, or barnacle and

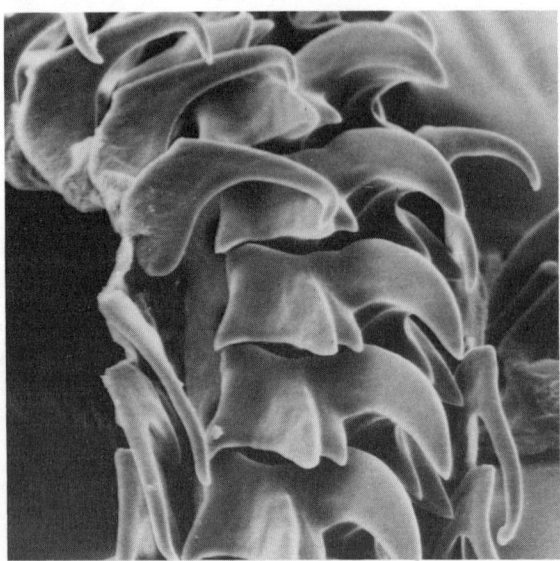

Portion of radula, *Muricopsis zeteki*, ×900, scanning electron micrograph (courtesy A. Solem).

TABLE 2
Feeding Data

Muricid predator	Prey species	Method(s) of feeding	Source
Chicoreus ramosus (as *Murex fortispina*)	*Ostrea cristagalli* and *Arca* sp.	Using ceratus as lever	François (1891); L. J. Bibbey (pers. comm.)
C. brevifrons	Fed unselectively on unfamiliar species of mollusks	Boring through shell or "smothering"	Raeihle (1967)
Murex tribulus	Carrion-unselective	Meat-cutting	L. J. Bibbey (pers. comm.)
Haustellum haustellum	Carrion-unselective	Meat-cutting	L. J. Bibbey (pers. comm.)
Muricanthus radix	Various bivalves and barnacles, apparently unselective	Chipping bivalve lip-margins, using outer apertural lip	Paine (1966)
Muricanthus fulvescens	Various bivalves, favoring *Crassostrea virginica*	Chipping valve margins, using outer lip; or prying, using powerful foot and shell; or boring through shell of prey	Wells (1958) Wells (1958) Radwin & Wells (1968)
Phyllonotus pomum	Large specimens of *C. virginica*	Boring through shell of prey	Menzel & Nichy (1958); Radwin & Wells (1968)
P. erythrostomus	Various bivalves, apparently unselective	Prying, using powerful foot and outer apertural lip	D. K. Mulliner (pers. comm.)
Ocenebra erinaceus	Various bivalves and gastropods	Boring through shell of prey	Orton (1929)
Urosalpinx cinerea	Various bivalves and barnacles, with preference for young *C. virginica*	Boring through shell of prey	Galtsoff, Prytherch & Engle (1937); Hancock (1954); Carriker (1955)
U. perrugata	Various bivalves, little apparent preference	Boring through shell of prey	Radwin & Wells (1968)
U. tampaensis	Bivalves, particularly *Brachidontes exustus*	Boring through shell of prey	Radwin & Wells (1968)
Eupleura caudata	Bivalves, preference for *C. virginica*	Boring through shell of prey	Chew (1960)
Favartia cellulosa	*Brachidontes exustus*	Boring through shell of prey	Radwin & Wells (1968)
Calotrophon ostrearum	Barnacles, especially *Balanus amphitrite niveus*	Boring through opercular plates	Radwin & Wells (1968)

begins to rasp a hole through its shell by alternate use of its radula and its accessory boring organ (ABO). The relationship between these two organs has been carefully studied; apparently both are essential to successful shell-boring (Carriker, 1961). The ABO is thought to produce a substance that softens and loosens the surface crystals of the calcium carbonate of the shell. The radula then mechanically scrapes the softened shell matter away (Carriker, 1961). The time required to achieve complete penetration of a shell depends in part on the thickness and hardness of the shell, but boring periods on the order of 50–150 hours are not uncommon, by all reports.

A great deal of attention has been given to the substance produced by the ABO. Earlier thought to be acidic, this secretion has been found to be neither strongly acidic nor strongly basic. Another suggestion, that it is an enzyme which attacks the conchiolin (protein) matrix of the shell, is contradicted by the fact that the substance etches nonbiological and presumably protein-free calcium carbonate. More recently, Carriker (1961, 1969) has suggested that the secretion of the ABO is a chelating agent that occupies sites in the calcium carbonate and thus destroys the physical integrity of the crystalline structure.

Although *Muricanthus fulvescens* is known to bore in this manner in some cases (Radwin & Wells, 1968), it has also been reported to pry apart oyster shells by using the considerable pull of its powerful foot against its outer apertural lip, which is employed as a brace (Wells, 1958). A similar technique is apparently used by *Phyllonotus erythrostomus*, as observed in captivity (D. K. Mulliner, personal communication). A third technique, also employed by *M. fulvescens*, may be used by other species of the same genus. The predator grips the bivalve shell tightly in its foot and delivers a series of sharp, hammerlike blows of its outer apertural lip to the lip-margin region of the bivalve shell. The resulting hole enables the proboscis to be inserted between the valves.

A fourth method of feeding involves the use of the long, sharp ceratus or labial spine that is found in several muricid genera, as well as in members of other families of gastropods. According to the most frequently cited reference (François, 1891) the predator may use the ceratus as a lever (so to speak, "a foot in the door") to permit it to insinuate its proboscis between the valves of the prey.

Before any feeding activity can take place, the predator must find the prey. The possibility of prey preference has been considered (Orton, 1929; Paine, 1963, 1966; Radwin & Wells, 1968), and although indications of specificity are clear in some species, others appear to be largely indiscriminate in their choice of prey. Orton (1929) found that *Ocenebra erinaceus* seemed to have different prey preferences in different parts of its range. He suggested that the recognition of food type was necessary for feeding to commence. Menzel and Nichy (1958) indicated that *Phyllonotus pomum* feeds solely on large specimens of *Crassostrea virginica*. Paine (1963) stated that *Chicoreus florifer* has the most specialized diet of the eight predatory species he studied. Radwin and Wells (1968) reported that *Phyllonotus pomum*, *Favartia cellulosa*, and *Calotrophon ostrearum* exhibited strict prey specificity, whereas *Muricanthus fulvescens*, *Chicoreus florifer*, *Urosalpinx perrugata*, and *U. tampaensis* were found to be less discriminating in choice of prey. Finally, Chew (1960) offered four bivalve species to *Ceratostoma inornatum* (as *Ocenebra japonica*) and found little prey preference by the predator.

Whatever the identity of the prey, the factors that attract a muricid predator bear investigation. Several such studies (Carriker, 1957; Haskin, 1940, 1950) have concentrated on *Urosalpinx cinerea*, the Atlantic oyster drill. This species, well-known as a predator on *Crassostrea virginica*, seems to prefer younger oysters to older ones, regardless of size. Although attempts have been made to correlate this discriminating ability directly with age or oxygen consumption, the most likely cue is some as yet unidentified metabolic by-product. The production of this metabolite is undoubtedly related to the age and rate of metabolism of the animal.

In the few species of muricids for which tests were made, feeding was dependent on water temperature. In *Urosalpinx cinerea*, feeding does not occur below 5°C; from 5° to 13°, feeding is desultory; and from 13° to 24°, the feeding rate increases with temperature. Feeding generally ceases above 24°. As a result, *U. cinerea*, throughout a goodly portion of its range, fasts during the winter months. In the spring, feeding commences with the arrival of warming water temperatures (Carriker, 1955). A similar phenomenon is found in *Ocenebra erinaceus* (Fretter & Graham, 1962). Exposure to air and/or water of excessively low salinity also inhibits feeding (i.e. drilling) in *U. cinerea* (Carriker, 1955).

Reproduction and Larval Development

As with other aspects of the biology and ecology of the Muricidae, the vast majority of the work on muricid reproduction has focused on a few species, and extrapolation to other species once again involves considerable risk.

Hargis and MacKenzie (1961) have described the intricate behavior of both sexes in the breeding of *Eupleura caudata* and *Urosalpinx cinerea*. Pairing and breeding begin with rising water temperatures in late March, copulation becoming prevalent in April. Indications are that the female emits an exocrine that attracts the male or males (promiscuous copulation is found in both species). Breeding continues until middle or late autumn, when water temperatures begin to decline.

Copulation itself is similar to that in other Neogastropoda and Mesogastropoda. In the two species studied by Hargis and MacKenzie, one or more males approach the female, each forming a sheath for its penis by folding a thin portion of its foot around it. Duration of copulation varies with species; *E. caudata* copulates intermittently over several days, whereas *U. cinerea* generally completes copulation in a few minutes. The females of both species can store viable sperm for a considerable period of time (8–14 months). The promiscuous nature of mating and copulation suggests that when the eggs are ultimately fertilized the resultant embryos might have diverse paternal hereditary compositions (Hargis & MacKenzie, 1961).

In many prosobranchs, each egg is surrounded by its own supply of nourishment and is encased in its own shell or capsule. In most stenoglossan groups, however, this capacity is lost and a variable number of eggs are encased in a single capsule composed of a parchmentlike substance. The egg-capsules are secreted in the pallial oviduct by the capsule gland. Groups of fertilized eggs embedded in albuminous fluid from the albumen gland arrive in the capsule gland, which secretes a wall around each group. These soft, egg-filled capsules are then passed into the ventral pedal gland, which molds and hardens them. The shape into which this gland molds the capsules is appar-

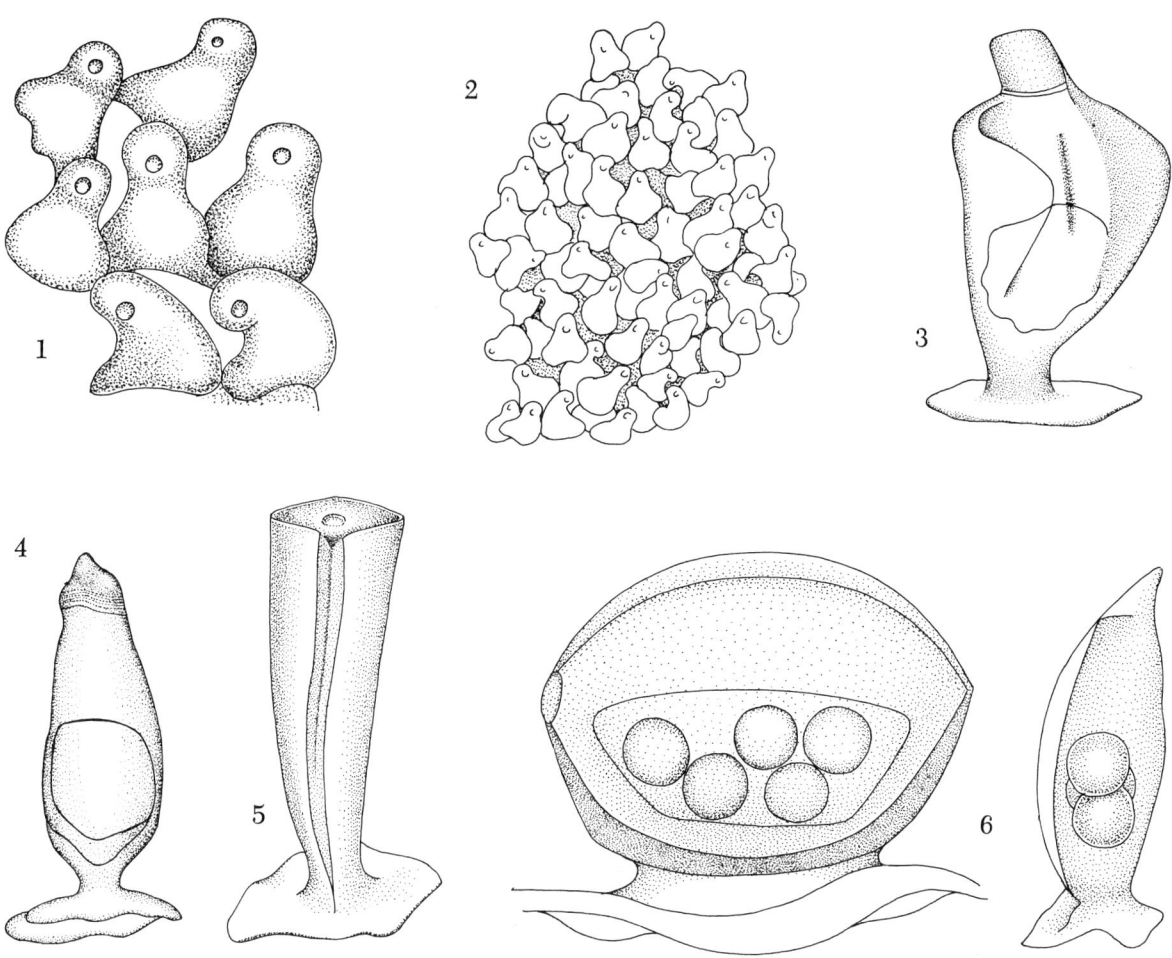

Muricid egg capsules: 1. *Phyllonotus pomum*, seven capsules from an egg mass. 2. *P. pomum*, small egg mass. 3. *Urosalpinx perrugata*, single egg capsule. 4. *U. tampaensis*, single egg capsule. 5. *Muricanthus fulvescens*, single egg capsule. 6. *Calotrophon ostrearum*, front and side views of a single egg capsule.

ently dependent on the shape of the pedal gland, and is thus genetically determined. Correlations can be made between egg-capsule morphology and other supposed taxonomic characters. After a variable period of time (a few minutes to a few hours) the capsule is expelled by the pedal gland, with the aid of muscular contractions in the gland-pore region, and is attached to a firm substratum (Fretter, 1941; Hyman, 1967).

The structure of the muricid egg capsule (see the accompanying figure) includes a fibrous outer layer, the fibers circular externally, longitudinal internally, overlying a homogeneous, semitransparent layer and a thin inner skin that surrounds the contents of the capsule. The outer two layers are of protein, probably conchiolin, and between the fibers is a mucoid substance (Fretter & Graham, 1962). Generally, one or more escape hatches are present in the apical region of each capsule. These hatches may be thinner than the surrounding capsule, but in some cases there appears to be a removable plug "glued" to the capsule proper (Hancock, 1956).

The duration of embryonic-larval incubation within the capsule varies with the species (see Table 3). A clear relationship also seems to exist between the time required for hatching and the form in which the young emerge from the capsule. Most muricids for which such data are available pass their entire larval development within the egg capsule, and the young emerge as tiny snails (see Table 3). In the few species that hatch as free-swimming veliger larvae, the time to hatching is reduced, since the release of larval forms reflects an abbreviated stay in the capsule.

Figures given for development time must be evaluated carefully, for many ecological factors can influence development. There have even been reports that some species pursue different modes of larval development (pelagic or nonpelagic) in

TABLE 3
Reproductive Data

Species	Spawning period	Gestation	Mode of development	Nurse-eggs	Source
Chicoreus territus		90 days	Nonpelagic	None	Murray & Goldsmith (1963)
C. brunneus			Nonpelagic	?Yes	Risbec (1932)
Muricanthus megacerus (as *Murex quadrifrons*)			Nonpelagic	Many	Knudsen (1950)
Phyllonotus pomum	May–July		?Nonpelagic	None	Radwin & Chamberlin (1973)
P. erythrostomus	June–July		Pelagic	None	D. K. Mulliner (pers. comm.)
Ocenebra erinaceus	March–July	ca. 90 days	Nonpelagic	Yes	Hancock (1956)
O. inermicosta (as *Murex fasciatus*)	Nov.–Dec. (southern hemisphere)		Nonpelagic		Knudsen (1950)
Eupleura caudata	May–July		Nonpelagic		MacKenzie (1961)
Urosalpinx cinerea	April–June	18–56 days	Nonpelagic	Yes	Carriker (1955)
U. perrugata	April–June		Nonpelagic	Many	Radwin & Chamberlin (1973)
Favartia cellulosa		29–31 days	Nonpelagic	?Yes	Raeihle (1966)
Bedeva paivae (as *B. hanleyi*)		30 days	Nonpelagic	Many	Anderson (1966)
Calotrophon ostrearum	May–June		Nonpelagic		Radwin & Chamberlin (1973)

different geographical regions (Thorson, 1950). Conceivably, such a pattern could be shown in aquarium experiments: temperature manipulation, perhaps, could cause the larvae of a species with typically nonpelagic development to hatch early (i.e. before the velum had been resorbed by the body). This has not been shown unequivocally, to our knowledge, and Thorson's evidence from field observations is not convincing.

According to Hancock (1956) the embryos of *Urosalpinx cinerea* develop to the crawling (i.e. hatching) stage in about two months at 16°C, and those of *Ocenebra erinaceus* do likewise in three months at 10°–19°C. It should be noted that these two cases are hardly typical: in England, where Hancock studied these species, *U. cinerea* is an introduced species; and *O. erinaceus* is near the lower limit of its range with respect to temperature.

The uniting of several eggs in a single capsule has permitted the evolution of embryonic cannibalism, and has contributed in turn to the suppression of a free-swimming larval stage. One function of this adaptation may be to permit the larvae to seek food abroad after the egg-capsule supply has been exhausted. The advent of abortive ova, or "nurse-eggs," as a source of in-capsule food for the normal embryos may enable the larvae to remain in the egg-capsule until they have completely metamorphosed into miniature snails. We may ask whether these eggs, arrested in development and fertilized or unfertilized, are genetically predetermined to abort or whether their abortion is accidental and random.

In at least two species of muricids we have information on parental brooding of an egg mass. According to Mr. Lawrence Thomas (personal communication), numerous females of *Phyllonotus regius* migrate into moderately shallow water in west Mexico to deposit their egg-capsules in a communal egg mass. Communal egg-laying has also been reported for *P. pomum* (Webb, 1942) and *P. erythrostomus* (Wolfson, 1968). In *P. regius*, however, the females remained on or near the rather large communal egg mass for several weeks after its deposition. When, after almost a month, several of these females were collected for food they were found to have severely atrophied livers (i.e. digestive glands), having apparently fasted during their vigil. This finding seems to support the opinion of Fretter and Graham (1962, p. 227) that the liver has a glycogen- or fat-storage function. Cernohorsky (1966) reports brooding of eggs in *Chicoreus torrefactus* (=*C. microphyllus*), which he says may involve either males or females. The claim is unconvincing, for there is no published evidence of male and female prosobranchs remaining paired after copulation; the deposition of egg capsules usually takes place some time after copulation (in some species as much as a year later!).

Other mass-spawning reports involve *Ceratostoma fournieri* and *Pteropurpura adunca* (both in Sagami Bay, Japan); in neither case was any brooding behavior noted (L. J. Bibbey, personal communication).

Hatching may occur in one of several ways. Typically, the hatchlings emerge through the thin opercular portion or portions of the capsule. The exit mode has been studied, and most workers have stated or implied that the young snails cut exit holes in the operculum (Fretter & Graham, 1962, p. 412). Hancock (1956), in investigating the hatching process in *Urosalpinx cinerea*, has determined that the larvae in the capsule apparently emit an as yet unidentified substance, perhaps an enzyme, that gradually dissolves the cement bonding the operculum to the remainder of the capsule. The synchrony of hatching readiness and deterioration of the opercular structure strongly suggests a functional and evolutionary relationship between the two.

According to Carriker (1957), most of the behavior of newly hatched *U. cinerea* is mediated by instinctive responses. The juvenile snails immediately move upstream, facilitating food-seeking. They also show a strong negative response to gravity and a strong positive response to moderate illumination, both of which impel them off the bottom and away from the danger of suffocation by suspended sediments. They also show a quick and marked positive response to potential prey.

Shell Formation

The muricid shell is deposited by the mantle, and as in many other prosobranchs the rates of growth of the shell and the mantle do not remain equal. As the animal becomes older, mantle breadth increases at a greater rate than mantle length. The mantle edge, therefore, becomes disproportionately broad for the size of the aperture in which it lies, and can only be accommodated there by being puckered. This folding of the mantle is reflected in a folding of the shell edge, since the shell is secreted by the mantle. The folding takes the form of spiral cords or ribs on the outer shell surface and denticles or lirae on the inner surface of the outer apertural lip (Fretter & Graham, 1962, p. 62).

Other events occurring in the formation of some shells are more complex, and seem to involve simultaneous change in rate of growth and rate of secretion. The resulting structures are chiefly varices and spines. A varix arises when the mantle edge turns outward while still secreting shell matter, producing an out-turned outer lip projecting more or less at right angles to the rest of the current whorl, ending smoothly or in a number of scales, points, or spines (Fretter & Graham, 1962, pp. 64–65).

In species such as *Murex pecten* and *Chicoreus palmarosae*, the varical spines assume a particularly elaborate form. Clearly, a very considerable growth in the mantle edge has occurred, leading to a great increase in the amount of calcareous matter produced.

The secretion of varices or spine-rows across the whole breadth of the current whorl obviously tends to complicate the formation of the shell when, in the process of growth, the next turn brings the columellar (inner) lip to lie alongside the former outer lip. In this position the varix would block much of the aperture and interfere with the movements of the animal in and out of the shell. In these circumstances it is vital that the spines or varix be removed from that part of the older whorl about to be overgrown by the younger (Fretter & Graham, 1962, p. 65).

In almost every individual shell in which axial ribs are normally found, one rib will be found to coincide with the outer lip of the shell aperture; this is known to some shell morphogeneticists as the labial rib or apertural varix.

The period between the secretion of one rib and the secretion of the next is very brief; shell growth is not regular but spasmodic, and in some species of "*Murex*" (Abbott, 1954b) only two days are required to form the intervening shell. In *Eupleura caudata*, according to MacKenzie (1961), the half-whorl interval between two varices is deposited in three weeks and fully reinforced in four weeks. He has suggested that in this species the amount of food available has a great influence on the rate of growth, and that growth appears to cease at sexual maturity.

Although number of varices is generally assumed to be an indication of the age of the snail, it is, in fact, of negligible value in this regard. MacKenzie (1960) has shown that no consistent number of varices is deposited each growing season. The secretion of ribs or varices may represent not so much an increased rate of secretion as a decreased rate of mantle growth, with the result that the shelly material produced piles up as the mantle edge remains relatively stationary (Fretter & Graham, 1962, p. 64).

Most molluscan shells are colored to one extent or another, and inspection shows the color to be limited to the outer layer of the shell. This location implies the presence of glands at the mantle edge that secrete pigments at the time (and near the place where) the calcareous material of the outer layer is deposited. The nature of the pigment produced in such a situation is often unknown, but it has been investigated in a number of animals. Most of the work on shell pigments has been done by Comfort (1951).

The pigments of higher prosobranch shells are bound to protein material contained in the shell. The chemical constituencies of these bound pigments have not been adequately investigated, since no methods of extraction have yet been developed, although Fretter and Graham (1962, pp. 135–36) suggest that they may be chromoproteins with melanin groups incorporated. Dietary factors can affect the color of the shell by altering the nature of the pigment that is laid down (Moore, 1936).

Like its ornamentation, the shell's color often shows specialization in space and time; and since the presence of color reflects the activity of chromogenic cells in the mantle skirt, there must be a spatial differentiation of that part of the body, with or without a superimposed temporal rhythm. For if the pigment glands lie uniformly along the length of the mantle skirt, then a uniformly colored shell will result. But if, as in many muricaceans, the manufacture of pigment is localized at points or stretches of the mantle edge that secrete continuously, then the result is a series of spiral lines or bands of color. And if the ability to manufacture pigment is present along the entire mantle edge, but pigment is produced only intermittently, axial lines of color will be produced (Fretter & Graham, 1962, p. 74). Finally, if color is produced intermittently and only at certain points or stretches that are not axially aligned, a spotted or blotched coloration will result.

Although much of the general structure, decoration, and sculpture of the muricids appears to be wholly unrelated to the environment, not all is. *Bolinus brandaris*, for example, develops long spines on muddy bottoms but only short ones on sand and rocks (Berner, 1942). Thus this adaptation may be more an individually acquired characteristic than a hereditary character.

The Purple Dye of the Muricacea

In the Muricidae, as in the entire superfamily Muricacea, the secretion of the hypobranchial gland is colored: greenish yellow when first liberated, purple in its ultimate form. The change depends on the presence of oxygen and light. Chemically, the purple pigment (the royal or Tyrian purple of the ancients, made in classical times from *Bolinus brandaris* and *Phyllonotus*

trunculus) is 4-4′ dibromindigo or 6-6′ dibromindigo, both of which are related to natural indigo. The chemical is presumably manufactured by the mollusk from a tryptophane source. The chromagen (i.e. precursor) varies from species to species, but the enzyme mediating the transformation is apparently the same—purpurase—in all species (Fretter & Graham, 1962, p. 127).

The secretion is reputed to be toxic and to be used in predation (Dubois, 1909; Clench, 1947). In addition to the dye, the secretion contains mercaptans (sulphated hydrocarbons), which are probably the source of the vile smell often reported, and choline esters, which are highly toxic to crabs, fish, and frogs, acting like curare, but appear to be harmless to mammals. This toxicity, which has been demonstrated in experiments involving injection, has no apparent offensive or defensive function, and does not diffuse to any appreciable extent from an uninjured animal. Even when injured, an animal gives off too little toxic secretion for the toxin to act as an external poison (Fretter & Graham, 1962, p. 121; Hyman, 1967, p. 387). (We may conjecture something akin to the mechanism of, for example, the brightly colored poisonous butterflies—the individual may be eaten, but the species benefits from the disinclination or inability of the predator to try another of these!)

Habitats and Distribution

Although muricids are sometimes called "rockshells," the term may be misleading. It is true that a moderately large number of species are typically inhabitants of rocky or rubble bottoms. It is also clear, however, that many muricids live on muddy bottoms, particularly those species living in depths of more than 200 meters, no doubt because most of the sea bottom below this depth is either mud or ooze suspended over mud. Other muricids, particularly several species of *Murex s.s.*, live on and in coarse sand. In general, one would not expect to find as many species or individuals of muricids on or in fine-grained sediment as on firmer substrata (e.g. rock, coral, or rubble).

Virtually no work has been done concerning the manner of distribution of muricid species. There are two basic ways of viewing the contemporary distributions and ranges of muricid species. In groups of relatively recent origin, geologically speaking, one might expect those species whose life cycles include a pelagic larval stage to have a greater potential for dispersal than is found in species lacking such a free-floating stage. If, however, we extrapolate from the data on mode of larval development (see Table 2) to the remainder of the family, we would have to conclude that as a family the Muricidae are unable to distribute themselves widely in a relatively short period of time. Such a conclusion, however, is at odds with the broad distributions of some muricid species (e.g. *Marchia elongata* and *Chicoreus brunneus*). In these cases, which reflect the second basic way of viewing distributions, we must assume that such a broad distribution pattern must have been arrived at via slow, stepwise migration over a great many generations, each generation producing a small extension and consolidation of the species' range.

Behavior

Little or nothing is known about the behavior of muricid gastropods, except as it relates to feeding or reproduction. It would appear that studies of competitive and defensive behavior may be a fertile field for ethological research.

One behavioral peculiarity, possibly related to a morphological or anatomical weakness, has been reported in *Urosalpinx cinerea*. Carriker (1955) and Fretter and Graham (1962) note, as a possible basis for controlling this oyster predator, that it has an apparent distaste for traversing soft substrate. A soft, muddy bottom lacking imbedded hard objects (e.g. rocks, shells) is said to present an effective barrier to the dispersal of this species.

The Fossil Record

Although it has been stated before, it cannot be overstressed that in dealing with the fossil record we are never aware of more than a small percentage of the totality of forms that have undoubtedly existed through the millions of years of muricid evolution. Further, the discovery of well-developed Paleocene forms that are essentially indistinguishable from Recent forms suggests an earlier derivation of the family and superfamily from a nonmuricacean stock.

The earliest appearance of the superfamily Muricacea, to judge from available evidence, is in the Cretaceous, with the advent of the *Rapana*-like genera *Morea* and *Sargana* and the strikingly *Latiaxis*-like *Lowenstamia funiculus* Sohl. The earliest unquestioned muricids first appear in the Paleocene (*Poirieria*, *Paziella*, and *Pterynotus*) (E. H. Vokes, 1971a, p. 42). In the Cenozoic the history of the Muricidae can be traced through its subfamilies. As noted above, we recognize five muricid subfamilies: the Muricinae, Ocenebrinae, Muricopsinae, Trophoninae, and Typhinae. In the Muricinae we perceive three major lineages (following Vokes, *ibid.*), the *Paziella-Poirieria* line, the *Pterynotus* line, and the *Hexaplex* line (first seen in the Eocene). Subsequent muricine evolution to the present has involved the derivation (in our opinion) of 29 extant genera and two genera now extinct.

The Ocenebrinae arose, it would seem, from an early muricopsine ancestor, in the middle or upper Oligocene. Subsequent evolution has seen the advent of 12 extant genera and six genera now extinct. The entity Muricopsinae has only recently been discerned (Radwin & D'Attilio, 1971), but indications are that two lineages, the *Murexsul* line and the *Murexiella* line, arose at approximately the same time (the middle Eocene). Subsequent evolution has seen the derivation of a total of ten extant genera and one genus now extinct. The Trophoninae constitute a subfamilial category we have used for the sake of convenience and for lack of a niche in which to place a rather large number of genera often assigned to the genus *Trophon*. Little is known about approximately one-third of these genera, even as regards familial placement, since no radular work has ever been done. Even among those that, on the basis of radular dentition, are clearly muricacean or muricid, there has been some speculation on the likely polyphyletic nature of the group. According to one authority, Dr. E. H. Vokes (personal communication), it appears likely that most northern trophons are derived from the *Paziella-Poirieria* line, and that the several austral forms that are unquestionably "trophonine" are probably derived from the Thaididae. Because of the types of habitats in which trophonine forms are found, fossil material is exceedingly rare. We therefore do not know, with any precision, the time of derivation of either trophonine component from its respective parent line.

The Typhinae, a group with a fossil record indicating greater specific and generic diversity (and thus possibly greater success) in the early-middle Cenozoic than seen today, appear first in the lower Eocene. Evolution over the 50 million years or so has seen the derivation of 16 extant genera and eight genera now extinct.

With the exception of the Typhinae and to a lesser degree the Ocenebrinae, the muricid subfamilies, and thus the family as a whole, appear to have undergone a gradual diversification leading, in our opinion, to 94 extant genera and only 19 genera that have become extinct during the progress of this Cenozoic trend—i.e., at least four-fifths of the genera known from the fossil record are represented in existing populations.

Methods of Treatment

A few comments are in order concerning various conventions and assumptions employed in the text proper.

Our classification of the entire family is given in the list on pp. 15–18; the list provides page-number references for subfamilies and genera. Genera within subfamilies, and species within genera, are given in text in alphabetical order. The principal morphological and distributional distinctions between the five subfamilies are given in Table 1 (pp. 4–5).

Of the 391 species treated, 340 are illustrated in color; because in many cases two or more variant forms of a given species are shown, there are actually 456 specimens illustrated in the color plates. In addition, many species not illustrated in color are illustrated in black-and-white, in text; most of these figures are photographs of type specimens or wash drawings taken from original published illustrations. Detailed data on all of the specimens shown—color and black-and-white—are given on p. 253.

The text also includes 179 line drawings of critical details—the rachidian tooth and one of the two flanking lateral teeth of the radula (70 species in 62 genera), the protoconch (34 species), and the intritacalx (11 species) and other microsculptural detail (3 species).

Except where otherwise indicated (in the synonymy), the use of parentheses around the author of a species name (in a boldface heading) indicates that the generic allocation of the species was either changed since its original description or is our own. The synonyms we have provided, whether placed in synonymy herein or by past authors, are only the names more frequently seen in the literature.

In most cases, morphological descriptions of species follow an unvarying sequence: overall shell size and shape, spire shape, numbers of nuclear and postnuclear whorls, suture form, body whorl size and shape, aperture size and shape, anal sulcus form, outer apertural lip shape, number and character of denticles on the outer apertural lip, character of the inner surface of the outer lip, shape of the columellar lip, form of the siphonal canal, axial and spiral sculpture (varices, spines, cords, and the like, in some detail), and coloration. In some cases, particularly where we have been unable to obtain access to type specimens (or where type specimens are not known to exist), we have departed from this standard approach, following closely the original published descriptions; to have attempted reformulations of these statements with modern terminology would have been to introduce possible misinterpretations and outright errors. In quoting or translating this material, we have altered only an occasional word or phrase for clarity.

All sources cited in the Introduction and in the main text and Appendix, whether as text references or as parts of recognized names or synonyms, are given in Literature Cited (p. 267). All epithets (species names) used in the book, whether recognized herein or considered synonymous, are given in the Index (p. 279). Finally, references to the color illustrations are given at the end of the text discussions; and the plates themselves are cross-referenced to the text.

Family Muricidae

RAFINESQUE, 1815

The shell of the muricids, basically the dextrally coiled sequence of nuclear and postnuclear whorls typical of the Gastropoda, varies greatly in size, shape, and ornamentation. Size ranges from the tiny (6 mm long) species of *Favartia* and *Ocinebrina* to huge, massive species such as *Siratus virgineus* (up to 250 mm) and *Chicoreus ramosus* (up to 300 mm and more). Form may be elongate and fusiform (*Naquetia, Roperia*) to club-shaped (*Murex, Bolinus, Haustellum*) or biconic (*Chicoreus, Homalocantha, Vitularia*), or may describe variations and combinations of these.

In ornamentation or sculpture the shells of the Muricidae range from those with almost smooth surfaces to those with strongly imbricate, scabrous, or lamellate textures, and from those with prominent, spinose varical projections of several types (*Chicoreus, Murex, Murexiella, Paziella*) to forms with low, nodose or nodulose prominences (*Attiliosa, Trachypollia, Evokesia*). Each varix is the outer margin of a former apertural lip.

The protoconch (see text figures) varies widely, even within a supposedly homogeneous genus, perhaps indicating differing lineages. Most are composed of few (one to two and one-half) smooth, convex whorls. A few are ornamented with transverse keels, nodules, papillae, or other features.

All muricids possess an operculum, so far as is known. Its form may be unguiculate, ovate, or rounded, and it may have a thickened peripheral callus on the inner side (Muricinae, Muricopsinae, Trophoninae, Typhinae) or it may lack one and have a thinner zone in its medial region (Ocenebrinae). The location of the nucleus appears to depend on the shape of the aperture and on several other factors, and seems to be unreliable as a diagnostic character (Clench, 1947).

The external morphology of the animal is not well known, owing at least in part to the muricid's habit of extending only minimally out of its shell. Muricids are assumed to have features much like those of other stenoglossan groups.

The muricids employ a complex, rasping feeding organ, the radula, consisting of multiple triseriate, transverse rows of teeth. Each transverse row contains a single three-, five-, or seven-cusped rachidian tooth and two flanking, sickle-shaped lateral teeth.

We consider the Muricidae to be divisible into five subfamilies. These are the Muricinae (p. 19), Ocenebrinae (p. 111), Muricopsinae (p. 141), Trophoninae (p. 175), and Typhinae (p. 193).

Classification of the Muricidae

All genera and species treated in this book are listed below in text sequence. The superscript ^{t} preceding a species name indicates that it is the type species of the genus; an asterisk (*) preceding a name indicates a new species described in the Appendix (p. 219); a double dagger (‡) preceding a name indicates a new name; and a question mark (?) preceding a name indicates that its genus assignment is questionable.

Subfamily MURICINAE (p. 19)

Acanthotrophon (p. 19)
  carduus
  sorenseni

Aspella (p. 21)
  acuticostata
  *castor
  *cryptica
  *mauritiana
  *morchi
  *platylaevis
  *pollux
  *ponderi
  producta
  pyramidalis
  senex
  ^{t}[*anceps*, species assignment uncertain]

Attiliosa (p. 25)
  aldridgei
  ^{t}*incompta*
  philippiana

Bedeva (p. 27)
  birileffi

16 MURICIDAE

    blosvillei
    livida
    ᵗ*paivae*
        [=*hanleyi*]
Bolinus (p. 28)
    ᵗ*brandaris*
    cornutus
Calotrophon (p. 30)
    ostrearum
    ᵗ*turritus*
        [=*bristolae*]
    velero
Chicoreus (p. 32)
    *akritos
    ‡*artemis*
    asianus
    axicornis
    banksii
    benedictinus
    brevifrons
    brunneus
    cnissodus
    cornucervi
    damicornis
    denudatus
    florifer
    gubbi
    insularum
    maurus
    microphyllus
    palmarosae
    penchinati
    ᵗ*ramosus*
    rossiteri
    rubescens
    rubiginosus
    saulii
    spectrum
    territus
    trivialis
Dermomurex (p. 44)
    abyssicola
    bakeri
    cunninghamae
    elizabethae
    indentatus
    myrakeenae
    obeliscus
    pauperculus
    ᵗ*scalaroides*
        [=*scalarinus*]
Ergalatax (p. 48)
    ᵗ*contracta*
        [=*recurrens*]
    tokugawai
Haustellum (p. 49)
    ᵗ*haustellum*
    wilsoni
Hexaplex (p. 50)
    ᵗ*cichoreum*
    stainforthi
Homalocantha (p. 52)
    anatomica

    melanamathos
    oxyacantha
    ᵗ*scorpio*
    secunda
    tortua
    zamboi
Lataxiena (p. 56)
    ᵗ*fimbriata*
        [=*lataxiena*]
Marchia (p. 57)
    barclayana
    *bibbeyi
    bipinnata
    ᵗ*elongata*
        [=*clavus*]
    laqueata
    martinetana
    ?*nodulifera*
    pellucida
    triptera
Murex (p. 60)
    anniae
    antelmei
    blakeanus
    brevispinus
    cabritii
    cervicornis
    chrysostoma
    coppingeri
    donmoorei
    elenensis
    gallinago
    hirasei
    kiiensis
    longicornis
    messorius
    mindanaoensis
    multiplicatus
    olssoni
    pecten
        [Lightfoot, 1786]
    *purdyae
    rectirostris
    recurvirostris
    rubidus
    scolopax
    serratospinosus
    trapa
    ᵗ*tribulus*
        [=*pecten* Montfort 1810]
    troscheli
    tryoni
    tweedianus
Muricanthus (p. 75)
    angularis
    fulvescens
    kusterianus
    megacerus
    princeps
    ᵗ*radix*
    saharicus
    varius

Naquetia (p. 79)
    annandalei
    barclayi
    capucina
    trigonula
    ᵗ*triquetra*
Nipponotrophon (p. 82)
    ᵗ*echinus*
    elegantulus
    galapaganus
    gorgon
    lasius
    pagodus
    scitulus
Paziella (p. 85)
    hystricina
    ᵗ*pazi*
Pazinotus (p. 86)
    smithi
    ᵗ*stimpsonii*
Phyllonotus (p. 87)
    brassica
    duplex
    erythrostomus
    laciniatus
    ᵗ*margaritensis*
        [=*imperialis*]
    peratus
    pomum
    regius
    superbus
    trunculus
Poirieria (p. 93)
    ᵗ*zelandica*
Prototyphis (p. 94)
    ᵗ*angasi*

Pterochelus (p. 95)
    ᵗ*acanthopterus*
    ariomus
    duffusi
    phillipsi
    triformis
Pterynotus (p. 98)
    ᵗ*alatus*
        [=*pinnatus*]
    bednalli
    leucas
    loebbeckei
    patagiatus
    phaneus
    phyllopterus
    vespertilio
Purpurellus (p. 101)
    ᵗ*gambiensis*
    macleani
    pinniger
Siratus (p. 103)
    alabaster
    articulatus
    beauii
    cailleti
    ciboney
    consuela
    formosus
    motacilla
    perelegans
    pliciferoides
    ᵗ*senegalensis*
    tenuivaricosus
    ?*virgineus*
Takia (p. 109)
    ᵗ*infrons*
        [=*inermis*]

Subfamily OCENEBRINAE (p. 111)

Ceratostoma (p. 111)
    burnetti
    foliatum
    fournieri
    inornatum
    lugubre
    ᵗ*nuttalli*
    rorifluum
Eupleura (p. 115)
    ᵗ*caudata*
    muriciformis
    nitida
    pectinata
    sulcidentata
    triquetra
Hadriania (p. 117)
    ᵗ*craticuloides*
        [=*craticulata*]
Jaton (p. 118)
    ᵗ*decussatus*
Ocenebra (p. 119)
    circumtexta

    ᵗ*erinaceus*
    erinaceoides
    foveolata
    gracillima
    grippi
    ?*hamata*
    inermicosta
    interfossa
    lurida
    ?*painei*
    seftoni
    vokesae
Ocinebrina (p. 125)
    ᵗ*aciculata*
        [=*corallina*]
    edwardsi
    ?*emipowlusi*
    hybrida
Poropteron (p. 126)
    incurvispina
    ?*sanctaehelenae*
    ᵗ*uncinarius*

MURICIDAE

Pteropurpura (p. 129)
 adunca
 bequaerti
 centrifuga
 esycha
 festiva
 leeana
 ᵗ*macroptera*
 modesta
 plorator
 trialata

Roperia (p. 133)
 ᵗ*poulsoni*

Trachypollia (p. 134)
 didyma
 lugubris

Subfamily MURICOPSINAE (p. 141)

Bizetiella (p. 141)
 ᵗ*carmen*
 micaela
 shaskyi

Evokesia (p. 143)
 ferruginosa
 grayi
 ᵗ*rufonotata*

Favartia (p. 144)
 alveata
 balteata
 ᵗ*brevicula*
 cellulosa
 confusa
 ?*crossei*
 cyclostoma
 ‡*emersoni*
 erosa
 funafutiensis
 garrettii
 incisa
 kurodai
 marjoriae
 ‡*minatauros*
 minirosea
 munda
 peasei
 planilirata
 *poormani
 rosea
 salmonea
 tetragona

Maxwellia (p. 154)
 angermeyerae
 ᵗ*gemma*
 ?*santarosana*

Murexiella (p. 155)
 bojadorensis
 cirrosa
 diomedaea
 ᵗ*hidalgoi*
 humilis
 nodulosa
 ᵗ[*sclera*, fossil]

Urosalpinx (p. 136)
 cala
 ᵗ*cinerea*
 haneti
 ?*macra*
 perrugata
 ?*puncturata*
 ?*purpuroides*
 ?*scrobiculata*
 ?*subangulata*
 tampaensis

Xanthochorus (p. 139)
 ?*buxeus*
 ᵗ*xanthostoma*

 jacquelinae
 lappa
 levicula
 macgintyi
 perita
 ?*phantom*
 radwini
 vittata

Murexsul (p. 161)
 ?*auratus*
 kieneri
 mariae
 ?*multispinosus*
 ᵗ*octogonus*
 ?*tokubeii*
 umbilicatus
 zonatus

Muricopsis (p. 165)
 angolensis
 armatus
 ᵗ*blainvillei*
 bombayanus
 brazieri
 cristatus
 cuspidatus
 *huberti
 infans
 jaliscoensis
 muricoides
 nicocheanus
 oxytata
 pauxillus
 roseus
 schrammi
 *tulensis
 zeteki

Subpterynotus (p. 172)
 ?*tatei*
 ᵗ[*textilis*, fossil]

Vitularia (p. 173)
 ᵗ*miliaris*
 salebrosa

Subfamily TROPHONINAE (p. 175)

Actinotrophon (p. 176)
 ᵗ*actinophorus*

Afritrophon (p. 177)
 ᵗ*kowieensis*

Anatrophon (p. 177)
 ᵗ*sarmentosus*

Apixystus (p. 177)
 ᵗ*stimuleus*

Axymene (p. 178)
 ᵗ*turbator*

Benthoxystus (p. 179)
 ᵗ*columnarius*

Boreotrophon (p. 179)
 ᵗ*clathratus*

Comptella (p. 180)
 ᵗ*curta*

Enatimene (p. 180)
 ᵗ*simplex*

Enixotrophon (p. 181)
 ᵗ*carduelis*

Fuegotrophon (p. 181)
 ᵗ*crispus*

Gemixystus (p. 181)
 ᵗ*laminatus*

Lenitrophon (p. 182)
 ᵗ*convexus*

Litozamia (p. 183)
 ᵗ*rudolphi*

Minortrophon (p. 183)
 ᵗ*crassiliratus*

Nodulotrophon (p. 184)
 ᵗ*dalli*

Pagodula (p. 184)
 ᵗ*vaginata*

Paratrophon (p. 184)
 ᵗ*cheesemani*

Pascula (p. 185)
 ᵗ*citrica*

Stramonitrophon (p. 186)
 ᵗ*laciniatus*

Terefundus (p. 186)
 ᵗ*crispulatus*

Tromina (p. 187)
 ᵗ*unicarinata*

Trophon (p. 187)
 ᵗ*geversianus*

Trophonopsis (p. 188)
 ᵗ*muricatus*

Xenotrophon (p. 188)
 ᵗ*euschema*

Xymene (p. 189)
 ᵗ*plebeius*

Xymenella (p. 189)
 ᵗ*pusilla*

Xymenopsis (p. 190)
 ᵗ*liratus*

Zeatrophon (p. 191)
 ᵗ*ambiguus*

Subfamily TYPHINAE (p. 193)

Cinclidotyphis (p. 193)
 ᵗ*myrae*

Distichotyphis (p. 194)
 ᵗ*vemae*

Haustellotyphis (p. 194)
 ᵗ*cumingii*

Laevityphis (p. 195)
 bullisi
 transcurrens
 tubuliger
 ᵗ[*coronarius*, fossil]

Monstrotyphis (p. 196)
 ᵗ*tosaensis*

Pterotyphis (p. 197)
 fimbriatus
 ᵗ*pinnatus*

Siphonochelus (p. 198)
 ᵗ*arcuatus*
 japonicus
 nipponensis
 pentaphasios
 solus
 syringianus

Talityphis (p. 201)
 *bengalensis
 *campbelli
 ᵗ*expansus*
 latipennis
 *perchardei

Tripterotyphis (p. 202)
 arcana
 fayae
 ᵗ*lowei*
 norfolkensis
 robustus
 triangularis

Trubatsa (p. 204)
 erythrostigma
 ᵗ*longicornis*
 pavlova

Typhina (p. 206)
 ᵗ*belcheri*

MURICIDAE

bivaricata
cleryi
imperialis
montforti
?nitens
pauperis
philippensis
ramosa
yatesi

Typhinellus (p. 210)
  occlusus
  ᵗsowerbii

Typhisala (p. 211)
  clarki
  ᵗgrandis

Typhisopsis (p. 212)
  ᵗcoronatus

INCERTAE SEDIS
(described on p. 215 but not assigned)

"Murex"
  alfredensis
  exquisitus
  pleurotomoides

SPECIES OF UNCERTAIN IDENTITY
(listed on p. 217 but not assigned)

alabastrum
baeticus
bandana
bituberculatus
briskasi
castus
clenchi
dearmatus
dentifer
duthiersi
exiguus
falcatiformis
flexirostris
fusiformis
hermanni
interserratus
jenksi
kopua
maculatus
medicago
natalensis
nitens
niveus
nucleus
oligocanthus
pallidus
percoides
pettardi
pudicus
puniceus
puteola
pyrrhias
rusticus
singaporensis
solidus
strigatus
sykesi
tumida

Subfamily Muricinae

RAFINESQUE, 1815

The muricine shell is the largest, on the average, in the family (6–300 mm in length), is generally fusiform to biconic in shape, and bears a color pattern generally consisting of a white or brown ground with markings or suffusions of brown, orange, red, or purple. The aperture varies in size and shape; the interior of the outer apertural lip is usually denticulate or lirate. The siphonal canal ranges from short to long and is generally narrowly open. Most forms have more or less prominent varices with simple or foliated spines and intervarical nodes. Spiral sculpture is fine. In almost half the genera the shell carries an intritacalx, this simple or lamellar (complex in *Aspella* and *Dermomurex*); in other groups the shell has a finely to coarsely scabrous surface texture.

Muricine protoconchs are generally short (two whorls or less), with simple, convex whorls; exceptions with additional ornamentation may be seen in a few species of *Murex s.s.*, *Pterynotus*, and *Homalocantha*.

The operculum is unguiculate and thickened marginally, with a depressed central area and irregular concentric rings.

The radula consists of numerous three-across transverse rows of teeth, each row consisting of a rachidian tooth with a single lateral tooth on each side. The rachidian is tiara-like, with a simple, shallow, gently curved, rectangular base bearing five cusps, the central cusp longest and not borne on a cowl, and all five independent (except in *Homalocantha* and *Purpurellus*); denticles are lacking.

Distribution: worldwide (primarily tropical and subtropical), in depths of 0 to 300 m.

We have included in the Muricinae a group of genera of uncertain subfamilial affinity. Many earlier authors have, by implication, assigned these genera to the Muricinae and, aberrant shell features notwithstanding, the radulae of these forms are indeed generally muricine in structure. This heterogeneous assemblage includes *Acanthotrophon*, *Attiliosa*, *Bedeva*, *Calotrophon*, *Ergalatax*, *Lataxiena*, *Nipponotrophon*, *Paziella*, *Pazinotus*, and *Poirieria*. Further study will be necessary before the subfamilial placement of these genera can be established with any confidence.

Genus ACANTHOTROPHON
Hertlein & Strong, 1951

TYPE SPECIES: *Trophon (Acanthotrophon) sorenseni* Hertlein & Strong, 1951, by original designation.

The following is taken, with modification, from Hertlein & Strong (1951):

"The shell is rather thin, biconic in outline; spiral sculpture consists of two or three rather weak, usually spinose cords below the shoulder on the body whorl and another cord, a bit more prominent, on the canal about halfway between the upper cords and the end of the canal; axial sculpture is of weak axially elongated nodes, these developed into a row of sharp, erect, guttered spines on the angulation of the body whorl; the earlier whorls bear a row of nodes rather than spines; a slight siphonal fasciole is present; the aperture is smooth interiorly."

Acanthotrophon carduus (Broderip, 1833)

Murex carduus Broderip, 1833: 175; *Acanthotrophon sentus* Berry, 1969: 162

The shell is moderately small (maximum length 28 mm) and biconic. The spire is high, consisting of five or six strongly shouldered postnuclear whorls and a protoconch of undetermined nature. The suture is indistinct. The body whorl is of moderate size and broadly fusoid. The aperture is of moderate size and ovate, with no apparent anal

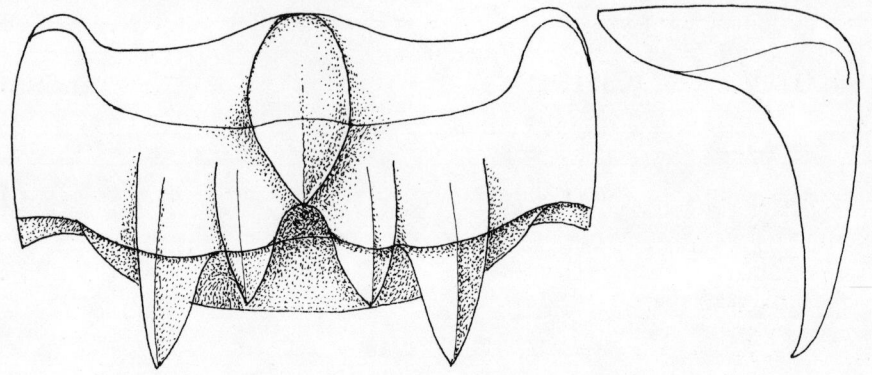

1. *Acanthotrophon carduus*, radular dentition

sulcus. The margin of the outer apertural lip is furrowed, the furrows opening into short, open spines; the inner surface of the outer lip is strongly lirate. The columellar lip is entirely adherent and smooth, except for one to three very weak plicae at its base. The siphonal canal is broad, moderately long, and open at the right.

The body whorl bears ten or eleven close-set, spinose varices, their thin, appressed leading edges crossing the shoulder obliquely. Spiral sculpture consists of a variable number of major and minor cords, these most prominent on the varices, where they form very short, sharp, open spines. Between the varices the cords are quite weak. The spines developed from the cord at the shoulder margin are two or three times as long as the others but nonetheless moderately short.

Shell color is white, with red-brown on the spines and just subsuturally. The aperture is white.

The typical form of this species, that figured by Sowerby (1834, fig. 22), has nine cords, six on the body (four majors, two minors) and three on the canal (all minor). Another form, more frequently encountered in collections today, especially from the Galápagos Islands, has fewer spiral cords and, thus, fewer rows of spines; it also bears a rose suffusion on portions of the body and canal.

Mazatlán to Peru and the Galápagos Islands.
See Pl. 14, fig. 1; Pl. 19, fig. 12.

Acanthotrophon sorenseni (Hertlein & Strong, 1951)

Trophon (Acanthotrophon) sorenseni Hertlein & Strong, 1951: 86

We have not seen a specimen of this species; the following is taken verbatim from Hertlein & Strong (1951):

"Shell thin, dingy white; only the last whorl of the nucleus remaining, apparently smooth; postnuclear whorls six, angulated, sculptured with axially elongated nodes on the upper whorls which on the last whorl are produced into ten narrow, radial, guttered spines; spiral sculpture consists of two faint cords immediately below the

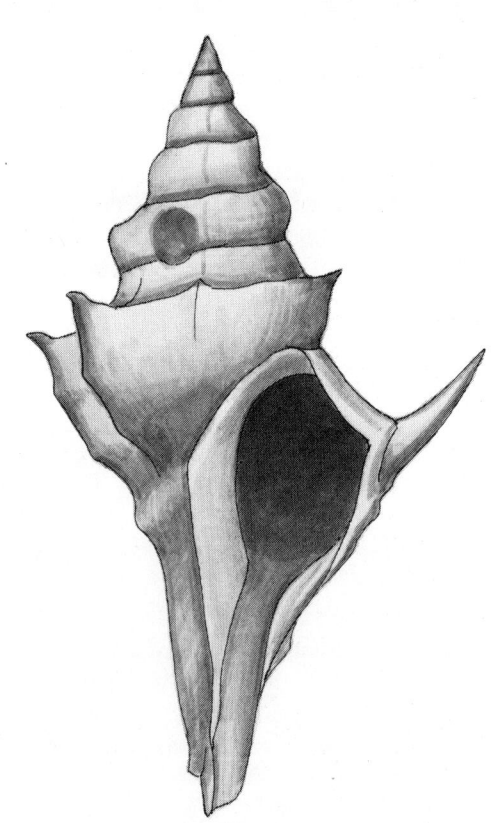

2. *Acanthotrophon sorenseni*

shoulder and a third, slightly more prominent, about halfway between the upper cords and the end of the canal; aperture ovate; canal narrow, open, distinctly recurved; outer [apertural] lip thin; [columellar] lip appressed to base, the enamel terminating some distance from the end of the canal, leaving an umbilical chink. The type measures: length 31 mm; length of aperture and canal 19 mm; maximum diameter (not including spines) 14 mm."

Southern end of the Gulf of California.

Genus ASPELLA Mörch, 1877

TYPE SPECIES: *Ranella anceps* (Lamarck) Mörch, 1877 (=*Aspella anceps* Lamarck, 1822), by monotypy.

This genus includes species with a small, moderately narrow, lanceolate shell, the latter whorls becoming dorsoventrally flattened. The spire is high and acute. The number of nuclear whorls ranges from one and one-half to three; postnuclear whorls, from five to ten. The body whorl is generally short and more or less broadly trigonal. The siphonal canal is short, open, and recurved, with a coarse siphonal fasciole. Early whorls bear six varices, each attached to varices on preceding and succeeding whorls. In the last two or three postnuclear whorls the two lateral varices are retained unchanged and become somewhat more prominent. Two or more of the four other varices, two dorsal and two ventral, are reduced to low costae or become obsolete, except for a buttresslike portion where the varix is appressed to the preceding whorl. Weak spiral sculpture may be present, with or without nodules at the intersection of the cords and the varices or varix positions. A moderately thick intritacalx, a consistent character of this genus, may have axial or both axial and spiral sculpture. This flat-white layer may be seen, at times, to be covered by a translucent tan or brown periostracum. Under the intritacalx the shell is waxy white or yellow-white with, in some instances, broad, diffuse, spiral brown bands. The radular dentition is muricine.

The assignment of valid names is difficult in *Aspella* because the types of such species as *A. anceps*, *A. pyramidalis*, and *A. hastula* are excessively beachworn. Because of strong superficial similarities in the shells of species in this group, identification often hinges on the number and features of the varices of the body, on the sculpture of the shell, and, in particular, on the nature of the intritacalx, especially where this differs from the underlying shell sculpture. As a result the shiny, smoothly worn type specimens are virtually worthless for identification purposes. The identities of the nominal species have been established herein for the most part on the basis of published descriptions and illustrations. This method avoids reliance on extant but unrecognizable types, and appears necessary to continued progress toward an understanding of the group.

Because of the difficulties involved in the determination of identities in previously described species of *Aspella*, we were faced with an insoluble taxonomic problem. The type species of *Aspella* was cited originally by Mörch (1877) as *Ranella anceps* (Lamarck, 1822). Gastropod species such as this one, referred to by Lamarck as in *"mon cabinet,"* are said to be in the Muséum d'Histoire Naturelle, Genève (Geneva, Switzerland). Investigation of this avenue has led to a dead end. Dr. E. Binder has informed us that it is essentially impossible to locate Lamarck's type specimens. No illustration of *A. anceps* was ever published by Lamarck, nor did he refer to any previously published figure. In addition, no locality was given, and Lamarck's description indicates that the specimen was badly eroded. Thus it is unlikely that the holotype, were it to come to light, would be useful in determining which, if any, of the 11 species treated in this book (four herein, seven in the Appendix) is the type species. Even Lamarck's description is so phrased that it could serve for any species in the genus. As it happens, then, little change in the generic concept would be occasioned regardless of the species determined to be *A. anceps*. Thus we have listed the type species as *A. anceps* for nomenclatural purposes, but it is likely that whatever Lamarck's *A. anceps* actually was has been treated herein under the name of one of the 11 species we *have* included, and the name is probably best considered a *nomen dubium*.

Improper assignment of *Favartia erosa* (Broderip, 1833) to *Aspella* has caused *Favartia* to be regarded as a subgenus of *Aspella*. Their respective radular dentitions indicate that these two genera are referable to separate muricid subfamilies (*Aspella* to Muricinae; *Favartia* to Muricopsinae). Another group more closely related to *Aspella* is *Dermomurex* Monterosato (type species: *Murex scalarinus* Bivona-Bernardi, 1832 [=*M. scalaroides* Blainville, 1829]). Some authors have treated *Dermomurex* as a subgenus; we consider it a closely related but distinct genus.

(See the Appendix for new species assignable to *Aspella*.)

Aspella acuticostata (Turton, 1932)

Ranella acuticostata Turton, 1932: 109

The shell is of moderate size for the genus (maximum length 13 mm) and lanceolate. The spire is high, consisting of one and one-half or two

translucent, convex nuclear whorls and five or six dorsoventrally flattened postnuclear whorls. The suture is moderately impressed but obscured by varical buttresses. The body whorl is moderately small and dorsoventrally flattened. The aperture is moderately small and ovate, with no perceptible anal sulcus. The outer apertural lip is smooth, moderately thickened, and nonerect, its inner surface smooth. The columellar lip is smooth and entirely adherent. The siphonal canal is long for the genus, narrowly open, bent slightly to the left, and dorsally recurved.

The body whorl bears two poorly developed major lateral varices, a minor varix ventral to the left major varix, and a weak costa indicating the position of a second minor varix dorsal to the right major varix. Earlier whorls show six varices of approximately equal strength. Spiral sculpture is not readily apparent, except for traces of several weak cords on the body.

The shell is translucent milk-white, covered by a flat-white, minutely axially striate intritacalx.

Although recently synonymized with another species (Ponder, 1972: 228), *A. acuticostata* is distinctive. It differs from all other species in its higher spire, its more strongly contracted and more elongate siphonal canal, and the extremely fine axial striations of its intritacalx.

South Africa (Fish Hoek Bay to Natal).

See Pl. 1, fig. 11.

Aspella producta (Pease, 1861)

Ranella producta Pease, 1861: 397

The shell is large for the genus (maximum length 20 mm) and lanceolate. The spire is high and acute, consisting of one and one-half translucent, polished nuclear whorls and eight or nine convex to subangulate postnuclear whorls. The suture, where visible, is strongly impressed. The

3. *Aspella acuticostata*, intritacalx

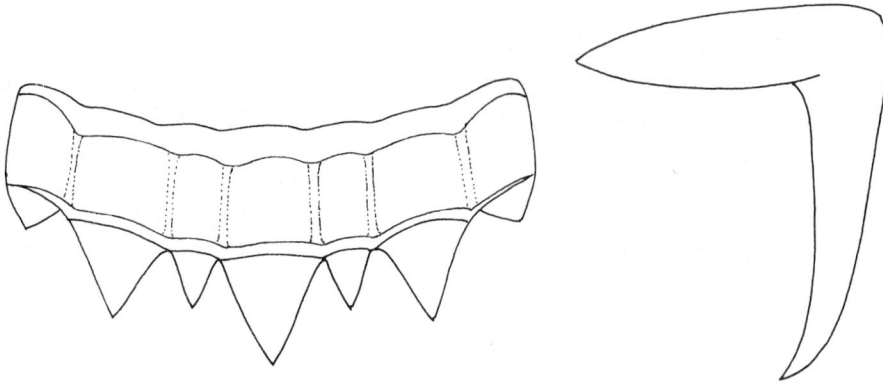

4. *Aspella acuticostata*, radular dentition

body whorl is relatively short and broadly trigonal. The aperture is small and ovate, with a weak anal sulcus. The outer apertural lip is barely erect, if at all, and bears on its inner surface a series of eight small denticles. The columellar lip is smooth and completely adherent. The siphonal canal is short, bent slightly to the left or right and dorsally, and narrowly open.

The body whorl bears four lateral varices, two on each side. The two main varices have receded to form low axial costae or have completely disappeared, leaving only buttresses at the suture. Considered in ventral aspect, the dorsal varix on the left and the ventral varix on the right are expanded into flanges; the ventral varix on the left and the dorsal varix on the right are relatively less expanded. Spiral sculpture consists of six major cords, a pair on the upper body (at the shoulder margin and shortly beneath it), a third cord at the base of the body, and two or three cords on the siphonal canal. Between the varices a series of three to five more or less strong pustules are apparent on the cords. The broad-based nature of these pustules may impart a more angulate whorl profile in some specimens than in others.

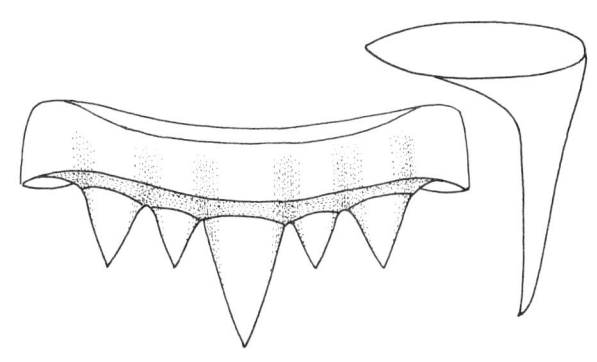

6. *Aspella producta*, radular dentition

The shell is white or yellow-white and is covered by a moderately thick, flat-white, finely cancellate intritacalx. The aperture is lustrous white or yellow-white.

This species differs from all its congeners in its larger average size, its strong, pustulose spiral sculpture, and its minutely cancellate intritacalx.

Tropical Indo-West Pacific, from eastern Africa (Zanzibar) to Taiwan and the Hawaiian Islands.

See Pl. 1, figs. 12–14.

Aspella pyramidalis (Broderip, 1833)
Ranella pyramidalis Broderip, 1833: 197

The shell is large for the genus (maximum length 21 mm) and lanceolate. The spire is high and acute, consisting of two and three-quarters smooth, convex, gradually increasing nuclear whorls and six to eight dorsoventrally flattened postnuclear whorls. The suture, where not obscured, is strongly impressed. The body whorl is relatively short and roughly fusoid. The aperture is small and ovate, with an imperceptible anal sulcus. The outer apertural lip is weakly erect, if at all, and bears a series of six weak denticles on its inner surface. The columellar lip is smooth and entirely adherent. The siphonal canal is short, narrowly open, and bent slightly to the left and dorsally.

The body whorl bears two well-developed varices laterally; each of these is thickened and narrowly expanded, if at all, and undulate. Two

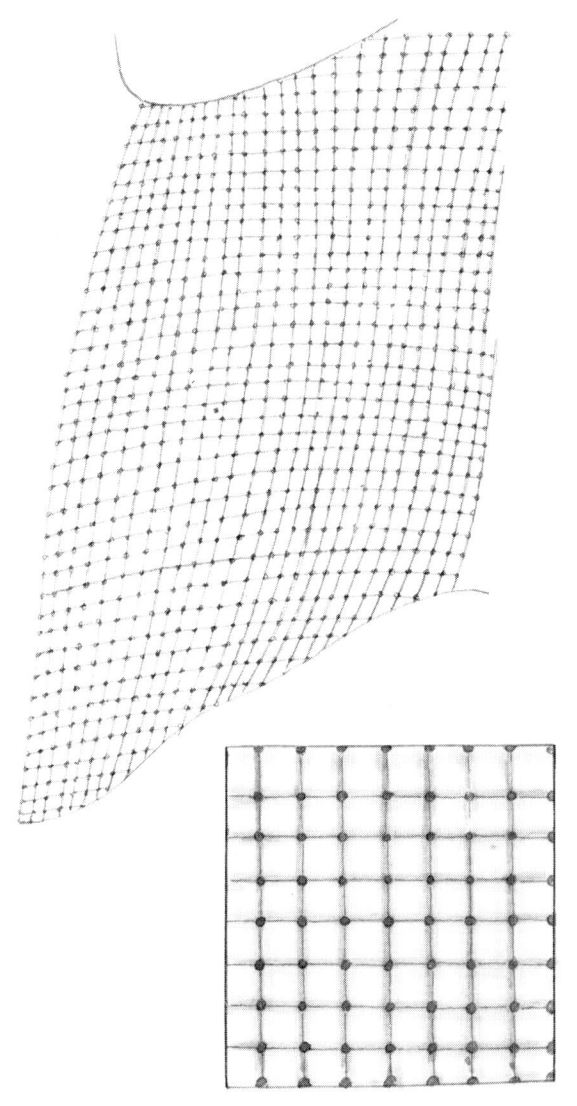

5. *Aspella producta*, intritacalx

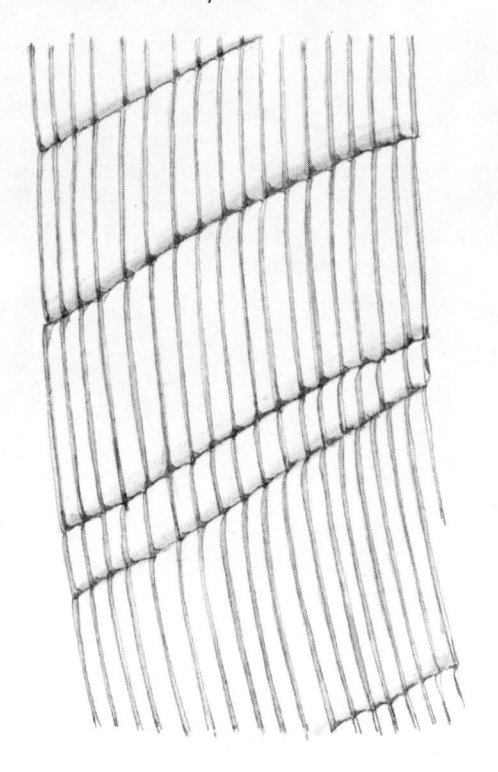

minor varices are also present, one dorsal to the right varix and one ventral to the left varix. In many specimens the minor varix dorsal to the right major varix becomes obsolete, leaving only three varices. Spiral sculpture consists of four to six low spiral cords on the body and ten to 12 cords of variable width on the siphonal canal. In well-preserved specimens from certain localities one or more rows of low, almost imperceptible pustules are apparent, following the weak spiral elements.

The shell is waxy yellow-white, in many specimens with a broad, red-brown spiral band on the upper half of each whorl. The aperture is porcelaneous white to yellowish, with red-brown staining on the labial denticles, especially in specimens with the spiral red-brown band. A layer of flat-white, finely axially striate intritacalx covers the shell in well-preserved specimens. The areas between the spiral cords are incised broadly into the intritacalx, this feature most evident on the leading edge of the varical flange.

A distinct form occurs endemically in the Galápagos Islands. Although almost certainly only a geographical variant of *A. pyramidalis* (Pl. 1, figs. 7 & 8), it can be seen to differ consistently from the mainland form in its shorter, coarser body whorl, its shorter, more bent siphonal canal, its almost complete loss of the two minor lateral varices, and in having comparatively strong spiral sculpture with its associated pustules. Keen (1971) has figured this form as *A. hastula* (Reeve, 1844) although Reeve's figure and description seem to indicate that he had the mainland form.

Although the identity of Broderip's species has been much discussed, Reeve's figure and description seem clearly to point to the form figured herein as *A. pyramidalis*. We cannot subscribe to the

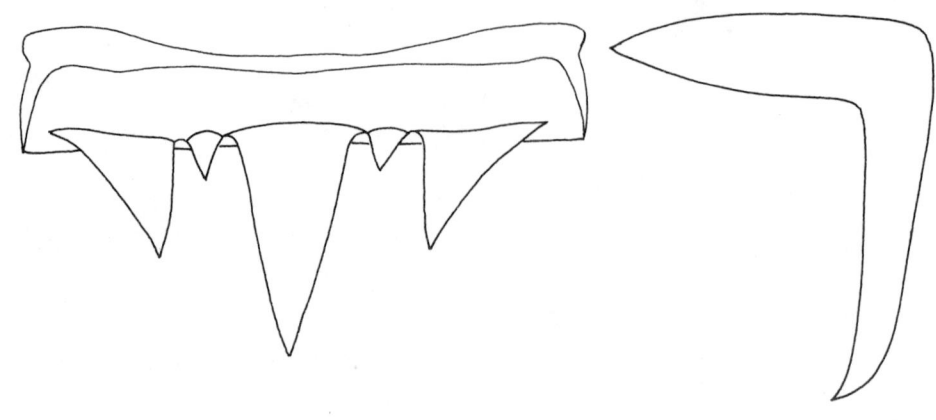

7. *Aspella pyramidalis*, intritacalx

8. *Aspella pyramidalis*, radular dentition

suggestions of Reeve or Ponder (1972) that this species is conspecific with *A. anceps*.

A. pyramidalis differs from other species of *Aspella* in its combination of large size and finely axially striate intritacalx, its color pattern (brown spiral band), and its long protoconch.

Panamic faunal province from the southern Gulf of California to Colombia and the Galápagos Islands.

See Pl. 1, figs. 4–8.

Aspella senex Dall, 1903

Aspella senex Dall, 1903: 1633

The shell is of moderate size for the genus (maximum length 14 mm) and broadly lanceolate. The spire is high and acute, consisting of six or seven broad, strongly dorsoventrally flattened postnuclear whorls and a protoconch of undetermined nature. The suture is deeply impressed but is largely obscured by varical buttresses. The body whorl is moderately large and broadly fusoid. The aperture is small and ovate, with a barely perceptible anal sulcus. The outer apertural lip is barely erect, its inner surface smooth. The columellar lip is smooth and entirely adherent. The siphonal canal is moderately long, narrowly open, and slightly dorsally recurved.

The body whorl bears two major lateral varices and two minor varices, one of these (the left) ventral to one lateral and the other (the right) dorsal to the other lateral. The varical flange at the growing edge is strongly constricted above the canal. Spiral sculpture consists of an axially striate and spirally incised intritacalx.

Shell color is waxy white. The apertural margin is porcelaneous white, and the interior of the aperture is golden orange to apricot.

Originally described in 1903 from a Pliocene specimen, this species was first recognized to have remained part of the living molluscan fauna by E. H. Vokes (1971b) as *A. senax*, a misspelling.

A. senex most closely resembles *A. pollux* (a new species, fully described in the Appendix), but differs from it in its proportionately larger aperture, the nondenticulate nature of the inner surface of the outer apertural lip, its adherent columellar lip, and in its less dorsally reflected, more angulate varical flanges.

Off the southeastern coast of the United States (off Cape Lookout, North Carolina) and the Gulf of Mexico (off western Florida).

See Pl. 1, figs. 1–2.

Genus **ATTILIOSA** Emerson, 1968

TYPE SPECIES: *Coralliophila incompta* Berry, 1960, by original designation.

The following is taken, with modifications, from Emerson (1968):

"The shell is stoutly biconic and of moderate size; spire acuminate, the aperture large, with spiral lirations within the outer apertural lip, and with small folds anteriorly placed on the columellar lip; anterior canal relatively long; base with siphonal fasciole."

Attiliosa aldridgei (Nowell-Usticke, 1968)

Vasum aldridgei Nowell-Usticke, 1968: 18

The following is taken, with modifications, from Nowell-Usticke (1968):

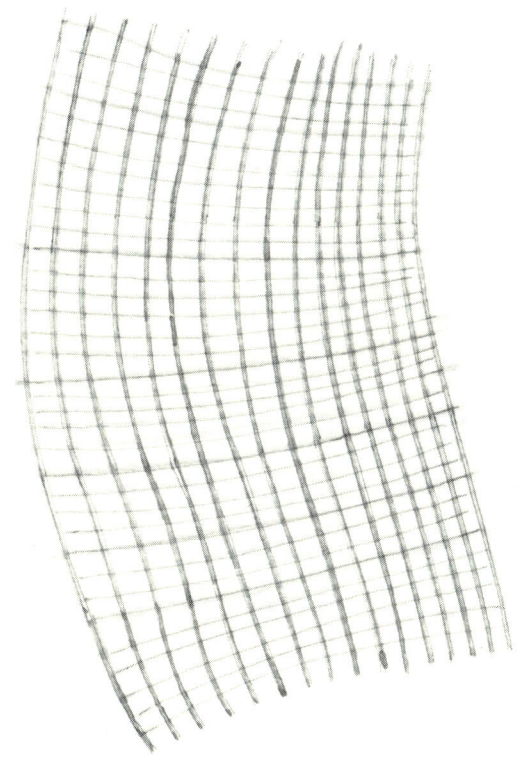

9. *Aspella senex*, intritacalx

"Shell smallish, solid, pointed, white, lacking prominent spines. The body appears to be smooth but is covered with faint spiral ribbing. There are seven strong, pointed, swollen, upright ribs, the tops of which are ornamented with orange patches on two strong horizontal lines just above the suture. There are also two of these orange lines about the middle of the body whorl and an orange splotch at the base. The shoulders slope sharply. There is a white callus on the parietal wall and there are three weak columellar folds lower down. The aperture is ovate to subcircular, with six strong teeth on the inside of the outer lip. The base is recurved."

Puerto Rico to Antigua.

See Pl. 28, fig. 5.

Attiliosa incompta (Berry, 1960)
Coralliophila incompta Berry, 1960: 119

The shell is of moderate size (maximum length 37 mm) and stoutly biconic. The spire is high, consisting of one and one-half convex nuclear whorls and six shouldered postnuclear whorls. The suture is weakly impressed and undulate. The body whorl is large, making up perhaps three-fifths of the entire shell length. The aperture is large and broadly ovate to subcircular, with a moderately broad and deep anal sulcus, extended into a short, callused spout. The outer apertural lip is thin, thickening quickly just behind the growing edge; the inner surface of the outer lip is strongly lirate in mature specimens. The columellar lip is broadly arcuate and entirely adherent, and bears two oblique plicae anteriorly. The siphonal canal is short to moderately long, open, and strongly recurved at its distal end.

The body whorl bears seven to ten axial ridges that may qualify as varices, depending on the definition used. In each case the ridge extends from a point on the shoulder to a point near the base of the body, where most become ephemeral. Spiral sculpture consists of four major cords, one at and one just below the shoulder margin, one medial, and one at the base of the body. The two in the region of the shoulder margin are prominent and are raised into transversely elongate swellings over the axial ridges.

Shell color is milky blue-white. In fresh examples the shell is covered with a moderately heavy intritacalx, causing the shell to appear "dead-white."

Central Gulf of California, especially off Isla Angel de la Guarda.

See Pl. 3, fig. 1.

Attiliosa philippiana (Dall, 1889)
Muricidea philippiana Dall, 1889: 213

The only specimen available for examination was a syntype, here designated as lectotype, an evidently immature example.

The shell is small (ca. 15 mm in length) and broadly biconic. The spire is high, consisting of five postnuclear whorls and a protoconch of undetermined nature. The suture is weakly impressed and undulate. The body whorl is slightly broader than high. The aperture is moderately

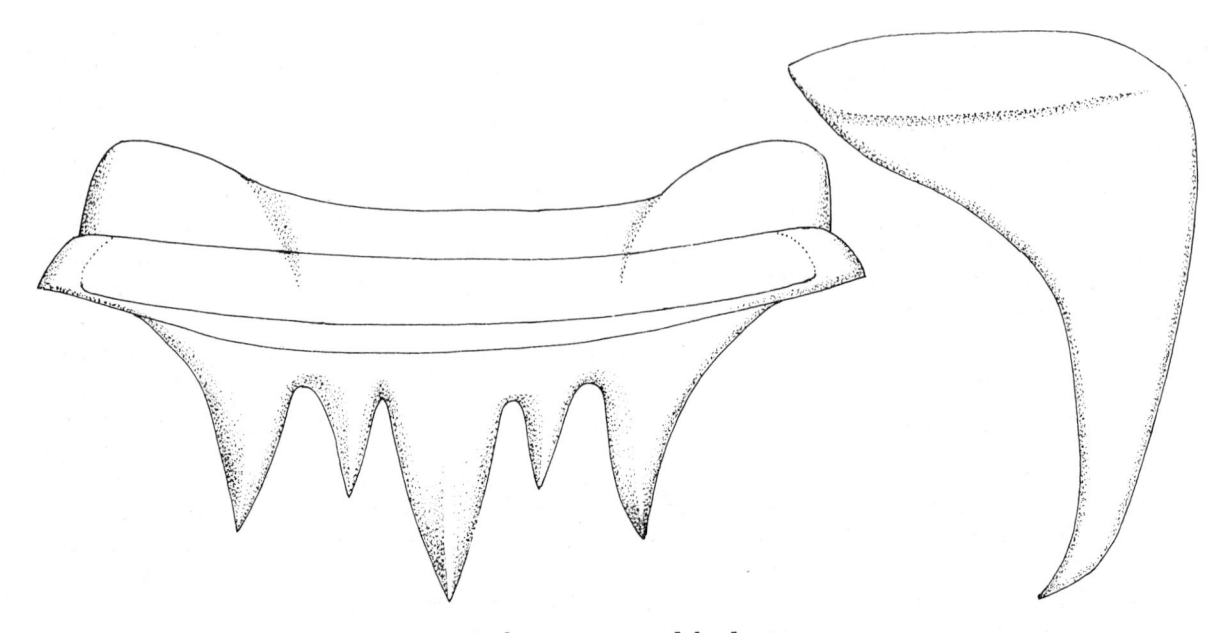

10. *Attiliosa incompta*, radular dentition

large and ovate, with a narrow, deep anal sulcus. The outer apertural lip is unthickened (?immature characteristic) and bears seven slender lirae on its inner surface. The columellar lip is adherent, the columella broadly arcuate. The siphonal canal is moderately short and broadly open.

The body whorl bears nine axial ridges (?varices), these confined almost entirely to the shoulder-margin region. Spiral sculpture consists of a variable number of weak to ephemeral cords, the two or three in the shoulder-margin region tending to become keeled or at least nodulose over the axial ridges.

Shell color is an almost translucent milky blue-white. The aperture is white and may have a minor rosy suffusion.

Isolated records from the fringes of the Gulf of Mexico and the northern Caribbean; off Cabo Catoche, Yucatán, Mexico; off Egmont Key, Florida, in the northeastern Gulf of Mexico; and Key West, Florida.

See Pl. 3, fig. 10.

Genus BEDEVA Iredale, 1936

TYPE SPECIES: *Trophon hanleyi* Angas, 1867 (=*T. paivae* Crosse, 1864), by original designation.

This genus includes species whose shells are generally small (most under 50 mm), fusiform, high-spired and nonvaricate. Most of them have strong, brief lirae on the inner surface of the outer lip and a moderately short, broadly open siphonal canal. The shell sculpture is generally fine, consisting of alternating elements of two sizes. The shell surface is generally finely scabrous and may be covered by a more or less evident intritacalx. In essence, this group appears to represent an Indo-Pacific counterpart of the tropical/subtropical trophonoid genera of the New World (*Calotrophon* and *Paziella*).

The genus *Bedevina* Habe, 1945, was established for *Fusus birileffi* Lischke, 1871, on the basis of differing radular characters. We have not studied this ourselves, and since the shells are indistinguishable at the generic level, we are retaining *birileffi* in *Bedeva*.

Bedeva birileffi (Lischke, 1871)

Trophon birileffi Lischke, 1871: 39

The shell is of average size for the genus (maximum length 25 mm) and fusiform. The spire is high, consisting of two and one-half nuclear whorls and five angulate postnuclear whorls. The suture is moderately impressed. The body whorl is of moderate size and fusoid. The aperture is ovate, with a moderately deep and wide anal sulcus. The outer apertural lip is sharp and minutely crenulate; its inner surface bears five brief, strong lirae. The columellar lip is smooth, almost straight, and entirely adherent. The siphonal canal is moderately short, straight, and open.

The body whorl is nonvaricate. Axial sculpture consists of eight ridges extending from just below the suture to the canal, these strongest over the shoulder margin. Spiral sculpture consists of numerous major and minor cords: four majors on the shoulder and 12 more majors, with one or two minors between each two majors, extending from the shoulder margin to the end of the canal.

The shell is light to medium brown, with the cord at the shoulder margin white and the remainder of the major cords light brown. The aperture is dirty white.

Central and southern Pacific coasts of Japan (Honshu to Kyushu).

See Pl. 2, fig. 6.

Bedeva blosvillei (Deshayes, 1832)

Fusus blosvillei Deshayes, 1832: 155

The shell is large for the genus (maximum length 50 mm) and fusiform. The spire is high, consisting of one and one-half nuclear whorls and six weakly subangulate postnuclear whorls. The suture is distinct and undulate. The body whorl is moderately large and fusoid. The aperture is large and ovate, with a broad, shallow anal sulcus, this delimited parietally by a low knob. The outer apertural lip rapidly thickens away from the growing edge; the lip margin is finely crenulate, reflecting the shell surface sculpture, and the inner surface is strongly lirate for a short distance into the aperture. The columellar lip is generally smooth and entirely adherent. The siphonal canal is quite long, moderately open, and recurved dorsally.

Axial sculpture consists of nine moderately prominent costae extending from just below the suture to the top of the siphonal canal. Spiral sculpture consists of 15 or 16 major cords alternating with minor cords.

The shell is pale chocolate-brown, with a white shoulder cord, two more white cords medial on the body, and the other cords pale brown. The aperture is creamy white with brown spiral lines. The columella may also have one or two suffusions of dark brown.

The Philippines to Queensland, Australia.

See Pl. 2, fig. 8.

Bedeva livida (Reeve, 1846)

Buccinum lividum Reeve, 1846: sp. 87

The shell is of moderate size (maximum length 35 mm) and fusiform. The spire is high and acute, consisting of seven or eight sharply angulate postnuclear whorls and a protoconch of undetermined nature. The suture is completely obscured. The body whorl is moderately large and fusoid. The aperture is of moderate size and ovate to lenticular, with a narrow, moderately deep anal sulcus. The outer apertural lip is sharp, but thickens quickly behind the growing edge; the lip margin is minutely crenulate, and the inner surface is denticulate or strongly, briefly lirate. The columellar lip is entirely adherent and smooth. The siphonal canal is short, straight, and open.

The body whorl is essentially nonvaricate, with nine axial ridges, the ridges beginning on the shoulder, sharply nodose at the shoulder margin, and extending to the siphonal canal, at which point they become obsolete. Spiral sculpture consists of a number of major and minor cords: seven minor cords on the shoulder; five major cords on the body, progressing anteriorly from the shoulder margin and intercalated by minor cords; and nine major cords on the lower portion of the body and the canal.

Shell color is uniform dark purple-brown or chocolate-brown. The aperture is purple-gray with suffusions of brown in some areas. The entire shell is covered by a thin intritacalx.

Known to us only from the Philippines (Mindoro, Cebu).

See Pl. 2, fig. 4.

Bedeva paivae (Crosse, 1864)

Trophon paivae Crosse, 1864: 278; *T. hanleyi* Angas, 1867: 110; *T. assisi* Tenison-Woods, 1876: 132

The extremely variable shell is of typical size for the genus (maximum length 32 mm) and fusiform. The spire is high, consisting of one nuclear whorl and seven sharply angulate postnuclear whorls. The suture is well-impressed. The body whorl is of moderate size and fusoid. The aperture is of moderate size and ovate to subovate, with the anterior margin somewhat flattened; the anal sulcus is narrow and very shallow. The outer apertural lip is sharp, but thickens quickly behind the growing edge; the lip margin is minutely crenulate, reflecting the shell surface sculpture, and the inner surface is strongly lirate. The columellar lip is smooth and entirely adherent. The siphonal canal is moderately short to moderately long, open, and bent slightly to the left and dorsally.

The body whorl is essentially nonvaricate and bears six more or less prominent axial ridges, these extending over the entire whorl. Spiral sculpture consists of 17 narrow cords, all of almost equal size: three on the shoulder, nine on the body, and five on the canal. In some specimens, intercalary secondary cords are found on the body.

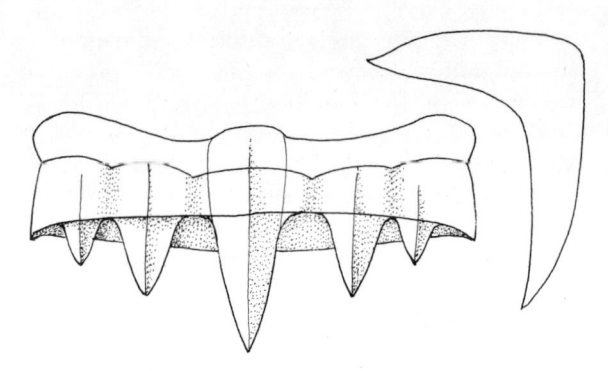

11. *Bedeva paivae*, radular dentition

Shell color varies from pale brown to cream, with light-brown or purple-gray suffusions. In some specimens two cream-colored cords, one at the shoulder margin and one at the base of the body, are slightly more prominent. The aperture is entirely white or may be suffused with mauve or purple-brown.

The variability of many shell features, such as spire height, canal length, degree of whorl angulation, color, size, etc., have led to the introduction of several superfluous names, as seen in the synonymy.

Southern Australia and Tasmania to southern Queensland.

See Pl. 2, figs. 2, 9; Pl. 14, fig. 9.

Genus BOLINUS Pusch, 1837

TYPE SPECIES: *Murex brandaris* Linné, 1758, by original designation.

A completely Old World genus, *Bolinus* includes two species, *B. brandaris* from the Mediterranean and *B. cornutus* from western Africa. The shells of both species are essentially club-shaped, and characterized by numerous spinose varices, a short spire, and an elongate, straight, or slightly recurved canal. Other characters include the well-developed parietal callus and inductura, features not unique to *Bolinus*.

Bolinus brandaris (Linné, 1758)

Murex brandaris Linné, 1758: 747

The shell is moderately large (maximum length 90 mm) and club-shaped. Its spire is moderately low, with two nuclear whorls and five shouldered postnuclear whorls. The suture is deeply impressed, and this feature is emphasized by a depressed area on the shoulder immediately abutting the suture. The body whorl is moderately large, as high as broad. The aperture is broadly ovate, with an anal sulcus posteriorly and a strong constriction anteriorly, at the top of the siphonal canal. The outer apertural lip is thickened, with a crenulate leading edge, the crenulations coinciding with short lirae that extend for some distance into the aperture. The columellar lip adheres to the body whorl above, forming a parietal callus that reaches the shoulder; below, the columellar lip is detached from the body whorl and developed into a prominent flaring inductura with a strongly concave inner surface. The siphonal canal is long, tubelike, narrowly open, and slightly recurved; to the side of the canal is a ridge composed of the vestiges of former canals.

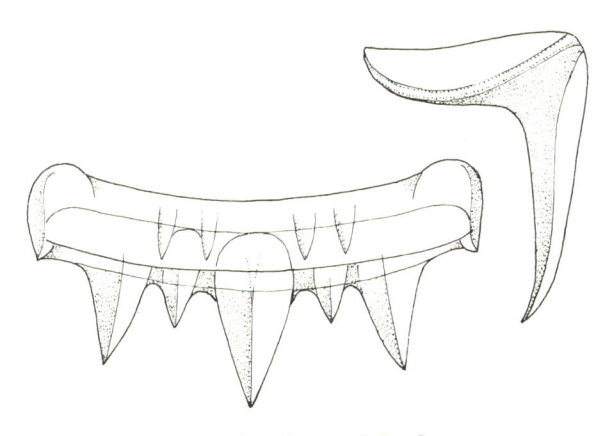

12. *Bolinus brandaris*, radular dentition

The body whorl bears six or seven varices, these proceeding obliquely across the shoulder to coincide with those on the former whorl. Spiral sculpture consists of many fine spiral threads and two or exceptionally three prominent cords. Where these cords cross the varices, short, broad-based, blunt or sharp spines are developed: the uppermost spiral row of spines, at the shoulder, is made up of moderately long, narrowly open spines; a second row, around the middle of the body whorl, is made up of shorter, completely closed spines; a third row of finer, narrowly open spines obliquely encircles the siphonal canal from just below the inductura to a point about one-third of the way down the canal.

Shell color is pale fleshy orange, with three faint brown spiral bands on the body whorl.

Central and western Mediterranean.

See Pl. 11, fig. 8.

Bolinus cornutus (Linné, 1758)

Murex cornutus Linné, 1758: 746

The shell is large (maximum length 200 mm) and club-shaped. Its spire is low, with two nuclear whorls and five shouldered postnuclear whorls. The suture is deeply impressed. The body whorl is very large and broader than high. The aperture is ovate, twice as high as broad, with a broad anal sulcus extending posteriorly onto the shoulder. The outer apertural lip is moderately thickened; its leading edge is crenulate, weakly above and more strongly below. The columellar lip forms a broad, polished parietal callus that extends posteriorly, crossing the shoulder to reach the suture; anteriorly, the columellar lip becomes detached from the body whorl, taking the form of a broad, thin, undulate inductura, this strongly concave over the columella. The siphonal canal is long, straight, and narrowly open; to the side of the canal is a ridge composed of the vestiges of former canals.

The body whorl bears seven oblique varices, these proceeding across the shoulder as low ridges. The varical margin is sharply raised. The varices are low, spineless ridges on the spire. On the body whorl the varical margin is crenulate, and the varix is composed of three crescentlike segments, the first proceeding from the suture to the edge of the shoulder, the second between the shoulder-edge and the middle of the body whorl, and the third extending to the base of the body whorl. Spiral sculpture consists of six or seven primary cords and secondary cords on the shoulder and on the posterior part of the body whorl. Where the top two primary cords cross the varices, on the shoulder-edge and medially on the body whorl, long, recurved, closed spines are developed. The entire shell surface is also decussated by fine axial and spiral scratches. Extensions of the varices form spinose axial ridges extending the full length of the canal. Two or three oblique rows of long, sharp spines encircle the canal starting immediately below the inductura. The upper row terminates above the midpoint of the canal, and the lower row ends below the midpoint; the third row, when present, terminates near the anterior end of the canal.

Shell color is tan or buff, with three darker, evenly spaced, brown spiral bands on the body whorl. The aperture is porcelaneous white, suffused with apricot orange on the lip-edge, parietal callus, and inductura.

Western coast of Africa, from Mauritania to Angola.

See Pl. 11, fig. 9.

Genus CALOTROPHON
Hertlein & Strong, 1951

TYPE SPECIES: *Calotrophon bristolae* Hertlein & Strong, 1951 (=*Tritonalia turrita* Dall, 1919), by original designation.

The shells of species assigned to this genus are generally solid and fusiform, with no apparent periostracum and a white intritacalx, thin, except on the shoulder where this chalky layer forms more or less erect lamellae. The whorls are shouldered, with strong axial ribs and moderately raised, imbricate spiral cords. The siphonal canal is of moderate length (equal to or shorter than the spire), and open. The aperture is moderately small and ovate; the outer apertural lip is dentate or lirate within, the columella generally smooth and gently arcuate. Nuclear whorls one and one-half.

Calotrophon ostrearum (Conrad, 1846)

Murex ostrearum Conrad, 1846: 25; *Urosalpinx floridana* Conrad, 1869: 106

The shell is of moderate size (maximum length 27 mm) and fusiform. The spire is high, consisting of one and one-half convex nuclear whorls and six shouldered postnuclear whorls. The suture is impressed and undulate. The body whorl is of moderate size and fusoid. The aperture is of moderate size and ovate, with a narrow, shallow anal sulcus. The outer apertural lip is thin, thickening rather quickly away from the growing edge; the inner surface of the outer lip bears seven weak, transversely elongate denticles, these becoming moderately weak lirae more deeply within the aperture. The columellar lip is weakly arcuate, smooth to pustulate anteriorly, and entirely adherent. The siphonal canal is moderately long, straight, open, and weakly recurved distally.

The body whorl bears seven or eight moderately prominent varices. Spiral sculpture consists of seven prominent cords, with or without intercalary minor cords on the body, and two major cords and a single minor cord on the canal. A moderately heavy intritacalx, strongest on the shoulder, covers the surface of the shell, imparting a stark white color to fresh specimens. Deep-water examples show noteworthy open spinelets formed from the expansion of fine axial lamellae over the major cords, especially at the shoulder margin.

Shell color is brown-purple, with flesh-colored spiral cords. The apertural margin and denticles are blue-white, pale purple, or mauve more deeply within the aperture. Deep-water examples have white apertures with pale-pink suffusions.

Northern and western Florida from Cape San Blas to Marco Island.

See Pl. 3, fig. 4.

Calotrophon turritus (Dall, 1919)

Tritonalia turrita Dall, 1919: 336; *Calotrophon bristolae* Hertlein & Strong, 1951: 87; *Hertleinella leucostephes* Berry, 1958: 95

The shell is moderately large (maximum length 41 mm) and fusiform. The spire is high, consisting of five or six shouldered postnuclear whorls and a protoconch of undetermined nature. The suture is impressed and undulate. The body whorl is of moderate size and fusoid. The aperture is moderately large and ovate, with a narrow, very shallow anal sulcus and a broadly open entrance into the siphonal canal. The outer apertural lip is thin, thickening rather quickly away from the growing edge; the inner surface of the outer lip bears four moderately strong denticles, these becoming moderately weak lirae more deeply within the aperture. The columellar lip is smooth, gently arcuate,

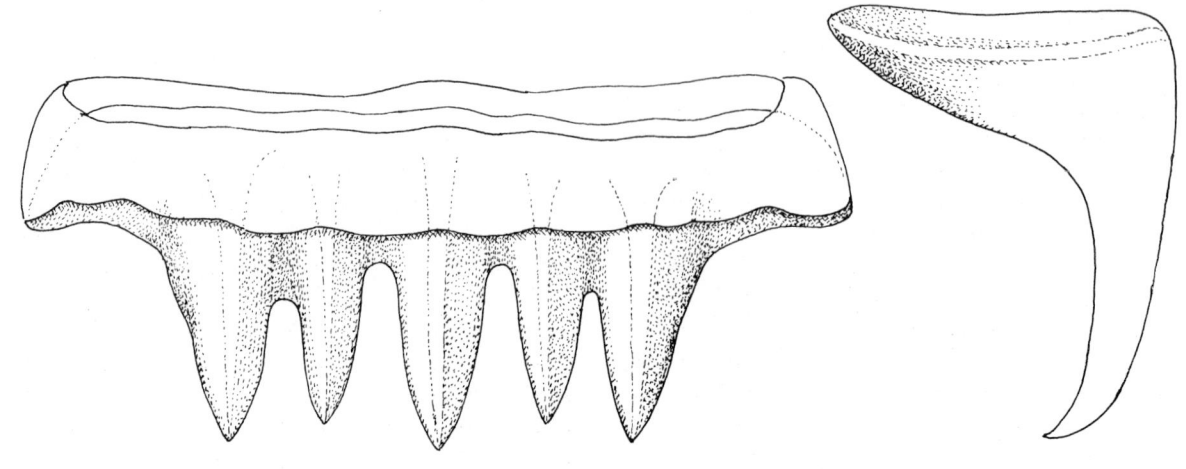

13. *Calotrophon turritus*, radular dentition

and completely adherent. The siphonal canal is of moderate length, straight, open, and more or less weakly dorsally recurved at its tip.

The body whorl bears seven heavy, fimbriate varices. Spiral sculpture consists of eight moderately strong cords bearing expansions of fine axial lamellae, these imparting a scabrous appearance to the cords. Five cords are apparent on the body, and three on the canal. The scabrous expansions on the shoulder margin cord are longer, and in some examples resemble spines. A moderately heavy intritacalx is apparent on most of the shell surface, but is strongest on the shoulder and between the spiral cords.

The intritacalx imparts a stark white ground color to fresh specimens. Below the intritacalx the shell is milky white, with gray to brown-black spiral cords.

Off both coasts of Baja California, Mexico, from Cedros Island and La Paz to Cabo San Lucas, in subtidal depths (17–30 m).

See Pl. 3, figs. 12–13.

Calotrophon velero (E. H. Vokes, 1970)

Poirieria velero E. H. Vokes, 1970: 47; *Panamurex velero* E. H. Vokes, 1971: 114

The shell is small (maximum length 15 mm) and fusiform. The spire is high, consisting of one and one-half smooth nuclear whorls (fide Vokes, 1970) and six convex to subangulate postnuclear whorls. The suture is impressed and strongly undulate. The body whorl is of moderate size and fusoid. The aperture is moderately small and ovate, with a narrow, moderately deep anal sulcus. The outer apertural lip is erect and finely serrate; its inner surface bears six or seven prominent lirae. The columellar lip is entirely adherent and bears several moderately strong, elongate-oblique, plaitlike pustules, three anteriorly and two posteriorly, the upper delimiting the left side of the anal sulcus. The siphonal canal is moderately short, open, and almost straight.

The body whorl bears six or seven strong varices. Spiral sculpture consists of nine major cords, these evenly distributed over the shell from the shoulder to the tip of the canal. A moderately thick, white intritacalx is deposited as innumerable microscopic axial lamellae, though these are not reflected in the underlying hard shell matter.

Shell color under the intritacalx is a warm purple-brown. The aperture is suffused with pale purple-brown; the denticles and pustules are a paler white-purple.

A problem arises concerning the genus *Panamurex* Woodring, 1959, to which Vokes (1970) has assigned this species, along with *P. carnicolor* Clench and Pérez Farfante, 1945, a name of dubious identity. (We have examined the supposed holotype of *P. carnicolor* on loan from the Museum of Comparative Zoology, and have concluded that it does not represent the specimen figured with the original description; indeed, it may not even represent the same species. The specimen figured by Vokes [1970] as this species is not from the type lot, although it does resemble the original figure.)

Woodring (ibid.) compares *Panamurex* (type species: *Murex gatunensis* Brown & Pilsbry, 1911) to *Dallimurex* Rehder, 1946, which we have determined to be an objective synonym of *Paziella* Jousseaume, 1880, on the basis of our synonymy of their respective type species (*Murex nuttingi* Dall, 1896; *M. pazi* Crosse, 1869). According to Woodring, "The strong spiral sculpture, strong elongate denticles on the basal part of the inner lip distinguish *Panamurex* from *Dallimurex*." Unfortunately, no comparison was made between *Panamurex* and *Calotrophon* Hertlein & Strong, 1951 (type species: *C. bristolae* Hertlein & Strong, 1951) nor any comment made on the similarity of its western Atlantic representative, *C. ostrearum* (Conrad, 1846), to several fossil species assigned to *Panamurex*.

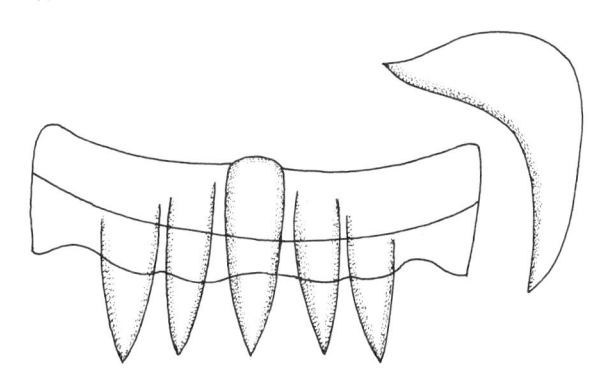

14. *Calotrophon velero*, radular dentition

Vokes (1970b) apparently bases her assignment of *C. velero* to *Panamurex* on two points, these being its similarity to "*Panamurex*" *mauryae* Vokes, 1970, and its possession of several denticles at the anterior end of the columella, a characteristic which, by implication, is lacking in related forms not assigned to *Panamurex* (i.e. *Calotrophon* spp.). An examination of several dozen specimens of *C. ostrearum* from Boca Ciega, Florida, has resulted in the discovery that fully one-third of the specimens had more or less well-marked denticles at the anterior end of the columella. It is thus strongly indicated that this character is of questionable value in assigning species to one or another of these genera.

For *Panamurex*, it may be suggested that in *P. gatunensis*, with its notable spines, etc., we have, on morphological grounds at least, a reasonable link between *Paziella* and *Calotrophon*. We could accept the continued use of *Panamurex* (as either a genus or a subgenus) for this species and several other Miocene species assigned there by Vokes [*P. lychnia* (Gardner, 1947); *P. mauryae* (E. H. Vokes, 1970); *P. fusinoides* (Gardner, 1947); etc.]. There does, however, seem to be a noticeable trend in this lineage toward the diminution or loss of columellar denticles and a reduction of spinosity into Recent times. Our position is that *Calotrophon* may well be a direct or almost direct descendent of a Miocene *Panamurex* form, and that this explains the absence of *Calotrophon* in earlier periods and the apparent paucity of Recent *Panamurex* species. With this assumption in mind, we would consider *C. velero* the *Calotrophon* species showing the greatest affinities with its presumed ancestral stock. Incidentally, the radulae of the type species of *Paziella* and *Calotrophon*, and of *C. velero*, show negligible differences, if any.

Northern South America; known only from the area southwest of Cabo de la Vela, Guajira Peninsula, Venezuela.

See Pl. 23, fig. 5.

Genus **CHICOREUS** Montfort, 1810

TYPE SPECIES: *Murex ramosus* Linné, 1758 (ICZN Opinion 911, 1970).

This genus, in numbers of species, is the largest in the subfamily Muricinae. The shells, varying in size from small to very large, are characterized by having three more or less foliaceous varices. The spire is generally moderately high. The body whorl may be capacious to moderate in size, with an aperture that may range from small to large; the aperture may bear a prominent labial tooth, as in the type species, or the tooth may be completely lacking. The canal ranges from short to quite long, depending on the species. Axial sculpture generally consists of three varices and one or more axial ridges in each intervarical space. Denticulation or liration of the interior of the outer apertural lip is generally lacking, although a few species do show this feature. The shells range in color from almost pure white to dark brown-black, with brown the predominant color in most species.

Tropical and subtropical portions of the Indo-West Pacific and Atlantic Oceans.

Chicoreus artemis, new name

Murex aculeatus Lamarck, 1822: 163 (not Schlotheim, 1820: 147)

The shell is small to moderate in size (maximum length 60 mm) and fusiform. Its spire is moderately high, consisting of nine postnuclear whorls and a protoconch of undetermined nature. The suture is impressed. The body whorl is small to moderate in size and suborbicular. The aperture is broadly ovate, with a posterior anal sulcus delimited on each side by an elongate spiral ridge. The outer apertural lip is erect and crenulate at its margin, with lirae extending from the crenulations into the interior. The columellar lip is detached and erect. The siphonal canal is short, moderately broad above, and tapering below.

The body whorl bears three varices, each ornamented with several short to moderately long, recurved spines. Other axial sculpture consists of one or two intervarical ridges, these strongly nodose at the shoulder. Spiral sculpture consists of several major cords, these intercalated with markedly imbricate minor cords. Where the major cords intersect the varices, the spines are developed. Where persistent, two spines per varix are present on the spire. Four or five major spines are generally developed on the body whorl. Two smaller, ventrally bent spines are found immediately below the shoulder spine. In addition, another smaller, ventrally bent spine may follow the second major spine.

Shell color ranges from pink to red-orange, the early whorls of deeper hue, with yellow suffusion. The more prominent spiral elements are red-brown on their crests. The aperture interior is white, suffused with rose-pink at the mouth.

Tosa Bay, Japan, to the Philippines.

See Pl. 4, fig. 4.

Chicoreus asianus Kuroda, 1942

Murex elongatus Lamarck, 1822: 161 (not Lightfoot, 1786); *Murex sinensis* Reeve, 1845: 25 (not Gmelin, 1791); *Chicoreus asianus* Kuroda, 1942: 80, new name for *Murex elongatus* Lamarck, 1822 (not Lightfoot, 1786)

The shell is large (maximum length 110 mm) and broadly fusiform. The spire is moderately high and consists of seven weakly shouldered, postnuclear whorls and a protoconch of undetermined nature. The suture is strongly impressed. The body whorl is large and broad. The aperture is moderately large and widely ovate, with a posterior anal sulcus. The outer apertural lip is strongly dentate and bears a prominent labial tooth near the junction of the body and the siphonal canal. The columellar lip is adherent above and slightly detached below. The siphonal canal is moderately long, moderately broad above, and tapering anteriorly to a narrow, tubelike, narrowly open distal portion.

The body whorl bears three varices, each ornamented with moderately long, slender, recurved foliated spines. Other axial sculpture consists of one or two short intervarical costae, these most prominent as tubercles in the shoulder region. Spiral sculpture consists of low spiral cords and minutely tuberculate threads. Where the spiral cords intersect the varices, the spines are developed. Two spines are persistent on the varices of the spire whorls and five are developed on each body-whorl varix. The shoulder spine is longest and is upturned; the remaining four are progressively shorter anteriorly. Three spines are developed on the siphonal canal, the posteriormost one the longest, the remaining two progressively shorter. In addition, small, ventrally bent spinelets alternate with the major spines.

Shell color is light brown or tan, with darker brown on the elevated, tuberculate portions of the spiral elements.

Southeastern Japan.

See Pl. 6, fig. 8.

Chicoreus axicornis (Lamarck, 1822)

Murex axicornis Lamarck, 1822: 163; *M. kawamurai* Shikama, 1964: 116

The shell is moderate in size (maximum length 70 mm) and fusiform. Its spire is high, consisting of nine convex postnuclear whorls and a protoconch of undetermined nature. The suture is deeply impressed. The body whorl is moderately small and fusoid. The aperture is ovate, with an inverted-U-shaped anal sulcus, strengthened on the left by a thickened spiral ridge. The outer apertural lip is erect and marginally dentate; its inner surface is lirate. The columellar lip is erect. The siphonal canal is long, moderately broad, tapering, narrowly medially open, and distally recurved.

The body whorl bears the three varices typical of *Chicoreus* and, generally, two prominent intervarical costae. Spiral sculpture consists of numerous major and minor cords and minutely tuberculate threads. Where the major cords intersect the varices, they turn vertically to become long, recurved, distally foliated spines. The shoulder spine is the longest, and a second, smaller spine is developed lower down on the body. Between these two spines and below the lower spine toward the canal there are a few very short, ventrally bent spines. Two moderately long, slender spines are developed on the canal, these intercalated with minor, ventrally bent spines.

Shell color is white or ochre to brown. The aperture is porcelaneous white.

Taiwan, the Philippines.

See Pl. 4, fig. 2.

Chicoreus banksii (Sowerby, 1841)

Murex banksii Sowerby, 1841: pl. 191, fig. 82; *M. bourguignati* Poirier, 1883: 48

The shell is moderately large (maximum length 100 mm) and fusiform. Its spire is high, consisting of one and three-quarter nuclear whorls and seven or eight shouldered postnuclear whorls. The suture is impressed. The body whorl is large and fusoid. The aperture is small and subcircular, with a shallow, inverted-V-shaped anal notch, this delimited by a small, strong callus on its parietal side. The outer apertural lip is barely erect beyond the varix and is composed of two parts: a shorter, finely crenulate portion between the suture and the shoulder, and a much longer, more coarsely dentate portion making up the remainder of the lip. The columellar lip is slightly detached and flaring anteriorly, and adherent posteriorly. The siphonal canal is moderately long and broad, narrowly medially open, and distally recurved.

The body whorl carries the three varices typical of *Chicoreus*. Other axial sculpture consists of one to three tubercles at the shoulder in each intervarical space. Spiral sculpture consists of numerous major and minor scabrous cords and finer threads. Where the major cords intersect the varices, they are developed into prominent distally foliated spines. The shoulder region is essentially devoid of spines. The longest spine, at the shoulder margin, is followed anteriorly by a much shorter, ventrally bent spine. Below this spine on the body are three recurved spines of approximately equal length and spacing. Another short, ventrally bent spine follows, below which is a spineless gap characteristic of this species. Below the gap, on the canal, a single recurved spine is followed by two straight, longer spines. Tiny, ventrally bent spinelets are intercalated with major spines in the body region.

The shell is tan to black, the aperture white.

This typical form is found primarily on the eastern African coast. In Queensland, eastern Australia, a more slender, attenuated form with much longer spines is prevalent. This is the form figured by Reeve (1845) as *M. axicornis* var. *b*. *C. banksii* may be distinguished from that species by its larger size, more numerous spines, more prominent spineless gap, and much less recurved spines. In western Australia this species has not been correctly identified because of its more compressed appearance—the spines are so densely crowded that all traces of the spineless gap have vanished and the spines in this region actually cross each other. All other features are readily recognizable as those of *C. banksii*.

Mozambique and Zanzibar to the west coast of Australia, the Sulu Sea, and Queensland, eastern Australia.

See Pl. 4, fig. 12.

Chicoreus benedictinus (Löbbecke, 1879)

Murex (Chicoreus) benedictinus Löbbecke, 1879: 79

The shell is moderately large (maximum length 90 mm) and fusiform. The spire is high, consisting of nine weakly subangulate postnuclear whorls and a protoconch of undetermined nature. The suture is impressed. The body whorl is of moderate size and fusoid. The aperture is of moderate size and ovate, with a narrow, moderately deep anal sulcus. The outer apertural lip is barely erect and crenulate, strongly lirate on its inner surface. The columellar lip is arched, adherent above, detached and erect below, and heavily callused. The siphonal canal is of moderate length, curved, and barely open.

The body whorl bears three briefly foliose varices. Intervarical axial sculpture consists of two costae of unequal prominence, the larger one always situated nearer the growing edge. Spiral sculpture consists of six primary cords, four on the body and two on the canal, and one or two intercalary cords between consecutive primary cords. Fine threads are apparent over the entire shell surface but are more densely distributed in three transverse bands, one above and on the shoulder margin, one medial, and one at the base of the body. The primary and secondary cords end at the varical margin in weakly foliated spines of different lengths, the longest, at the shoulder margin, open ventrally and bent back, as are all the primary spines, the other spines bent ventrally. The two anteriormost spines are joined by a webbing.

Shell color is white, with diffuse brown coloration in some areas. The crests of the spiral threads are dark chestnut-brown, imparting to the three areas of greatest thread density the appearance of transverse brown bands.

This description was drawn in part from a Latin description by Th. Löbbecke. The details are based on two specimens in Mr. D'Attilio's collection that had been unidentified and that seem to closely fit Löbbecke's description.

If we have correctly associated Löbbecke's name with the D'Attilio specimens, the species is indigenous to the Red Sea area (the specimens are from the Gulf of Aqaba).

See Pl. 23, fig. 10.

Chicoreus brevifrons (Lamarck, 1822)

Murex brevifrons Lamarck, 1822: 161; *M. calcitrapa* Lamarck, 1822: 162; *M. purpuratus* Reeve, 1846: sp. 183

The shell is large (maximum length 140 mm) and broadly fusiform. The spire is high and consists of two convex nuclear whorls and eight barely shouldered, postnuclear whorls. The suture is unimpressed, but the region immediately below the suture is depressed. The body whorl is large and broadly fusoid. The aperture is large and ovate, with a deep, inverted-U-shaped anal notch, delimited parietally by a small, heavy callus. The outer apertural lip is barely, if at all, erect, and strongly dentate, the bifid teeth representing the spaces between varical spines. The columellar lip is thin and entirely adherent. The siphonal canal is moderately long, broad, narrowly open to the right, and distally recurved.

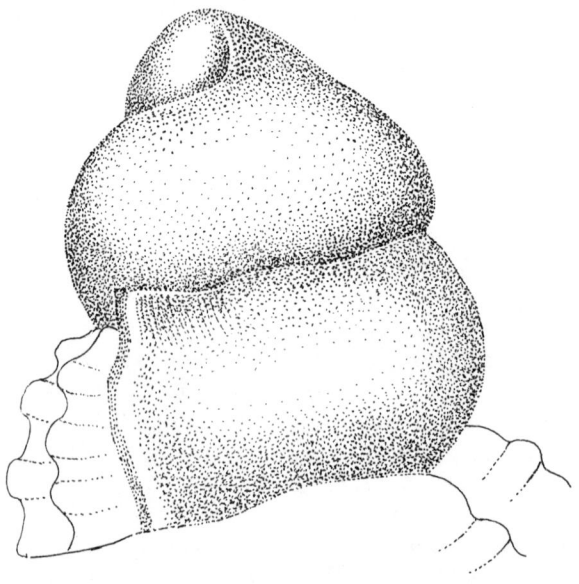

15. *Chicoreus brevifrons*, protoconch

The body whorl bears the three varices typical of *Chicoreus*. Other axial sculpture consists of one or two prominent, elongate tubercles in each intervarical space. Spiral sculpture consists of finely imbricate major and minor cords and threads. Where the cords intersect the varices, long, stout, distally foliated spines are developed. The shoulder region is devoid of spines. The heavy, straight, shoulder-margin spine is much the longest. Immediately below this is a small, ventrally bent spine, followed by a second long, straight spine. Below this there is a smaller, dorsally bent spine, followed by two ventrally bent spines of equal length. In the region of the junction of the body and the canal there is a gap in the spination, the gap bearing only two or three tiny, ventrally bent spinelets. Three long spines developed on the canal diminish slightly in length toward the anterior.

Shell color is light to dark brown, with tan to white on the major and minor spiral cords. The proportion of light to dark coloration determines whether the shell appears dark brown with light spiral bands or vice-versa.

Southern Caribbean Sea.

See Pl. 4, fig. 10.

Chicoreus brunneus (Link, 1807)

Purpura brunnea Link, 1807: 121; *Murex adustus* Lamarck, 1822: 162; *M. despectus* A. Adams, 1854: 72; *M. huttoniae* Wright, 1878: 85

The shell is moderately large (maximum length 90 mm) and solidly rhomboid. The spire is high, consisting of one and one-half nuclear whorls, and seven weakly angulate postnuclear whorls. The suture is impressed. The body whorl is large, broad, and strong. The aperture is small, subcircular, and almost entire, and is interrupted by a small anal sulcus. The outer apertural lip is erect and finely dentate; on its inner surface, lirae extend from these teeth into the aperture. The columellar lip is narrow and slightly erect, with a parietal callus. The siphonal canal is shorter than the spire, narrowly open, and distally recurved.

The body whorl bears three densely foliaceous varices. Additional axial sculpture consists of a single broad, very prominent node in each intervarical space. Spiral sculpture on the body whorl consists of about 12 cords of moderate development. In addition, the entire shell is covered with finely tuberculate threads. Where the cords intersect the varices, prominent, distally foliated spines are developed. The three or four uppermost spines are recurved and progressively more dorsally bent toward the anterior, forming a gradual arc in that direction. The three shorter spines immediately below this arc are bent progressively more ventrally toward the anterior, forming an arc in a direction opposite to the upper arc. A single small spine marks the junction of the body and the canal. On the canal, four long recurved spines form a progressively ventrally oriented arc in which the spines diminish in length toward the anterior.

Shell color is blackish-brown to jet black. Populations with yellow-orange shells are known from several western Pacific localities (Guam, New Caledonia, etc.). The interior of the aperture is white, except for the margin, which is generally yellow (East African populations) or pinkish-red (Pacific populations).

In young specimens, especially those we have seen from the Solomon Islands, the entire shell surface is scabrous or laminate, the intervarical node is less prominent (two may be present), and the shell is more slender and elongate.

Occurs intertidally throughout the Indo-West Pacific.

See Pl. 4, fig. 9.

Chicoreus cnissodus (Euthyme, 1889)

Murex cnissodus Euthyme, 1889: 263

The shell is moderate in size (maximum length 75 mm) and broadly fusiform. The spire is high, consisting of two and one-half nuclear whorls and seven weakly shouldered postnuclear whorls. The suture is deeply impressed. The body whorl is moderately large and fusoid. The aperture is moderately large and ovate, with an anal sulcus bounded parietally by a spiral ridge extending into the aperture. The outer apertural lip is erect and finely dentate. The columellar lip is adherent for a short distance above, but detached for more than half its length. The siphonal canal is shorter than the spire and narrowly open.

The body whorl bears the typical three foliaceous varices of *Chicoreus*. Additional axial sculpture consists of two or three intervarical costae; these are enlarged and nodose at the shoulder. Spiral sculpture consists of low major and minor cords, these most prominent over the intervarical tubercles. In addition, the entire surface is covered with finely tuberculate threads. Where the cords intersect the varices, moderately long, open, distally foliated spines are developed; the longest, at the shoulder, is recurved. Below this are four or five spines on the body and two or three on the canal, all of which are straight. Smaller, ventrally bent spinelets are intercalated with the spines on the body.

Shell color is white, with the crest of each cord brown. The intervarical costae and the ends of the spines may be lightly suffused with brown. A periostracum preserved on one specimen is cocoa-brown and minutely hairy.

Southeastern Japan to New Caledonia (including Taiwan and the Philippines).

See Pl. 5, fig. 3.

Chicoreus cornucervi (Röding, 1798)

Purpura cornucervi Röding, 1798: 142; *Murex monodon* Sowerby, 1825: Append. p. 19

The shell is moderately large (maximum length 110 mm) and the spire is moderately high, comprising eight or nine strongly convex postnuclear whorls and a protoconch of undetermined nature. The suture is strongly impressed. The body whorl is moderately large and broadly fusoid. The aperture is large and subcircular, with a broad, shallow anal sulcus. The outer apertural lip bears a few strong denticles and a large, very prominent labial tooth, anteriorly on the body. The columellar lip is detached and prominently erect. The siphonal canal is relatively short, tapering from its moderately broad posterior portion to its more slender anterior end.

The body whorl bears three foliaceous varices. Additional axial sculpture, if any, consists of one weak intervarical ridge. Spiral sculpture consists of weak major and minor cords and numerous finely nodulose threads covering the entire shell. Where the major cords intersect the varices, very long, strongly recurved, narrowly open, foliated spines are developed. On the body whorl there are three spines intercalated with smaller spinelets. Below this the point of origin of the large labial tooth is followed by two additional varical spines of intermediate length. The upper three spines may be so strongly recurved that they touch the body.

Shell color varies from pure white to dark brown. The aperture is light to dark pink marginally, white more deeply within.

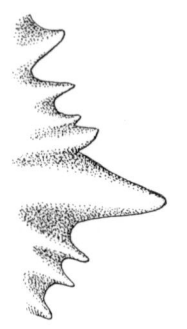

16. *Chicoreus cornucervi*, labial tooth (ceratus)

Specimens from the Torres Straits population (Thursday Island) are smaller (maximum length 75 mm) and more delicately formed, and are found in 20–40 m. The larger, northwestern Australian specimens (Broome) are collected in shallow water under overhanging rock ledges.

Torres Straits (off northeastern Australia) to northwestern Australia.

See Pl. 4, fig. 11.

Chicoreus damicornis (Hedley, 1903)

Murex damicornis Hedley, 1903: 378

The shell is moderate in size (maximum length 70 mm) and fusiform. The spire is moderately high to high, consisting of two polished nuclear whorls and six convex postnuclear whorls. The suture is relatively unimpressed. The body whorl is small to moderate in size and fusoid. The aperture is ovate, with an inverted-V-shaped anal sulcus, the V pointing toward the columella and bounded parietally by a strong spiral ridge. The outer apertural lip is erect and finely dentate. The columellar lip is adherent above, slightly detached below. The siphonal canal is shorter than the spire, narrowly open, and distally recurved.

The body whorl bears three foliaceous varices. Additional axial sculpture consists of two or three intervarical ridges, one prominent, the other one or two somewhat reduced. Spiral sculpture consists of major and minor cords and numerous scabrous or finely nodulose threads. Where the cords intersect the varices, open, weakly foliated spines are developed. The shoulder spine is very long and broadly, medially open, with its end broadly bifurcated. Below the shoulder are four major spines and minor intercalating spinelets. The lower two spines are often connected at their bases by a webbing. The canal bears two or three spines.

Shell color is white to pale yellow or buff, in coalescing axial streaks or in a simple suffusion. The aperture is porcelaneous white.

New South Wales to the Gulf of Carpenteria. In Queensland, specimens generally have a significantly shorter spire.

See Pl. 4, fig. 3.

Chicoreus denudatus (Perry, 1811)

Triplex denudata Perry, 1811: pl. 7, fig. 2; *Murex corrugatus* Sowerby, 1841: pl. 189, fig. 72; *M. palmiferus* Sowerby, 1841: pl. 195, fig. 104; *M. australiensis* A. Adams, 1854: 72; *Torvamurex extraneus* Iredale, 1936: 324; *Torvamurex immunitus* Iredale, 1936: 324

The shell is small (maximum length 50 mm) and broadly fusiform. Its spire is high, consisting of two and one-half nuclear whorls and six strongly convex postnuclear whorls. The suture is strongly impressed, and is emphasized by a concave region below the suture. The body whorl is moderately large and broadly fusoid. The aperture is ovate, with a narrow, inverted-V-shaped anal sulcus, the V pointing toward the columella, and its parietal boundary is formed by a thickened spiral ridge. The outer apertural lip is erect, extending a short distance beyond the last varix, and is finely dentate; its inner surface is lirate.

The columellar lip is detached and weakly erect. The siphonal canal is relatively short, tapering anteriorly, and recurved distally.

The body whorl bears three foliaceously ornamented varices. Other axial sculpture consists of two elongate, finely nodulose intervarical costae. Spiral sculpture consists of numerous major and minor, scabrous or finely nodulose threads. Where groups of these threads coalesce and intersect the varices, short, distally foliated, open spines are developed. The spines are much reduced on the spire. The body whorl bears six spines, none above the shoulder; the siphonal canal bears an additional three or four spines of equal length. Small intercalating spinelets may be present between the spines on the body.

17. *Chicoreus denudatus*, protoconch

Shell color is generally light to moderately dark rusty brown, strongest on the nodules of the spiral elements and the intervarical costae. A lighter band generally girdles the body region at its equator. The interior of the aperture is porcelaneous white.

Australia, New South Wales to south Queensland.

See Pl. 4, fig. 5.

Chicoreus florifer (Reeve, 1846)

Murex rufus Lamarck, 1822: 162 (not Montagu, 1803); *M. florifer* Reeve, 1846: sp. 188; *M. salleanus* A. Adams, 1854: 70; *M. dilectus* A. Adams, 1855: 120; *M. florifer arenarius* Clench & Pérez Farfante, 1945: 34

The shell is moderately large (maximum length 90 mm) and fusoid. The spire is high, consisting of two nuclear whorls and seven convex postnuclear whorls. The suture is impressed. The body whorl is moderately large and fusoid. The aperture is relatively small and subcircular, with a deep, narrow, flask-shaped anal sulcus that is almost closed at the apertural edge. The outer apertural lip is erect and coarsely dentate; its interior is broadly lirate, each lira extending in-

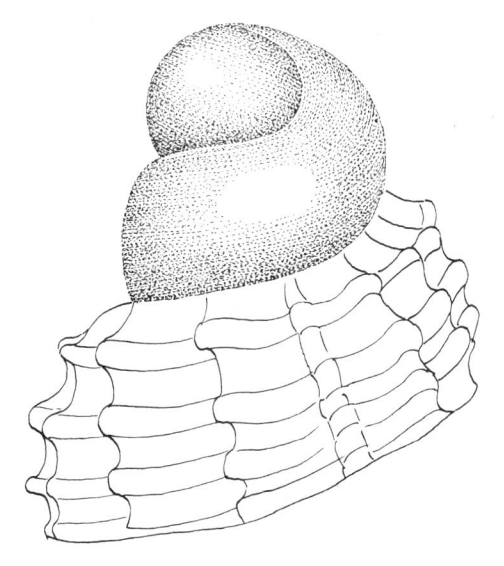

18. *Chicoreus florifer*, protoconch

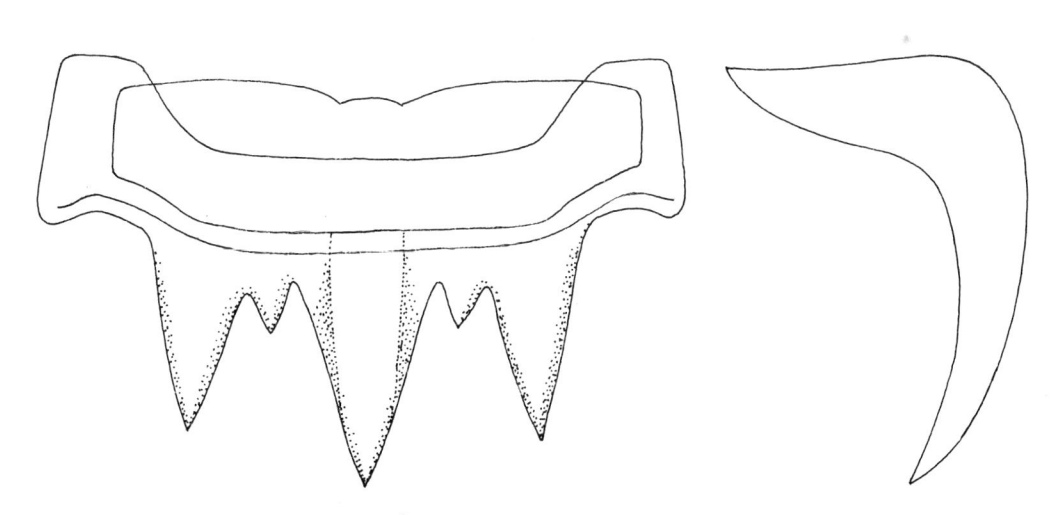

19. *Chicoreus florifer*, radular dentition

ward from one of the coarse teeth. The columellar lip is arched and weakly erect. The siphonal canal is moderately broad above, tapering below to a distal tubelike portion, narrowly, medially open, and terminally recurved.

The body whorl bears three foliaceous varices. Other axial sculpture consists of one major costa and one or two minor intervarical costae, these most prominent at the shoulder. Spiral sculpture consists of numerous spiral cords and minutely tuberculate threads. Where the strongest cords intersect the varices, numerous short to moderately long, foliaceous, open spines are developed, the shoulder spine the longest. Above this, between the shoulder edge and the suture, there are three or four moderately long, straight spines. Below the shoulder, on the body, six moderately long, ventrally bent spines are developed. Four longer, straight spines are developed on the canal. In addition, all regions bear small intercalating spinelets.

The shell is white through pinkish to pale rust-brown and dark purple-brown, the varices sometimes darker. The interior of the aperture is often suffused with pink or vivid purple.

Specimens from Caribbean populations are darker brown and have a longer shoulder spine, and all spines are unbent.

Cape Hatteras, North Carolina, and the northern Gulf of Mexico to northern Cuba and the northwestern Bahama Islands.

See Pl. 6, figs. 6–7.

Chicoreus gubbi (Reeve, 1849)
Murex gubbi Reeve, 1849: sp. 193

The shell is moderately small (maximum length 50 mm) and fusiform. Its spire is high, consisting of eight shouldered postnuclear whorls and a protoconch of undetermined nature. The suture is impressed. The body whorl is large, and trigonal in outline. The aperture is subovate, with its parietal margin almost straight and its anal sulcus delimited by a strong tubercle at the posterior end of the outer lip. The outer apertural lip is thickened and weakly, marginally dentate, its inner surface bearing six large, medially grooved tubercles; above these tubercles is a deep channel leading into the open shoulder spine. The columellar lip is smooth, completely adherent above, and partially detached and weakly erect below. The siphonal canal is moderately short, narrowly open, and straight, except for its distally recurved end.

The body whorl bears three foliaceously ornamented varices. Additional axial sculpture consists of a single prominent intervarical costa, this strongly nodose at the shoulder. Spiral sculpture consists of strong cords and major and minor threads. Where the cords intersect the varices, moderately long, distally foliated spines are developed. The upturned and dorsally bent shoulder spine is by far the longest. Below it on the body, four shorter, straight spines are developed, and the canal bears two similar spines. On the spire only the long shoulder spine is retained.

The shell is a uniform light chocolate-brown, the ventral surfaces of the varices much lighter.

West Africa. Little is known about the distribution of this species. According to recently received information, native fishing boats have collected *C. gubbi* off Ghana, West Africa.

See Pl. 6, fig. 11.

Chicoreus insularum (Pilsbry, 1921)
Murex torrefactus var. *insularum* Pilsbry, 1921: 319

The shell is moderately large (maximum length 95 mm), heavy, and rhomboid. The spire is high, consisting of one and one-half nuclear whorls and seven convex postnuclear whorls. The suture is impressed. The body whorl is solid and very heavy. The aperture is subcircular, with an anal sulcus delimited parietally by a strong, knobby spiral ridge. The outer apertural lip is erect and marginally finely dentate, its interior lirate. The columellar lip is detached and moderately erect. The siphonal canal is short, bent to the left, tapering anteriorly, and distally recurved.

The body whorl bears three foliose varices. Other axial ornamentation consists of a single very large, knoblike intervarical ridge. Spiral sculpture consists of cords of varying degrees of strength and fine, scabrous threads. Where the cords intersect the varices, stout, straight, moderately long, foliated spines are developed. The shoulder spine, the longest, is bent posteriorly. The second and third spines are progressively more dorsally oriented, forming, as in *C. brunneus*, an arc of spines. Below this arc, on the body, is a pair of straight spines. Two moderately long, straight spines are developed on the canal.

Shell color is light brown, with darker rusty brown on the spiral elements. The aperture is porcelaneous white.

Apparently endemic in the Hawaiian Island chain.

See Pl. 5, fig. 4.

Chicoreus maurus (Broderip, 1833)

Murex maurus Broderip, 1833: 174; *M. steeriae* Reeve, 1845: sp. 16; *M. thomasi* Crosse, 1872: 212

The shell is moderately large (maximum length 90 mm) and broadly rhomboid. The spire is high, with eight weakly convex postnuclear whorls and a protoconch of undetermined nature. The suture is impressed. The body whorl is heavy and broadly fusoid. The aperture is ovate and moderately broad, with a narrow, deep, inverted-V-shaped anal sulcus, this delimited parietally by a strong spiral ridge. The outer apertural lip is erect, arising briefly from the last varix, and strongly dentate; the teeth extend into the aperture as strong lirations, and between the teeth the lip margin is minutely crenulate. The columellar lip is essentially completely adherent and bears, in addition to the strong ridge mentioned, a series of brief, moderately weak denticles in the parietal region. The siphonal canal is moderately short, anteriorly tapering, and distally recurved.

The body whorl bears three foliaceously ornamented varices. Additional axial sculpture consists of a single, strong, nodose intervarical ridge. Spiral sculpture consists of major and minor cords and numerous fine threads. All spiral elements bear low, vaulted scales, these represented in mature specimens by minute tubercles. Where the major cords cross the varices, moderately well-developed foliaceous spines are present. On the body whorl the shoulder spine is the longest, the second spine the most strongly recurved. In all, four major spines are evident, these decreasing in length anteriorly. On the spire only the shoulder spine is retained. At the base of the body whorl there is a short spineless gap, followed by three smaller spines on the siphonal canal.

Shell color consists of alternating white and dark-brown bands, the white bands much broader. The apertural margin and the ventral portion and cavities of the varical spines are red-violet.

Marquesas Islands, New Caledonia, Tuamotu Islands.

See Pl. 5, fig. 5.

Chicoreus microphyllus (Lamarck, 1816)

Murex microphyllus Lamarck, 1816: pl. 415, Liste p. 5; *M. torrefactus* Sowerby, 1841: pl. 199, fig. 120; *M. poirieri* Jousseaume, 1881: 349; *M. jousseaumei* Poirier, 1883: 58

The shell is moderately large (maximum length 110 mm) and fusiform. The spire is high, consisting of two and one-half nuclear whorls and nine convex postnuclear whorls. The suture is impressed. The body whorl is moderately large and somewhat elongate. The aperture is broadly ovate, with a broad, moderately deep anal sulcus, this reinforced by a spiral parietal ridge; in some cases, one or two other elongate ridges follow the topmost parietal ridge. The interior of the outer apertural lip, above the shoulder spine, bears three or four small, sharp lirae; below, the lip is slightly erect and finely denticulate, with lirations leading from these fine teeth into the aperture. The columellar lip is adherent except for its extreme anterior portion, which is slightly detached; the margin of the inner lip may be smooth, but in some cases numerous small nodules or denticles occur along its entire length. The siphonal canal is moderately long, strongly recurved, tapering anteriorly, and narrowly, centrally open.

The body whorl bears three low, foliose varices. Other axial sculpture consists of one to three intervarical ridges, these more or less tuberculate at the shoulder. Spiral sculpture consists of primary and secondary cords and numerous fine threads

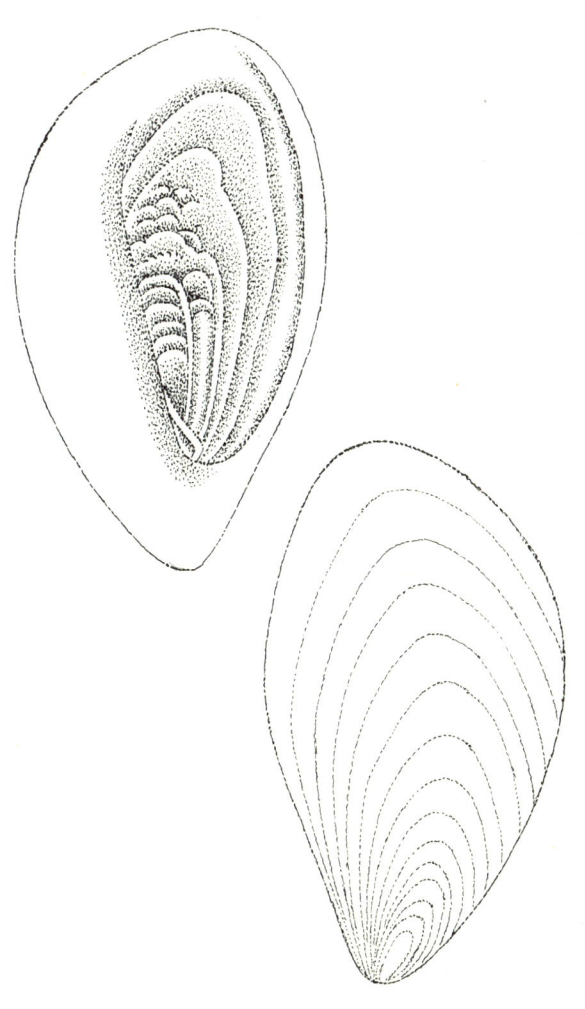

20. *Chicoreus microphyllus*, operculum

that may bear close-set scales or fine nodes. Where the cords intersect the varices, five or six primary and secondary short, foliated spines are developed, their length increasing anteriorly. A gap in spination occurs at the base of the body. Three spines found on the canal are similar to the spines above except that they arise closer to the rear edge of the varix. The uppermost of the three canal spines is sharply recurved.

Shell color is light brown to dark chestnut-brown, with darker color on the spiral cords. The aperture is generally white within, yellow-orange marginally.

Generally throughout the entire Indo-West Pacific.

See Pl. 4, fig. 7; Pl. 5, fig. 7.

Chicoreus palmarosae (Lamarck, 1822)

Triplex rosaria Perry, 1811: pl. 6, fig. 3; *Murex palmarosae* Lamarck, 1822: 161 (placed on ICZN official list, Opinion 911, 1970)

The shell is moderately large (maximum length 115 mm) and fusiform. The spire is high, consisting of nine convex postnuclear whorls and a protoconch of undetermined nature. The suture is impressed. The body whorl is moderate in size and fusoid. The aperture is broadly ovate, with an anal sulcus reinforced on both sides by a knobby ridge. The outer apertural lip is erect and finely dentate, with lirae extending into the aperture. The columellar lip is entirely adherent and bears numerous short, close-set, elongate denticles. The siphonal canal is long, moderately broad, and distally recurved.

The body whorl bears three ornately foliaceous varices. Additional axial sculpture consists of three low ridges in each intervarical space. Spiral sculpture consists primarily of weak cords of various widths, and fine, scabrous striae. The body portion of the shell bears four moderately long, broad, foliose spines. The shoulder spine, the longest, is hollow, distally bifurcate, and recurved. Below it there are three somewhat shorter spines. A wide gap divides the body spines from the three canal spines.

Shell color is ochre to light or dark brown, with the crests of the spiral elements darker. The apertural margin, including the spaces between the columellar denticles, is stained brown. In specimens from the vicinity of Ceylon, the interior of the frondose spines is suffused with lavender or violet. Specimens from other localities have brown-stained spines.

Ceylon to the Philippines and southwestern Japan.

See Pl. 5, fig. 2.

Chicoreus penchinati (Crosse, 1861)

Murex penchinati Crosse, 1861: 351

The shell is moderate in size (maximum length 50 mm) and fusiform. The spire is high, consisting of eight or nine convex postnuclear whorls and a protoconch of undetermined nature. The suture is impressed. The body whorl is moderately large and fusoid. The aperture is ovate, with an anal sulcus delimited parietally by a strong spiral ridge followed by two weaker ones. The outer apertural lip is slightly erect and finely dentate, its interior surface bearing short lirae extending from the teeth into the aperture. The columellar lip is barely detached. The siphonal canal is moderately short, broad, narrowly open, slightly bent, and distally recurved.

The body whorl bears three foliaceous varices. Other axial sculpture consists of a single moderately strong intervarical ridge, this nodose at the shoulder, and one or two weaker costae. Spiral sculpture consists of major and minor cords and numerous threads. Where the cords intersect the varices, short, open, foliaceous spines of equal length are developed. The major spines, arising from the major cords, are slightly ventrally bent. Intercalating minor spines arise from the minor cords and are more ventrally bent. Seven spines occur on the body, and three or four may be developed on the canal. All spines bear three to five fine striae.

Ground color of the shell is rusty pink, with the varical spines more intensely colored and the spiral cords red-brown. The apertural margin is bright pink.

Ryukyu Islands and seas between Japan and the northern Philippines.

See Pl. 6, fig. 4.

Chicoreus ramosus (Linné, 1758)

Murex ramosus Linné, 1758: 747; *Purpura incarnata* Röding, 1798: 142

The shell is very large (maximum length 300 mm) and massively fusiform. The spire is low, consisting of one and one-half nuclear whorls and nine strongly convex postnuclear whorls. The suture is impressed. The body whorl is large and inflated. The aperture is large and broadly ovate, with a broad anal sulcus, this delimited parietally by a strong spiral ridge. The outer apertural lip is erect, projecting more or less strongly beyond the last varix, and strongly, coarsely dentate, bearing a large, triangular labial tooth anteriorly; the lip interior is briefly, weakly lirate. The columellar lip is adherent above, detached and weakly erect below. The siphonal canal is broad, moderately long, tapering anteriorly, distally recurved, and narrowly open at its extreme right side.

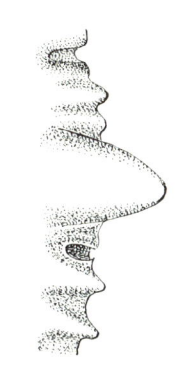

21. *Chicoreus ramosus*, labial tooth (ceratus)

The body whorl bears three foliaceously ornamented varices. Additional axial sculpture consists of one narrow major intervarical ridge and, generally, one or two minor ones. Spiral sculpture consists of broad, weak, spiral cords and fine, scabrous threads. Where the cords intersect the varices, strong, moderately long, distally foliated, closed spines are developed. The leading edge of each spine is filled with thin lamellae. The shoulder spine, the longest, is distally recurved. Below this are four somewhat shorter, straighter spines of equal length. Two similar spines are developed on the canal. Smaller intercalating spinelets are bent ventrally. On the spire whorls only the long shoulder spine is retained.

Shell color is white, stained with pale rusty pink, the color strongest on the intervarical ridges and on the crests of the spiral threads. The apertural margin is suffused with light to medium red or red-orange, the color covering the entire columella and a narrower band at the edge of the interior of the outer lip.

Generally throughout the entire Indo-West Pacific.

See Pl. 4, fig. 8.

Chicoreus rossiteri (Crosse, 1872)

Murex rossiteri Crosse, 1872: 74; *Chicoreus saltatrix* Kuroda, 1964: 129

The shell is moderately small (maximum length 55 mm) and fusiform. The spire is moderately high, consisting of seven convex postnuclear whorls and a protoconch of undetermined nature. The suture is impressed. The body whorl is moderately small and fusiform. The aperture is broadly ovate, with a small anal sulcus, this reinforced parietally by a major and a minor spiral ridge. The outer apertural lip bears several fine lirae immediately below the anal sulcus, and is erect and finely dentate, the teeth becoming lirae extending into the aperture. The columellar lip is erect and marginally denticulate, the size of the denticles diminishing anteriorly; the last three or four denticles follow an oblique line from the lip margin to a point deeper in the aperture. The siphonal canal is long, arched to the left, and distally recurved.

The body whorl bears three low, foliaceous varices. Other axial sculpture consists of a large intervarical ridge, nodose at the shoulder to the right and a smaller ridge, not nodose, to the left. Spiral sculpture consists of numerous finely scabrous spiral threads. A small number of these threads are more prominent; where these intersect the varices, short to moderately long foliose spines are developed. On the upper portion of the body, four small, weak, tightly bunched spines are developed. Below this on the body are two moderately long, open spines. A moderately broad space separates the body spines from the two or three moderately long, open, somewhat recurved, canal spines.

Shell color is pinkish-orange, strongest on the varices and the intervarical ridges, paler on the spire. The apertural margin is bright red-violet.

Southeastern Japan to the Fiji Islands and Lifou, Loyalty Islands.

See Pl. 4, fig. 6.

Chicoreus rubescens (Broderip, 1833)

Murex rubescens Broderip, 1833: 174

The shell is small (maximum length 45 mm) and biconic. The spire is moderately high, consisting of six or seven shouldered postnuclear whorls and a protoconch of undetermined nature. The suture is weakly impressed. The body whorl is small and fusoid. The aperture is moderately small and ovate, with a small, shallow anal sulcus, this delimited parietally by a spiral ridge extending more deeply into the aperture. The outer apertural lip is nonerect and weakly dentate, its interior bearing elongate denticles. The columellar lip is slightly detached and barely erect. The siphonal canal is moderately long, tapering anteriorly, and bent to the left.

The body whorl bears three strong, broad,

rounded varices, which are spinose only anteriorly and bent to the left. Other axial sculpture consists of a single broad, strongly developed costa in each intervarical space, almost completely occupying the space. Spiral sculpture consists of five strong, rounded cords on the body: one on the shoulder slope, one at the shoulder edge, one medial, and two more, closely spaced at the base of the body. There are also two cords on the canal. The entire surface of the shell is finely, spirally striate. Where the paired spirals at the base of the body and on the canal intersect the varices, moderately short, closed spines are developed.

Shell color is deep orange-red, suffused with red-brown on the spiral cords where they cross the axial sculptural elements.

Originally said to have been collected by Hugh Cuming "ad insulam Taheiten" (Tahiti Island); no live-collected specimens have come to our attention.

See Pl. 6, fig. 5.

Chicoreus rubiginosus (Reeve, 1845)

Murex rubiginosus Reeve, 1845: sp. 32

The shell is large (maximum length 130 mm) and robustly fusiform. The spire is high, consisting of eight or nine postnuclear whorls and a protoconch of undetermined nature. The suture is impressed. The body whorl is moderately large and fusoid. The aperture is broadly ovate, with an anal sulcus delimited by a parietal spiral ridge. The outer apertural lip is weakly erect and finely dentate, the teeth becoming short lirae extending into the aperture; there is a deep furrow into the shoulder spine. The columellar lip is adherent, smooth, and somewhat thickened. The siphonal canal is moderately short, narrowly open, bent to the left, and distally recurved.

The body whorl bears three foliaceous varices. Other axial sculpture consists of one moderately strong intervarical ridge, tuberculate at the shoulder. Spiral sculpture consists of major and minor cords and finely nodulose spiral threads. Where the cords cross the varices short, distally foliated spines are developed. The body whorl bears five strong, slightly recurved spines, these intercalated with ventrally bent smaller spinelets. The canal bears three straight, major spines.

Shell color ranges from pale flesh to rich orange and to dark chestnut, the color most intense on the varices, spines, and spiral elements. The interior of the spines is often a golden yellow, rich vermilion-pink, or violet. The interior of the aperture is yellow-orange, strongest on the columella.

Southeastern Japan to Australia, most common in northwestern Australia.

See Pl. 6, fig. 10.

Chicoreus saulii (Sowerby, 1841)

Murex saulii Sowerby, 1841: pl. 190, fig. 77

The shell is moderately large (maximum length 100 mm) and fusiform. The spire is high, consisting of nine convex postnuclear whorls and a protoconch of undetermined nature. The suture is impressed. The body whorl is moderate in size, elongate, and relatively slender. The aperture is broadly ovate, with a deep, thick-walled U-shaped anal sulcus, this reinforced on both sides by two strong denticles; to the left of the anal sulcus a smooth, white, thickened callus pad extends to the uppermost varical spine of the corresponding varix of the previous whorl. The outer apertural lip is erect and dentate, with lirae extending from the fine marginal teeth into the interior of the aperture; the margin of the outer lip is notably indented at the point of development of each varical spine. The columellar lip is briefly detached and barely erect. The siphonal canal is moderately long, narrowly open to the right, and strongly, distally recurved.

The body whorl bears three prominent, foliaceous varices. Additional axial sculpture consists of a strong ridge centrally placed in each intervarical space and one or two weak costae flanking it. The costae, including the ridge noted above, are nodose at the shoulder. Spiral sculpture consists of major and minor cords covered with fine, minutely scabrous threads, these most numerous on the major cords. Where the cords intersect the varices, moderately long, foliose, open spines are developed. Four primary, weakly recurved spines are developed on the body, the shoulder spine much the strongest and somewhat longer than the rest. Intercalated with these are five small, ventrally bent secondary spinelets. In addition, two secondary spinelets occur between the shoulder spine and the second spine, and a single spinelet is found after each of the other major spines. Following a broad spine-free gap, three major and two minute minor spines are developed on the canal; the upper major spine is moderately long, slender, and recurved, the middle one is longer and stronger, and the third is short and bent anteriorly.

Shell color is light rusty orange-brown, with the apertural margin and the interior of the spines a bright purple-pink. The crests of the spiral threads are dark brown.

Ryukyu Islands, perhaps south to New Guinea. See Pl. 5, fig. 8.

Chicoreus spectrum (Reeve, 1846)

Murex spectrum Reeve, 1846: sp. 187; *M. imbricatus* Higgins & Marrat, 1878: 413 (not Brocchi, 1814); *M. argo* Clench & Pérez Farfante, 1945: 31, new name for *M. imbricatus* Higgins & Marrat, 1878 (not Brocchi, 1814)

The shell is large (maximum length 120 mm) and elongate-fusiform. The spire is high, consisting of eight or nine convex postnuclear whorls and a protoconch of undetermined nature. The suture is deeply impressed. The body whorl is comparatively small, elongate, relatively slender, and fusoid. The aperture is ovate, with a narrow, U-shaped anal sulcus on the shoulder, close to the suture. The outer apertural lip is erect and coarsely dentate, with brief, ephemeral lirae extending from these teeth into the aperture. The columellar lip is detached and weakly erect. The siphonal canal is moderately long, narrowly open to the right, and distally tapering.

The body whorl bears three prominent, foliaceous varices. Other axial sculpture consists of four to six low costae in each intervarical space. Spiral sculpture consists of four to six low cords in each intervarical space and numerous, finely nodulose, major and minor spiral threads, these grouped into stronger cords. Where the cords intersect the varices, moderately long, slightly recurved, distally foliated spines are developed. On the body whorl, the shoulder spine is the longest and heaviest. Below this are, in succession, a small spine, another major spine, another small spine, and two moderately long major spines. Between the body and the canal, a region that is spineless in many species of *Chicoreus*, are two very small spinelets. The canal bears three major spines, these decreasing anteriorly in both length and degree of recurvature.

Shell color is ochre-yellow, overlaid by a deep brown imparted by the darker coloration of the spiral threads. Some dead-collected specimens are rich red-brown. The aperture is white.

Greater Antilles to south-central Brazil.

See Pl. 5, fig. 1.

Chicoreus territus (Reeve, 1845)

Murex territus Reeve, 1845: sp. 167

The shell is of moderate size (maximum length 75 mm) and fusiform. The spire is high, consisting of two nuclear whorls and seven convex postnuclear whorls. The suture is impressed. The body whorl is comparatively large. The aperture is moderately large and ovate, with a moderately shallow, inverted-V-shaped anal sulcus, this parietally delimited by a spiral ridge. The outer apertural lip is strongly erect and finely dentate, with lirae extending into the aperture from the denticles. The columellar lip is detached and barely erect. The siphonal canal is moderately long, narrowly open to the right, bent to the right, and distally recurved.

The body whorl bears three frondose varices. Other axial sculpture consists of major and minor cords separated by deep channels, and numerous fine threads covering the entire shell. Where the cords intersect the varices, four moderately long, open, recurved spines and several smaller intercalary spines are developed. For about half of their length, these spines are fused to form a prominent varical webbing, fringing the entire body region. The shoulder spine is the longest. Canal spinatation follows that of the body without the typical spine-free gap. There are three or four moderately long, unfused, anteriorly bent spines on the canal.

The shell is white to pinkish brown, with darker, rust-colored maculations scattered over the surface on the crests of the spiral cords.

Queensland and New South Wales, Australia.

See Pl. 6, fig. 9.

Chicoreus trivialis (A. Adams, 1854)

Murex trivialis A. Adams, 1854: 71

The shell is moderately small (maximum length 55 mm) and rhomboid. The spire is high, consisting of nine convex postnuclear whorls and a protoconch of undetermined nature. The suture is obscured by the extension of the succeeding whorl. The body whorl is moderately large and broadly fusoid. The aperture is small and ovate, with a small, shallow anal sulcus, this delimited by a spiral parietal ridge. The outer apertural lip is barely erect and finely dentate, with short lirae extending from the denticles briefly into the aperture. The columellar lip is smooth and entirely adherent. The siphonal canal is narrowly open to the right and distally recurved.

The body whorl bears three prominently foliaceous varices. Other axial sculpture consists of a single intervarical ridge, this nodose at the shoulder. Spiral sculpture consists of major cords and threads of primary and secondary strength. Where the cords and primary threads intersect the varices, short to moderately long foliose spines are developed. The orientation of the spines suggests that of *C. brunneus*. Following two very small major spines on the shoulder slope, three open, foliose spines form a progressively dorsally bent arc. Below this arc, three similar spines form the reverse (i.e. ventrally bent) arc. The crowded spination has the appearance of a varical fringe or webbing, though the spines are separate. Small, ventrally bent spinelets alternate with the major spines on the body.

Shell color is dark brown, with the spiral threads, varices, and intervarical ridges entirely black. A pale brown to white suprasutural band is a prominent feature, as is the rosy pink apertural margin.

This species may be readily distinguished from *C. brunneus* Link, 1807, which it superficially resembles, by its higher spire and the light-colored suprasutural band obscuring the suture.

Northwestern Australia.

See Pl. 6, fig. 12.

Genus **DERMOMUREX** Monterosato, 1890

TYPE SPECIES: *Murex scalarinus* Bivona-Bernardi, 1832 (=*M. scalaroides* Blainville, 1829), by original designation.

This genus includes species with moderately small, solid, generally fusiform shells. The first few postnuclear whorls resemble those of *Aspella*; subsequent whorls are more circular in cross section than in that genus. The spire is high and moderately to strongly acute. The body whorl is of moderate size (half the total shell length) and moderately broad. The siphonal canal is of moderate length and more or less dorsally recurved. The body whorl bears three or four more or less heavy, ropelike varices. Earlier whorls have six varices, two or three becoming reduced to weak costae or completely disappearing on the body whorl. Spiral sculpture generally consists of five to eight more or less well-developed cords which may be heavy and ropelike (*D. pauperculus, D. myrakeenae*) or narrower and more sharply bladelike (*D. scalaroides, D. cunninghamae*). A series of finer threads may be present on the siphonal canal. Shell color is generally translucent milk-white to waxy yellow-white, in some species with narrow, red-brown spiral bands alternating with the spiral cords. A thick, white, finely axially striate or minutely reticulate intritacalx is covered, in uneroded specimens, by a fine, thin, pale-yellow or buff periostracum.

Dermomurex abyssicola (Crosse, 1865)

Murex abyssicola Crosse, 1865: 30

The shell, to judge from the original illustration, is small (ca. 12 mm long) and broadly fusiform. The spire is moderately high, consisting of five or six convex or weakly shouldered postnuclear whorls and a protoconch reportedly of one and one-half whorls. The suture is impressed. The body whorl is moderately large and broadly trigonal. The aperture is moderately large and ovate, with no perceptible anal sulcus. The outer apertural lip is barely erect, if at all. The columellar lip is adherent. The siphonal canal is moderately long, narrowly open, and bent weakly to the right and dorsally at the tip.

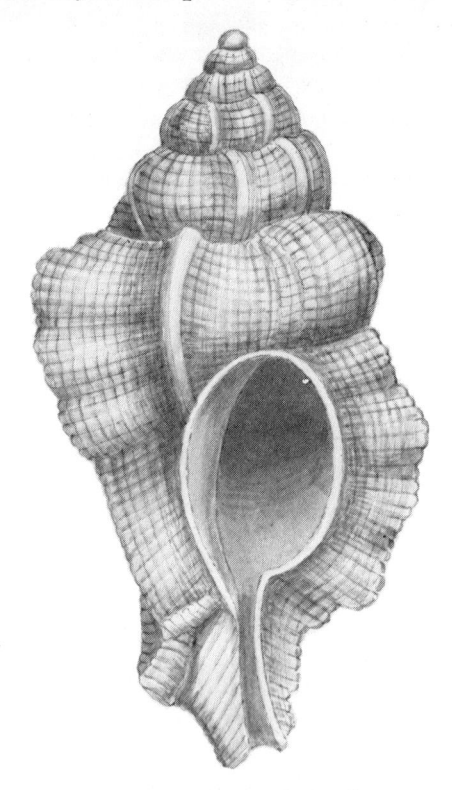

22. Dermomurex abyssicola

The body whorl bears three weakly developed varical flanges. Earlier whorls bear six varices. Spiral sculpture is limited to four broad cords, these apparent only on the receding side of each varix.

The shell color is reportedly corneous brown, in places seemingly whitish. The fine scratches mentioned in the description and shown in the figure probably are indicative of a fine, flat-white, minutely reticulate intritacalx, covered by a buff-colored periostracum, much like that seen in related species.

The figure suggests that this species is closest to *D. cunninghamae* (Berry) and may prove to be a western Atlantic cognate of that species.

Known to us only from the type locality, Guadeloupe, French West Indies.

Dermomurex bakeri (Hertlein & Strong, 1951)

Aspella bakeri Hertlein & Strong, 1951: 79

The shell is of moderate size for the genus (maximum length 22 mm) and lanceolate. The spire is high and acute, consisting of two and one-half nuclear whorls and six or seven moderately dorsoventrally flattened postnuclear whorls. The suture is impressed but is largely obscured by varical buttresses. The body whorl is of moderate size (about one-half of the total shell length) and fusoid. The aperture is ovate and moderately large for the genus, with a barely perceptible anal sulcus. The outer apertural lip is strongly thickened and somewhat flaring, its interior bearing a series of five weak denticles, these diminishing in strength posteriorly; the uppermost denticle, interior to the shoulder margin, is generally obsolete. The columellar lip is smooth and entirely adherent. The siphonal canal is moderately long, narrowly open, bent slightly to the left, and dorsally recurved.

The varices are eight on the early whorls, diminishing in number to two or three on the body whorl. In unusual specimens as many as six of the eight original varices are persistent in the form of more or less prominent axial costae. Spiral sculpture consists of five cords on the body and three or four finer cords on the canal.

The shell is translucent white, with brown bands, the upper portion of the body entirely suffused with red-brown; the remaining three spiral cords are also red-brown, but the interspaces are white. A thick, flat-white, axially striate intritacalx covers the shell when not eroded; fine spiral tunnels honeycomb the intritacalx, and these are apparent as it erodes along fine spiral tracks. In specimens in which the axial costae are persistent on the body whorl, the intritacalx follows the costae to form erect lamellae on the canal.

Southern Gulf of California (Danizante I., Cabo Pulmo, Escondido Bay, La Paz, Cerralvo I.). See Pl. 1, figs. 18–19.

Dermomurex cunninghamae (Berry, 1964)

Trialatella cunninghamae Berry, 1964: 149

The shell is of moderate size (maximum length 16.5 mm) and broadly fusiform. The spire is high and acute, consisting of two and one-half tightly wound, convex nuclear whorls and five moderately shouldered postnuclear whorls. The suture is deeply impressed. The body whorl is moderately large (more than one-half the total shell length) and broadly fusoid. The aperture is of moderate size and roughly ovate, with no perceptible anal sulcus. The outer apertural lip is barely erect and scalloped in a pattern reflecting the spiral sculpture of the shell; just behind the lip the varix is moderately developed into thin, sharp varical "wings" or flanges, the scalloping again corresponding to the shell's spiral sculpture. The columellar lip is smooth and entirely adherent. The siphonal canal is moderately long, narrowly open, and dorsally recurved.

The body whorl bears three bladelike varices. Spiral sculpture consists of seven weak cords on the body, these more prominent on the varices and ephemeral between them.

The shell is pale waxy yellow-brown, covered by a moderately thick, flat-white, microscopically reticulate intritacalx. The aperture is porcelaneous pale brownish-white.

Berry (1964), in describing this species, made it the type species of a new genus, *Trialatella*. Although differing in species-level characters, *D. cunninghamae* does not differ generically from such forms as *D. myrakeenae*.

Known to us only from off San Carlos Bay, Sonora, Mexico, in 40 m or more.

See Pl. 1, fig. 20.

Dermomurex elizabethae (McGinty, 1940)

Aspella elizabethae McGinty, 1940: 63

The shell is of moderate size (maximum length 18 mm) and roughly lanceolate. The spire is high and acute, consisting of one and one-half convex, nuclear whorls and five slightly dorsoventrally flattened postnuclear whorls. The suture is impressed and is partly obscured by varical buttresses. The body whorl is of moderate size and roughly fusoid. The aperture is moderately small and ovate, with no perceptible anal sulcus. The outer apertural lip is not noticeably erect; its inner surface is smooth. The columellar lip is smooth and entirely adherent. The siphonal canal is moderately short, narrowly open, and more or less dorsally recurved.

The body whorl bears three moderately expanded varices. Spiral sculpture consists of four weak cords on the body and three finer threads on the canal.

The shell is translucent blue-white, covered by a thick, flat-white, predominantly axially striate intritacalx. The nuclear whorls are milk-white, and the aperture is a lustrous white.

This species differs in size, proportions, and number of varices from *D. pauperculus*, the only other western Atlantic *Dermomurex* with which it could be confused.

Known only from Middle Sambo Shoals (the type locality) and Sand Key, both off Key West, Florida and Bermuda.

See Pl. 1, figs. 15–16.

Dermomurex indentatus (Carpenter, 1857)

Murex erinaceoides var. *indentata* Carpenter, 1857: 527; *Aspella perplexa* Keen, 1958: 248

The shell is large for the genus (maximum length 31 mm), heavily fusiform and robust. The spire is high and acute, consisting of six or seven convex postnuclear whorls and a protoconch of undetermined nature. The suture is weakly impressed, where it is not completely obscured by strong, broad varical buttresses. The body whorl is of moderate size (one-half the total shell length) and broadly fusoid. The aperture is small and ovate, with a well-marked anal sulcus. The outer apertural lip is erect and flaring, and crenulated in a pattern reflecting the spiral shell sculpture; the inner surface of the outer lip bears six prominent denticles, the anterior and the most posterior both heavier and more prominent than the middle four (the posterior denticle is actually a reinforced knob delimiting the anal sulcus from the aperture). The columellar lip is smooth and entirely adherent. The siphonal canal is long, broad, narrowly open, and weakly dorsally recurved at its tip.

The body whorl bears three long, massive, ropelike varices and three secondary axial costae, these alternating with the varices. Spiral sculpture consists of seven moderate to very prominent cords on the body and four other, weaker cords on the canal.

Shell color is a dull, translucent, dirty white, with red-brown markings on the axial sculptural elements and a solid red-brown band at the shoulder margin. The shell is covered by a moderately thick, flat-white to brown-white, microscopically axially striate intritacalx; where axial growth lines in the intritacalx cross the spiral threads in the intritacalx, the entire layer appears minutely cancellate. A thin, pale-brown periostracum covers the entire shell.

Although long confused with *D. obeliscus*, just as that species has been confounded with *D. pauperculus*, this species has within recent years been recognized and collected alive in Panamá.

Mazatlán, Mexico, to Panamá.

See Pl. 1, fig. 17.

Dermomurex myrakeenae (Emerson & D'Attilio, 1970)

Aspella myrakeenae Emerson & D'Attilio, 1970: 89

The shell is of moderate size (maximum length 23 mm) and broadly fusiform. The spire is high and acute, consisting of one and one-half translucent, convex nuclear whorls and six or seven convex postnuclear whorls. The suture is impressed but is partially obscured by varical buttresses. The body whorl is large (more than one-half the total shell length) and fusoid. The aperture is moderately large for the genus and ovate, with a weak anal sulcus. The outer apertural lip is simple, with a cordlike outer surface. The inner surface of the outer apertural lip bears six low denticles, these increasing in prominence anteriorly; on the inner surface, in the shoulder region, there is a broad, low swelling. The columellar lip is smooth and entirely adherent, and bears a prominent, sharp, angular projection at the entrance to the canal. The siphonal canal is moderately long, narrowly open, and weakly dorsally recurved.

The body whorl bears four heavy, ropelike varices and one or two more or less prominent intervarical costae. On the earlier whorls all six axial elements are of equal strength. Spiral sculpture consists of six moderately heavy cords on the body and two or three on the canal; these are ephemeral in the narrow intervarical spaces and more prominent on each varix and on its receding leading edge.

Shell color is pale brown, broken up into spiral lines by the white coloration of the spiral cords; the brown color is strongest on the shoulder and may form a continuous red-brown band. The shell is covered by a moderately thick, flat-white, microscopically reticulate intritacalx, which in turn is covered by a transparent tan periostracum. The aperture is porcelaneous white.

Western Mexico (Mazatlán to Acapulco).

See Pl. 1, fig. 28.

Dermomurex obeliscus (A. Adams, 1853)

Murex obeliscus A. Adams, 1853: 269

The shell is large for the genus (maximum length 30 mm) and obelisk-shaped. The spire is high and subacute, consisting of one and one-half to two and one-half translucent, convex, rapidly enlarging nuclear whorls and seven or eight convex postnuclear whorls; these expand rapidly, imparting an exceptionally convex aspect to the overall spire. The suture is impressed and is obscured almost entirely by broad, heavy varical buttresses extending over the shoulder to the body of the earlier whorl. The body whorl is fusoid and of moderate size; its proportion of the shell length decreases in larger shells. The aperture is of moderate size and ovate, with a narrow, shallow anal sulcus. The outer apertural lip is barely, if at all, erect, and broadly, obtusely crenulate; the inner surface of the outer lip bears six spirally elongate denticles. The columellar lip is smooth and entirely adherent. The siphonal canal is moderately short, straight, narrowly open, and strongly dorsally bent.

The early whorls bear six equally prominent, heavy, ropelike varices. In the last two or three whorls, the alternate varices are reduced, leaving three, these also heavy and alternating with three more or less prominent axial costae. Spiral sculpture consists of five low, broad cords, these prominent before and on each varix and obsolete between them. In addition, numerous fine threads cover the shell.

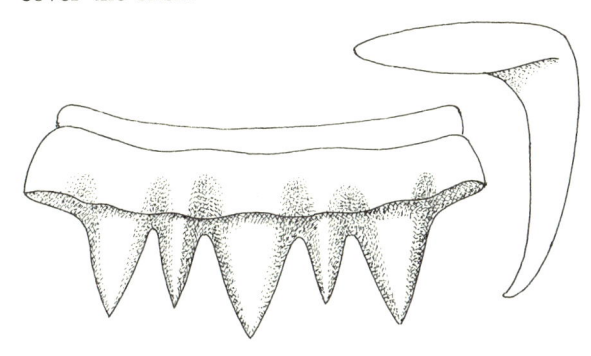

23. *Dermomurex obeliscus*, radular dentition

Shell color is white, with narrow, interrupted, red-brown bands following the cords; the bands are apparent where the cords are prominent, i.e. on and around varices and costae and on varical buttresses. The entire shell is covered by a thick, flat-white, minutely reticulate intritacalx; the thickness of this layer imparts a grossness to the coarsely wrinkled surface, an appearance that is enhanced by the strong emphasis produced on all sculptural elements by this deposition.

Mazatlán, Mexico, to Puntarenas, Costa Rica.
See Pl. 1, figs. 21–24.

Dermomurex pauperculus (C. B. Adams, 1850)

Murex pauperculus C. B. Adams, 1850: 60

The shell is moderately large for the genus (maximum length 24 mm) and roughly fusiform. The spire is high, consisting of one and one-half convex, translucent nuclear whorls and five convex postnuclear whorls. The suture is impressed where it is not covered by buttresslike expansions of the varices. The body whorl is moderately large and fusoid. The aperture is moderately large and ovate, with a broad, very shallow anal sulcus. The outer apertural lip is barely, if at all, erect; the inner surface of the outer lip bears ten spirally elongate, weak denticles. The columellar lip is smooth and entirely adherent. The siphonal canal is of moderate length, narrowly open, and strongly dorsally recurved.

The body whorl bears three heavy, ropelike varices, with a weaker intervarical costa between each two varices. Spiral sculpture consists of five strong cords on the body, three somewhat weaker ones on the upper canal, and four threads on the lower canal. All spiral elements are strongest before and on each varix but are not much weaker intervarically.

The shell is a translucent milk-white, covered with a thick, flat-white, microscopically reticulate or cancellate intritacalx. The aperture is porcelaneous white.

Miami and St. Petersburg, Florida, to Cyril's Bay, Trinidad.
See Pl. 1, figs. 25–26.

Dermomurex scalaroides (Blainville, 1829)

Murex scalaroides Blainville, 1829: 131; *M. scalarinus* Bivona-Bernardi, 1832: 22; *M. distinctus* Cristofori & Jan, 1832: 11; *M. leucoderma* Scacchi, 1836: 11; *M. scalariformis* Locard, 1886: 224

The shell is of moderate size (maximum length 18 mm) and roughly fusiform. The spire is high, consisting of two convex nuclear whorls and six convex, shouldered postnuclear whorls. The suture is impressed but partially obscured by weak varical buttresses. The body whorl is of moderate size and roughly fusoid. The aperture is moderately small and ovate, with a barely perceptible anal sulcus. The outer apertural lip is barely, if at all, erect; its inner surface bears seven low denticles, five evenly spaced and the anterior pair closely bunched, the denticles increasing in prominence anteriorly. The columellar lip is smooth and entirely adherent. The siphonal canal is moderately short and slender, straight, narrowly open, and slightly dorsally recurved.

The body whorl bears three to six varices. The strongest three (those that are never missing) are: one at the apertural margin, one opposite it on the left of the aperture, and a third midway on the dorsum. One or more of the other varices may be more or less prominent. Spiral sculpture consists of five or six more or less heavy, broad, low cords on the body, these ephemeral between the varices and strongly developed just before and on the receding edge of the moderately expanded flange of the latest varix.

The shell is a translucent milky-white, covered by a thick, flat-white, minutely cancellate intritacalx and a thin, pale-brown periostracum. The aperture is porcelaneous white.

Known to us from the Mediterranean in the area around Sicily.

See Pl. 1, fig. 27.

Genus **ERGALATAX** Iredale, 1931

TYPE SPECIES: *E. recurrens* Iredale, 1931 (=*Buccinum contractum* Reeve, 1846), by original designation.

The shell in this genus is small to moderate in size, solid, and roughly fusiform. The varices, numbering one to four, are low and appear at erratic intervals. The aperture is weakly emarginate, the anal sulcus more or less well-developed. The moderately short siphonal canal is open. Sculpture consists primarily of spiral cords and finer striae crossed by varices.

Kuroda and Habe (1971) have erected a new subfamily, Ergalataxinae, in which they have placed members of the genera *Ergalatax*, *Bedevina* Habe, 1946, and *Cytharomorula* Kuroda, 1953. There seems to be some likelihood that this is a heterogeneous taxon; in any case, in our opinion the diagnosis does not suggest a group of sufficient distinctness to warrant its own subfamilial name.

Ergalatax contracta (Reeve, 1846)

Buccinum contractum Reeve, 1846: sp. 53; *Urosalpinx innotabilis* E. A. Smith, 1879: 201; *U. smithi* Schepman, 1911: 351; *Ergalatax recurrens* Iredale, 1931: 231

The shell is of moderate size (maximum length 42 mm) and fusiform. The spire is high, consisting of six or seven subangulate postnuclear whorls and a protoconch of undetermined nature. The suture is impressed. The body whorl is of moderate size and fusoid. The aperture is moderately large and ovate, with a prominent anal sulcus, this very briefly extended posteriorly. The outer apertural lip is barely erect and minutely serrate; its inner surface bears seven transversely elongate denticles, the spaces between which diminish anteriorly. The columellar lip is lightly callused and entirely adherent, the anterior end of the columella bearing three more or less well-developed pustules. The siphonal canal is moderately short, open, straight, and dorsally recurved at its tip.

The body whorl bears one to four low, ropelike varices, these occurring at erratic intervals. Intervarical axial sculpture consists of varying numbers (zero to two) of low, ropelike ridges, these distinguished from the varices by their failure to swell into brief, spoutlike anal canals at their points of contact with the body whorl. Spiral sculpture consists of numerous cords of various strengths, these covering the shell from the suture to the tip of the canal. Growth lines in the form of fine lamellae are thrown into fine, scalelike projections between the spiral cords.

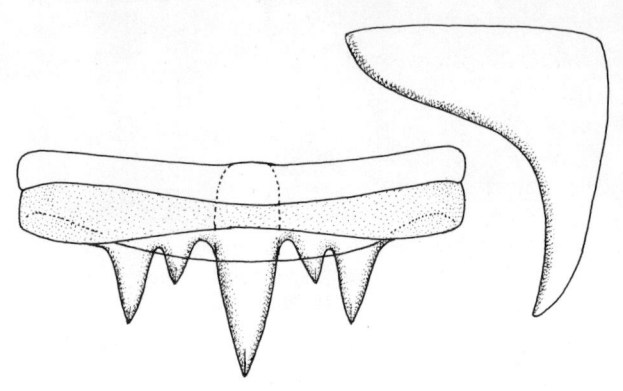

24. Ergalatax contracta, radular dentition

Shell color is variable, ranging from yellow-brown with darker red-brown stains on the strongest spiral cords and subsuturally, to purple-brown or blackish-brown with pale axial elements and alternating white-crested and dark-brown-black-crested strong spiral cords. The aperture is white or blue-white.

A chunky, truncate form from Japan (the typical form also occurs in Japan) has been named *Ergalatax calcareus* (Dunker, 1860) (Pl. 2, fig. 11, herein). Several different size ranges are exhibited.

The Indo-West Pacific, from Japan (Japan Sea and Kii) to Australia (New South Wales) and New Caledonia and to East Africa (Zanzibar).

See Pl. 2, figs. 10–12; Pl. 19, figs. 13, 18.

Ergalatax tokugawai Kuroda & Habe *in* Kuroda, Habe & Oyama, 1971

Ergalatax tokugawai Kuroda & Habe *in* Kuroda, Habe & Oyama, 1971: 151

The shell is of average size for the genus (ca. 18 mm in length) and fusiform. The spire is high and acute, consisting of two and one-half rounded, conical nuclear whorls and five subangulate to convex postnuclear whorls. The suture is impressed. The body whorl is of moderate size and fusoid. The aperture is of moderate size and narrowly ovate, with a shallow, moderately broad anal sulcus. The outer apertural lip is briefly erect and finely serrate, reflecting the spiral sculpture of the outer shell surface. The columellar lip is entirely adherent. The siphonal canal is very short, open, and weakly dorsally recurved.

The body whorl bears eight apparent varices, none of which shows a trace of the former apertural margin. The intervarical spaces are about equal to the varices in width. Spiral sculpture consists of about eight primary cords, these distributed from the shoulder to the tip of the canal and alternating with, for the first three primary cords, a series of three secondary cords. The remaining primary cords alternate with single secondary cords.

Shell color is pale yellow-brown, with transverse red-brown bands on the shoulder and just below the periphery of each whorl; the bands are interrupted by the ground-colored varices.

There is some question about the correct spelling of the trivial name of this species. It was originally described in *The Sea Shells of Sagami Bay*, a work printed in both Japanese and English. In the first (Japanese) section of the book the species was cited as *Ergalatax tokugawai* Kuroda & Habe (nov.); in the second section (English) it is cited as *Ergalatax tokugawa* Kuroda & Habe (nov.); and in the illustration section it is cited as it is in the Japanese section. In addition, the label of the type specimen we have seen employed the spelling with the final "i." It must be assumed that the omission of the letter "i" in the English-language section is a typographical error.

Honshu (Sagami Bay and Enshu-Nada), Japan. See Pl. 14, fig. 4.

Genus HAUSTELLUM Schumacher, 1817

TYPE SPECIES: *Murex haustellum* Linné, 1758, by tautonymy.

Variability in relatively minor characters, from one population to another and throughout the broad Indo-Pacific range of the type species of this genus, has led to the introduction of several superfluous specific names. The genus, typified by *M. haustellum* Linné, has a characteristically club-shaped shell with three varices. The two species now placed in *Bolinus*, a superficially similar genus, are restricted to the eastern Atlantic, and *Haustellum* is found only in the Indo-Pacific.

Haustellum haustellum (Linné, 1758)

Murex haustellum Linné, 1758: 746; *Murex longicaudus* F. C. Baker, 1891: 56; *Murex fallax* E. A. Smith, 1901: 113; *Murex kurodai* Shikama, 1964: 34

The shell is large (maximum length 150 mm) and club-shaped. Its spire is moderately low, with two and one-half nuclear whorls and seven shouldered postnuclear whorls. The suture is undulate and impressed. The body whorl is large, globose, and somewhat higher than broad. The aperture is subcircular; the narrowly U-shaped anal notch is constricted at its open end, and there is a very narrow opening anteriorly into the siphonal canal. The outer apertural lip is greatly thickened and a thinner shelf projects beyond it; the edge of this shelf bears 12 to 14 widely spaced crenulations corresponding in number to the lirae within the aperture. The columellar lip is adherent posteriorly; anteriorly, the lip is detached from the body whorl, forming a strongly erect inductura. The inner surface of the inductura as well as the columella is smooth and polished; the outer surface is unpolished and strongly sculptured with irregular ridges and bumps. The siphonal canal is longer than the remainder of the shell, straight, and barely open on the right side; on its left side is a strong ridge composed of the fused vestiges of former canals.

The body whorl bears three varices and three or four low axial costae in each intervarical space. The varices are rounded and aligned from whorl to whorl, raised and slightly sinuous above the shoulder and concave on their trailing edges. Spiral sculpture consists of five to seven primary spi-

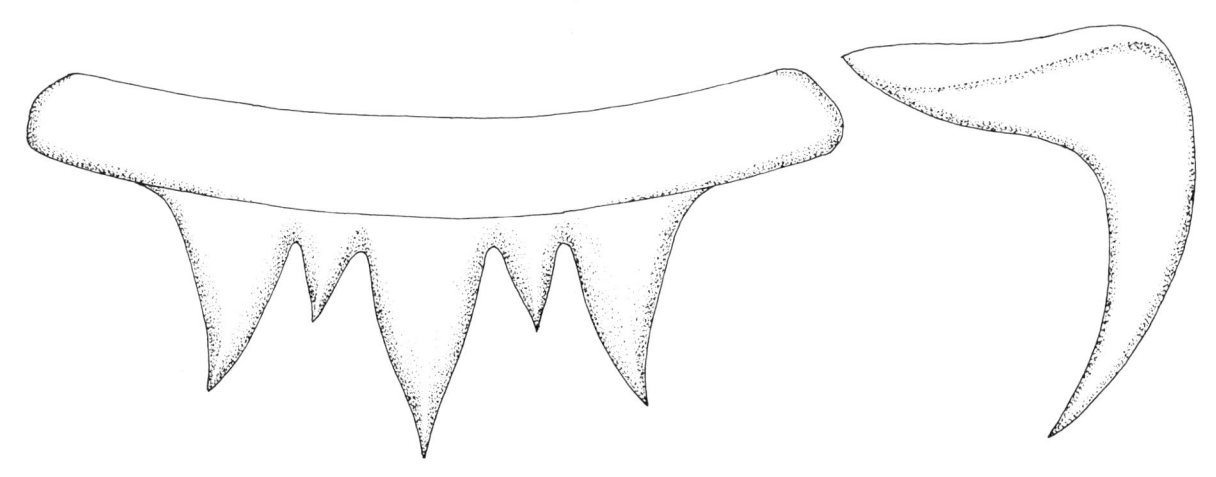

25. *Haustellum haustellum*, radular dentition

ral cords interspersed with numerous secondary threads. Where the primary cords cross the axial costae, prominent tubercles are developed. Five to seven spiral rows of sharp tubercles correspond to the primary spiral cords on the body whorl. The strongest row is at the shoulder-edge; four to six rows of weaker nodes are evenly spaced below it. The secondary threads cover the entire shell, including the surface of the varices. Axial canal sculpture consists of two axial grooves representing previous canal slits; spiral canal sculpture includes a continuation of the corded and threaded texture of the body whorl to a point less than halfway down the canal.

The ground color of the shell is white or warm flesh color. Three spiral bands of fine, chestnut-brown spiral lines are evenly spaced on the body whorl, most strongly and solidly developed on the varices and on the nodes of the intervarical axial costae. Isolated spiral brown lines may be found between these bands. The interior of the aperture is pale peach-pink.

Certain populations differ in several characters from the typical form. In these populations, given the names *H. longicaudus* (F. C. Baker, 1891), and *H. kurodai* Shikama, 1964, shells differ from those of the typical *H. haustellum* in having a channeled suture, in having developed a varical spine at the shoulder-edge and two spirally revolving rows of canal spines beginning immediately behind the inductura, and most prominently in a marked diminution of the secondary spiral threads and their associated brown lines. Specimens from some East African localities (*H. fallax*) show characters intermediate to both extreme forms.

Japan to eastern Australia, Red Sea (eastern Africa) to Fiji Islands (Cernohorsky, 1967).

See Pl. 11, fig. 10.

Haustellum wilsoni D'Attilio & Old, 1971

Haustellum wilsoni D'Attilio & Old, 1971: 316

The shell is of moderate size (maximum length 75 mm) and club-shaped. The spire is moderately high, consisting of two convex, polished nuclear whorls and seven strongly convex postnuclear whorls. The suture is impressed and situated in a deeply cut channel. The body whorl is moderately large and swollen. The aperture is ovate, its greatest diameter oriented at an angle to the long axis of the shell; the anal sulcus is small and shallow. The outer apertural lip is weakly erect and finely crenulate; its inner surface bears brief lirations. The columellar lip is callused and adherent above, detached and erect below. The siphonal canal is moderately short, straight, and barely open.

The body whorl bears three heavy, ropelike varices, these aligned up the spire to its apex. Intervarical axial sculpture consists of five broad, low costae, these moderately prominent at the shoulder, ephemeral on the lower half of the body, and nodulose over the major spiral cords. Spiral sculpture consists of eight major cords, these starting on the edge of the sutural channel and alternating with finer, non-nodulose cords. The entire shell surface appears finely malleated from innumerable irregularities in the axial and spiral elements.

The shell is pinkish-brown, with paler nodules. Three faint, transverse, brown bands may be seen, one at the shoulder margin, one medial on the body, and one basal. The aperture is pinkish-brown with a white margin. The edge of the outer lip bears an axial line of 12 red-brown dots, imparting a stitched appearance to the lip; this feature persists on preceding varices.

Central and southern coasts of western Australia.

See Pl. 23, fig. 15.

Genus HEXAPLEX Perry, 1811

TYPE SPECIES: *Hexaplex foliacea* Perry, 1811 (=*Murex cichoreum* Gmelin, 1791), by subsequent designation, Iredale, 1915.

The shell of *Hexaplex*, as typified by *H. cichoreum*, is solid and globose, with five to eight more or less foliaceous varices. The spire is moderate in height and the aperture is subcircular. The siphonal canal is moderately broad. Shell color generally consists of three darker bands on the body, although adult specimens may lack these.

The type species of *Hexaplex* strongly resembles many *Chicoreus* species, except for its larger number of varices. The radula also substantially resembles that found in *Chicoreus*. Future work may determine that these two groups should be united under the earliest available name, *Chicoreus* Montfort, 1810.

Hexaplex cichoreum (Gmelin, 1791)

Murex cichoreum Gmelin, 1791: 3530; *Hexaplex foliacea* Perry, 1811: pl. 8, fig. 4; *M. endivia* Lamarck, 1822: 168; *M. saxicola* Broderip, 1825: 202

The shell is moderately large (maximum length 130 mm). The spire is moderately high and acute, consisting of two nuclear whorls and six or seven convex postnuclear whorls. The suture is strongly

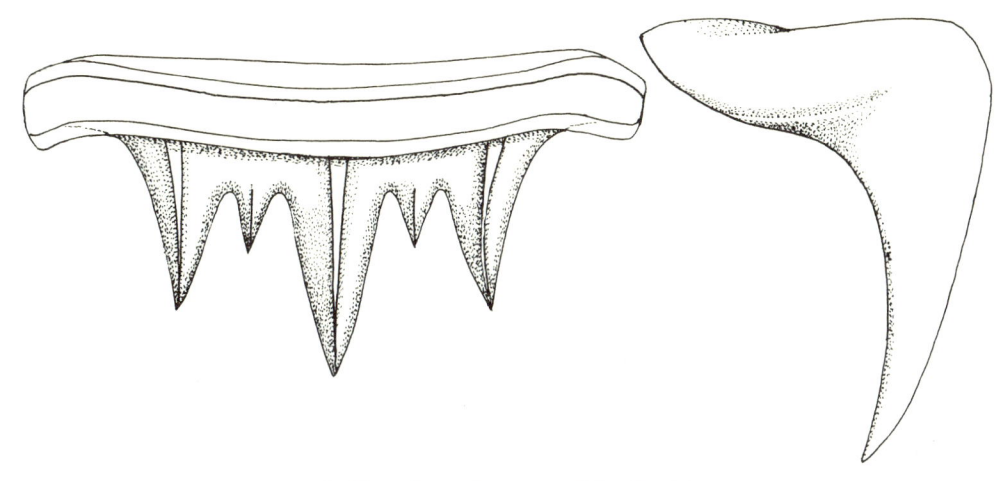

26. *Hexaplex cichoreum*, radular dentition

impressed. The body whorl is large and globose. The aperture is large and subcircular, with a broad, deep anal sulcus. The outer apertural lip is not erect, except for the coarsely dentate margin; the interior of the outer lip is smooth, and a prominent labial tooth is apparent toward the base of the body. The columellar lip is adherent above, weakly detached and barely erect below; its surface is smooth. The canal is short to moderately long, broad to moderately slender, bent to the right and dorsally, and very narrowly open to the right.

27. *Hexaplex cichoreum*, labial tooth (ceratus)

The body whorl bears five to eight (generally six) foliaceous varices. Intervarical axial sculpture consists of a single nodose ridge, this sometimes lacking in the newer portions of the shell. Spiral sculpture consists of five major cords alternating with six minor cords. Numerous fine threads cover the entire surface of the shell. Where the major and minor cords cross the varices, moderate to long foliated spines are developed. Major spines are strongly recurved; minor spines are ventrally bent.

Shell color is white or off-white, with broad, dark-brown transverse bands at the shoulder, medial on the body, and at the base of the body. The last of these bands covers the dorsal surface of the siphonal canal. The spines are predominantly brown. The color varies, occasional specimens being completely white. The aperture is white, and the apertural margin is fleshy pink-orange.

Limited to the Philippines.

See Pl. 7, figs. 16–17.

Hexaplex stainforthi (Reeve, 1843)

Murex stainforthi Reeve, 1843: 104

The shell is moderate in size (maximum length 65 mm) and globose-fusiform. The spire is of moderate height, consisting of two nuclear whorls and six convex postnuclear whorls. The suture is impressed in the earlier whorls, obscured by the succeeding whorl in the later whorls. The body whorl is large and globose. The aperture is subcircular, with a shallow, briefly spoutlike anal sulcus, this delimited parietally by a thickened ridge. The outer apertural lip is somewhat erect and finely dentate at its margin, with shallow lirae extending into the aperture. The columellar lip is entirely adherent and smooth. The siphonal canal is short and broad, essentially straight, and narrowly open to the right.

The body whorl bears eight low, briefly foliaceous varices. Intervarical axial sculpture is lacking. Spiral sculpture consists of numerous major and minor cords: two consecutive major cords in the shoulder region, five major cords alternating with minor cords, and two consecutive majors again at the base of the body. Where the cords intersect the varices, very short, briefly foliaceous spines are developed. The major spines are strongly recurved, the minor cords bent ventrally. The canal bears three or four somewhat longer recurved spines, these diminishing in length anteriorly. Numerous fine threads cover the cords.

Shell color is white or off-white, with dark-brown threads coloring the spines. At times the shell may be almost entirely orange or black. The aperture is pink to orange.

Northwestern Australia in shallow water.

See Pl. 7, figs. 1–2.

Genus HOMALOCANTHA Mörch, 1852

TYPE SPECIES: *Murex scorpio* Linné, 1758, by monotypy.

On the basis of the radula, operculum, and selected features of shell morphology, the concept of this genus has been broadened to include not only those species with palmately digitate shell projections, as in the type species, but also those with nonpalmate spines, such as *H. oxyacantha*.

The shells are of moderate size (maximum length 70 mm), and robustly or more narrowly fusiform. The spire is moderately low to moderately high, consisting of a comparatively extensive protoconch and three to five shouldered postnuclear whorls. The body whorl bears five to ten spinose varices. The spines may be distally palmate or nonpalmate. The suture is unimpressed but is set in an excavated region that is most apparent behind each strongly buttressed varical shoulder portion. The aperture is small to moderate in size and generally subcircular. The canal is lightly sealed by overlapping, or is very narrowly open. The anal sulcus is weakly indicated or entirely lacking. The columellar lip is detached, weakly erect, and smooth; at its anterior end it is thickened into a knob, the thickening resulting in the formation of an oblique sulcus leading directly into the siphonal canal. In profile, the ventral surface is more or less broadly arcuate.

The ocenebrine operculum is generally subcircular. The nucleus on its exterior surface is more or less near the right margin and halfway between the anterior and posterior ends. Opposite the nucleus, the interior surface has an oval, depressed area, and is irregularly, concentrically ridged; the remainder of the interior is somewhat thickened and polished.

The lateral radular teeth are typically muricoid and not unusual in size or other features. The rachidian tooth is muricine but is remarkable for the shortness and bluntness of its cusps. The central cusp is the longest, the laterals are almost as long, and the intermediates are so small and have become fused to such an extent with the laterals that they are generally little more than short appendages or simple lumps on their inner edges.

Homalocantha anatomica (Perry, 1811)

Hexaplex anatomica Perry, 1811: pl. 8, fig. 2; *Murex rota* Mawe, 1823: 131; *M. pele* Pilsbry *in* Pilsbry & Bryan, 1918: pl. 9, figs. 9, 12

The shell is moderately large for the genus (maximum length 60 mm) and fusiform. The spire is moderately low to moderately high, consisting of three and one-half smooth nuclear whorls, the first depressed into the second, and three and one-half shouldered postnuclear whorls. The suture is unimpressed, but the region surrounding the suture is deeply excavated. The body whorl is large, making up most of the visible shell, and fusoid. The aperture is subcircular to ovate, with a barely discernible anal sulcus. The outer apertural lip is strongly erect and finely dentate, and bears two or three coarser denticles reflecting the varical spines. The columellar lip is detached, weakly erect, and smooth; at its anterior end is an oblique sulcus followed by a thickening. The siphonal canal is moderately long, overlapping, very narrowly open to the right, and distally recurved.

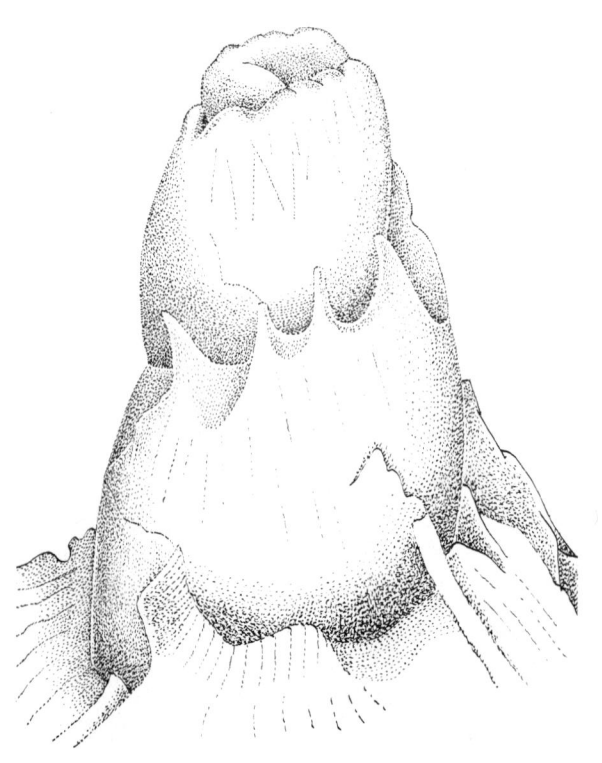

28. *Homalocantha anatomica*, protoconch

The body whorl bears five spinose varices. Other axial sculpture is lacking. Spiral sculpture consists of major and minor cords, these ephemeral between the varices, prominent only over the varices, where they are developed into moderately long, very narrowly open, distally broadly palmate digitations, the ends of these projections serrate. Starting immediately above the shoulder margin there is a spine of variable development, followed at the shoulder margin by the longest, broadest projection. Below this on the body there is another major digitation, followed by a fourth projection of variable development. Three spines, sharply diminishing in length anteriorly, may be found on the canal. On the shoulder, a thin, smooth webbing connects the uppermost spine to the preceding whorl. Segments of coarsely fimbriate webbing connect the ventral surfaces of the major spines and extend beyond the lowest spine.

Shell color is typically white, but in some individuals, especially those from Western Pacific populations, the shell may be suffused with violet or red-orange.

The Indian Ocean form, the most typical, generally exhibits four primary palmate digitations and a relatively broader body whorl. The form from Japan, the Hawaiian Islands, and elsewhere in the Western Pacific, distinguished by Pilsbry (1918) as *Murex pele,* differs in having only the second and third digitations strongly developed, although the first and fourth digitations are very variable in development and may be quite large in some specimens.

Eastern Africa and the Indian Ocean, throughout the western Pacific and the Hawaiian Islands. See Pl. 8, figs. 6–10.

Homalocantha melanamathos (Gmelin, 1791)

Murex melanamathos Gmelin, 1791: 3527

The shell is moderately small for the genus (maximum length 45 mm) and broadly fusiform. The spire is low, consisting of four or five convex postnuclear whorls and a protoconch of undetermined nature. The suture is obscured by the succeeding whorl, and the region around the suture is excavated, though not as broadly or as deeply as in other species of the genus. The body whorl is large and fusoid. The aperture is ovate, with a very shallow, almost imperceptible anal sulcus. The outer apertural lip is barely erect and finely dentate, with lirae extending from its margin into the aperture. The columellar lip is entirely adherent and smooth, with a thin callus extending over the parietal region; at its anterior end are an oblique sulcus and a tubercle. The siphonal canal is moderately long, narrowly open at the right, and distally recurved.

The body whorl bears seven spinose varices. Other axial sculpture is lacking. Spiral sculpture consists of cords of primary, secondary, and tertiary strength, and of finely scabrous threads. Where the cords intersect the varices, short, sharp, laterally compressed, narrowly open spines are developed, the prominence of the spines dependent on the type of cord from which they originate. Between spines, on the ventral surface of the varix, many horizontal laminae form a fimbriate webbing of the entire varical fringe, this webbing starting at the suture. On the body whorl are six primary spines, five secondary spines, and four tertiary spines; on the canal are two primary spines and one secondary spine.

Shell color is white, with the spiral elements brown between the varices, becoming black on the varix. The aperture and the upper half of the siphonal canal are white; the lower half of the canal is black-brown.

Western Africa (Dahomey to Angola). See Pl. 8, fig. 3.

Homalocantha oxyacantha (Broderip, 1833)

Murex oxyacantha Broderip, 1833: 176; *M. (Phyllonotus) stearnsii* Dall, 1918: 26

The shell is large for the genus (maximum length 60 mm) and broadly fusiform. The spire is moderately low, consisting of five shouldered postnuclear whorls and a protoconch of undetermined nature. The suture is obscured by the succeeding whorl, but the region surrounding the suture is deeply and broadly excavated. The body whorl is moderately large and fusoid. The aperture is small and subcircular, with no indication of an anal sulcus. The outer apertural lip is more or less erect and marginally, finely dentate, with brief lirae extending from the labial denticles into the aperture. The columellar lip is adherent, entire, and smooth; at its anterior end are an oblique sulcus and a knob. The siphonal canal is moderately long, very narrowly open at the right, and distally recurved.

The body whorl bears six to eight spinose varices. Other axial sculpture is lacking. Primary and secondary spiral cords become most prominent where they intersect the varices and are raised up to form short to moderately long, narrowly open, slender, sharply pointed spines, the first of these at the shoulder margin. Much finer tertiary cords are also present. Five primary, dorsally bent spines alternate with six smaller secondary, ventrally bent ones. Tertiary spinelets are interspersed, apparently randomly, among the spines, and finely squamose threads cover the varical area. The canal bears three or four primary spines, these diminishing in length anteriorly. The intervarical spaces are unusually narrow.

The shell is white on the spire and between the varices, and rusty brown on the varices and the spines. The aperture is white.

Guaymas, Mexico, to southern Ecuador.

See Pl. 8, figs. 14–15.

Homalocantha scorpio (Linné, 1758)

Murex scorpio Linné, 1758: 747; *M. varicosus* Sowerby, 1834: pl. 65, fig. 49; *M. digitatus* Sowerby, 1841: pl. 198, fig. 114; *Homalocantha fauroti* Jousseaume, 1888: 180

The shell is moderately large for the genus (maximum length 55 mm) and fusiform. The spire is moderately high to moderately low, consisting of four and one-half shouldered postnuclear whorls and a protoconch of undetermined nature. The suture is unimpressed, but the region surrounding the suture is deeply excavated. The body whorl is large, constituting 70 to 80 percent of the entire shell, and roughly fusoid. The aperture is subcircular, with no indication of an anal sulcus. The outer apertural lip is strongly erect and finely dentate; five short, bluntly bifid projections on the lip reflect the varical spines, and weak lirations extend into the aperture from the labial denticles. The columellar lip is detached, weakly erect, smooth, and regular; at its anterior end is an oblique sulcus followed by a thickening. The siphonal canal is moderately long, narrowly open to the right, and strongly, distally recurved.

The body whorl bears six spinose varices. Other axial sculpture is lacking. Spiral sculpture consists of alternating major and minor cords and numerous low, scabrous threads. Where the major cords intersect the varices, moderately long, narrowly open, distally palmate, digitate projections are developed. Starting at the shoulder margin there are generally five such major projections of almost equal length on the body and four on the canal, these sharply diminishing in length anteriorly. Above the first spine, on the shoulder, a ventrally fimbriate webbing connects the uppermost spine with the preceding whorl. A moderately developed, ventrally fimbriate webbing also connects all the spines on the body. The minor cords develop tiny, ventrally bent spinelets. There are two or three tiny spinelets between the body and the canal.

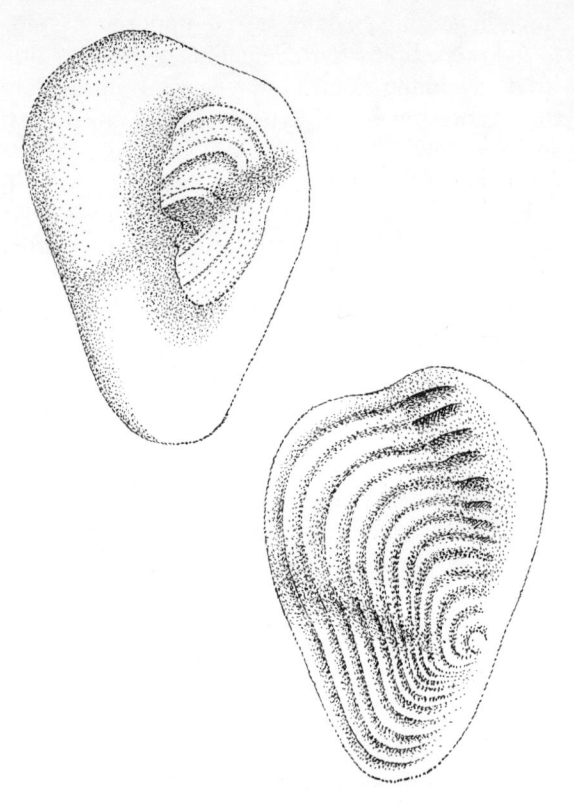

30. *Homalocantha scorpio*, operculum

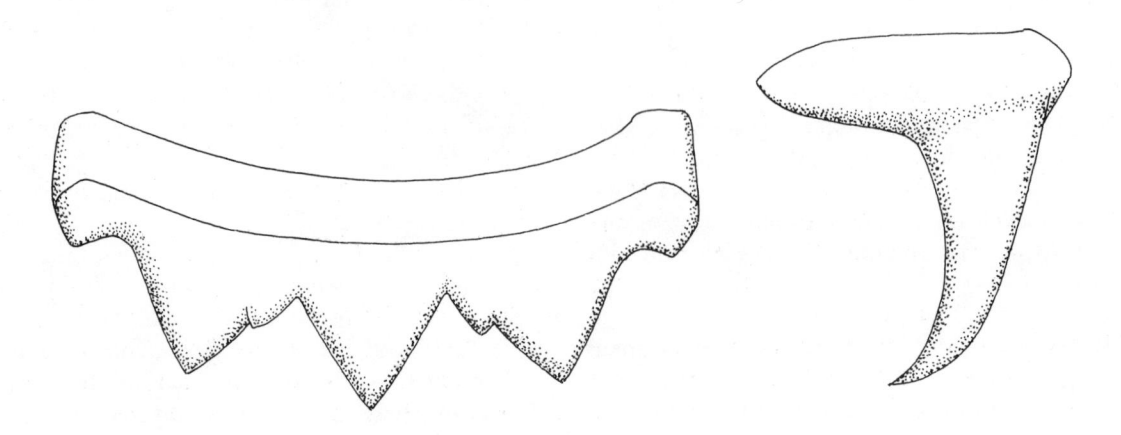

29. *Homalocantha scorpio*, radular dentition

Shell color ranges from blackish-brown to chestnut-brown to almost white, generally with some white following each varix.

Specimens from old (nineteenth-century) collections differ in having the webbing between the shoulder spine and the preceding whorl less well-developed, giving the spire a peculiarly slender, isolated appearance. They also have four, rather than five, spines on the body.

Known to us from the Philippines, Indonesia, and the Red Sea.

See Pl. 8, figs. 11–13.

Homalocantha secunda (Lamarck, 1822)

Murex secundus Lamarck, 1822: 169; *M. lamberti* Poirier, 1883: 86

The shell is moderately small for the genus (maximum length 40 mm) and broadly fusiform. Its spire is moderate in height, consisting of one nuclear whorl and five or six shouldered postnuclear whorls. The suture is obscured by the succeeding whorl. The body whorl is large and roughly fusoid. The aperture is small and subcircular, with no trace of an anal sulcus. The outer apertural lip is barely erect posteriorly, more strongly erect anteriorly, and finely dentate, with brief lirae extending from the labial teeth into the aperture. The columellar lip is adherent, entire, and smooth; at its anterior end are a sharply oblique sulcus and a knob. The canal is moderately long, barely open to the right, and distally recurved.

The body whorl bears five to seven varices, only the most recently formed of these strongly developed. At the shoulder, each varix is connected to the preceding whorl by a ventrally fimbriate webbing. Behind this webbing, the sutural area is deeply excavated. The most recently formed varix bears four major body spines; these are laminate, closed ventrally, distally narrowly palmate, and bear numerous laterally compressed scales on their dorsal surfaces. These major spines alternate with smaller spinelets. The canal bears two major and two minor projections. Spinose ornamentation on older varices is slight, and other axial sculpture is lacking. Spiral sculpture consists of major and minor, laterally undercut cords, these developing into spinose projections where they intersect the varices.

Shell color is variable, ranging from uniform dark purple-brown, to tan with dark-brown varices and spines, to white with spiral bands of orange-brown.

Generally considered rare or uncommon, this species has apparently eluded collectors as a result of its tendency to become heavily encrusted. A specimen in the field often looks like a lump of stone or calcareous algae.

Northwestern Australia to Indonesia and New Caledonia.

See Pl. 8, figs. 1–2, 5.

Homalocantha tortua (Sowerby, 1834)

Murex crispus Broderip, 1833: 176 (not Lamarck, 1803); *M. tortuus* "Brod." Sowerby, 1834: pl. 59, fig. 8; *M. multicrispatus* Dunker, 1869: 126, new name for *M. crispus* Broderip, 1833 (not Lamarck, 1803)

The shell is large for the genus (maximum length 60 mm) and broadly fusiform. The spire is moderately low, consisting of four or five shouldered postnuclear whorls and a protoconch of undetermined nature. The suture is obscured by the succeeding whorl, and the region around the suture is deeply and broadly excavated. The body whorl is large and broadly fusoid. The aperture is moderately large and broad and ovate to subcircular. The outer apertural lip is not mature in the one available specimen and thus is not here described. The columellar lip is completely adherent and smooth; at its anterior end are a sulcus and a tubercle. The siphonal canal is moderately long and weakly, distally recurved.

The body whorl bears ten spinose varices. Other axial sculpture is lacking. Spiral sculpture consists of alternating major and minor cords and numerous fine threads. Where the cords intersect the varices, short, partially open, flat-topped spines are developed. The two longest spines are developed at the shoulder margin. Below this, on the shoulder, four major spines alternate with four or five minor ones. The siphonal canal bears two major spines. The spiral threads cover most of the shell surface but are strongest on the sides of the spines and entirely lacking on their flat tops.

Shell color is pale tan, with fleshy purple-pink on the tops of the cords and spines.

Originally described by Broderip using a preoccupied name, this species has been little reported since that time. The type locality is "... twelve miles from Pacosmayo [Pacasmayo] (Peru) in twenty-five fathoms water."

See Pl. 8, fig. 16.

Homalocantha zamboi (Burch & Burch, 1960)

Murex anatomica var. *zamboi* Burch & Burch, 1960: 7

The shell is moderately large for the genus (maximum length ca. 58 mm) and fusiform. The spire is high, consisting of three or four roundly shouldered postnuclear whorls and a protoconch of undetermined nature. The suture is impressed, but is obscured by the strong buttresses extending over it and connecting the two whorls. The body whorl is large and fusoid. The aperture is of moderate size and ovate, with a flattened posterior margin and a barely perceptible anal sulcus. The outer apertural lip is erect and marginally crenulate; its inner surface is smooth. The columellar lip is adherent at its posterior end, detached and barely erect for its remaining extent. The siphonal canal is long, bent to the left and then to the right, and narrowly open.

The body whorl bears five thick varices, these spaced broadly at the shoulder margin but crowded on the canal. Spiral sculpture is not apparent. Each varix bears four long, terminally broadly palmate spine projections of differing lengths. The two longest, arising medially on the body, are considerably longer than the other two and form a V-shape as a result of their respective posterior and anterior angles relative to the long axis of the shell. The shorter two spines, arising from the canal, are shorter than the posterior pair and the anteriormost spine is shortest of all. The margin of the leading edge of the last varix is folded to form numerous short, open spinelets, and shows traces of what must be a fairly thick, simple intritacalx, this apparently removed in cleaning these typically heavily encrusted shells. The palmate ends of the spine projections are divided by dorsal grooves to form a digitate structure.

Shell color is white, with a purple intervarical suffusion. The aperture and the lumen of the siphonal canal are salmon-pink.

The shell of *H. zamboi* differs from that of the superficially similar *H. anatomica* in its development of two longer and two shorter spine projections (compared to four equally short ones in *H. anatomica*), its more slender shell, its higher, more slender spire, and the salmon-pink coloration of the aperture and the siphon interior.

The Philippines; a few records from the Solomon Islands.

See Pl. 8, fig. 3.

Genus **LATAXIENA** Jousseaume, 1883

TYPE SPECIES: *L. lataxiena* Jousseaume, 1883 (=*Trophon fimbriatus* Hinds, 1844), by tautonymy.

The shell in this genus is of moderate size (22–48 mm) and fusiform to biconic. The aperture is of moderate size and ovate to lenticular, with a shallow, broad anal sulcus and a short siphonal spout projecting posteriorly. The outer apertural lip is thin, becoming abruptly thicker behind; the posterior end of the outer lip may be elevated immediately before it joins the body. The columellar lip is smooth, except for one to three very weak plicae at its anterior end. Axial shell sculpture consists of numerous fimbriae or lamellae that are thrown into prominent, open, scalelike projections at their intersections with a series of broad spiral cords.

Lataxiena fimbriata (Hinds, 1844)

Trophon fimbriatus Hinds, 1844: 14; *Murex luculentus* Reeve, 1845: sp. 127; *Fusus imbricatus* E. A. Smith, 1876: 540; *Lataxiena elegans* Jousseaume, 1883: 187; *L. lataxiena* Jousseaume, 1883: 187

The shell is of moderate size (maximum length 48 mm) and roughly fusiform. The spire is high, consisting of two and one-half convex nuclear whorls and six or seven strongly shouldered postnuclear whorls. The suture is moderately impressed. The body whorl is moderately large and roughly fusoid. The aperture is moderate in size and ovate, with a broad, shallow to moderately deep anal sulcus, this extended to form a more or less brief, spoutlike posterior canal. The outer apertural lip is thin to moderately thickened, and its inner surface is strongly lirate. The columellar lip is generally entirely adherent, but may on

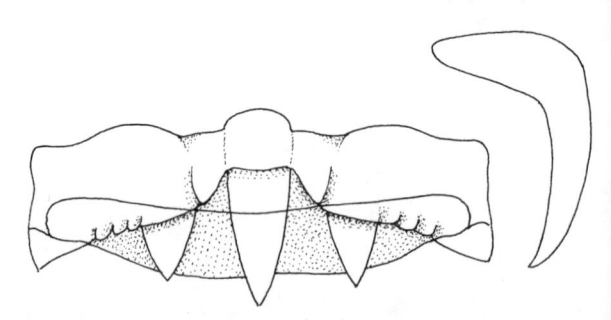

31. *Lataxiena fimbriata*, radular dentition

occasion be detached and weakly erect; the columella bears one to three weak anterior plaits but is otherwise smooth. The siphonal canal is broad, moderately long, straight, open, and slightly recurved dorsally at its tip.

The body whorl bears numerous fine lamellae or fimbriae, these sometimes concentrated in varixlike axial ridges. Spiral sculpture consists of seven major cords, one very strong one on the shoulder and six on the body; and eight minor cords, the anterior five alternating with the major cords. Where the cords intersect the lamellae, prominent, scalelike expansions of the lamellae are formed. The strength of development of the lamellae and scales varies.

Shell color is yellow-brown to white, with purple-brown bands at the shoulder and at the base of the body whorl. The aperture is whitish-yellow marginally, with brownish-purple showing through from the outer surface. The interior of the aperture is blue-gray.

Southeastern Japan to Queensland, Australia, and New Caledonia.

See Pl. 19, figs. 10–11.

Genus **MARCHIA** Jousseaume, 1880

TYPE SPECIES: *Murex clavus* Kiener, 1843 (=*M. elongatus* Lightfoot, 1786), by original designation.

The species presently assigned to *Marchia* are closely related to *Pterynotus*, but differ in having more numerous denticles surrounding the aperture and, in some species, a higher spire and a reduction of the varical blades on the spire to low costae. The shells are generally white, suffused in exceptional specimens with yellow, pink, or violet. The species have very wide geographical ranges, extending in several cases over the entire Indo-West Pacific region, though they are never abundant in a given area.

(See Appendix for a new species assignable to *Marchia*.)

Marchia barclayana (H. Adams, 1873)

Coralliophila barclayanus H. Adams, 1873: 205; *Murex lienardi* Crosse, 1873: 284

The shell is small (maximum length 35 mm) and fusiform. Its spire is high, with six or seven barely shouldered postnuclear whorls and a protoconch of undetermined nature. The suture is shallow and weakly defined. The body whorl is moderately large. The aperture is moderately small and ovate, with a broad shallow anal sulcus and a strongly constricted anterior end. The outer apertural lip is barely erect and weakly crenulate, with six moderately strong denticles on its inner surface. The columellar lip is adherent, or at most barely erect at its anterior end, and bears two weak denticles at its anterior end. The siphonal canal is short, open, and weakly recurved, and vestiges of former canals ornament the region to the left of the canal.

The body whorl bears four moderately broad, undulate, winglike varices, these entire from the suture to the tip of the siphonal canal. Varices on the spire are reduced in size to form, together with one or two intervarical costae, a series of eight nodes of equal strength per whorl. Spiral sculpture consists of eight to ten major cords, the strongest medial on the body whorl. Many minor spiral elements are interspersed with the major cords. The surface of the shell is covered with fine, densely distributed lamellae.

Shell color is light to dark brown; the interior of the aperture and siphonal canal is violet.

Apparently subtidal, known to us only from Mauritius, the Philippines, and the Solomon Islands.

See Pl. 9, fig. 9.

Marchia bipinnata (Reeve, 1845)

Murex bipinnatus Reeve, 1845: sp. 6

The shell is of moderate size (maximum length 55 mm) and fusiform. Its spire is high, with seven weakly shouldered postnuclear whorls and a protoconch of undetermined nature. The suture is shallow and weakly defined. The body whorl is proportionately large and slender. The aperture is small and ovate, with no discernible anal sulcus and a marked constriction immediately above the entrance to the siphonal canal. The outer apertural lip is erect, with a crenulate margin, and bears five to nine strong denticles on its inner surface. The columellar lip is weakly erect posteriorly, more so anteriorly, with three to five denticles immediately above the canal. The siphonal canal is moderately long, narrowly open, and generally straight; vestiges of former canals ornament the region to the left of the canal.

The body whorl bears three winglike varices, these greatly expanded in the shoulder region and for a short distance anteriorly. From the posterior end of the canal to its tip, the varix diminishes in width. On the spire axial sculpture consists of eight low costae of equal prominence, these representing the three varices and one or two intervarical nodes between each two varices. Spiral sculpture on the body whorl consists of several cords, the strongest about midway on the whorl. The shell is scabrous, owing to the presence of strong, crowded lamellae over the entire surface, these thrown into a series of axially aligned folds or ruffles.

Shell color is generally white. The interior of the aperture and canal is pinkish-violet.

Intertidal to subtidal, generally throughout the entire Indo-West Pacific.

See Pl. 9, fig. 11.

Marchia elongata (Lightfoot, 1786)

Murex elongatus Lightfoot, 1786: 65; *M. clavus* Kiener, 1842: 111 (not Michelotti, 1841)

The shell is moderately large (maximum length 90 mm) and elongate-fusiform. Its spire is high, with nine shouldered postnuclear whorls and a protoconch of undetermined nature. The suture is impressed. The body whorl is moderately large. The aperture is sublenticular, with the upper right portion flattened, and the anal sulcus is broad and very shallow. The outer apertural lip is erect, crenulated at its margin by the ends of the spiral sculptural elements, and denticulate on its inner surface. The columellar lip is detached anteriorly and erect, with three or four denticles at its anterior end. The siphonal canal is moderately short, narrowly open, and slightly recurved; to the left of the canal is a prominent ridge bearing the vestiges of former canals.

The body whorl bears three broad, winglike varices. Other axial sculpture consists of a single medial, intervarical ridge, this strongest at the shoulder. On the spire, the winglike varices are reduced except for their uppermost corners, these developed into upturned, flattened hooks. The margin of the last varix is undulate, sometimes recurved in one or more regions, and generally indented anteriorly, between the body whorl and the canal. The posterior portion of the varical "wing" is ventrally folded and adheres to the remainder of the varix. The ventral surface of the extended varix is richly lamellose. Spiral sculpture consists of many primary and secondary, fine, densely arranged scabrous threads, these coalescing, at times, into heavier cords.

Shell color is white, exceptionally fleshy pink or violet.

This species has also been known as *Murex clavus* Kiener, 1842, and *M. uncinarius* "Lamarck" of authors. Although the shell length given by Lamarck and recently by Cernohorsky (1970) indicates that the name *M. uncinarius* Lamarck, 1822, refers to the species we now assign to *Poropteron*, the figures Lamarck cited in Martini & Chemnitz (1785) are of the present species. Cernohorsky's assertion of having located this and other Lamarckian types is open to question, for Dr. Binder, of the Muséum d'Histoire Naturelle, Geneva, has stated (*in litteris*) to both of us separately that it is essentially impossible to determine the identity of Lamarck's types. Kiener, with Lamarck's collection in his possession, described *Murex clavus*, indicating that Lamarck had, indeed, referred to the small *Poropteron* species in his description of *M. uncinarius*.

Intertidal to subtidal, southeastern Japan, the Philippines, and generally throughout the entire Indo-West Pacific.

See Pl. 9, fig. 10.

Marchia laqueata (Sowerby, 1841)

Murex laqueatus Sowerby, 1841: pl. 190, fig. 78

The shell is moderately small for the genus (length 37 mm) and broadly fusiform. The spire is high, consisting of seven or eight subangulate, postnuclear whorls and a protoconch of undetermined nature. The suture is impressed. The body whorl is moderately large and fusoid. The aperture is small and ovate, with a narrow, shallow, callused anal sulcus, this parietally delimited by a strong, transverse tubercle. The outer apertural lip is erect and marginally serrate, and its inner surface bears 11 strong denticles: four in the shoulder region and seven below, in the body region. The columellar lip is detached and erect, with three elongate, oblique pustules, increasing in size anteriorly. The siphonal canal is sealed, moderately broad and short, straight, and dorsally recurved at its tip.

The body whorl bears four webbed varices. Additional axial sculpture consists of two costae, a prominent one close to the older varix, a less prominent one at the trailing edge of the next

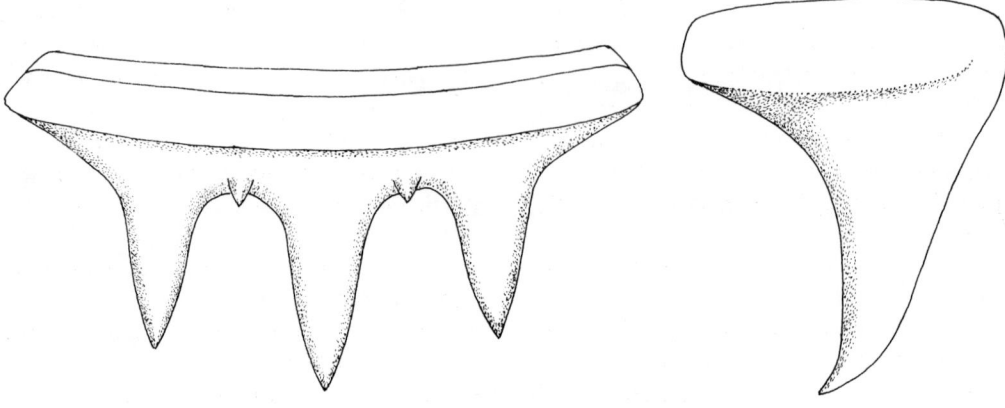

32. *Marchia elongata*, radular dentition

varix. Spaces between the axial elements are deep. Spiral sculpture consists of two groups of major cords, one starting just below the shoulder margin, the other near the base of the body. There are also two minor cords on the shoulder, a single minor cord between the two groups of majors, and another minor cord below the lower group. Three major cords are evident on the canal, following a notable sculptural gap at the base of the body. Where the spiral cords intersect the varices, there are two groups of short spines, these corresponding to the cords. The major development of spines is seen only on the last varix, where the spines in each group, becoming slightly more separated toward their free ends, are connected to each other by a thin webbing. The three canal cords end in moderately long, unconnected, oblique spines.

Shell color is pinkish-white, with suffusions of deeper rose-pink in various areas. The cords are deep golden orange. The aperture is white, with a rose-pink suffusion on the columella and on the densely fimbriate leading edge of the varix.

This extremely rare species has been reported, to our knowledge, only from Guam and Taiwan.
See Pl. 9, fig. 5.

Marchia martinetana (Röding, 1798)
Purpura martinetana Röding, 1798: 141; *Murex fenestratus* Dillwyn, 1817: 716

The shell is moderately small for the genus (maximum length 42 mm) and broadly fusiform. The spire is high, with a generally convex profile, and consists of six weakly convex to subangulate postnuclear whorls and a protoconch of undetermined nature. The suture is undulate and weakly impressed. The body whorl is moderately large and fusoid. The aperture is small and ovate, with a narrow, moderately deep anal sulcus, this delimited parietally by a transverse ridge. The margin of the outer apertural lip is barely erect and minutely serrate; the inner surface of the outer lip bears six strong denticles, one in the shoulder region and five in the body region. The columellar lip is thinly callused, detached, and erect; a series of three or four pustules is apparent at the anterior end of the columella, the two nearest the siphonal canal generally crowded together. The siphonal canal is moderately long, narrowly open, and dorsally recurved.

The body whorl bears four rugose varices. Additional axial sculpture consists of a single ropelike ridge midway in each intervarical space. Spiral sculpture consists of three distinct groups of major cords: the uppermost, at the shoulder margin, consists of three cords; that at the middle, of a single cord; and that at the base of the body, of two cords. A sharply defined sculptural gap is followed by two cords on the canal. Numerous scabrous threads cover the shell, the cords, and the spaces between them. Where the major cords intersect the varices, three groups of short to moderately long spines, corresponding to the spiral sculpture, diverge distally from each other within each group. In most cases a thin webbing connects the groups of spines. The spines on all but the last varix are generally very short and appear undeveloped. The prominence of the sculptural elements lends to the rectangular spaces between the major axial and spiral elements a depressed appearance and to the shell surface a reticulate or fenestrate appearance. Numerous ruffled axial lamellae impart a minutely scabrous texture to the shell. The leading edge of the last varix is densely fimbriate.

Shell color is white to ivory, with rust-colored varices. The region just before the varix is suffused with gold ochre, and the rectangular, fenestrate depressions appear deeper by being colored dark chestnut-brown. The aperture is golden yellow, with white denticles and pustules.

The Red Sea to the Ryukyus.
See Pl. 9, fig. 1.

?Marchia nodulifera (Sowerby, 1841)
Murex noduliferus Sowerby, 1841: pl. 194, fig. 94; *Muricidea caledonica* Jousseaume, 1881: 349

The shell is small for the genus (maximum length 30 mm) and roughly fusiform. The spire is high and acute, consisting of seven shouldered postnuclear whorls and a protoconch of undetermined nature. The suture is impressed. The body whorl is of moderate size and roughly trigonal. The aperture is moderately large and ovate, with a shallow, barely discernible anal sulcus. The outer apertural lip is erect and finely serrate at its margin; its inner surface bears seven or eight transversely elongate denticles. The columellar lip is entirely adherent, except for its extreme anterior portion, which is detached and erect; at its anterior end, over the columella, is a series of three strong, oblique pustules. The siphonal canal is moderately short, narrowly open, and almost straight.

The body whorl bears five varices, these separated by moderately broad interspaces. Spiral sculpture consists of three major cords, a pair at the shoulder margin and a single one near the base of the body. A single minor cord is apparent on the shoulder, another one in the space between the paired cords and the single cord. Where the major cords intersect the varices, short, dorsally recurved, distally foliated spines are developed. The paired spines at the shoulder margin are generally coalescent, forming a single strong, short, bifid spine.

Shell color is white or pale yellow-white, with red-brown to purple-brown staining on the varices and particularly on the spines. The aperture is white or ochre-yellow. In all specimens a heavy encrustation obscures the color pattern.

The Philippines to the Solomons and the Fiji Islands.

See Pl. 27, fig. 3.

Marchia pellucida (Reeve, 1845)
Murex pellucidus Reeve, 1845: sp. 54

The shell is moderate in size (maximum length 52 mm) and fusiform. Its spire is high, with eight or nine shouldered postnuclear whorls and a protoconch of undetermined nature. The suture is impressed. The body whorl is large. The aperture is sublenticular, with the upper portion flattened, and the anal sulcus broad and shallow. The outer apertural lip is erect, with a crenulate margin and denticulate interior surface. The columellar lip is adherent above, detached and erect below, and bears three or four denticles on the anterior end of the columella. The siphonal canal is moderately short, narrowly open, and distally recurved; to the left of the canal is a prominent ridge bearing the vestiges of former canals.

The body whorl bears three broad, winglike varices. Other axial sculpture consists of a single prominent, elongate ridge. The varices on the spire are reduced, forming slender, upturned, pointed and somewhat recurved extensions. The final varix is broad, upturned at the shoulder, and connected to the varix of the preceding whorl; below, it extends outward and reaches the distal portion of the siphonal canal. Spiral sculpture consists of fine, scabrous major and minor threads over the entire shell. The edge of the varix is finely scalloped, the prominent points of the scalloping corresponding to the major spiral threads. The ventral surface of the last varix is richly lamellose.

Shell color is generally white, occasionally pinkish.

Although specimens of *M. pellucida* appear superficially to be small specimens of *M. elongata*, their small shells have the same number of whorls as mature specimens of *M. elongata*. In addition, the shell is proportionately stouter, the varices do not form flattened hooks on the spire, and the last varix is broad and never folded ventrally.

Southeastern Japan to East Africa.

See Pl. 9, fig. 7.

Marchia triptera (Born, 1778)
Murex tripterus Born, 1778: 287

The shell is moderately small (maximum length 50 mm) and stoutly fusiform. Its spire is moderately high, with one and one-half nuclear whorls and seven or eight moderately shouldered postnuclear whorls. The suture is shallow and weakly defined. The body whorl is large and moderately broad. The aperture is moderate in size and subovate, with a weak anal sulcus and a strongly constricted anterior end. The outer apertural lip is erect, with a crenulate margin and eight strong denticles within. The columellar lip is adherent posteriorly, becoming progressively more erect anteriorly and bearing five to nine strong denticles distributed along its entire length. The siphonal canal is moderately short, narrowly open, and generally straight; vestiges of former canals ornament the region to the left of the canal.

The body whorl bears three broad, winglike varices, each well-developed across the shoulder, their margins indented to form two or three lobes. The varices on the spire are reduced in size and are entire rather than lobate. Intervarical axial sculpture consists of one or two more or less developed costae. Spiral sculpture consists of numerous cords, the strongest medial on the body whorl. In unworn specimens the entire surface of the shell is finely, densely lamellose, most strongly so on the ventral surface of the last varix.

Shell color is white or cream. The aperture is pale to deep yellow-orange.

Intertidal to subtidal, throughout the Indo-West Pacific.

See Pl. 9, fig. 12.

Genus MUREX Linné, 1758

TYPE SPECIES: *Murex pecten* Montfort, 1810 (not Lightfoot, 1786) (=*M. tribulus* Linné, 1758), by subsequent designation, Montfort, 1810.

Species correctly assigned to this genus have spindle or club-shaped shells and three varices per whorl, these bearing a variable number of short to long, simple, partially or entirely closed spines. The spire is moderately high to quite high but never comparable to the canal length. The siphonal canal, also generally bearing spines, is moderate in length to very long. The aperture is broadly ovate or lenticular to subcircular, with or without an anal sulcus. The columellar lip is generally produced into an inductura of moderate size. In some species the outer apertural lip bears a prominent labial tooth formed from the enlargement of one to three of the points crenulating the outer margin.

(See the Appendix for a new species assignable to *Murex*.)

Murex anniae M. Smith, 1940

Murex anniae M. Smith, 1940: 44; *M. (M.) recurvirostris sallasi* Rehder & Abbott, 1951: 58; *M. anniae belleglandensis* E. H. Vokes, 1963: 111

The shell is small (maximum length 54 mm) and stoutly club-shaped. The spire is high, consisting of one and one-half convex nuclear whorls and five heavy, barely shouldered postnuclear whorls. The suture is impressed and undulate. The body whorl is large, inflated, and sharply constricted just above the siphonal canal. The aperture is small and ovate, with a narrow, moderately deep anal sulcus, the sulcus angled toward the inner lip and delimited parietally by a short, sharp, transverse ridge. The outer apertural lip is erect and marginally crenulate, the crenulations above the shoulder margin swollen to form prominent marginal denticles; the inner surface of the outer lip bears seven weak, elongate denticles, these becoming more prominent anteriorly. The columellar lip is smooth and adherent at its posterior end, detached and erect for its remaining length. The siphonal canal is short, straight, and narrowly open to the right.

The body whorl bears three heavy, rounded varices, deeply sulcate on their trailing edges. Intervarical axial sculpture consists of three or four costae of moderate strength that are sharply nodulose over the major spiral cords. Spiral sculpture consists of major and minor cords. The shoulder bears a single major cord flanked by single minors above and below it. Proceeding anteriorly from the major cord at the shoulder margin, seven major cords alternate with minor cords on the body. A single major cord near the top of the siphonal canal is flanked on each side by three minor cords. Where the major cords intersect the varices, very short, closed spines are developed; except for the slightly longer straight one at the shoulder margin, these are all strongly ventrally bent.

The shell's white ground color is overlaid with two wide, poorly defined, spiral bands of bright rose-pink, one covering the entire shoulder region to just below the shoulder margin, and one at the base of the body. The siphonal canal is suffused with rose-pink. All the major cords and several of the anterior minor cords bear yellow-brown crests.

Gulf of Mexico from off Yucatán to off western and northern Florida in 40–100 m.

See Pl. 7, fig. 15; Pl. 11, fig. 6.

Murex antelmei Viader, 1938

Murex antelmei Viader, 1938: 6

We have never seen a specimen of this species; the following is based on the original description and figure:

The shell is moderate in size (average length 70 mm) and fusiform. The spire is high, consisting of three glossy, convex nuclear whorls and five subangulate postnuclear whorls. The suture is moderately impressed. The body whorl is moderately small and fusoid. The aperture is of moderate size and ovate, with a small, shallow anal sulcus. The outer apertural lip is erect and finely, marginally crenulate. The columellar lip is briefly adherent above, detached and erect for its remaining length. The siphonal canal is long, barely open to the right, and weakly dorsally bent.

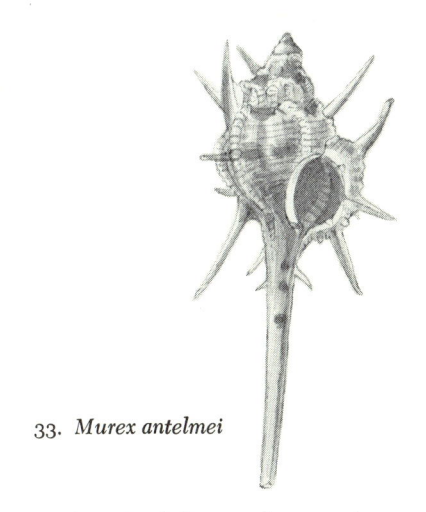

33. *Murex antelmei*

The body whorl bears three spinose varices. Intervarical axial sculpture consists of irregular, fine threads, these in some instances nodulose over submicroscopic, oblique, undulate striae. Three spiral threads become more prominent over the varices, where they give rise to slender, moderately long, straight, closed spines, one at the shoulder margin, one medial on the body, and one basal. The direction of the spines depends on their place of origin: the uppermost points up at about 45°, the medial is roughly horizontal, and the basal points downward at 45°. One or two short, straight spines are apparent at the top of the siphonal canal.

Shell color is whitish, with weak brown markings.

Known only from off Port Louis, Mauritius, in 120 m.

Murex blakeanus E. H. Vokes, 1967

Murex blakeanus E. H. Vokes, 1967: 88

The only specimen of this species at our disposal is so worn that its details are unrecognizable; the following is based on the original description and figure:

The shell is small (maximum length 50 mm) and club-shaped. The spire is high, consisting of one and one-half bulbous nuclear whorls and five convex, subangulate postnuclear whorls. The suture is strongly impressed. The body whorl is moderately large and inflated. The aperture is very large and subcircular, with a barely perceptible anal sulcus. The outer apertural lip is erect and microscopically, marginally crenulate; its inner surface is almost smooth, except in the shoulder region, where it is finely denticulate.

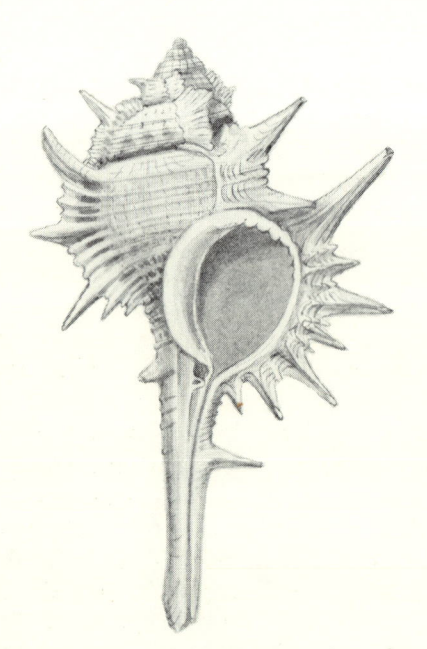

34. *Murex blakeanus*

The columellar lip is briefly adherent above, detached and strongly erect for its remaining extent; its inner surface is weakly, irregularly wrinkled. The siphonal canal is broad, straight and short for the genus and is apparently briefly sealed at its top.

The body whorl bears three spinose varices, these somewhat sulcate on their trailing edges. Intervarical axial sculpture consists of five or six weak costae, these nodulose over the major spiral elements. The weak spiral elements are of primary, secondary, and tertiary comparative strengths. Three primary cords are found on the body, each giving rise to a moderately short, rapidly tapering, closed spine, one at the shoulder margin, one medial, and one basal. Single secondary cords alternate with the primaries, giving rise to slightly shorter intercalary spines between the primaries. The spines are oriented according to their points of origin; spines on the upper third of the body point upward at 45°. A single short spine is evident at the top of the siphonal canal.

Shell color is uniform white or gray.

This is the species erroneously figured by Clench and Pérez Farfante (1945) as *M. tryoni*.

Southern Caribbean Sea; Trinidad and Grenada to Colombia.

Murex brevispinus Lamarck, 1822

Murex brevispinus Lamarck, 1822: 159; *M. macgillivrayi* Dohrn, 1862: 202; *M. acanthodes* Watson, 1882: 599

The shell is moderate in size for the genus (maximum length 70 mm) and club-shaped. The spire is low to moderately high, consisting of two and one-half smooth, polished, horn-colored nuclear whorls and seven angulate postnuclear whorls. The spire is moderately high. The suture is impressed. The body whorl is small and quadrate. The aperture is moderately large and broadly lenticular, with a narrow, moderately deep, inverted-V-shaped anal sulcus, angled toward the parietal region of the shell. The outer apertural lip is strongly erect and denticulate: above the shoulder margin it is thickened and bears four closely spaced denticles; below the shoulder margin five or six somewhat more broadly spaced denticles are followed by a large, blunt, labial tooth; below this tooth, three or four more denticles occur; and the position of a varical spine is marked on the inner surface of the outer lip by an indentation. The columellar lip is broadly adherent above, expanded into a thin, extensive callus, and for the lower two-thirds of its length detached and forming a strongly erect inductura; the columella is smooth. The siphonal canal is moderately long, straight, and narrowly open to the right.

The body whorl bears three more or less spinose varices, their trailing edges excavated. Intervarical axial sculpture consists of two equidistant ridges, these more or less nodose over the primary spiral cords. Spiral sculpture is made up of primary, secondary, and tertiary cords. The primary cords number three: one at the shoulder margin, one medial, and one basal on the body. These cords develop short, apically curved, ventrally closed and grooved spines where they intersect the varices. Four secondary cords, followed by a tertiary, occupy the shoulder. Below the shoulder a pattern of one tertiary, four secondaries, and another tertiary is the rule. The siphonal canal bears numerous secondary cords and a single primary, this forming a straight spine about one-fourth of the way down the length.

Shell color is gray-white or pale ochre-brown. The aperture is white, brown more deeply within. A speckled appearance is imparted to many specimens by a darker brown in the form of fine dots on the spiral elements and between denticles at the current and previous apertural margins.

Eastern Africa (Durban, South Africa, to Zanzibar) and Northwest Cape, Western Australia, to central Queensland, Australia.

See Pl. 11, fig. 2.

Murex cabritii Bernardi, 1858

Murex cabritii Bernardi, 1858: 301

The shell is of moderate size (maximum length 75 mm) and club-shaped. The spire is moderately high and subacute, consisting of two and one-half nuclear whorls and six convex postnuclear whorls. The suture is impressed. The body whorl is small and subhemispherical. The aperture is ovate to lenticular, with a short, narrow anal sulcus, this delimited parietally by a weak nodule. The outer apertural lip is erect and finely dentate, each pair of fine teeth separated from neighboring pairs by a deeper indentation; the inner surface of the outer lip is very weakly lirate. The columellar lip is adherent above and more or less heavily callused; the remaining two-thirds of the columellar lip is detached and strongly erect. The siphonal canal is long and straight.

The body whorl bears three thickened, spinose varices, these excavated on their receding edges. Intervarical axial sculpture consists of three or four costae, these most prominent as strong nodules over the major spiral elements. Spiral sculpture on the body consists of two secondary cords on the shoulder, two at the base, and six primary cords alternating with tertiary cords. The canal bears five primary cords; above the uppermost one and between each two is a secondary cord, flanked by two tertiary elements. Where the primary cords cross the varices, short to long, sharp, ventrally closed and ventrally curved spines are developed. Those on the canal are exceptionally long.

Ground color is pastel fleshy pink; the spines and varices are white tinged with pink; the spire is yellow at its origin, grading into white and finally into the ground color on the penultimate whorl; the spiral cords are yellow-pink where they are developed into spirally elongate nodes, except for single node-rows on the shoulder, medial on the body, and at the base of the body, these being almost white. The aperture is pale pink-white marginally, and deeper pink within, where the color of the outer surface shows through.

Gulf of Mexico (Florida Keys to Yucatán, Mexico), eastern coast of Florida (Pompano Beach to Florida Keys), and Barbados (fide Clench & Pérez Farfante, 1945).

See Pl. 10, fig. 12.

Murex cervicornis Lamarck, 1822

Murex cervicornis Lamarck, 1822: 163

The shell is of moderate size (maximum length 65 mm) and fusiform. The spire is high, consisting of two and one-half rounded nuclear whorls and six peripherally angulate postnuclear whorls. The suture is impressed. The body whorl is moderately small. The aperture is ovate, with a small, shallow anal sulcus, this delimited on both sides by an elongate transverse ridge. The outer apertural lip is erect and weakly crenulate. The columellar lip is detached and strongly erect. The siphonal canal is long, narrowly open to the right, arched to the left, and dorsally recurved.

The body whorl bears three spinose varices, these slightly excavated on their trailing edges. Intervarical axial sculpture consists of three to five weak to ephemeral ridges, these strongest over the major spiral elements. Spiral sculpture consists of primary and secondary cords and threads of two strengths. Above the shoulder margin, three or four coarse threads are evident, with three to five finer threads in each interspace and extending onto the varical spines. At the shoulder margin is a pair of primary cords, with fine threads between the two. Below this, several fine and coarse threads are followed by two or three secondary cords, a second pair of primary cords with accompanying threads, and several additional secondary cords and fine threads. The siphonal canal bears two primary cords and many fine threads. Where the two pairs of primary body cords intersect the varices, long, antlerlike, bifurcated, ventrally closed spines are developed. The lower fork of the uppermost spine extends directly outward, curving gently in a posterior direction. The upper branch is sharply dorsally bent. The two rami (branches of the lower spine) are divergent but unrecurved. Secondary cords form short, sharp, ventrally bent spines on the varices. The two major cords on the canal develop two moderately long, slender, sharp, straight spines. The persistent shoulder spines of older whorls appear to add additional spines at the posterior end of each varix.

Shell color is pale fleshy tan to white. The aperture is white.

Our placement of this species and of *M. longicornis* in *Murex* is based on the lack of spinefoliations and the overall *Murex*-like form of the body whorl.

Queensland, Australia, north and west to northwestern Australia.

See Pl. 11, fig. 5.

Murex chrysostoma Sowerby, 1834

Murex chrysostoma Sowerby, 1834: pl. 58, fig. 1; *M. bellus* Reeve, 1845: sp. 83

The shell is moderate in size (maximum length 80 mm) and heavily club-shaped. The spire is moderately high, consisting of one and one-half nuclear whorls and six convex to weakly angulate postnuclear whorls. The suture is impressed. The body whorl is large and goblet-shaped. The aperture is large, with a narrow anal sulcus, this delimited by a transverse parietal ridge. The outer apertural lip is crenulate and erect, most prominently just below the shoulder margin and decreasingly so anteriorly. The columellar lip is adherent above, detached and strongly erect below; a shallow, medial, longitudinal furrow marks the point at which the columellar lip loses contact with the body, and beyond this furrow, more deeply recessed within the aperture, numerous elongate denticles may range over the entire length of the columella. The siphonal canal is moderately long, open, essentially straight, and tapering anteriorly.

The body whorl bears three strong, rounded varices, each deeply furrowed on its receding side. Intervarical axial sculpture consists of a single short ridge, strongly nodose at the shoulder margin, and two similar but weaker costae closer to the newest varix. Spiral sculpture consists of numerous cords of major and minor strength, these weaker in intervarical areas, stronger on the varices, and nodose at the intersection of spiral and axial elements. A few spiral cords extend onto the canal. Where the major cord on the shoulder margin intersects a varix, a single blunt, spinelike projection is developed.

Shell color is light tan. The aperture is white within; the apertural margin is either uniformly or interruptedly suffused with a golden-orange color. Some individuals show two faint brown spiral bands, one on the shoulder and one at the base of the body.

A distinctive population (Pl. 10, fig. 11) has been called *Murex bellus* Reeve, 1845. This form, found in Curaçao, differs from typical *M. chrysostoma* in having sharp, upturned, hooklike spines at the shoulder margin and on the upper canal, and in having the crests of the spiral cords colored redbrown. In addition, this form generally reaches only 55 mm in length and has a darker orange-red suffusion in the aperture.

The southern Caribbean Sea, from Barbados and Tobago to Curaçao and the northern coast of South America.

See Pl. 10, figs. 10–11.

Murex coppingeri E. A. Smith, 1884

Murex coppingeri E. A. Smith, 1884: 42

The shell is moderately small for the genus (maximum length 60 mm) and club-shaped. The spire is moderately high, consisting of three weakly convex nuclear whorls and seven strongly shouldered postnuclear whorls. The suture is impressed and undulate. The body whorl is of moderate size and almost trigonal in cross section. The aper-

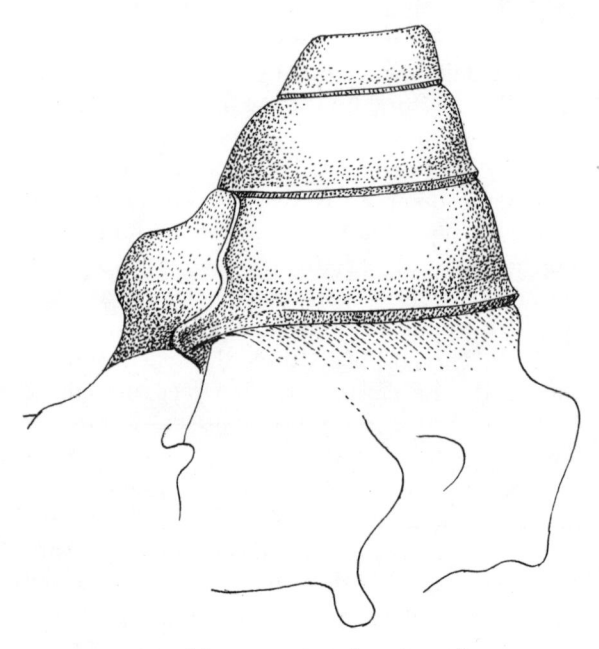

35. *Murex coppingeri*, protoconch

ture is ovate, but flattened in the shoulder region, with a broad, shallow anal sulcus. The outer apertural lip is erect and crenulate, with a narrow opening into the shoulder spine. The columellar lip is adherent above, detached and erect below. The siphonal canal is moderately long, essentially straight, and weakly, dorsally recurved at its distal end.

The body whorl bears three spinose varices. Intervarical axial sculpture consists of two evenly spaced low costae originating at the shoulder margin. Spiral sculpture consists of cords of four different strengths. Three primary cords on the body and five on the canal give rise to moderately long, solid, barely open spines on the varices. The longest spine, at the shoulder margin, and the two lower body spines are hooked posteriorly. The five canal spines are ventrally arched and diminish in length anteriorly. Secondary cords alternate with the primaries on both the body and the canal and give rise to short, sharp, ventrally bent spinelets on the varices. Tertiary cords are found on the shoulder and between each primary cord and its neighboring secondary. Numerous finer threads are found over the entire shell, and fine scabrous lamellae are distributed over the entire shell surface, imparting an unpolished look to the shell.

Shell color is whitish to light tan, with darker tan on the spiral elements. Three obscure brown spiral bands are apparent, one subsutural, one at the shoulder margin, and one at the base of the body, the last band extending onto the upper portion of the canal. The aperture is white, with brown markings showing through from the exterior.

Northern Australia in moderate depths (type locality, Torres Straits).

See Pl. 11, fig. 1.

Murex donmoorei Bullis, 1964

Murex donmoorei Bullis, 1964: 101

The shell is small (maximum length 40 mm) and club-shaped. The spire is moderately high, consisting of two and one-half horn-colored nuclear whorls and five convex postnuclear whorls. The suture is impressed. The body whorl is moderate in size and subhemispherical. The aperture is ovate, with a narrow, shallow, parietally angled anal sulcus, this delimited to the left by a strong, transverse, elongate ridge. The outer apertural lip is weakly erect and strongly denticulate, and bears six strong nodes in the shoulder region, below which it is weakly crenulate. The columellar lip is adherent above and very weakly callused, detached and weakly erect below; the anterior portion of the columella bears four or five weak, oblique, elongate, ridgelike nodes. The siphonal canal is moderately long, narrowly open, and essentially straight.

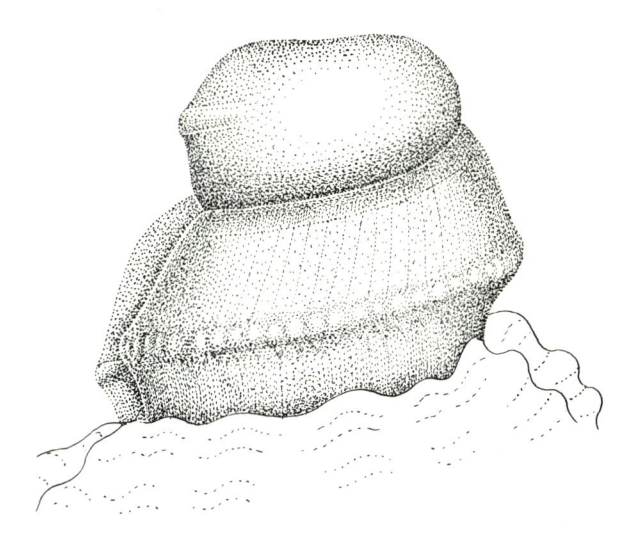

36. *Murex donmoorei*, protoconch

The body whorl bears three weakly spinose varices, these strongly furrowed on their receding edges. Intervarical axial sculpture consists of three or four nodulose costae, the fourth one, nearest the newest varix, when present, weaker than the others. Spiral sculpture consists of a series of cords of equal strength, some of which become more prominent on the varices and develop short, straight, ventrally closed spines. Three cords on the shoulder are followed by the shoulder-margin cord, this developing a spine at the varix. Below this another group of three cords is followed by a spiniferous one. A third triad of cords is followed by two that form a peculiar bifid spine at the varix. Five cords in the transition zone between the body and canal are followed, at the top of the canal, by two spine-bearing cords, these separated once again by three minor cords. On the body the second of each group of three intercalary cords bears a tiny spinelet arising away from the varical margin and closer to the aperture.

Shell color is light fleshy tan, with three diffuse darker-brown body bands, one at the shoulder margin, one medial, and one basal. The crests of the spiral cords are red-brown. The aperture is white.

Off French Guiana (type locality), and off western Trinidad in 60 m.

See Plate 10, fig. 3.

Murex elenensis Dall, 1909

Murex plicatus Sowerby, 1834: pl. 58, fig. 6 (not Gmelin, 1791); *M. recurvirostris* var. *lividus* Carpenter, 1857: 519; *M. elenensis* Dall, 1909: 218, new name for *M. plicatus* Sowerby, 1834 (not Gmelin, 1791); *M. tricoronis* Berry, 1960: 119

The shell is moderate in size (maximum length 90 mm) and roughly club-shaped. The spire is moderately high, consisting of two and one-half nuclear whorls and seven or eight convex postnuclear whorls. The suture is moderately impressed. The body whorl is moderately small to moderately large. The aperture is moderately large and ovate, with a moderate-sized anal sulcus, this delimited parietally by a double-noded transverse ridge and a smaller single-noded one. The sinuous outer apertural lip is crenulate, barely erect above the shoulder margin, and strongly erect below it. The columellar lip is adherent above and detached and erect below, its margin reflected. The siphonal canal is moderately long, narrowly open to the right, primarily straight, but strongly dorsally bent for the distal one-third of its length.

The body whorl bears three high, rounded, spinose varices, each furrowed on its trailing edge. Intervarical axial sculpture consists of three or four costae, these nodose over the major spiral elements. Spiral sculpture on the body consists of three or four tertiary cords on the shoulder, a heavy primary cord at the shoulder margin, and three somewhat finer primary cords intercalated with secondary cords on the body below the shoulder margin. The canal bears four or five primary cords. Where the primary cords cross the varices, short to moderate-sized, essentially straight, ventrally closed spines are developed The spine at the shoulder margin is generally stouter and more posteriorly hooked than the rest. Below the shoulder spine are three body spines, one medial and two basal. The spines on the canal are generally somewhat longer than the body spines. The intercalary secondary cords on the body develop small ventrally bent spinelets on the varices. The number and heaviness of spines on the body and especially on the canal vary with the age of the specimens and the population from which they come.

Shell color is pale tan to flesh to purple-gray in some specimens, with a darker band at the shoulder margin and at the base of the body. The crests of the spiral elements are pale orange to rusty brown. The aperture is white.

Scammon's Lagoon, Baja California, to Ecuador, including the entire Gulf of California.

See Pl. 11, fig. 13; Pl. 13, fig. 1.

Murex gallinago Sowerby, 1903

Murex gallinago Sowerby, 1903: 496

The shell is moderately small (maximum length 50 mm) and fusiform. The spire is high, consisting of one and three-fourths convex nuclear whorls and six weakly convex postnuclear whorls. The suture is strongly undulate and weakly impressed. The body whorl is moderately large. The aperture is wide and ovate to lenticular, with a broad, shallow anal sulcus, this delimited on each side by a single strong ridge or node. The outer apertural lip is erect, weakly crenulate, and marginally reflected on its anterior portion. The columellar lip is adherent above, detached and moderately erect below; close to the reflected edge of the columellar lip is a longitudinal furrow; slightly more deeply recessed into the aperture is a series of elongate denticles, four above, on the adherent portion of the lip, six below, on the detached portion. The siphonal canal is moderately long, narrowly open, and weakly recurved at its distal end.

The body whorl bears three strong, rounded varices. Intervarical axial sculpture consists of two strong costae and numerous very fine, scabrous lamellae. Spiral sculpture consists of primary, secondary, and tertiary elements. Narrow primary cords alternate on the body with secondaries; between each primary and secondary, a tertiary is evident. The canal bears only primary cords. Minute spines, occasionally linked by a brief webbing, arise at the base of the body on the varix.

Shell color is pale fleshy cream, with two diffuse transverse brown bands: at the shoulder margin and the base of the body. The aperture is white.

Known only from the type locality (Ogasawara, Japan).

See Pl. 7, fig. 11.

Murex hirasei "Dautzenberg" Hirase, 1915

Murex hirasei "Dautzenberg" Hirase, 1915: pl. 47, fig. 232

The shell is moderately large for the genus (maximum length 90 mm) and spindle-shaped. The spire is moderately high and acute, consisting of two and one-half nuclear whorls and eight flat-sided, subangulate postnuclear whorls. The sutures are undulate and impressed and lie below the margin of the excavated shoulder region. The body whorl is moderately large and fusoid. The aperture is ovate, with a moderately deep anal sulcus, this parietally delimited by a small transverse ridge. The outer apertural lip is erect below the shoulder margin and weakly, marginally crenulate; its inner surface is lirate. The columellar lip is adherent above and developed into a moderate, reflected inductura below, the inductura strongly concave over the columella and ornamented near this furrow with elongate, oblique ridges. The siphonal canal is long, slender, closed for the upper two-thirds of its length, and distally recurved.

The body whorl bears three moderately prominent varices, these sulcate on their trailing edges and essentially aligned up the spire. Intervarical axial sculpture consists of three or four moderately prominent costae. Spiral sculpture consists of numerous major and minor cords distributed over the entire shell surface. A small, spurlike spine is apparent at the shoulder on all but the final varix. Two other similar spines are found on the upper canal.

Shell color is creamy, more or less tinged with fleshy hues. The spiral elements are rust-red on their crests. The aperture is white.

Hirase credited Dautzenberg with the description of this species, but Dautzenberg never published a description of it. The name must thus be attributed to Hirase.

Known to us only from southeastern Japan in approximately 200 m.

See Pl. 11, fig. 12.

Murex kiiensis Kira, 1959

Murex kiiensis Kira, 1959: 58

The shell is of moderate size (maximum length 60 mm) and spindle-shaped. The spire is high, consisting of eight convex postnuclear whorls and a protoconch of undetermined nature. The body whorl is moderate in size to large. The aperture is moderately small and ovate, with a small, shallow anal sulcus, this delimited by a small knob. The outer apertural lip is erect and finely, marginally crenulate; its inner surface bears seven or eight denticles, these recessed into the aperture. The columellar lip is adherent above, detached and erect below, the anterior end bearing four denticles. The siphonal canal is tapered anteriorly, distally recurved, and closed for the upper two-thirds of its length.

The body whorl bears three rounded, strongly elevated, weakly spinose varices, these deeply sulcate on their trailing edges. Intervarical axial sculpture consists of two or three low costae. Spiral sculpture consists of numerous sharp-crested, low, spiral cords, these alternating with finer spiral threads over the entire shell, except for the anterior end of the canal. Where certain of the major cords intersect the varices, at the shoulder margin and twice more near the base of the body, short, sharp spines are developed, the spine at the shoulder margin stronger than the other two. The upper portion of the canal bears two additional short spines.

Shell color is white to pale tan, with deep red-brown on the major spiral elements. Three faint brown transverse bands are evident on the body, one at the shoulder margin, one medial, and one basal. The aperture is white, at times with a line of brown spots on the outer lip margin representing a cross section of the spiral cords.

Northwestern Pacific from the Philippines (a more delicate form with proportionately smaller, more convex whorls, Pl. 11, fig. 12) to southeastern Japan (a heavier, coarser form with less spination and larger, less convex whorls, Pl. 13, fig. 5).

See Pl. 11, fig. 14; Pl. 13, fig. 5.

Murex longicornis Dunker, 1864

Murex longicornis Dunker, 1864: 99; *M. recticornis* von Martens *in* Löbbecke & Kobelt, 1880: 81; *Poirieria kurranulla* Garrard, 1961: 27

The shell is small (maximum length 45 mm) and essentially spindle-shaped. The spire is high, consisting of two and one-half convex nuclear whorls and five angulate postnuclear whorls. The suture is impressed. The body whorl is small and fusoid. The aperture is broadly ovate, with a moderately deep anal sulcus, delimited by a strong, elongate tubercle on its parietal side. The outer apertural lip is erect and weakly, marginally crenulate. The columellar lip is barely erect above, detached and strongly erect below. The siphonal canal is arched to the left, dorsally recurved, and narrowly open.

The body whorl bears three spinose varices. Intervarical axial sculpture consists of two or three costae, these prominently nodulose where they intersect spiral sculptural elements. Spiral sculpture consists of numerous major and minor cords. The major cords occur at the shoulder margin and medially on the body. One minor cord and two finer threads occur between the two major cords. Three minor cords occur at the base of the body. Where the major cords intersect the varices, long, closed, straight spines are developed. The minor cord between the two majors gives rise to a short, ventrally bent spinelet, and the three minor cords at the base of the body each give rise to a fine, short, straight spinelet.

Our placement of this species and of *M. cervicornis* in *Murex* is based on the lack of spinefoliations and the overall *Murex*-like form of the body whorl.

Shell color is uniformly white, tan, or pink. The aperture is white.

Amboina, Molucca Islands (type locality) to southern Queensland, Australia.

See Pl. 11, fig. 4.

Murex messorius Sowerby, 1841

Murex messorius Sowerby, 1841: pl. 194, fig. 93;
M. woodringi Clench & Pérez Farfante, 1945: 9

The shell is moderately small (maximum length 65 mm) and club-shaped. The spire is high, consisting of one and one-half nuclear whorls and seven convex postnuclear whorls. The suture is moderately impressed. The body whorl is moderate in size and suborbicular. The aperture is moderately large and lenticular, with a small, shallow anal sulcus. The outer apertural lip is sinuous and crenulate, erect below the shoulder margin; its inner surface is denticulate. The columellar lip is adherent above, erect below, and bears a single knoblike node on the upper portion and several others near the margin on the lower portion. The siphonal canal is moderate in length, distally recurved, and narrowly open.

The body whorl bears three rounded varices, these sulcate on their trailing edges. Intervarical axial sculpture consists of three or four weak costae, nodulose where they intersect the major spiral cords. Spiral sculpture consists of ten major cords, intercalated with minor cords on the body and canal. Where each alternate major cord, beginning at the shoulder margin, intersects the varix, a short, closed, more or less posteriorly curved spine is evident. One such spine is developed at the top of the canal.

Shell color is pale tan to medium brown, with a darker transverse band at the shoulder margin. In some specimens, additional darker-brown color is present on the spiral cords. The aperture is grayish-brown within, white at the margin.

Throughout the Caribbean, most common in the southern half.

See Pl. 11, fig. 7.

Murex mindanaoensis Sowerby, 1841

Murex mindanaoensis Sowerby, 1841: pl. 194, fig. 92

The shell is moderately large (maximum length 110 mm) and spindle-shaped. The spire is high, consisting of two and one-half polished, convex nuclear whorls and seven convex postnuclear whorls. The suture is impressed. The body whorl is moderate in size. The aperture is moderately large and ovate, with a small, transversely elongate tubercle delimiting its parietal margin. The outer apertural lip is erect and finely crenulate at its margin; its inner surface is lirate. The columellar lip is adherent above, detached and erect below; at its free edge, reflecting the underlying spiral sculpture, is a thin, wrinkled parietal callus. The siphonal canal is long, narrowly open, and distally recurved.

The body whorl bears three moderate, rounded varices, these sulcate on their trailing edges. Intervarical axial sculpture consists of four or five weak costae. Spiral sculpture consists of numerous low cords, these intercalated with finer threads. Where the shoulder margin cord and four lower body cords intersect the varix, short, barely open, spurlike spines are developed. Between these spines, tiny, ventrally bent spinelets are evident. On the upper canal are two or three short spines.

Shell color is light to medium rust-brown, darker on the upper part of each whorl. The aperture is white.

Known at present only from the area around Tayabas Bay, Quezon, and Marinduque Islands, in the Philippines, in depths of approximately 150–200 m.

See Pl. 10, fig. 4.

Murex multiplicatus Sowerby, 1895

Murex multiplicatus Sowerby, 1895: 216

The shell is moderately small for the genus (maximum length 55 mm) and club-shaped. The spire is moderately high, consisting of two and one-half polished nuclear whorls, the last of which has a subperipheral carina, and seven convex postnuclear whorls. The suture is impressed. The body whorl is moderately small and subglobular. The aperture is ovate, with a weak anal sulcus, this bounded parietally by a weak transverse ridge.

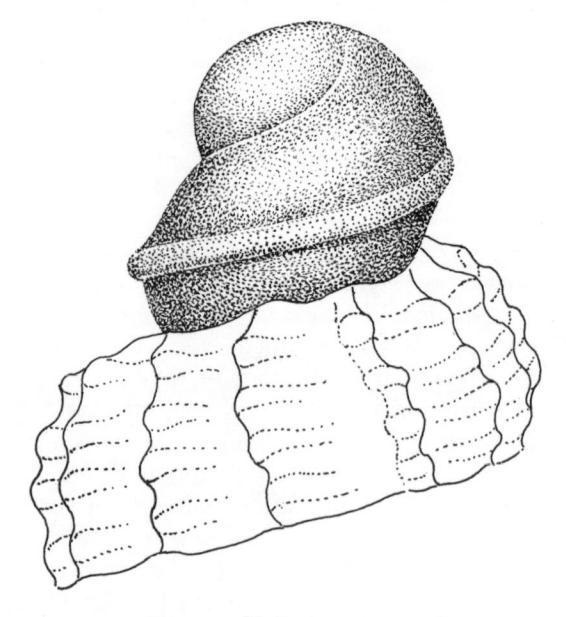

37. *Murex multiplicatus*, protoconch

The outer apertural lip is erect, with a finely crenulate margin and a lirate inner surface. The columellar lip is weakly erect above, detached and strongly erect below. The siphonal canal is long and narrowly open.

The body whorl bears three elevated, generally nonspinose ridges, these sulcate on their trailing edges. Intervarical axial sculpture consists of three or four costae extending from the suture to the base of the body. Spiral sculpture consists of numerous equidistant primary cords. The intersections of these cords with the costae and the varices are marked by small nodes. Occasionally, a short shoulder spine and/or one or two small body-base spines are developed on the varix.

Shell color is gray-white, encircled by purple-brown bands, a dark one at the shoulder margin, one medial, and one basal. The aperture is porcelaneous white.

Western Australia (Port Hedland and Broome) to Rabaul, New Britain.

See Pl. 11, fig. 16.

Murex olssoni E. H. Vokes, 1967

Murex olssoni E. H. Vokes, 1967: 84

The shell is small for the genus (maximum length 52 mm) and roughly club-shaped. The spire is high, consisting of one and one-half nuclear whorls and six barely subangulate or convex postnuclear whorls. The suture is weakly impressed. The body whorl is moderately large (two-thirds of the shell length, exclusive of the siphonal canal) and roughly fusoid. The aperture is moderate in size and ovate, with a moderately weak anal sulcus, this angled severely toward the parietal region of the shell. The outer apertural lip is erect and finely serrate, and is arched in such a way that the portion just posterior to the anterior end of the lip projects the most; the inner surface of the outer lip bears a series of spirally elongate denticles that decrease in size with anterior progress; the strongest of these, internal to the shoulder margin spine, is set off from the others by a notable space, the others being all evenly spaced. The columellar lip is detached and erect and bears five or more oblique and more or less irregularly oriented elongate pustules. At the posterior end of the outer lip, just posterior to the point at which the columellar lip becomes adherent to form a brief callus, is a moderately strong denticle, this recessed a short distance within the aperture and delimiting the anal sulcus parietally. The siphonal canal is of moderate length, straight, and narrowly open to the right.

The body whorl bears the three heavy, cord-like varices typical of the genus. Intervarical axial sculpture consists of two or three heavy, rounded, ropelike costae; the third costa, where present nearest the most recently formed varix, is generally narrower and less prominent than the other two. Spiral sculpture consists of numerous cords of at least two levels of prominence. There are 11 primary cords, one on the shoulder, seven on the body, and three on the canal. All of these except two on the canal terminate on the varix as short to moderately long, almost completely closed, slightly dorsally curved spines. Alternating with the primary cords are significantly less prominent secondary threads. All the spiral elements are weak between the axial elements but form prominent, sharp-crested nodes over the varices and the axial costae. The trailing edge of each varix is moderately deeply sulcate.

Shell color is white, with off-white nodes. A thin, flat-white frosting of intritacalx is apparent over the entire shell in specimens that have not been eroded. The nuclear whorls and early postnuclear whorls are pale horn-colored. The aperture is porcelaneous white.

Southwestern Caribbean, from Punta San Blas, Panamá, to Gulf of Morrosquillo, Colombia.

See Pl. 7, fig. 6; Pl. 14, fig. 8.

Murex pecten Lightfoot, 1786

Murex pecten Lightfoot, 1786: 188; *Aranea triremis* Perry, 1811: pl. 45, fig. 3; *M. tenuispina* Lamarck, 1822: 158; not *M. pecten* Montfort, 1810, which is *M. tribulus* Linné, 1758

The shell is large (maximum length 150 mm) and subfusiform. The spire is high and acute, consisting of two and one-half rounded nuclear whorls and seven or eight convex postnuclear whorls. The suture is well impressed, exaggerated by excavated regions immediately above and below it. The body whorl is moderately large and elongately fusoid. The aperture is ovate to lenticular, with a broad, shallow anal sulcus angled toward the left. The outer apertural lip is strongly erect and coarsely dentate, the teeth very weak above the shoulder margin; four pairs of thick, blunt teeth occur below, on the body, followed by a fifth pair about twice the size of the others, forming a labial tooth of sorts; the sixth and seventh pairs are very weak. The inner surface of the outer lip is essentially smooth, except for some brief, shallow furrows. The columellar lip is adherent and callused for one-third of its length, detached and strongly erect below this; the lower half of the columellar lip bears a broad, shallow, longitudinal furrow.

The siphonal canal is long, straight, and very narrowly open.

The body whorl bears three excessively spinose varices. Intervarical axial sculpture consists of numerous (three to nine) low to ephemeral costae, these weakly nodulose at their intersections with spiral elements. Spiral sculpture consists of primary, secondary, and tertiary cords. Where these cords intersect the varices, moderately long to very long, solid, curving spines are developed. Five major cords occur on the body, 11 on the canal. The longest spine is derived from the primary cord at the shoulder margin. Another long spine is found medially on the body, and three others with curved tips are developed at or near the base of the body. On the body, secondary and tertiary ventrally curving spines generally are intercalated with the primaries. Thus, between the uppermost large spine and next primary are two tertiaries flanking a secondary. Between the next two major spines we find only one tertiary and one secondary. A single tertiary occurs at the base of the body. Each major cord on the canal bears a very long, ventrally curving spine, these spines diminishing in size anteriorly. A second tier or row of shorter, sharply ventrally bent spines are found between the primary canal spines.

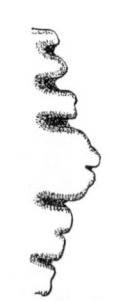

38. *Murex pecten*, labial tooth (ceratus)

Shell color is fleshy ochre, with pale tan between the spiral elements. Notches on the outer lip margin, reflecting the primary and secondary spiral cords, are colored deep red-brown.

Throughout the tropical western Pacific (southeastern Japan to Queensland, Australia, and the Solomon Islands).

See Pl. 10, fig. 1.

Murex rectirostris Sowerby, 1841

Murex rectirostris Sowerby, 1841: pl. 197, fig. 111; *M. sobrinus* A. Adams, 1863: 370

The shell is moderate in size (maximum length 80 mm) and club-shaped. The spire is high, consisting of two and one-half smooth nuclear whorls and seven obsoletely angulate postnuclear whorls. The suture is impressed. The body whorl is small to moderate in size and subfusoid. The aperture is subcircular, with no apparent anal sulcus. The outer apertural lip is erect and marginally crenulate; its inner surface is lirate. The columellar lip is briefly adherent above, detached and strongly erect for its remaining length. The siphonal canal is open, tubelike, and slightly recurved.

The body whorl bears three heavy, rounded varices, these deeply sulcate on their trailing edges. Intervarical axial sculpture consists of three or four prominent costae, these nodulose over the major spiral cords. Spiral sculpture consists of alternating major and minor cords, except on the shoulder, where four minor cords are apparent. Eight major and minor cords are found on the body. The uppermost major cord, at the shoulder margin, and two or three others at the base of the body form short, stout, closed spines on the varices. A single open, scalelike spine sometimes arises near the top of the siphonal canal.

Shell color is light brown or tan, with a lighter transverse band on the lower portion of the body, and at times another lighter band on the shoulder. The aperture is porcelaneous white.

The Japanese form, known by most people as *M. sobrinus* A. Adams, 1863 (Pl. 13, fig. 2, herein), is typically smaller, more delicate, and more spinose. The form from Taiwan, most common in older collections, is considerably larger and more robust, with shorter spines.

Southeastern Japan to Taiwan.

See Pl. 11, fig. 3; Pl. 13, fig. 2.

Murex recurvirostris Broderip, 1833

Murex recurvirostris Broderip, 1833: 174; *M. nigrescens* Sowerby, 1841: 138

The shell is moderately small (maximum length 60 mm) and spindle-shaped. The spire is moderately high, consisting of one and one-half translucent, weakly convex nuclear whorls and five convex, barely shouldered postnuclear whorls. The suture is well-impressed. The body whorl is moderately large and swollen. The aperture is moderately large and ovate, with a narrow, deep anal sulcus, this angled to the left and its parietal margin formed by a moderately large tubercle. The outer apertural lip is undulate and erect below the shoulder margin; above the shoulder margin are two pairs of small denticles, and the inner surface of the outer lip bears seven small denticles, these recessed a short distance into the aperture and reflecting the major spiral sculpture. The columellar lip is adherent above, detached and strongly erect below; over the columella its anterior half bears eight or nine oblique denticles. The siphonal canal is moderate in length, straight, and narrowly open.

The body whorl bears three large, heavy varices, these strongly sulcate on their trailing edges and often nonspinose. Intervarical axial sculpture consists of three or four moderately strong costae, these nodulose over the major spiral cords. Spiral sculpture consists of seven major cords, these alternating with minor cords, beginning on the shoulder. The canal bears a single major cord and many minor elements. A single short, straight, closed spine may be developed at the shoulder margin, and two or three more at the base of the body; one may also be developed near the top of the siphonal canal.

Shell color is pale brown, with three darker purple-brown transverse bands, one at the shoulder margin, one medial, and one basal. Most major spiral cords and a few minor ones are red-brown. The aperture is blue-white within and white on the margin.

Scammon's Lagoon, Baja California, to Ecuador.
See Pl. 11, fig. 11.

Murex rubidus F. C. Baker, 1897

Murex messorius var. *rubidum* F. C. Baker, 1897: 377; *M. recurvirostris rubidus* "F. C. Baker" Abbott, 1954: 202

The shell is moderately small for the genus (maximum length 55 mm) and spindle-shaped. The spire is moderately high, consisting of two and one-half polished, convex nuclear whorls and five subangulate postnuclear whorls. The suture is impressed and undulate. The body whorl is small to moderate in size and subglobose. The aperture is ovate, with a moderately broad, shallow anal sulcus, this delimited parietally by a strong transverse ridge. The outer apertural lip is weakly erect, marginally crenulate, and denticulate within. The columellar lip is adherent posteriorly, detached and moderately erect anteriorly; over the columella it bears eight oblique denticles, starting anteriorly. The siphonal canal is moderately long, narrowly open, and distally recurved.

The body whorl bears three sparsely spined varices, more or less weakly sulcate on their trailing edges. Intervarical axial sculpture consists of two prominent costae. Spiral sculpture consists of six cords of equal size that are nodulose over the costae and on the varices. Three cords, one at the shoulder margin and two at the base of the body, form short, sharp spines on the varices. The shoulder-margin spine is closed and posteriorly hooked; the two lower spines are straight and ventrally open. One or two cords on the upper portion of the canal are developed into short, sharp, straight, closed spines. Fine threads alternate with the cords over the entire shell.

Shell color is variable, ranging from bright orange or yellow through yellow-green and pink. Some specimens show a white ground color banded with pink.

East and west coasts of Florida and the Bahama Islands, in 20–160 m (see Clench & Pérez Farfante, 1945).
See Pl. 11, fig. 15.

Murex scolopax Dillwyn, 1817

Murex scolopax Dillwyn, 1817: 681; *M. occa* Sowerby, 1834: pl. 64, fig. 45

The shell is large (maximum length 145 mm) and club-shaped. The spire is moderately high and acute, consisting of two and one-half subangular nuclear whorls and eight convex postnuclear whorls. The suture is deeply impressed. The body whorl is moderate in size and subglobose. The aperture is broadly lenticular, with a moderately broad, deep anal sulcus. The outer apertural lip is slightly erect and bears five broad marginal teeth below the shoulder margin; of these, the fourth one down is enlarged, forming a prominent labial tooth. The columellar lip is adherent above, detached and erect below. The siphonal canal is essentially straight, narrowly open, and dorsally recurved at its distal end.

39. *Murex scolopax*, labial tooth (ceratus)

The body whorl bears three strongly spinose varices. Intervarical axial sculpture is lacking. Spiral sculpture consists of strong cords and threads. There are four cords on the body and six on the canal. The shoulder bears four ephemeral threads. The space between each two major cords is occupied by two to four very fine threads. Where the major cords intersect the varices, long, solid, ventrally curved spines are developed. As in *Murex pecten,* a second row of spines, turned ventrally at right angles to the row above, arises on the canal.

Shell color is pale gray-brown, with red-brown on the major spiral cords and at the base of the spines. The aperture is white. The interior of the aperture is pale red-brown.

Northern Indian Ocean, from the Red Sea to northwestern Australia and the Philippines.

See Pl. 10, figs. 6–7.

Murex serratospinosus Dunker, 1883

Murex serratospinosus Dunker, 1883: 35; *M. malabaricus* E. A. Smith, 1894: 162

The shell is moderately large (maximum length 100 mm) and spindle-shaped. The spire is high, consisting of two and one-half polished, convex nuclear whorls and eight or nine convex postnuclear whorls. The suture is moderately impressed. The body whorl is moderately large and fusoid. The aperture is moderately large and ovate, with no perceptible anal sulcus. The outer apertural lip is erect and minutely, marginally crenulate. The columellar lip is adherent at its posterior end, detached and strongly erect for the remainder of its length; at its anterior end are three elongate, oblique denticles. The siphonal canal is long, slender, narrowly and sinuously open, and dorsally recurved.

The body whorl bears three prominent varices. Intervarical axial sculpture consists of three to six moderately low costae that are sharply nodulose over the major spiral cords. Spiral sculpture consists of 22 primary cords: four on the shoulder, ten on the body, and eight on the upper half of the canal. Between each two primary cords is a single secondary cord flanked by two tertiaries, except on the canal, where the two secondary cords occupy this space. The major spiral cords on the body, at their intersections with the varices, are produced into short, open, dorsally recurved spines, the largest of these at the shoulder margin. These spines are connected to each other, imparting a briefly webbed appearance to the varix. Five short, straight, open spines alternate with very short spinelets on the upper portion of the canal.

Shell color is pale tan, with three darker-brown transverse bands, one at the shoulder margin, one medial, and one basal. The crests of the spiral elements are deep red-brown, continuously in banded regions, interruptedly in the paler regions. The aperture is porcelaneous white, with some exterior color showing through.

Northern Indian Ocean, from Bushehr, Iran, to the Bay of Bengal.

See Pl. 10, fig. 2.

Murex trapa Röding, 1798

Murex trapa Röding, 1798: 145; *M. rarispina* Lamarck, 1822: 158; *M. martinianus* Reeve, 1845: sp. 72

The shell is moderately large (maximum length 100 mm) and fusiform. The spire is high and acute, consisting of two and one-half convex nuclear whorls and seven or eight postnuclear whorls. The suture is not impressed. The body whorl is moderate-sized and fusoid. The aperture is lenticular but somewhat flattened posteriorly and to the left, with a moderately broad anal sulcus. The outer apertural lip is erect and weakly, marginally crenulate; near the base of the body two crenulations have coalesced to form a strong, bifid labial tooth, the posterior segment longer than the anterior one. The columellar lip is adherent and weakly callused above, detached and weakly erect below. The siphonal canal is moderately long, straight, and narrowly open.

The body whorl bears three spinose varices. Intervarical axial sculpture consists of four or five low to ephemeral costae, barely nodulose on the spiral elements. Spiral sculpture consists of primary, secondary, and tertiary elements. Three primary cords occur on the body, one at the shoulder margin, one medial, and one basal. Each is flanked by an upper and a lower tertiary thread. Three secondary cords are apparent on the shoulder, another three between the first two primaries. Between the medial and basal primary cords, two secondaries are present, separated by a tertiary. Below the basal primary cord is a secondary cord followed by three tertiary threads. The canal bears a secondary cord and three tertiary threads, these followed by a thrice-repeated pattern of a primary and three tertiaries. Where the primary cords intersect the varices, short, stout, almost straight, closed spines are developed. Three secondary cords on the lower half of the body also give rise to very short, straight intercalary spinelets.

Shell color is blue-gray, with some yellow-brown on the spiral cords and on the spines. The aperture is porcelaneous white at the margin, deep red-brown within.

The region surrounding the South China Sea: Taiwan, southern China, northwestern Philippine Islands, and the Malayan and Indo-Chinese areas.

See Pl. 10, fig. 14.

Murex tribulus Linné, 1758

Murex tribulus Linné, 1758: 746; *M. pecten* Montfort, 1810 (not Lightfoot, 1786); *M. ternispina* Lamarck, 1822: 158; *M. aduncospinosus* Sowerby, 1841: pl. 197, fig. 110; *M. nigrispinosus* Reeve, 1845: sp. 79; *Acupurpura carbonnieri* Jousseaume, 1881: 349

The shell is highly variable. The following describes one of the most prevalent forms, generally collected in the Philippines. Additional information on variants follows the standard treatment.

The shell is strong, coarsely sculptured, moderately large (maximum length 110 mm) and club-shaped. The spire is moderately high, consisting of two and one-half convex nuclear whorls and seven convex postnuclear whorls. The suture is strongly impressed, reinforced in some specimens by a subsutural channel in some parts of the shell. The body whorl is subhemispherical and moderate in size. The aperture is moderately large and sublenticular, with a broad, shallow anal sulcus. The outer apertural lip is erect and crenulate, most erect below the shoulder margin; two or three coalescent crenulations near the base of the body are enlarged to form a prominent labial tooth, and the inner surface of the outer lip is lirate. The columellar lip is adherent and callused above, extending above the anal sulcus, and detached and strongly erect below. The siphonal canal is long, straight, narrowly open, and bent to the left and dorsally at its distal end.

40. *Murex tribulus*, protoconch

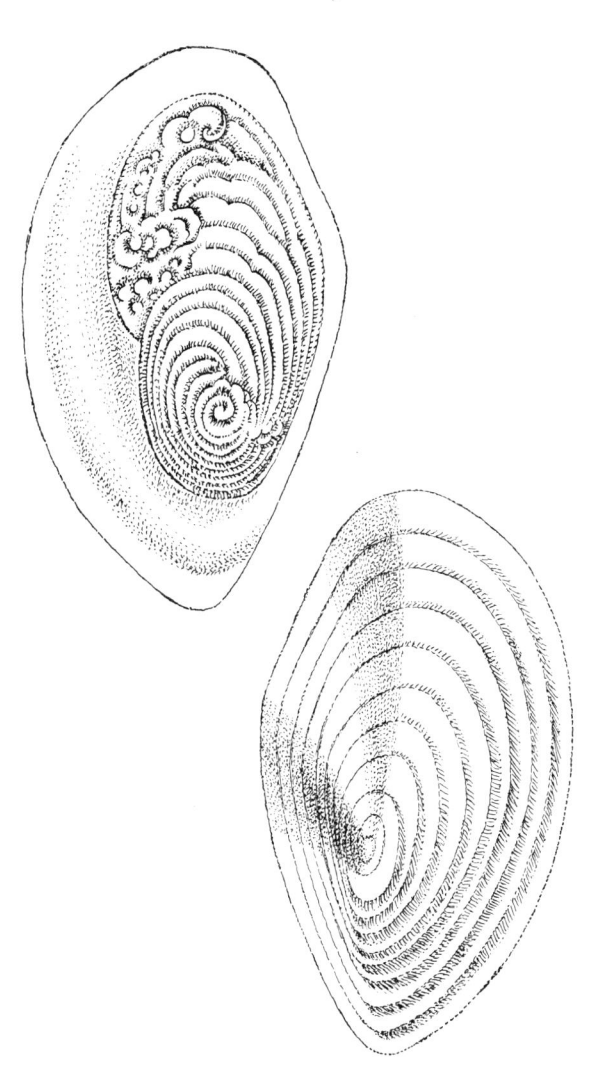

42. *Murex tribulus*, operculum

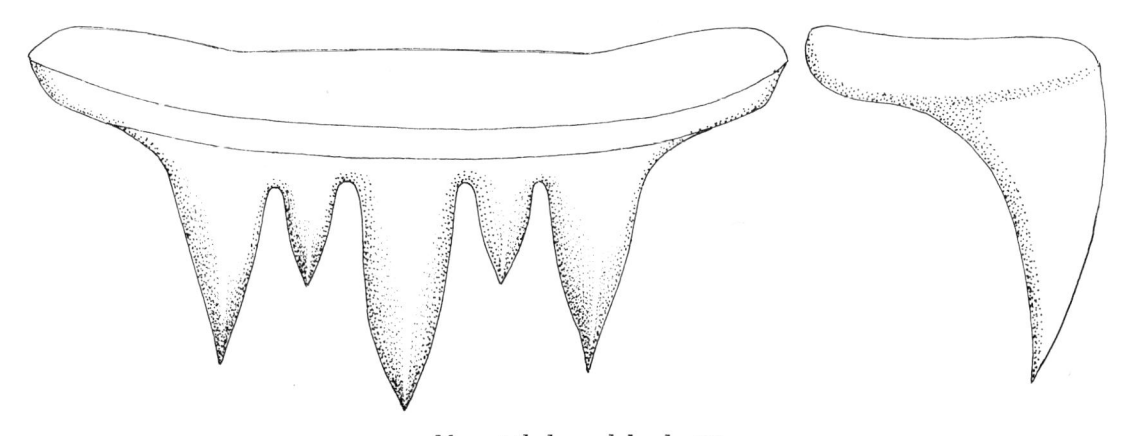

41. *Murex tribulus*, radular dentition

The body whorl bears three rounded, strongly spinose varices, sulcate on their trailing edges. Intervarical axial sculpture consists of three or four costae, strongly nodose over the spiral cords. Spiral sculpture consists of three major cords on the body and seven on the canal. Between each two of these major cords on the body are two minor cords. Numerous finer cords and threads occur between these elements over the entire shell. Where the major cords on the body intersect the varices, heavy, long, almost straight, closed spines arise. Minor cords on the body give rise to short, closed, tapering, ventrally curving spines, these diminishing in length anteriorly along the canal's entire length.

Shell color is creamy white to pale tan. The tips of the spines are dark purple, brown, or black. The aperture is white.

This widely distributed species exhibits striking polymorphism in shell features, as the following list of variable characters demonstrates:

1. The length of the spine at the shoulder margin may be much exaggerated.

2. A reduction in the size and an increase in the number of axial costae may yield much smaller nodes.

3. The number of canal spines may be reduced from six to five, producing, in the process, an additional row of ventrally turned spines, these oriented 90° to the typical row of canal spines.

4. The tips of the spines may lack the dark coloration.

5. Shell structure may be generally lighter and thinner.

6. A red-brown color may be present between the spiral sculptural elements.

The entire Indo-West Pacific region, from southeastern Japan to northeastern Australia and from eastern Africa to Fiji.

See Pl. 10, figs. 8–9.

Murex troscheli Lischke, 1868

Murex troscheli Lischke, 1868: 219; *M. heros* Fulton, 1936: 9

The shell is large (maximum length 160 mm), solid, and club-shaped. The spire is high, consisting of two and one-half convex nuclear whorls and eight strongly convex postnuclear whorls. The suture is strongly impressed, forming a very narrow, sharp channel. The body whorl is moderately large and globose. The aperture is moderately large and ovate, with a broad, moderately shallow anal sulcus. The outer apertural lip is erect and coarsely, marginally crenulate; near the base of the body two coalescent crenulations are enlarged to form a broad, blunt labial tooth, and the inner surface of the outer lip is weakly lirate. The smooth columellar lip is adherent and briefly spreading above, detached and obliquely erect below. The siphonal canal is long, barely open to the right, and straight, except for its dorsally recurved distal end.

The body whorl bears three strongly spinose varices. Intervarical axial sculpture consists of numerous weak costae, these becoming ephemeral on the later whorls and retained only as low irregularities on the spiral elements. Spiral sculpture consists of elements of four different strengths. Secondary, tertiary, and quaternary elements are apparent on the shoulder. Three primary cords on the body alternate with secondary cords, these in turn alternating with tertiary cords, and the tertiaries alternating with quaternary threads. All four types of elements are developed into spines at their intersections with the varices. Spines arising from primary cords are long, straight or barely ventrally curved, and barely open ventrally. Secondary through quaternary elements are also produced into varical spines, the ventral curvature of these progressively greater with diminution of cord strength. The canal is sculptured similarly, except that quaternary threads and their associated spines are lacking. Eight barely ventrally curved spines are borne on the canal, these diminishing in length anteriorly. Secondary spines alternate with the primaries, and tertiaries alternate with the secondaries.

Shell color is creamy white, with rust-brown on the crests of the primary, secondary, and tertiary cords, the brown coloring lacking on the ventral (apertural) portion of each whorl, which is white. The aperture is also white.

Southeastern Japan to the central Philippines. See Pl. 10, fig. 5.

Murex tryoni Hidalgo, 1880

Murex tryoni Hidalgo *in* Tryon, 1880: 134

The shell is small for the genus (maximum length 55 mm), short, and club-shaped. The spire is high, consisting of one and one-half convex nuclear whorls and six subangulate postnuclear whorls. The suture is strongly impressed. The body whorl is moderately large and subglobose. The aperture is small and ovate, with a narrow, very shallow anal sulcus. The outer apertural lip is erect and finely marginally crenulate; its inner surface is very weakly lirate. The columellar lip is adherent above, bearing a small knob delimiting the left side of the anal sulcus; the remainder of the columellar lip is detached and strongly erect, bearing, over the columella, a series of six to eight weak, irregular wrinkles. The siphonal canal is moderately long, barely open to the right, and straight.

The body whorl bears three spinose varices. Intervarical axial sculpture consists of six narrow, low costae that are finely nodulose over the spiral cords. Spiral sculpture on the body consists of weaker cords and fine intercalary threads. The shoulder bears three cords followed by a thread. The cord at the shoulder margin is followed anteriorly by six other cords alternating with threads. The siphonal canal carries four to six weaker cords, alternating with threads. Each varix bears three short, sharp, closed body spines where the cords cross the varix, one at the shoulder margin, one medial on the body, and one basal. The shoulder-margin spine is twice as long as the other two and is more upward-curving. The canal bears a single spine, near the top.

Shell color is white to pale fleshy pink. The crests of the spiral cords are pale red-brown. The canal is suffused with purple-brown. The aperture is pale fleshy pink.

Gulf of Mexico and the Caribbean in 150 m.

See Pl. 7, fig. 18.

Murex tweedianus Macpherson, 1962

Murex espinosus Macpherson, 1959: 51 (not Hutton, 1886); *M. tweedianus* Macpherson, 1962: 176, new name for *M. espinosus* Macpherson, 1959: 51 (not Hutton, 1886)

The shell is moderate in size (maximum length 70 mm) and club-shaped. The spire is moderately high, consisting of one and one-half convex, basally keeled nuclear whorls and seven globose postnuclear whorls. The suture is not impressed, and each whorl is obscured by a portion of the subsequent whorl. The body whorl is large (for the genus) and globose. The aperture is moderate in size and ovate, with a deep, narrow anal sulcus. The outer apertural lip is briefly erect, the margin bearing prominent, toothlike points. The smooth columellar lip is adherent and thinly callused above, detached and strongly erect below. The siphonal canal is straight and (for the genus) moderately short.

The body whorl bears three largely nonspinose varices, the last one with a thin weblike flange on its leading edge that is most prominent anteriorly and thrown into spinelike folds. This may be retained on some earlier varices. Intervarical axial sculpture consists of three moderately prominent costae, these sharply nodose over the major spiral cords and diminishing progressively in prominence toward the newest varix. Spiral sculpture consists of major and minor cords. Three minor cords on the shoulder are followed by six major body cords alternating with minor cords. A sculptureless space separates the body from the canal. Three major cords are apparent on the upper half of the siphonal canal. Aside from the spinelike folds where several anterior spiral cords intersect the varical webbing, the only spines are two or three short, dorsally recurved, ventrally open spurlike spines on the upper half of the canal. The spiral elements are minutely nodulose, and the spaces between these elements are microscopically wrinkled.

Shell color is a fleshy pink or purple-pink suffusion overlain by irregular rust-brown markings. The crests of the varical and intervarical nodes are white; one darker-brown blotch occurs medially on the body before and on each varix. The aperture is white.

Southern Queensland, Australia, in moderate depths (ca. 40 m).

See Pl. 10, fig. 13.

Genus MURICANTHUS Swainson, 1833

TYPE SPECIES: *Murex radix* Gmelin, 1791 (ICZN Opinion 888, 1969).

This genus and *Chicoreus* Montfort, 1810, are apparently directly descended from *Hexaplex* Perry, 1811, a genus with a longer geological history.

The problems involved in the type designation for *Muricanthus* have been reviewed by Vokes (1964). In a recent paper (Keen, 1969), *Murex radix* Gmelin, 1791, was specified as type species.

The shell in *Muricanthus* ranges from moderately small to large and is characterized by the possession of six to 11 varices bearing short to moderately long foliaceous spines. It has a large, globose body whorl, a large aperture with a generally strong, serrate outer apertural lip, and a narrowly open, moderately long canal. The shell is generally white, with a greater or lesser proportion of brown or black markings following the spiral elements and on the spines. The aperture is porcelaneous white. A labial tooth is present in some species.

The West African species herein assigned to *Muricanthus* (*M. megacerus*, *M. saharicus*, *M. varius*, and *M. angularis*) represent a distinctive species group that fits equally well in *Chicoreus* or in *Muricanthus*. Our placement, therefore, is tentative, and may require alteration on the basis of new data.

Muricanthus angularis (Lamarck, 1822)

Murex angularis Lamarck, 1822: 174; *Murex lyratus* A. Adams, 1853: 269; *Murex inornatus* A. Adams, 1853: 269 (not Récluz, 1851); *Murex densus* H. & A. Adams, 1853: 75, new name for *Murex inornatus* A. Adams, 1853 (not Récluz, 1851); *Murex adamsi* Sowerby, 1879: 38, 53, new name for *Murex inornatus* A. Adams, 1853 (not Récluz, 1851); *Murex hirsutus* Poirier, 1883: 83; *Murex goniophorus* Euthyme, 1889: 259

The shell is small for the genus (maximum length 50 mm) and broadly fusiform. The spire is moderately high, with six moderately shouldered postnuclear whorls and a protoconch of undetermined nature. The suture is indistinct and generally obscured by the succeeding whorl. The body whorl is large, globose, and weakly shouldered. The aperture is subcircular and broadly open, with a shallow, inverted-V-shaped anal sulcus. The outer apertural lip is dentate and generally unthickened. The columellar lip is entirely adherent, with a single spiral, parietal ridge extending into the aperture. The siphonal canal is moderately short and narrowly open to the right.

The body whorl bears six to eight varices, these ascending the shoulder obliquely. Spiral sculpture consists of several weak cords on the shoulder and nine or ten strong cords interspersed with finer threads on the body whorl and canal. Where the strong cords intersect the varices, short, blunt, weakly foliated spines are developed. The small portion of each spire whorl that is exposed shows only the sparse shoulder sculpture.

Shell color varies from a uniform white to white with brown on the varices. The interior of the aperture is porcelaneous white. Long-dead specimens from certain localities may be colored pale to deep orange.

Western Africa: Senegal to Gabon.

See Pl. 12, fig. 4; Pl. 13, fig. 3.

Muricanthus fulvescens (Sowerby, 1834)

Murex fulvescens Sowerby, 1834: pl. 62, fig. 30; *Murex spinicosta* "Val." Kiener, 1843: 49 (not Bronn, 1828)

The shell is large (maximum length 200 mm) and massive. Its spire is moderately low, with two nuclear whorls and six shouldered postnuclear whorls. The suture is indistinct and generally obscured by the succeeding whorl. The body whorl is massive. The aperture is moderately large and ovate. The outer apertural lip is unthickened and dentate, with an open shoulder spine and a compound labial tooth at the periphery of the body whorl. The columellar lip is entirely adherent. The siphonal canal is rather long, broad, narrowly open, and weakly, distally recurved.

The body whorl bears seven to nine varices, depending on the age or size of the individual specimen. The varices are spinose and extend obliquely over the shoulder to the preceding whorl. Spiral sculpture consists of numerous major and minor cords; on the body whorl are one major and two minor cords on the shoulder, and four majors on the body, these interspersed with one or two minor cords and numerous spiral threads; the canal bears three major spiral cords. Where these spiral elements intersect the varices, sharp, triangular, moderately foliated spines are developed.

Shell color is white, with rust-colored markings on the spiral elements and on the spines. The interior of the aperture is porcelaneous white.

Cape Hatteras, North Carolina, to Cape Canaveral, Florida, and the northeastern Gulf of Mexico, from off Cedar Key, Florida, to off southwestern Texas.

See Pl. 12, fig. 3.

Muricanthus kusterianus (Tapparone-Canefri, 1875)

Murex spinosus A. Adams, 1853: 268 (not Molina, 1782); *Murex kusterianus* Tapparone-Canefri, 1875: 635

The shell is moderately large and massive (maximum length 120 mm). The spire is low and broad, with one and one-half nuclear whorls and five shouldered postnuclear whorls; the spire is flat-sided, the shoulder region alone being visible on the spire. The suture is obscured by the succeeding whorl. The body whorl is large and broad. The broad, ovate aperture has a broad, shallow anal sulcus posteriorly, this strengthened by a spiral ridge extending some distance into the aperture. The outer apertural lip is unthickened and strongly dentate, with a partially open shoulder spine and an inconspicuous labial tooth. The columellar lip is almost completely adherent, with a brief anterior portion slightly detached. The siphonal canal is short, very broad, narrowly open at the right, and weakly distally recurved.

The body whorl bears seven or eight heavy, rounded, spineless varices. Spiral sculpture consists of numerous alternate major and minor cords incised by numerous fine threads. Where these intersect the varices on the shoulder and body whorl, low knobs or low, pyramidal, open spines are developed.

Shell color is white, with a greater or lesser number of fine purplish-brown spiral lines, primarily on the most recently formed intervarical areas. In some individuals, especially younger ones, two broad, spiral, purple-brown bands are evident, one on the shoulder, the other near the base of the body. The interior of the aperture is porcelaneous white.

Gulf of Oman and adjacent regions.

See Pl. 12, fig. 7.

Muricanthus megacerus (Sowerby, 1834)

Murex megacerus Sowerby, 1834: pl. 60, fig. 18; *Murex moquinianus* Duval, 1853: 203

The shell is of moderate size (maximum length 110 mm) and broadly fusiform. The spire is moderately high, with six to eight weakly shouldered postnuclear whorls and a protoconch of undetermined nature. The suture is weakly impressed and generally obscured by the succeeding whorl. The body whorl is large and solid. The aperture is ovate, with an inverted-V-shaped anal sulcus, this delimited parietally by a spiral ridge extending into the aperture. The outer apertural lip is erect and finely denticulate, and projects briefly beyond the thickened varix; its interior is lirate, each lira ending in a labial denticle (a primary labial tooth is lacking). The columellar lip is entirely adherent. The siphonal canal is moderately short, broad, moderately open, and weakly recurved distally.

The body whorl bears four or five prominent spinose varices and a single axial ridge in each intervarical space. Spiral sculpture consists of numerous major and minor cords, all of these covered with fine, scaly threads. Where the cords intersect the varices, short foliated spines are developed, the shoulder spine the longest. Immediately below this a slightly weaker cord ends in a smaller, ventrally bent spine. Below that is a large straight spine, followed by a second smaller, ventrally bent spine and two large straight spines.

Shell color is white, with more or less brown marking on the spiral cord and spines. The interior of the aperture is porcelaneous white.

Canary Islands and West Africa from Mauritania to Luanda, Angola.

See Pl. 12, fig. 8.

Muricanthus princeps (Broderip, 1833)

Murex princeps Broderip, 1833:175

The shell is moderately large (maximum length 140 mm) and broadly fusiform. Its spire is moderately high, with three nuclear whorls and seven weakly shouldered postnuclear whorls. The suture is moderately impressed and partially obscured by the succeeding whorl. The body whorl is large and massive, but less globose than that of *M. radix*. The aperture is large, moderately broad, and ovate, with a shallow, inverted-V-shaped anal sulcus and a moderately broad opening into the siphonal canal. The outer margin of the outer apertural lip is moderately strongly crenulate, with shallow channels between the points; a deeper channel penetrates the open shoulder spine. The columellar lip is entirely adherent. The siphonal canal is broad, long, and distally recurved, with its narrow opening placed far to the right, almost on the right edge of the canal; to the left of the canal, the fused vestiges of former canals form a ridge.

The body whorl bears five or six spinose varices. The shoulder region is devoid of spiral sculpture. At the shoulder edge is a single dominant cord, and on the canal are two additional cords, the three interspersed with minor cords. Where each spiral element crosses a varix, a spine is present, the size depending on the prominence of the cord.

Shell color is white, with more or less chestnut-brown markings on the spiral cords and on the foliated spines. The interior of the aperture is porcelaneous white.

Although rarely confused with any other species from the tropical eastern Pacific, this species at full size is inevitably heavily encrusted with calcareous algae and bryozoans. Because of this, many salient adult characters are obscured and have never been adequately described. This species, in contrast to *M. radix*, exhibits little form variation throughout its geographical range.

Guaymas, Mexico, to Ecuador and Galápagos Islands.

See Pl. 12, fig. 10.

Muricanthus radix (Gmelin, 1791)

Murex radix Gmelin, 1791: 3527; *Murex nitidus* Broderip, 1833: 176; *Murex ambiguus* Reeve, 1845: sp. 51; *Murex nigritus*, Philippi, 1845: 191; *Murex callidinus* Berry, 1958: 84

The shell is large (maximum length 150 mm) and massive. Its spire is low, with two and one-fourth nuclear whorls and seven weakly shouldered postnuclear whorls. The suture is shallow and generally obliterated by the succeeding whorl. The body whorl is very large and globose. The aperture is large, broad, and ovate, with a broad, moderately shallow anal sulcus and a broad opening anteriorly into the siphonal canal. The margin of the outer apertural lip is strongly dentate, with a deep indentation at the shoulder spine, and projecting most strongly where it forms a compound labial tooth near the anterior end of the aperture. The columellar lip is completely adherent and bears a spiral ridge from the outer margin of the parietal region to within the posterior portion of the aperture. The siphonal canal is broad, moderately long, narrowly open on the right side, and slightly recurved; the region adjacent to the canal bears sizable portions of former canals forming a strong ridge, beneath which there is a deep false umbilicus.

The body whorl bears six to 11 strongly spinose varices. Spiral sculpture consists of several major cords interspersed with minor cords: two majors are developed on the shoulder, one is appressed to the suture, and one lies nearer the shoulder edge; below the shoulder are five additional cords of more or less equal development; and the canal bears two additional major cords. Where the major cords intersect the varices they are developed into coarse, slender, erect, foliaceous projections. The foliated portions of these projections are recurved and may be short and blunt or extended into spinose processes. Sculpture is diminished on the spire, largely because of the limited exposure of each whorl. Visible axial sculpture proceeds obliquely across the spire.

The shell is white, with blackish-brown on the spiral elements and foliations. The proportion of white to black is variable.

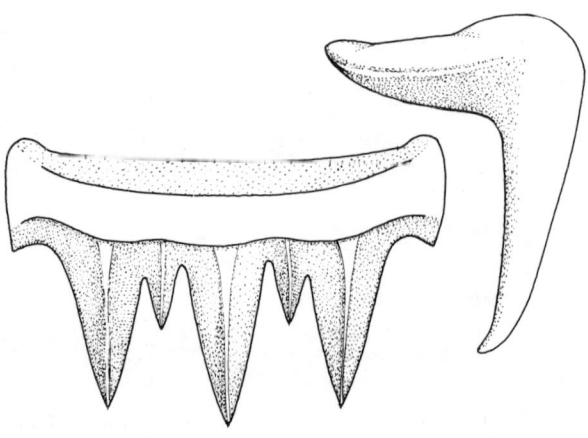

43. *Muricanthus radix*, radular dentition

A high degree of polymorphism is exhibited in the shell of this species. The northernmost form (Pl. 12, fig. 2), known as *M. nigritus* Philippi, 1845, is relatively high-spired, with six to nine varices. The form from the center of the range (north of Mazatlán, Mexico, to somewhat south of Manzanillo, Mexico; Pl. 12, fig. 1), which is known as *M. ambiguus* Reeve, 1845, has a somewhat lower spire, eight to ten varices, and a proportionately more massive body whorl. Specimens from the southern portion of the Panamic province, known as *M. radix*, have a still heavier, more globose body whorl and eight to 11 densely arranged varices. Other names given to this species,

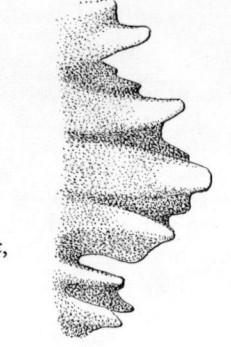

44. *Muricanthus radix*, labial tooth (ceratus)

based primarily on young shells with long, beautifully developed spines, are *M. nitidus* Broderip, 1833, and *M. callidinus* Berry, 1958; in all other characters these forms are indistinguishable.

Upper portion of the Gulf of California to Peru. See Pl. 12, figs. 1–2, 9.

Muricanthus saharicus (Locard, 1897)
Murex saharicus Locard, 1897: 305

The shell is moderately small (maximum length 70 mm) and fusiform. The spire is high and acute, consisting of two and one-half convex nuclear whorls and six subangulate postnuclear whorls. The suture is moderately impressed. The body whorl is moderate in size and fusoid. The aperture is subovate, with a flattened posterior margin and a narrow, deep anal sulcus, this angled toward the parietal portion of the shell and delimited parietally by a sharp transverse ridge. The outer apertural lip is somewhat erect and marginally crenulate, the crenulations reflecting the outer shell sculpture. The columellar lip is entirely adherent. The siphonal canal is moderately long, open, and weakly bent to the right and dorsally.

The body whorl bears four spinose varices. Intervarical axial sculpture consists of one or two narrow ridges, these most prominent on the earlier whorls. Spiral sculpture consists of primary, secondary, and tertiary elements. The shoulder is covered with fine threads. On the body, anterior to the shoulder margin, are five primary cords alternating with secondary cords, these stronger elements interspersed with many fine threads. Low, scabrous axial lamellae impart an imbricate appearance to the shell surface. Where the primary cords cross the varices, moderately long, ventrally open spines are developed. The shoulder-margin spine is much longer than the others and may be straight or recurved. The remaining four shorter spines are straight, rather blunt, and weakly, distally foliated. Two or three tiny spinelets mark the transition of the body to the canal and the canal itself bears two widely spaced, short, straight spines.

Shell color is creamy white, with two faint brown spiral bands, one at the shoulder margin and one at the base of the body. The upper band is most prominent just after each varix, fading away as the next varix is developed.

This species has been confused with *M. megacerus* Sowerby, 1834, from which it differs in many ways, such as the pattern of varical spination.

Western Africa from the Canary Islands to Mauritania.

See Pl. 7, fig. 10.

Muricanthus varius (Sowerby, 1834)

Murex varius Sowerby, 1834: pl. 67, fig. 57; *Murex clausi* Dunker, 1879: 215

The shell is small for this genus (maximum length 65 mm) and fusoid. Its spire is high, with three nuclear whorls and five or six shouldered postnuclear whorls. The suture is weakly delimited and generally obscured by the succeeding whorl. The body whorl is moderately large and fusoid. The aperture is of moderate size and ovate, with a narrow, very shallow anal sulcus posteriorly, this strengthened by a spiral ridge. The outer apertural lip is moderately to strongly thickened, and its interior is briefly lirate. The columellar lip is entirely adherent. The siphonal canal is broad and narrowly open to the right.

The body whorl bears four to seven weakly spinose varices. In addition, one or more intervarical spaces bear a prominent axial ridge. Spiral sculpture consists of numerous cords and threads of various strengths. Where the strongest spiral elements intersect the varices, short, stout, partially open spines are developed, the longest one at the shoulder edge and another prominent spine at the anterior end of the body whorl; below this are two shorter, ventrally bent spines and a single moderately long spine on the canal; and some specimens carry one or two additional prominent spines between the shoulder spine and the basal body-whorl spine. A series of much smaller, ventrally bent spines may alternate with these longer spines on the body whorl.

The shell is pale flesh-colored, with darker brown on the spiral cords and a brown suffusion at the end of the siphonal canal.

In a short note, Sowerby (1841) stated that "a variety occurs with more than three varices." However, the original illustration and all subsequent figures but one have shown the form with five varices. Knudsen (1956) figured a form with

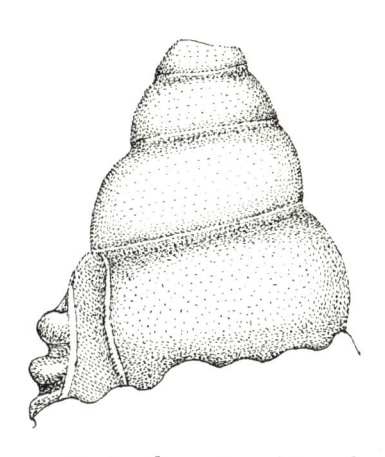

45. *Muricanthus varius*, protoconch

three varices (Pl. 12, fig. 5, herein) from the west coast of Africa under the name *Murex senegalensis* Gmelin, 1791, a species limited to the Brazilian coast. This form with three varices differs consistently from the more typical "multivaricate-form" of *M. varius* in its smaller number of varices, its possession of a persistent intervarical node, its proportionately longer canal, and its shorter spire. In general, these two forms differ largely in terms of greater or lesser development of the same elements (see *Siratus senegalensis*, p. 107, for additional explanation).

Western Africa: Senegal to Angola.

See Pl. 12, figs. 5–6.

Genus NAQUETIA Jousseaume, 1880

TYPE SPECIES: *Murex triqueter* Born, 1778, by original designation.

Because of its close relationship to *Chicoreus*, *Phyllonotus*, and *Siratus*, *Naquetia* has often been considered a subgenus of one or another of these groups. In having three varices per whorl and certain other features it most closely resembles the first of these genera; it differs from it, however, in the sparseness of its varical extensions. It resembles some *Phyllonotus* species in having a varical webbing or flange, composed of fused fronds, along the entire varix, but generally most prominent anteriorly. The shell is generally slender, but the proportion of spire to body whorl and canal varies from species to species.

The radula resembles that of *Chicoreus* in the general shape of the lateral and rachidian teeth. It may be distinguished by its generally smaller size, by the heaviness and broadness of the laterals, and by the proportionately smaller size of the intermediate cusps of the rachidian tooth.

The genus appears to be restricted to the Indo-West Pacific, although a western Atlantic species, *Siratus consuela* (A. H. Verrill, 1950), has been placed here by several authors.

Naquetia annandalei (Preston, 1910)
Pteronotus annandalei Preston, 1910: 118

The shell is moderately large for the genus (maximum length 80 mm) and fusiform. The spire is high, consisting of one and one-half smooth, convex nuclear whorls and eight subangulate postnuclear whorls. The suture is impressed. The body whorl is large and fusoid. The aperture is moderate in size and ovate to lenticular, with a narrow, deeply cut anal sulcus. The mature outer apertural lip is thickened and strongly lirate within, the lirae arranged in pairs anteriorly, becoming heavier and single at the posterior end, where an inner and an outer node delimit the anal sulcus. The columellar lip is adherent posteriorly, detached and weakly erect anteriorly, where there is a weak, oblique fold. The siphonal canal is long, moderately broad, narrowly open, and slightly bent, first to the left and then to the right.

The body whorl bears three broadly thickened varices, with well-developed undulate webbings limited to the anterior portion of the body and the siphonal canal. Additional axial sculpture consists of two to four intervarical ridges. Spiral sculpture consists of seven to nine heavy primary cords on the body, these intercalated by several secondary and tertiary sculptural elements, and three primary cords and several minor cords and threads on the canal. Where the primary and secondary cords intersect the axial sculptural elements they are thrown into prominent nodes.

Shell ground color is tan-pink, with tan-white on the summits of most spiral cords. Three spiral bands of red-brown are evident, one at the shoulder margin, one medial, and one basal. The aperture and the central portion of the siphonal canal are white.

Bay of Bengal, in 76 m (type locality), off East Africa, and in the Red Sea.

See Pl. 15, figs. 9–10.

Naquetia barclayi (Reeve, 1858)
Murex barclayi Reeve, 1858: 209

The shell is large for the genus (maximum length 90 mm) and fusiform. The spire is high, consisting of seven or eight convex to weakly shouldered postnuclear whorls and a protoconch of undetermined nature. The suture is moderately impressed. The body whorl is large and fusoid. The aperture is large and ovate, with a deep, looped anal sulcus, this strengthened by a weak parietal ridge. The outer apertural lip is somewhat erect and marginally crenulate, the crenulations extending very briefly into the aperture as ephemeral lirae; where the outer lip abuts the anal sulcus, two or three strong denticles are developed. The columellar lip is adherent above, spreading into a thin parietal callus; below, the lip is detached and somewhat erect. The siphonal canal is narrow and moderately long, straight, and minutely open to the right.

The body whorl bears three low varices. Additional axial sculpture consists of two or three slender ridges, these most prominent at the shoulder margin, and finer nodulose threads. In addition, fine axial scratches cover the entire shell. The varices develop an extensive webbing, this extending from the suture to the midpoint of the siphonal canal: the webbing is most broadly expanded in the region of the siphonal canal and is generally best preserved on the last varix; it is also pleated, the pleats reflecting the spiral cords, these most strongly developed on the dorsal surface of the webbing.

Shell color is a fleshy purple-brown, with three spiral brown bands, these most prominent on the varices. The apertural margin is white; the interior of the aperture is pale violet.

N. barclayi differs from *N. annandalei* in its larger, broader aperture, larger anal notch, more weakly lirate interior surface of its outer apertural lip, broader, more globose body whorl, more extensive webbing of its varix, finer sculpture, and more subdued shell coloration.

Mauritius (type locality), Taiwan (figured specimen), southeastern Japan, and Queensland, Australia.

See Pl. 15, fig. 8.

Naquetia capucina (Lamarck, 1822)
Murex capucinus Lamarck, 1822: 164; *M. permaestus* Hedley, 1915: 745, unnecessary new name for *M. capucinus* of authors, not of Lamarck, 1822

The shell is moderately large for the genus (maximum length 85 mm) and fusiform. The spire is high, consisting of six convex postnuclear whorls and a protoconch of undetermined nature. The suture is generally obscured by the succeeding whorl. The body whorl is fusoid and moderate in size. The aperture is moderately large and ovate to subcircular, with a narrow, shallow anal sulcus. The outer apertural lip is thickened, flaring, nonerect, and finely crenulate, with strong but brief lirae extending into the aperture. The columellar lip is smooth and entirely adherent. The siphonal canal is moderate in length, broad, narrowly open to the right, and weakly distally recurved.

The body whorl bears three fimbriate varices. Other axial sculpture consists of two or three ephemeral ridges in each intervarical space. Fine lamellae cover the entire shell. Spiral sculpture consists of alternating major and minor cords. Where the cords intersect the varices, the lamellae covering the varix are thrown into frilly folds or pleats. In well-developed shells the anterior portion of the last varix is expanded into a pleated webbing, scalloped with points representing the positions of the spiral cords.

Shell color is uniform in the individual, ranging from light chestnut-brown to dark umber-brown. The uniform coloration of the shell is the clearest diagnostic character of this species.

The Philippines and Singapore to western Australia.

See Pl. 15, fig. 13.

Naquetia trigonula (Lamarck, 1816)

Murex trigonulus Lamarck, 1816: pl. 417, fig. 4, Liste, p. 5; *M. triqueter* var. *amanuensis* Couturier, 1907: 142

The shell is moderately small (maximum length 55 mm) and fusiform. The spire is moderately high to high, consisting of one and one-half nuclear whorls and five or six convex postnuclear whorls. The suture is impressed. The body whorl is large and fusoid. The aperture is moderately small and ovate, with a moderately small, shallow, parietally demarcated anal sulcus. The outer apertural lip is essentially nonerect and finely crenulate. The columellar lip is smooth and entirely adherent. The siphonal canal is moderately long, exceedingly narrowly open to the right, and distally recurved.

The body whorl bears three varices, all of which are low and rounded posteriorly, more developed anteriorly. Other intervarical axial sculpture consists of two or three narrow costae. Spiral sculpture consists of ten broadly spaced major cords, these starting at the shoulder margin and extending to the tip of the canal. In the space between each two major cords are one or two minor cords and numerous fine spiral threads. The entire shell, when unworn, is covered with fine axial lamellae, these becoming raised over the spiral elements and imparting a finely scabrous appearance to the shell surface. Where the cords intersect the axial elements, prominent nodes are formed. The anterior half of each varix is developed into a moderately broad, thin, pleated webbing. There is a sharp demarcation between the webbing, which appears to be an extension of the dorsal sculpture, and the remainder of the outer apertural lip, which is densely fimbriate on its ventral surface.

Shell color is yellow to buff, with two or three spiral brown bands on the body and irregular brown blotches scattered at random over the shell surface.

Although the range of this species overlaps that of *N. triquetra* throughout the entire Indian

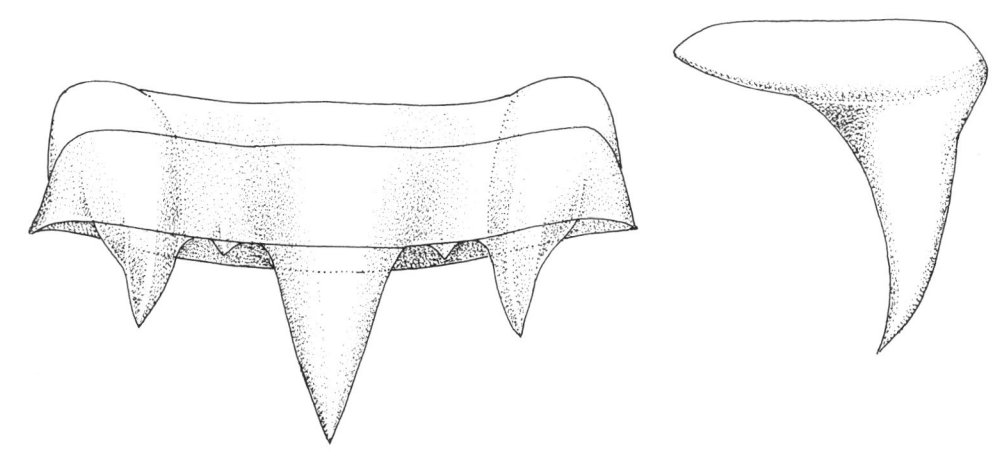

46. *Naquetia trigonula*, radular dentition

Ocean, *N. triquetra* is apparently more common in the Indian Ocean; *N. trigonula* is more common in the western Pacific, with the point of greatest overlap being in the Philippines. Isolated examples of rarely occurring forms intermediate between *N. trigonula* and *N. triquetra,* presumably hybrids, have been brought to our attention.

Eastern Africa (Mozambique) to the Fiji Islands.

See Pl. 15, fig. 12.

Naquetia triquetra (Born, 1778)
Murex triqueter Born, 1778: 288; *M. roseotinctus* Sowerby, 1860: 429

The shell is small to moderate in size (maximum length 70 mm) and fusiform. The spire is high, consisting of one and one-half nuclear whorls and eight or nine convex postnuclear whorls. The suture is impressed. The body whorl is moderately large and fusoid. The aperture is moderate in size and ovate, with a small, shallow anal sulcus. The outer apertural lip is barely erect and minutely dentate; its interior is finely lirate. The columellar lip is weakly denticulate at its posterior end and adherent for its entire length. The siphonal canal is moderate in length, broad, very narrowly open to the right, and distally recurved.

The body whorl bears three low varices. Additional axial sculpture consists of three or four low ridges, these strongest at the shoulder, in each intervarical space. Spiral sculpture consists of numerous low cords of equal strength. Where the cords cross the intervarical ridges, nodules are formed, these enhancing the reticulate pattern. Almost no projection is produced where the cords cross the varix, except anteriorly, where a more or less well-defined webbing or flange is produced on each varix.

The final varix is much more developed than the earlier varices. The entire shell is covered with fine threads, these crossed by fine axial lamellae. The ventral surface of the final varix is richly laminate.

Shell color is variable, consisting generally of a white base, spiral bands of chestnut-brown, purple-brown, or gray-brown, and brown blotches distributed at random over the shell. Some eastern African populations have pure white individuals intermingled with typically colored specimens.

Eastern Africa (Zanzibar, Mozambique) to the Philippines and Okinawa.

See Pl. 15, fig. 11.

Genus NIPPONOTROPHON
Kuroda & Habe, 1971

TYPE SPECIES: *Boreotrophon echinus* Dall, 1918, by original designation

The shell is moderate-sized to moderately large (30–52 mm in length) and fusiform. The spire is quite high, consisting of one and one-half to two and one-half convex nuclear whorls and six to eight postnuclear whorls. The shoulder is characteristically broad and obtusely angulate or subangulate. The aperture is moderately large and ovate, with a weak anal sulcus. The outer apertural lip is thin and weakly crenulate, weakly furrowed on its inner surface, and flaring at its margin. The columellar lip is adherent above and generally detached and erect for the anterior two-thirds of its length. The siphonal canal is moderately long to very long.

The body whorl bears five or six low, sharp, more or less briefly and sparsely spinose varices. Spiral sculpture consists of four to seven weak cords, these sometimes obsolete between the varices. At their intersections with the varices the cords are produced into short to moderately long, open, dorsally curved spines resembling extended scales; the longest such spines are developed on the shoulder-margin cord.

Shell color is gray-white or yellow-white. Fresh examples of some species may bear a thin, flat-white intritacalx.

The operculum is light brown, roughly unguiculate (hoof-shaped), and moderately strongly annulate on its interior surface, with a terminal nucleus.

The radular dentition is muricoid, with each transverse row consisting of a coronate rachidian tooth flanked on each side by a sickle-shaped lateral tooth. The rachidian is very simple, with five very sharp cusps, evenly spaced on the base, these all of approximately equal length.

Nipponotrophon echinus (Dall, 1918)
Boreotrophon echinus Dall, 1918: 232

The shell is small for the genus (maximum length 35 mm) and fusiform. The spire is high, consisting of two nuclear whorls and five or six angulate postnuclear whorls. The suture is weakly impressed and undulate. The body whorl is of moderate size and fusoid. The aperture is moderately large and ovate, with a narrow, shallow anal sulcus and a moderately broad opening into the siphonal canal. The outer apertural lip is erect, barely crenulate marginally, and weakly flaring; its inner surface is weakly furrowed. The columellar lip is weakly callused and adherent posteriorly, detached and erect anteriorly. The siphonal canal is moderately long, bent to the left, and open.

The body whorl bears five or six spinose varices. Spiral sculpture consists of five weak cords, all on the body. Where these cords intersect the varices, short, open, slightly dorsally recurved spines are produced. The shoulder-margin spine is longer than the four other spines.

Shell color is gray-white, with a porcelaneous white aperture.

Known to us only from southeastern Japan in deep water (ca. 200 m).

See Pl. 3, fig. 2.

Nipponotrophon elegantulus (Dall, 1907)
Boreotrophon elegantulus Dall, 1907: 165

The shell is small for the genus (maximum length 31.5 mm) and fusiform. The spire is high and acute, consisting of two nuclear whorls and five postnuclear whorls. The suture is distinct but not deeply impressed. The body whorl is moderately large and fusoid. The aperture is moderately large and ovate, with a shallow, narrow anal sulcus. The outer apertural lip is thin, erect, and dorsally reflected. The columellar lip is detached and erect, except parietally, where it forms a small, transparent callus. The siphonal canal is moderately long, essentially straight, and narrowly open.

The body whorl bears ten to 12 thin, lamellate, dorsally reflected varices. Spiral sculpture consists of three or four weak cords on the early whorls, these obsolete on the later whorls. Numerous fine spiral striae cover the entire shell.

Shell color is pellucid white, with one nebulous brown band just below the suture, a second at the periphery, and a third on the canal.

Off Attu Island (type locality), Aleutian Islands.

Nipponotrophon galapaganus (Emerson & D'Attilio, 1970)
"Murex" galapaganus Emerson & D'Attilio, 1970: 271

The shell is moderately large (maximum length 46 mm) and roughly fusiform. The spire is high, consisting of two and one-half smooth nuclear whorls and seven weakly shouldered postnuclear whorls. The suture is moderately impressed and more or less obscured. The body whorl is moderately large and fusoid. The aperture is moderately large and ovate, with a broad, very shallow anal sulcus. The outer apertural lip is erect, flaring, and weakly furrowed on its inner surface, this bearing eight weak denticles. The columellar lip is smooth and arcuate, more or less strongly callused and detached, and weakly erect. The siphonal canal is moderately long and open, bent to the left, then to the right, and dorsally recurved at its tip.

The body whorl bears six low, sharp, spinose varices. Spiral sculpture consists of four weak to ephemeral cords, these developed into moderately long, open, dorsally recurved spines at their intersections with the varices.

Shell color is white, covered with a thick, flat-white intritacalx. The aperture is porcelaneous white.

Known only from Santa Cruz and Hood Islands, Galápagos Islands (Ecuador), in deep water (150–200 m).

See Pl. 3, fig. 6.

Nipponotrophon gorgon (Dall, 1913)
Boreotrophon gorgon Dall, 1913: 588

The shell is large for the genus (maximum length 52 mm) and fusiform. The spire is high and acute, consisting of about two nuclear whorls and six obtusely angulate postnuclear whorls. The suture is weakly impressed. The body whorl is long and fusoid. The aperture is large and ovate

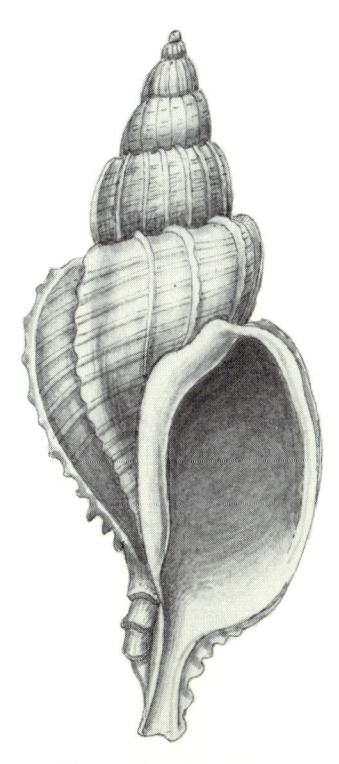

47. *Nipponotrophon elegantulus*

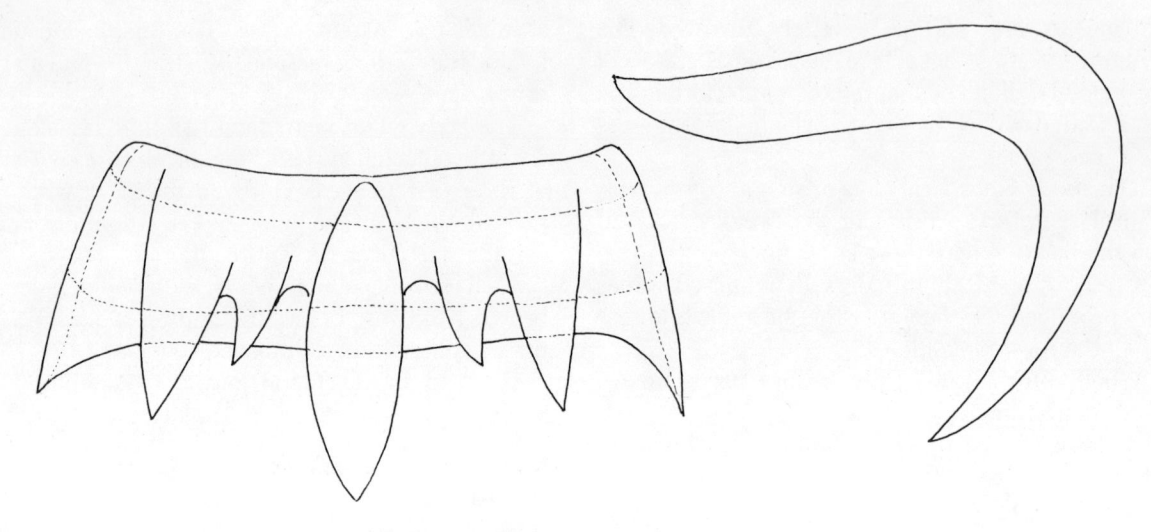

48. Nipponotrophon gorgon, radular dentition

to lenticular, with a shallow, narrow anal sulcus. The outer apertural lip is thin and very weakly crenulate. The columellar lip is detached and erect, except parietally, where it is represented by a moderately broad callus. The siphonal canal is long, narrowly open, bent to the left and distally to the right, and curved dorsally at its tip.

The body whorl bears five or six thin, lamellate, spiny varices. Spiral sculpture consists of seven weak cords, four on the body and three on the canal. At the intersection of each cord with a varix, a thin-walled, moderately sharp, open, dorsally curving spine is formed. The spine formed by the shoulder-margin cord is twice as long and strong as any other, and is bent not only dorsally but also weakly posteriorly.

Shell color is white to pale fleshy yellow-white. The spines and the aperture are white. Indications of a thin, flat-white intritacalx persist on the specimens we have seen.

Known to us from off southern Japan (Hondo, type locality) and from off southeastern Japan (Kii).

See Pl. 3, fig. 14.

Nipponotrophon lasius (Dall, 1919)

Neptunea (Trophonopsis) lasia Dall, 1919: 338

The shell is large (maximum length 50 mm) and variable in sculpture. The spire is high and acute, consisting of six or seven angulate to convex postnuclear whorls and a protoconch of undetermined nature. The suture is distinct but not impressed. The body whorl is moderately large and fusoid. The aperture is moderately large and ovate, with a shallow, narrow anal sulcus. The outer apertural lip is very slightly erect, if at all. The columellar lip is detached, erect anteriorly, and adherent posteriorly, in some cases forming a brief parietal callus. The siphonal canal is moderately long, narrowly open, and generally bent to the left.

The body whorl bears up to 11 more or less prominent varices. In most specimens we have seen, these varices are low, heavy axial ridges with a former outer apertural margin projecting moderately from the growth plane. In some cases the varices are much less broad but project more prominently (Pl. 13, fig. 7). Numerous fine spiral threads cover the shell, and fimbriations are produced over the varices. In strongly sculptured forms, at the intersections of spiral and axial elements, brief spines are produced, these longest at the shoulder margin; in addition, in these forms, the spiral threads are stronger and are packed together so tightly that little if any space may be seen between them. Although the two extremes differ substantially, other specimens show an apparently unbroken intergradation between them.

Shell color is blue-white, with a thin, flat-white intritacalx, a dirty-brown periostracum, and a porcelaneous white aperture.

Southeastern Bering Sea to Todos Santos Bay, Baja California (fide Dall, 1921).

See Pl. 13, figs. 6–8.

Nipponotrophon pagodus (Hayashi & Habe, 1965)

Boreotrophon pagodus Hayashi & Habe, 1965: 12

The shell is moderately large (maximum length 52 mm) and narrowly fusiform. The spire is high, consisting of two convex nuclear whorls and six weakly shouldered postnuclear whorls; the shoulder is characteristically broad and obtusely sloping. The suture is more or less impressed and undulate. The body whorl is long (about three-fifths of the entire shell length) and narrowly fusoid. The aperture is large and ovate to sublenticular, with a weak anal sulcus. The outer apertural lip is thin and flaring marginally; its inner surface is weakly furrowed. The columellar lip is adherent and weakly callused posteriorly, attached and moderately erect anteriorly. The siphonal canal is quite long, open to the right, bent first to the left and then to the right, and dorsally recurved at its tip.

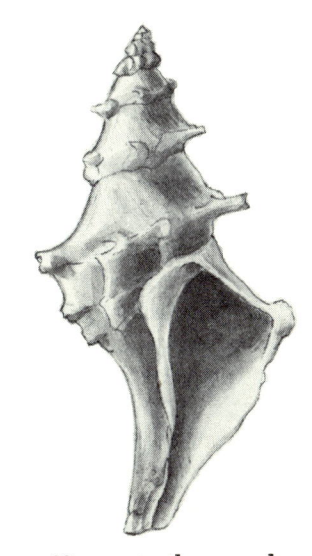

49. Nipponotrophon pagodus

The body whorl bears five low, sharp varices. The intersections of the varices with the five weak to ephemeral spiral cords produce short to moderately long, open, dorsally curved spines, the spines at the shoulder margin being much the longest.

Shell color is white to yellow-white, the aperture colored much the same as the remainder of the shell.

Known to us only from the southeastern coast of Japan in deep water (ca. 300 m).

See Pl. 14, fig. 7.

Nipponotrophon scitulus (Dall, 1891)

Trophon (Boreotrophon) scitulus Dall, 1891: 188

The shell is moderately large for the genus (maximum length 40 mm) and fusiform. The spire is high, consisting of a bulbous, asymmetrical protoconch of one and one-half whorls and five or six shouldered postnuclear whorls. The suture is weakly impressed. The body whorl is of moderate size and fusoid. The aperture is of moderate size and ovate, with a narrow, moderately shallow anal sulcus. The outer apertural lip is more or less erect and weakly crenulate. The smooth columellar lip is detached and erect anteriorly, and forms an adherent, moderately well-developed callus posteriorly. The siphonal canal is moderately long to quite long and slender, narrowly open, and bent slightly to the left.

The body whorl bears nine or more thin, lamellate, spiny varices. Spiral sculpture consists of seven or eight weak cords, four or five on the body and three on the canal. At the intersections of these cords and the varices, short, subacute, open, weakly dorsally recurved spines are developed.

Shell color is translucent blue-white, covered by a thin, flat-white intritacalx.

Bering Sea [cited by Dall (1921) as from the Pribilof Islands to Unalaska Island].

See Pl. 14, figs. 10–11.

Genus PAZIELLA Jousseaume, 1880

TYPE SPECIES: *Murex pazi* Crosse, 1869, by original designation.

The shell is fusiform, with a high spire. The suture is strongly impressed. The aperture is ovate and moderately large, the outer apertural lip flaring marginally and more or less strongly lirate within. The siphonal canal is of moderate length. The body whorl bears low spinose varices, these originating at the suture. Weak spiral cords are developed into short, sharp, open, dorsally recurved spines where they intersect the varices. In some instances a double axial row of spines is developed on the varices. The spines developed from the shoulder-margin cord are almost twice as long as those on the other cords. A notable gap in spiral sculpture is apparent at the base of the body, the gap followed on the canal by one or two strong spiral cords produced into moderately long spines on the varices.

Shell color is white or gray-white, with a thick intritacalx. The aperture is porcelaneous white.

Paziella hystricina (Dall, 1889)

Murex hystricinus Dall, 1889: 200

The shell is small (maximum length 21 mm) and biconical. The spire is high, consisting of one and one-half convex nuclear whorls and six or seven shouldered postnuclear whorls. The suture is impressed. The body whorl is moderate in size and roughly trigonal. The aperture is ovate or subovate, the posterior margin somewhat flattened, with a broad, shallow anal sulcus. The outer apertural lip is erect and weakly crenulate, its inner surface bearing five or six notable denticles. The columellar lip is detached, erect, and flaring. The siphonal canal is of moderate length, open, and bent strongly to the right.

The body whorl bears six strongly spinose varices. Other axial sculpture is lacking. Spiral sculpture consists of four weak cords on the body and two still weaker ones on the canal. Additionally, innumerable microscopic lamellae crossed by equally fine spiral threads impart the appearance of an exceedingly fine latticework to the unworn portions of the shell. Where the spiral cords intersect the varices, long, slender, more or less dorsally recurved spines are produced, those at the shoulder margin by far the longest. A brief, thin webbing connects all the spines of a given varix.

Shell color is white. The aperture is porcelaneous white.

Off Cuba and Puerto Rico to Martinique in very deep water (296–552 m).

See Pl. 25, fig. 12.

Paziella pazi (Crosse, 1869)

Murex pazi Crosse, 1869: 183; *M. nuttingi* Dall, 1896: 13; *M. atlantis* Clench & Pérez Farfante, 1945: 41; *M. oregonia* Bullis, 1964: 106

The shell is variable in size but reaches a maximum length of 90 mm. The spire is high, consisting of six or seven square-shouldered postnuclear whorls and a protoconch of undetermined nature. The suture is strongly impressed. The body whorl is of moderate size and roughly fusoid. The aperture is moderately large and subovate, the posterior margin flattened; the anal sulcus is broad and shallow. The outer apertural lip is thin and erect, with no marginal serration; its inner surface is strongly lirate. The columellar lip is adherent above, detached or adherent below. The siphonal canal is moderately short, open at the extreme right, and dorsally recurved at its tip.

The body whorl bears six to eight low, spinose varices. Spiral sculpture consists of four to eight weak cords on the body and one or two stronger ones on the canal. Where each spiral cord intersects the varices, one or two short, sharp, open, dorsally recurved spines are developed, the longest of these at the shoulder margin. A gap in spiral sculpture below the base of the body is followed by one or two stronger spiral cords on the canal, these giving rise to moderately long, straight, open spines.

Shell color is uniform white or gray-white. The aperture is porcelaneous white, blue-white, or yellow-white.

Apparently mature shells occur in two or three distinct size ranges.

M. nuttingi is the type species of *Dallimurex* Rehder, 1946, and *M. atlantis* is the type species of *Bathymurex* Clench & Pérez Farfante, 1945.

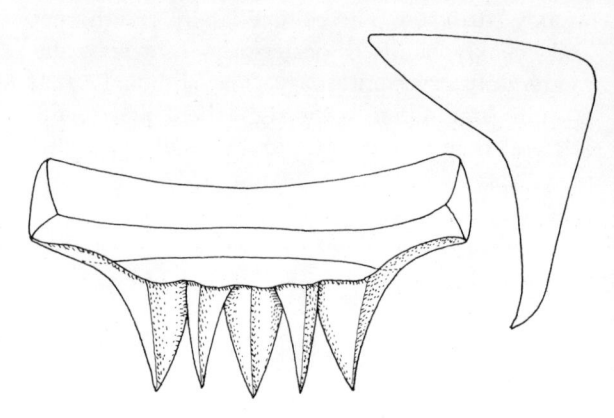

50. *Paziella pazi*, radular dentition

Because we consider both of these species to be synonyms of *Paziella pazi*, these genera are thus objective junior synonyms of *Paziella*.

Caribbean Sea, from the Florida Keys and Cuba to the coast of French Guiana in moderately deep to quite deep water (30–550 m).

See Pl. 26, figs. 1–3.

Genus PAZINOTUS E. H. Vokes, 1970

TYPE SPECIES: *Eupleura stimpsonii* Dall, 1889, by original designation.

The shell is small (10–15 mm long) and broadly fusiform. The spire is high, and the suture is strongly impressed. The aperture is small and ovate, with a shallow, narrow to broad anal sulcus, three to five prominent denticles on the inner surface of the outer apertural lip, and two or three weak, oblique, elongate, plica-like pustules on the anterior end of the columella.

Axial ornamentation consists of four to seven more or less winglike varices, formed by lamellar flanges connecting varical spines. These spines, a reflection of spiral sculptural elements, are weakly to moderately developed.

Pazinotus smithi (Schepman, 1911)

Ocinebra smithi Schepman, 1911: 349

We have not seen a specimen of this species; the following is taken from Schepman (1911):

"Shell shortly fusiform with rather long, acute

spire, thin, yellowish brown. Whorls about seven or eight (in the finest specimen the upper whorls are incrustated [sic], in the other one worn), convex, slightly flattened above, separated by a deep suture. Shell rather smooth, with eight varices on the upper whorls, six on the last; these varices have two hollow spines on the upper whorls, three on the penultimate [whorl], and six on the last one. The upper spine of each varix is longest and elegantly turned up; the other ones are only slightly upturned; the spines are connected on the intermediate areas by rather inconspicuous spiral ribs or lirae. Aperture subtriangular, upper margin horizontal, outer margin convexly curved, the spines not very prominent, [since] in the apertural varix they are connected by a very fine wall, [this] consisting on the front side of fine, angular scales, which are, moreover, undulate. Interior margin with four tubercles, the columellar margin smooth, with a thin, free lamina, the columellar side and outer border of upper and right margins light violet, interior of aperture brown, canal moderately long, a little open, directed toward the right and upturned, with an external row of scales at its origin, formed by the ends of the varices.

51. *Pazinotus smithi*

"Alt. 15 mm, lat. 8 mm (without spines of opposite varix), apert. alt., with canal, 8.5 mm, lat. 2 mm.

"Known only from 'Siboga' Station 105, 6°8' N. lat. 121°19' E. long., Eastern Sulu Archipelago, in 274 meters."

Pazinotus stimpsonii (Dall, 1889)

Eupleura stimpsonii Dall, 1889: 204

The shell is small (maximum length 14 mm) and broadly fusiform. The spire is high, consisting of two smooth, convex nuclear whorls and five shouldered postnuclear whorls. The suture is impressed. The body whorl is moderate in size to moderately large and subtrigonal. The aperture is small and ovate, with a narrow, shallow anal sulcus. The outer apertural lip is weakly erect; its inner surface is flared at the margin and bears five prominent denticles, the posteriormost one in the shoulder margin region. The columellar lip is slightly callused and adherent and bears two or three oblique, anterior pustules. The siphonal canal is moderately short, is narrowly open to the right, and is dorsally recurved at its tip.

The body whorl bears four to six more or less broad winglike varices extending from the suture to a point just above the tip of the siphonal canal. Spiral sculpture consists of five weak to ephemeral cords produced into small to tiny points on the varical margin. The shoulder-margin spine, the longest, is hooked posteriorly.

Shell color is waxy yellow-white. The aperture is porcelaneous white.

Off Egmont Key, western Florida, and Palm Beach, eastern Florida, to Barbados (type locality) in deep water (120–200 m).

See Pl. 23, fig. 3.

Genus **PHYLLONOTUS** Swainson, 1833

TYPE SPECIES: *Murex imperialis* Swainson, 1833 (=*M. margaritensis* Abbott, 1958), by subsequent designation, Swainson, 1833.

The shell is generally large, solid, and globose. The spire is low to moderately high. The suture is moderately impressed but usually obscured by the succeeding whorl. The body whorl is large and globose. The aperture is subcircular, with a deep, broad anal sulcus. The outer apertural lip is erect, most strongly so anteriorly, and strongly crenate; the interior of the outer lip is strongly lirate. The columellar lip is smooth and adherent above, expanded into a moderate parietal callus; below, it is detached, forming an erect inductura of greater or lesser extent. In several species, a series of denticles may be found over the anterior end of the columella. The siphonal canal is broad, narrowly open to the right, and strongly, distally recurved. The shells of most species bear three broad, spiral, brown bands, these most visible on the varices and on the interior of the outer lip. In addition, the apertural margin is heavily enameled and generally bears pink, orange, yellow, or brown markings or a combination of these colors.

Arakawa (1964) has introduced the generic taxon *Chicomurex* for *Murex superbus* Sowerby, 1889. We do not consider it distinct from *Phyllonotus*. If it should prove to be distinct, *M. laci-*

niatus Sowerby, 1841, would also be assigned to *Chicomurex*.

Phyllonotus brassica (Lamarck, 1822)
Murex brassica Lamarck, 1822: 167; *M. ducalis* Broderip & Sowerby, 1829: 377

The shell is very large (maximum length 205 mm) and globose. The spire is moderate in height, consisting of two nuclear whorls and six or seven convex postnuclear whorls. The suture is partially to entirely obscured by the succeeding whorl. The body whorl is large and globose. The aperture is moderately large and ovate, with a moderately deep, broad anal sulcus, delimited parietally by a heavy spiral ridge. The outer apertural lip is erect and coarsely dentate: four or five wedge-shaped denticles occur on the shoulder portion of the outer lip, followed by a prominent notch, below which more typical labial dentition is the rule; the interior of the lip is barely lirate. The columellar lip is adherent and briefly spreading above (forming a small parietal callus), marginally detached and briefly erect below; three to five weak bumps or pustules occur at its anterior end. The siphonal canal is short to moderate in length, moderately broad, narrowly open at the right, and weakly, distally recurved.

The body whorl bears seven or eight varices. Other axial sculpture is generally lacking, although in some specimens, some intervarical spaces are ornamented with nodose ridges. Spiral sculpture consists of ephemeral cords, which, as they cross the varices, are strongly elevated to form heavy, blunt, anteroposteriorly flattened, closed protuberances. The area above the shoulder margin lacks spinose ornamentation. The shoulder spine, much the longest, is followed by a gap. A series of low protuberances, increasing in length anteriorly, follows the gap. At the base of the body and extending onto the canal is a series of five short, sharp, open spines. The solid body spines, representing the true varix, are set back some distance from the outer apertural lip. The entire shell is covered with a very fine microsculpture consisting of numerous dense, fine spiral threads, these minutely tuberculate.

The ground color of the shell is buff-brown. There are also three spiral brown bands, one at the shoulder margin, one medial, and one basal. The aperture is yellow-white within; the apertural margin is orange-pink. The margin of each varix is slightly raised above the shell surface, exposing the pink coloration of previous outer lips.

Southern Baja California and Mazatlán, Mexico, to Peru.
See Pl. 16, fig. 5.

Phyllonotus duplex (Röding, 1798)
Purpura duplex Röding, 1798: 141; *Purpura rosarium* Röding, 1798: 140; *Murex melonulus* Lamarck, 1822: 171; *M. ananas* Hinds, 1844: 127; *M. beckii* Philippi, 1847: pl. 2, fig. 1; *M. bifasciata* A. Adams, 1853: 269; *M. hoplites* Fischer, 1876: 236

The shell is large (maximum length 165 mm) and fusiform to globose-fusiform. The spire is moderately low to moderately high, consisting of two nuclear whorls and seven or eight weakly shouldered postnuclear whorls. The suture is generally obscured by the succeeding whorl. The body whorl is large and globose to fusiform. The aperture is large and ovate, with a moderately deep and broad anal sulcus, this delimited parietally by a strong spiral ridge. The outer apertural lip is coarsely dentate and somewhat erect, most notably anteriorly. The columellar lip is adherent for its entire length, with a few weak or ephemeral pustules at its anterior end. The siphonal canal is generally broad, moderately short, narrowly open to the right, and weakly, distally recurved.

The body whorl bears six to eight varices, these sometimes spinose or nodose. Other axial sculpture consists of one to three ridges in each intervarical space. Spiral sculpture consists of alternating major and minor cords, these producing very short to moderately long projections where they cross the varices. There are generally two long, open or partially open projections (whether long spines or short, blunt nodes), the longer at the shoulder margin and a slightly shorter one just below it. A series of four shorter spines is followed by a gap and then by two short, open spines on the canal. Microsculpture, consisting of numerous fine, irregular spiral threads, crossed by fine axial lamellae, covers the entire shell.

Shell color is yellow-brown to pinkish-brown, with three spiral brown bands on the body, one at the shoulder margin, one medial, and one basal, these most noticeable on the varices and on the interior of the outer lip, where the color changes to pale pink or dark salmon-pink. The aperture is white within; the apertural margin is suffused with pale pinkish-orange or deep salmon.

In the form common to nineteenth-century collections (Pl. 16, fig. 7), the spines are moderately long, broadly open, and straight to strongly recurved. This form, which grows to the listed maximum size, is the *M. saxatilis* of authors. Actually, Linné's concept of *M. saxatilis* is a composite of several species and is generally considered a dubious name. Another form, named *Purpura rosarium* Röding, 1798 (Pl. 16, fig. 1, herein), has a much smaller shell (65–70 mm) and low, closed, nodelike shell projections. In this form almost all shell sculpture is reduced. To judge from the number of shell whorls present, the specimens to which this name is attached are generally immature.

Cape Verde Islands to Angola, western Africa. See Pl. 16, figs. 1, 7.

Phyllonotus erythrostomus (Swainson, 1831)

Murex erythrostomus Swainson, 1831: pl. 73; *M. bicolor* Valenciennes, 1832: 301; *M. hippocastanum* Philippi, 1845: 191

The shell is large (maximum length 150 mm) and globose. The spire is moderately low, consisting of two and one-half nuclear whorls and six convex postnuclear whorls. The suture is obscured by the succeeding whorl. The body whorl is large and globose. The aperture is large and ovate, with a deep, broad anal sulcus extending posteriorly to the shoulder of the preceding whorl. The outer apertural lip is coarsely dentate and strongly erect; its interior is moderately to weakly lirate. The columellar lip is expanded posteriorly into an adherent parietal callus, this detached and strongly erect anteriorly, forming a prominent inductura, the edge of which is horizontally furrowed or crumpled; along the columellar axis are six to ten weakly to moderately well-developed denticles. The siphonal canal is moderately long, slender (for the genus), narrowly open at the right, and strongly recurved for one-half its length.

The body whorl bears four or five spinose varices. Axial sculpture otherwise consists of a single slender, knobbed ridge in each intervarical space. Spiral sculpture consists of six or seven prominent cords, these forming raised knobs on the intervarical ridges and turning up into sharp, open spines over the varices; the uppermost spine, at the shoulder margin, is much longer than the others, and its hollow body is confluent with the aperture. There is also a microsculpture consisting of fine, irregular spiral threads and fine axial lamellae, these elevated into fine scales where they cross the threads.

Shell color is flat white, exaggerated in its flatness by the microsculpture. The interior of the aperture, the inductura, and the interior of the upper portion of the canal are rich pink. In young specimens the three brown spiral bands typical of the genus are apparent, particularly the upper and lower bands; these are not visible in mature shells.

Northern Gulf of California to Peru. See Pl. 16, fig. 4.

Phyllonotus laciniatus (Sowerby, 1841)

Murex laciniatus Sowerby, 1841: pl. 187, fig. 59; *M. scabrosus* Sowerby, 1841: pl. 189, fig. 73; *M. jickelii* Tapparone-Canefri, 1875: 582

The shell is small for the genus (maximum length 55 mm) and heavily fusiform. The spire is high, consisting of two and one-half nuclear whorls and seven or eight convex postnuclear whorls. The suture is deeply impressed. The body whorl is moderately large and globose. The aperture is moderately large and subcircular, with a very small, shallow anal sulcus. The outer apertural lip is erect and finely dentate, with brief lirations extending into the aperture from the denticles. The columellar lip is entirely detached, nonerect posteriorly, and strongly erect anteriorly. The siphonal canal is of moderate length, broad, narrowly open to the right, and bent to the right.

The body whorl bears three lamellose varices. Other axial sculpture consists of two or three weak axial costae, these strongest at the shoulder, and more or less well-developed axial lamellae over the entire shell surface. Spiral sculpture consists of six or seven major cords and numerous weak threads. Where the cords intersect the lamellae forming the body of each varix, the lamellae are elevated. The most marginal of these lamellose folds is developed separately from its neighbors, forming a recurved, spinelike growth; the strongest of these projections is located anteriorly on the body. In traversing a broad gap between the body and the canal, the continuously fringed varices and their spinose projections are much diminished. On the canal, three separate, strongly recurved spines are developed, followed by a straight, bifid spine. The strongly sculptured anterior portion of each spire whorl is obscured by the succeeding whorl, only the upper portion being visible.

Shell color is predominantly warm, fleshy ochre or brown, with three weak, darker brown spiral bands, one at the shoulder edge, one in the midbody region, and one anterior on the body. These bands are darkest on the varices. The aperture is porcelaneous white, except for the columellar margin and the edge of the inner surface of the outer apertural lip, which are suffused with a deep rosy pink to violet.

For *Murex laciniatus* of Japanese authors, see *Phyllonotus superbus* (Sowerby, 1889).

The Philippines (intertidal) to north Queensland, Australia (subtidal).

See Pl. 6, fig. 3.

Phyllonotus margaritensis (Abbott, 1958)

Murex imperialis Swainson, 1831: ser. 2, vol. 2, p. 67, pl. 67 (not Fischer de Waldheim, 1807); *M. margaritensis* Abbott, 1958: 61, new name for *M. imperialis* Swainson, 1831 (not Fischer de Waldheim, 1807).

The shell is moderately large (maximum length 115 mm) and obese-fusiform. The spire is moderate in length, consisting of six or seven convex postnuclear whorls and a protoconch of undetermined nature. The suture is generally obscured by the succeeding whorl. The body whorl is large and globose. The aperture is large, broadly open, and ovate, with a deep, moderately broad anal sulcus, this extending for some distance posteriorly and delimited parietally by a broad, low spiral ridge. The outer apertural lip is erect (most strongly anteriorly) and coarsely crenate; its interior is strongly lirate. The columellar lip is detached and erect, and may be developed into a moderate inductura; along the columellar line are five to 12 denticles. The siphonal canal is broad, moderate in length, narrowly open at the right, and sharply, distally recurved.

The body whorl bears four or rarely five low, knobby varices. Axial sculpture otherwise consists of a single prominent node in each intervarical space. Spiral sculpture consists of six prominent major cords, these forming knobs over the varices and the intervarical nodes, and seven minor cords, forming smaller knobs between each pair of large knobs; in addition, numerous fine spiral threads and axial lamellae cover the entire shell.

Ground color of the shell is white to buff-brown or yellow-brown. Three interrupted dark-brown spiral bands may occur on the body, and are then most prominent on the leading edges of the varices and inside the outer lip. The upper band may cover the entire shoulder, the second is medial, and the third is basal, extending in some instances onto the canal. The interior of the aperture varies in color: individuals from most populations have a pale apricot-orange or a paler yellow-orange aperture; unusually brightly marked shells (such as the figured specimen, from Porlamar, Venezuela) have a deep fleshy-pink aperture, with a dark-brown blotch of greater or lesser extent in the parietal region.

The southern Caribbean, from Trinidad to western Venezuela and northern Brazil.

See Pl. 16, fig. 6.

Phyllonotus peratus Keen, 1960

Phyllonotus peratus Keen, 1960: 105; *P. peratus decoris* Keen, 1960: 107

The shell is small for the genus (maximum length 65 mm) and broadly fusiform. The spire is high and acute, consisting of three nuclear whorls and six or seven subangulate to convex postnuclear whorls. The suture is well-impressed. The body whorl is moderately large and globose. The aperture is large and ovate, with a deep, moderately broad anal sulcus. The outer apertural lip is erect and coarsely dentate, the teeth arranged, for the most part, in groups of two; the inner surface of the outer lip bears many prominent

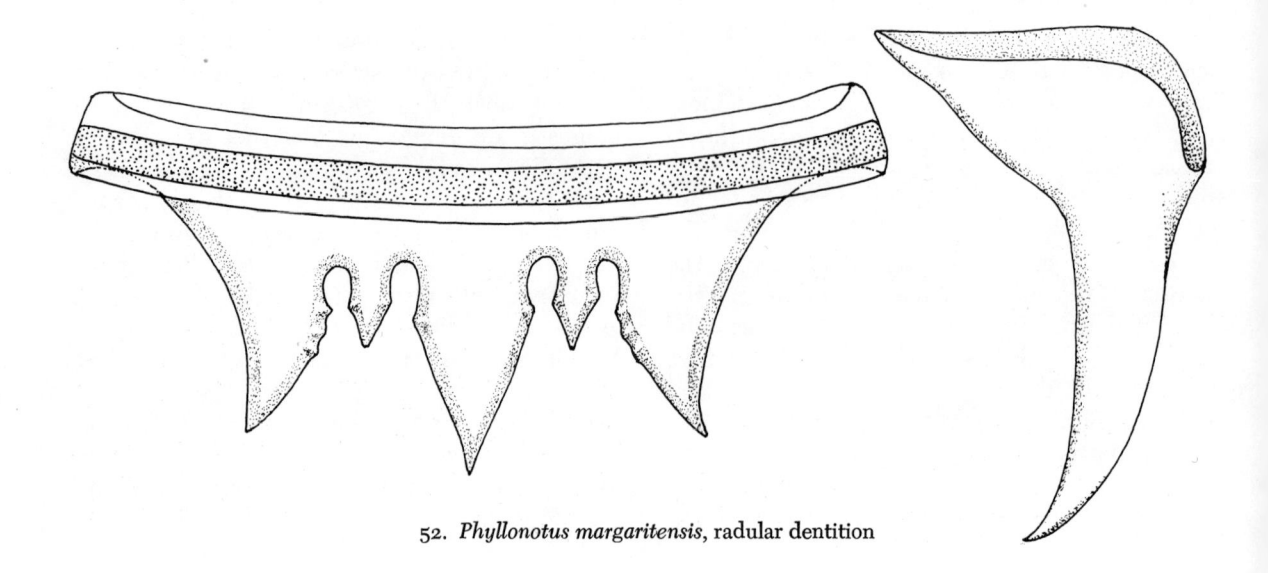

52. *Phyllonotus margaritensis*, radular dentition

lirae, each reflecting a tooth on the lip margin. The columellar lip is adherent posteriorly, detached and erect anteriorly, and bears a row of three to six more or less prominent pustules. The siphonal canal is short, narrowly open, and bent to the left and dorsally.

The body whorl bears three or four more or less prominent varices and two or three axial rows of nodes between each two consecutive varices. Spiral sculpture consists of six major cords, these prominent on the varices, where they form short, open, triangular spines, and of many fine threads. The leading edge of each varix is elevated out of the plane of shell growth, forming a frilly ornament in each case.

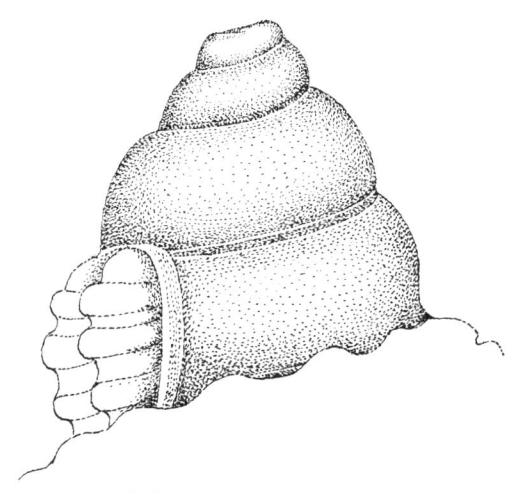

53. *Phyllonotus peratus*, protoconch

Shell ground color is pale yellow-brown to pink-brown. In addition there are four interrupted, darker brown spiral bands, one subsutural on the shoulder, one at the shoulder-margin site, one medial, and one basal; these are most prominent on the varices, less so on the intervarical nodes. The aperture is pale yellow, with four darker-brown spots on the interior of the outer lip at the end-positions of each brown color band.

This is apparently an eastern Pacific cognate of *Phyllonotus pomum*. It differs from that species in its generally smaller average size, larger protoconch (three whorls, as opposed to two), and its generally deeper habitat.

Mazatlán, Mexico, to Panamá, in 40 m or more. See Pl. 16, fig. 3.

Phyllonotus pomum (Gmelin, 1791)

Murex pomum Gmelin, 1791: 3527; *M. asperrimus* Lamarck, 1822: 164 (not Gmelin, 1791); *M. oculatus* Reeve, 1845: sp. 36; *M. mexicanus* Petit de la Saussaye, 1852: 51; *M. pomiformis* Mörch, 1852: 96

The shell is moderately large (maximum length 120 mm) and globose-fusiform. The spire is moderately high to high, consisting of two smooth nuclear whorls and seven convex postnuclear whorls. The suture is generally obscured by the succeeding whorl. The body whorl is large and globose. The aperture is large and ovate, with a broad, shallow anal sulcus, this delimited parietally by a spiral ridge. The outer apertural lip is coarsely crenate and erect, most prominently anteriorly; its interior is strongly but briefly lirate. The columellar lip is adherent and spreading, detached and erect below to form a moderate inductura; a long series of pustules of varying size and shape is found over the columellar region. The siphonal canal is broad, moderate in length, narrowly open to the right, and strongly, distally recurved.

The body whorl bears three or four nodose or briefly spinose varices. Other axial sculpture consists of one or two elongate nodes in each intervarical space. Spiral sculpture consists of alternating major and minor cords, these developed into knobs where they intersect the intervarical nodes, and into short, open, sharp spines where they intersect the varices. In addition, minute spiral threads and axial lamellae cover the entire shell.

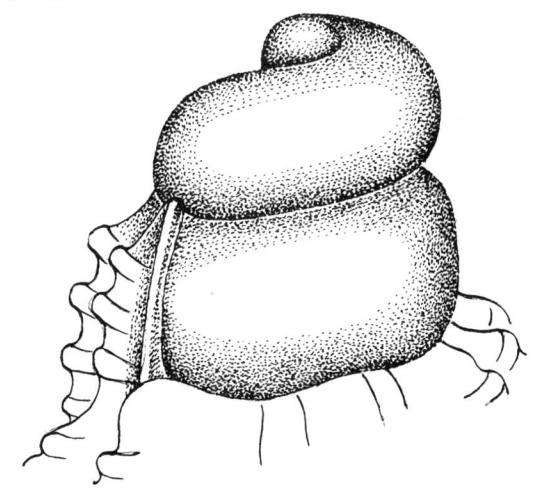

54. *Phyllonotus pomum*, protoconch

The ground color of the shell is gray-brown to yellow-brown. Three interrupted brown spiral bands on the body are most apparent on the leading edge of each varix and on the interior of the outer apertural lip. The color of the aperture varies from pale yellow to yellow-brown, with a brown blotch of greater or lesser extent in the parietal region.

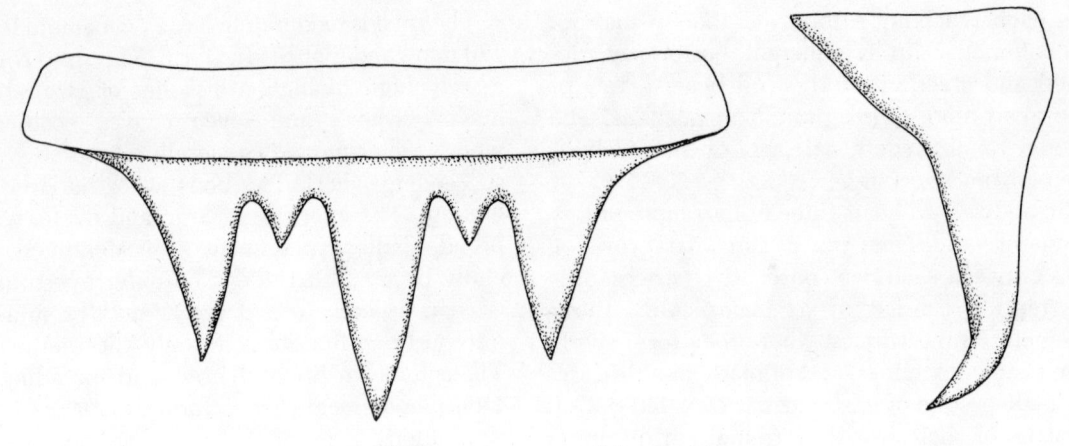

55. *Phyllonotus pomum*, radular dentition

Cape Hatteras, North Carolina, and the northern Gulf of Mexico to the southern Caribbean and northern Brazil, generally intertidal.

See Pl. 16, fig. 8.

Phyllonotus regius (Swainson, 1821)
Murex regius Swainson, 1821: 5

The shell is large (maximum length 170 mm) and globose-fusiform. The spire is moderate in height, consisting of three nuclear whorls and six or seven convex postnuclear whorls. The suture is generally obscured by the succeeding whorl. The body whorl is very large and globose. The aperture is broad and ovate, with a deep, angular anal sulcus extending posteriorly for some distance, its parietal border formed by two strong ridges, one axial and one spiral, which meet at almost right angles. The outer apertural lip is erect, most strongly so anteriorly, and coarsely dentate; its interior is briefly, strongly lirate. The columellar lip is expanded into a broad, adherent parietal callus, detached and marginally erect below to form a moderate inductura, the edge of which may be crumpled or folded; three to five small denticles may be present on the anterior end of the columellar lip. The siphonal canal is moderately short, broad, narrowly open to the right, and distally recurved.

The body whorl bears six or seven prominently spinose varices. Axial sculpture consists of major and minor cords and numerous fine, irregular threads, these crossed by equally irregular wrinkles: the minor cords are persistent between the varices and develop into minor spines on the varices; the major cords are ephemeral between the varices, arising just previous to the varix to form moderately long, stout, sharp, recurved, open spines, the longest the uppermost, at the shoulder margin. The open faces of this shoulder spine and the one just below it are confluent with the aperture. Immediately below the second open spine the outer apertural lip begins to project to a considerable extent beyond the varix proper. The shell margin, in notches between the labial teeth, is thrown into a series of spinelike folds, thus imparting to the varix the appearance of a double row of spines. The canal bears one major spine flanked by two minor ones.

Shell color is pale fleshy brown, with thin spiral brown lines and three interrupted spiral brown bands, these most prominent on the varices and inside the outer lip. The aperture is bright pink, with an extensive brown blotch extending from the parietal region into the anal sulcus and the siphonal canal; this brown coloration extends so far onto the previous whorl that most spire whorls show a brown band immediately above the suture.

Southern Gulf of California to Peru.

See Pl. 16, fig. 2.

Phyllonotus superbus (Sowerby, 1889)
Murex superbus Sowerby, 1889: 565

The shell is moderate in size for the genus (maximum length 76 mm) and fusiform. The spire is high, consisting of seven or eight weakly shouldered postnuclear whorls and a protoconch of undetermined nature. The suture is weakly impressed. The body whorl is moderate in size and fusoid. The aperture is moderately large and ovate, with a narrow, shallow anal sulcus. The outer apertural lip is erect and serrate; its inner surface is lirate, the lirae forming weak, transversely elongate denticles near the apertural margin. The columellar lip is adherent and more or less callused posteriorly, detached and erect anteriorly; the anterior end of the columella may bear up to three weak pustules. The siphonal canal is moderate in length, barely open, and dorsally recurved at its distal end.

The body whorl bears three fimbriate and briefly spinose varices. The anterior end of the varix generally bears a short to moderately long webbing. Intervarical axial sculpture consists of two or three ridges, these most prominent at the shoulder margin and becoming weak to ephemeral anteriorly. Spiral sculpture consists of seven scabrous major cords on the body and three on the canal, all of these intercalated by minor cords. The major cords on the body are produced into short, dorsally bent, open spines on the varices; the cords on the siphonal canal are developed into moderately long, more or less straight, open spines. In fresh examples many fine axial lamellae cover the shell and are thrown into scalelike projections over the spiral cords.

Shell color is whitish, with pale-orange or purple-pink suffusions and interrupted red-brown lines on the major spiral cords. The aperture is porcelaneous white.

The typical form of this species (Pl. 6, fig. 2) is found in deep water (140–160 m). Another form (Pl. 6, fig. 1), found in shallower water (40 m), has been identified as *P. laciniatus* (Sowerby, 1841), a species found in Australian and Philippine waters, but not occurring in Japan. Indeed, the shallower-dwelling form does superficially resemble *P. laciniatus*, a species of undoubtedly close relationship. It is distinct from true *P. laciniatus* in its larger size, differing color pattern, differing geographical range, larger, less circular aperture, and differing spire form. It differs from typical *P. superbus* in having a lower, broader spire, each whorl being less elevated, and in having generally a much more scabrous shell surface.

Southeastern Japan (Kii and Tosa).

See Pl. 6, figs. 1–2.

Phyllonotus trunculus (Linné, 1758)

Murex trunculus Linné, 1758: 747; *M. turbinatus* Lamarck, 1822: 170; *M. yoldii* Mörch, 1852: 95

The shell of this well-known and variable species is moderate in size for the genus (up to 80 mm in length) and broadly fusiform. The spire is high, consisting of two and one-half convex nuclear whorls and seven or more angulate postnuclear whorls. The suture is almost completely obscured. The body whorl is moderately large and broadly fusoid. The aperture is large and broadly ovate, with, in most instances, a flattened posterior margin. The outer apertural lip is serrate and strongly erect beyond a more or less well-developed varical thickening; the inner surface of the outer lip is corrugated, reflecting the outer shell sculpture. The columellar lip is entirely adherent. The siphonal canal is of moderate length, narrowly open to the right, strongly bent to the left, and dorsally recurved.

The body whorl bears five or six more or less well-developed varices. A single poorly developed axial ridge may be present intervarically. Spiral sculpture consists of six major cords on the body, the largest the one at the shoulder margin, and two on the canal; minor cords may be intercalated with the majors on the body and are generally the main sculpture on the canal. Where cords intersect varices and costae, protuberances ranging from low knobs to substantial straight, open spines arise. There are numerous fine threads covering the entire shell.

Shell color is generally gray-white or yellow-white, with three chestnut-brown spiral bands, a broad one covering the shoulder and the upper quarter of the whorl, a narrow medial one, and a broad basal one (this, however, narrower than the shoulder band). These bands appear strongly on the porcelaneous-white background of the interior of the aperture.

Several generic names have been erected with this species as type. These include *Trunculariopsis* Cossmann, 1921, and others.

As with other Mediterranean species, multiple variations of shell sculpture and, more rarely, form, have inspired several names for this species and engendered much confusion regarding its generic placement. In some forms the fine spiral threads are much stronger and more scabrous. One such form, from the Canary Islands, is called *M. turbinatus* Lamarck. Other forms, some in which the knobs are produced into long spines, and some in which almost all sculpture is lost, have caused the introduction of other, less well-known synonymous names.

The Mediterranean and the Atlantic coasts of Europe and Africa (Spain and Portugal, Morocco, and the Canary Islands).

See Pl. 5, fig. 6; Pl. 7, fig. 3.

Genus POIRIERIA Jousseaume, 1880

TYPE SPECIES: *Murex zelandicus* Quoy & Gaimard, 1833, by original designation.

The shell in this genus, as typified by its monotype, is of moderate size and roughly fusiform.

The spire is high, the suture impressed. The body whorl is moderately large; the aperture is large and broadly open. The siphonal canal is moderately long and slender.

The body whorl bears five thin, erect, fluted, lamella-like varices. Spiral cords, although subobsolete, give rise to long, straight, open spines where they cross the varices, those at the shoulder margin the longest and stoutest.

Shell color is yellow-white, overlaid with a moderately thick layer of simple white intritacalx.

Poirieria zelandica (Quoy & Gaimard, 1833)

Murex zelandicus Quoy & Gaimard, 1833: 529

The shell is moderate in size (maximum length 62 mm) and roughly fusiform. The spire is high, consisting of one and one-fourth bulbous, convex nuclear whorls and six or seven shouldered postnuclear whorls. The suture is strongly impressed. The body whorl is moderately large and fusoid. The aperture is large and ovate, with a broad, shallow anal sulcus, angled slightly to the left. The outer apertural lip is thin and thrown into a series of broad folds by the development of spines whose margins are continuous with the apertural margin; the inner surface of the outer lip is smooth. The columellar lip is entirely adherent and expanded briefly at its posterior end to form a moderately thick callus. The siphonal canal is moderately long, slender, narrowly open to the right, and dorsally recurved at its tip.

The body whorl bears five thin, lamella-like varices. Spiral sculpture consists of four to seven weak to obsolete cords, each of which, at its intersection with a varix, gives rise to a moderately short to long, more or less straight, open spine. Four spines, one at the shoulder and three others below, are most prominent. Anteriorly, secondary spines alternate with the first, second, and third long spines. No secondary spine separates the two longish spines at the base of the body. The shoulder-margin spine is much the longest.

Shell color is yellow-white, but this is generally obscured by a thick, white, simple intritacalx. The aperture is porcelaneous white.

Known to us only from northeastern New Zealand (Hauraki Gulf, Bay of Plenty).

See Pl. 26, fig. 9.

Genus PROTOTYPHIS Ponder, 1972

TYPE SPECIES: *Typhis angasi* Crosse, 1863, by original designation.

The shell is moderately small (under 45 mm maximum length) and roughly biconical. The spire is high, the whorls angulate and moderately broad. Each whorl bears three winged varices, each produced into a point or spine at the shoulder angle. This hollow spine communicates with the aperture and is either open at the ventral surface, as in the typical form of the type species, or closed, as in at least one other form. The aperture has smooth margins. The short protoconch is flat-topped and peripherally angulate; the operculum is simple, with a terminal nucleus. The radular dentition consists of a single five-cusped

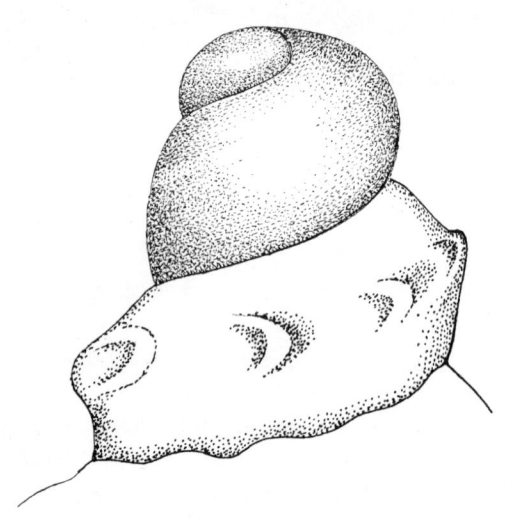

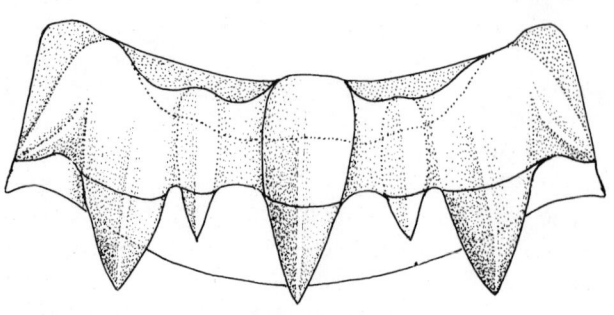

56. *Poirieria zelandica*, protoconch

57. *Poirieria zelandica*, radular dentition

rachidian tooth and two sickle-shaped laterals, one on each side of the rachidian.

Although named originally as a *Typhis*, the type species has until recently been grouped either with the superficially similar South African genus *Poropteron* or the Australian genus *Pterochelus*. It differs from the former in many shell features and in its muricine radular dentition (that of *Poropteron* is ocenebrine); it differs from the latter in the finer shell details, details of radular dentition, and the protoconch morphology.

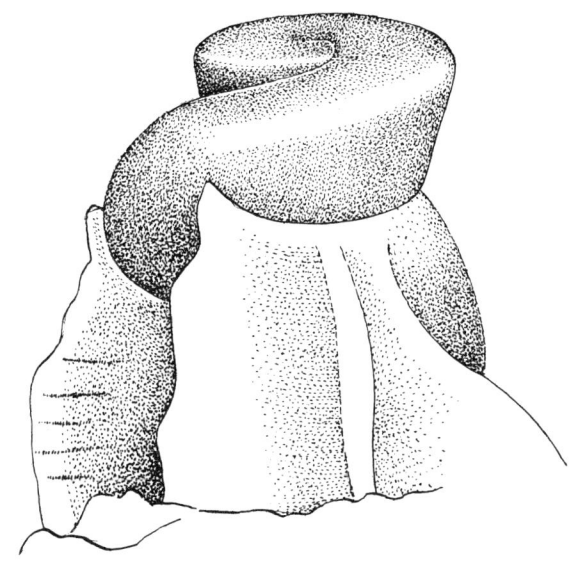

58. *Prototyphis angasi*, protoconch

Prototyphis angasi (Crosse, 1863)

Typhis angasi Crosse, 1863: 86; *Murex eos* Hutton, 1873: 8; *T. zealandica* Hutton, 1873: 2; *M. zonatus* Tenison-Woods, 1877: 132; *Pterynotus* (*Pterochelus*) *zealandicus iredalei* C. A. Fleming, 1962: 116

The shell is small (maximum length 23 mm) and fusiform. The spire is high and acute, and consists of one and one-fourth nuclear whorls and six weakly shouldered postnuclear whorls; the nuclear whorls are flattened, tabulate, and canted opposite to the cant of the postnuclear whorls. The suture is weakly, if at all, impressed. The body whorl is large and fusoid. The aperture is small and ovate. The outer apertural lip is unthickened and briefly erect, arising from a moderately broad, entire varical webbing on the periphery of the body and extending to the tip of the canal; the ventral surface of the webbing is finely lamellose, and the interior of the outer lip is weakly crenulate. The columellar lip is entirely smooth and adherent. The siphonal canal is moderately short and centrally narrowly open.

The body whorl bears three entire, winged varices. At the shoulder edge of each varix is a single long, recurved spine, this connecting with the aperture by an open channel. Other axial sculpture consists of two or three irregularly placed ridges at the shoulder in each intervarical space. Spiral sculpture is almost entirely lacking. On the dorsal surface of the varical webbing, several vague, low cords may be developed.

In *Prototyphis zealandicus* (Hutton, 1873) and *Prototyphis zealandicus iredalei* (Fleming, 1962), the shoulder-spine furrow is closed; Fleming also notes one or two other minor differences.

Shell color is variable: white to pink to orange to wax-yellow. The aperture is white.

Southeastern Australia to New Zealand.

See Pl. 15, fig. 4.

Genus **PTEROCHELUS** Jousseaume, 1880

TYPE SPECIES: *Murex acanthopterus* Lamarck, 1816, by original designation.

This genus, with a large and widespread fossil record, is represented in the Recent period by three species from Australia, one from the western Atlantic, and one from the eastern Pacific.

The shell is small to moderate in size (maximum length 80 mm) and bears three winged varices, as in *Pterynotus*. The varical webbing ends at the shoulder in a spine with a well-developed median channel. The aperture is moderately small and ovate to subtrigonal; the outer apertural lip is briefly lirate on its interior surface.

Pterochelus acanthopterus (Lamarck, 1816)

Murex acanthopterus Lamarck, 1816: pl. 417, fig. 2, Liste p. 5

This species, with the largest shell in the genus, has a fusoid shell reaching a maximum length of 80 mm. Its spire is high and acute, consisting of two and one-half nuclear whorls and five weakly shouldered postnuclear whorls. The suture is strongly impressed. The body whorl is large, fusiform, and longer than broad. The aperture is subtrigonal and rather small, with a very shallow anal sulcus. The outer apertural lip is slightly thickened and briefly erect, arising from a broad, undulate varical webbing whose edges may be recurved. This webbing extends from the shoulder region over the shoulder spine, is more or less indented immediately below the spine, and resumes its full character along the edge of the body; it is strongly indented at the top of the canal, after which it expands again to its termination at the tip of the canal. The interior of the outer lip is weakly lirate. The columellar lip is erect and unornamented, except for a slight callus in the parietal region. The siphonal canal is long and centrally narrowly open.

The body whorl bears three prominent winged varices. A single long shoulder spine may have an open channel running into the aperture, but in most mature specimens the channel is partially sealed, leaving a troughlike vestige. Additional axial sculpture consists of weak intervarical nodes, three on the earlier whorls and one or two on the later whorls. Spiral sculpture consists of numerous cords, these bifurcate where they extend over the dorsal portion of the varical webbing. The ventral surface of the webbing is lamellose.

Shell color is generally yellowish white, with more or less brown marking, primarily on the shoulder and the varical webbing.

Comparatively shallow water along the entire western coast of Australia (dwarf populations in the Port Hedland and Cape Preston region may attain only one-half the maximum shell length).

See Pl. 15, figs. 1–3.

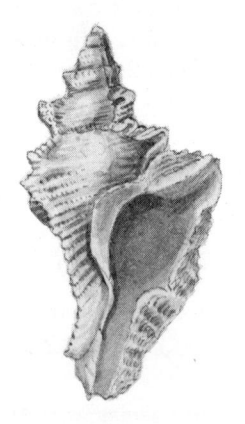

59. *Pterochelus ariomus*

Pterochelus ariomus (Clench & Pérez Farfante, 1945)

Murex (Pterynotus) ariomus Clench & Pérez Farfante, 1945: 39

The shell is small for the genus (the unique holotype is about 24 mm in length) and roughly biconic. The spire is high, consisting of one and one-half small, convex nuclear whorls and six and one-half subangulate postnuclear whorls. The suture is deeply impressed. The body whorl is moderately large and trigonal. The aperture is moderately large, with a weak anal sulcus and an open trough in the rounded point at the shoulder margin. The outer apertural lip of the holotype is not mature. The columellar lip is adherent posteriorly, detached and somewhat erect anteriorly. The siphonal canal is of moderate length, open, and bent slightly to the left.

The body whorl bears three weakly developed, winglike varices with crenulate margins; a single low, intervarical node is also apparent. Spiral sculpture consists of numerous rather fine cords, these thrown into numerous fine scales where they are crossed by fine growth lamellae.

Shell color is dull white.

Known only from the type locality, off Hollywood, Florida, in 100–120 m.

Pterochelus duffusi Iredale, 1936

Pterochelus duffusi Iredale, 1936: 323

The shell is moderate in size for the genus (maximum length 63 mm) and roughly biconic. The spire is high, consisting of one or two convex nuclear whorls and five or six subangulate postnuclear whorls. The suture is impressed. The body whorl is moderately large and trigonal. The aperture is subovate, with a flattened posterior margin, a weak, narrow anal sulcus, and an open channel extending from the aperture the entire length of the moderately long shoulder spine. The columellar lip is adherent, except for a small portion anteriorly. The siphonal canal is moderately long, narrowly open, and bent to the right and dorsally at its tip.

The body whorl bears three more or less well-developed winged varices, each encompassing the channelled shoulder spine and each marginally crenulate and folded into pleats. The shoulder spine is moderately long and acute. A single inter-

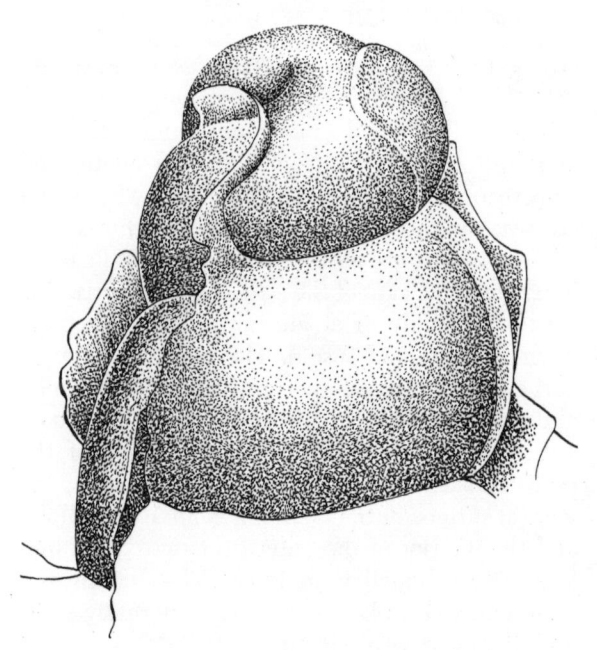

60. *Pterochelus duffusi*, protoconch

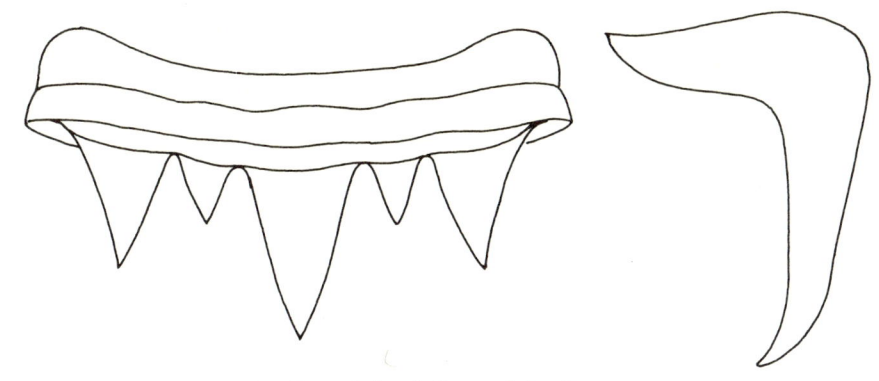

61. *Pterochelus duffusi*, radular dentition

varical node is apparent; spiral sculpture consists of several (three to five) cords giving rise to brief points on the varix margin, and numerous finer threads, these thrown into a multitude of fine scales where they cross fine axial-growth lines.

Shell color is pale fleshy tan with red-brown maculations.

Queensland and northern New South Wales, Australia.

See Pl. 15, fig. 5.

Pterochelus phillipsi (E. H. Vokes, 1966)

Pterynotus (Pterochelus) phillipsi E. H. Vokes, 1966: 165

The shell is small for the genus (the unique holotype is 28.4 mm in length) and biconic. The spire is high, consisting of seven postnuclear whorls and a protoconch of undetermined nature. The suture is impressed. The body whorl is moderately large and trigonal. The moderate-sized aperture would be ovate except for a flattened posterior margin; the anal sulcus is shallow but evident and an open channel runs the length of the moderately long shoulder-margin spine and opens into the aperture. The outer apertural lip is erect and marginally crenulate. The columellar lip is adherent, except at its anterior end. The siphonal canal is moderately long, straight, and narrowly open.

The body whorl bears three rather well-developed, winglike varices, each with a ventrally channeled shoulder spine and a well-developed crenulate webbing extending from the spine to the preceding whorl and anteriorly, with an indentation near the top of the canal extending almost to the tip of the canal. A single intervarical node is apparent. Spiral sculpture consists of four or five cords, these becoming points at the varix margin, and faint spiral threads crossed by fine axial growth lines on the receding sides of the varices, thus forming a weakly imbricate surface texture.

The shell is a pale flesh color.

The original describer concedes that this form is hardly distinguishable from *Pterochelus duffusi* Iredale, 1936, an eastern Australian form.

62. *Pterochelus phillipsi*

Known only from the type locality, Santa Barbara Channel, between Port Hueneme and Anacapa Island, California, in about 200 m.

Pterochelus triformis (Reeve, 1845)

Murex triformis Reeve, 1845: sp. 53

The shell is somewhat smaller than that of *P. acanthopterus* (maximum length 60 mm) and is coarser and more solid. The spire is high, not as acute as in *P. acanthopterus*, and consists of five weakly shouldered postnuclear whorls and a protoconch of undetermined nature. The suture is generally less impressed than in *P. acanthopterus*. The body whorl is large and fusiform. The aperture is small and subtrigonal, with a sagging posterior margin and a very shallow anal sulcus. The outer apertural lip is more or less thickened and briefly erect, arising from a broad, undulate varical webbing whose edges may be recurved.

The webbing, lamellose on its ventral surface, extends from the shoulder, over the shoulder spine, to the tip of the siphonal canal, and is slightly, if at all, indented at the top of the siphonal canal. The interior of the outer lip is briefly denticulate. The columellar lip is erect and unornamented except for a slight callus in the parietal region. The siphonal canal is long and centrally narrowly open.

The body whorl bears three prominent, winged varices. A single relatively inconspicuous projection at the shoulder may have an open channel, connecting with the aperture, although this channel is generally sealed in specimens with mature features. Other axial sculpture consists of intervarical nodes, one or two on the earlier whorls, two or three on the later whorls. Spiral sculpture consists of numerous cords connected by fine axial lamellae, these becoming bifurcate on the dorsal region of the webbing.

Shell color is light to dark brown, exceptionally with white on the ventral side of the varical webbing and on the canal. The interior of the aperture is porcelaneous white.

Southern Australia from New South Wales to Albany, Western Australia.

See Pl. 15, figs. 6–7.

Genus **PTERYNOTUS** Swainson, 1833

TYPE SPECIES: *Murex pinnatus* Swainson, 1822 (=*Purpura alata* Röding, 1798), by subsequent designation, Swainson, 1833 (text to pl. 122).

Muricine species with trivaricate shells and more or less expanded varical flanges are generally assigned to *Pterynotus, Pterochelus,* and *Marchia,* and are very closely related. Either *Pterochelus* or *Marchia* could be treated as of equal rank with, or as a subgenus of, *Pterynotus,* depending on the interpretation of the worker. Species assigned here to *Pterynotus* also have a small to moderate-sized fusiform shape, an adherent columellar lip, and a smoothly laminate ventral surface of the varical "wing." The operculum is generally muricoid. The radula is generally muricine, but the central radular tooth exhibits a marked diminution of the intermediate cusps, and the lateral teeth are large and broad-based.

Pterynotus alatus (Röding, 1798)

Purpura alata Röding, 1798: 144; *Murex pinnatus* Swainson, 1822: 17

The shell is moderately large for the genus (maximum length 75 mm) and fusiform. The spire is high, consisting of ten moderately convex postnuclear whorls and a protoconch of undetermined nature. The suture is very shallow. The body whorl is moderately large and fusoid. The aperture is ovate and broadly open, with a very shallow, almost imperceptible anal sulcus. The outer apertural lip is erect and finely dentate; fine lirae extend into the aperture from the denticles. The columellar lip is adherent and briefly, parietally expanded above, detached and weakly erect below. The siphonal canal is narrowly, centrally open, strongly bent to the right, and distally recurved.

The body whorl bears three winged varices. Each varical "wing" is sinuous at its margin, developed into a broad point at its shoulder, strongly laminate at its uppermost extremity, and attached to and following the contour of the body and the canal. Other axial sculpture consists of a low ridge, nodose at the shoulder, in each intervarical space. Spiral sculpture consists of numerous finely scabrous major and minor cords.

Shell color is white, with a faint axial, flesh-colored stripe on the dorsal side of each varical wing.

Subtidal, western Pacific (southeastern Japan, Taiwan, and elsewhere) and eastern Indian Ocean.

See Pl. 9, fig. 6.

Pterynotus bednalli (Brazier, 1878)

Murex bednalli Brazier, 1878: 6

The shell is moderately large (maximum length 85 mm) and fusiform. The spire is high, consisting of one and one-half smooth nuclear whorls and seven or eight angulate postnuclear whorls. The suture is obscured by a flangelike extension of the succeeding whorl. The body whorl is large and fusoid. The aperture is small and lenticular, with a moderately shallow anal sulcus. The flaring outer apertural lip is weakly erect above, more strongly erect below, and strongly, coarsely dentate; the nine labial denticles extend for a short distance into the aperture as prominent lirae. The columellar lip is smooth, adherent and expanded into a thin parietal callus for the upper one-third of its length, detached and weakly erect for the lower two-thirds. The aperture is strongly constricted at its point of entrance into the siphonal canal; the canal is moderately long, narrowly open to the right, and strongly, distally recurved.

The body whorl bears three broad, winglike varices. Each "wing" is appressed in its uppermost portion to the corresponding varical wing of the preceding whorl, upswept in its shoulder portion, richly laminate on its ventral surface, and scalloped on its margin by 15 to 18 broad, shallow grooves corresponding to spiral cords on its dorsal surface; its margin does not follow the contour of the body whorl. Axial sculpture consists of one to three weak intervarical ridges.

Shell color is pale to dark fleshy yellow-brown or orange, with interrupted brown spiral bands, these most visible on the varices. The interior of the aperture is white.

Northwestern Australia.

See Pl. 9, figs. 4, 8.

Pterynotus leucas (Locard, 1897)

Murex leucas Locard, 1897: 306

We have not seen a specimen of this species; the following is translated, without change, from the original description:

"Shell rather large with a somewhat elongate, tripterous, fusiform shape, better developed below than above. Spire high and acute, composed of nine or ten whorls; the first ones, after the embryonic whorls, strongly angulate, the three last ones rather convex, growing quickly in height and slowly in diameter. Body whorl rounded above, terminating below in an open, elongate, slender canal, and bent dorsally and to the left at its tip. Sutures straight and well-impressed. Apex somewhat swollen (mammillate), with one or two rounded, almost smooth nuclear whorls. Aperture ovate-pyriform, higher than wide, somewhat rounded above, ending below in a foliaceous, open, quite short canal. Peristome interrupted, the columellar margin formed by a large, foliated expansion, this fringed at its periphery, plicate within as well as without, slender and sharp, flaring outward with a laterally rounded profile, swinging posteriorly near its junction with the body of the shell, the columellar margin strong, slightly pustulose anteriorly, accompanied by a poorly defined callus. Shell solid, rather thin, almost transparent, bearing varices and spiral cords. Three varices present on the penultimate whorl, two on the body whorl. Development of the peristome suggests the beginning of the third varix, the peristome very thin, very high, foliaceous, the leading edge more or less imbricate; very vague spiral cords indicated on base of body whorl, these forming, by their elongation into the varical webbing, straight costulations, these reproduced on the leading edge of the varix.

"Shell color is white, with a trace of yellow. The aperture is porcelaneous white.

"Dimensions: total length 48 mm; maximum diameter 27 mm."

Off the northwestern coast of Africa ("à l'Ouest du Sahara") in deep water (640 m).

Pterynotus loebbeckei (Kobelt, 1879)

Murex (Pteronotus) löbbeckei Kobelt, 1879: 78

The shell is moderately large (maximum length 75 mm) and broadly fusiform. The spire is high, consisting of eight or nine convex postnuclear whorls and a protoconch of undetermined nature. The suture is shallow. The body whorl is large and broadly fusoid. The aperture is moderately large and ovate, with a small, very shallow anal sulcus. The outer apertural lip is erect and finely dentate, the denticles extending strongly into the aperture. The columellar lip is adherent above, detached and erect below. The siphonal canal is moderately short, narrowly open to the right, weakly bent to the right, and distally recurved.

The body whorl bears three winglike varices. The margin of each varical "wing" follows the contour of the shell. Each wing is most expanded at the shoulder margin, is attached to the base of a varix of the preceding whorl, extends almost to the end of the canal, bears a small indentation corresponding to the anterior end of the body, and is richly laminate on its ventral surface. The entire "wing" is finely rippled. Axial sculpture consists otherwise of two rounded, knoblike ridges in each intervarical space. Spiral sculpture consists of numerous minutely scabrous cords, which are strongest on the dorsal surface of the varix.

Shell color is pink to fleshy orange, strongest on the earliest whorls.

63. *Pterynotus leucas*

Known only from the type locality, "Oceano Indochinensis," and southeastern Japan.

See Pl. 9, fig. 14.

Pterynotus patagiatus (Hedley, 1912)

Murex patagiatus Hedley, 1912: 151

The shell is moderate in size for the genus (maximum length 50 mm) and broadly fusiform. The spire is high, consisting of one and one-half nuclear whorls and seven convex postnuclear whorls. The suture is very shallow. The body whorl is broadly fusoid. The aperture is small and ovate, with a broad, shallow anal sulcus recessed a short distance into the aperture. The outer apertural lip is barely erect and finely crenulate, the crenulations extending into the aperture as brief lirae. The upper one-third of the columellar lip is adherent and broadened into a thin parietal callus; below, the lip is detached and strongly erect. The siphonal canal is relatively long, narrowly open to the right, bent to the right, and distally recurved.

The body whorl bears three frilly, winglike varices. The varices here, in contrast to those in other species of *Pterynotus*, do not extend along the siphonal canal but end at the base of the body. The varical "wing" is not appressed to the varix above it but is drawn into a pointed projection at the shoulder margin and otherwise generally follows the contour of the shell. The outer portion of the ventral surface of the varix is richly laminate; the inner portion is scabrous along spiral lines corresponding to 16 richly scabrous spiral cords on the dorsal surface. Axial sculpture consists, besides the varices, of a single ridge, this nodose at the shoulder.

Shell color is light fleshy orange, strongest in the intervarical spaces. The varical wings are translucent white. The interior of the aperture is pale pink.

Queensland to northern New South Wales, Australia.

See Pl. 9, fig. 13.

Pterynotus phaneus (Dall, 1889)

Murex phaneus Dall, 1889: 201; *M. tristichus* Dall, 1889: 202 (not Beyrich, 1854); *M. pygmaeus* Bush, 1893: 213 (not Schlotheim, 1820); *Pterynotus havanensis* E. H. Vokes, 1970: 13, new name for *M. tristichus* Dall, 1889 (not Beyrich, 1854); *P. bushae* E. H. Vokes, 1970: 13, new name for *M. pygmaeus* Bush, 1893 (not Schlotheim, 1820)

This is the smallest of all known *Pterynotus* species (maximum length 20 mm), and its shell is thin, translucent, and fusiform. The spire is moderately high, consisting of one and one-half polished nuclear whorls canted opposite to the cant of the remaining four weakly convex postnuclear whorls. The suture is distinct but not impressed. The body whorl is broadly fusoid. The aperture is lenticular, with a sharp, narrow anal sulcus, this bounded on each side by a node. The outer apertural lip is erect. The columellar lip is adherent. The siphonal canal is moderate in length, narrowly open, and distally recurved.

The body whorl bears three winglike varices, each of which generally follows the contours of the shell. Each "wing" is appressed above to a varical wing on the preceding whorl, drawn outward and upward at the shoulder margin into a sharp point, as in *P. vespertilio*, extending anteriorly no further than the base of the body, gently undulate on its ventral surface, reflecting low spiral cords on the dorsal surface, and laminate. The dorsal surface is given an undulate character by a series of low spiral cords, each cord extending into a recurved point on the margin of the wing. Axial sculpture consists of numerous faint growth striae. Spiral sculpture, in addition to the low cords mentioned above, consists of innumerable scratches crossing the growth striae to impart to the shell surface a microscopically cross-hatched effect.

Shell color is uniform white.

The form figured is *P. tristichus* (Dall, 1889), a preoccupied name that Vokes (1970b) has replaced with *P. havanensis*. Upon close examination, the holotype of *P. phaneus* does not differ significantly from *P. tristichus*. It appears, from the specimens we have seen, that *P. phaneus* was described from a specimen in which the sharp shoulder projection on the body whorl, fragile to begin with, had broken off. The same projection is persistent on the penultimate whorl. In addition, the intervarical costae are moderately prominent on the holotype of *P. phaneus*, but lacking on the three specimens of *P. tristichus* we have seen. The name *Murex phaneus* is not preoccupied, and this is the earliest available name for the species.

Deep water (200–800 m) off Charleston, South Carolina, to off Havana, Cuba.

See Pl. 9, fig. 3.

Pterynotus phyllopterus (Lamarck, 1822)

Murex phyllopterus Lamarck, 1822: 164; *M. rubridentatus* Reeve, 1846: sp. 186

The shell of this recently rediscovered species is rather large (length about 80 mm) and trigonal. The spire is high, consisting of six or seven convex to barely subangulate postnuclear whorls and a protoconch of undetermined nature. The suture

Plate 1. 1 & 2: *Aspella senex*, p. 25. 3: *A. pollux*, p. 225. 4–8: *A. pyramidalis*, p. 23. 9: *A. morchi*, . 223. 10: *A. cryptica*, p. 220. 11: *A. acuticostata*, p. 21. 12–14: *A. producta*, p. 22.
5 & 16: *Dermomurex elizabethae*, p. 25. 17: *D. indentatus*, p. 46. 18 & 19: *D. bakeri*, p. 45.
0: *D. cunninghamae*, p. 45. 21–24: *D. obeliscus*, p. 46. 25 & 26: *D. pauperculus*, p. 47. 27: *D.
calaroides*, p. 47. 28: *D. myrakeenae*, p. 46. 29: *A. pollux*, p. 225. 30 & 31: *Takia infrons*, p. 109.

Plate 2.   1: *Muricopsis schrammi*, p. 171.   2: *Bedeva paivae*, p. 28.   3: *Muricopsis muricoides*, p. 168.   4: *Bedeva livida*, p. 28.   5: *Muricopsis roseus*, p. 170.   6: *Bedeva birileffi*, p. 27. 7: *Murexsul umbilicatus*, p. 164.   8: *Bedeva blosvillei*, p. 27.   9: *Bedeva paivae*, p. 28. 10–12: *Ergalatax contracta*, p. 48.

Plate 3. 1: *Attiliosa incompta*, p. 26.   2: *Nipponotrophon echinus*, p. 82.   3: *Muricopsis infans*, p. 168.   4: *Calotrophon ostrearum*, p. 30.   5: *Evokesia ferruginosa*, p. 143. 6: *Nipponotrophon galapaganus*, p. 83.   7: *Trachypollia lugubris*, p. 134.   8: *T. didyma*, p. 134. 9: *T. nodulosa*, p. 135.   10: *Attiliosa philippiana*, p. 26.   11: *Evokesia rufonotata*, p. 144. 12 & 13: *Calotrophon turritus*, p. 30.   14: *Nipponotrophon gorgon*, p. 83.

Plate 4. 1: *Chicoreus akritos*, p. 228. 2: *C. axicornis*, p. 33. 3: *C. damicornis*, p. 36.
4: *C. artemis*, p. 32. 5: *C. denudatus*, p. 36. 6: *C. rossiteri*, p. 41. 7: *C. microphyllus*, p. 39.
8: *C. ramosus*, p. 40. 9: *C. brunneus*, p. 35. 10: *C. brevifrons*, p. 34. 11: *C. cornucervi*, p. 36.
12: *C. banksii*, p. 33.

Plate 5. 1: *Chicoreus spectrum*, p. 43. 2: *C. palmarosae*, p. 40. 3: *C. cnissodus*, p. 35.
4: *C. insularum*, p. 38. 5: *C. maurus*, p. 39. 6: *Phyllonotus trunculus*, p. 93. 7: *Chicoreus microphyllus*, p. 39. 8: *C. saulii*, p. 42.

Plate 6. 1&2: *Phyllonotus superbus*, p. 92.   3: *P. laciniatus*, p. 89.   4: *Chicoreus penchinati*, p. 40.   5: *C. rubescens*, p. 41.   6&7: *C. florifer*, p. 37.   8: *C. asianus*, p. 32.   9: *C. territus*, p. 43.   10: *C. rubiginosus*, p. 42.   11: *C. gubbi*, p. 38.   12: *C. trivialis*, p. 43.

Plate 7. 1 & 2: *Hexaplex stainforthi*, p. 51.   3: *Phyllonotus trunculus*, p. 93.   4 & 5: *Xanthochorus xanthostoma*, p. 140.   6: *Murex olssoni*, p. 69.   7: *Vitularia miliaris*, p. 173.   8: *Pterynotus phyllopterus*, p. 100.   9: *Murexsul mariae*, p. 162.   10: *Muricanthus saharicus*, p. 78.   11: *Murex gallinago*, p. 66.   12 & 13: *Vitularia miliaris*, p. 173.   14: *V. salebrosa*, p. 173.   15: *Murex anniae*, p. 61.   16 & 17: *Hexaplex cichoreum*, p. 50.   18: *Murex tryoni*, p. 74.

Plate 8. 1 & 2: *Homalocantha secunda*, p. 55. 3: *H. zamboi*, p. 55. 4: *H. melanamathos*, p. 53. 5. *H. secunda*, p. 55. 6–10: *H. anatomica*, p. 52. 11–13: *H. scorpio*, p. 54. 14 & 15: *H. oxyacantha*, p. 53. 16: *H. tortua*, p. 55.

Plate 9. 1: *Marchia martinetana*, p. 59.   2: *Pterynotus vespertilio*, p. 10.   3: *P. phaneus*, p. 100.
4: *P. bednalli*, p. 98.   5: *Marchia laqueata*, p. 58.   6: *Pterynotus alatus*, p. 98.   7: *Marchia pellucida*, p. 60.   8: *Pterynotus bednalli*, p. 98.   9: *Marchia barclayana*, p. 57.   10: *M. elongata*, p. 57.   11: *M. bipinnata*, p. 57.   12: *M. triptera*, p. 60.   13: *Pterynotus patagiatus*, p. 100.
14: *P. loebbeckei*, p. 99.

Plate 10. 1: *Murex pecten*, p. 69. 2: *M. serratospinosus*, p. 72. 3: *M. donmoorei*, p. 65. 4: *M. mindanaoensis*, p. 68. 5: *M. troscheli*, p. 74. 6 & 7: *M. scolopax*, p. 71. 8 & 9: *M. tribulus*, p. 72. 10 & 11: *M. chrysostoma*, p. 64. 12: *M. cabritii*, p. 63. 13: *M. tweedianus*, p. 75. 14: *M. trapa*, p. 72.

Plate 11. 1: *Murex coppingeri*, p. 64. 2: *M. brevispinus*, p. 62. 3: *M. rectirostris*, p. 70. 4: *M. longicornis*, p. 67. 5: *M. cervicornis*, p. 63. 6: *M. anniae*, p. 61. 7: *M. messorius*, p. 68. 8: *Bolinus brandaris*, p. 28. 9: *B. cornutus*, p. 29. 10: *Haustellum haustellum*, p. 49. 11: *Murex recurvirostris*, p. 70. 12: *M. hirasei*, p. 66. 13: *M. elenensis*, p. 66. 14: *M. kiiensis*, p. 67. 15: *M. rubidus*, p. 71. 16: *M. multiplicatus*, p. 68.

Plate 12. 1 & 2: *Muricanthus radix*, p. 77. 3: *M. fulvescens*, p. 76. 4: *M. angularis*, p. 76. 5 & 6: *M. varius*, p. 79. 7: *M. kusterianus*, p. 76. 8: *M. megacerus*, p. 77. 9: *M. radix*, p. 77. 10: *M. princeps*, p. 77.

Plate 13. 1: *Murex elenensis*, p. 66. 2: *Murex rectirostris*, p. 70. 3: *Muricanthus angularis*, p. 76.
4: *Murexiella bojadorensis*, p. 156. 5: *Murex kiiensis*, p. 67. 6–8: *Nipponotrophon lasius*, p. 84.

Plate 14. 1: *Acanthotrophon carduus*, p. 19. 2: ?*Ocenebra hamata*, p. 121. 3: *Favartia tetragona*, p. 153. 4: *Ergalatax tokugawai*, p. 48. 5: ?*Murexsul auratus*, p. 161. 6: *Favartia planilirata*, p. 152. 7: *Nipponotrophon pagodus*, p. 84. 8: *Murex olssoni*, p. 69. 9: *Bedeva paivae*, p. 28. 10 & 11: *Nipponotrophon scitulus*, p. 85. 12: *Favartia kurodai*, p. 149.

Plate 15. 1–3: *Pterochelus acanthopterus*, p. 95. 4: *Prototyphis angasi*, p. 95. 5: *Pterochelus tuffusi*, p. 96. 6 & 7: *Pterochelus triformis*, p. 97. 8: *Naquetia barclayi*, p. 80. 9 & 10: *N. annandalei*, p. 80. 11: *N. triquetra*, p. 82. 12: *N. trigonula*, p. 81. 13: *N. capucina*, p. 80.

Plate 16. 1: *Phyllonotus duplex*, p. 88. 2: *P. regius*, p. 92. 3: *P. peratus*, p. 90. 4: *P. erythrostomus*, p. 89. 5: *P. brassica*, p. 88. 6: *P. margaritensis*, p. 90. 7: *P. duplex*, p. 88. 8: *P. pomum*, p. 91.

Plate 17. 1: *Siratus senegalensis*, p. 107. 2 & 3: *S. articulatus*, p. 104. 4–6: *S. cailleti*, p. 105. 7: *S. senegalensis*, p. 107. 8: *S. beauii*, p. 104. 9: *S. formosus*, p. 106. 10: *S. alabaster*, p. 103. 11: *S. perelegans*, p. 107. 12: *S. ciboney*, p. 105. 13: *S. consuela*, p. 106. 14: *S. motacilla*, p. 106. 15: ?*Siratus virgineus*, p. 108. 16: *S. tenuivaricosus*, p. 108. 17: *S. pliciferoides*, p. 107.

Plate 18. 1&2: *Ceratostoma foliatum*, p. 112. 3: *Ocenebra erinaceoides*, p. 120. 4&5: *O. erinaceus*, p. 119. 6&7: *Ceratostoma burnetti*, p. 111. 8: *C. fournieri*, p. 112. 9: *Ocenebra vokesae*, p. 124. 10–12: *C. inornatum*, p. 113. 13: *C. rorifluum*, p. 114. 14&15: *C. nuttalli*, p. 114.

Plate 19. 1: *Eupleura triquetra*, p. 117.   2: *E. sulcidentata*, p. 117.   3 & 4: *E. caudata*, p. 115.
5: *E. muriciformis*, p. 115.   6: *E. nitida*, p. 116.   7: *E. pectinata*, p. 116.   8 & 9: *Roperia poulsoni*, p. 133.   10 & 11: *Lataxiena fimbriata*, p. 56.   12: *Acanthotrophon carduus*, p. 19.
13: *Ergalatax contracta*, p. 48.   14: *Maxwellia angermeyerae*, p. 154.   15 & 16: ?*Maxwellia santarosana*, p. 155.   17: *M. gemma*, p. 154.   18: *Ergalatax contracta*, p. 48.

Plate 20. 1: *Ocenebra inermicosta*, p. 122. 2: *O. grippi*, p. 121. 3: *O circumtexta*, p. 119.
4 & 5: *O. lurida*, p. 123. 6: *O. interfossa*, p. 122. 7: *O. seftoni*, p. 124. 8: ?*Ocenebra painei*,
p. 123. 9: *Ocenebra foveolata*, p. 120. 10: *O. gracillima*, p. 121. 11–13: *O. interfossa*, p. 122.
14–17: *O. foveolata*, p. 120.

Plate 21. 1: ?*Urosalpinx purpuroides*, p. 138. 2: ?*Urosalpinx scrobiculata*, p. 138. 3: *U. cala*, p. 136. 4 & 5: *U. cinerea*, p. 136. 6: *U. haneti*, p. 137. 7: *Ocinebrina edwardsi*, p. 125. 8: *O. aciculata*, p. 125. 9: ?*Ocinebrina emipowlusi*, p. 126. 10: *O. hybrida*, p. 126. 11: ?*Urosalpinx puncturata*, p. 137. 12: *U. tampaensis*, p. 139. 13: ?*Urosalpinx subangulata*, p. 138. 14: *U. perrugata*, p. 137.

Plate 22. 1: *Pteropurpura bequaerti*, p. 129.   2: *Poropteron uncinarius*, p. 128.   3: *Poropteron incurvispina*, p. 127.   4: *Pteropurpura modesta*, p. 132.   5: *Pteropurpura esycha*, p. 130. 6: *Pteropurpura trialata*, p. 132.   7: *Pteropurpura leeana*, p. 131.   8: *Pteropurpura plorator*, p. 132.   9: *Pteropurpura festiva*, p. 130.   10: *Pteropurpura adunca*, p. 129.   11: *Pteropurpura centrifuga*, p. 130.   12: *Jaton decussatus*, p. 118.   13: *Pteropurpura macroptera*, p. 131.

Plate 23. 1: *Bizetiella shaskyi*, p. 142. 2: *Murexsul kieneri*, p. 162. 3: *Pazinotus stimpsonii*, p. 87. 4: *Evokesia grayi*, p. 143. 5: *Calotrophon velero*, p. 31. 6: *Bizetiella micaela*, p. 142. 7: *B. carmen*, p. 141. 8&9: *Ceratostoma lugubre*, p. 113. 10: *Chicoreus benedictinus*, p. 34. 11: *Favartia brevicula*, p. 145. 12: *Muricopsis nicocheanus*, p. 169. 13: *Pteropurpura macroptera*, p. 131. 14: *Muricopsis blainvillei*, p. 165. 15: *Haustellum wilsoni*, p. 50.

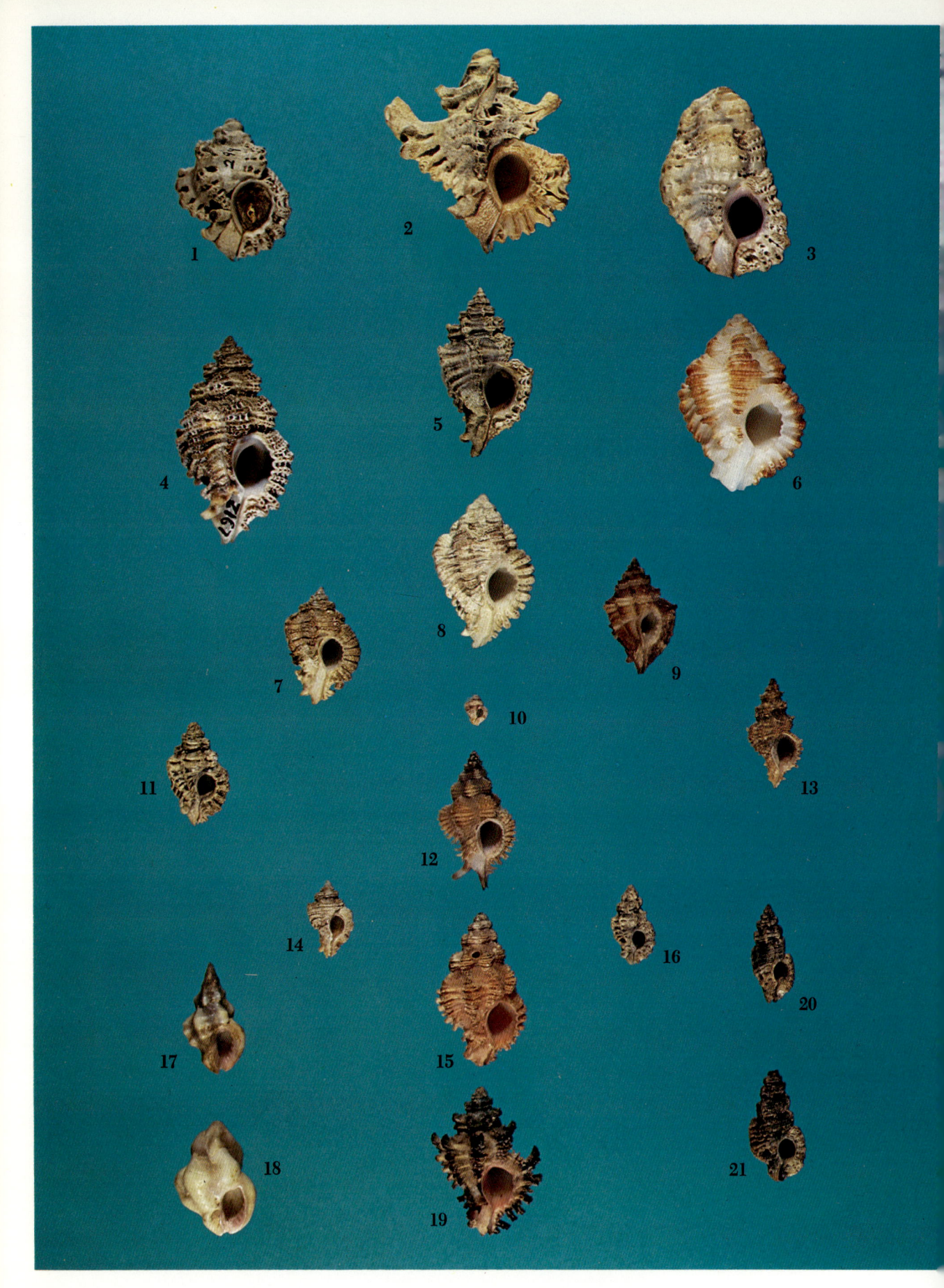

Plate 24. 1 & 2: *Favartia brevicula*, p. 145. 3: *F. minatauros*, p. 150. 4–6: *F. cellulosa*, p. 146. 7: *F. emersoni*, p. 147. 8: *F. incisa*, p. 149. 9: *F. poormani*, p. 231. 10: *F. garrettii*, p. 149. 11: *F. cyclostoma*, p. 147. 12: *F. rosea*, p. 152. 13: *Muricopsis brazieri*, p. 166. 14: *Favartia munda*, p. 151. 15: *F. salmonea*, p. 153. 16: *F. alveata*, p. 144. 17 & 18: ?*Favartia crossei*, p. 146. 19: *F. balteata*, p. 145. 20 & 21: *F. erosa*, p. 148.

Plate 25. 1: *Murexiella diomedaea*, p. 157. 2: ?*Murexsul tokubeii*, p. 163. 3–5: *Murexiella
umilis*, p. 157. 6: ?*Murexsul multispinosus*, p. 162. 7: "*Murex*" *pleurotomoides*, p. 216.
: *Murexiella hidalgoi*, p. 157. 9: *Murexiella radwini*, p. 160. 10 & 11: *Murexiella macgintyi*,
. 159. 12: *Paziella hystricina*, p. 85. 13: *Murexiella cirrosa*, p. 156.

Plate 26. 1–3: *Paziella pazi*, p. 86. 4: *Murexiella vittata*, p. 161. 5: *Murexiella lappa*, p. 158. 6 & 7: *Murexsul octogonus*, p. 163. 8: *Murexiella perita*, p. 159. 9: *Poirieria zelandica*, p. 94. 10: *Murexiella levicula*, p. 159. 11 & 12: *Murexiella jacquelinae*, p. 158. 13: *Purpurellus macleani*, p. 102. 14: *Purpurellus pinniger*, p. 102. 15: *Purpurellus gambiensis*, p. 102.

Plate 27. 1 & 2: *Muricopsis armatus*, p. 165. 3: *Marchia nodulifera*, p. 59. 4: *Muricopsis jaliscoensis*, p. 168. 5: *Muricopsis oxytata*, p. 169. 6: *Muricopsis bombayanus*, p. 166. 7 & 8: *Muricopsis pauxillus*, p. 169. 9: *Muricopsis cuspidatus*, p. 167. 10: *Muricopsis cristatus*, p. 167. 11: *Muricopsis angolensis*, p. 165. 12–14: *Muricopsis zeteki*, p. 171. 15: *Muricopsis blainvillei*, p. 165.

Plate 28. 1: *Aspella castor*, p. 219. 2: *Tripterotyphis norfolkensis*, p. 203. 3: *Aspella platylaevis*, p. 224. 4: *Aspella mauritiana*, p. 221. 5: *Attiliosa aldridgei*, p. 25. 6: *Aspella ponderi*, p. 227. 7: *Murexsul zonatus*, p. 164. 8: *Pagodula vaginata*, p. 184. 9: *Boreotrophon clathratus*, p. 179. 10 & 11: *Trophon geversianus*, p. 187. 12: *Nodulotrophon dalli*, p. 184.

Plate 29. 1: *Typhisala grandis*, p. 211. 2: *Trophon geversianus*, p. 187. 3: *Xenotrophon euschema*, p. 189. 4: *Hadriania craticuloides*, p. 118. 5: ?*Subpterynotus tatei*, p. 172. 6 & 7: *Favartia peasei*, p. 151. 8: ?*Typhina nitens*, p. 208. 9 & 10: *Zeatrophon ambiguus*, p. 191. 11: *Tripterotyphis robustus*, p. 204. 12: *Gemixystus laminatus*, p. 182. 13: *Anatrophon sarmentosus*, p. 177. 14: *Xymene plebeius*, p. 189. 15: "*Murex*" *alfredensis*, p. 215. 16. *Favartia minirosea*, p. 151.

Plate 30. 1: *Pterotyphis fimbriatus*, p. 197. 2: *P. pinnatus*, p. 197. 3 & 4: *Cinclidotyphis myrae*, p. 193. 5 & 6: *Tripterotyphis lowei*, p. 203. 7: *Tripterotyphis triangularis*, p. 204. 8 & 9: *Tripterotyphis arcana*, p. 202. 10 & 11: *Tripterotyphis fayae*, p. 202. 12: *Laevityphis bullisi*, p. 195. 13 & 14: *Talityphis latipennis*, p. 201. 15: *Talityphis perchardei*, p. 236.

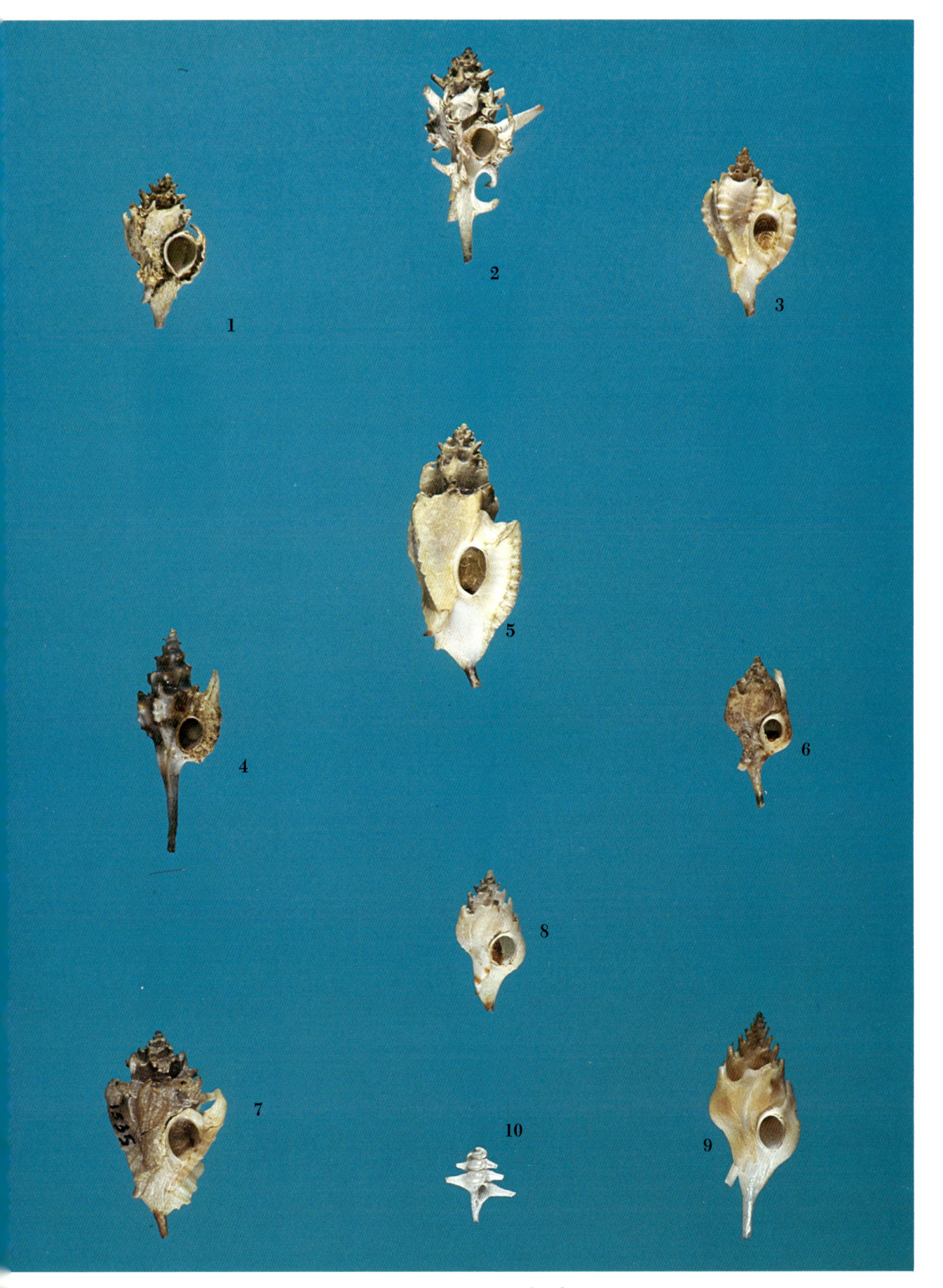

Plate 31. 1: *Typhina yatesi*, p. 209.   2: *Monstrotyphis tosaensis*, p. 196.   3: *Talityphis expansus*, p. 201.   4: *Haustellotyphis cumingii*, p. 195.   5: *Typhisala clarki*, p. 211.   6: *Trubatsa pavlova*, p. 205.   7: *Typhinellus sowerbii*, p. 210.   8: *Trubatsa erythrostigma*, p. 204.   9: *Trubatsa longicornis*, p. 205.   10: *Distichotyphis vemae*, p. 194.

Plate 32. 1: *Siphonochelus japonicus*, p. 198. 2: *S. syringianus*, p. 200. 3: *Typhinellus occlusum*, p. 210. 4: *Typhina ramosa*, p. 209. 5: *Typhina montforti*, p. 207. 6: *Typhina cleryi*, p. 207. 7: *Typhina philippensis*, p. 209. 8: *Typhina imperialis*, p. 207. 9: *Siphonochelus nipponensis*, p. 199. 10–12: *Typhisopsis coronatus*, p. 212.

is indistinct. The body whorl is moderately large and trigonal. The aperture is smallish and lenticular, with a narrow, moderately deep anal sulcus, and the entire aperture is oriented out of the plane of the outer apertural lip; the inner apertural margin is sunken relative to the outer apertural margin. The outer apertural lip is broadly flaring, weakly erect, and thrown into a series of broadly spaced short points or cusps; the inner surface of the outer lip, almost completely exposed at the outer apertural margin, bears a series of eight prominent tubercles, these decreasing in size anteriorly. The columellar lip is adherent and thinly callused, barely detached and nonerect at its anterior end. The siphonal canal is of moderate length, broad, barely open, and distally recurved.

The body whorl bears three broad, ruffled varices upswept posteriorly to fuse with the varix of the preceding whorl. The winglike flanges thus extend from the suture and from the fusion of the varix with a varix of a preceding whorl to the point near the tip of the canal at which the canal turns dorsally. Intervarical axial sculpture consists of two or three low ridges, these strongest at the shoulder margin and extending to about midway on the body. Spiral sculpture consists of a single weak cord on the shoulder, seven stronger cords on the body, and three strong cords on the canal, the cords corresponding to the dorsally upraised portions of the ruffled varical margin.

Shell color is orange-brown, with irregular whitish blotches. The leading edge of the varix is white, with a brown line running along the ventrally folded portions of the ruffled varix. The inner surface of the outer apertural lip is suffused with fleshy pinkish-orange; the tubercles on the inner surface of the outer lip are rosy pink to darker rosy red, grading to white at their inner ends. The remainder of the aperture is white.

Known to us only from off Martinique, Windward Islands (Caribbean), in 30 m.

See Pl. 7, fig. 8.

Pterynotus vespertilio (Kira, 1959)

Ceratostoma (Pteropurpura) vespertilio Kira, 1959: 61

The shell is of moderate size for the genus (maximum length 50 mm), fusiform, thin, and fragile. The spire is high, consisting of one full, convex nuclear whorl and six weakly shouldered postnuclear whorls. The suture is unimpressed. The body whorl is proportionately large and fusoid. The aperture is ovate to lenticular, with a very shallow, almost imperceptible anal sulcus. The outer apertural lip is slightly erect and smooth within. The columellar lip is adherent and briefly, parietally expanded into a thin callus above, detached and barely erect below. The siphonal canal is moderately long, narrowly, centrally open, strongly bent to the right, and distally recurved.

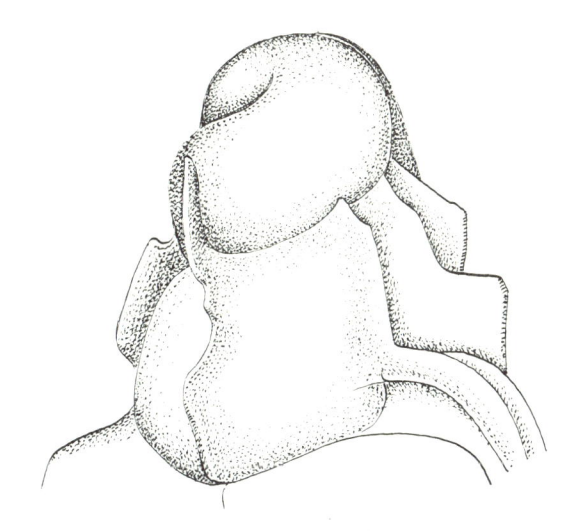

64. *Pterynotus vespertilio*, protoconch

The body whorl bears three winged varices. The margin of each varical "wing" is scalloped, its scalloping reflecting the presence of spiral elements on its dorsal surface, each of which ends in a point; each such point is separated from the next by a moderately sharp, V-shaped notch, and at the uppermost point each wing overlaps and is fused to the wing of the corresponding varix of the preceding whorl. Each wing is produced at the shoulder into a long, sharply pointed spine; anteriorly it reaches the midpoint of the siphonal canal and is intricately laminate on its ventral surface. Other axial sculpture consists of four or five ephemeral ridges in each intervarical space. Spiral sculpture consists of seven low cords, these strongest on the dorsal surface of the varical wing. the most prominent the uppermost one at the shoulder margin.

The shell is pale fleshy brown, erratically marked with small, red-brown blotches. The ventral surface of each varical "wing" and the interior of the aperture are glossy white.

Known only from southeastern Japan in 100–200 m.

See Pl. 9, fig. 2.

Genus PURPURELLUS Jousseaume, 1880

TYPE SPECIES: *Murex gambiensis* Reeve, 1845, by original designation.

The shells are generally of moderate size (30–65 mm) and subfusiform. The spire is high and acute, with a completely obscured suture. The body whorl is moderately large. The aperture is entire and ovate to subcircular. The siphonal canal is long, broad, and sealed, its left margin overlapping its right.

The body whorl bears three moderately broad, winglike varices, these sometimes entire or indented at the base of the body. The varix is drawn into an upward-hooked point at the shoulder margin, and the leading edge of the varix at the shoulder spine is overlapped by a fold from above. Portions of each varix are retained on the spire, forming a continuous, spinose ridge from the body whorl to the apex.

According to Emerson & D'Attilio (1969), "The available distribution data ... indicate that the living representatives of this group are surviving, relict elements of the older Tertiary West-Tethyan faunas." This would explain the present, apparently discontinuous distribution, with species now living in the tropical eastern Atlantic (*P. gambiensis* Reeve, 1845) and eastern Pacific oceans (*P. pinniger* Broderip, 1833; *P. macleani* Emerson & D'Attilio, 1969). Fossils representing several species are known from both Europe and North America.

Purpurellus gambiensis (Reeve, 1845)

Murex gambiensis Reeve, 1845: sp. 65; *M. osseus* Reeve, 1845: sp. 73

The shell is moderately small (maximum length 38 mm) and subfusiform. The spire is high, consisting of six weakly shouldered postnuclear whorls and a protoconch of undetermined nature. The suture is completely obscured by the succeeding whorl. The body whorl is moderately large and fusoid. The aperture is ovate to subcircular and entire, with no perceptible anal sulcus. The outer apertural lip is weakly erect and faintly crenulate. The columellar lip is adherent but may be briefly erect anteriorly. The siphonal canal is moderately long, fused (except at its tip), and weakly bent to the right and dorsally.

The body whorl bears three winglike varices, these continuous from the suture to just above the tip of the canal. A more or less deep embayment is evident near the midpoint of the canal. Additional axial sculpture consists of a single sharp node midway along the shoulder margin in each intervarical space. Spiral sculpture consists of 11 weak cords, eight on the body, three on the canal. These cords are weakest intervarically and strongest on the varix, and end at the varical margin as short, dorsally reflected spinelets. The spine at the shoulder margin is large and posteriorly hooked. An overlapping fold on the upper portion of the shoulder spine is characteristic of the genus.

Shell color is pale mauve to violet-white. Erratic brown markings may be found on the shell, particularly just postvarically.

Western Africa: Senegal and Gambia.
See Pl. 26, fig. 15.

Purpurellus macleani (Emerson & D'Attilio, 1969)

Pterynotus (*Purpurellus*) *macleani* Emerson & D'Attilio, 1969: 147

The shell of this species is small for the genus (maximum length 30 mm) and subfusiform. The spire is moderately high, consisting of one and one-half nuclear whorls and seven weakly shouldered postnuclear whorls. The suture is entirely obscured by the subsequent whorl. The body whorl is large and fusoid. The aperture is ovate, with no perceptible anal sulcus. The outer apertural lip is weakly erect. The columellar lip is adherent to barely erect. The siphonal canal is broad, fused in mature specimens, and bent to the right and dorsally.

The body whorl bears three broadly winged varices, these extending from the suture to a point near the tip of the canal, without a break or indentation. Additional axial sculpture consists of a single large tubercle at the shoulder margin, midway in each intervarical space. Spiral sculpture consists of barely discernible cords ending in tiny, dorsally recurved points at the varical margin. The uppermost portion of the varix forms a large, broad, posteriorly hooked spine, this having, on its ventral surface, the overlapping, tightly appressed, folded-over layer typical of the genus.

Shell color is pale brownish-pink, with several gradually weakening red-brown spiral bands, these persisting at the leading edge of each varix. The aperture is porcelaneous white.

Known at present only from Loreto Channel, Baja California, and off Secas Island, Panamá.
See Pl. 26, fig. 13.

Purpurellus pinniger (Broderip, 1833)

Murex pinniger Broderip, 1833: 174

The shell is moderate in size (maximum length 65 mm) and subfusiform. The spire is high, consisting of six or seven weakly shouldered postnuclear whorls and a protoconch of undetermined nature. The suture is entirely obscured by the succeeding whorl. The body whorl is moderately large and fusoid. The aperture is ovate to sub-

65. *Purpurellus pinniger*, radular dentition

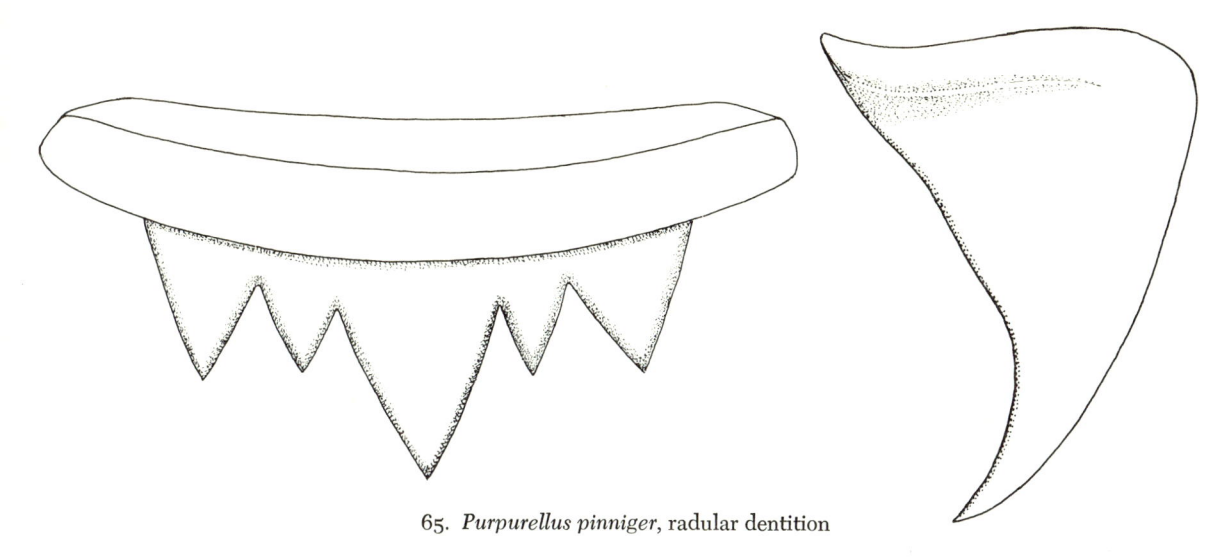

circular, with an imperceptible anal sulcus. The outer apertural lip is barely erect and essentially smooth at its margin. The columellar lip is entirely adherent to barely erect. The siphonal canal is moderately broad and long, and bent weakly to the right and dorsally.

The body whorl bears three undulate, winglike varices, these continuous from the suture to a point near the tip of the canal. In most specimens there is a more or less deep embayment near the midpoint of the canal. Additional axial sculpture consists of a single sharp, medial node at the shoulder margin of each intervarical space. Spiral sculpture consists of 11 ephemeral cords, these almost obsolete between varices, becoming slightly stronger on the trailing edge of each varix, and ending on the varical margin as a series of sharp, more or less dorsally reflected folds or ruffles. The point at the shoulder margin is curved posteriorly. An additional layer or "fold" overlaps this varical point, originating near its apex.

Shell color varies from white, with irregular, chestnut-brown blotches, to pinkish-white, with faint brown lines following the spiral cords. In the latter case most of the brown coloration is apparent immediately after each varix.

Guaymas, Mexico, to Panamá.

See Pl. 26, fig. 14.

Genus **SIRATUS** Jousseaume, 1880

TYPE SPECIES: "*Purpura sirat* Adanson" (=*Murex senegalensis* Gmelin, 1791), by original designation.

The shell is small to large (35–250 mm) and fusiform. Its spire is moderately high and acute, consisting of one and one-half or two smooth nuclear whorls and six to nine globose, more or less shouldered postnuclear whorls. The suture is moderately to strongly impressed. The body whorl is moderately large and globose. The aperture is moderately large and ovate, with a shallow, moderately broad anal sulcus. The outer apertural lip is erect and marginally, finely to coarsely dentate; the interior of the lip is generally weakly lirate. The columellar lip is generally detached and weakly erect, with a few prominent elongate denticles posteriorly, these forming the parietal margin of the anal sulcus, and three or four weaker denticles anteriorly. The canal is moderately long to very long and strongly bent to the right. The body whorl bears three more or less spinose varices. The length of the medially open varical spines varies with the species. The varices also develop more or less broad, webbing-like extensions, these better developed in some species than in others.

This genus seems to have evolved a considerable number of very closely related species. Their similarity has caused a great confusion in identification. Attempts to diminish the number of names have convinced us that these resemblances, especially in the Caribbean forms, are based on generic, rather than specific, characters. Caribbean forms of *Siratus* differ from those of *Murex* s.s. in their more globose whorls, notably bent siphonal canal, and varical webbing.

Siratus alabaster (Reeve, 1845)

Murex alabaster Reeve, 1845: sp. 39

The shell is very large (maximum length 200 mm) and fusiform. The spire is high and acute, consisting of one and one-half nuclear whorls and nine shouldered postnuclear whorls. The suture is moderately impressed. The body whorl is large and globosely angulate. The aperture is broad and ovate, with a broad, very shallow anal sulcus. The outer apertural lip is erect and weakly, marginally crenulate; its interior is briefly, weakly lirate. The columellar lip is detached and weakly erect, with no denticles or other features. The siphonal canal is long and slender, bent to the right, and minimally open to the right.

The body whorl bears three prominent winged varices. A single strong spiral keel at the shoulder margin is extended into a single moderately long, straight, medially open shoulder spine. Other sculpture consists of numerous major and minor threads. Each varix is expanded into a thin, bladelike webbing, extending in two sections, one from the suture to the tip of the shoulder spine (which is distinct as a spine only from the ventral side) and the other from the spine to the uppermost quarter of the siphonal canal. Immediately below the webbing on the siphonal canal is a moderately short, broadly open spine.

Shell color is stark white to ivory, although several live-collected specimens we have seen (D'Attilio and SDSNH collections) have a black or gray stain, probably of environmental origin, over the entire shell.

Southeastern Japan and Taiwan to the Philippines.

See Pl. 17, fig. 10.

Siratus articulatus (Reeve, 1845)

Murex motacilla var. Sowerby, 1841: pl. 189, fig. 169; *M. articulatus* Reeve, 1845: note under sp. 88; *M. nodatus* Reeve, 1845: sp. 107 (not Gmelin, 1791)

The shell is moderately small (maximum length 55 mm) and fusiform. The spire is high and acute, consisting of one and one-half nuclear whorls and six convex postnuclear whorls. The suture is moderately impressed. The body whorl is moderate in size. The aperture is moderately small, with a moderately broad and deep anal sulcus, this directed toward the parietal region. The outer apertural lip is erect and finely, marginally denticulate; its interior is barely lirate for a very short distance. The columellar lip is detached and somewhat erect, and bears two teeth at its posterior end, one at the lip margin, and one recessed into the aperture, these parietally delimiting the anal sulcus; at its anterior end the columellar lip bears three to five elongate, oblique pustules. The siphonal canal is long, more or less bent to the right, and narrowly open to the right.

The body whorl bears three spinose varices. Intervarical axial sculpture consists of three to five slender, elongate, nodulose ridges. Spiral sculpture consists of six major spiral cords, the uppermost one at the shoulder margin. Other spiral sculpture consists of intercalating minor cords and numerous threads. Where the major cords intersect the varices, short to moderately long, sharp, medially grooved spines are developed: the uppermost spine is the longest; the third and fifth spines below this are also strong and are essentially straight; the second, fourth, and sixth spines are shorter, sharper, and bent ventrally. A thin webbing of minor extent connects the last two spines and extends briefly below them. The canal bears a short and a longer spine.

Shell color is purple-brown, with thin, interrupted brown spiral lines following the crests of the major cords.

The appearance of this species varies with locality: a slender form with longer spines (Pl. 17, fig. 7) was named *M. nodatus* Reeve, 1845 (not Gmelin, 1791). The heavier, shorter-spined form (Pl. 17, fig. 2) is the typical *M. articulatus* Reeve, 1845, and this is the earliest valid name.

Moderately deep water in the central and southern Caribbean.

See Pl. 17, figs. 2–3.

Siratus beauii (Fischer & Bernardi, 1857)

Murex beauii Fischer & Bernardi, 1857: 295; *M. branchi* Clench, 1953: 360

The shell is moderately large (maximum length 120 mm) and fusiform. The spire is high and sharp, consisting of eight or nine postnuclear whorls and a protoconch of undetermined nature. The suture is strongly impressed. The body whorl is small and globose. The aperture is small and ovate, with a shallow, moderately broad anal sulcus. The outer apertural lip is strongly flaring and coarsely crenulate, except on the shoulder portion, where it is finely crenulate. The columellar lip is detached and erect, with a series of weak to ephemeral denticles extending its entire length. The siphonal canal is quite long, bent to the right and dorsally, and narrowly open to the right.

The body whorl bears three more or less winged varices. Intervarical axial sculpture consists of four to seven nodulose axial ridges. Spiral sculpture consists of five major cords, the uppermost one at the shoulder margin. Intercalated with these are minor cords, and interspersed over the entire shell are finer threads. Where the major cords cross the varices, long to moderately short, ventrally open spines are developed, the uppermost one by far the longest, the remainder of about equal size. Between these, a delicate webbing of variable extent may be developed, the upper portion extending from the suture to the shoulder spine, the lower portion extending from the shoulder spine to the base of the body. The upper third of the siphonal canal bears three sharp, moderately short, open spines.

Shell color is white or off-white, with three broad, brown spiral bands on the body, these most prominent on the varices.

This species is not uncommon at about 200 m in the eastern and central Gulf of Mexico. Reports of numerous specimens in each dredge or trawl haul indicate that it may be one of the dominant predators at that depth. Collectors, however, are rarely satisfied with the condition of any of the vast majority of specimens collected, for most have little or no varical webbing and are partially eroded or heavily encrusted. The few relatively clean specimens with extensive varical webbing are in great demand.

Northern Gulf of Mexico to the Lesser Antilles (St. Vincent), Brazil, and Uruguay in 170–235 m. See Pl. 17, fig. 8.

Siratus cailleti (Petit de la Saussaye, 1856)

Murex similis Sowerby, 1841: pl. 89, fig. 70 (not Schroeter, 1805); *M. cailleti* Petit de la Saussaye, 1856: 87; *M. cailleti* var. *kugleri* Clench & Pérez Farfante, 1945: 19

The shell is moderately small (maximum length 70 mm) and fusiform to club-shaped. The spire is moderately high and acute, consisting of one and one-half smooth nuclear whorls and six weakly shouldered postnuclear whorls. The suture is weak to indistinct. The body whorl is small and globose. The aperture is small and ovate, with a moderately broad and deep anal sulcus, this heavily callused and delimited parietally by two small knobs, one at the apertural margin and one recessed. The outer apertural lip is strongly erect and finely, marginally crenulate, fine lirae extending into the aperture on its inner surface. The columellar lip is adherent for the upper one-third of its length, detached and weakly erect for the remainder, and bears three or four oblique, elongate denticles at its anterior end, the uppermost much weaker than the others; several irregular denticles may also be developed in the parietal region. The siphonal canal is moderately long, bent to the right and dorsally, and narrowly open to the right.

The body whorl bears three low, rounded, weakly spinose varices. Sculpture varies considerably from one population to another. Intervarical axial sculpture generally consists of two or three heavy, knobby ridges. Where three ridges are developed, the one closest to the newest varix is much weaker than the others. Spiral sculpture consists of three major cords, the uppermost one at the shoulder margin, and numerous minor cords in groups of three between each two major cords. Where the major cords cross the varices, short, sharp spines may be developed. The anterior end of the varix generally develops a brief, webbing-like expansion. The canal bears one or rarely two sharp spines, these somewhat longer than those on the body.

Shell color is ivory to wax yellow-brown, with three diffuse, brown spiral bands on the body and fine red-brown lines following the crests of the spiral cords.

Southeastern Florida to Barbados in deep water. See Pl. 17, figs. 4–6.

Siratus ciboney (Clench & Pérez Farfante, 1945)

Murex trilineatus Reeve, 1845: sp. 103 (not Sowerby, 1813: 80); *M. ciboney* Clench & Pérez Farfante, 1945: 20; *Chicoreus reevei* E. H. Vokes, 1965: 196, new name for *M. trilineatus* Reeve, 1845 (not Sowerby, 1813)

The shell is moderately small (maximum length 55 mm) and fusiform. Its spire is high and acute, consisting of seven or eight convex postnuclear whorls and a protoconch of undetermined nature. The suture is impressed. The body whorl is small to moderate in size. The aperture is small and ovate, with a narrow, moderately shallow anal sulcus delimited on each side by a small sharp denticle. The outer apertural lip is erect and finely denticulate, its interior lirate. The columellar lip is adherent most of its length, is briefly detached and erect at its anterior end, and bears three or four weak, oblique, elongate denticles, the uppermost much the weakest. The siphonal canal is of moderate length, weakly bent to the right, narrowly open to the right, and strongly dorsally recurved.

The body whorl bears three weakly spinose varices. Intervarical axial sculpture consists of two to four nodose ridges. Spiral sculpture consists of seven primary cords, these alternating with secondary cords and many tertiaries. Where the primary cords intersect the varices, very short, ventrally bent, open spines are developed; the longest of these is at the shoulder, followed by three that are barely discernible and three others that are shorter than the first but longer than the middle three. The upper third of the canal bears one or two small spines.

Shell color is white to ivory, with three fine brown spiral lines, one at the shoulder margin, one medial, and one basal.

Cuba and Jamaica to the Lesser Antilles (St. Kitts) in considerable depths (180–300 m).

See Pl. 17, fig. 12.

Siratus consuela (A. H. Verrill, 1950)

Murex pulcher A. Adams, 1853: 270 (not Sowerby, 1813: 63); *M. pulcher* var. *consuela* A. H. Verrill, 1950: 7

The shell is moderate in size (maximum length 65 mm) and fusiform. The spire is high and acute, consisting of two smooth nuclear whorls and six or seven weakly shouldered postnuclear whorls. The suture is indistinct or obscured. The body whorl is moderate in size and fusoid. The aperture is small and ovate, with a small, shallow anal sulcus. The outer apertural lip is marginally, weakly crenulate and smooth within, except for two or three somewhat stronger denticles on the shoulder portion. The columellar lip is adherent parietally, detached and weakly erect for most of its length, and one or two parietal denticles delimit the anal sulcus on the left side; below this are seven to ten denticles, these becoming stronger anteriorly. The siphonal canal is moderately long, weakly bent to the right, barely open to the right, and strongly, dorsally recurved.

The body whorl bears three varices. Intervarical axial sculpture consists of two, or more commonly three nodose ridges, the one nearest the newest varix much less prominent than the other two. Spiral sculpture consists of seven major cords intercalated with minor cords. Where the major cords cross the intervarical ridges and varices, prominent nodes are developed. The uppermost major cord, at the shoulder margin, is drawn out into a spinelike point on the varix. On the varix, at about the midpoint of the body, a thin pleated webbing is developed, extending anteriorly to the midpoint of the canal. On the canal the webbing is drawn into two or three spinose points.

Shell color is purple-pink, with three spiral brown bands and other lines of brown markings following the spiral elements. The nuclear and early postnuclear whorls are bright pink.

St. Croix, Virgin Islands, to Trinidad; a single record from Texas, on offshore reefs.

See Pl. 17, fig. 13.

Siratus formosus (Sowerby, 1841)

Murex formosus Sowerby, 1841: pl. 97, fig. 112; *M. antillarum* Hinds, 1844: 126; *M. aguayoi* Clench & Pérez Farfante, 1945: 15; *M. finlayi* Clench, 1955: 1

The shell is moderate in size (maximum length 90 mm) and fusiform. The spire is high, consisting of one and one-half smooth, brown nuclear whorls and seven or eight weakly shouldered postnuclear whorls. The suture is moderately to weakly impressed. The body whorl is moderate in size and fusoid. The aperture is moderately large and ovate, with a broad, shallow anal sulcus. The outer apertural lip is somewhat erect and coarsely dentate at its margin. The columellar lip is adherent above, detached and erect below, and bears four moderately strong denticles at its anterior end and two strong denticles at the posterior end, one at the margin and one recessed and parietally delimiting the anal sulcus. The siphonal canal is long, weakly bent to the right and dorsally, and narrowly open to the right.

The body whorl bears three spinose varices. Intervarical axial sculpture consists of three nodulose ridges, these becoming progressively weaker in the direction of growth. Spiral sculpture consists of primary, secondary, and tertiary cords and of numerous intercalating threads. Where the primary and secondary cords intersect the varices, sharp, short to moderately long, straight spines are developed; of these, four are major, the uppermost one, at the shoulder margin, the longest. A thin varical webbing connects most or rarely all of the varical spines and is most prominent at the anterior end of the varix. The siphonal canal bears two or three spines, the uppermost minute, the middle one short but longest of the three, and the lowermost almost as long as the middle.

Shell color is pale brown, with thin white lines following the crests of the primary cords, and three diffuse, brown spiral bands. The aperture is white.

The Dry Tortugas, Florida to Barbados in moderately deep water (54–380 m).

See Pl. 17, fig. 9.

Siratus motacilla (Gmelin, 1791)

Murex motacilla Gmelin, 1791: 3530

The shell is moderate in size (maximum length 65 mm) and broadly fusiform or club-shaped. The spire is moderately high, consisting of two nuclear whorls and six or seven globose, broadly shouldered postnuclear whorls. The suture is very shallow where not obscured. The body whorl is large and globose. The aperture is moderate in size and ovate, wtih a moderately developed anal sulcus. The outer apertural lip is strongly erect and its margin is coarsely, marginally crenulate. The columellar lip is adherent at its posterior end, detached and weakly erect for the remainder of its length, and its surface is denticulate; three strong, oblique, elongate denticles at its anterior end are followed posteriorly by seven or eight weaker denticles. The siphonal canal is moderately long, strongly bent to the right and dorsally, and narrowly open on its right.

The body whorl bears three heavy, moderately spinose varices. Intervarical axial sculpture consists of two or three nodose ridges; where three are present, the one nearest the growing edge is much the weakest of the three. Spiral sculpture consists of alternating major and minor cords and numerous threads. Where the five major cords intersect the varices, short, sharp, ventrally open spines are generally developed on the body. A single short, open, triangular spine is developed at the top of the canal. The anterior portion of each varix bears a brief, thin, shelflike projection, this apparently a vestige of the varical webbing better developed in related species.

The shell is white or ivory, suffused with a deep fleshy orange-brown. On the shoulder there is generally a medial brown blotch, and three diffuse brown bands encircle the body, these becoming more distinct on the varices. The interior of the aperture is white.

The Lesser Antilles: Dominica to Barbados.
See Pl. 17, fig. 14.

Siratus perelegans (E. H. Vokes, 1965)

Murex elegans Sowerby, 1841: pl. 92, fig. 84 (not *M. elegans* Donovan, 1804; *Chicoreus perelegans* E. H. Vokes, 1965: 196, new name for *M. elegans* Sowerby, 1841 (not Donovan, 1804)

The shell is moderate in size (maximum length 65 mm) and broadly fusiform. The spire is moderate in height, consisting of six postnuclear whorls and a protoconch of undetermined nature. The suture is obscured by the succeeding whorl. The body whorl is large, solid, and globose. The aperture is moderately small and ovate, with a small, shallow anal sulcus. The outer apertural lip is strongly erect and coarsely dentate; its interior is briefly lirate. The columellar lip is adherent above, detached and weakly erect below; its anterior end bears two prominent, oblique, elongate denticles, and one or two prominent denticles parietally delimit the anal sulcus. The siphonal canal is moderately long, strongly bent to the right and dorsally, and narrowly open to the right.

The body whorl bears three heavy, rounded varices. Intervarical axial sculpture consists of two knoblike ridges, these either of equal size or the one nearer the growing edge smaller. Spiral sculpture consists of 16 cords of approximately equal strength, these slightly raised where they intersect the intervarical ridges and the varices, although no spines are evident on the body. A single short, ventrally open spine is developed at the top of the canal.

Shell color is white or ivory. The summit of each spiral cord is red-brown, this imparting a spirally pin-striped appearance to the shell.

Caribbean Sea: Hispaniola to Barbados.
See Pl. 17, fig. 11.

Siratus pliciferoides (Kuroda, 1942)

Murex pliciferus Sowerby, 1841: pl. 195, fig. 101 (not Bivona-Bernardi, 1832: 22); *Chicoreus pliciferoides* Kuroda, 1942: 80, new name for *M. pliciferus* Sowerby, 1841 (not Bivona-Bernardi, 1832); *M. (Siratus) propinquus* Kuroda & Azuma, in Azuma, 1961: 300

The shell is large (maximum length 120 mm) and roughly fusiform. The spire is high and acute, consisting of seven or eight weakly shouldered postnuclear whorls and a protoconch of undetermined nature. The suture is weakly defined. The body whorl is large and fusoid. The aperture is large and ovate, with a broad, shallow anal sulcus. The outer apertural lip is erect, finely dentate, and briefly lirate within. The columellar lip is smooth and adherent for most of its length, erect at its anterior end. The siphonal canal is moderate in length, weakly bent to the right and dorsally, and narrowly open to the right.

The body whorl bears three spinose varices. Intervarical axial sculpture consists of one to three knoblike ridges. Spiral sculpture consists of seven primary cords and numerous secondary and tertiary cords. Where the primary cords intersect the varices, short, sharp, ventrally open spines are developed. Two spines arise from secondary spiral cords on the shoulder. The longest true spine arises at the shoulder margin; below this, the six remaining spines are progressively longer anteriorly. The canal bears two spines of moderate length.

Shell color is ivory, with three diffuse brown spiral bands on the body, these most prominent on the varices.

The Philippines to southeastern Japan.
See Pl. 17, fig. 17.

Siratus senegalensis (Gmelin, 1791)

Murex senegalensis Gmelin, 1791: 3537; *M. springeri* Bullis, 1964: 104

The shell is moderately small (maximum length 60 mm) and broadly fusiform. The spire is high and acute, consisting of six or seven shouldered postnuclear whorls and a protoconch of undetermined nature. The suture is weakly impressed.

The body whorl is large and fusoid. The aperture is moderately large and ovate to subcircular, with a moderately broad, shallow anal sulcus. The outer apertural lip is erect and finely dentate, and its interior is briefly lirate. The columellar lip is entirely adherent and bears five to eight tiny denticles at its anterior end; a single small node parietally delimits the anal sulcus. The siphonal canal is moderately short, almost straight, and narrowly open to the right.

The body whorl bears three rounded, almost spineless varices. Intervarical axial sculpture consists of two or three ridges of moderate strength. Spiral sculpture consists of numerous, seemingly scabrous primary, secondary, and tertiary cords in the pattern 1-3-2-3-1. Where the strongest primary cord, at the shoulder margin, crosses the varix, a short, stout, recurved spine is apparent. The entire varical margin bears a thin, poorly developed erect webbing, this strongest anteriorly on the body and at the top of the canal. Below this, on the canal, one or two short, ventrally open spines are developed.

Shell color is white to ivory or light tan, with three spiral brown bands on the body. The interior of the aperture is white.

This species has been known for many years but has persistently been located in West Africa by certain workers, apparently as a result of an erroneous locality in Adanson (1757), a nonbinominal work in which it was first described and figured. Additional confusion has led some recent authors to call a slender, trivaricate form of the West African *Muricanthus varius* by this name (i.e. *S. senegalensis*). Another superficially similar species is *S. tenuivaricosus* (Dautzenberg, 1927), about which more is said below. *S. springeri* (Bullis, 1964) appears to be a more coarsely sculptured form of this species from the southern Caribbean and northern Brazil (Pl. 17, fig. 1).

The southern Caribbean to southern Brazil.
See Pl. 17, figs. 1, 7.

Siratus tenuivaricosus (Dautzenberg, 1927)

Murex calcar Kiener, 1842: 107 (not J. de C. Sowerby, 1823: 7); *M. tenuivaricosus* (Dautzenberg, 1927: 94, new name for *M. calcar* Kiener, 1842 (not Sowerby, 1823: 7); *Chicoreus carioca* E. H. Vokes, 1968: 39, new name for *M. calcar* Kiener, 1842 (not Sowerby, 1823)

The shell is moderately large (maximum length 105 mm) and broadly fusiform. The spire is high, consisting of two nuclear whorls and seven or eight convex postnuclear whorls. The suture is moderately impressed. The body whorl is large and broadly fusoid. The aperture is moderately large and ovate, with a moderately broad, shallow anal sulcus angling toward the parietal region. The outer apertural lip is weakly to moderately erect and minutely denticulate; its interior is smooth. The columellar lip is adherent for most of its length, weakly detached and barely erect just above the origin of the canal; on its anterior end are four moderately weak denticles, and posteriorly, the columellar lip bears four irregularly placed elongate denticles, the uppermost most prominent and parietally delimiting the anal sulcus. The siphonal canal is moderate in length, bent to the right, and narrowly open at the right.

The body whorl bears three winged varices. Intervarical axial sculpture consists of very numerous, minutely nodulose ribs of varying strengths. The body whorl bears four major spiral cords. Where the major cord at the shoulder margin intersects a varix, a long, finely tapering, dorsally and posteriorly curved spine is developed. The entire varix is fringed by a thin, fluted webbing, the upper part extending from the suture to midway along the shoulder spine, the lower part extending from midway along the shoulder spine to the upper portion of the canal. Where each of the other three major cords intersects a varix, a short, recurved, ventrally open point is developed. The canal bears two anteriorly pointing, ventrally open spines.

The shell is flesh-colored, with three rust-brown spiral bands on the body. The webbing and aperture are pale pink.

S. tenuivaricosus differs from its congener and fellow inhabitant of the Brazilian coast, *S. senegalensis*, in having longer spines, a much more extensive webbing, one or two more whorls at maturity, and a much less solid shell, and in being both ecologically distinct (deeper-water habitat) and much larger when full-grown.

The central and southern coasts of Brazil.
See Pl. 17, fig. 16.

?Siratus virgineus (Röding, 1798)

Purpura virginea Röding, 1798: 141; *Murex anguliferus* Lamarck, 1822: 171; *M. erythraeus* Fischer, 1870: 176; *M. cyacantha* Sowerby, 1879: 11; *M. ponderosus* Sowerby, 1879: 12

The shell is moderately large to very large (maximum length 160 mm) and robustly fusiform. The spire is moderately low and acute, consisting of seven or eight strongly shouldered postnuclear whorls and a protoconch of undetermined nature. The suture is essentially obscured by the succeeding whorl. The body whorl is large and fusoid. The aperture is of moderate size and ovate, with a narrow, moderately deep anal sulcus. The outer apertural lip is weakly erect, dentate, and smooth within, with a weak labial tooth toward its anterior end. The columellar lip is entirely adherent and smooth, except for a strong parietal ridge running into the aperture and delimiting the anal sulcus. The siphonal canal is moderate in length, broad, weakly bent to the right and dorsally, and narrowly open to the right.

The body whorl bears three or four heavy, rounded varices. Intervarical axial sculpture consists of a single heavy, pointedly knobby ridge, generally closer to the growing edge of the shell. Spiral sculpture consists of five or six major cords, these alternating with minor cords, and a multitude of finer cords and threads. Where the major cord at the shoulder margin intersects the varix, a short, stout, sharply pointed, and more or less recurved spine is developed. Toward the anterior end of the body a moderately broad spiral depression reflects the position of the tooth on the varical margin. Immediately below this, a series of three or four broadly, ventrally open, scalelike spines are developed, these sometimes coalescent, forming a webbing of sorts. The canal bears two short, ventrally open spines.

Shell color ranges from white to light chocolate-brown, most commonly white with scattered brown flecks, the flecks sometimes arranged in diffuse spiral bands, these most prominent on the intervarical ridges and just before a varix. The aperture is white, generally rimmed with fleshy pink.

Northwestern Indian Ocean, from eastern Africa to the Bay of Bengal.

See Pl. 17, fig. 15.

Genus **TAKIA** Kuroda, 1953

TYPE SPECIES: *Murex inermis* (Sowerby, 1841) (=*Takia infrons* E. H. Vokes, 1974), by original designation.

The shell in *Takia* is larger than in other related forms (30–40 mm); the body whorl is broadly fusiform; the siphonal canal is proportionately longer than in other aspelloid forms; and the low denticles characteristic of the inner surface of the outer apertural lip have fused to form a low ridge. The genus seems to be limited to the Indo-West Pacific region.

Takia infrons (E. H. Vokes, 1974)

Murex inermis Sowerby, 1841: pl. 192, fig. 87 (not Philippi, 1836: 209); *Dermomurex* (*Takia*) *infrons* E. H. Vokes, 1974: 2, new name for *M. inermis* Sowerby, 1841 (not Philippi, 1836)

The shell is large (maximum length 35 mm) and roughly fusiform. The spire is high and acute, consisting of almost two convex nuclear whorls and five strongly convex postnuclear whorls. The suture is impressed, obscured at times by varical buttresses. The body whorl is large (about three-fifths of total shell length) and broadly fusoid. The aperture is large, ovate, and broadly open, with a barely perceptible anal sulcus. The outer apertural lip is essentially nonerect, and its inner surface bears a series of low denticles, the anteriormost one or two most apparent; above this, the denticles merge to form a low labial ridge. The columellar lip is smooth, except for a weak pustule at its anterior end, and is almost entirely adherent, with a thin, spreading columellar callus. The siphonal canal is long, narrowly open, and bent to the right.

The body whorl generally bears three moderately strong and sharp varices. Earlier whorls bear six varices of equal strength; three of these typically are reduced to secondary axial elements or disappear on the body whorl. In some specimens a six-varixed condition persists in adult specimens. Each varix is roughly triangular in cross section and sharply, if briefly, bladelike at its edge. Spiral sculpture consists of five weak cords on the body that are barely visible between varices.

Shell color is translucent blue-white, covered by a moderately thick, flat-white intritacalx. The aperture is porcelaneous white.

Southeastern Japan in 67–132 m.

See Pl. 1, figs. 30–31.

Subfamily Ocenebrinae

COSSMANN, 1903

The shell ranges in size from small to moderately large (10–150 mm in length), is trigonal or stoutly fusiform in shape, and generally bears a color pattern of brown markings over a brown or tan ground, the colors generally more subdued than in the Muricinae. The aperture varies in size and shape and forms an entire peristome. The siphonal canal is generally fused, without overlap. Ocenebrine forms sometimes lack varices, but commonly bear three winged varices per whorl, sometimes with short points or spines. Spiral sculpture is very fine. The surface in most species is finely to coarsely scabrous or imbricate; a simple intritacalx is present in scattered species in several genera, but no consistent pattern of incidence is apparent.

Ocenebrine protoconchs are generally short, in many cases with sharply angulate whorls. The operculum is generally thin and trapezoidal, the center not depressed; there is an oblique zone of weakness along which it folds when dried.

The radula consists of the typical series of three-across rows of teeth, each row with a rachidian tooth and two lateral teeth. The rachidian has a moderately deep rectangular base with strong double endpoints and a strong, prominent, slender cowl bearing the central cusp; the remaining four cusps are smaller and dependent, the intermediates appended to the laterals, and two to four denticles are apparent between each lateral cusp and the base endpoint.

Distribution: worldwide (primarily temperate), in depths of 0 to 100 m.

Genus CERATOSTOMA Herrmannsen, 1846

TYPE SPECIES: *Murex nuttalli* Conrad, 1837, by monotypy.

The variability of key characters in this genus prevents its concise definition. The shells of the type species, *C. nuttalli* (Conrad), and of *C. fournieri* (Crosse) have three winglike varices, strong denticulation on the inner surface of the outer apertural lip, and a stout tooth at the margin of the outer lip. Two other species, *C. foliatum* (Gmelin) and *C. burnetti* (Adams & Reeve), have similar shell features but lack the apertural denticles. Still other species, *C. rorifluum* (Adams & Reeve) and *C. inornatum* (Récluz), differ from the typical form in other respects: *C. rorifluum* has four rather than three varices, and *C. inornatum* has from two to ten varices, depending on the population. The varices in some specimens may develop as projecting lamellae, and in others they may be reduced to simple, low, axial ridges. In addition, specimens of *C. inornatum* may lack a labial tooth, a feature of apparently sporadic incidence in the species.

Ceratostoma burnetti (Adams & Reeve, 1849)

Murex burnetti Adams & Reeve (*in* Reeve), 1849: sp. 192; *M. coreanicus* A. Adams, 1854: 72

The shell is large (maximum length 130 mm) and broadly fusiform. The spire is high and acute, consisting of six convex to weakly shouldered postnuclear whorls and a protoconch of undetermined nature. The suture is obscured by the succeeding whorl. The body whorl is large and broadly fusoid. The aperture is moderate in size and ovate, with a shallow anal sulcus. The outer apertural lip is strongly erect and coarsely crenulate, the second or third crenulation up from the base of the body being developed into a long, stout, medially grooved ceratus; the inner surface of the outer lip is weakly lirate to smooth. The columellar lip is adherent and weakly callused above, detached and somewhat erect for the lower two-thirds of its extent. The siphonal canal is fused for the upper two-thirds of its length, moderately long, weakly bent to the right, and dorsally recurved.

The body whorl bears three marginally digitate winglike varices. Additional intervarical sculpture consists of a single axial row of low swellings on the primary spiral cords, these swellings closer to the older of any two consecutive varices. Spiral sculpture consists of seven primary cords, each ending in a prominent, dorsally recurved, digitate projection at the varix margin; the uppermost cord above the shoulder margin, the lowest at the base of the body, and the fifth, sixth, and seventh cords are each followed by a more or less discernible secondary cord.

Shell color is pale pink-brown to red-brown, with patches of dark red-brown immediately following each varix.

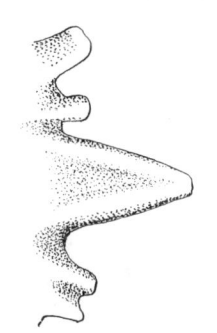

66. *Ceratostoma burnetti*, labial tooth (ceratus)

The western coast of Japan and the Japan Sea coasts of Korea and the U.S.S.R.

See Pl. 18, figs. 6–7.

Ceratostoma foliatum (Gmelin, 1791)

Murex foliatus Gmelin, 1791: 3529

The shell is moderately large to large (maximum length 110 mm) and broadly fusiform. The spire is high and acute, consisting of six shouldered postnuclear whorls and a protoconch of undetermined nature. The suture is generally obscured by the succeeding whorl. The body is moderately large and broad and roughly fusoid. The aperture is moderately small and ovate, with a weak anal sulcus angled toward the parietal region of the shell. The outer apertural lip is coarsely and bluntly crenulate, one of these blunt bumps near the base of the body being developed into a long, thornlike, medially grooved ceratus; the inner surface of the outer lip is generally smooth in fully mature specimens, although in specimens with immature outer lips a row of low, fused denticles may be present. The columellar lip is adherent above, detached and strongly erect for most of its extent; the columella is twisted through about 40 degrees where the siphonal canal begins. The siphonal canal is moderately long, fused for the upper two-thirds of its length, and strongly bent to the right and dorsally at its open distal end.

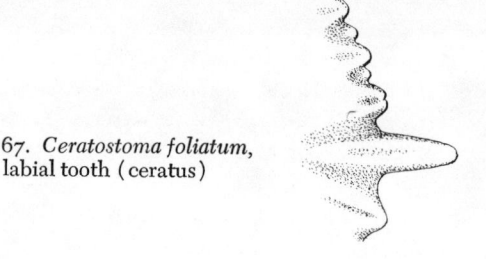

67. *Ceratostoma foliatum*, labial tooth (ceratus)

The body whorl bears three winged varices with broadly digitate margins. Intervarical axial sculpture consists of a single axially arranged row of knobs on the spiral cords. Spiral sculpture consists of prominent primary, secondary, and tertiary cords. A single secondary cord above the shoulder margin is followed by three primary cords, the uppermost one at the shoulder margin; following these are a low tertiary cord, a secondary, a primary, and another tertiary cord. The leading edge of each varix is richly fimbriate. The lateral extent of the varical wings varies with the population and with water depth.

Shell color is white, with brown mottling between the varices and especially on the spiral cords; the leading edges of the varices are white. A randomly occurring all-white variant is a novelty among collectors.

Alaska in shallow, subtidal depths to Santa Cruz Island, California, in deeper (25–70 m) subtidal situations.

See Pl. 18, figs. 1–2.

Ceratostoma fournieri (Crosse, 1861)

Murex emarginatus Sowerby, 1841: pl. 193, figs. 98, 100 (not Donovan, 1804); *M. fournieri* Crosse, 1861: 352

The shell is moderately small for the genus (maximum length 60 mm) and roughly fusiform. The spire is high and acute, consisting of seven shouldered postnuclear whorls and a protoconch of undetermined nature. The suture is obscured by the succeeding whorl. The body whorl is moderately large and fusoid. The aperture is moderate in size and ovate, with an all but imperceptible anal sulcus. The outer apertural lip is moderately erect and finely crenulate, the third crenulation from the base of the body being larger and forming a moderately long, slender ceratus; the inner surface of the outer lip is smooth to weakly denticulate. The columellar lip is adherent and slightly callused above, erect below; the columella is smooth and has a sinuous twist of about 70 degrees where it enters the siphonal canal. The siphonal canal is moderate in length, fused for two-thirds of its extent, and dorsally recurved.

The body whorl bears three crenulate varices. Intervarical axial sculpture consists of a single prominent knob at the shoulder, this closer to the older of two consecutive varices. Spiral sculpture consists of four major cords, the uppermost and strongest at the shoulder margin. In addition, numerous scabrous spiral threads cover the entire shell surface. The major cords arise abruptly from the essentially unsculptured intervarical area, thus emphasizing the depressed webbing between them and forming large, rectangular pits. The leading edges of the varices are notably fimbriate.

Shell color is white, with varying degrees of brown on the varices and intervarical nodes. In some cases the whole shell is light to moderately dark brown, except for the aperture and the leading edges of the varices, which are generally white.

Eastern coast of Japan from 33° to 37° north latitude.

See Pl. 18, fig. 8.

Ceratostoma inornatum (Récluz, 1851)

Murex inornatus Récluz, 1851: 207; *M. crassus* A. Adams, 1853: 269; *M. japonicus* Dunker, 1860: 230; *M. talienwhanensis* Crosse, 1862: 56; *M. endermonis* E. A. Smith, 1875: 420; *Ocinebra monoptera* Pilsbry, 1904: 17; *O. lumaria* Yokoyama, 1926: 270

The shell is so variable that a simple description will not suffice for a clear understanding of the species. The shell is moderately small to quite small (maximum length 45 mm) and broadly fusiform. The spire is high and acute, consisting of five or six postnuclear whorls and a protoconch of undetermined nature. The suture is moderately impressed. The aperture is moderate in size and ovate, with a very shallow to indiscernible anal sulcus. The outer apertural lip is weakly erect, if at all, and minutely serrate, one of these minute serrations, on the margin near the base of the body, being developed into a small, sharp ceratus; the inner surface of the outer lip is generally weakly denticulate. The columellar lip is smooth and adherent, except for its anterior one-fourth, where it is sharply twisted as it enters the canal. The siphonal canal is moderate in length, fused for the upper three-fourths of its extent, and weakly, dorsally recurved.

The body whorl bears two to five varices, which, when maximally developed, are thin, perpendicular, recurved, lamellose structures; in some populations, however, most varices are reduced to low, rounded axial ridges. The edge of each varix in a well-developed specimen bears short, sharp spinelets, representing the ends of the major spiral cords. Intervarical axial sculpture is lacking where many varices are developed. Spiral sculpture consists of primary, secondary, and tertiary cords: four primary cords are evident, the uppermost one at the shoulder margin; midway between each two primaries, a secondary may be seen; a tertiary cord occurs between each primary and secondary.

Shell color varies from dirty white through dirty brown, red-brown with or without white markings, to dark purple-brown with cream-colored varices.

The variability in size and sculpture of this species has led to the introduction of numerous superfluous names based on ecological or genetic variants. Certain populations from northern Japan produce dwarfed specimens that reach only one-third to one-half the size of typical mature shells. In some populations all sculpture except the primary spiral cords and the last one or two varices is suppressed. The problem has been compounded by the introduction of this species to the northwestern coast of North America, together with Japanese oysters.

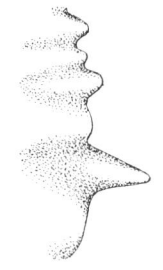

68. *Ceratostoma inornatum*, labial tooth (ceratus)

Eastern and western coasts of temperate Japan and mainland Asia from 33° to 51° north latitude; also the coasts of Oregon, Washington, and British Columbia, particularly in Puget Sound (there introduced).

See Pl. 18, figs. 10–12.

Ceratostoma lugubre (Broderip, 1833)

Murex lugubris Broderip, 1833: 175; *M. monoceros* Orbigny, 1841: 454 (not Sowerby, 1841); *M. fontainei* Tryon, 1880: 126, new name for *M. monoceros* Orbigny, 1841 (not Sowerby, 1841)

The shell is small (maximum length 35 mm) and stoutly fusiform. The spire is moderately high, consisting of four or five angulate postnuclear whorls and a protoconch of undetermined nature. The suture is indistinct. The body whorl is moderately large and broad. The aperture is ovate to lenticular, with a broad, shallow anal sulcus. The outer apertural lip is barely erect and marginally crenulate, reflecting the sculptural pattern on the outer shell surface. At the base of the body is a moderately long, slender labial ceratus, grooved on its dorsal surface; just below the shoulder region, and for a short distance anteriorly, the inner surface of the outer lip bears five or six denticles. The columellar lip is adherent above, detached and weakly erect below. The siphonal canal is short, weakly recurved, and closed.

The body whorl bears six or seven strong, recurved, scabrously lamellate varices extending over the shoulder and attached, buttresslike, to the preceding whorl. Immediately below the persistent labial tooth there is a notchlike separation in the varix, the portion of the varix below this slightly offset dorsally (i.e. away from the direction of growth). Spiral sculpture consists of four primary cords on the body, alternating with secondaries and with a tertiary cord between a secondary and each primary. Secondary and tertiary cords are also found on the canal. Where the primary cords cross the varices, short, open, recurved, spinelike points are developed, all of these connected by a thick, ventrally fimbriate varical flange.

Shell color is light brown. The aperture is white, tinged with deeper gray-blue within.

Puerto Potrero, Costa Rica (type locality of *M. lugubris*), southern Ecuador to Peru.

See Pl. 23, figs. 8–9.

Ceratostoma nuttalli (Conrad, 1837)

Murex nuttalli Conrad, 1837: 264; *M. monoceros* Sowerby, 1841: pl. 188, figs. 64, 65

The shell is moderate in size (maximum length 70 mm) and fusiform. The spire is high and acute, consisting of one and one-half nuclear whorls and six or seven shouldered postnuclear whorls. The suture is weakly impressed. The body whorl is large and fusoid. The aperture is moderately large and ovate, with a moderately deep, sharply cut anal sulcus angling toward the parietal region of the shell and delimited there by a weak transverse ridge. The outer apertural lip is weakly erect above, more so below, and coarsely crenulate along its full extent; the second or third tooth above the canal is developed into a prominent labial ceratus, and the inner surface of the outer lip bears a series of denticles recessed about 3 or 4 mm from the lip margin and reflecting the spaces between the spiral cords. The columellar lip is smooth, and the columella twists through about 70 degrees where it passes into the siphonal canal. The siphonal canal is moderate in length, dorsally recurved, and sealed along all but its recurved distal portion.

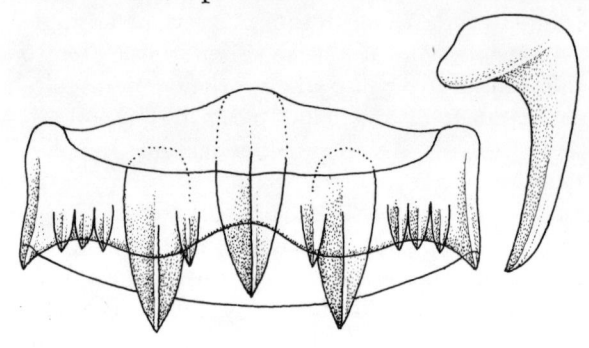

69. *Ceratostoma nuttalli*, radular dentition

The body whorl bears three winglike varices. Intervarical axial sculpture consists of a single ridge that is sharply prominent at the shoulder and generally nearest the older of two consecutive varices. In addition, swellings of the spiral elements, just behind each varical margin, are axially aligned to form another axial ridge. Spiral sculpture consists of five to seven cords, all originating on the body portion of the shell. A single weak cord on the shoulder is followed by another much more prominent one at the shoulder margin. The remaining cords diminish in strength anteriorly. The leading edges of the varices are markedly fimbriate or laminate.

Shell color varies from white, to tan, to rich chestnut-brown or brown with transverse white bands. The leading edges of the varices in the typical form are generally white or cream-colored. The aperture is white.

A form from Baja California (*M. monoceros* Sowerby) differs from the typical form in lacking the winglike extensions of the varices and in developing numerous finely squamose spiral threads between the cords.

Pt. Conception, California, to Santa María Bay, Baja California.

See Pl. 18, figs. 14–15.

Ceratostoma rorifluum (Adams & Reeve, 1849)

Murex rorifluus Adams & Reeve *in* Reeve, 1849: sp. 190; *M. monachus* Crosse, 1862: 55

The shell is small (maximum length 40 mm) and heavily fusiform. The spire is high and acute, consisting of four or five convex to weakly shouldered postnuclear whorls and a protoconch of undetermined nature. The suture is completely obscured by succeeding whorls. The aperture is moderately large and ovate, with an almost imperceptible anal sulcus, this angled toward the columella. The outer apertural lip is barely erect and finely, marginally serrate; the third point up from the base of the body may be developed into a small ceratus. The columellar lip is smooth, adherent for the upper three-fourths of its extent, and detached and weakly erect for the lower one-fourth. The siphonal canal is moderately short, fused for most of its length, and open and dorsally recurved at its distal end.

The body whorl bears four low, rounded varices. Intervarical axial sculpture consists of a single low, knoblike ridge midway in each intervarical space. Spiral sculpture consists of primary, secondary, and tertiary cords: above the shoulder margin a single secondary cord is generally evident; a series of three primary cords follows, the uppermost one at the shoulder margin; below this are three more primaries, each alternating with a tertiary. Canal sculpture is essentially lacking.

Shell color is moderately dark chestnut-brown. Most shells have a worn appearance, owing to the partial erosion of a thick, white, chalky intritacalx that exposes patches of the underlying color.

Japan Sea, on the coasts of China and Korea (33° to 39° north latitude) and western Japan.

See Pl. 18, fig. 13.

Genus EUPLEURA H. & A. Adams, 1853

TYPE SPECIES: *Ranella caudata* Say, 1822, by subsequent designation, F. C. Baker, 1895.

Shells in this genus are moderately small (up to 55 mm) and broadly fusiform. The early whorls bear multiple varices. The body whorl is dorsoventrally flattened and bears two expanded, more or less spinose varices on opposite sides of the shell's ventral surface. The intervarical nodes on the body whorl represent vestiges of multiple varices present on the first few whorls. The slender, moderately long, open siphonal canal and the pointed ends of the two varices impart to the shell a trigonal form. The tip of the canal is stained purple-brown.

Eupleura caudata (Say, 1822)

Ranella caudata Say, 1822: 236; *Eupleura caudata* var. *etterae* B. B. Baker, 1951: 76

The shell is moderately small to moderately large (maximum length 36 mm) and fusiform. The spire is high, consisting of one and one-half nuclear whorls and four or five shouldered postnuclear whorls. The body whorl is moderate in size and fusoid. The aperture is of moderate size and ovate, with a narrow, shallow anal sulcus. The outer apertural lip is thickened, nonerect, and marginally crenulate; its inner surface bears six moderately strong denticles, these extending into the aperture as weak lirae. The columellar lip is smooth and entirely adherent, with a slight swelling at its anterior end. The siphonal canal is of moderate length, straight, and narrowly open.

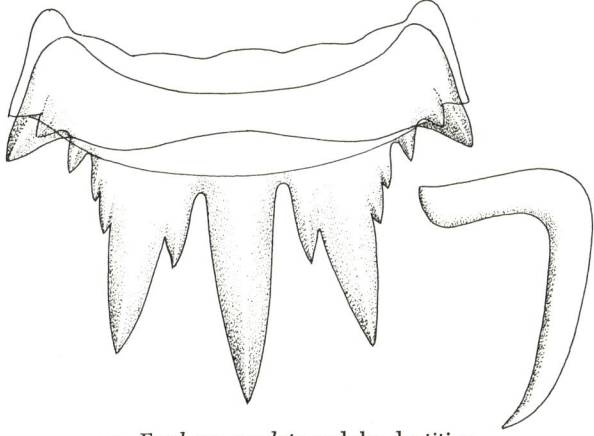

70. *Eupleura caudata*, radular dentition

The body whorl bears two or three varices, one at the growing edge, the other one or two on the far side of the moderately flattened ventral surface of the shell. Intervarical axial sculpture consists of three or four nodes at the shoulder margin. Spiral sculpture consists of 11 major cords, one on the shoulder, six on the body, and four weaker ones on the canal. The cord at the shoulder margin ends on the varix in a trigonal point. The remaining cords end on the tightly fimbriate varix as thickened horizontal ridges.

Shell color is gray-brown, with a thin, white intritacalx. The aperture is a pale, creamy flesh color. The tip of the canal is stained red-brown.

Another name, applied variously as a distinct species and as a subspecies of *E. caudata*, is *E. etterae* B. B. Baker, 1951, a form differing from the typical form only in its larger size, and thus constituting the higher end of the maximum length reference above.

Cape Cod, Massachusetts, to southeastern Florida.

See Pl. 19, figs. 3–4.

Eupleura muriciformis (Broderip, 1833)

Ranella muriciformis Broderip, 1833: 179

The shell is of moderate size (maximum length 35 mm) and broadly fusiform. The spire is high, consisting of one and one-half nuclear whorls and six or rarely seven weakly shouldered postnuclear whorls. The suture is shallow and undulate. The body whorl is large and broadly fusoid. The aperture is moderately small and ovate to lenticular, with a narrow, moderately shallow anal sulcus, delimited to the left by a weak transverse ridge. The outer apertural lip is thickened, barely erect, and broadly crenulate, its inner surface bearing five weak, elongate denticles. The columellar lip is smooth, moderately thickly callused, and completely adherent, with a faint, oblique indentation just above the top of the canal. The siphonal canal is moderately long, straight, narrowly open, and weakly, dorsally recurved.

The body whorl bears two expanded, more or less spinose varices, these situated opposite each other on the ventral surface of the shell. Additional axial sculpture consists of two or three knobs at the shoulder margin. Spiral sculpture consists of ten or 11 moderately strong cords, these evenly distributed over the shell from the shoulder margin to the midpoint of the siphonal canal, the top three or four cords ephemeral between varices, the uppermost five or six spiral cords developed on the varices into short, sharp, dorsally recurved spines. A webbing, thick at its base and thin at the varical margin, connects the spines and produces a winglike varix. The leading edge of the varix is tightly laminate, with narrow grooves extending from the varix to the ventral surfaces of the spines.

Shell color is gray-brown, with pale tan varices, gray-brown spiral cords, a white apertural margin, and a darker purple-brown stain at the tip of the siphonal canal.

This species has been confused with *Eupleura triquetra* Reeve, 1845, many workers considering the two synonymous. Others have applied names to forms without reference to the original figures (the types have not been located in recent years), resulting in mistaken identity. The adult *E. muriciformis* has a broadly trigonal, flattened shell with expanded varices, and the shell color is predominantly brown, whereas *E. triquetra* has a more narrowly trigonal, unflattened shell with essentially unexpanded varices, and the shell color is predominantly blue-gray. Significant radular differences corroborate these shell distinctions.

Southern Baja California (Isla Cedros to Cabo San Lucas) and the Gulf of California to Ecuador.

See Pl. 19, fig. 5.

Eupleura nitida (Broderip, 1833)

Ranella nitida Broderip, 1833: 179

The shell is moderately small for the genus (maximum length 25 mm) and broadly fusiform. The spire is high, consisting of five weakly angulate postnuclear whorls and a protoconch of undetermined nature. The suture is completely obscured. The body whorl is large, dorsoventrally flattened, and broadly fusoid. The aperture is small and ovate, with a narrow, shallow anal sulcus. The outer apertural lip is thickened, non-erect, and weakly crenulate at its margin, its inner surface bearing five strong denticles. The columellar lip is entirely adherent and smooth, except for a low node at its anterior end. The siphonal canal is moderate in length, open, slightly bent to the left, and weakly, dorsally recurved.

The body whorl bears two expanded, opposite varices, these extending from the suture to the midpoint of the canal. Intervarical axial sculpture consists of five moderately strong costae, extending over the entire whorl. Spiral sculpture consists of seven major cords, five on the body, starting at the shoulder margin, and two weaker cords on the canal. Where the cords intersect the intervarical costae, prominent nodules are formed. The cords end at the varical margin as short, sharp, triangular points, those on the canal weaker than those on the body. Numerous fine spiral threads cover the shell surface; where these intersect very numerous fine lamellae, prominent scale-like expansions of the lamellae are formed.

Shell color is dark purple-gray, with white on the varices and the aperture and purple-brown on the crests of the spiral cords. The multitude of almost microscopic lamellae cause the shell to look worn, even in the freshest condition, by muting the color.

Mazatlán, Mexico, to Panamá.

See Pl. 19, fig. 6.

Eupleura pectinata (Hinds, 1844)

Ranella pectinata Hinds, 1844: 13

The shell is moderate in size (maximum length 37 mm) and roughly club-shaped. The spire is high, consisting of five weakly shouldered postnuclear whorls and a protoconch of undetermined nature. The aperture is small and lenticular, with a narrow, deep anal sulcus that is delimited on the left by a weak transverse ridge. The outer apertural lip is barely erect; its inner surface bears six weak pustules, two singles followed by two pairs, all in the body region. The columellar lip is entirely adherent. The siphonal canal is moderately long, open, and straight.

The body whorl bears two weakly expanded, oppositely situated, briefly spinose varices. Intervarical axial sculpture consists of three or four more or less prominent knobs at the shoulder margin. Spiral sculpture consists of five major cords on the body, alternating with minor threads. Five threads are evident on the upper portion of the canal. The major cords end on the varices, where they are developed into short, straight or ventrally hooked spines. Parts of the earlier varices, showing the upper three spines, persist on the spire.

Shell color is mauve to pale purple-brown, with darker-brown intervarical nodes. The spiral cords are the same pale mauve as the ground color and stand out in sharp contrast where they cross the darker-brown intervarical nodes. The thickly callused apertural margin is porcelaneous white.

Southern Mexico to southern Central America. See Pl. 19, fig. 7.

Eupleura sulcidentata Dall, 1890

Eupleura caudata var. *sulcidentata* Dall, 1890: 144

The shell is small (maximum length 20 mm), flattened, and fusiform. The spire is high, consisting of one and one-half nuclear whorls and five shouldered postnuclear whorls. The suture is completely obscured. The body whorl is of moderate size and fusoid. The aperture is moderately small and ovate, with a narrow, moderately deep anal sulcus that is lightly callused. The outer apertural lip is thickened, nonerect, and weakly, marginally crenulate; its inner surface bears five moderately strong denticles. The columellar lip is entirely adherent and smooth, except for a low swelling at the anterior end of the columella. The siphonal canal is moderately long, narrowly open, straight, and dorsally recurved at its distal end.

The body whorl bears two weakly expanded, opposite varices. Intervarical axial sculpture consists of two or three more or less weak nodes at and just below the shoulder margin. Spiral sculpture consists of six cords, obsolete intervarically and becoming slightly more prominent on the two sides of the varix. These cords are developed at the varical margin into tiny, dorsally recurved points.

Shell color is fleshy purple-brown overlaid with a thin, white intritacalx. The varices are flesh-colored to ivory or white. The interior of the aperture is ivory-colored and stained red-brown between the denticles and beneath the spiral cords.

Gulf of Mexico, western and northwestern coasts of Florida.

See Pl. 19, fig. 2.

Eupleura triquetra (Reeve, 1844)

Ranella triquetra Reeve, 1844: sp. 41; *R. plicata* Reeve, 1844: sp. 33

The shell is large (maximum length 55 mm) and fusiform. The spire is high, consisting of one and one-half nuclear whorls and six shouldered postnuclear whorls. The suture is undulate and weakly impressed. The body whorl is large, trigonal, and fusoid. The aperture is moderately large and ovate to subtrigonal, with a flattened anterior margin; the anal sulcus is narrow, very shallow, and angled toward the left, its parietal margin formed by a very weak transverse ridge running into the aperture. The outer apertural lip is barely erect and marginally crenulate, thickening abruptly behind the margin; its inner surface bears six evenly spaced denticles, the uppermost one situated interior to the shoulder margin. The columellar lip is lightly callused and entirely adherent, with a barely discernible indentation and a weak swelling at its anterior end. The siphonal canal is of moderate length, broad, open, and weakly, dorsally recurved.

The body whorl bears two moderately developed lateral varices; between the varices, at the shoulder margin, are three low bumps. Spiral sculpture consists of nine subobsolete cords, one on the shoulder slope, four generally obsolete on the canal, and four on the body. Except for the shoulder cord, which gives rise to a strong, short, dorsally hooked point at each varix, all cords produce minute points on the margin of the heavily thickened varix. The leading edge of the varix shows these cords most strongly.

Shell color is predominantly blue-gray, with cream-colored portions on the varices and below the suture. The intervarical knobs may be pale gray-brown. The apertural margin is porcelaneous white; the interior and the tip of the canal are suffused with purple-brown.

Cabo San Lucas, Baja California, to Panamá. See Pl. 19, fig. 1.

Genus HADRIANIA
Bucquoy & Dautzenberg, 1882

TYPE SPECIES: *Murex craticulatus* Brocchi, 1814 (not Linné, 1758) (=*Tritonalia* (*Hadriania*) *craticuloides* E. H. Vokes, 1964), by original designation.

The following, translated from Bucquoy et al., 1882, is taken verbatim from Vokes, (1964):

"Shell fusiform, with pointed conical spire. Whorls angular in the upper portion, ornamented by rather numerous, rounded, varicose longitudinal ribs, and rugose decurrent striae. Last whorl very convex. Aperture oval, terminated at the base by a rather long, stout canal slightly twisted and closed anteriorly. Labium subsalient, angular at the apex. Color grayish or fawn, aperture whitish."

Hadriania craticuloides (E. H. Vokes, 1964)

Murex craticulatus Brocchi, 1814: 406 (not *M. craticulatus* Linné, 1758); *M. brocchii* Monterosato, 1875: 39 (not Cantraine, 1835), new name for *M. craticulatus* Brocchi, 1814: 406 (not Linné, 1758); *Tritonalia (Hadriania) craticuloides* E. H. Vokes, 1964: 20, new name for *M. craticulatus* Brocchi, 1814 (not Linné, 1758)

The shell is of moderate size for the subfamily (maximum length 36 mm) and strongly fusiform. The spire is high and acute, consisting of one and one-half moderately bulbous nuclear whorls and seven strongly angulate postnuclear whorls. The suture is deeply impressed. The body whorl is of moderate size and fusoid. The aperture is moderately long, broadly open, and subovate, with a very narrow, shallow anal sulcus. The outer apertural lip is slightly erect and marginally serrate; its inner surface is weakly lirate. The columellar lip is arcuate, smooth, and entirely adherent. The siphonal canal is moderately long, narrow, bent to the left, and dorsally recurved, and is almost entirely fused, the two margins meeting simply and fusing.

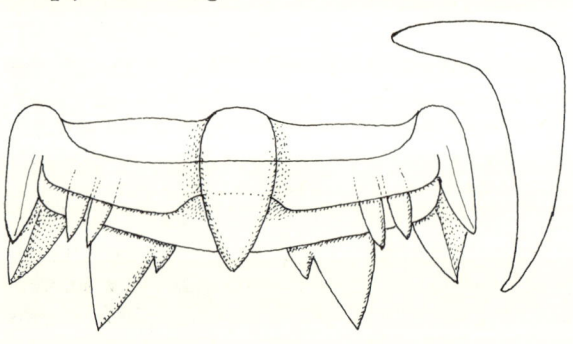

71. *Hadriania craticuloides*, radular dentition

The body whorl bears nine low to moderately prominent axial ribs. Spiral sculpture consists of a series of primary and secondary cords, two on the shoulder, the stronger one at the shoulder margin, a major space with a secondary cord, five primaries on the body, these alternating with secondaries, and nine or more secondaries on the canal. Five axial lamellae impart a densely scabrous texture to the cords.

Shell color is off-white to fleshy yellow-pink; the tips of all canals, the current one as well as the former ones retained on the left side of the siphonal canal, are suffused with purple-brown.

Throughout the Mediterranean, especially in the western half.
See Pl. 29, fig. 4.

Genus JATON Pusch, 1837

TYPE SPECIES: *Murex decussatus* "Linné" (=*M. decussatus* Gmelin, 1791), by original designation.

The following is translated, essentially without change, from Pusch (1837):

"Shell oblong, subturreted, with five distinct whorls, deeply canaliculate above, with three or four transverse plications, the plicae (or costae) wide, smooth, rounded, separated by deep, slightly striated grooves; aperture oval, the labrum with three or four plications, the canal short, scarcely recurved."

This genus, as represented by its type species, has been associated at times with *Shaskyus* Burch & Campbell, 1963 (type species: *Murex festivus* Hinds, 1844), because of superficial resemblance of shell form and sculpture. We consider the shell of "*M.*" *festivus* to represent an extreme expression of the basic *Pteropurpura* pattern. "*M.*" *decussatus* may be distinguished, at a generic level, by the fact that young specimens are miniature replicas of the adults, whereas young "*M.*" *festivus* show the typically entire outer apertural lip of a *Pteropurpura*; many specimens of "*M.*" *decussatus* have a more or less well-developed ceratus on the outer apertural lip. As Vokes (1964) has noted, "*Jaton* is the Recent member of an evolutionary sequence which goes back to the upper Miocene subgenus *Pterorytis*" (with a prominent ceratus). "*M.*" *festivus* has no indication of such a structure.

Jaton decussatus (Gmelin, 1791)

Murex decussatus Gmelin, 1791: 3527; *M. hemitripterus* Lamarck, 1816: pl. 418, fig. 4, Liste p. 5; *M. jatonus* Lamarck, 1816: pl. 418, fig. 1, Liste p. 5; *M. lingua* Dillwyn, 1817: 688; *M. gibbosus* Lamarck, 1822: 166 (not Born, 1778); *M. linguavervecina* Reeve, 1845: sp. 121

The shell is of moderate size (maximum length 45 mm) and fusiform. The spire is low to moderately high, consisting of four or five postnuclear whorls and a protoconch of undetermined nature. The suture is entirely obscured and is situated in a deep furrow. The body whorl is large and fusoid. The aperture is small and ovate, with an almost imperceptible anal sulcus. The outer apertural lip is erect and marginally serrate, in some instances with a moderately long ceratus anteriorly. The columellar lip is entirely adherent, except at its anterior end, where it is briefly detached. The siphonal canal is moderate in length, fused, and more or less bent to the right.

The body whorl bears three bladelike varices, each much broader at its base than at its free margin, and thickest posteriorly, where it is appressed to the preceding whorl almost at its shoulder margin; anteriorly the varices extend to the midpoint of the siphonal canal. Intervarical axial sculpture consists of a single, massive knob, filling almost the entire intervarical space. Spiral sculpture consists of seven weak major cords and numerous fine intercalary threads. The leading edge of each varix is richly fimbriate.

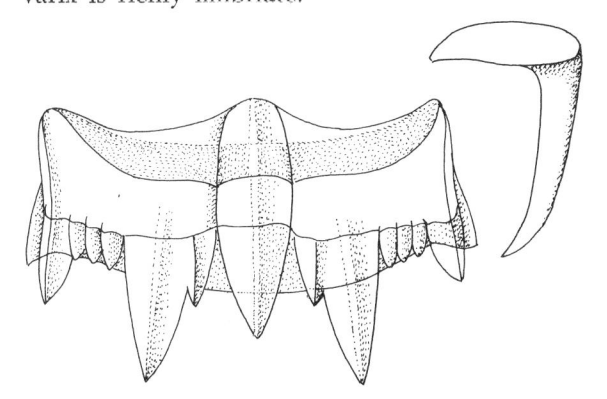

72. *Jaton decussatus*, radular dentition

Shell color is white or off-white, with chestnut-brown markings. The aperture is porcelaneous white to pale yellow.

Western Africa from Mauritania to Angola.

See Pl. 22, fig. 12.

Genus OCENEBRA Gray, 1847

TYPE SPECIES: *Murex erinaceus* Linné, 1758, by monotypy.

The shell in this genus may be characterized by its oblong or fusiform shape, its convex to strongly shouldered whorls, a generally closed canal, and its strongly scabrous shell surface. Details of shell morphology are extremely variable. Size range in the genus varies from moderate (70 mm long) to very small (10 mm long) and may even vary within a species. Although *Ocenebra* species are found in the eastern Atlantic and are prominent faunal elements in the eastern Pacific, no such species are known from the western Atlantic.

Ocenebra circumtexta (Stearns, 1871)

Ocinebra circumtexta Stearns, 1871: 172

The shell is of moderate size for the genus (maximum length 30 mm) and ovoid to stoutly fusiform. The spire is low to moderate in height, consisting of one and one-fourth convex to very weakly angulate nuclear whorls and four or five moderately convex postnuclear whorls. The suture is distinct. The body whorl is large and ovate, with a weak anal sulcus. The outer apertural lip is weakly erect in the central portion of older shells; its inner surface bears six strong, evenly spaced denticles. The columellar lip is entirely adherent. The siphonal canal is short and broad, its closure evident only in completely mature specimens.

The body whorl bears eight to ten low varices. Axial sculpture otherwise consists of lamellar growth striae, these present between and on the varices and most prominent on the spiral cords. Spiral sculpture consists of 12 or 13 equal-sized, closely spaced major cords, spread evenly over the body. A single subsutural secondary cord is generally present.

Shell color is generally white, with two broad, interrupted, brown transverse bands on the body. In certain populations the entire shell is brown. The aperture is white at its margin, grading into a darker rich creamy yellow or brown or purple-brown to a dark purple.

Monterey, California, to Scammon's Lagoon, Baja California.

See Pl. 20, fig. 3.

Ocenebra erinaceus (Linné, 1758)

Murex erinaceus Linné, 1758: 748; *M. torosus* Lamarck, 1816: pl. 441, fig. 5, Liste p. 9; *M. tarentinus* Lamarck, 1822: 173

The shell is of moderate size (maximum length 50 mm) and stoutly fusiform. The spire is high, consisting of seven or eight strongly shouldered or tabulate postnuclear whorls and a protoconch of undetermined nature. The suture is distinct. The body whorl is moderately large and fusoid. The aperture is ovate, with a very weak to indis-

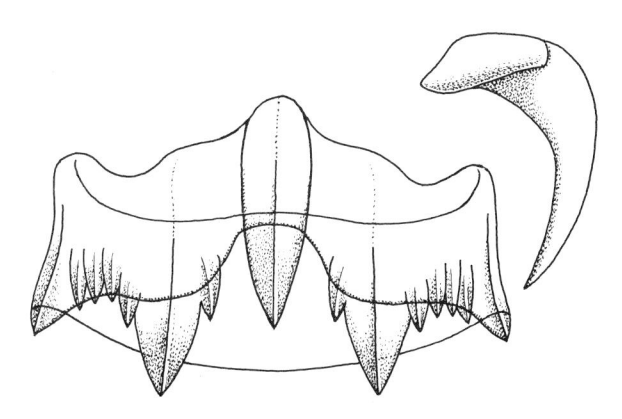

73. *Ocenebra erinaceus*, radular dentition

tinct anal sulcus. The outer apertural lip is erect and marginally crenulate; its inner surface bears six or seven weak to moderately strong denticles. The columellar lip is adherent above, detached and erect below. The siphonal canal is moderately short, broad, closed, and dorsally recurved.

The body whorl bears three to nine varices. In some specimens every second varix is reduced to a secondary axial ridge. The entire shell surface is scabrously laminate, with vaulted scales of varying size over the spiral elements. Spiral sculpture consists of six to eight strongly raised primary cords, these generally alternating with secondary and tertiary cords. Where the spiral elements intersect the axial sculpture, they are elevated into short, open, scalelike spines.

Shell color is pale yellow-ochre tinged with brown. The aperture is white.

As in the genus as a whole, this species shows a great deal of variability in its shell morphology. The numerous variants that have been named can, however, be shown to intergrade.

Western Mediterranean basin to the British Isles.

See Pl. 18, figs. 4–5.

Ocenebra erinaceoides (Valenciennes, 1832)

Murex erinaceoides Valenciennes, 1832: 302;
M. californicus Hinds, 1844: 128

The shell is of moderate size (maximum length 60 mm) and strongly angulate-fusiform. The spire is high, consisting of two and one-half nuclear whorls and six or seven shouldered postnuclear whorls. The suture is distinct. The body whorl is moderately large and fusoid. The aperture is ovate, with a weak anal sulcus. The outer apertural lip is weakly, if at all, erect, and finely, marginally crenulate. The columellar lip is adherent above, detached and moderately erect below. The siphonal canal is moderate in length, closed, broad above, tapering below, and dorsally recurved at its tip.

The body whorl bears three erect, fimbriate, frequently backswept varices. Intervarical axial sculpture consists of a single centrally placed ridge. The entire shell is covered with scabrous lamellae, these rising as vaulted scales on the cords. On the leading edge of the varix, between the cords and their associated backswept spiny processes, the scabrous sculpture is strongly marked. Spiral sculpture on the body and upper canal consists of seven or eight primary cords; about eight incised lines cover each cord. Numerous scabrous threads are found on the shoulder.

The primary cords terminate on the varices as short, open, dorsally recurved spines, the one at the shoulder margin the largest.

Shell color is more or less uniform yellow or brown-ochre. The aperture is white.

Gulf of California and the outer coast of Baja California as far north as Bahía Magdalena, Mexico.

See Pl. 18, fig. 3.

Ocenebra foveolata (Hinds, 1844)

Murex foveolatus Hinds, 1844: 127; *M. barbarensis* Gabb, 1865: 183; *Trophon squamulifer* Carpenter, *in* Gabb, 1869: 44; *Tritonalia beta* Dall, 1919: 250; *Tritonalia epiphanea* Dall, 1919: 335; *Tritonalia fusconotata* Dall, 1919: 333; *Ocenebra keenae* Bormann, 1946: 40; *O. crispatissima* Berry, 1953: 414

The exceedingly variable shell is moderately large (maximum length 40 mm) and stoutly to narrowly fusiform. The spire is high, consisting of one and one-fourth subtabulate nuclear whorls and five and one-half convex to subangulate postnuclear whorls. The suture is distinct. The body whorl is moderate in size and fusoid. The aperture is of moderate size and ovate, with a weak anal sulcus, this delimited on each side by a tubercle. The outer apertural lip is briefly erect, abruptly thickening shortly before its thin, erect margin; the lip margin is undulate, reflecting the spiral sculpture of the shell surface, and the inner surface of the outer lip bears eight strong denticles. The columellar lip is adherent above, detached and erect below. The siphonal canal is broad, closed, and distally recurved.

The body whorl bears five or six varices, these more or less prominent, with a more or less well-defined leading edge. The entire shell surface is scabrously lamellose. Spiral sculpture consists of 15 to 20 major cords of roughly equal size below the shoulder margin and four or five on the shoulder. In many specimens the scales are produced into short spines, generally most prominent on the early whorls and often reduced or lacking on the body whorl.

Shell color ranges from all dirty white to all brown or light brown, with bands of yellow-ochre, darker brown, and white. These color forms seem to be randomly distributed in any sizable population.

Several distinctive morphological variants seem to appear in spatially distinct populations. These forms differ from the typical form, itself quite variable, in the height of the spire relative to total shell length, degree of angulation or tabulation of whorls, degree of development of the scabrous surface texture and spination, relative size and shape of the aperture, strength of the apertural dentition, and overall size.

The degree of variability of the shell in this complex has encouraged the introduction of several names for the more distinctive forms. It must be emphasized that the above synonymy is a product of lengthy examination of a reasonably large series of specimens. One or more of these forms may be a distinct and valid taxon, though we are inclined to doubt it. In any case, a serious conclusion concerning this complex should not be reached without the aid of considerable material from varied habitats and localities.

Monterey Bay, California, to Bahía Magdalena, Baja California.

See Pl. 20, figs. 9, 14–17.

Ocenebra gracillima (Stearns, 1871)

Ocinebra gracillima Stearns, 1871: 172

The shell is small (maximum length 17 mm), strong, and stoutly fusiform. The spire is high and acute, consisting of one and one-half tabulate nuclear whorls and six weakly convex postnuclear whorls. The suture is distinct. The body whorl is broadly fusoid. The aperture is moderately small and ovate, with a weak anal sulcus. The outer apertural lip is erect, the shell portion just previous being abruptly thicker; the inner surface of the outer lip bears four strong denticles. The columellar lip is entirely adherent. The siphonal canal is short, broad, closed, and weakly, distally recurved.

Although 14 varices are evident on the earlier whorls, the body whorl in mature specimens lacks varices or other axial sculpture. Scabrous lamellae, prominent on the earlier whorls, persist on the body whorl in the spaces between spiral cords; where these lamellae are sufficiently separated, the spaces between them may take the form of deep, square pits. Spiral sculpture consists of 17 or 18 low, flat-topped cords of primary and secondary prominence.

Shell ground color is rust-brown. The spiral cords bear alternating spots of blue-gray and red-brown. Two paler transverse bands, one at what would be the shoulder margin and one at the base of the body, are produced where the cords bear fewer, more distantly placed brown blotches, resulting in a preponderance of blue-gray. The canal is pale yellow-white.

Monterey, California, to Bahía Todos Santos, Baja California.

See Pl. 20, fig. 10.

Ocenebra grippi (Dall, 1911)

Eupleura grippi Dall, 1911: 87

The shell is moderately small (maximum length 25 mm) and broadly fusiform. The spire is high, consisting of one and one-fourth convex nuclear whorls and four convex to weakly angulate postnuclear whorls. The suture is distinct. The body whorl is moderately large and fusoid. The aperture is large and ovate, with a very weak anal sulcus. The outer apertural lip is thin at its margin, thick immediately behind; its inner surface bears six to ten weak to moderately strong denticles. The columellar lip is entirely adherent or, in some individuals, detached and weakly erect below. The siphonal canal is moderately short and closed in most fully mature specimens.

The body whorl bears five or six nodose axial ridges, these most prominent at the shoulder margin, where protruding knobs may be developed. Spiral sculpture consists of 15 to 30 close-set, scabrous cords, all of about the same size, and separated from each other by sharply cut grooves.

Shell color varies from dark purple-brown to golden yellow. In some brown-colored individuals, three to eight of the spiral cords, just below the shoulder margin, are lighter in color, with evenly spaced, red-brown spots. The aperture is violet-brown within, white at the margin. The columella is generally suffused with violet.

Originally described as *Eupleura grippi*, this species was known for many years from a single specimen, the "unique" holotype. This specimen is a large, gerontic individual with a greatly thickened apertural margin, imparting to it a superficial resemblance to some species of *Eupleura*.

Southern California (Pt. Conception to San Diego).

See Pl. 20, fig. 2.

?Ocenebra hamata (Hinds, 1844)

Murex hamatus Hinds, 1844: 128

The shell is moderately large for the genus (ca. 45.5 mm in length) and trigonofusiform. The spire is high and acute, consisting of about two broad nuclear whorls and five subangulate postnuclear whorls. The suture is barely impressed, if at all. The body whorl is moderately large and trigonal. The aperture is large and subovate, with an obliquely flattened posterior margin. The outer apertural lip is erect, with crenulations extending from the margin into the interior; one of the larger projections of the outer lip, near its anterior end, appears, in younger specimens, to form a substantial ceratus, but in the specimens we examined it was not well developed. The columellar lip is adherent and covered with a thin but extensive callus. The siphonal canal is moderately long, closed (except at its anterior end), and bent to the right and dorsally.

The body whorl bears three to five prominent, spinose varices. Intervarical axial sculpture is lacking. Spiral sculpture consists of cords of three different strengths: on the body there are five primary cords, these ephemeral between varices and prominent just before and on the varices, where they form moderately short, open, dorsally recurved spines; secondary cords alternate with the three anteriormost primary cords, and on the canal are two secondary cords; on the shoulder there are three tertiary cords, a single secondary cord, and three more tertiary threads. Numerous fine, scalelike axial-growth lamellae, apparent on the canal, are represented on the body and spire by remnants, these imparting a superficially malleated surface to the shell. The leading edge of the varical flange is densely fimbriate, the fimbriae arranged in a "draped" fashion.

Shell color is tan to brown, with extensive suffusions of purple-brown on the spire and the body, especially immediately before, on, and after each varix.

Some paleontologists may wish to assign this species to the otherwise extinct genus *Pterorytis* on the basis of its possessing more than three varices. Not only is this an apparently variable character, but this single feature does not seem to us to warrant resurrecting an otherwise extinct genus for a very rare species.

Known to us from the west coast of South America (the studied specimen was collected in Peruvian waters).

See Pl. 14, fig. 2.

Ocenebra inermicosta (E. H. Vokes, 1964)

Murex fasciatus Sowerby, 1841: pl. 192, fig. 86 (not Gmelin, 1791); *Tritonalia inermicosta* E. H. Vokes, 1964: 20, new name for *M. fasciatus* Sowerby, 1841 (not Gmelin, 1791)

The shell is of moderate size for the genus (maximum length 30 mm) and stoutly fusiform. The spire is high, consisting of two and one-half nuclear whorls and five subangulate to convex postnuclear whorls. The suture is obscured by the succeeding whorl. The body whorl is moderate in size and fusoid. The aperture is ovate and moderately large; the outer apertural lip is erect and marginally crenulate; its inner surface is adherent at its upper extremity, detached and erect below. The columellar lip is smooth, gently arcuate, and entirely adherent. The siphonal canal is short, broad, closed, and distally recurved.

The body whorl bears three prominent, rounded varices with more or less well-developed tubercles at their points of junction with the major spiral cords. Intervarical axial sculpture consists of a single prominent costa. Spiral sculpture consists of seven major body cords and, below these, three or four secondary cords. The canal bears a single primary cord and two anterior secondaries. Numerous scabrous threads fill the cord interspaces. The major cord at the shoulder margin is variable in its development of tubercles.

Shell color is brown, with the spiral cords generally white. The edges of the varices may also be white, sometimes with a paler band at the shoulder margin. The aperture is cream-colored to yellow-ochre.

Western Africa, from Senegal to Angola.

See Pl. 20, fig. 1.

Ocenebra interfossa (Carpenter, 1864)

Ocinebra interfossa Carpenter, 1864: 663; *O. interfossa* var. *atropurpurea* Carpenter, 1865: 64; *Tritonalia fraseri* Oldroyd, 1920: 135

The variable shell is moderately small (maximum length 25 mm) and fusiform. The spire is high and acute, consisting of one and one-fourth tabulate nuclear whorls and five more or less angulate postnuclear whorls. The suture is weakly impressed. The body whorl is of moderate size and fusoid. The aperture is ovate and moderately small, with no apparent anal sulcus. The erect margin of the outer apertural lip is thin and finely crenulate, abruptly thicker just behind the margin; the interior of the outer lip bears six weak to moderately strong denticles, these distributed evenly over the entire length of the aperture. The columellar lip is generally entirely adherent. The siphonal canal is broad, moderately short, and closed.

The body whorl bears seven or eight more or less prominent axial costae (whose relationship to varices is impossible for us to interpret). Spiral sculpture consists of major and minor cords: beginning at the shoulder margin there are six major cords on the body and three on the canal; above the shoulder margin and between each two major cords is a minor cord. These cords, in the typical form, are as prominent between the axial costae as they are over them. Numerous fine lamellae cover the remainder of the shell surface.

Shell color is red-brown, with white on the spiral elements.

The above description refers to what has been

called the "typical" form, figured in Dall (1921, Pl. 11, fig. 8). The remarkable variability of the shell of this species has, as in the case of *O. foveolata* (Hinds, 1844), encouraged the introduction of several superfluous names.

In the San Diego, California, area an endemic, dwarf population, called *O. minor* Dall, 1919 (Pl. 20, fig. 11, herein), differs primarily in size (maximum length 10 mm) and in a reduction in the number of spiral elements.

In the San Pedro, California, area a somewhat stouter form differs from the typical form in having an increased number of axial costae (up to 11) and a partial to complete loss of intercalary minor spiral cords. This pattern doubles the size of the spaces formed by the intersection of the axial and spiral sculptural elements and imparts a reticulate or waffled appearance to the shell sculpture. This form, given the name *O. atropurpurea* Carpenter, 1865 (Pl. 20, fig. 12, herein), is also generally dark purple-brown, often with two transverse bands of orange, one medial on the body and one on the canal.

A third variant form is found at the northern end of the range. This form, named *O. interfossa fraseri* (Oldroyd, 1920) (Pl. 20, fig. 6, herein), is larger than the typical form and develops short, sharp spinelike nodes at the intersections of axial and spiral elements. The shell is also paler in color, under a thin intritacalx.

Scammon's Lagoon, Baja California, to Sitka, Alaska.

See Pl. 20, figs. 6, 11–13.

Ocenebra lurida (Middendorff, 1848)

Tritonium (Fusus) luridum Middendorff, 1848: 244; *Vitularia asper* Baird, 1863: 66; *Ocinebra lurida* var. *munda* Carpenter, 1864: 663; *Tritonalia sclera* Dall, 1919: 334

The shell is exceedingly variable in size, ranging from small (10–20 mm) in the southern portion of its range to moderately large (30–40 mm) in the northern portion. The shell is more or less fusiform. The spire is high, consisting of one and one-half nuclear whorls and five or six convex postnuclear whorls. The suture is moderately impressed. The body whorl is of moderate size and fusoid. The aperture is ovate and moderately large, with a barely perceptible anal sulcus. The outer apertural lip is erect and finely, marginally undulate; its inner surface bears six or seven denticles. The columellar lip is adherent above, detached and erect below. The siphonal canal is short, closed, and distally recurved.

The body whorl bears six to ten low, rounded varices. Additional axial sculpture, where present, consists of more or less strong, scabrous lamellae. Spiral sculpture consists of 17 major cords. The spaces between cords are broader than the cords themselves, and in mature specimens intercalary minor cords may occur sporadically in the broadest of these interspaces.

Shell color is white, yellow-ochre, or brown, or occasionally white transversely banded with one or both of these other colors. The entire shell, in fresh specimens, is covered with a thick intritacalx, laid down as numerous growth striae.

The variability of shell form and size seems to follow a latitudinal pattern in *O. lurida*. The southern representatives are generally small, the specimens becoming progressively larger to the north and reaching maximum size in British Columbia and Alaska. The incidence of other parameters of shell variability, such as color pattern and relative stoutness, is not correlated with variation in size. As with *O. interfossa* and *O. foveolata*, the extreme variability of shell form has led to the introduction of several superfluous names.

Sitka, Alaska, to Santo Tomas, Baja California. See Pl. 20, figs. 4–5.

?Ocenebra painei (Dall, 1903)

Murex (Ocinebra?) painei Dall, 1903: 174

The shell is small (maximum length 15 mm) and stoutly fusiform. The spire is moderately high, consisting of one nuclear whorl and four or five convex postnuclear whorls. The suture is unimpressed. The body whorl is of moderate size and broadly fusoid. The aperture is of moderate size, with a shallow, narrow anal sulcus. The outer apertural lip is slightly erect and smooth, both at its margin and within. The columellar lip is entirely adherent, smooth, and weakly callused. The siphonal canal is moderately short, fused, almost straight, and sharply, dorsally recurved.

The body whorl bears 11 or 12 delicate varices, these shaped like erect lamellae; one or two on each whorl may be double. Spiral sculpture consists of six moderately strong major cords on the body, two on the canal, and minor cords between consecutive major cords. At an imaginary shoulder margin on an essentially unshouldered shell the lamelliform varices each make a right angle, imparting the appearance of a shouldered whorl.

Shell color is white to dirty ivory.

The lamellose shell sculpture and short, stout form suggest affinity with the southern trophons (e.g. *T. geversianus* Pallas, 1774); the fused canal implies an ocenebrine relationship; and the radula favors neither of these possibilities. Thus, this species is placed here conditionally.

Dundas Bay, Alaska, to San Diego, California (fide Oldroyd, 1927).

See Pl. 20, fig. 8.

Ocenebra seftoni Chace, 1958

Ocenebra seftoni Chace, 1958: 331

The shell is small (maximum length 12 mm) and fusiform. The spire is high, consisting of one and one-half nearly flat-sided, tabulate nuclear whorls and four or five weakly angulate postnuclear whorls. The body whorl is of moderate size and fusoid. The aperture is small and ovate, with no apparent anal sulcus. The outer apertural lip is erect, abruptly thicker immediately behind; its inner surface bears four weak denticles anteriorly. The columellar lip is adherent above, detached and erect below. The siphonal canal is moderately long, closed, and weakly, distally recurved.

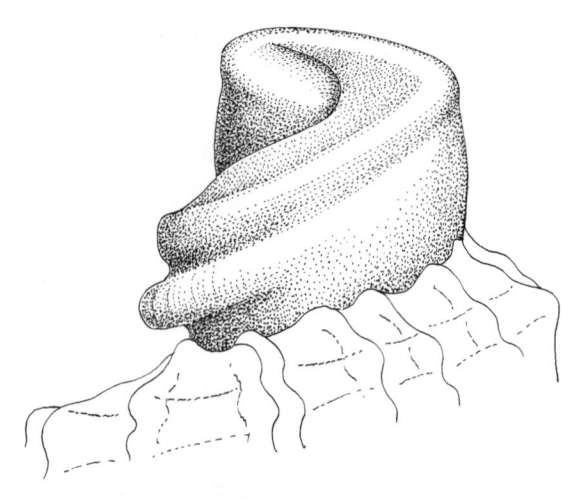

74. *Ocenebra seftoni*, protoconch

The body whorl bears nine moderately prominent varices that are triangulate in cross section. The free edge of each varix forms a thin, erect lamella. The entire surface is finely lamellose, the lamellae raised over the spiral elements to form small to large scalelike extensions. Spiral sculpture on the body consists of three major scabrous cords on the shoulder and five below the shoulder margin; the canal bears three primary cords; intercalary secondary cords alternate with the primary cords on the body below the shoulder.

Shell ground color varies from white to buff or tan. The scalelike expansions of the surface lamellae that occur on the primary cords are generally white, alternating with unraised red-brown marks, these imparting a dappled appearance.

Apparently endemic to Isla Guadalupe, Mexico. See Pl. 20, fig. 7.

Ocenebra vokesae (Emerson, 1964)

Murex (Pteropurpura) petri Dall, 1902: pl. 34, fig. 7 (not Dall, 1900); *M. (Alipurpura) rhyssus* Dall, 1919: 332 (not Tate, 1888); *Pteropurpura (Pteropurpura) vokesae* Emerson, 1964: 5, new name for *M. rhyssus* Dall, 1919 (not Tate, 1888)

The shell is of moderate size (maximum length 70 mm) and angulate-fusiform. The spire is high, consisting of seven or eight weakly shouldered postnuclear whorls and a protoconch of undetermined nature. The suture is distinct. The body whorl is moderately large and fusoid. The aperture is ovate and somewhat smaller than that of the closely related *O. erinaceoides*; a barely perceptible anal sulcus is situated far to the left and angled to the left. The outer apertural lip is barely detached and nonerect above, weakly erect below; its inner surface is nondenticulate; the columellar lip is essentially smooth. The siphonal canal is moderately long, closed, moderately broad, and almost straight.

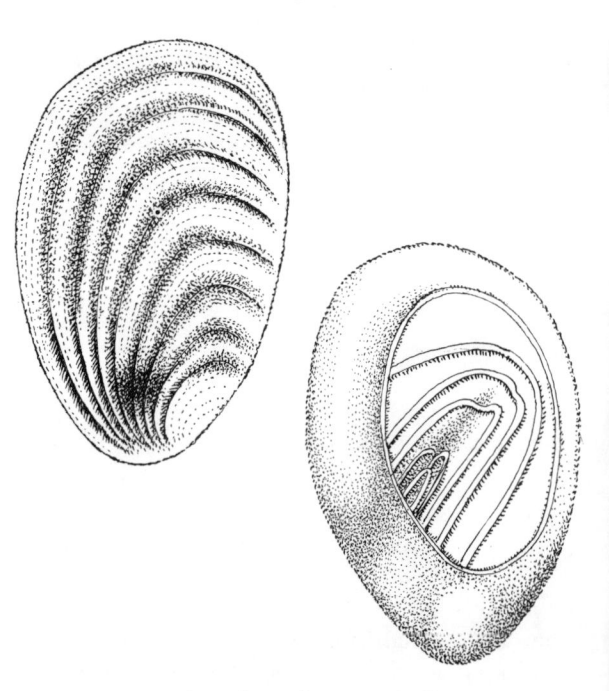

75. *Ocenebra vokesae*, operculum

The body whorl bears three erect, fimbriate, winglike varices, these backswept at their margins. Intervarical axial sculpture consists of a single roughly central ridge. The entire shell is covered with strongly scabrous lamellae, these arising as vaulted scales over the spiral cords. Spiral sculpture consists of ten primary cords on the body and canal, five or six secondary cords distributed between each two primaries, and nine secondary cords on the shoulder. The primary cords terminate as short, open, dorsally recurved spines at the margin of each varix, the largest at the shoulder margin.

Shell color is more or less uniform yellow or brown-ochre. The aperture is porcelaneous white.

This species and the very closely related *O. erinaceoides* differ in few substantive morphological features. *O. erinaceoides* occurs intertidally in the relatively warm waters of the Gulf of California, whereas the present species is found subtidally (to 33 m) in the cooler waters off the southern California and Baja California coasts. The exact distribution of these two species on the central Baja California coast is not clear; when known, it may allow a clearer understanding of their interrelationship.

Santa Rosa Island, California, to Bahía San Bartolomé, Baja California.

See Pl. 18, fig. 9.

Genus OCINEBRINA Jousseaume, 1880

TYPE SPECIES: *Murex corallinus* Scacchi, 1836 (=*M. aciculatus* Lamarck, 1822), by original designation.

The shell in this genus is generally small (5–20 mm in length) and stoutly fusiform, with a convex protoconch and a small number (four to six) of unshouldered whorls. The outer apertural lip is denticulate on its inner surface; the columellar lip may be detached and erect. Numerous rounded varices are crossed by weaker spiral elements. The siphonal canal is almost always fused. Shell microsculpture is invariably finely scabrous.

Although closely approaching *Ocenebra* (especially its eastern Pacific representatives) in shell form, the genus is set apart by its distinctive radula and protoconch.

Ocinebrina aciculata (Lamarck, 1822)

Murex aciculatus Lamarck, 1822: 176; *Fusus corallinus* Scacchi, 1836: 11; *M. badius* Reeve, 1845: sp. 159

The shell is moderately small (maximum length 16 mm) and stoutly fusiform. The spire is high, consisting of one and one-half convex nuclear whorls and five or six convex postnuclear whorls. The suture is distinct and weakly impressed. The body whorl is of moderate size and fusoid. The aperture is small and ovate to lenticular, with a shallow, moderately broad anal sulcus. The outer apertural lip is thickened, essentially nonerect, and minutely serrate; its inner surface bears six moderately strong denticles. The columellar lip is adherent posteriorly, more or less detached and weakly erect anteriorly. The siphonal canal is moderately short and fused.

The body whorl bears eight prominent axial ridges that may qualify as varices, depending on the definition used. Spiral sculpture consists of 18 prominent spiral cords, three on the shoulder, 12 on the body, and three on the canal, these cords as prominent between the axial ridges as on them. Numerous fine axial lamellae are thrown into scalelike expansions on the spiral cords.

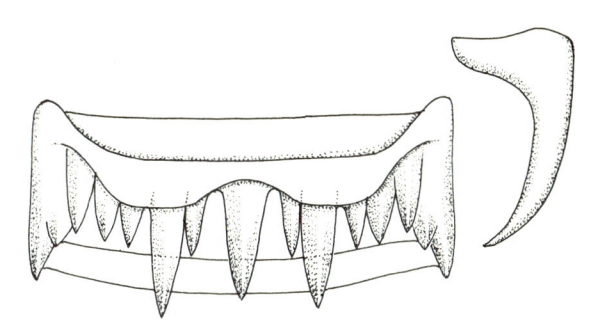

76. Ocinebrina aciculata, radular dentition

Shell color is uniform orange-brown through red-brown to purple-brown. The aperture is porcelaneous white.

Lusitanian Province, from the central Mediterranean (Adriatic Sea) to the British Isles and Madeira.

See Pl. 21, fig. 8.

Ocinebrina edwardsi (Payraudeau, 1826)

Purpura edwardsi Payraudeau, 1826: 155; *Murex inglorius* Crosse, 1865: 213; *M. semiclausus* Küster, 1870: 111; *M. requieni* Locard, 1899: 72

The shell is moderately small (maximum length 22 mm) and broadly fusiform. The spire is high, consisting of barely one convex nuclear whorl and five or six convex to barely shouldered postnuclear whorls. The suture is impressed. The body whorl is of moderate size and fusoid. The aperture is moderately large and ovate, with a barely-perceptible anal sulcus. The outer apertural lip is essentially nonerect; its inner surface bears five or six weak denticles. The columellar lip is slightly flaring, lightly callused, and largely adherent. The siphonal canal is moderately short and fused.

The body whorl bears ten axial ridges that may be considered varices. In some individuals these ridges are no more than nodes extending to just above and just below the shoulder margin. Spiral sculpture consists of ten strong major cords, two on the canal, two on the shoulder, and six on the body. Between each two major cords a single strong minor cord is apparent.

The variability of shell form and sculpture seen in this species, and so typical of many Mediterranean species, has led to the introduction of a large number of synonymous names.

Shell color is yellow-brown to purple-brown or purplish-gray, with a porcelaneous white aperture.

Western Mediterranean (Adriatic Sea and elsewhere) to Madeira and the British Isles.

See Pl. 21, fig. 7.

?Ocinebrina emipowlusi (Abbott, 1954)

Ocenebra (Ocinebrina) emipowlusi Abbott, 1954: 41

The shell is tiny (maximum length 8 mm) and broadly fusiform. The spire is high, consisting of one and one-half keeled nuclear whorls and four or five convex to subangulate postnuclear whorls. The body whorl is of moderate size, broad posteriorly, but much constricted above the siphonal canal. The aperture is moderately small and ovate, with an extremely small anal sulcus. The outer apertural lip is weakly erect and minutely crenulate beyond a strong, thickened varix; the inner surface of the outer lip is smooth to weakly lirate. The columellar lip is smooth, adherent posteriorly, and barely detached and suberect anteriorly. The siphonal canal is of moderate length, slanted to the left, and barely open; the upper portion of the canal is almost fused in the specimens examined.

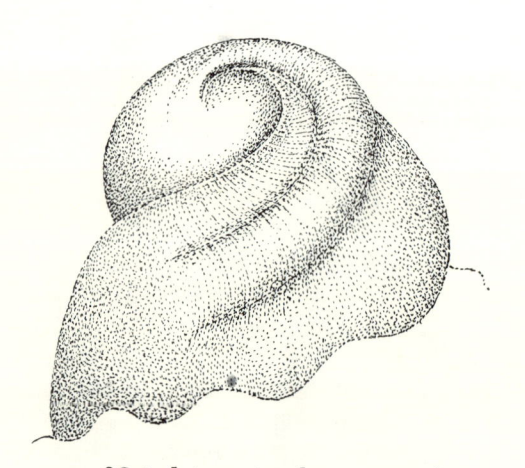

77. ?*Ocinebrina emipowlusi*, protoconch

The body whorl bears six heavy varices. Additional axial sculpture is lacking. Spiral sculpture consists of seven distinct major cords of equal strength on the body, beginning at the suture, and six minor cords on the canal.

Shell color is generally a shade of pinkish-orange, but may be as light as pale, waxy yellow or white.

The placement of this species will remain in doubt until we are able to examine its radula.

Moderately deep water (ca. 100–140 m) in the eastern Gulf of Mexico.

See Pl. 21, fig. 9.

Ocinebrina hybrida (Aradas & Benoit, 1870)

Murex hybridus Aradas & Benoit, 1870: 272

The shell is of moderate size (maximum length 15 mm) and roughly fusiform. The spire is high and acute, consisting of five or six sharply shouldered postnuclear whorls and a protoconch of undetermined nature. The suture is strongly impressed. The body whorl is of moderate size and fusoid. The aperture is ovate and of moderate size, with a very small, weak anal sulcus. The outer apertural lip is more or less weakly erect and coarsely serrate; its inner surface bears five weak denticles. The columellar lip is smooth and entirely adherent. The siphonal canal is rather short and fused.

The body whorl bears two or three prickly varices arising briefly at right angles to the shell surface, and several intervarical ridges of greater or lesser extent. Spiral sculpture consists of eight weak major cords, five on the body and three on the canal. These cords are somewhat stronger on the axial sculptural elements, where they are developed into very short, sharp prickles. The prickles at the shoulder margin form a crown around each whorl.

Shell color is pale waxy white-yellow to dark rust-brown. The aperture is white.

Reported only from the area around Sicily.

See Pl. 21, fig. 10.

Genus POROPTERON Jousseaume, 1880

TYPE SPECIES: *Murex uncinarius* Lamarck, 1822, by original designation.

Shells of the three species assigned to this genus are small and roughly fusiform. The spire is high, acute, and strongly shouldered. The body whorl is moderately large and fusoid, with an almost imperceptible anal sulcus. The aperture is moderate in size and ovate to subcircular. The siphonal canal is of moderate length and its margins are fused. The body whorl bears three briefly spinose varices. The shoulder spine is exaggeratedly curved upward. Other macrosculpture is reduced, but the entire shell surface exhibits an unusual microsculpture resembling minute, oblique chisel marks.

This small genus has two representatives from South Africa and one from St. Helena Island in the South Atlantic. All three species bear a superficial resemblance to *Prototyphis angasi* (Crosse, 1863). *Poropteron* differs from *Prototyphis* in its sealed canal, its microsculpture, its ovate, entire aperture, and its ocenebrine (as opposed to muricine) radular dentition.

Poropteron incurvispina (Kilburn, 1970)

Murex mitraeformis Sowerby, 1841: pl. 190, fig. 75 (not Brocchi, 1814); *M. mitriformis* Sowerby, 1841: Cat. p. 4 (not Wood, 1828); *Pteropurpura (Poropteron) incurvispina* Kilburn, 1970: 44, new name for *M. mitraeformis* Sowerby, 1841 (not Brocchi, 1814)

The shell is small (maximum length 25 mm) and roughly fusiform. The spire is high and acute, consisting of one full nuclear whorl and six strongly shouldered, excavated postnuclear whorls. The suture is weakly impressed. The body whorl is large and fusoid. The aperture is subcircular to ovate, with a barely discernible anal sulcus. The outer apertural lip is weakly erect and broadly crenulate; its inner surface is smooth. The columellar lip is also entirely smooth. The siphonal canal is moderate in length, with fused margins.

The body whorl bears three briefly spinose varices. Intervarical axial sculpture consists of a single knob, closer to the older of any two consecutive varices. Spiral sculpture consists of a weak cord at the shoulder margin and seven obsolete cords below it, the last two on the canal. Where the cords intersect the varices, short, sharp, curved, ventrally fused spines are developed. The spine at the shoulder margin is much the longest, hooking sharply posteriorly to touch the preceding whorl. Of the remaining six ventrally curving spines, three arise on the lower body and three on the canal. The entire shell surface is covered with minute, oblique "chisel-holes."

Shell color varies from cream and pale orange-pink to dark purple-brown.

Numerous authors have suggested that this species is conspecific with *P. uncinarius*. The differences are as follows:

P. uncinarius	*P. incurvispina*
1. Shoulder spine hooked posteriorly and bent dorsally	1. Shoulder spine hooked posteriorly, dorsal curvature lacking
2. Shoulder spine not touching previous whorl	2. Shoulder spine bent posteriorly, touching previous whorl
3. Varix bears five straight or dorsally bent spines	3. Varix bears seven spines, the lower six ventrally curved
4. Shoulder region sloping and unexcavated	4. Shoulder region sharply angular, excavated
5. Occurs subtidally	5. Occurs intertidally

Sowerby, in introducing his name for this species, spelled it "*mitraeformis*" in his "Index to the Figures..." and "*mitriformis*" in his "A Catalogue of Recent Species," each dated 1841. The

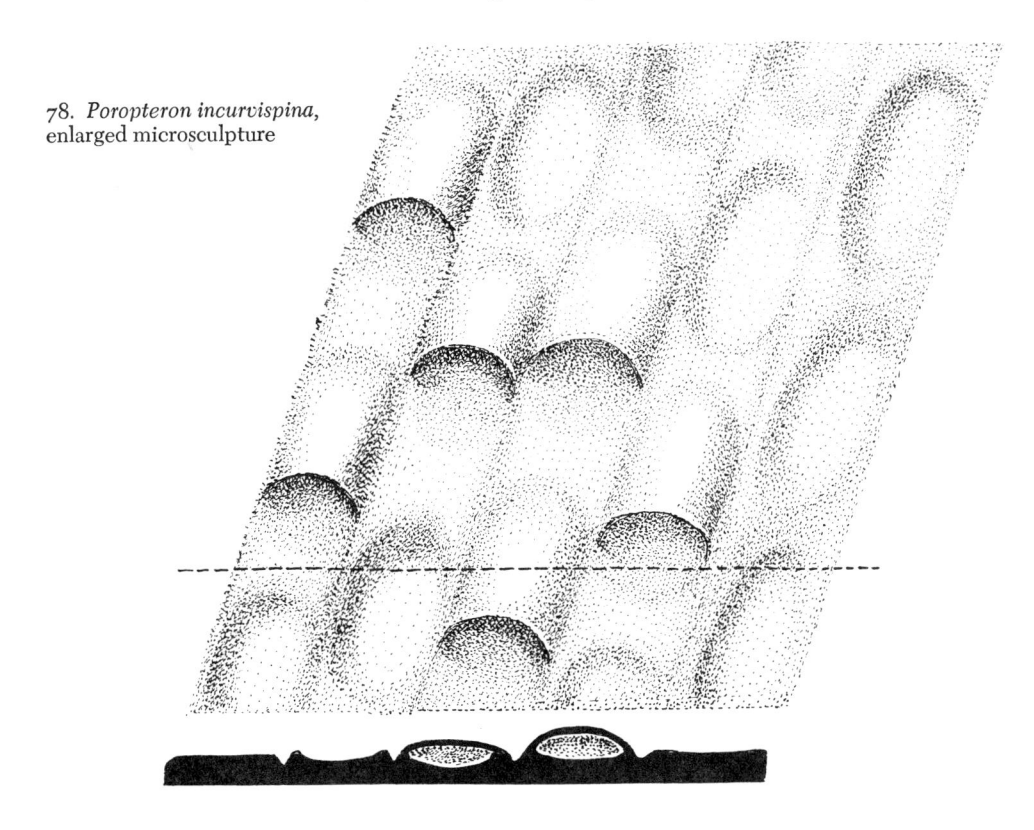

78. *Poropteron incurvispina*, enlarged microsculpture

name preoccupying Sowerby's (*mitraeformis* Brocchi, 1814, or *mitriformis* Wood, 1828) depends on the spelling one uses.

South Africa from East London to Port Alfred. See Pl. 22, fig. 3.

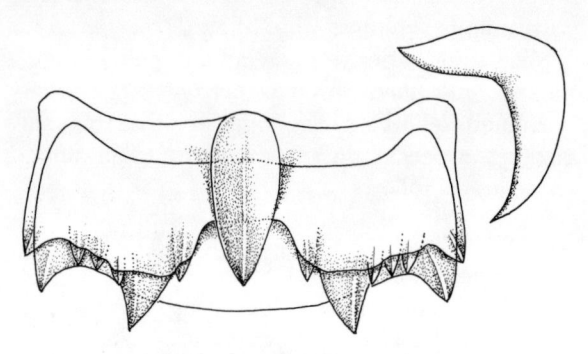

79. *Poropteron incurvispina*, radular dentition

?Poropteron sanctaehelenae (E. A. Smith, 1891)

Murex sanctaehelenae E. A. Smith, 1891: 258

We have not seen a specimen of this species. The following is based on the original description and a photograph of the holotype.

The shell is of average size for the genus (ca. 30 mm in length) and fusiform. The spire is high and acute, consisting of ten postnuclear whorls and a protoconch of undetermined nature. The suture is moderately impressed, but appears deeply impressed, owing to the excavated nature of the shoulder. The body whorl is moderately large and fusoid. The aperture is subovate, with an insignificant anal sulcus. The outer apertural lip is barely erect and coarsely crenulate; its inner surface is smooth. The columellar lip is adherent above, and barely detached below. The siphonal canal is moderate in length and is narrowly open to fused.

The body whorl bears three briefly winged varices. Intervarical axial sculpture is lacking. Spiral sculpture consists of nine cords of varying strength: four strong ones on the body, three weak ones in the space between the body and the canal, and two weak ones on the canal.

80. *Poropteron sanctaehelenae*

Where these cords intersect the varices, short to moderately long, dorsally recurved hollow spines are developed. A thin webbing arises between the spines of the body and the interspace, and extends as far from the surface of the whorl as the spines do. On the dorsal side of the body portion of the varix, the cords appear so abruptly from the unsculptured body surface and are so strongly raised that the spaces between them have the appearance of deep pits.

The shell is white.

Apparently restricted to the island of St. Helena.

Poropteron uncinarius (Lamarck, 1822)

Murex uncinarius Lamarck, 1822: 166; *M. capensis* Sowerby, 1841: pl. 190, fig. 76; *M. quinquelobatus* Sowerby, 1879: 22

The shell reaches a maximum length of 30 mm and is fusiform. The spire is high and acute, consisting of four strongly shouldered postnuclear whorls and a protoconch of undetermined nature. The suture is weakly impressed. The body whorl is moderately large and fusoid. The aperture is ovate and moderately small, with an obsolete anal sulcus. The outer apertural lip is weakly erect and smooth, its inner surface also smooth. The columellar lip is smooth and erect. The siphonal canal is moderate in length and its margins are fused.

The body whorl bears three briefly spinose varices. Intervarical axial sculpture consists of a single knob, closer to the older of any two consecutive varices. Spiral sculpture is lacking on the shoulder. The body bears three obsolete cords, one at the shoulder margin and two below it. Two other cords are found on the canal. Where these cords intersect the varices, comparatively short, sharp, posteriorly hooked, ventrally fused spines are developed. The spine at the shoulder margin is much the longest; the remainder are shorter and become progressively shorter anteriorly. The entire shell surface is covered with a microsculpture imparting the appearance of oblique chisel punctures.

Shell color is pale rusty orange; the aperture is white.

Lamarck, in his description of *Murex uncinarius*, referred to figures in Martini & Chemnitz (1785) that are clearly of the species now known as *Marchia elongata* (Lightfoot, 1786). His description and measurements are, however, just as clearly referable to the South African species now assigned to the genus *Poropteron* Jousseaume, 1880. This ambiguity has, perhaps, been cleared up with the recent publication (Cernohorsky, 1971) of the ostensible holotype in the Muséum d'Histoire Naturelle, Geneva; this proved to be a specimen of *Poropteron uncinarius*, whose measurements and description were first given by Lamarck.

False Bay to Cape Natal, South Africa, apparently in moderately deep water.

See Pl. 22, fig. 2.

Genus PTEROPURPURA Jousseaume, 1880

TYPE SPECIES: *Murex macropterus* Deshayes, 1839, by original designation.

Shells of most species in this group superficially resemble those of *Pterynotus* species in having three winged varices per whorl. However, in *Pteropurpura* the operculum and radula show affinities to those of *Ocenebra*; moreover, the siphonal canals are fused, as in *Ocenebra*. With one exception (*P. bequaerti*), all species of the group inhabit the North Pacific. Some species show little variability in shell form or color throughout their range. In a few species, however, a marked color range is apparent in specimens from different regions. Surface sculpture may also range from almost smooth to richly imbricate. At times these sculptural differences may coincide with divergences in shell proportion. No correlation has been shown as yet between these differences, on the one hand, and latitudinal distribution, water depth, or other ecological parameters, on the other.

Pteropurpura adunca (Sowerby, 1834)

Murex aduncus Sowerby, 1834: pl. 62, fig. 35; *M. falcatus* Sowerby, 1834: pl. 62, fig. 31; *M. eurypteron* Reeve, 1845: sp. 76; *M. speciosus* A. Adams, 1855: 121; *M. expansus* Sowerby, 1860: 428; *Phyllonotus acanthophorus* A. Adams, 1863: 372

The shell is moderately large (maximum length 75 mm) and broadly fusiform. The spire is high, consisting of one and one-half nuclear whorls and six strongly shouldered postnuclear whorls. The suture is impressed. The body whorl is moderately large and broadly fusoid. The aperture is of moderate size and ovate, with no perceptible anal sulcus. The outer apertural lip is erect and finely crenulate marginally, and smooth on its inner surface. The columellar lip is entirely adherent in most specimens, heavily callused and somewhat detached in very large specimens. The siphonal canal is sealed, weakly bent to the right, and dorsally recurved.

The body whorl bears four winglike varices, each of which extends from the suture to the upper half of the siphonal canal. Intervarical axial sculpture is lacking. Spiral sculpture consists of five more or less prominent major cords on the body and numerous more or less strong intercalary threads. Each major cord terminates at the varical margin as a pucker in the margin, the five thus giving the varical margin a ruffled appearance. The leading edge of the varix is more or less laminate.

Shell color is white, cream, or light red-brown, with darker red-brown markings, generally in the form of transverse bands. The aperture is white.

The shell of this species is exceedingly variable, with each bay in southern Honshu Island having its own endemic form. Certain striking forms have been given distinct names: one has much reduced spiral sculpture and develops enormously expanded varical "wings"; another is generally a uniform brown, with strong spiral sculpture.

The existence of a persistent fourth varix has prompted the introduction of the generic (or subgeneric) category *Ocinebrellus* Jousseaume, 1880; if this taxon is necessary, we feel that it is, at best, of subgeneric rank.

Southeastern coasts of Japan, north to Tokyo Bay.

See Pl. 22, fig. 10.

Pteropurpura bequaerti (Clench & Pérez Farfante, 1945)

Murex bequaerti Clench & Pérez Farfante, 1945: 40

The shell is small for the genus (maximum length 42 mm) and fusiform. The spire is high, consisting of one and one-half nuclear whorls and six or seven postnuclear whorls. The suture is indistinct to completely obscured. The body whorl is of moderate size and fusoid. The aperture is small and ovate, with no perceptible anal sulcus. The outer apertural lip is erect and finely crenulate marginally, and smooth on its inner surface. The columellar lip is largely adherent, but at its anterior end it is slightly detached and barely erect. The siphonal canal is moderately long, fused, and bent to the right.

The body whorl bears three bladelike varices that are broader at their base than at their edge. Intervarical axial sculpture consists of a single low knob, midway in each space. Spiral sculpture consists of five weak major cords and numerous minor cords: between each two consecutive cords are three minor cords, the middle one the most prominent; on the canal several low minor cords are apparent; and the major and minor cords on the body end in small, toothlike points on the varical margin, the largest of these being at the shoulder margin.

Shell color is dirty white, with tinges of blue-gray on the spire, where retained animal matter or mud shows through. The aperture is white, and the tip of the canal is generally suffused with brown-purple.

Off Cape Hatteras, North Carolina, to off the Dry Tortugas, in 100 or more meters.

See Pl. 22, fig. 1.

Pteropurpura centrifuga (Hinds, 1844)

Murex centrifuga Hinds, 1844: 126; *Pterynotus swansoni* Hertlein & Strong, 1951: 85; *Pteropurpura deroyana* Berry, 1968: 156

The shell reaches a maximum length of 80 mm and is fusiform. The spire is high, consisting of two bulbous nuclear whorls and eight weakly shouldered postnuclear whorls. The suture is indistinct or weakly impressed. The body whorl is large and fusoid, and appears very large because of its broad varical flange. The aperture is of moderate size and ovate, with a barely perceptible anal sulcus. The outer apertural lip is erect and smooth marginally, except for three brief bumps reflecting spiral cords; its inner surface is smooth. The columellar lip is smooth and thickened, adherent at its upper end, detached and erect for its remaining length. The siphonal canal is sealed, moderately long, and almost straight.

The body whorl bears three winged varices. Intervarical axial sculpture consists of a single prominent node extending from the shoulder margin to shortly below it. Spiral sculpture consists of five major cords ending at the varical margin as partially open spines, and numerous fine threads, that are ephemeral between varices, becoming much stronger between and on the varical spines. The leading edge of the varix is richly laminate.

Shell color is uniform pale yellow-buff, in some instances with light-brown blotches.

Central Gulf of California (often trawled by shrimp fishermen docking at Guaymas, Mexico) to the Galápagos Islands.

See Pl. 22, fig. 11.

Pteropurpura esycha (Dall, 1925)

Murex esychus Dall, 1925: 21

The shell is small for the genus (maximum length 35 mm) and stoutly fusiform. The spire is moderately high and subacute, consisting of one and one-third nuclear whorls and three or four weakly shouldered postnuclear whorls. The suture is moderately impressed. The body whorl is large and broadly fusoid. The aperture is of moderate size and ovate, with no clear indication of an anal sulcus. The outer apertural lip is barely erect, if at all, and faintly crenulate marginally, and smooth on its inner surface. The columellar lip is entirely adherent. The siphonal canal is moderately short, fused, and strongly, dorsally bent.

The body whorl bears three broad, winged varices, each with a single prominent point at the shoulder margin. Intervarical axial sculpture consists of a single more or less weak node at the shoulder margin. Spiral sculpture consists of nine major cords, seven on the body and two on the canal, and numerous minor, intercalary threads; each major spiral element and several of the minor ones end in weak projections at the varical margin. The leading edge of the varix is richly laminate. Irregular growth lines crossing the finer spiral elements impart a rough appearance to the shell.

Shell color is white or tan, with irregular light-brown markings. The aperture is white.

Known to us only from southeastern Japan.

See Pl. 22, fig. 5.

Pteropurpura festiva (Hinds, 1844)

Murex festivus Hinds, 1844: 127

The shell is moderately large (maximum length 60 mm) and fusiform. The spire is high, consisting of one and one-third nuclear whorls and five or six angulate postnuclear whorls. The suture is obscured by the subsequent whorl. The body whorl is relatively large and fusoid. The aperture is of moderate size and ovate, with a shallow, moderately broad anal sulcus. The outer apertural lip is erect and dentate; its inner surface bears six sharp, elongate denticles. The columellar lip is entirely adherent, and in large specimens heavily callused. The upper two-thirds of the siphonal canal is sealed; the lower third is open and dorsally recurved.

The body whorl bears three prominent varices with their free margins reflected dorsally along their entire length, but otherwise typical for the genus. The varices extend from the suture to the anteriormost sealed portion of the canal. Intervarical axial sculpture consists of a single abrupt, prominent medial knob. Spiral sculpture consists of numerous minor cords, separated by fine, sharply cut grooves, the cords apparent immediately before and after the varix but becoming ephemeral over the intervarical node. The leading edge of each varix is richly fimbriate.

Shell color is white to yellow-brown, with numerous transverse, red-brown lines between the spiral cords, these persisting where the cords become ephemeral. The aperture is porcelaneous white.

Although never in doubt at the species level, this species has been shuffled among several different genera in recent years. Eventually the genus *Shaskyus*, based on radular dentition as well as shell distinctions, was erected by Burch & Campbell (1963). We find, however, that the radular distinctions hold up no better than the shell distinctions.

Santa Barbara, California, to Bahía Magdalena, Baja California.

See Pl. 22, fig. 9.

Pteropurpura leeana (Dall, 1890)

Murex (Chicoreus) leeanus Dall, 1890: 329

The shell is moderately large (maximum length 75 mm) and fusiform. The spire is high and acute, consisting of one and one-half nuclear whorls and six or seven shouldered postnuclear whorls. The body whorl is fusoid and small, but appears larger because of the long spines projecting from the shoulder margin. The aperture is of moderate size and ovate, with a moderately broad, very shallow anal sulcus. The outer apertural lip is briefly erect and smooth marginally, as well as on its inner surface. The columellar lip is more or less callused and entirely adherent. The siphonal canal is fused and moderately long and straight.

The body whorl bears three thickened, ropelike varices; these are not prominent except at the shoulder margin. Intervarical axial sculpture consists of a single knoblike node, situated closer to the earlier of any two consecutive varices. Spiral sculpture consists of a single heavy cord, ephemeral over the intervarical node but becoming prominent on the varix, where it gives rise to a long, straight to recurved spine, almost closed on its leading edge. In addition, the entire shell surface is covered with very fine threads, scabrous at their intersection with microscopic axial growth striae.

Shell color is waxy yellow to yellow-brown, overlaid by a chalky white intritacalx.

Although the specific name of this species has never been in doubt, its generic placement has troubled some workers. The genus *Calcitrapessa* Berry, 1959, was introduced for this aberrant *Pteropurpura*. Other workers, their attention drawn to the exaggeratedly long shoulder spines, have erroneously concluded that it belonged with the "trophons."

Off the west coast of Baja California to Cabo San Lucas, and in the southern half of the Gulf of California.

See Pl. 22, fig. 7.

Pteropurpura macroptera (Deshayes, 1839)

Murex macropterus Deshayes, 1839: 360; *Pteronotus carpenteri* Dall, 1899: 138; *M. petri* Dall, 1900: 37

The shell is moderately large (maximum length 75 mm) and fusiform. The spire is high, consisting of one angulate nuclear whorl and six or seven convex postnuclear whorls. The suture is impressed. The body whorl is fusoid and of moderate size, but with an exaggeratedly large appearance owing to its large, winged varices. The aperture is subcircular, with a barely perceptible anal sulcus. The outer apertural lip is erect and smooth to broadly undulate; its inner surface is very weakly denticulate. The columellar lip is smooth, adherent above, and detached and strongly erect below. The siphonal canal is moderately long, sealed, bent to the right, and dorsally recurved.

The body whorl bears three broad, digitate, winglike varices. Intervarical axial sculpture is lacking. Spiral sculpture consists of five broad major cords, these ephemeral intervarically, apparent on the trailing edge of the varix, and ending in short to moderately long marginal digitations. Several minor cords are erratically distributed over the shell surface, one generally associated with the

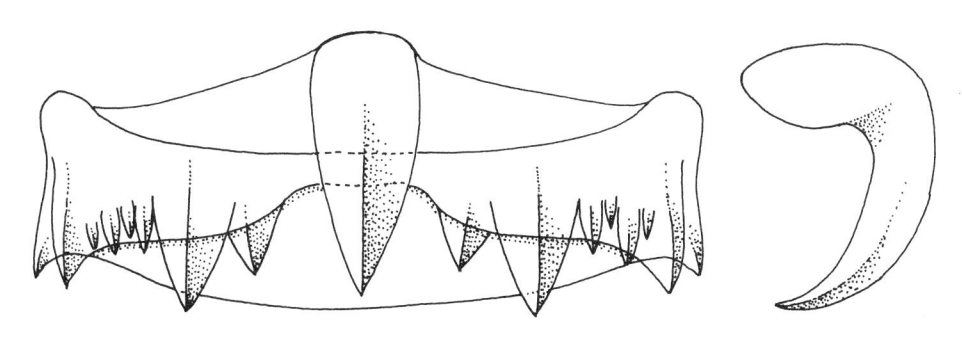

81. *Pteropurpura macroptera*, radular dentition

anteriormost major cord. The leading edge of each varix is laminate.

Two forms of this species are known: one form is smooth, with very broad varical flanges and broad, rather brief, varical digitations; the other has a more scabrous shell surface and moderately broad varical flanges with longer, more slender digitations.

Shell color is generally brown, varying from dark purple-brown in the form with long varical digitations to pale tan-brown in the more broadly winged form. The brown color is consistently strongest on the spiral cords over the varices. The aperture is porcelaneous white.

Monterey Bay, California, to Bahía Todos Santos, Baja California.

See Pl. 22, fig. 13; Pl. 23, fig. 13.

Pteropurpura modesta (Fulton, 1936)

Ocenebra (Ocinebrellus) modesta Fulton, 1936: 10

The shell is small for the genus (maximum length 35 mm) and fusiform. The spire is high, consisting of one and one-half angulate nuclear whorls and six shouldered postnuclear whorls. The suture is obscured by the subsequent whorl. The body whorl is of moderate size and fusoid. The aperture is moderately small and ovate, with no apparent anal sulcus. The outer apertural lip is erect and crenulate marginally, and smooth on its inner surface. The columellar lip is entirely adherent. The siphonal canal is moderately long, fused, and sharply bent to the right toward its end.

The body whorl bears three winglike varices, these extending from the suture to midway on the canal. Intervarical axial sculpture consists of a single small, knoblike node at the shoulder margin immediately following each varix. Spiral sculpture consists of four primary cords on the body, with numerous intercalary threads between each two consecutive primary cords; the uppermost primary cord, at the shoulder margin, gives rise to a moderately long, spinelike projection at the varical margin, and below the fourth primary is a series of seven to nine secondary cords, intercalated with finer threads. The leading edge of the varix is ruffled and weakly laminate.

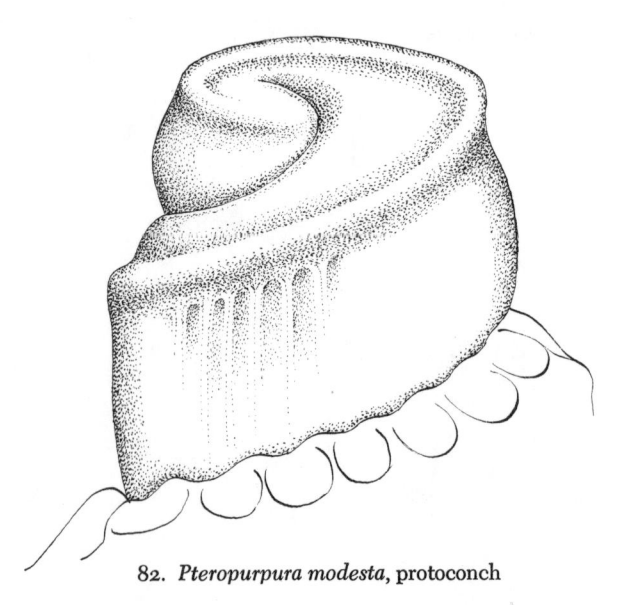

Shell color is yellow-brown. The aperture is porcelaneous white.

Known to us only from southeastern Japan.

See Pl. 22, fig. 4.

Pteropurpura plorator (Adams & Reeve, 1849)

Murex plorator Adams & Reeve *in* Reeve, 1849: sp. 191

The shell is of moderate size (maximum length 52 mm) and fusiform. The spire is high, consisting of one and one-fourth nuclear whorls and five or six weakly shouldered postnuclear whorls. The suture is obscured by part of the subsequent whorl. The body whorl is large and fusoid, and appears broader than it is because of its broad, winglike varices. The aperture is moderately small and ovate, with a barely perceptible anal sulcus. The outer apertural lip is weakly, broadly crenulate, and its inner surface is smooth. The columellar lip is smooth and essentially adherent for its entire extent. The siphonal canal is moderately long, sealed, and weakly, dorsally recurved.

The body whorl bears three winglike varices, each of these extending slightly more than one-half the length of the siphonal canal. Intervarical axial sculpture consists of a single prominent, knoblike node almost midway in the intervarical space. Spiral sculpture consists of five major cords, these ephemeral over the intervarical node and more prominent on the varix and just after it.

Ground color of the shell is white or pale tan, generally overlaid with chestnut-brown markings; these may be spiral bands between the spiral cords or axial flammules, and in some cases both patterns are present.

Known to us only from southeastern Japan.

See Pl. 22, fig. 8.

Pteropurpura trialata (Sowerby, 1834)

Murex trialatus Sowerby, 1834: pl. 62, fig. 33

The shell is large (maximum length 93 mm) and fusiform. The spire is high, consisting of one and one-half nuclear whorls and seven or eight weakly shouldered postnuclear whorls. The suture

82. *Pteropurpura modesta*, protoconch

is weakly impressed to obscure. The body whorl is large and fusoid, and appears broader than it is because of its winglike varices. The aperture is of moderate size and ovate, with a negligible anal sulcus. The outer apertural lip is briefly erect and finely dentate, reflecting the shell's spiral sculptural elements; the inner surface of the outer lip is smooth or weakly undulate. The columellar lip is entirely adherent. The siphonal canal is moderately long, slender, gradually curved dorsally, and sealed.

The body whorl bears three broad, flat, winglike varices, each extending from the suture to two-thirds the length of the siphonal canal. The leading edge of the varix is laminate. Otherwise, axial sculpture consists solely of microscopic growth lines. Spiral sculpture consists of eight broad cords, obsolete intervarically, more prominent on the varix, where they terminate as broad digitations at the varical margin; between each two major cords are six fine spiral threads, and other fine threads continue over the surface of the obsolete major cords.

Shell color is white to cream, with dark-brown spiral bands corresponding to the spaces between the major cords; in many individuals a lighter-brown coloration suffuses these spaces; exceptionally, a pure white or pure dark-brown individual is encountered. The varices are almost entirely white, and the aperture is white.

This species was erroneously called *Murex phyllopterus* Lamarck, 1822, by Reeve (1845).

Palos Verdes, California, to Isla Cedros, Baja California.

See Pl. 22, fig. 6.

Genus **ROPERIA** Dall, 1898

TYPE SPECIES: *Fusus roperi* Dall, 1898 (=*Ocenebra poulsoni* Carpenter, 1864), by monotypy.

The shell in this genus, as represented by the monotype, *R. poulsoni*, is moderately large and fusiform. The spire is high, the body whorl moderately large and fusoid. The aperture is moderately large and ovate, with a well-developed anal sulcus. The outer apertural lip thickens abruptly behind the margin; the interior surface bears a number of strong denticles. The columellar lip is generally smooth, except for a posterior node, delimiting the left side of the anal sulcus. The siphonal canal is short, broad, and open. Axial sculpture consists of few, erratically placed varices and long, heavy, axial ridges, about equal in prominence to the varices. Spiral sculpture consists of fine, incised lines and subobsolete, ropelike cords.

Roperia poulsoni (Carpenter, 1864)

Ocenebra poulsoni Carpenter, 1864: 663; *Fusus roperi* Dall, 1898: 4

The shell is moderately large (maximum length 65 mm) and fusiform. The spire is high, consisting of one and one-half nuclear whorls and seven or eight weakly shouldered postnuclear whorls. The suture is obscured by posterior expansions of the

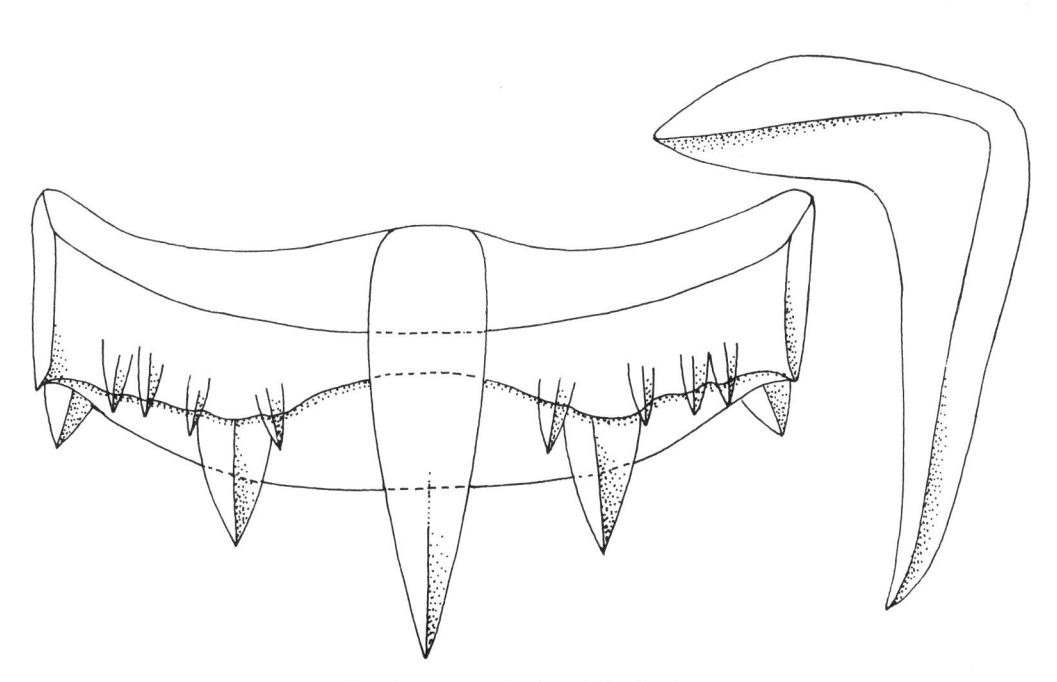

83. *Roperia poulsoni*, radular dentition

subsequent whorl. The body whorl is moderately large and fusoid. The aperture is moderately large and ovate, with a deep, moderately narrow anal sulcus. The outer apertural lip is thin and coarsely crenulate marginally, thickening immediately behind the growing edge; the inner surface of the outer lip bears six or seven strong denticles. The columellar lip is entirely adherent and smooth, except for a prominent posterior node, delimiting the left side of the anal sulcus. The siphonal canal is short, open, and dorsally recurved at its tip.

The body whorl bears one to four erratically placed varices and an additional seven strong axial ridges. Spiral sculpture consists of five or six prominent ropelike cords and numerous fine, incised lines covering the entire shell; fine axial lamellae produce microscopic pits where they cross these incised lines. Where the spiral cords cross the axial sculptural elements, raised nodes are formed, imparting a corrugated appearance to the shell.

Shell color is pale waxy yellow, with red-brown in the troughs of the incised lines; in most individuals this pattern occurs only between the spiral cords, forming transverse bands of red-brown. The aperture is porcelaneous white. In some instances portions of the aperture, including the labial denticles, are suffused with an apricot-orange color.

Santa Barbara, California, to Bahía Magdalena, Baja California, in intertidal depths.

See Pl. 19, figs. 8–9.

Genus **TRACHYPOLLIA** Woodring, 1928

TYPE SPECIES: *Trachypollia sclera* Woodring, 1928 (fossil), by original designation.

The small (12–20 mm long) and essentially nonvaricate shell is fusoid to moruloid in form, with a finely nodulose surface. The edge of the outer apertural lip may be thin or thickened and denticulate within. The columellar lip is entirely adherent and bears two or three elongate tubercles at its anterior end. The siphonal canal is moderately short and open.

The three species assigned here have previously been placed in *Morula* (type species: *Purpura uva* Röding, 1798), from which they differ in their more slender overall form, the thin outer apertural lip present in two of the three species, and significant radular differences. We consider *Trachypollia* to be ocenebrine, whereas *Morula* appears to us to be more accurately assigned to Wenz's subfamily Drupinae, which we place in the Thaididae.

Trachypollia didyma (Schwengel, 1943)
Drupa didyma Schwengel, 1943: 76

The shell is small (maximum length 12 mm) and fusiform. The spire is high, consisting of three and one-half papillose, convex nuclear whorls and six strongly nodulose postnuclear whorls. The suture is impressed. The body whorl is moderately large and fusoid. The aperture is ovate to lenticular, with a well-marked U-shaped anal sulcus, the parietal margin of the sulcus delimited by a moderately strong transverse ridge. The outer apertural lip is unthickened and finely crenulate at its margin; on the inner surface of the outer lip, recessed a short distance into the aperture, are five moderately weak denticles, diminishing in size anteriorly. The columellar lip is adherent at its posterior extremity, detached and weakly erect for its remaining length; at its anterior end the columellar lip bears two elongate, oblique denticles. The siphonal canal is moderately short, open, and weakly bent to the left and dorsally.

The nonvaricate shell bears axial sculpture consisting of 13 low costae, sharply nodulose over the major and minor cords. Of the major cords, one is subsutural, two are located at the shoulder margin, three are distributed evenly over the anterior half of the body, and one or two occur on the canal; two minor cords lie between the subsutural major cord and the paired major cords at the shoulder margin, and additional single minor cords alternate with the major cords on the remainder of the body and canal.

Shell color is yellow-ochre, with red-brown on the major spiral cords, strongest on the nodules. The aperture is fleshy white, with deeper fleshy pink on the columellar denticles.

Known from the southeastern coast of Florida (at the type locality, Palm Beach, in 68 m to off Miami in 40 m), and from Texas (offshore reefs).

See Pl. 3, fig. 8.

Trachypollia lugubris (C. B. Adams, 1852)
Buccinum lugubre C. B. Adams, 1852: 293

The shell is moderately large (maximum length 18 mm) and fusiform. The spire is quite high, consisting of three and one-half nuclear whorls and five or six subangulate postnuclear whorls (see Burch, 1940). The suture is well-defined. The body whorl is moderately large and fusoid. The aperture is moderately large and broadly ovate, with a narrow, deep anal sulcus. The outer apertural lip is thin and minutely crenulate at its margin, reflecting the spiral sculpture; the inner surface of the outer lip bears six weak denticles recessed into the aperture, each corresponding to the trough between two major spiral cords. The columellar lip is completely adherent, bearing a small knob delimiting the parietal extent of the anal sulcus, and a series of three moderately strong denticles at its anterior end; of these three denticles the anterior two are closer together. The siphonal canal is moderately short, open, and bent to the left.

The shell is essentially nonvaricate. Axial sculpture consists of eight to ten costae with shallow interspaces, the costae most prominent over the major spiral cords. Spiral sculpture consists of primary, secondary, and tertiary scabrous cords: the shoulder bears three or four undulate tertiary cords; one primary cord is evident immediately subsuturally, a pair are at the shoulder margin, and three single primaries are distributed evenly over the lower half of the body; between the pair of primary cords at the shoulder margin and the primary immediately below them, and between each two succeeding primaries, are three secondaries, the outside two each appended to the neighboring primary; two secondary cords are found at the top of the siphonal canal; the bottom half is smooth. Where the primary cords intersect the axial costae, small, sharp nodules are developed.

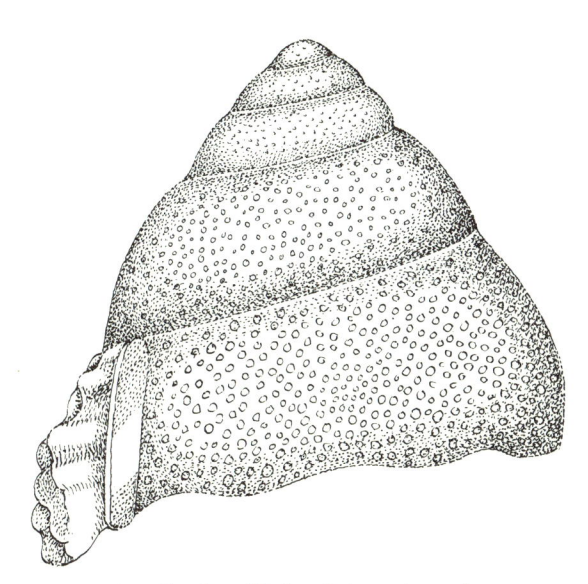

84. *Trachypollia lugubris*, protoconch

Shell color is light tan to pale fleshy brown on the shell and in the aperture. The nodules are dark red-brown.

Considerable variation in size and overall proportions may be found, particularly in association with geographical (i.e. population) differences.

Redondo Beach, California (Burch, 1940), to Panamá.

See Pl. 3, fig. 7.

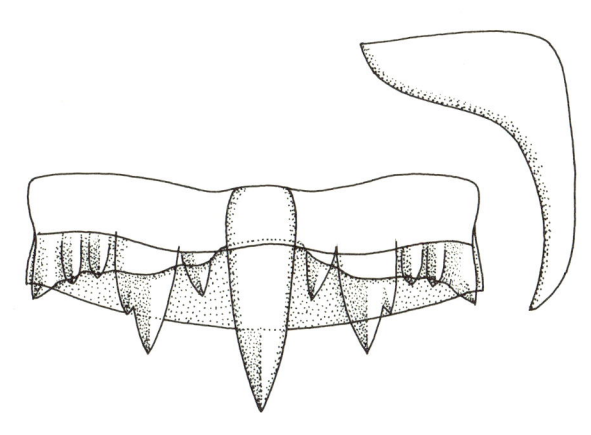

85. *Trachypollia lugubris*, radular dentition

Trachypollia nodulosa (C. B. Adams, 1845)

Purpura nodulosa C. B. Adams, 1845: 2

The shell is large for the genus (maximum length 20 mm) and moruloid to fusiform. The spire is high and acute, consisting of two and one-half convex, papillose nuclear whorls and five or six weakly convex postnuclear whorls. The suture is weakly marked. The body whorl is moderately large and roughly fusoid. The aperture is narrow and subovate, with a narrow, moderately shallow anal sulcus, this parietally delimited by a broad low node. The outer apertural lip is nonerect and smooth at its margin; the inner surface of the outer lip bears four prominent denticles recessed a short distance from the apertural margin, the denticles diminishing in prominence anteriorly. The columellar lip is entirely adherent, and bears three oblique, elongate denticles at its anterior end. The siphonal canal is moderately short, open, and barely bent to the left.

The existence of varices is difficult to determine; one or more apparent varices may occur erratically on the shell, but their number and position are never consistent. The animal does apparently pause briefly after the formation of each costa, but these do not constitute varices by our definition of the term. Axial sculpture consists of seven to ten low ridges, prominent where they intersect the spiral elements. Spiral sculpture consists of five major cords on the body and one or two on the canal: one cord is subsutural, one is at the shoulder margin, and the remaining three are distributed evenly over the lower half of the body. Where these cords intersect the costae, sharp nodules are developed. Between each two major cords is a series of six to ten fine threads.

Shell color is dark brown-black or blue-black, darkest on the nodules. In some specimens the shoulder-margin major cord and another cord at the base of the body bear white spots between the nodules. The aperture is blue-gray, with brown markings at its margin. The denticles in the aperture are white.

Southeastern Florida to southern Brazil; Texas (offshore reefs).

See Pl. 3, fig. 9.

Genus UROSALPINX Stimpson, 1865

TYPE SPECIES: *Fusus cinereus* Say, 1822, by original designation.

The shells in this widespread genus are generally small to moderate in size (7–45 mm long) and fusiform. The spire is high, the suture impressed, and the aperture ovate, with a poorly developed anal sulcus and an unthickened outer apertural lip. The siphonal canal is short to moderately short and open. The body whorl is generally nonvaricate, with obsolete, subdued, or strongly squamoid sculpture. Color is generally muted, in tones of gray, brown, or pale yellow. In all but the open canal and the generally weak shell sculpture, these are typical ocenebrine forms, a relationship corroborated by the form of the operculum and radular dentition.

Urosalpinx cala (Pilsbry, 1897)

Ocinebra cala Pilsbry, 1897: 296

The shell is small (maximum length 13 mm) and fusiform. The spire is high, consisting of one and one-fourth nuclear whorls and three convex postnuclear whorls. The suture is strongly impressed. The body whorl is of moderate size and fusoid. The aperture is of moderate size and ovate, with a relatively broad, shallow anal sulcus. The outer apertural lip is thickened and flaring at its margin; its inner surface bears seven strong denticles, recessed a short distance into the aperture. The columellar lip is entirely adherent and smooth. The siphonal canal is short, slanted to the left, and narrowly open.

The body whorl bears eight strong axial costae. Spiral sculpture consists of 12 narrow, depressed cords, these persistent between the axial costae.

Shell color is white with tinges of pink or yellow.

Known to us only from the coast of Uruguay.

See Pl. 21, fig. 3.

Urosalpinx cinerea (Say, 1822)

Fusus cinereus Say, 1822: 236; *Urosalpinx cinerea* var. *follyensis* B. B. Baker, 1951: 75

The shell is large for the genus (maximum length 45 mm) and fusiform. The spire is high, consisting of one and one-half nuclear whorls and five barely shouldered to convex postnuclear whorls. The suture is weakly impressed. The body whorl is of moderate size and fusoid. The aperture is moderately large, with a narrow, shallow anal sulcus angled toward the left. The outer apertural lip is unthickened and barely crenulate; its inner surface is moderately strongly lirate. The columellar lip is entirely adherent and smooth, except for a barely discernible swelling at its anterior end. The siphonal canal is moderately short, straight, narrowly open to the extreme right, and barely recurved at its distal end.

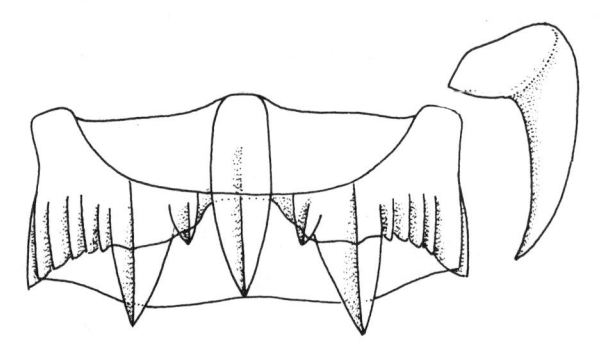

86. *Urosalpinx cinerea*, radular dentition

The body whorl bears eight to 12 axial ridges, ranging, even on a single whorl, from strongly prominent to completely obsolete. No true varices are present. Spiral sculpture consists of seven weak major cords, one on the shoulder and six on the body; between consecutive major cords there is generally a single minor cord, and the canal bears four to six minor cords. The intersection of the spiral cords and axial ridges is marked by the development of weak nodules.

Shell color is yellow-gray to blue-gray, becoming brown where worn. The aperture is pale fleshy yellow; within the aperture three transverse bands of brown-purple overlay the yellow color.

The eastern coast of North America from Prince Edward Island to the central portion of the eastern coast of Florida. Reports of this species from the western coast of Florida have never been verified. A giant form is found on the outer coast of Virginia (e.g. Wachapreague, Va.). *U. cinerea* has also been introduced with oysters into several localities on the west coast of the United States, particularly in the San Francisco Bay area; although these populations are apparently self-sustaining, little range expansion has been reported.

See Pl. 21, figs. 4–5.

Urosalpinx haneti (Petit de la Saussaye, 1856)

Murex haneti Petiti de la Saussaye, 1856: 90;
Urosalpinx rushi Pilsbry, 1897: 297

The shell is of moderate size for the genus (maximum length 24 mm) and stoutly fusiform. The spire is high and acute, consisting of one and one-half nuclear whorls and five convex postnuclear whorls. The suture is moderately impressed. The body whorl is moderately large and broadly fusoid. The aperture is moderately large and ovate, with a narrow, moderately deep anal sulcus. The outer apertural lip is unthickened; its inner surface bears seven denticles of varying strengths, the uppermost very small and followed by three pairs of moderately strong denticles. The columellar lip is entirely adherent and smooth. The siphonal canal is rather short, open, and bent to the left.

The body whorl bears nine low, rounded axial costae. Spiral sculpture consists of eight primary cords, six on the body and two on the siphonal canal, and five secondary cords between each two primary cords.

Shell color is white to red-brown. The aperture is porcelaneous white. The shell is covered with a fuzzy, tan periostracum, and in many cases there is a thin intritacalx under the periostracum.

This species is the type species of the genus *Hanetia* Jousseaume, 1880, which is thus synonymized herein in *Urosalpinx* Stimpson, 1865.

Central Brazil to southern Uruguay.

See Pl. 21, fig. 6.

?Urosalpinx macra A. E. Verrill, 1884

Urosalpinx macra A. E. Verrill, 1884: 237

The shell is small (maximum length 15 mm) and fusiform. The spire is high, consisting of two convex nuclear whorls and five convex postnuclear whorls. The suture is weakly impressed and situated in a moderately deep furrow. The body whorl is moderately small and fusoid. The aperture is ovate, with a narrow, moderately shallow anal sulcus. The outer apertural lip is erect and broadly serrate marginally; its inner surface is smooth. The columellar lip is smooth and entirely adherent. The siphonal canal is short, bent to the left, and narrowly open.

The body whorl bears nine low axial costae. Spiral sculpture consists of seven major cords on the body and two on the canal; between each two major cords are six fine threads. Where the major spiral cords intersect the axial costae, moderately prominent nodules are developed.

Shell color is uniformly waxy yellow-white.

Southeastern United States: off Cape Hatteras to Cape Florida, in moderately deep water (150–200 m).

Urosalpinx perrugata (Conrad, 1846)

Fusus perrugatus Conrad, 1846: 397

The shell is of moderate size (maximum length 25 mm) and fusiform. The spire is high and acute, consisting of one and one-half nuclear whorls and four shouldered postnuclear whorls. The suture is weakly impressed. The body whorl is of moderate size and fusoid. The aperture is ovate, with a shallow, narrow anal sulcus. The outer apertural lip is thickened, nonerect, and minutely serrate; its inner surface is more or less strongly lirate. The columellar lip is entirely adherent and smooth. The siphonal canal is of moderate length, narrowly open, and weakly dorsally recurved.

The body whorl bears seven strong axial costae, extending from the shoulder region to the canal. Spiral sculpture consists of major and minor cords, seven majors on the body and three on the canal, progressing anteriorly from the shoulder margin. Between adjacent cords, a single minor cord is generally present.

Shell color is blue-gray, with pale-yellow axial costae. One to three evenly spaced, red-brown, interrupted transverse lines encircle the body. The aperture is pale yellow marginally, grading to deep red-brown or purple-brown within.

Sanibel Island to Cape San Blas, Florida.

See Pl. 21, fig. 14.

?Urosalpinx puncturata (Sowerby, 1886)

Cominella puncturata Sowerby, 1886: 2

The shell is small (maximum length 16 mm) and fusiform. The spire is high, consisting of two and one-half nuclear whorls and four or five convex to very weakly shouldered postnuclear whorls. The suture is weakly impressed. The body whorl is of moderate size and fusoid. The aperture is moderately large and ovate, with a weak anal sulcus. The outer apertural lip is unthickened, slightly flaring, and finely crenulate at its margin; the inner surface of the outer lip bears fine lirations extending just beyond the flaring portion of the lip. The columellar lip is smooth and entirely adherent. The siphonal canal is short, narrowly open, and bent dorsally.

The body whorl is nonvaricate and bears 15 to 20 low to obsolete axial costae. Spiral sculpture consists of numerous fine cords of various sizes and strengths. Six fine cords are evident on the shoulder and a strong shoulder-margin cord is followed by a secondary thread and seven moderately strong cords; at the base of the body another secondary thread is followed by four to six moderately prominent cords on the canal. The moderately deep spaces between the cords are bridged by fine, erect, axial lamellae, these obsolete over the cords, the combination imparting a microscopically pitted appearance to the shell surface, particularly in a broad band just below the shoulder margin.

Shell color is pale fleshy yellow to fleshy tan. Several spiral cords show an interrupted pattern of small brown and white blotches, this being strongest on the cord at the shoulder margin.

South Africa (our specimens are from False Bay).

See Pl. 21, fig. 11.

?Urosalpinx purpuroides (Reeve, 1845)

Murex purpuroides Reeve, 1845: sp. 158; *M. dunkeri* Krauss, 1848: 112

The shell is small (maximum length 15 mm) and fusiform. The spire is high and acute, with a single nuclear whorl and six or seven sharply shouldered postnuclear whorls. The suture is largely obscured. The body whorl is of moderate size and fusoid. The aperture is moderately small and ovate, with a narrow, moderately deep anal sulcus, delimited on its left side by a narrow, sharp knob. The outer apertural lip is thickened, nonerect, "ruffled" by the ends of the spiral cords, and barely crenulate at its margin; the inner surface of the outer lip is briefly flaring and more or less strongly lirate. The columellar lip is smooth and entirely adherent. The siphonal canal is moderately short, straight, and barely open.

The body whorl bears 11 sharp-crested axial ridges. No true varices are present. Spiral sculpture consists of five strong cords on the body, each separated from the next by a very narrow cleft. In addition, the shoulder bears two or three weak cords, and the canal bears two minor cords, one on each side of a single major. A moderately prominent lamella extends from each axial ridge to the sutural region. The axial ridges are actually moderately strong lamellae developed into numerous scalelike expansions where they intersect the spiral cords.

Shell color is uniformly white, in rare exceptions with pale transverse bands of gold-ochre on the body.

This species has often been considered to be conspecific with ?*U. scrobiculata* (Philippi, 1846), from the same region. It differs from this species in its more sloping shoulder, its erect, less flattened, and laterally expanded scales, its color pattern, its much weaker spiral sculpture (particularly on the shoulder), and in numerous minor details of radular dentition and opercular morphology.

South Africa (the Cape region).

See Pl. 21, fig. 1.

?Urosalpinx scrobiculata (Philippi, 1846)

Fusus scrobiculatus Philippi, 1846: 118; *Murex babingtoni* Sowerby, 1892: 2; *M. crawfordi* Sowerby, 1892: 2

The shell is small (maximum length 15 mm) and fusiform. The spire is high, consisting of one and one-half nuclear whorls and four or five weakly shouldered postnuclear whorls. The suture is deeply impressed but indistinct and interrupted by axial striae. The body whorl is of moderate size and fusoid. The aperture is moderately small and ovate, with a narrow, moderately shallow anal sulcus, the left side of which is formed by a low, transverse ridge extending into the aperture. The outer apertural lip is unthickened, and crenulate at its margin; its inner surface is smooth. The columellar lip is entirely adherent and smooth. The siphonal canal is moderately short, narrowly open, bent to the left, and distally recurved.

The body whorl bears no true varices. Numerous axial growth striae are developed into prominent, laterally expanded, scalelike structures where they intersect the four spiral cords on the body and the two on the canal. A single cord on the shoulder also bears numerous scalelike expansions of the growth striae; the striae are continuous between the cords, where they are relatively unexpanded.

Shell color is pale violet-brown. The aperture is tan at its margin and mauve within.

South Africa (Cape region).

See Pl. 21, fig. 2.

?Urosalpinx subangulata (Stearns, 1873)

Muricidea subangulata Stearns, 1873: 81; *Ocinebra michaeli* Ford, 1888: 188

The shell is moderately small (maximum length 22 mm) and fusiform. The spire is high, consisting of five or six strongly shouldered postnuclear whorls and a protoconch of undetermined nature.

The suture is weakly impressed and undulate. The body whorl is of moderate size and fusoid. The aperture is ovate and of moderate size, with a very narrow, shallow anal sulcus that extends deeply into the aperture. The outer apertural lip is unthickened and minutely serrate; its inner surface bears five moderately weak denticles. The columellar lip is entirely adherent and smooth. The siphonal canal is of moderate length, straight, and open.

The body whorl is nonvaricate. Axial sculpture consists of seven moderately prominent costae. Spiral sculpture consists of numerous primary and secondary cords: the shoulder bears four minor cords, these progressively stronger toward the shoulder margin; a single primary cord at the shoulder margin is followed by three secondary cords and a second primary cord midway on the body; below this are three secondary cords on the body and six on the canal.

Shell color is white. The three secondary cords between primary cords on the body and the one or two such cords at the base of the body are dark red-brown. The aperture is porcelaneous white.

Middle California coast from Pt. Conception to Ft. Ross (Mendocino County), California (fide Strong, 1945, *Min. Conch. Club S. Calif.*, vol. 51, p. 50).

See Pl. 21, fig. 13.

Urosalpinx tampaensis (Conrad, 1846)

Murex tampaensis Conrad, 1846: 25

The shell is of moderate size (maximum length 25 mm) and fusiform. The spire is high, consisting of one and one-half nuclear whorls and five shouldered postnuclear whorls. The suture is completely obscured by posterior projections of the subsequent whorl. The body whorl is moderately large and fusoid. The aperture is of moderate size and ovate, with a moderately broad anal sulcus. The outer apertural lip is thickened, nonerect, and weakly notched at broadly spaced intervals; the inner surface of the outer lip bears five strong denticles, a sharply cut groove running between adjacent denticles. The columellar lip is entirely adherent and smooth, except for a low, rounded swelling at its anterior end. The siphonal canal is moderately short and straight, narrowly open, and weakly, dorsally recurved.

The body whorl bears a single true varix at the outer apertural margin. Other axial sculpture consists of nine strong costae extending from the shoulder margin to the tip of the canal. On the shoulder, thin, suberect lamellae correspond in position to the axial costae. Spiral sculpture consists of eight strong cords, five on the body and three on the canal. The spiral cords are produced into low, transversely elongate nodules where they intersect the axial costae. The costae bear suberect lamellae on the canal, reminiscent of those on the shoulder. The depressed, rectangular interspaces formed by the strong sculptural elements impart a strongly reticulate appearance to the shell surface.

Shell color is blue-gray, with gray-white sculptural elements. The aperture is stained a rusty brown.

Western Florida (Tampa Bay region to Franklin County).

See Pl. 21, fig. 12.

Genus **XANTHOCHORUS** Fischer, 1884

TYPE SPECIES: *Purpura xanthostoma* Broderip, 1833, by monotypy.

The shell in this genus, as typified by *X. xanthostoma*, is moderately large (although several size groups of full-grown specimens may be found) and broadly fusoid. The aperture is large, with a lirate inner surface to the outer apertural lip and, in some specimens, a short, blunt ceratus near its anterior end. The canal is moderately short and open. Sculpture is rather variable, ranging from strongly reticulate to almost obsolete.

?Xanthochorus buxeus (Broderip, 1833)

Murex buxeus Broderip, 1833: 194

The shell is moderately small for the genus (length of specimen studied 35 mm) and roughly fusiform. The spire is high and acute, consisting of four or five subangulate postnuclear whorls and a protoconch of undetermined nature. The suture is not impressed. The body whorl is moderately large (about three-fifths of total shell length) and fusoid. The aperture is moderately large and ovate, with the outer lip flaring, thus causing the apertural opening to be larger at the point of last growth than it is immediately behind it; the anal sulcus is narrow and deep, made so by virtue of the thickenings both on the outer lip side and in the parietal region. The outer apertural lip is not erect beyond the varical thickening and is coarsely serrate; the inner surface of the outer lip bears a series of five broad, shallow transverse grooves reflecting the raised spiral elements of the outer shell sculpture; between these grooves the shell is thrown into low, transverse denticles that are, in some cases, bifurcated by a slender, shallower groove. The columellar lip is entirely adherent and somewhat excavated in the parietal region. The siphonal canal is moderately short, broadly open, and bent slightly dorsally.

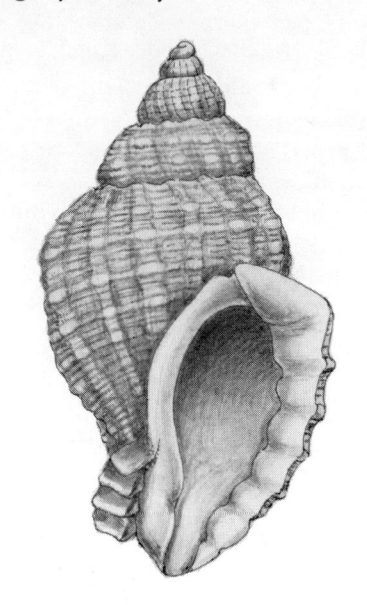

87. *Xanthochorus buxeus*

The body whorl bears eight to ten low, heavy, ropelike varices, the intervarical spaces in many cases completely obscured by the heaviness of the varices and the great density of them in a relatively limited area. Spiral sculpture consists of five major cords, one at the shoulder margin and the remainder distributed evenly over the body region; between each two consecutive major cords three or four finer cords are apparent, and similar fine cords are apparent on the shoulder (five or six) and on the canal (ten to 12).

Color is yellow-brown, with the major cords and the apertural region an off-white.

Pacasmayo, Peru, to Antofagasta, Chile.

Xanthochorus xanthostoma (Broderip, 1833)

Purpura xanthostoma Broderip, 1833: 8; *Murex horridus* Broderip, 1833: 176 (not Brocchi, 1814); *M. boivini* Kiener, 1842: 81

The shell is moderately large (maximum length 75 mm) and pyriform, although several size classes of full-grown specimens are demonstrable. The spire is high in smaller specimens, moderately low in larger specimens, consisting of six convex to more or less weakly shouldered postnuclear whorls and a protoconch of undetermined nature. The suture is moderately impressed. The body whorl is large and fusoid. The aperture is large and ovate, with a broad, shallow anal sulcus and a broad entrance into the siphonal canal. The outer apertural lip is thin, thickening abruptly behind the margin; the inner surface of the outer lip bears six to 13 moderately weak denticles. The columellar lip is entirely adherent and smooth. The siphonal canal is moderate in length, open, and weakly, dorsally bent at its tip.

The body whorl bears six to eight heavy varices. Spiral sculpture consists of six primary cords, five on the body and one on the canal, and secondary, tertiary, and quaternary sculptural elements alternating with the primaries in a distinct pattern; on the shoulder are a primary cord, two secondaries, and numerous tertiaries and quaternaries. Innumerable fine axial lamellae form scalelike projections at their intersections with the spiral cords. In some populations, sculpture is almost lacking; in others, spiral or axial sculpture may predominate.

Shell color varies from white to yellow-white. The aperture is generally porcelaneous white, but may be suffused with pale yellow-orange.

Northern Peru to southern Chile.

See Pl. 7, figs. 4–5.

Subfamily Muricopsinae

RADWIN & D'ATTILIO, 1971

The shell is moderately small (5–85 mm in length) and fusiform to biconic, as in the Muricinae, and bears a color pattern as in the Muricinae (white or brown ground with brown, orange, red, or purple suffusions or markings), but in more subdued shades. The aperture is ovate and of variable size, the anal sulcus weaker than in the Muricinae. The siphonal canal is of moderate length and narrowly open. Most forms bear a number of prominent varices per whorl, the number variable but generally four or more, each varix bearing spinose or foliaceous projections. A prominent gap in the spiral sculpture marks the junction of the body and the canal; the spiral sculpture itself is fine. The shell surface texture is characterized by many fine growth lamellae that are thrown into fine imbrications where they intersect spiral threads. In at least half the genera, the shell bears a simple intritacalx.

Muricopsine protoconchs are variable, some with strongly tabulate whorls, as in the Ocenebrinae, others with typically convex whorls, as in the Muricinae. The operculum, essentially indistinguishable from that of the Muricinae, is unguiculate, thickened marginally, and depressed and annulate centrally.

The radula is similar to that of the Ocenebrinae, but differs in the larger, broader, more prominent cowl on which the central cusp of the rachidian tooth is borne, the deeper (from front to back) base of the rachidian, its strong, single (rather than double) endpoints, and its independent intermediate cusps; denticles may be present as wrinkles or folds between the lateral cusps and the base endpoints.

Distribution: worldwide (primarily tropical and subtropical), in depths of 0 to 300 m.

Genus **BIZETIELLA** Radwin & D'Attilio, 1972

TYPE SPECIES: *Tritonalia carmen* Lowe, 1935, by original designation.

The shell in this genus is small (9–15 mm long) and fusiform. The spire is high and acute. The aperture is moderately large and ovate, with a weakly thickened outer apertural lip that is lirate to weakly denticulate within. The columellar lip is entirely adherent and smooth. Sculpture consists of two to four strong cords on the body, these knobby over the indistinct varices.

Bizetiella carmen (Lowe, 1935)

Tritonalia carmen Lowe, 1935: 20

The shell is small (maximum length 10 mm) and fusiform. The spire is high and acute, consisting of three convex nuclear whorls and four or five strongly shouldered postnuclear whorls. The suture is impressed. The body whorl is moderately large, fusoid, and strongly contracted below the periphery. The aperture is subovate, with a broad entrance into the open siphonal canal, and no perceptible anal sulcus. The outer apertural lip is nonerect and weakly, broadly crenulate; its inner surface bears eight moderately weak lirations, two in the shoulder region and six below it. The columellar lip is entirely adherent and smooth. The siphonal canal is moderately short and open, bent to the left, and dorsally recurved.

The body whorl bears five erect, subspinose varices. Intervarical axial sculpture is lacking, except for weak growth lamellae. Spiral sculpture consists of major and minor cords: three strong major cords on the body diminish in prominence anteriorly, one at the shoulder margin, one medial, and one basal; a single minor cord, between the upper two majors, is visible only on the varix; and on the upper canal is a series of two or three minor cords.

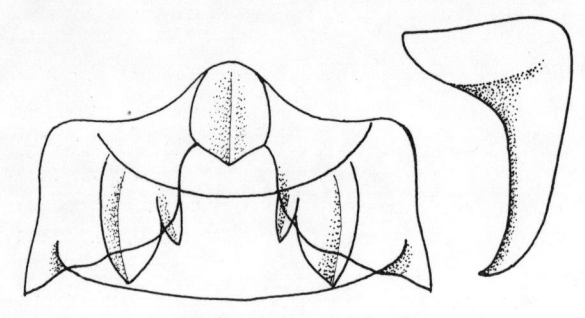

88. *Bizetiella carmen*, radular dentition

Shell color is white to waxy yellow-orange. In some specimens, intervarical blotches of brown are evident on the shoulder.

Central Gulf of California: Isla Angel de la Guarda to La Paz, and at Guaymas, Mexico.

See Pl. 23, fig. 7.

Bizetiella micaela Radwin & D'Attilio, 1972

Bizetiella micaela Radwin & D'Attilio, 1972: 343

The shell is small (maximum length 9 mm) and broadly fusiform. The spire is high and acute, consisting of two and one-half convex nuclear whorls and four and one-half strongly angulate postnuclear whorls. The suture is strongly impressed. The body whorl is moderately large and broadly fusoid. The aperture is moderately broad and ovate, with a broad, shallow anal sulcus. The posterior end of the outer apertural lip is arcuate, almost reaching the shoulder margin of the previous whorl; the margin of the outer apertural lip is erect, moderately thickened, and broadly, gently undulate, and eight denticles are apparent on the inner surface of the outer lip, two in the shoulder region and six below, the anteriormost the most prominent. The columellar lip is entirely adherent and smooth, except for a knoblike protuberance where the lip makes a sharp angle entering the siphonal canal. The siphonal canal is moderately short and open, bent to the right, and dorsally recurved.

The body whorl bears five low to moderately prominent varices. Spiral sculpture consists of two major cords of about equal size on the body, one at the shoulder margin and one near the base of the body, these intervarically ephemeral, prominent only immediately before and on the varices. Other sculpture is lacking.

Shell color is white, with two broad, transverse, interrupted, pale-red-brown bands, one just above the shoulder margin and one between the two spiral cords; the interrupted nature of these bands derives from their disappearance immediately after each varix, the markings being apparent just before and on each varix. The aperture is white, with a rosy-pink suffusion on the columella.

Known only from Bahía Coastocomate and Tamarindo Cove, Jalisco, Mexico.

See Pl. 23, fig. 6.

Bizetiella shaskyi Radwin & D'Attilio, 1972

Bizetiella shaskyi Radwin & D'Attilio, 1972: 347

The shell is moderately small (maximum length 13.5 mm) and rhomboid. The spire is high, consisting of three and one-half weakly convex nuclear whorls and five shouldered postnuclear whorls, and the shoulder region of each whorl is weakly concave. The suture is impressed and strongly undulate. The body whorl is moderately large and broadly fusoid. The aperture is broadly ovate, with a broad, shallow anal sulcus. The outer apertural lip is weakly thickened and nonerect; the inner surface of the outer apertural lip bears five lirae and a knobby swelling at the anterior end. The columellar lip is adherent, with a weak transverse ridge delimiting the left side of the anal sulcus, and with another ridge at the anterior end of the lip. The siphonal canal is open and short, the opening moderately broad; the canal is weakly bent to the left, and dorsally recurved.

The body whorl bears eight weakly defined varices. Intervarical axial sculpture is lacking. Spiral sculpture consists of major and minor cords; the shoulder region lacks sculpture. Anteriorly from the shoulder margin are a pair of major cords, a single minor, and another major, followed by another minor and a final major. Where the major cords intersect the varices, sharp, transversely elongate nodes are developed, most strongly on the uppermost pair of cords. The siphonal canal bears no spiral sculpture.

Shell color is pale blue-white, with spiral bands of cream-color subsuturally and on the canal. Numerous brown markings are apparent between the spiral cords, just before and on each varix.

Cabo Pulmo, Baja California, Islas Tres Marías and Bahía Banderas, Jalisco, Mexico, to Panamá and the Galápagos Islands, Ecuador.

See Pl. 23, fig. 1.

Genus EVOKESIA Radwin & D'Attilio, 1972

TYPE SPECIES: *Sistrum rufonotatum* Carpenter, 1864, by original designation.

The shell in this genus is small to moderately small (15–30 mm long), thin to moderately thick, fusiform to subfusiform, and nonvaricate. The spire is moderately high to very high and acute. The aperture is ovate and more or less constricted anteriorly. The outer apertural lip is thin to moderately thickened marginally and lirate to weakly denticulate within. The columellar lip is entirely adherent and smooth. Shell sculpture consists of sharply raised, transversely elongate nodes.

Although in many ways members of this genus resemble those in *Trachypollia*, a primary distinction may be seen in the radular dentition of the representative species of each (figs. 85 & 89).

Evokesia ferruginosa (Reeve, 1846)
Ricinula ferruginosa Reeve, 1846: sp. 50

The shell is moderately large (maximum length 23–30 mm) and fusiform. The spire is high and acute, consisting of three and one-half rapidly expanding, papillose nuclear whorls and six weakly angulate postnuclear whorls. The suture is weakly impressed to completely obscured. The body whorl is moderately large and subovate. The aperture is of moderate size and ovate, with a narrow, moderately deep anal sulcus angled toward the columella and a very weak transverse ridge forming the left side of the anal sulcus. The outer apertural lip is unthickened to weakly thickened and minutely marginally crenulate; its inner surface bears four more or less weakly developed denticles, these recessed a short distance into the aperture. The columellar lip is entirely adherent and smooth. The siphonal canal is short, open, bent to the left, and dorsally recurved.

The shell is essentially nonvaricate. Axial sculpture consists of seven to nine low costae, most prominent over the major spiral cords. Spiral sculpture consists of six major cords and numerous minor cords: immediately below the suture a single major cord; a cord at the shoulder margin, the most prominent major; three other majors distributed evenly over the lower half of the body; a single major at the top of the short siphonal canal; six minors separating the shoulder margin cord from the major cord below it; and in all other cases, four minors occupying the space between each two consecutive majors. Where the major cords intersect the costae, sharp, transversely elongate knobs are developed.

Shell color is uniformly dark brown-black, except for white areas on the major cords immediately after the knobs. These white areas are present erratically on all cords except the one at the shoulder margin, where they are consistent. The aperture is blue-gray, except for a dark-brown margin and white denticles. Typically, the shell is encrusted with coralline algae, and mature specimens frequently have a soft brown surface deposit on the spire.

Bahía Magdalena, Baja California, along the entire western shore of the Gulf of California, and on the eastern shore south to Guaymas (Sonora), Mexico.

See Pl. 3, fig. 5.

Evokesia grayi (Dall, 1889)
Nassaria (Nassarina) grayi Dall, 1889: 183

The shell is small for the genus (maximum length 16 mm) and broadly fusiform. The spire is high, consisting of two and one-half convex, granulose to minutely papillose nuclear whorls and five subangulate postnuclear whorls. The suture is weakly impressed and undulate. The body whorl is of moderate size and broadly fusoid. The aperture is ovate to lenticular, with a narrow, moderately deep anal sulcus. The outer apertural lip is thickened and barely erect; its inner surface bears six denticles of varying strengths. The columellar lip is adherent at its posterior end, becoming more or less detached and erect anteriorly. At the anterior end of the columella are three low pustules, the anteriormost of these extending along the left side of the opening of the siphonal canal as a low ridge. The siphonal canal is short, open, and dorsally recurved.

The body whorl bears seven prominent, rounded axial costae, the most prominent of these at the growing edge. Spiral sculpture consists of 14 weak cords, two on the shoulder, eight on the body, and four on the canal.

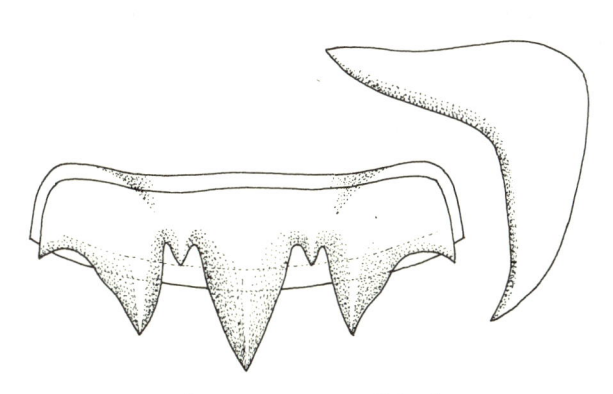

89. *Evokesia ferruginosa*, radular dentition

Shell color is pale waxy yellow, with a moderately broad, diffuse shoulder margin. The spiral cords are red-brown.

This species was originally named *Nassarina grayi* in Dall's (1889) "Blake Report," a presumptive familial placement (Columbellidae) that radular examination has proved untenable.

Off Barbados in moderately deep water (60–160 m).

See Pl. 23, fig. 4.

Evokesia rufonotata (Carpenter, 1864)

Sistrum (?*Ochrostoma* var.) *rufonotatum* Carpenter, 1864: 48

The shell is of moderate size (maximum length 20 mm) and heavily fusiform. The spire is high, consisting of three and one-half convex, rapidly expanding, granulose nuclear whorls and four to six weakly angulate postnuclear whorls. The suture is weakly impressed. The body whorl is moderately large and more or less swollen. The aperture is subovate and of moderate size, with a broad, moderately deep anal sulcus. The outer apertural lip is weakly erect and minutely crenulate; its inner surface bears five or six moderately weak lirae, these diminishing in strength anteriorly. The columellar lip is entirely adherent and smooth. The siphonal canal is short, open, weakly bent to the left, and dorsally recurved.

The essentially nonvaricate shell bears axial sculpture consisting of six to eight more or less strong costae, these most prominent at their intersections with the major spiral cords. Spiral sculpture consists of major and minor cords, these apparent only over the axial costae; the interspaces are devoid of spiral sculpture. The bare shoulder is followed by three major cords, one at the shoulder margin, one medial on the body, and one at the base of the body; minor cords alternate with these majors on the body, the upper half of the canal bearing two or three minor cords as well. Where the major spiral cords intersect the costae, moderately sharp, more or less prominent knobs are developed.

Shell color is white to light tan, with more or less consistent darker-brown markings on the receding slopes of the knobs. The apertural margin is white, with a marked gold suffusion more deeply within.

Shell proportions may vary with the population, since some specimens are short and obese and other specimens are more slender and more fusoid in shape.

Cabo Pulmo, Baja California, and Islas Tres Marías to Manzanillo and Islas Revillagigedo, Mexico, and the Galápagos Islands.

See Pl. 3, fig. 11.

Genus FAVARTIA Jousseaume, 1880

TYPE SPECIES: *Murex breviculus* Sowerby, 1834, by original designation.

This genus is composed of species with small (5–30 mm long), broadly fusiform shells. The spire is generally moderately high to high. The aperture is typically moderately small, and ovate and lirate within. The anal sulcus is weak, and the siphonal canal is generally short to moderate in length, narrowly open to the right, and more or less dorsally recurved. The body whorl bears three to seven flattened varices oriented perpendicularly to the shell surface, and more or less prominent. The spiral cords are usually scabrously laminate and may extend beyond the varical margin as short spines. In some species a gap in the spiral and axial sculpture is evident between the body and the siphonal canal.

Shell color ranges from gray to orange-pink or white. The aperture is white, in some species suffused with pink or red.

(See the Appendix for treatment of a new species assignable to *Favartia*.)

Favartia alveata (Kiener, 1842)

Murex alveatus Kiener, 1842: 94; *M. intermedius* C. B. Adams, 1850: 60 (not Brocchi, 1814: 400); *Aspella elegans* Perrilliat Montoya, in Vokes, 1971: 44, new name for *M. intermedius* C. B. Adams, 1850 (not Brocchi, 1814)

The shell is moderately small for the genus (maximum length 15 mm) and fusiform. The spire is high, consisting of one and one-half smooth, bulbous nuclear whorls and six weakly convex postnuclear whorls. The suture is strongly impressed. The body whorl is moderately small and fusoid. The aperture is small and subcircular, with no apparent anal sulcus. The outer apertural lip is erect and finely crenulate, reflecting the endings of the spiral sculptural elements. The columellar lip is detached and moderately erect. The siphonal canal is short, narrowly open to the right, and sharply, dorsally recurved at its distal end.

The body whorl bears five to seven well-elevated, rounded varices, these separated by broad interspaces. The varices are appressed to the preceding whorl in the shoulder region and are sharply undercut on their trailing edges. Spiral sculpture consists of six cords of equal size, five on the body and one on the canal. The sides of these cords bear laterally compressed, vaulted scales constituting expansions of axial lamellae that traverse the entire shell but are inconspicuous between the cords. Five fine, spiral striae incise the surface of each cord and the scales appressed to it. The leading edge of each varix is densely fimbriate.

Shell color is pale purple-brown, with two transverse brown bands, one at the suture and one on the lower half of the body. In nature, the presence of a moderately thick intritacalx, laid down as simple growth striae, frosts the entire shell in unworn specimens, imparting to the shell an all-white appearance. The aperture is white at its margin, two brown bands showing through in its recesses.

Bermuda to Brazil and offshore in the western Gulf of Mexico (Texas coast).

See Pl. 24, fig. 16.

Favartia balteata (Sowerby, 1841)

Murex balteatus Sowerby, 1841: pl. 191, fig. 83; *Ocinebra fuscofrondosa* Schepman, 1911: 349

The shell is large for the genus (maximum length 25 mm) and broadly fusiform. The spire is moderately high, consisting of one and one-half nuclear whorls and five or six angulate postnuclear whorls. The suture is impressed. The body whorl is moderately large and fusoid. The aperture is ovate, with a broad, shallow anal sulcus. The outer apertural lip is flattened above the shoulder margin, erect below it, and undulate at its margin; the inner surface of the outer lip is lirate. The columellar lip is adherent above, erect below. The siphonal canal is broad, short, narrowly open, and weakly recurved at its tip.

The body whorl bears five or six briefly frondose varices. Intervarical axial sculpture consists entirely of fine scabrous lamellae. Spiral sculpture consists of seven medially grooved major cords, five on the body and two on the canal. Intercalary cords of varying strengths alternate with these, except in the area between the body and the canal, where three or four consecutive minor cords are found. Where the cords intersect the varices, frondose, open spines are developed. Spines arising from major cords are dorsally recurved and diminish in strength anteriorly; spines arising from minor cords are generally bent ventrally.

Shell color is white to pale pink, with the tips of the foliated spines brown. A fine frosting of intritacalx is apparent in fresh specimens. The aperture is deep red-pink, most strongly on the columella.

Western Pacific from the Philippines to Queensland, Australia, in subtidal depths.

See Pl. 24, fig. 19.

Favartia brevicula (Sowerby, 1834)

Murex breviculus Sowerby, 1834: pl. 63, fig. 37

The shell is large for the genus (maximum length 25 mm, gerontic specimens to 35 mm) and massively rhomboidal. The spire is moderately high, consisting of five subangulate postnuclear whorls and a protoconch of undetermined nature. The suture is impressed. The body whorl is short and very heavy. The aperture is relatively small and ovate to subcircular, with a barely perceptible anal sulcus. The outer apertural lip is erect and broadly crenulate, reflecting the spiral sculptural elements; the inner surface of the outer lip is more or less lirate. The columellar lip is weakly detached and erect anteriorly. The siphonal canal is moderately long, barely open to the right, and strongly, dorsally recurved at its distal end.

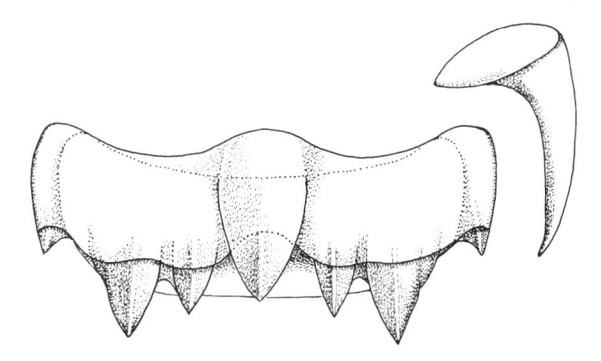

90. *Favartia brevicula*, radular dentition

The body whorl bears four broad varices that are bladelike on the shoulder, heavier below, and fimbriate on their leading edges. Spiral sculpture consists of five or six major cords, diminishing in strength anteriorly, the cords weak to ephemeral between the varices, strongly erect and recurved on the varix, imparting a deeply excavated aspect to the areas between the cords on the trailing edge of each varix.

Shell color is a dull chalky white, this derived from the hard shell itself and from a moderately thick intritacalx covering the unworn portions of the shell; in some cases the shell may be a dull gray. The aperture is porcelaneous white.

An unusual form of this species occurs at Ata'a, Malaita, British Solomon Islands, apparently living with the typical form and differing from it in having the ends of the spiral cords greatly elongated to form prolonged, open, blunt spines, these especially prominent at the shoulder margin.

Indo-West Pacific from Zanzibar, eastern Africa, to southeastern Japan and Fiji in shallow (intertidal) situations.

See Pl. 23, fig. 11; Pl. 24, figs. 1–2.

Favartia cellulosa (Conrad, 1846)

Murex cellulosus Conrad, 1846: 25; *M. nuceus* Mörch, 1850: 31; *M. jamaicensis* Sowerby, 1879: 39

The shell is moderately large for the genus (maximum length 28 mm) and broadly fusiform. The spire is high, consisting of one and one-half bulbous nuclear whorls and five to seven subangulate postnuclear whorls. The suture is well-marked but not impressed. The body whorl is of moderate size and fusoid. The aperture is of moderate size and ovate, with a moderately deep, U-shaped anal sulcus. The outer apertural lip is erect and crenulate marginally, the crenulations reflecting the spiral sculpture of the shell. The inner surface of the outer lip is undulate, the undulations corresponding to the crenulations on the lip margin. The columellar lip is adherent above, erect below. The siphonal canal is broad above, tapering distally, and narrowly open to the right.

The body whorl bears five varices, these blade-edged at the shoulder margin. Fine axial lamellae of varying strengths occur over the entire shell surface. Spiral sculpture consists of five major cords on the body and one on the canal; a few minor cords are evident on the shoulder, alternating at times with stronger elements. On the trailing edge of each varix the cords are strongly raised, causing the interspaces to appear deeply excavated.

Shell color is pale brown, strongest on the varices. This is covered in unworn specimens by a flat-white frosting of intritacalx, laid down in axial growth striae.

The shell of this species exhibits a good deal of variability in form. Its proportion of width to height (slenderness vs. obesity) and the development of the varices (large, rounded, thickly imbricate vs. slender, bladelike) are both variable. The heavy, thick form, approximating in appearance that of *Favartia incisa* (Broderip, 1833), has been called *F. cellulosa nucea* (Mörch, 1877) (Pl. 24, fig. 6).

Bermuda, the northeastern and western coasts of Florida offshore, and the Texas coast to southern Brazil.

See Pl. 24, figs. 4–6.

Favartia confusa (Brazier, 1877)

Pterynotus confusus Brazier, 1877: 172

We have not seen a specimen of this species; the following is taken, verbatim, from the original description:

"Shell somewhat pyriformly ovate, rather rough, spire short, sharp-pointed, whorls five and one-half, five varicose, on the whorl ending in the form of a canal, varices laminated, interstices between the varices crossed with four laminated ribs; on the last whorl below somewhat smooth, forming hollow pits, suture minutely laminated, the varices on the upper whorls small, more like rounded nodules, laminated and excavated behind, white stained with brown between the varices, aperture roundly ovate, interior of the aperture glossy white, edge of peristome denticulated, canal rather short, attenuated and recurved. Length: 13.5 lines. Breadth: 7.5 lines. Height: 6.5 lines [1 line equals 2.11 mm].

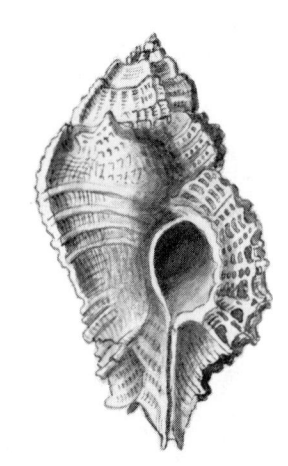

91. *Favartia confusa*

"This beautiful shell was brought up in the tangles from the depth of thirty fathoms (60 m), white sand and coral bottom."

Darnley Island, Torres Strait.

?Favartia crossei (Lienard, 1873)

Murex crossei Lienard, 1873: 285

The shell is small (maximum length 15 mm) and stoutly biconical. The spire is high and slender, consisting of five or six convex to barely angulate, ventricose postnuclear whorls and a protoconch of undetermined nature. The suture is moderately impressed. The body whorl is small to moderate in size and stoutly trigonal. The aperture is moderately small and ovate, with a moderately deep and broad anal sulcus. The outer apertural lip is barely erect, if at all; its inner surface bears six moderately strong denticles, these becoming lirae more deeply within. The columellar lip is entirely adherent; a weak node delimits the left side of the anal sulcus at its posterior end, a single weak plica is evident at the midpoint of the anal sulcus, and a pair of weak, oblique-elongate pustules are apparent at its anterior end. The siphonal canal is very short, open, and slightly bent to the right and dorsally.

The body whorl bears four sharp-crested, oblique varices separated by moderately broad interspaces. Spiral sculpture consists of four major cords, these moderately strong just before and on the varices and obsolete between them; the two posterior cords are close together, the cords otherwise evenly spaced.

The ground color of the shell is white, with pale-brown markings between cords on the lower part of the body. The aperture is suffused with violet.

In gerontic individuals the shell has quite a different character: it becomes exaggeratedly coarse and heavy, and all the varices become huge and thickened, imparting an obtuse appearance to the typically slender spire.

Our specimens are from the Line Islands (Christmas Island and Palmyra Island); the type locality is Mauritius.

See Pl. 24, figs. 17–18.

Favartia cyclostoma (Sowerby, 1841)

Murex cyclostomus Sowerby, 1841: pl. 194, fig. 95;
M. nucula Reeve, 1845: sp. 31

The shell is moderately small for the genus (maximum length 15 mm) and broadly fusiform. The spire is high, consisting of five or six angulate postnuclear whorls and a protoconch of undetermined nature. The suture is impressed. The body whorl is of moderate size and fusoid. The aperture is moderately small and ovate, with a shallow anal sulcus. The outer apertural lip is erect and strongly, marginally undulate; its inner surface bears several pairs of weak denticles. The columellar lip is weakly erect above, detached and erect below. The siphonal canal is moderately short, narrowly open to the right, and distally recurved.

The body whorl bears six or seven varices. Other axial sculpture consists of fine axial lamellae, close-set between the cords, developing into scales on the cords. Spiral sculpture consists of six strong cords, equally spaced on the body; the cord at the shoulder margin and the two on the shoulder are the most prominent of those on the body whorl; the canal bears two cords, which terminate on the varices as short, recurved spines.

The leading edge of each varix is markedly fimbriate; the trailing edge is deeply excavated between spiral cords, the cords themselves finely, spirally striate.

Shell color is white, with scattered brown blotches. The entire shell, when unworn, is covered with a moderately thick intritacalx, laid down as axial growth striae.

Reported by Reeve and Sowerby from the Philippines. Known to us from Zanzibar, East Africa.

See Pl. 24, fig. 11.

Favartia emersoni, new name

Murex gravidus Hinds, 1844: 128 (not Dujardin, 1837)

The shell is moderately small for the genus (maximum length 16 mm) and broadly fusiform. The spire is high, consisting of about two and one-fourth nuclear whorls and four weakly convex postnuclear whorls. The suture is weakly impressed. The body whorl is moderately large and rounded. The aperture is small and ovate, with a broad and very shallow anal sulcus. The outer apertural lip is erect and strongly undulate at its margin; the inner surface of the outer lip is strongly lirate. The columellar lip is detached and strongly erect. The siphonal canal is moderately long, narrowly open to the right, and distally recurved.

The body whorl bears five heavy, fimbriate varices, reflected away from the direction of growth, producing a concavity in the receding edge. Axial growth striae composed mainly of intritacalx may be seen between the varices. Spiral sculpture consists of seven cords on the body below the shoulder margin, three major and four minor intercalary cords, and a few almost obsolete cords on the shoulder. Between the body and the canal there is a marked gap in prominent sculpture, the area bearing only six low threads. The canal bears two major cords. All cords are scabrous, but on the leading edge of each varix they become densely imbricate; in this area the scales coalesce to form undulate lamellae.

Shell color is white, overlaid with a thick frosting of flat-white intritacalx. The aperture is porcelaneous white.

This species was originally described as *Murex gravidus* Hinds, 1844, a name preoccupied by *M. gravidus* Dujardin, 1837, a fossil species. The present replacement name is here introduced in honor of Dr. William K. Emerson, American Museum of Natural History.

Western coast of Africa: Cape Blanco, Mauritania, to Luanda Harbor, Angola.

See Pl. 24, fig. 7.

Favartia erosa (Broderip, 1833)

Murex erosus Broderip, 1833: 174

The shell is of moderate size (maximum length 15 mm), fusiform, and somewhat flattened dorsoventrally. The spire is high, consisting of two and one-half nuclear whorls and six or seven weakly convex postnuclear whorls. The suture is impressed. The body whorl is fusoid but somewhat truncate. The aperture is relatively small and ovate, with a shallow anal sulcus. The outer apertural lip is marginally erect below the shoulder margin, with crenulations reflecting the crests of the spiral sculptural elements; the inner surface of the outer lip is weakly lirate. The columellar lip is smooth. The siphonal canal is short, truncate, narrowly open, and distally recurved.

92. *Favartia erosa*, enlarged microsculpture

The spire whorls bear six strongly raised varices. On the body whorl the last varix and the one opposite it are more strongly developed, causing the remaining four varices, all of equal size, to appear weak. The varices are raised in buttresses and cross the shoulder to adhere to the preceding whorl. The growth lines are raised to form fine lamellae between the spiral cords. Spiral sculpture consists of six strongly raised, concave-sided cords on the body whorl, distributed from the shoulder margin to the base of the body. Between the body and the siphonal canal there is a broad, excavated gap in spiral sculpture, traversed by the axial elements (varices). The axial-growth lamellae are laterally flattened on each side of the base and at the crest of each cord, this imparting a bilaterally squamose appearance to the intersection of a lamella and a cord. The leading edge of each varix is moderately densely fimbriate.

Shell color is generally purple-gray or purple-brown, with varying proportions of creamy-white transverse banding; the varices and the aperture are also predominantly creamy white. On mature, unworn specimens the entire shell is often covered by a translucent intritacalx.

Mazatlán, Mexico, to Panamá and the Galápagos Islands.

See Pl. 24, figs. 20–21.

Favartia funafutiensis (Hedley, 1899)

Murex funafutiensis Hedley, 1899: 458

We have not seen a specimen of this shell; the following is taken, verbatim, from the original description:

"Shell small, biconical. Colour ochraceous buff, banded with chocolate, interior of aperture pale lilac. Whorls seven, sculptured each with seven prominent varices, which mount the spire continuously and obliquely. On the spire each varix presents a hollow spine above a blunt tubercle. Between and parallel to the varices are a series of imbricating lamellae. Five spiral ridges run round the shoulder of the shell, and undulate both the blades and the interstices of the varices. The

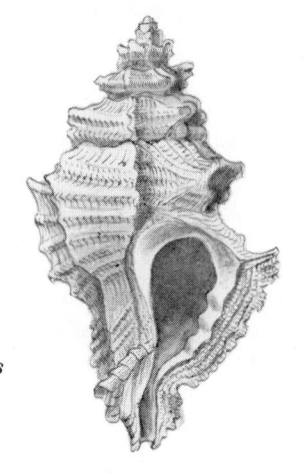

93. *Favartia funafutiensis*

lamellae are likewise microscopically beaded by minute spiral threads. The aperture is oblique, ovate, choked by an inner tuberculate ridge and by the great development of the columella; the latter is arched, deeply obliquely entering, anteriorly with two incipient tubercles, and truncate below. Canal short, open, and recurved; above it are two series of disused canals, corresponding to the ultimate and penultimate varices. Length 9 mm, breadth 5 mm.

"One specimen, taken by tangles, at a depth of 40–80 fathoms [80–160 m], on the western slope of Funafuti [Atoll, southwestern Pacific]."

Favartia garrettii (Pease, 1868)
Murex garrettii Pease, 1868: 103, new name for *M. exiguus* Garrett, 1857: 102 (not Broderip, 1833: 175)

The tiny, obese shell may reach 5 mm in length. The spire is high, consisting of four shouldered postnuclear whorls and a protoconch of undetermined nature. The suture is impressed. The body whorl is ventricose and of moderate size. The aperture is of moderate size and ovate, with little or no perceptible anal sulcus. The outer apertural lip is thickened and nonerect; its inner surface is weakly, spirally grooved, this imparting to the lip a weakly lirate appearance. The columellar lip is entirely adherent and smooth. The siphonal canal is short and rather sharply bent to the left.

The body whorl bears six weak varices, each consisting of a single low ridge extending from the suture to the tip of the canal, or of an interrupted ridge made up of aligned nodes on the spiral cords. The leading edge of the varix is fimbriate. Spiral sculpture consists of five rather strong cords on the body, the uppermost one at the shoulder margin, and a single cord on the canal. Between the body and the canal there is a brief but notable gap in spiral sculpture. A series of fine, erect lamellae may connect consecutive spiral cords between the varices.

Shell color is waxy white, with a single diffuse red-brown band on the shoulder and one at the base of the body.

Known to us only from the Hawaiian Islands.
See Pl. 24, fig. 10.

Favartia incisa (Broderip, 1833)
Murex incisus Broderip, 1833: 176

The shell is large for the genus (maximum length 30 mm) and obese-fusiform. The spire is moderately high, consisting of two and one-half nuclear whorls and five weakly convex postnuclear whorls. The suture is, for the most part, obscured by the massive varices. The body whorl is obese. The aperture is moderately small and ovate, with an insignificant anal sulcus. The outer apertural lip is barely erect and finely crenulate, the crenulations reflecting the spiral sculpture of the shell; the inner surface of the outer lip is strongly lirate. The columellar lip is adherent above, detached and weakly erect below. The siphonal canal is broad, narrowly open to the right, and distally recurved.

The body whorl bears six or seven large, rounded varices of such breadth that intervarical areas are obliterated. The uppermost portion of each varix, as it crosses the shoulder, is excavated on its receding edge and reaches the next whorl. The areas between varices on the shoulder are depressed and basinlike. Spiral sculpture on the body consists of nine strong, rounded, tightly fimbriate cords, distributed from the suture to the base of the body. The siphonal canal bears three or four cords. The body sculpture is set off from that of the canal by a narrow gap carrying either no spiral sculpture or spiral elements of much diminished strength. The body bears from one to three minor, erratically occurring cords.

Shell color is chalky white, at times stained with red-brown on the varices or on the spiral cords. The entire surface of unworn specimens bears a frosting of white intritacalx laid down in the form of growth striae. The aperture is porcelaneous white.

Bahía Banderas, Mexico, to Ecuador and the Galápagos Islands.
See Pl. 24, fig. 8.

Favartia kurodai Nakamigawa & Habe, 1964
Favartia kurodai Nakamigawa & Habe, 1964: 25, 27

We have not seen a specimen of this species; the following is taken, verbatim, from the original description:

"The shell is small, solid, [resembling an] elongated pentagonal pyramid in shape, [this appearance imparted] by the five strong axial varices. The surface is strongly sculptured and light brown in color, but usually soiled by calcareous dust [?intritacalx]. The whorls are six in number, the two embryonic ones smooth and polished, but generally eroded in adult [individuals]. The succeeding four whorls each have three spiral cords, the upper one being weak and the other two very strong, with a deep groove between them. The varices are five on each whorl and beset with equal intervals, and the growth threads are distinct and somewhat lamellate crossing the spiral cords and grooves. The body whorl is large, higher than broad, occupying about three-fifths of the length of the shell, and narrowed toward the anterior end, and has nine spiral cords and five strong varices and many weak growth lines. The aperture is rather small, ovate in shape, narrowing towards the rather long and narrow anterior siphonal canal. The outer side of the columellar margin is expanded by the last varix, forming short scales corresponding with the grooves on the outer surface, and its inner wall has six white teeth regularly arranged. The inner margin is edged by the erect lip, and extends over the parietal wall. The siphonal canal is narrow and rather long and open. The umbilical chink between the fasciole and columellar wall of the canal is narrow.

"Height, 11.7 mm; breadth, 5.8 mm (holotype). Height, 9.8 mm; breadth, 5.5 mm (paratype). Height, 9.7 mm; breadth, 5.0 mm (paratype)."

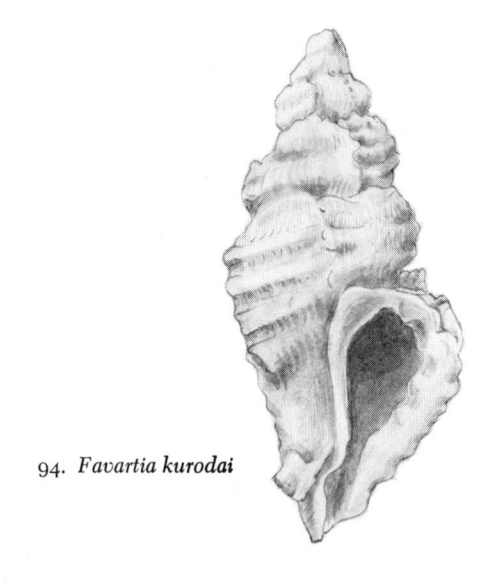

94. *Favartia kurodai*

95. *Favartia marjoriae*

aperture is rotundly ovate; the outer apertural lip is prettily multifimbriate, white to straw-colored, coarse [solid], the inner surface is shining [white], bearing nine or ten crenulations; siphonal canal briefly rostrate, almost closed."

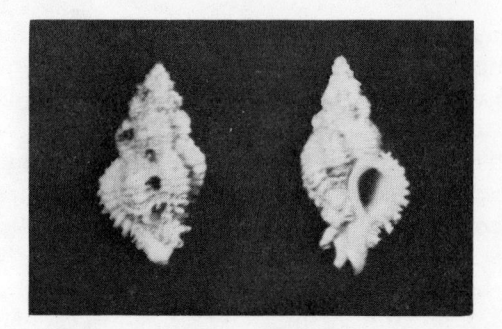

Known only from the Persian Gulf (type locality).

Favartia minatauros, new name

Murex obtusus Sowerby, 1894: 41 (not Bellardi, 1872, or Sowerby, 1879)

The shell is moderately large (maximum length 25 mm) and ovate in general form. The spire is high, blunt, and barely convex, with five poorly defined postnuclear whorls and a protoconch of undetermined nature. The suture is almost completely obscured. The body whorl is short and heavy. The aperture is small and subcircular, with a barely perceptible anal sulcus. The outer apertural lip is not appreciably erect beyond the thickened varix but is weakly crenulate, the crenulations reflecting the spiral cords on the shell surface; its inner surface is smooth. The columellar lip is adherent above, detached and strongly erect below. The siphonal canal is short, very broad, narrowly open to the right, and strongly distally recurved.

The body whorl bears three large, heavy, rounded, thickened varices, nonaligned from whorl to whorl. Each varix on a given whorl is about midway between two varices on the preceding whorl. The varices project laterally most strongly near the base of the body, the steeply sloping shoulder region occupying more than half of the body. Intervarical spaces are not depressed, as is typical for the genus, this tending to diminish the distinction between the varices and the spaces between them. Each varix crosses the shoulder and is appressed to the preceding whorl. Spiral sculpture consists of six major cords of approximately equal size. Axial lamellae are obsolete over the spiral cords but are strongly in evidence between

Known to us only from Minatu, Izu Peninsula, Honshu, Japan (type locality).

See Pl. 14, fig. 12.

Favartia marjoriae (Melvill & Standen, 1903)

Murex marjoriae Melvill & Standen, 1903: 308

We have not seen a specimen of this shell; the following is translated from the original Latin:

"Murex, the shell solid, ovate-oblong, whitish gray, the whorls six, entirely costate, the costae very solid, varicose [i.e. forming varices], each composed of six fimbriae [leaves or layers]; each of five moderately angulate postnuclear whorls bears heavy, solid, squamate-lirate cords; the them, imparting a reticulate texture to the shell surface.

Shell color is white to light gray, covered with a moderately thin, white, finely spirally striate intritacalx. The aperture is pale violet.

Known to us only from the type locality, Mauritius.

See Pl. 24, fig. 3.

Favartia minirosea (Abbott, 1954)

Ocenebra (Ocinebrina) minirosea Abbott, 1954: 43

The shell is tiny (maximum length 10 mm) and fusiform. The spire is high, consisting of one and one-half convex nuclear whorls and four or five convex postnuclear whorls. The suture is well-impressed. The body whorl is of moderate size and fusoid. The aperture is moderately small and ovate to subcircular, with a bare indication of an anal sulcus. The outer apertural lip is erect and weakly crenulate at its margin; its inner surface is weakly lirate. The columellar lip is adherent at its posterior end but detached and weakly erect for its remaining length. The siphonal canal is moderately long, bent to the left, and barely open.

The body whorl bears seven moderately weak varices. Spiral sculpture consists of seven weak major cords on the shoulder and the body; between adjacent major cords is a single minor cord of almost the same size as a major. The canal bears four minor cords.

Shell color is pale fleshy pink to pale orange or yellow. The aperture is white.

Known only from the eastern Gulf of Mexico in moderately deep water (50–100 m).

See Pl. 29, fig. 16.

Favartia munda (Reeve, 1849)

Murex mundus Reeve, 1849: *Murex errata*, new name for *M. exiguus* Reeve, 1845 (not Broderip, 1833: 175)

The shell is small (maximum length 13 mm) and fusiform. The spire is moderately high, consisting of one and one-half nuclear whorls and four angulate postnuclear whorls. The suture is impressed. The body whorl is broadly fusoid. The aperture is of moderate size and ovate, with a wide, inverted-V-shaped anal sulcus. The outer apertural lip is weakly erect and undulate on its inner surface. The columellar lip is adherent above, weakly erect below. The siphonal canal is relatively very short, narrowly open, and weakly, distally recurved.

The body whorl bears four or five relatively weak varices. The intervarical areas are broad and bald, except immediately before and after each varix. Spiral sculpture consists of five cords on the body, a single weaker cord between the body and the canal, two others on the canal, and another weak cord on the shoulder, this bent back to form a spinelike projection; the cords are weak to ephemeral between varices, stronger just before and after each varix.

Shell color is pale rusty brown, strongest on the varices and on the spiral cords. A thin intritacalx covers unworn specimens. The aperture is white.

Known only from southeastern Japan.

See Pl. 24, fig. 14.

Favartia peasei (Tryon, 1880)

Murex peasei Tryon, 1880: 129, new name for *M. foveolatus* Pease, 1869 (not Hinds, 1844)

The shell is small for the genus (maximum length 16 mm) and roughly fusiform or narrowly biconic. The spire is high and subacute, consisting of five convex postnuclear whorls and a protoconch of undetermined nature. The suture is obscured by strong sculptural elements on the shoulder. The body whorl is stoutly fusoid. The aperture is small and ovate, with a very narrow, shallow anal sulcus. The outer apertural lip is somewhat erect and weakly, marginally crenulate; the inner surface is weakly undulate, corresponding to the crenulations on the lip margin. The columellar lip is detached and erect, except for a tiny adherent area at its posterior end. The siphonal canal is short and stout, barely open, and abruptly, dorsally turned at its distal end; at its upper (i.e. posterior) end, the right margin briefly overlaps the left but is not fused with it.

The body whorl bears six heavy, low varices. Earlier whorls bear seven varices. Spiral sculpture consists chiefly of five coarse, heavy major cords: one on the shoulder, three on the body, and one on the canal. Otherwise, there are several finer cords or threads on the shoulder and on the canal. Numerous fine axial lamellae cover the shell; where these intersect the major cords, marked, laterally compressed, vaulted scales are produced. Rather deep spaces separate the major cords, and large, excavated areas are apparent on the shoulder and at the base of the body. The last varix is moderately well-developed into a rather broad, flangelike structure, briefly dorsally reflected at its margin; the leading edge of the last varix is densely fimbriate, the fimbriae producing a draped effect, this imparted by the undulations of the fimbriae, and radial struts that correspond to the major spiral cords. Earlier varices are not as well-developed as the last.

Shell color is pale yellow-white, overlaid by a thick, flat-white intritacalx. The aperture is porcelaneous white.

The true identity of *Favartia peasei* (Tryon, 1880) is a subject requiring some discussion. *F. peasei* was first described by Pease (1869) as *Murex foveolatus*, with the type locality given as "La Paz, in sinu Californica." Tryon (1880), recognizing the homonymy of this name with the earlier *M. foveolatus* Hinds, 1844 (now assigned to *Ocenebra*), introduced a new name for the species, *M. peasei* Tryon, 1880. Subsequent authors have searched for the identity of this species among Panamic species without much success until Keen (1958) suggested that *Tritonalia margaritensis* Dall MS, a Panamic form, as illustrated in M. Smith (1939), might be *M. peasei*. Subsequent collectors of that form have thus identified it as "*Murex*" *peasei*. Recently we encountered, in the collection of the Academy of Natural Sciences, Philadelphia, where most of Pease's types are deposited, a specimen clearly labeled as the holotype of *Murex foveolatus* Pease (automatically the type of *M. peasei*, since a name change would not occasion the selection of a distinct type). Interestingly, no locality was given on the label, but a second lot with a label written in the same handwriting and identical ink contains conspecific specimens and is localized as "Viti [i.e. Fiji] Islands." This led to a reexamination of one lot of unidentified specimens in the D'Attilio collection from Ata'a, Malaita, British Solomon Islands, and the realization that these, too, are conspecific. Apparently, the type locality given with the original description is erroneous, probably because Pease was working concurrently on a paper on Polynesian mollusks.

This leaves the Panamic form, misidentified as *Favartia peasei*, without a valid name. The reader is requested to turn to the appendix for a treatment of *F. poormani* sp. nov., as we propose to call this form.

Known only from the western Pacific (type locality not noted; other specimens studied from Fiji and from Ata'a, Malaita, British Solomon Islands).

See Pl. 29, figs. 6–7.

Favartia planilirata (Reeve, 1845)

Murex planiliratus Reeve, 1845: sp. 149

The shell is of moderate size for the genus (maximum length 26 mm) and broadly fusiform. The spire is high and acute and consists of one and one-half sharply shouldered nuclear whorls and five weakly subangulate postnuclear whorls. The suture is well-impressed. The body whorl is of moderate size and fusoid. The aperture is of moderate size and ovate, with a moderately broad, shallow anal sulcus. The outer apertural lip is briefly erect and finely serrate, the serrations reflecting the sculpture of the shell. The columellar lip is largely detached and erect, but adherent at its posterior end; one or two low pustules may be apparent at the anterior end of the inner lip. The siphonal canal is of moderate length, slender, narrowly open, and bent dorsally.

The body whorl bears six moderately low, rather sharp-crested varices. Spiral sculpture consists of 13 moderately strong cords, almost square in cross section; each cord is separated from its neighbors by a deeply cut channel. The shell is covered with numerous fine axial-growth lamellae; and where the cords intersect the lamellae, partially erect scales are formed, these imparting a finely scabrous texture to the entire shell.

Shell color is off-white to pale tan-white, with a longitudinal band of purple-white after each varix and extending one-half to two-thirds of the distance across the intervarical space. The apertural margin is porcelaneous white; the above-mentioned darker longitudinal band is apparent more deeply within the aperture.

According to Ponder (1972), *F. planilirata* is distributed on the southern coast of Australia from Wilson's Promontory to Perth, Western Australia. Our specimens are from Woodman's Point, Cockburn Sound, ca. 4 km south of Fremantle (just south of Perth), Western Australia.

See Pl. 14, fig. 6.

Favartia rosea Habe, 1961

Favartia rosea Habe, 1961: 49

The shell is of moderate size (maximum length 20 mm) and broadly fusiform. The spire is high, consisting of six convex postnuclear whorls and a protoconch of undetermined nature. The suture is deeply impressed and undulate. The body whorl is of moderate size and fusoid. The aperture is ovate, with a barely discernible anal sulcus. The outer apertural lip is minutely crenulate, the crenulations reflecting the surface sculpture; the inner surface of the outer lip is weakly lirate. The columellar lip is adherent above, detached and erect below; three to five weak pustules are apparent on the lip at the base of the columella. The siphonal canal is slender, tubular, barely open to the right, and dorsally recurved.

The body whorl bears four or five strong, widely

spaced varices, triangular in cross section (broad at the base, sharp at the apex). Intervarical axial sculpture, where present, consists of weak ridges. Spiral sculpture consists of two major cords on the shoulder and seven on the body; the cords are strong just before and on the varices and ephemeral between them; each cord is divided in half lengthwise by a strongly incised groove. Between the canal and the body there is a gap in major spiral sculpture; several minor cords in the gap are followed by two major cords and several minor ones on the canal. The leading edge of each varix is finely but densely fimbriate.

Shell color is pale fleshy orange-yellow to coral-pink, darkest on the varices; in unworn specimens this is overlaid between the varices by a thin, frosting-like intritacalx. The aperture is white marginally, pale purple-pink within.

Known only from southeastern Japan.
See Pl. 24, fig. 12.

Favartia salmonea (Melvill & Standen, 1899)

Murex pumilus A. Adams, 1854: 70 (not Broderip, 1833: 175); *M. (Ocinebra) salmoneus* Melvill & Standen, 1899: 162

The shell is of moderate size (maximum length 21 mm) and broadly fusiform. The spire is high, consisting of one and one-half nuclear whorls and six moderately convex postnuclear whorls. The suture is distinct but not impressed. The body whorl is moderately large and broadly fusoid. The aperture is ovate to subcircular, with a barely perceptible anal sulcus. The outer apertural lip is minutely crenulate, the crenulations reflecting the spiral shell sculpture; the inner surface of the outer lip is weakly, briefly lirate. The columellar lip is adherent above, detached and erect below, and smooth over the columella. The siphonal canal is moderately short and broad, narrowly open to the right, and briefly recurved at its tip.

The body whorl bears six prominent, widely spaced varices. Spiral sculpture consists of five major cords, these occurring from the shoulder margin to the base of the body; two or three ephemeral minor cords may be present on the shoulder, and another one may occur between the third and fourth major cords from the shoulder margin. A gap in the spiral sculpture is followed on the canal by one or two major cords. The cords are evident between the varices and are strongly elevated on the trailing edge of each varix. The leading edge of each varix is strongly fimbriate.

Shell color is fleshy pinkish-orange, darkest on the varices; the intervarical areas are paler, owing to the presence of a thin, white intritacalx. The aperture is orange-pink.

Known to occur in eastern Africa (Zanzibar, Mozambique), Mauritius, and off northeastern and eastern Australia (Queensland).
See Pl. 24, fig. 15.

Favartia tetragona (Broderip, 1833)

Murex tetragonus Broderip, 1833: 174

The shell is of moderate size for the genus (maximum length 20 mm) and broadly fusiform. The spire is high, consisting of five subangulate postnuclear whorls and a protoconch of undetermined nature. The suture is well-impressed. The body whorl is broadly fusiform and of moderate size. The aperture is moderately small and ovate, with little or no trace of an anal sulcus. The outer apertural lip is erect and marginally serrate or crenulate, the projections forming this edge reflecting the spiral sculpture of the shell surface, as do the crenulations on the inner surface of the outer lip. The columellar lip is erect, except at its posterior end, where it is adherent and forms a tiny callus. The siphonal canal is moderately short, barely open, and dorsally recurved at its tip.

96. *Favartia tetragona*

The body whorl bears three broad, flangelike varices of broadly triangular cross section. Each varix is brief on the shoulder, most prominent at the shoulder margin and below, and extends to the point at which the canal bends sharply dorsally. Earlier whorls appear to have four varices, and the first few postnuclear whorls bear five or six varices. Each varix extends posteriorly over the shoulder and is appressed to the former whorl, thus forming a buttress that interrupts the continuity of the shoulder. Spiral sculpture consists of four major cords, one on the shoulder and three on the body; one or two minor cords are apparent above the major cord on the shoulder, and another one is apparent between the shoulder-margin cord and the major cord anterior to it. The canal bears five to seven minor cords. Each of the major cords is divided into parts by incised lines on its crest and sides: the shoulder-margin cord bears two such lines on its crest and one on its anterior flank; the shoulder cord bears two lines on its crest; the other two cords bear one or two lines in the same position. The leading edge of the last varix is densely fimbriate, the fimbriae arranged in a draped fashion between straight radial lines, the lines not corresponding to the spiral sculptural elements on the outer (trailing) edge of the varix.

Shell color is translucent blue-white, under a flat-white, lamellose intritacalx.

Known to us from Wading Island, Fiji Islands, and Bohol and Luzon Islands, Philippine Islands.

See Pl. 14, fig. 3.

Genus MAXWELLIA Baily, 1950

TYPE SPECIES: *Murex gemma* Sowerby, 1879, by original designation.

Species in this genus generally have small to moderate-sized fusiform shells, with some unusual features of shell morphology held in common. Generally the spire is low to moderately high. The siphonal canal is moderately long, curved to the left, fused at the top, and barely open below. The varices, five or six per whorl, are very long, extending from the shoulder margin to the tip of the siphonal canal. Each varix is well-developed, more or less strongly reflected dorsally, and generally deflected or twisted at the base of the body. On the shoulder the dorsal reflection of each varix causes a small pointed spine to closely approach the preceding varix; this feature, together with the otherwise shallow intervarical spaces, imparts a sunken or excavated appearance to the intervarical space on the shoulder. The varical margin may bear numerous more or less prominent spines, and the leading edge of the varix is more or less finely or coarsely fimbriate.

Maxwellia angermeyerae (Emerson & D'Attilio, 1965)

Aspella (Favartia) angermeyerae Emerson & D'Attilio, 1965: 1

The shell is small for the genus (maximum length 25 mm) and subfusiform. The spire is of moderate height, consisting of two and one-half nuclear whorls rising towerlike from the first of four shouldered postnuclear whorls. The suture is entirely obscured by the subsequent whorl, which reaches to just above the shoulder margin of the previous whorl. The body whorl is large and subfusoid. The aperture is ovate, with a narrow, shallow anal sulcus that is swept into a posterior-pointing, V-shaped callus. The outer apertural lip is strongly erect and coarsely crenulate, its inner surface essentially completely smooth. The columellar lip is essentially entirely adherent and callused. The siphonal canal is moderately long, fused above, barely open below, and bent to the left and dorsally.

The body whorl bears five low, heavy varices, twisted and swollen at the base of the body. Intervarical axial sculpture is lacking. Spiral sculpture consists of eight or nine major cords: one on the shoulder, six on the body, and one or two on the canal. The cords are almost obsolete intervarically, becoming subnodose over the varix. Between the major cords and climbing their flanks almost to their crests there are numerous low threads.

Shell color is white, with dark purple-black varical nodes; the entire shell is covered with a thin, simple, white intritacalx, through which the nodes appear blue-white.

Apparently limited to the Galápagos Islands.

See Pl. 19, fig. 14.

Maxwellia gemma (Sowerby, 1879)

Murex gemma Sowerby, 1879: 32

The shell is of moderate size (maximum length 40 mm) and fusiform. The spire is moderately high and subacute, consisting of five convex postnuclear whorls and a protoconch of undetermined nature. The suture is deeply impressed where not obscured by the subsequent whorl. The body whorl is moderately large and fusoid. The aperture is subcircular, with no apparent anal sulcus. The outer apertural lip is more or less weakly erect and obsoletely crenulate; its inner surface is broadly undulate, the troughs reflecting the spiral cords on the shell's outer surface. The columellar lip is almost entirely detached and erect and is generally well callused. The siphonal canal is

97. *Maxwellia gemma*, radular dentition

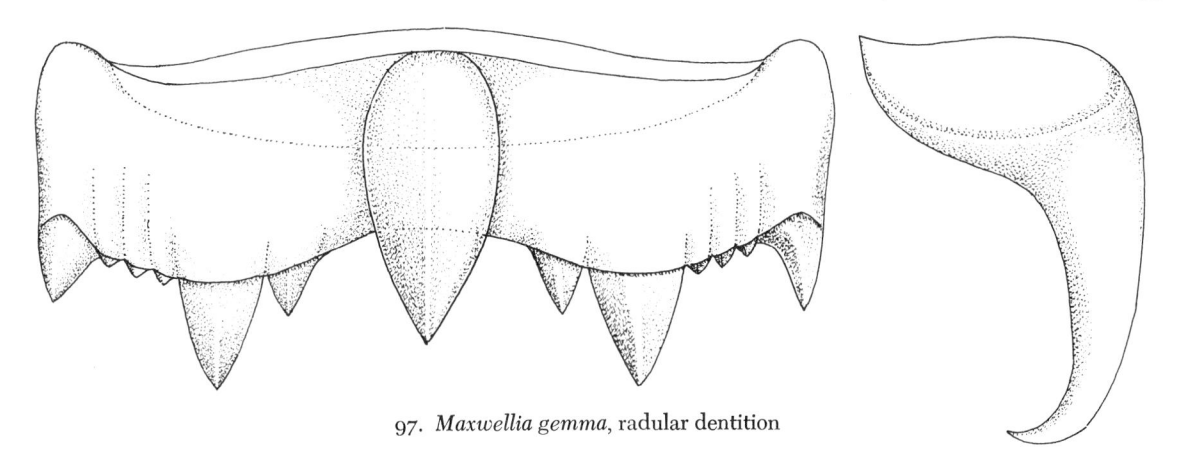

moderately long, barely open (or fused at the body end), and curved to the left and dorsally.

The body whorl bears five heavy, strongly dorsally reflected varices, each extending from its point of contact near the shoulder margin of the preceding whorl to the tip of the canal. The narrow intervarical space lacks additional axial sculpture. Spiral sculpture consists of ten low cords: two on the shoulder, six on the body, and two on the canal. Many of these cords, especially those on the shoulder and at the base of the body, end at the varical margin in short, largely closed, strongly dorsally reflected spines. The leading edge of each varix is very finely to obsoletely fimbriate.

Shell color is white, with a single broad, transverse brown band at and just below the shoulder margin. Over this area and over the remainder of the shell is a series of dark-brown spiral lines corresponding to the spiral cords. In unworn shells a thin to moderately thick, white intritacalx covers all this coloration.

Santa Barbara, California, to Isla Asunción, Baja California.

See Pl. 19, fig. 17.

?Maxwellia santarosana (Dall, 1905)

Murex fimbriatus A. Adams, 1854: 71 (not Brocchi, 1814, Lamarck, 1822, De France, 1827, or Michelotti, 1841); *Murex (Phyllonotus) santarosana* Dall, 1905: 14

The shell is of moderate size (maximum length 42 mm) and fusiform. The spire is high, consisting of six postnuclear whorls and a protoconch of undetermined nature. The suture is well-impressed where not obscured by the subsequent whorl. The body whorl is moderately large and fusoid. The aperture is subcircular to ovate, with a barely perceptible anal sulcus. The outer apertural lip is barely erect and finely crenulate. Except for the small crenulations at its margin, the inner surface of the outer apertural lip is smooth. The columellar lip is smooth, entirely adherent to weakly erect, and callused. The siphonal canal is moderately long, fused above, barely open below, and bent to the left and dorsally.

The body whorl bears six prominent, strongly dorsally reflected varices, each extending from the shoulder margin of the preceding whorl to the end of the canal. Intervarical axial sculpture is lacking. Spiral sculpture consists of major and minor cords. The major cords end at the varical margin in short, strongly reflected spines, the strongest at the shoulder margin. Spiral sculpture is also lacking intervarically but is apparent on the varices. The very shallow intervarical spaces become excavated on the shoulder and are partially covered by the shoulder-margin spine and the remainder of the exaggeratedly reflected shoulder portion of the varix. The leading edge of the varix is richly, finely fimbriate.

Shell color is white, with the leading edge of each varix stained ochre-brown. The intervarical spaces and the canal may be covered by a simple, moderately thick, white intritacalx. The aperture is porcelaneous white.

Point Estero, California, to Bahía San Bartolomé, Baja California; reported (questionably) from the Gulf of California.

See Pl. 19, figs. 15–16.

Genus MUREXIELLA
Clench & Pérez Farfante, 1945

TYPE SPECIES: *Murex hidalgoi* Crosse, 1869, by original designation.

The shell is moderately small for the family (maximum length 40 mm) and somewhat stoutly fusiform. The aperture is small, and the outer apertural lip is generally edentulate on its inner surface. The anal sulcus is small to indistinct. The four to eight varices bear several short to long, open, more or less foliaceous spines. In some species each varix is coalescent between the spines, forming a webbing of moderate extent on its leading edge. The shell surface is more or less scabrously laminate, this most pronounced over the spiral elements. The spire is moderately high to high. The canal is long, narrowly open to the right, and dorsally recurved. Shell color is generally in shades of ochre, brown, or purple-pink.

Ponder (1972) has named three new species in this genus. He has made *Murexiella* a subgenus of *Favartia*. We have not yet studied specimens of these species.

Murexiella bojadorensis (Locard, 1897)

Murex bojadorensis Locard, 1897: 304; *Murex asteriae* Nicolay, 1972: 43

The following is translated, with slight change, from the original description: "The shell is of moderate height, with an inverted pyriform shape, short and broad posteriorly, straight and very elongate anteriorly. The spire is very short and obtuse, and consists of eight or nine indistinct whorls that are little elevated, increasing rapidly in diameter, and with a convex profile. The body whorl is very large and rounded, ending in a very elongate canal that is straight, closed, and dorsally recurved at or near its tip. The suture is undulate and indistinct. The apex is small, subacute, and swollen [mammillate]. The aperture is subcircular, smaller than the remainder of the whorl and oriented in a vertical plane. The peristome is thin and sharp, interrupted posteriorly at the point of attachment of the outer apertural lip and at the upper end of the canal. The outer apertural lip is well-arched, accompanied by the last varix, which extends from the uppermost portion of the whorl to the base of the canal. The columellar margin is arcuate and adherent above, detached and sharply erect below. The shell is solid, stout, and subopaque, with axial varices and spiral cords. The penultimate and body whorls each bear five varices. The body whorl bears eight strong, solid, spiral cords of equal prominence, each made up of a cluster of finer, regular, imbricate cords. These strong cords form, at their intersections with the varices, elongate, straight, bi- or trilobed digitations. The superior (i.e. uppermost) digitation is the largest and strongest, and is the only one persisting on the other whorls.

"Shell color white with a rose tinge or . . . in shades of light to dark brown.

"Dimensions: total length 37 mm; maximum diameter, 26 mm."

Off northwestern Africa (Cape Bojador) in deep water (200 m). Recently received information indicates that specimens of this species are being collected off Ghana in 100 m.

See Pl. 13, fig. 4.

Murexiella cirrosa (Hinds, 1844)

Murex cirrosus Hinds, 1844: 118

The shell is small (maximum length 17 mm) and broadly fusiform. The spire is moderately high, consisting of six subangulate postnuclear whorls and a protoconch of undetermined nature. The suture is impressed. The body whorl is broadly fusoid. The aperture is broadly ovate, with a very shallow anal sulcus, strongly turned to the left. The margin of the outer apertural lip is both finely and coarsely dentate, reflecting spiral shell sculpture; the inner surface is weakly crenulate or smooth. The columellar lip is adherent above, detached and erect below. The siphonal canal is of moderate length, open, and dorsally recurved.

The body whorl bears eight strongly raised and frilled varices. Spiral sculpture consists of six cords on the body, these diminishing in strength anteriorly. Following a marked gap in sculpture at the base of the body, the canal bears a single bifid cord. Minor cords and threads occur at irregular intervals. Where the cords intersect the varices, moderately short, strongly recurved, open, weakly foliated spines are developed. Three or four irregular lamellae are developed on the leading edge of each varix.

Type locality "Straits of Macassar." Our specimen, from the D'Attilio Collection, has no locality. Recently received information indicates that specimens of this species are being collected off Somalia, eastern Africa, in 100 m.

See Pl. 25, fig. 13.

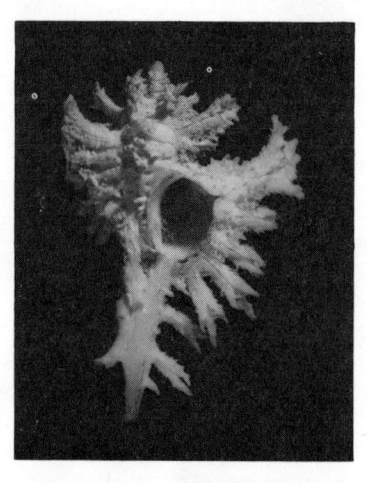

98. *Murexiella bojadorensis*

Murexiella diomedaea (Dall, 1908)

Murex diomedaeus Dall, 1908: 313

The shell is of moderate size (maximum length 25 mm) and fusiform. The spire is moderately high, consisting of two and one-half nuclear whorls and four postnuclear whorls. The suture is impressed. The body whorl is moderately small, roughly fusoid, and triangular in cross section. The aperture is ovate, with a flattened posterior margin; the anal sulcus is shallow, very broad, and oriented to the left. The outer apertural lip is erect and marginally crenulate; its inner surface is smooth or weakly crenulate. The columellar lip is adherent above, detached and erect below. The siphonal canal is long, slender, dorsally recurved, and narrowly open to the right.

The body whorl bears six pyramidal, strongly erect varices, with comparatively broad interspaces. Intervarical axial sculpture is lacking. Spiral sculpture consists of five major cords on the body and two more on the canal, and two minor cords in the space between the body and the canal. The major cords are large, prominent, and tripartite, consisting of a single major ridge flanked on each side by a minor one. The entire shell surface is scabrously laminate, the edges of the laminae erect. The leading edge of each varix is richly fimbriate. Where the spiral cords intersect the varices, moderately long, weakly foliaceous spines are developed. The spine at the shoulder margin, much the longest, is strongly upturned and recurved; the spines are otherwise of equal length.

Shell color is pinkish-brown, with a thin, white, chalky surface layer.

Punta Gorda, Baja California, to the Gulf of Panamá in moderately deep water (100–200 m).

See Pl. 25, fig. 1.

Murexiella hidalgoi (Crosse, 1869)

Murex hidalgoi Crosse, 1869: 408

The shell is of moderate size (maximum length 35 mm) and broadly fusiform. The spire is moderately high, consisting of two and one-half nuclear whorls and five strongly shouldered postnuclear whorls. The suture is moderately impressed. The body whorl is large and broadly fusoid. The aperture is subovate, its posterior margin flattened; the anal sulcus is imperceptible. The outer apertural lip is strongly erect and coarsely crenulate, its inner surface crenulate marginally, smooth within. The columellar lip is detached and erect. The siphonal canal is long, very narrowly open to the right, and dorsally recurved.

The body whorl bears five spinose varices. Intervarical axial sculpture is lacking. Spiral sculpture consists of five major cords on the body, these beginning at the shoulder margin, three more in the space between the body and the canal, and two others on the canal; minor cords alternate with the majors on the body. The major cords are very weakly marked in the intervarical spaces; over the varices, however, they are developed into long, narrow, foliaceous spines of equal length that are narrowly open on their leading edges. A webbinglike expansion of the varix extends to about one-half the length of the spines. Where they are extended into spines the major cords become transversely tripartite, with a single major, transverse ridge flanked on each side by a single minor ridge. The entire shell surface is covered with fine spiral threads and scabrous laminae.

Shell color is pale yellow-ochre to rich purple-brown, with a white aperture.

Gulf of Mexico to the southern Caribbean in moderately deep water.

See Pl. 25, fig. 8.

Murexiella humilis (Broderip, 1833)

Murex humilis Broderip, 1833: 175; *Murex norrisii* Reeve, 1845: sp. 129; *Murex octogonus* Sowerby, 1860: 428 (not Quoy & Gaimard, 1833: 53); *Murex sowerbyi* Kobelt, 1877: 248, new name for *Murex octogonus* Sowerby, 1860 (not Quoy & Gaimard, 1833); *Murex obtusus* Sowerby, 1879: 30 (not Bellardi, 1872: 82), new name for *Murex octogonus* Sowerby, 1860 (not Quoy & Gaimard, 1833); *Murexiella keenae* E. H. Vokes, 1970: 328; *Murexiella laurae* E. H. Vokes, 1970: 328

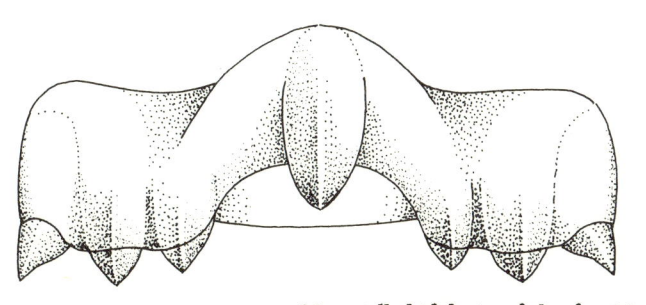

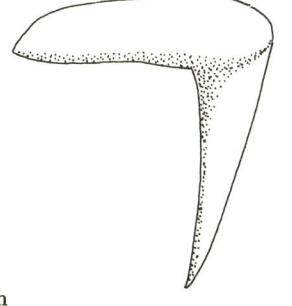

99. *Murexiella hidalgoi*, radular dentition

The shell is large for the genus (maximum length 40 mm) and stoutly fusiform. The spire is moderately high, consisting of two and one-half nuclear whorls and six convex to weakly shouldered postnuclear whorls. The suture is impressed. The body whorl is moderately globose and fusoid. The aperture is subcircular, with no discernible anal sulcus. The outer apertural lip is finely dentate at its margin, weakly undulate to smooth within. The columellar lip is primarily adherent above, detached and strongly erect below. The siphonal canal is long, narrowly open to the right, and dorsally recurved.

The body whorl bears seven or eight well-developed varices. Additional axial sculpture consists of numerous scabrous laminae. Spiral sculpture consists of eight major cords, five on the body and three on the canal; the cords are tripartite, consisting of a strong medial ridge flanked on each side by a weaker one. An evident unsculptured gap is apparent between the body and the canal. Where the cords intersect the varices, short, recurved, open, foliated spines are developed. The leading edge of the varix is richly fimbriate.

Shell color is off-white, with a medium-brown band on the shoulder, the white coloration persisting on the leading edges of the varices, the spaces between the cords as they surmount the varices, and the area between the body and the canal; the intervarical space and the spines are generally suffused with a deep fleshy pink. The aperture is porcelaneous white.

Specimens from Panamá are typical. Shells of specimens from the Guaymas, Mexico, region are less robust and more strongly shouldered, lack the pinkish-purple suffusion, and have a less globose body. Shells of specimens from the Manzanillo, Mexico, area are dwarfed, lack strong coloration, and are lacking much of the scabrous lamination of typical specimens.

Northern Gulf of California (eastern side) to Panamá, the Galápagos Islands, and Ecuador.

See Pl. 25, figs. 3–5.

Murexiella jacquelinae (Emerson & D'Attilio, 1969)

Murexsul jacquelinae Emerson & D'Attilio, 1969: 324

The shell is small for the genus (maximum length 25 mm) and fusiform. The spire is high, consisting of one and one-half nuclear whorls and six weakly shouldered postnuclear whorls. The suture is indistinct. The body whorl is of moderate size and fusoid. The aperture is moderately small and ovate, with an all but indiscernible anal sulcus. The outer apertural lip is weakly erect and minutely denticulate; its inner surface is weakly lirate, the lirae reflecting spaces between spiral elements on the shell's outer surface. The columellar lip is smooth, adherent at its posterior end, and detached and erect for the anterior three-fourths of its length. The siphonal canal is moderately long, minutely open to the right, and dorsally recurved.

The body whorl bears six or seven densely spinose varices. Intervarical axial sculpture is lacking. Spiral sculpture consists of numerous narrow cords, each separated from its neighbor by a deep channel: three cords above the shoulder margin, one at the shoulder margin, and three immediately below it are all of equal strength; below this, two minor and two major cords alternate, these followed by three minor cords at the base of the body; the canal bears three major cords, these diminishing in strength anteriorly. Where the spiral cords intersect the varices, short, sharp, slender, ventrally open spines are developed. Anteriorly from the shoulder margin, the first six spines on each varix form a dorsally curved arc; below this, the spines form an arc in the opposite direction. The minor spines at the base of the body, and those on the canal, are bent sharply ventrally.

Shell color is pale buff or tan. The interior of the aperture is suffused with pale rosy violet.

Apparently limited to the Galápagos Islands.

See Pl. 26, figs. 11–12.

Murexiella lappa (Broderip, 1833)

Murex lappa Broderip, 1833: 177; *Murex dipsacus* Broderip, 1833: 194; *Murex radicatus* Hinds, 1844: 128

The shell is of moderate size (maximum length 30 mm) and rhomboid to fusiform. The spire is high, consisting of three and one-half polished, horn-colored nuclear whorls and six angulate postnuclear whorls. The suture is somewhat indistinct. The body whorl is moderate in size and fusoid. The aperture is comparatively small and ovate, with an indistinct anal sulcus. The outer apertural lip is erect and finely dentate, its inner surface weakly crenulate. The columellar lip is adherent above, detached and erect below. The siphonal canal is moderately long, narrowly open to the right, and dorsally recurved.

The body whorl bears five or six spinose varices. Additional axial sculpture is lacking. Spiral sculpture consists of primary, secondary, and tertiary cords: on the shoulder is a medial secondary cord flanked on each side by a pair of tertiaries; the body bears five primary cords alternating with tertiaries; the canal bears four secondaries. In addition, the surface of each primary cord is incised by five to seven fine grooves. Where the cords intersect the varices, short to moderately long, sharp, open, slightly foliated spines are developed. The entire shell surface is finely, scabrously laminate.

Shell color is generally white, stained with orange-brown to orange-ochre, particularly on the varical spines and on one transverse band, this medial on the body.

Mazatlán, Mexico, and Socorro Island, Mexico, to Ecuador.

See Pl. 26, fig. 5.

Murexiella levicula (Dall, 1889)

Ocinebra (Favartia) (cellulosa var.?) *levicula* Dall, 1889: 211; *Murex glyptus* M. Smith, 1938: 89

The shell is small (maximum length 17 mm) and fusiform. The spire is high, consisting of two and three-fourths polished, convex nuclear whorls and five angulate postnuclear whorls. The suture is impressed. The body whorl is fusoid. The aperture is moderately small and ovate, with a broad, shallow anal sulcus. The outer apertural lip is strongly erect and gently, marginally undulate, its inner surface smooth to weakly crenulate. The columellar lip is adherent above, detached and erect below. The siphonal canal is comparatively long, straight, and narrowly open to the right.

The body whorl bears four or five narrow, erect, spinose varices. Spiral sculpture consists of five weak cords of equal size on the body and four or five others on the canal. Where they cross the varices these cords become very prominent and are developed into moderately long, weakly foliaceous spines. An expansion of the varix extends to almost the midpoint of the spines to form a webbing between them. The spines on the body are incised by a medial groove and are weakly scabrous.

Shell color is very pale brown to ochre. The aperture is cream-colored.

Gulf of Mexico, in 100–120 m.

See Pl. 26, fig. 10.

Murexiella macgintyi (M. Smith, 1938)

Murex macgintyi M. Smith, 1938: 88

The shell is small (maximum length 25 mm) and broadly, angulately fusiform. The spire is moderately high, consisting of one and one-half nuclear whorls and five angulate postnuclear whorls. The suture is impressed. The body whorl is moderately small and globose. The aperture is small and subcircular, with a very shallow, indistinct anal sulcus. The outer apertural lip is erect and strongly crenulate, its inner surface weakly lirate or undulate. The columellar lip is adherent at its posterior end, detached and strongly erect anteriorly. The siphonal canal is long, narrowly open to the right, and dorsally recurved at its tip.

100. *Murexiella macgintyi*, protoconch

Axial sculpture on the body whorl consists of six or seven spinose varices. Spiral sculpture consists of five strong cords on the body and two weaker ones on the canal. Between these two regions is a notably sculpture-free gap. Between the varices the cords are almost completely obsolete; where the body cords ascend the varices, however, short, open, recurved, foliaceous spines are developed. The cords, where prominent, and the spines are incised by fine grooves, these imparting to the spines a compound appearance. The secondary cords on the canal also give rise to spines on the varices, but these are longer, less open, and less foliated; a weak cord on the shoulder also develops a spinelike projection on the varix.

Shell color is fleshy pink, most intense subsuturally and in the excavated area on the dorsal side of each varix.

Eastern and western coasts of Florida, and the Bahamas to the southern Caribbean (Aruba); fossil in the Plio-Pleistocene of southern Florida.

See Pl. 25, figs. 10–11.

Murexiella perita (Hinds, 1844)

Murex peritus Hinds, 1844: 129

The shell is small (maximum length 20 mm) and fusiform. The spire is high, consisting of two and three-fourths convex nuclear whorls and five shouldered postnuclear whorls. The suture is indistinct or weakly marked. The body whorl is of moderate size and fusoid. The aperture is small and ovate, with an indistinct anal sulcus. The outer apertural lip is erect and coarsely crenulate at its margin. The columellar lip is adherent above, detached and somewhat erect below. The siphonal canal is long, moderately open, and dorsally recurved.

The body whorl bears six weakly spinose varices. A varical expansion forms a webbing between the spines to about one-half their length. Intervarical axial sculpture is lacking. Spiral sculpture consists chiefly of four major cords on the body, these noticeable only over the varices, where they are finely incised by five to nine fine grooves. Alternating with the major cords are pairs of threads, and a series of four or five single threads occurs on the anterior end of the body. The canal bears two inconspicuous minor cords. Where the spiral elements cross the varix, low, sharp, dorsally recurved spines are formed. The entire shell is covered with weak scabrous laminae, these most prominent on the cords and on the leading edge of each varix.

Shell color is pale orange to yellow ochre-brown.

Bahía Magdalena, Baja California, to the Gulf of Tehuántepec, Mexico.

See Pl. 26, fig. 8.

?**Murexiella phantom** (Woolacott, 1957)

Minnimurex phantom Woolacott, 1957: 115

We have not seen a specimen of this species; the following is taken, verbatim, from the original description:

"A small, broad shell, 11 x 7 mm, of a cream color, with approximately six strong, thick spiral ribs on the body whorl and two on the remaining whorls. The ribs frequently guttered centrally and bearing seminodulose scales projecting laterally and lamellose in part. Interstices narrow, deep and reticulated, with deep pits behind the varices; these pits sometimes brown in color. There are four adult whorls and a glassy, one-and-one-half-whorled protoconch. The beautifully frilled varices number four on the body whorl and five on the preceding whorls, and they project upward sharply. The area between the periphery and the well-defined sutures is practically flat. Aperture oval, canal medium and partly open.

"Found in shell drift from Eden to Angourie, New South Wales, Australia."

Murexiella radwini Emerson & D'Attilio, 1970

Murexiella radwini Emerson & D'Attilio, 1970: 270

The shell is moderately large for the genus (maximum length 33.5 mm) and broadly fusiform. The spire is high, consisting of two and one-half nuclear whorls and seven convex to barely shouldered postnuclear whorls. The suture is strongly impressed. The body whorl is moderately large and roughly fusoid. The aperture is moderately small and ovate, with a broad, shallow anal sulcus. The outer apertural lip is erect and strongly crenulate, the crenulations reflecting the sculpture on the outer shell surface; the inner surface of the outer lip is smooth to weakly crenulate. The columellar lip is adherent above, slightly erect below. The siphonal canal is moderately long, barely open at the right, and essentially straight.

The body whorl bears five foliose varices. Intervarical axial sculpture is lacking. Spiral sculpture consists of six broad, intervarically ephemeral

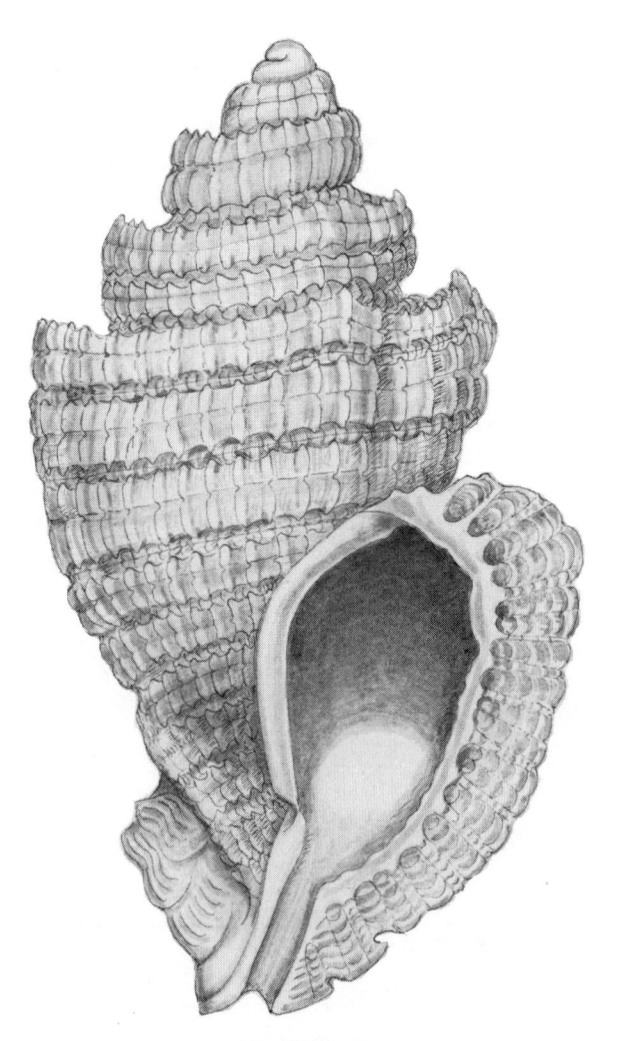

101. *Murexiella phantom*

cords on the body and two on the canal. Where the cords intersect the varices, they are developed into moderately long, foliose spines; the upper three spines on the body are dorsally recurved, and the lower three on the body and the two on the canal are essentially straight. The two uppermost cords of earlier whorls and their associated spines are persistent. Smaller, intercalary spines alternating with the major ones are derived from faint minor cords. The major cords and spines are covered with five or seven fine scabrous threads, a major thread at the crest and two or three on each flank. A notable gap in varical sculpture is apparent between the body and the canal. The leading edge of the varix is richly fimbriate.

Shell color is a warm, fleshy violet except on the varices, which are pinkish-tan. The aperture is light violet.

Only a single mature specimen, the holotype, has ever been collected. Three juvenile specimens have also been found.

Known only from the Galápagos Islands in deep water (100 m).

See Pl. 25, fig. 9.

Murexiella vittata (Broderip, 1833)

Murex vittatus Broderip, 1833: 176; *Murex lepidus* Reeve, 1845: sp. 113; *Murex taeniatus* Sowerby, 1860: 428

The shell is large for the genus (maximum length 35 mm) and stoutly fusiform. The spire is high, consisting of two and three-fourths convex nuclear whorls and six or seven postnuclear whorls. The suture is distinct but not impressed. The body whorl is large and globosely fusoid. The aperture is moderately small and ovate, with a shallow, moderately narrow anal sulcus. The outer apertural lip is strongly erect and coarsely, marginally dentate; its inner surface bears deep grooves, these reflecting the lip-margin dentition and, ultimately, the spiral sculpture of the shell. The columellar lip is briefly adherent at its extreme upper end, detached and erect for most of its length. The siphonal canal is moderately long, barely open to the right, and dorsally recurved.

The body whorl bears six or seven prickly varices. Intervarical axial sculpture is lacking. Spiral sculpture consists of six primary cords on the body: one above the shoulder margin, one at the shoulder, and four below it. Between the body and the canal, a brief gap in prominent spiral sculpture is marked by a reduction in the prominence of the varices and by a weak tertiary cord. The canal bears three secondary cords, alternating with tertiaries. Where the spiral elements intersect the varices, short, prickly, partially open, weakly recurved spines are developed. Ventral to each primary body spine, two or three low, scalelike spinelets are developed, these extending almost to the margin of the outer apertural lip.

Shell color is white to cream-colored, with three interrupted transverse brown-black bands, one on the shoulder, one medial on the body, and one between the body and the canal. The aperture is white.

Bahía Magdalena, Baja California, and the Gulf of California to Guayaquil, Ecuador.

See Pl. 26, fig. 4.

Genus MUREXSUL Iredale, 1915

TYPE SPECIES: *Murex octogonus* Quoy & Gaimard, 1833, by original designation.

Shells are all small to moderately large, with a high spire and a short to moderately long siphonal canal. The sculpture is important in distinguishing *Murexsul* species from those of other muricid groups. In the type species and in unworn examples of other species the varices are composed of numerous erect lamellae. Even more significant is the gap in spiral sculpture apparent immediately below the base of the body—a gap found, as well, in *Murexiella* and *Favartia*. The canal generally bears several longish, straight spines.

The radula, protoconch, and internal anatomy corroborate the above shell-based distinctions.

?Murexsul auratus Kuroda & Habe, 1971

Murexsul auratus Kuroda & Habe, 1971: 215, 141

The shell is tiny (holotype length 7.5 mm) and roughly fusiform. The spire is high, consisting of one and one-half horn-colored nuclear whorls, the first half whorl of which is sunken into the next, and four subangulate postnuclear whorls. The suture is moderately impressed and interrupted by spiral and axial sculptural elements. The body whorl is of moderate size and roughly fusoid. The aperture is small and subcircular, with a poorly defined anal sulcus. The margin of the outer apertural lip is erect and crenulate, the crenulations reflecting the outer shell sculpture. The columellar lip is also erect. The siphonal canal is short, open, and weakly dorsally recurved.

The body whorl bears seven varices, oriented slightly obliquely to the long axis of the shell and raised and moderately broad, the intervarical spaces approximately equal to the varices in width. Spiral sculpture consists of five broad cords on the body, intercalary elements of secondary strength on the body, and one primary and two secondary elements on the canal. The body cords are medially incised as they traverse the intervarical spaces, and all spiral elements become nodulose over the varices. The entire shell presents a cancellate appearance.

Shell color is pale flesh overall.

Known only from the holotype (type locality Sagami Bay, Japan).

See Pl. 14, fig. 5.

Murexsul kieneri (Reeve, 1845)

Murex exiguus Kiener, 1842: 97 (not Broderip, 1833);
Murex kieneri Reeve, 1845: sp. 172, new name for *Murex exiguus* Kiener, 1842 (not Broderip, 1833)

The shell is very small (maximum length 9 mm) and roughly fusiform. The spire is moderately high, consisting of one and one-half nuclear whorls and four tabulate postnuclear whorls, with the vertical portion of each whorl being convex in outline. The suture is deeply impressed. The body whorl is of moderate size and ovate and is sharply contracted where it passes into the siphonal canal. The aperture is small and subovate, with a barely perceptible anal sulcus angled toward the left. The outer apertural lip is nonerect and finely crenulate; its inner surface is sparsely lirate. The columellar lip is entirely adherent and smooth. The siphonal canal is of moderate length, open, and curved first to the left and then to the right.

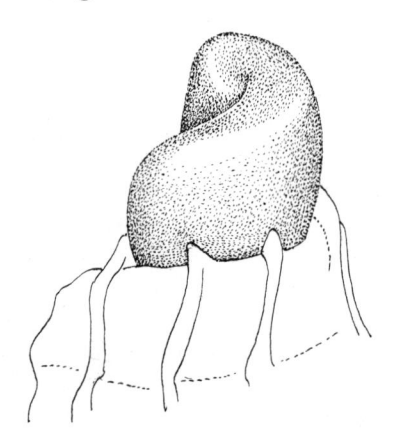

102. *Murexsul kieneri*, protoconch

The body whorl bears ten densely fimbriate varices, which are produced into posteriorly and dorsally hooked spines at the shoulder margin. The spaces between the varices are very narrow and deep. Spiral sculpture consists of six low cords, most apparent in the narrow intervarical spaces. Where the spiral cords intersect the varices, the lamellae forming the varix are thrown into short, dorsally reflected points. Just below the base of the body there is a notable "bald" zone formed by the complete absence of spiral sculpture and by a diminution of the varices. The sculpture above is so prominent that the sparseness of sculpture in this zone imparts to it a furrowlike appearance. The siphonal canal bears a single spiral cord ending in a single short, straight, open spine.

Shell color is waxy yellow, with red-brown spots on the varix corresponding to the spaces between spiral cords.

South Africa (eastern section); we have seen specimens from Port Alfred and East London.

See Pl. 23, fig. 2.

Murexsul mariae Finlay, 1930

Murexsul mariae Finlay, 1930: 237

The shell is small (about 15–20 mm in length) and roughly fusiform. The spire is high, consisting of five convex postnuclear whorls and a protoconch of undetermined nature. The suture is distinct. The body whorl is of moderate size and roughly fusoid. The aperture is of moderate size and ovate, with a weak to barely perceptible anal sulcus. The outer apertural lip is barely erect and weakly crenulate; its inner surface bears four swollen tubercles, the uppermost at the shoulder margin. The columellar lip is smooth and entirely adherent. The siphonal canal is short, broad, open, and weakly, distally recurved.

The body whorl bears eight to 11 moderately prominent varices. Spiral sculpture consists of five or six major spiral cords with minor intercalary cords. Between the body and the canal is a moderately broad gap in axial sculpture.

Shell color is white to tan, with darker purple-brown spiral cords. The aperture is gray-white with a purplish tinge.

New Zealand.

See Pl. 7, fig. 9.

?Murexsul multispinosus (Sowerby, 1904)

Murex multispinosus Sowerby, 1904: 8; *Poirieria azami* Kuroda, 1929: 91, 95

The shell is moderately small (maximum length 25 mm) and club-shaped. The spire is high, consisting of one and one-half convex nuclear whorls and five or six convex to weakly shouldered postnuclear whorls. The suture is deeply impressed. The body whorl is moderately large and elongate-fusoid. The aperture is small and ovate, with a barely discernible anal sulcus. The outer apertural lip is erect and finely serrate, its inner surface weakly crenulate. The columellar lip is detached and erect, with a weak swelling and a twisted groove anteriorly, leading into the siphonal canal. The siphonal canal is long and straight, or slightly bent to the right near its tip.

The body whorl bears eight densely spinose varices. Spiral sculpture consists of five major cords on the body and two or three on the canal; in some major-cord interspaces, minor cords are apparent. Where the cords intersect the varices, short to moderately long, open spines are developed: the longest spines, those developed from the shoulder-margin cord, are straight or curving posteriorly; other spines are shorter and dorsally recurved.

Shell color ranges from all white to white with two transverse, orange-brown bands, one on the shoulder and one medial on the body. The aperture is white.

Although this species' shell morphology is quite unique, its radular dentition indicates its probable relationship to *Murexsul* Iredale.

Known to us only from southeastern Japan and the Philippines.

See Pl. 25, fig. 6.

Murexsul octogonus (Quoy & Gaimard, 1833)

Murex octogonus Quoy & Gaimard, 1833: 531; *Murex peruvianus* Sowerby, 1841: pl. 195, fig. 103; *Murexsul cuvierensis* Finlay, 1927: 487; *Murex ednae* M. Smith, 1940: 43; *Murexsul conatus* McMichael, 1964: 31

The shell is moderate in size to moderately large (maximum length 57 mm) and narrowly to stoutly fusiform. The spire is high, consisting of one and one-half nuclear whorls and five to seven weakly to more or less strongly shouldered postnuclear whorls; the first half whorl of the nucleus

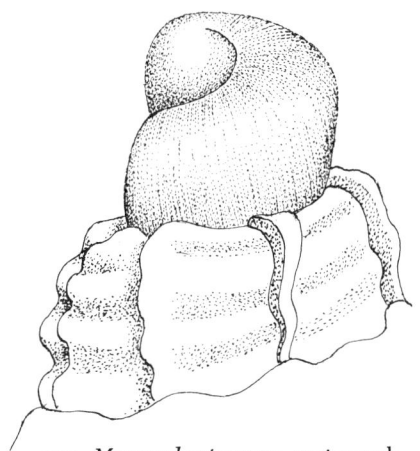

103. *Murexsul octogonus*, protoconch

is depressed and tabulate, the remainder convex. The suture is weakly impressed, if at all. The body whorl is moderately large and narrowly to broadly fusoid. The aperture is of moderate size and subovate, with a flattened posterior margin and a narrow, shallow anal sulcus angled to the left. The outer apertural lip is strongly erect and sharply serrate, the serrations reflecting the ends of the spiral sculptural elements at the lip margin; the inner surface of the outer lip is strongly lirate for a short distance into the aperture. The columellar lip is smooth, adherent and weakly callused at its posterior end, detached and more or less strongly erect for its remaining extent. The siphonal canal is moderately short to moderately long, bent to the left, and narrowly open to the right.

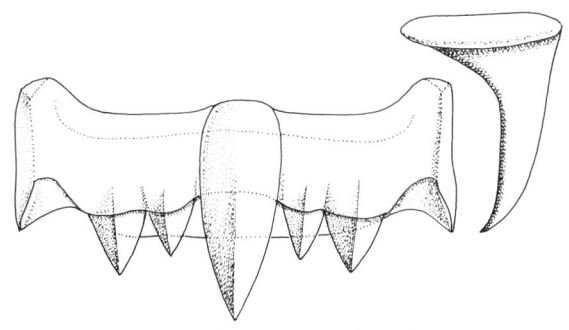

104. *Murexsul octogonus*, radular dentition

The body whorl bears seven or eight more or less prickly varices, each extending from the shoulder margin to, or almost to, the tip of the siphonal canal. Spiral sculpture on the body consists of seven primary cords, these intercalated with an equal number of secondary cords. Below the base of the body is a zone depauperate in spiral and, to a lesser extent, axial sculpture. The canal bears two primary cords. Where the primary and secondary cords intersect the varices, they project perpendicular to the shell surface to form one to four axial rows of short, prickly, open spinelets.

Shell color is yellow-white, with yellow-brown on the spiral cords, grading on the cords into darker red-brown just prior to each varix. The aperture is porcelaneous white.

New Zealand waters in moderate subtidal depths.

See Pl. 26, figs. 6–7.

?Murexsul tokubeii Nakamigawa & Habe, 1964

Murexsul tokubeii Nakamigawa & Habe, 1964: 26, 28

The shell is small (maximum length 23 mm) and fusiform. The spire is high, consisting of one and one-third convex nuclear whorls and six barely shouldered postnuclear whorls. The suture is impressed. The body whorl is of moderate size and fusoid. The aperture is moderately small and ovate, with a barely perceptible anal sulcus. The outer apertural lip is distinctly erect and marginally serrate; its inner surface bears five transversely elongate denticles, recessed a short distance into the aperture. The columellar lip is smooth, gently arcuate, detached, and strongly erect, except at its posterior end. The siphonal canal is long, slender, narrowly open, and gradually, dorsally recurved.

The body whorl bears five or six briefly spinose varices, the earlier whorls seven or eight varices. Spiral sculpture consists of five major cords on the body, one on the canal, and innumerable fine, spiral threads and axial lamellae covering the shell. A brief gap in spiral sculpture is apparent at the base of the body. Where the major cords cross the varices, short, open, straight, foliaceous spines are produced.

Shell color is white to waxy yellow, with darker yellow-brown on the tips of the spines. The aperture is porcelaneous white.

Known to us only from southeastern Japan, in deep water (50–100 m).

See Pl. 25, fig. 2.

Murexsul umbilicatus (Tenison-Woods, 1876)
Trophon umbilicatus Tenison-Woods, 1876: 135

The shell is of moderate size for the genus (maximum length 25 mm) and broadly fusiform. The spire is high, consisting of one convex nuclear whorl and four shouldered postnuclear whorls. The suture is moderately impressed. The body whorl is moderately large and broadly fusoid. The aperture is broad and ovate, with the barest hint of an anal sulcus. The outer apertural lip is briefly erect and finely crenulate; its inner surface is slightly flaring and weakly lirate. The columellar lip is smooth, adherent anteriorly, detached and weakly erect for its remaining length. The siphonal canal is short, bent to the left, and open at the right.

The body whorl bears eight prominent varices, each consisting of prominent portions of the spiral cords. Spiral sculpture on the body consists of six major cords and six intercalary minor cords. The canal bears a single major cord and a single minor one. Between the canal and the body is a moderately broad gap in spiral and axial sculpture. Where the cords intersect the varices, each is expanded and lifted to form a moderately prominent, blunt fold or ruffle.

Shell color is white, with red-brown on the expanded portion of each varix. The aperture is white.

Southeastern and south-central Australia and northern Tasmania.

See Pl. 2, fig. 7.

Murexsul zonatus Hayashi & Habe, 1965
Murexsul zonatus Hayashi & Habe, 1965: 11, 13

The following is taken with modifications from the original description:

"The shell is small, rather solid, and elongate-biconic in shape. The spire is elevated and consists of the seven stepped whorls. Each whorl except the two smooth and polished embryonic whorls is shouldered by a strong spiral cord with seven to nine strongly upturned tubercular spines, and bears two cords and narrow interstitial cords below it, these crossed by the densely set lamellate growth lines and seven to nine low longitudinal ribs forming short spines on the spiral cords. The body whorl is large and strongly shouldered, with tubercular spines (these occurring as well on other whorls), and gradually narrowing toward the siphonal canal, which bears a distinct fasciole. The aperture is roundly oval in shape and somewhat constricted at the siphonal canal. The coloration is white, with a broad brown band below the suture and two narrow brown bands on the base of the body whorl.

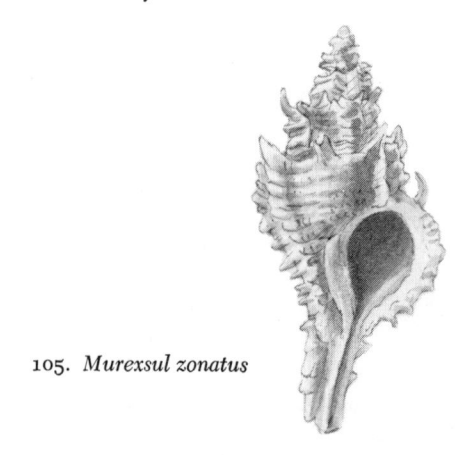

105. *Murexsul zonatus*

"Height 20.1 mm, breadth 9.7 mm (type specimen, preserved in the National Science Museum).

"Height 18.9 mm, breadth 9.1 mm (paratype specimen #1).

"Height 19.5 mm, breadth 9.6 mm (paratype specimen #2).

"Known only from the type locality: Enshu-Nada, off Honshu, Japan, at a depth of about 200 m."

See Pl. 28, fig. 7.

Genus **MURICOPSIS** Bucquoy & Dautzenberg, 1882

TYPE SPECIES: *Murex blainvillei* Payraudeau, 1826, by original designation.

The shell is generally small (maximum length 45 mm) and fusiform. The spire is high, and the whorls are more or less shouldered. The protoconch is generally small (one and one-half whorls), convex or tabulate, and distally canted in the direction opposite to that of the postnuclear whorls. The body whorl is moderately large, and the aperture is ovate to lenticular. The outer apertural lip is denticulate on its inner surface, and the columellar lip is denticulate or pustulose anteriorly. Numerous varices (five to eight) bear short to moderately long, scalelike spines whose ventral surfaces are lamellose and thus not open. Other sculpture consists of spiral cords and numerous thin laminae, the whole imparting a scabrous appearance to fresh shells.

We have determined, from an examination of shell, radula, and protoconch, that three species formerly constituting the genus *Risomurex* Olsson & McGinty, 1958, are actually assignable here, thus synonymizing that genus with *Muricopsis*.

(See the Appendix for treatment of new species assignable to *Muricopsis*.)

Muricopsis angolensis (Odhner, 1922)

Ocinebra angolensis Odhner, 1922: 13

The shell is small (maximum length 10 mm) and fusiform. The spire is high, consisting of six weakly convex postnuclear whorls. The suture is weakly impressed. The body whorl is moderately large and fusoid. The aperture is ovate, with an indistinct anal sulcus. The outer apertural lip is erect and coarsely, marginally dentate; its inner surface bears five strong, knobby denticles, one above the shoulder margin and four evenly spaced below it. The columellar lip is adherent above, detached and weakly erect below. The siphonal canal is short, broad, moderately open, and distally recurved.

The body whorl bears seven tuberculate varices, equal in breadth to the interspaces. The varices are somewhat rounded dorsally, richly laminate ventrally. Other axial sculpture is lacking. Spiral sculpture consists of major cords, five on the body and two on the canal, and numerous fine striae. Where the major cords intersect the varices, short, open, scalelike, ventrally bent spines are developed.

Shell color is pale buff-yellow, except for three dark-brown spiral bands, these most intense over the varices: one at the shoulder margin, one at the base of the body, and one on the canal. The interior of the aperture is a polished brown.

Tropical West Africa (Isla Fernando Po to northern Angola).

See Pl. 27, fig. 11.

Muricopsis armatus (A. Adams, 1854)

Murex armatus A. Adams, 1854: 71; *Muricidea squamulata* Carpenter, 1866: 281 (not *Murex squamulatus* Brocchi, 1814: 422, or Risso, 1826: 199)

The shell is of moderate size (maximum length 40 mm) and fusiform. The spire is high and acute, consisting of one and one-fourth smooth, tabulate nuclear whorls and six to eight angulate postnuclear whorls; the apex of the protoconch is depressed and canted opposite to the cant of the postnuclear whorls. The suture is weakly defined. The body whorl is of moderate size. The aperture is of moderate size and ovate, with a broad, very shallow anal sulcus. The outer apertural lip is nonerect and finely, marginally crenulate; its inner surface bears five moderately weak denticles, these increasing in prominence anteriorly. The columellar lip is adherent above, detached and weakly erect below; on the columella, immediately above the canal, is one weak, knoblike denticle. The siphonal canal is moderately broad and open, comparatively short, and dorsally recurved at its end.

The body whorl bears seven spinose varices. Intervarical axial sculpture is lacking. Spiral sculpture consists of four scabrous major cords alternating with minor cords. Spiral sculpture is lacking on the shoulder. Where the spiral elements intersect the ventrally fimbriate varices, short to moderately long, essentially straight, closed, medially grooved spines are developed.

Shell color is yellow-brown to dead white. The aperture is entirely porcelaneous white.

Northern Gulf of California to Islas Tres Marías, Mexico (records for Panamá have been impossible to substantiate).

See Pl. 27, figs. 1–2.

Muricopsis blainvillei (Payraudeau, 1826)

Murex blainvillei Payraudeau, 1826: 149

The shell is of moderate size for the genus (maximum length 30 mm) and fusiform. The spire is high, consisting of one and one-half translucent, glassy nuclear whorls and seven weakly shouldered postnuclear whorls. The suture is weakly impressed. The body whorl is moderately large and fusoid. The aperture is lenticular to ovate, with a weakly defined anal sulcus. The

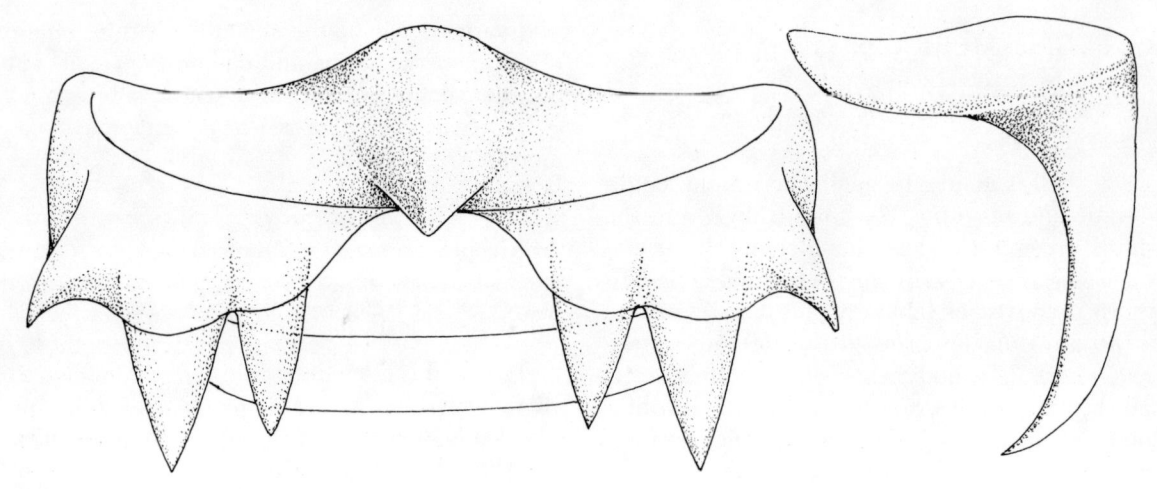

106. *Muricopsis blainvillei*, radular dentition

outer apertural lip is thickened and finely, marginally crenulate; its inner surface flares anteriorly and is strongly dentate, bearing six strong denticles, the uppermost (interior to the shoulder slope) followed by a much smaller, at times ephemeral denticle, and immediately below this by a large, broad denticle and three smaller, equal-sized denticles. The columellar lip is adherent parietally, detached and weakly erect below; near the anterior end of the columella are two more or less strongly developed oblique pustules. The siphonal canal is moderately short and weakly recurved.

The body whorl bears six or seven more or less prominent varices. Spiral sculpture consists of numerous major cords alternating with minor ones, as well as fine, weak, spiral threads covering the shell.

Shell color is generally orange-brown to purple-brown, with two bands of lighter orange, one at the shoulder, one at the base of the body. The margin of the aperture is pinkish-purple.

The shell of this species shows the polymorphism so well known in other Mediterranean species. Most of the localized specimens we have seen are from Sicily.

Eastern Greece (Athens), Sicily, and southern Italy to ?Atlantic coasts of Portugal and Spain, and ?Madeira.

See Pl. 23, fig. 14; Pl. 27, fig. 15.

Muricopsis bombayanus (Melvill, 1893)

Murex bombayanus Melvill, 1893: 52

The shell is of moderate size (maximum length 30 mm) and fusiform. The spire is high and acute, consisting of two and one-half nuclear whorls and six angulate postnuclear whorls. The suture is impressed. The body whorl is of moderate size. The aperture is moderately small and ovate, with an inverted-U-shaped anal sulcus, delimited on each side by a transverse ridge. The outer apertural lip is moderately erect and coarsely dentate; on its inner surface, in addition to the ridge demarcating the anal sulcus, five elongate denticles extend from the anterior to the posterior end. The columellar lip is entirely adherent; the columellar surface bears three denticles immediately above the canal. The siphonal canal is moderately short, broad, open, and dorsally recurved.

The body whorl bears seven or eight varices, each of these produced into a prominent axial ridge that weakens at the shoulder margin. The varices and the intervarical spaces are of approximately equal width. The leading edge of each varix is laminose. Spiral sculpture consists of four primary cords on the body and two secondary and two tertiary cords on the canal. Where the spiral and axial elements intersect, very short, broad-based, scalelike spines are developed, these most prominent on the shoulder.

Shell color is dull tan, with a few of the spiral cords colored brown. The aperture is pale flesh-color, with a grayish suffusion on the columella and three faint gray transverse bands within.

Bombay, India.

See Pl. 27, fig. 6.

Muricopsis brazieri (Angas, 1878)

Murex brazieri Angas, 1878: 171

The shell is small (maximum length 15 mm), thin, and fusiform. The spire is high and acute, with one nuclear whorl and five weakly shouldered postnuclear whorls; the first half-turn of the protoconch is sharply shouldered and depressed below the second half-turn. The suture is weakly impressed. The body whorl is of moderate size and fusoid. The aperture is small and ovate, with a small, inverted-U-shaped anal sulcus, this delimited parietally by a low transverse knob. The outer apertural lip is erect, the margin weakly crenulate; on the inner surface are six denticles, one above the shoulder margin and five below (in some specimens some of these denticles may be bifid). The columellar lip is adherent above, detached and erect below, and bears one knoblike denticle on its anterior end, directly above the canal. The canal is of moderate length, open, and dorsally recurved.

The body whorl bears seven moderately prominent varices, these stronger anteriorly. The entire shell is also scabrously laminate, this feature most strongly developed on the leading edges of the varices. Intervarical axial sculpture is lacking. Spiral sculpture consists of four major cords on the body alternating with minor cords. The canal bears a single median major cord flanked on each side by three or four minor ones. Where the cords intersect the varices, small, scalelike spines are developed, the one at the shoulder margin generally the most prominent.

Shell color is pale fleshy pink, slightly stronger on the varical crest. The aperture is translucent white.

Australia (New South Wales, South Australia, and Tasmania).

See Pl. 24, fig. 13.

Muricopsis cristatus (Brocchi, 1814)

Murex cristatus Brocchi, 1814: 394; *Murex cataphractus* Sowerby, 1834: pl. 63, fig. 40 (not Brocchi, 1814); *Murex inermis* Philippi, 1836: pl. 11, fig. 25

The shell is, except for an unlocalized giant race, moderately small (maximum length ca. 20 mm) and fusiform. The spire is high, consisting of one and one-half convex nuclear whorls and six or seven shouldered postnuclear whorls. The suture is impressed. The body whorl is of moderate size and fusoid. The aperture is small and lenticular to kidney-shaped, with a deep, moderately broad anal sulcus. The outer apertural lip is barely erect, if at all, and crenulate; its inner surface bears five strong denticles, four grouped evenly anteriorly, and a fifth internal to the shoulder of the whorl. As is typical for the genus, the penultimate denticle, anterior to the shoulder angle, is the largest. The columellar lip is almost entirely adherent and bears two or more strong, oblique pustules on its barely erect anterior end. The siphonal canal is short, straight, and rather broadly open.

The body whorl bears six more or less prominent varices. Spiral sculpture consists of eight equally strong and evenly spaced cords, one on the shoulder, six on the body, and one on the canal. Where the cords cross the varices they are developed into short, open, triangular spines, the longest at the shoulder margin.

Shell color is pale brownish-white, with dark blue-purple undertones. The aperture is maroon to purple-brown, with white denticles and pustules.

Sowerby (1834) figured a giant example of this species as *Murex cataphractus*, and we figure what we believe to be the same specimen (ex Calvert Collection) (Pl. 23, fig. 14, herein). It represents a form that is much larger than typical *M. cristatus* but that is otherwise indistinguishable.

Sicilian region of the Mediterranean (our figured specimen is from the Gulf of Salerno).

See Pl. 27, fig. 10.

Muricopsis cuspidatus (Sowerby, 1879)

Murex cuspidatus Sowerby, 1879: 36

The shell is of moderate size (maximum length 25 mm) and broadly fusiform. The spire is moderately high and acute, consisting of six or seven angulate postnuclear whorls and a protoconch of undetermined nature. The suture is weakly marked. The body whorl is large and moderately inflated. The aperture is moderately large and ovate, with a broad, inverted-U-shaped anal sulcus, parietally demarcated by a strong transverse ridge. The outer apertural lip is erect and weakly, coarsely crenulate; its inner surface is markedly denticulate, with one strong denticle situated above the shoulder margin and six others below it, these decreasing in size anteriorly. The columellar lip is adherent above, detached below; two confluent denticles are apparent at the base of the columella, followed by a single denticle above the base. The siphonal canal is moderately short, broad, open, and dorsally recurved.

The body whorl bears seven briefly spinose varices. Intervarical axial sculpture is lacking. Spiral sculpture consists of five major cords on the body and one on the canal. Three minor cords arise on the shoulder and others alternate with the major cords over the remainder of the body, two or three preceding the major cord on the canal. All cords develop into open, weakly foliaceous spines on the varices, most prominently at the shoulder margin. The leading edge of each varix is richly laminose.

Shell color is white, the varices a scorched brown. The aperture is porcelaneous white.

Japan (type locality), New Caledonia (figured specimen).

See Pl. 27, fig. 9.

Muricopsis infans (E. A. Smith, 1884)
Murex infans E. A. Smith, 1884: 491

The shell is large (maximum length 32.5 mm), robust, and broadly fusoid. The spire is high, consisting of one and one-fourth rounded nuclear whorls and seven or eight obliquely shouldered postnuclear whorls. The suture is moderately impressed and undulate. The body whorl is moderately large and broadly fusoid. The aperture is of moderate size and ovate, with a narrow, shallow anal sulcus posteriorly and a narrow entrance to the siphonal canal anteriorly. The outer apertural lip is thin, crenulate, and erect; its inner surface bears six to eight sharply, spirally elongate denticles, the anteriormost one at times double. The columellar lip is adherent posteriorly, expanding in this region into a moderately thick callus, detached and erect for the anterior two-thirds of its length; the posterior end bears two or three oblique pustules. The siphonal canal is moderately long, narrowly open, and slightly bent, if at all.

The body whorl bears five or six spinose varices. Spiral sculpture consists of four major cords, the two outer ones larger than the medial two, and numerous minor cords: three on the shoulder, two between the heavy shoulder spine and the next spine, single minors alternating with the anterior three majors, and five minors on the canal. Where the major and the strongest minor cords intersect the varices, straight, open spines are developed, their length varying with the prominence of the cord. Extremely fine axial growth lamellae produce microscopic scales over the spiral elements, the scales imparting a finely scabrous texture to the shell.

Shell ground color varies widely from uniform rust-brown, to rust-brown with darker-brown intervarices and cord interspaces, to pale violet-brown or yellow-brown. The apertural region is white, suffused with violet or pink, the same color staining all or the distal portions of the spines.

Known to us from the Andaman Islands region of the Indian Ocean in depths of 60–70 m.

See Pl. 3, fig. 3.

Muricopsis jaliscoensis Radwin & D'Attilio, 1970
Muricopsis jaliscoensis Radwin & D'Attilio, 1970: 353

The shell is small to moderate in size (maximum length 28 mm) and roughly fusiform. The spire is high, consisting of two depressed, tabulate nuclear whorls and six weakly shouldered postnuclear whorls. The suture is obscured by the posterior expansion of the subsequent whorl. The body whorl is moderately small and ovate, with a narrow, shallow anal sulcus, this weakly delimited by a spiral parietal ridge. The outer apertural lip is nonerect, finely, marginally denticulate, somewhat thickened, and plicate to strongly dentate on its inner surface. The columellar lip is essentially completely adherent; on the columella, directly above the siphonal canal, are three contiguous denticles in a posterior-anterior orientation, the posteriormost one most prominent. The siphonal canal is moderately long, narrowly open, and dorsally recurved.

The body whorl bears five briefly spinose varices. Intervarical axial sculpture is generally lacking. Spiral sculpture on the body whorl consists of five primary cords, four equi-distant and the fifth more remote on the canal. Interspersed with these are secondary cords, one or two between each two primaries, and fine tertiary cords or threads cover the entire shell. Where the primary and secondary cords intersect the varices, low conical, scalelike, ventrally bent spines are developed; the smaller, secondary spines are more ventrally bent than the others. On the spire the varical edge and its spines are obliterated.

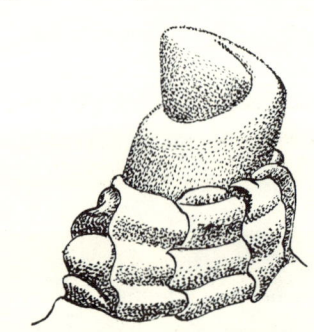

107. *Muricopsis jaliscoensis*, protoconch

Shell color is light sienna-brown to tan. The aperture is bluish-white.

Mexico (Bahía Banderas to Manzanillo).
See Pl. 27, fig. 4.

Muricopsis muricoides (C. B. Adams, 1845)
Fusus muricoides C. B. Adams, 1845: 3; *Tritonalia caribbaea* Bartsch & Rehder, 1939: 7; *Risomurex muricoides* (C. B. Adams) Olsson & McGinty, 1958: 41

The shell is small (maximum length 11 mm) and roughly fusiform or biconic. The spire is high, consisting of one or one and one-half keeled nuclear whorls and four convex postnuclear whorls. The suture is weakly impressed to indistinct. The body whorl is of moderate size, fusoid, and strongly constricted above the canal. The aperture is small, emarginate, and subovate, the posterior margin flattened; the anal sulcus is deep and narrow. The outer apertural lip is thickened, erect, and coarsely serrate; its inner surface bears five strong denticles, the strongest being the second from the anal sulcus. The columellar lip is entirely adherent and bears a number of pustules, apparently reflecting the nodulose sculpture of the shell's outer surface. The siphonal canal is short, narrowly open, and bent to the left.

The body whorl bears eight apparent varices, these extending, as low axial ridges, from the suture to the tip of the siphonal canal. Spiral sculpture consists of eight major cords, six on the body and two on the canal, each cord divided into three parts by two fine transverse grooves; a single thread separates each major cord from its neighbor. Where the major cords cross the varices, moderately large, nodulose swellings are developed.

Shell color is red-brown to yellow-brown; the spiral cord at the shoulder margin, one at the midpoint of the body, and two on the canal are white (on the other cords only the nodules are white). The aperture reflects the brown and white banding of the outer shell surface.

Caribbean Sea: Jamaica to Panamá and Barbados.

See Pl. 2, fig. 3.

Muricopsis nicocheanus (Pilsbry, 1900)

Sistrum nicocheanum Pilsbry, 1900: 3

The shell is moderately small (maximum length 20 mm) and fusiform. The spire is high, consisting of five moderately convex postnuclear whorls and a protoconch of undetermined nature. The suture is moderately impressed. The aperture is ovate, with a moderately deep, U-shaped anal sulcus. The outer apertural lip is thickened and marginally crenulate; its inner surface bears six prominent denticles, the third one down being the largest. The columellar lip is adherent above, detached and erect below; the anterior end of the columella bears a single elongate plait extending into the upper canal. The siphonal canal is of moderate length, broad, moderately open, and weakly, dorsally recurved.

The body whorl bears seven strong, rounded, nodulose varices. The interspaces are approximately as wide as the varices. Intervarical axial sculpture is lacking. Spiral sculpture consists of nine major cords: one above the shoulder margin, six on the body, and three on the canal. The cords diminish in size anteriorly. Three or four raised threads occur between the major cords. Where the major cords intersect the varices, strong, transversely expanded nodes are developed.

Shell color is light fleshy orange-brown. The aperture is white.

South Atlantic, from southern Brazil to mid-Argentina.

See Pl. 23, fig. 12.

Muricopsis oxytata (M. Smith, 1938)

Murex hexagonus Lamarck, 1816: pl. 418, fig. 3, Liste p. 5 (not Gmelin, 1791: 3565); *Murex hexagonus oxytata* M. Smith, 1938: 89

The shell is moderately large for the genus (maximum length 45 mm) and fusiform. The spire is high and acute, consisting of one and one-half nuclear whorls and six angulate postnuclear whorls. The suture is weakly impressed. The body whorl is moderately long and slender. The aperture is moderately small and ovate, with a wide, moderately shallow anal sulcus. The outer apertural lip is erect and coarsely dentate; its inner surface bears seven prominent denticles, the uppermost one more prominent than the rest. The columellar lip is adherent above, detached and erect below; the lower end of the columella may bear a single weak denticle. The siphonal canal is moderately long and dorsally recurved.

The body whorl bears six or seven spinose varices. The entire surface of the shell is squamately lamellose, the leading edges of the varices most strongly so. Spiral sculpture consists of numerous major and minor cords: minor cords on the shoulder, a single major cord at the shoulder margin, and three evenly spaced major cords and intercalary minor cords on the body. A large, spine-free gap at the anterior end of the body is followed on the canal by two major cords and a single intercalary minor one. Where the cords intersect the varices, low, sharp, closed, and ventrally grooved spines are developed.

Shell color is cream to fleshy pink; the varices, in some specimens, are stained brown. The aperture is white to pale creamy yellow.

Southern Florida to the southern Caribbean.

See Pl. 27, fig. 5.

Muricopsis pauxillus (A. Adams, 1854)

Murex pauxillus A. Adams, 1854: 71

The shell is small (maximum length 18 mm) and fusiform. The spire is high and acute, consisting of one and one-half strongly angulate nuclear whorls and six weakly angulate postnuclear whorls; the protoconch is apically depressed and

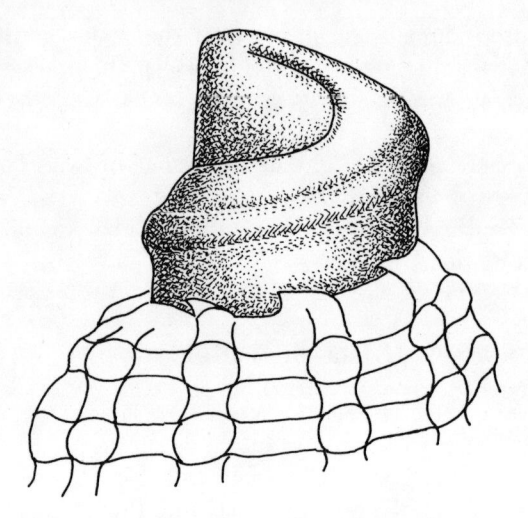

108. *Muricopsis pauxillus*, protoconch

canted opposite to the cant of the other whorls. The suture is weakly marked. The body whorl is of moderate size. The aperture is small and ovate, with a large, inverted-U-shaped anal sulcus. The outer apertural lip is erect and weakly, coarsely crenulate; its inner surface bears five large, knoblike denticles, one above the shoulder margin and four evenly spaced along the remainder of the lip surface. The columellar lip is adherent above, detached and weakly erect below; on the columella, a short distance above the canal, is a single tubercle. The siphonal canal is moderately short, moderately open, and weakly, dorsally recurved.

The body whorl bears six or seven prickly varices, these broader anteriorly, more slender over the shoulder. Intervarical axial sculpture is lacking. Primary spiral sculpture consists of four cords, at times bifid, the upper one of each pair the more prominent; there are minor intercalary cords on the body and on the canal. The intersection of these cords with the varices is marked by the development of short, scalelike spines.

Shell color is chocolate-brown, with two gray-white to yellow-white spiral bands, one at the shoulder margin and one at the base of the body. The aperture is suffused with blue-gray.

Southern Gulf of California to Central America. See Pl. 27, figs. 7–8.

Muricopsis roseus (Reeve, 1846)

Ricinula rosea Reeve, 1846: sp. 46; *Risomurex roseus* (Reeve) Olsson & McGinty, 1958: 41

The shell is small (maximum length 13 mm) and biconic. The spire is high, consisting of a keeled protoconch of one and one-half nuclear whorls and four or five rounded postnuclear whorls. The suture is impressed and undulate. The body whorl is of moderate size, fusoid, and strongly constricted above the canal. The aperture is small, emarginate, and subovate, the posterior margin flattened; the anal sulcus is narrow and rather shallow, and is extended posteriorly into a brief spout. The outer apertural lip is thin and finely, marginally serrate; its inner surface bears five denticles, four moderately weak; only the second from the posterior end is prominent. The columellar lip is entirely adherent and bears two weak, plaitlike ridges, formed by the impression of two rows of pustules from the outer

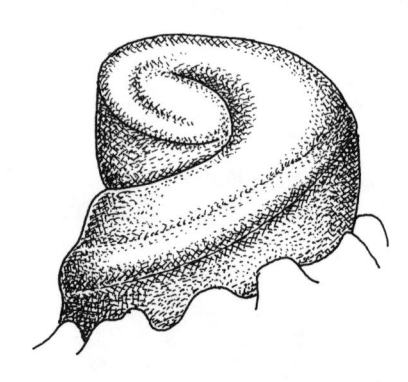

109. *Muricopsis roseus*, protoconch

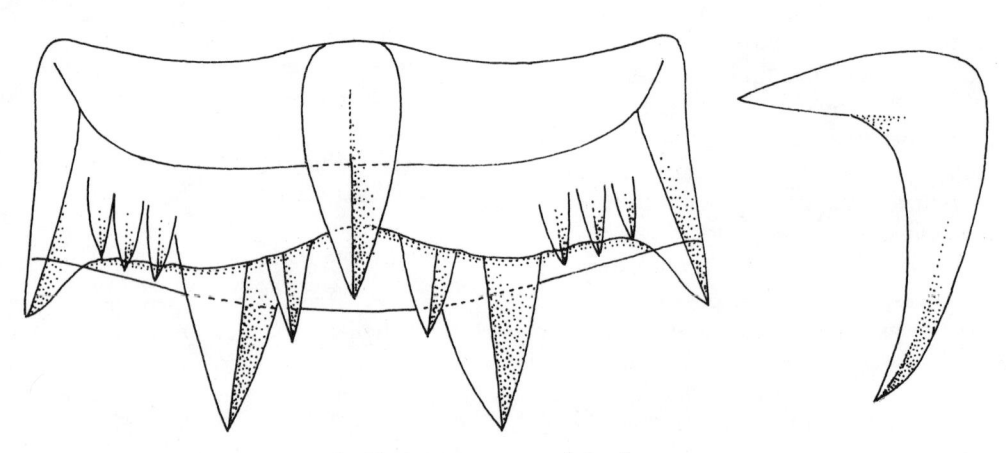

110. *Muricopsis roseus*, radular dentition

surface of the previous whorl on the columellar surface. The siphonal canal is moderate in length, open, and bent to the left.

The body whorl bears eight low varices, extending from the suture to the tip of the siphonal canal. Additional axial sculpture consists of numerous fine, undulate lamellae, these most apparent between the spiral cords. Spiral sculpture consists of eight major cords, six on the body and two weaker ones on the canal. Where the major cords intersect the varices, moderately prominent, sharp-crested nodules are formed.

Shell color is white, with three spiral brown bands, one on the shoulder, one medial on the body, and one at the base of the body. The crests of the nodules on the body are suffused with rosy pink, as is the entire apertural margin and the siphonal canal. The denticles on the outer apertural lip are white.

Caribbean: Bahamas to Hispaniola, St. Thomas, and Antigua.

See Pl. 2, fig. 5.

Muricopsis schrammi (Crosse, 1863)

Engina schrammi Crosse, 1863: 82; *Sistrum ferrugineum rubidum* Dall, 1889: 217; *Risomurex schrammi* (Crosse) Olsson & McGinty, 1958: 41

The shell is small (maximum length 11 mm) and biconic. The spire is high, consisting of one and one-fourth angled, tabulate nuclear whorls and five convex postnuclear whorls. The suture is weakly impressed and undulate. The body whorl is of moderate size, fusoid, and strongly constricted above the siphonal canal. The aperture is small, strongly emarginate, and subovate, the posterior margin flattened; the anal sulcus is narrow and shallow, and is extended to form a brief spout. The outer apertural lip is barely erect and minutely serrate; its inner surface bears five denticles, the second from the posterior end very

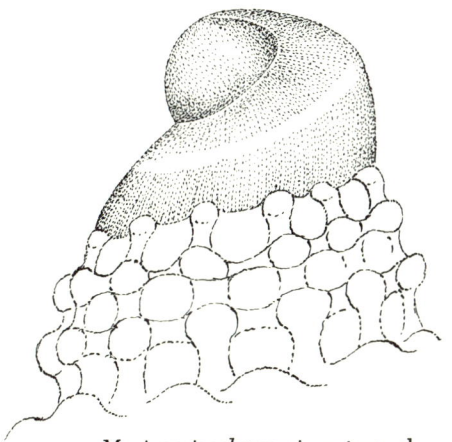

111. *Muricopsis schrammi*, protoconch

large. The columellar lip is adherent at its posterior end, barely detached and weakly erect for most of its length; a series of pustules on the outer shell surface of the previous whorl is reflected on the columella. The siphonal canal is moderately short, almost closed, and bent to the left.

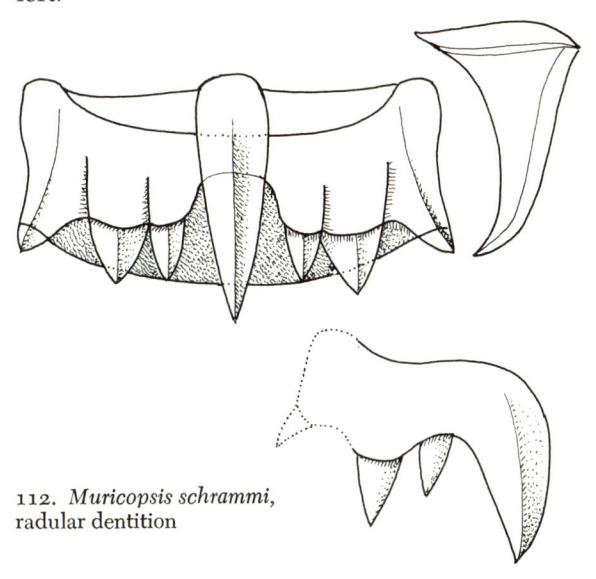

112. *Muricopsis schrammi*, radular dentition

The body whorl bears seven or eight low varices. Additional axial sculpture consists of numerous fine lamellae, thrown into scalelike projections over the spiral sculptural elements. Spiral sculpture consists of eight major cords, six on the body and two weaker ones on the canal; there may be a single intercalary minor cord between each two major cords. Where the major cords intersect the varices, moderately prominent, transversely elongate nodules are formed.

Shell color is blue-black and blue-gray, or red-brown in sun-bleached specimens; the nodules are colored rosy pink. The aperture is purple or blue-gray, with white denticles and pustules. In faded specimens the nodules and the aperture are white.

Caribbean: Guadeloupe to Venezuela and Panamá.

See Pl. 2, fig. 1.

Muricopsis zeteki Hertlein & Strong, 1951

Murex aculeatus Wood, 1828: 15 (not Perry, 1811: pl. 46, fig. 2; Schlotheim, 1820: 147; or Lamarck, 1822: 163); *Murex dubius* Sowerby, 1841: pl. 61, fig. 23, new name for *Murex aculeatus* Wood, 1828 (not Dillwyn, 1817: 716); *Muricopsis zeteki* Hertlein & Strong, 1951: 85, new name (sp. nov. [sic]) for *Murex dubius* Sowerby, 1841 (not Dillwyn, 1817)

The shell is of moderate size (maximum length 28 mm) and broadly fusiform. The spire is moderately high and acute, consisting of six or seven angular postnuclear whorls and a protoconch of undetermined nature. The suture is very weakly marked. The body whorl is moderately large and fusoid. The aperture is of moderate size and ovate, with a broad, inverted-U-shaped anal sulcus. The outer apertural lip is erect and finely dentate; its inner surface is denticulate, the uppermost denticle above the shoulder margin, and of four evenly spaced denticles below the shoulder margin the first is generally the largest. The columellar lip is adherent above, detached and erect below; the columella has a few knobby tubercles, a single low, recessed fold at its anterior end, and a shallow groove between this fold and another fold at the entrance to the canal. The siphonal canal is moderate in length, moderately open to the right, and weakly, dorsally recurved.

The body whorl bears eight spinose varices. Intervarical axial sculpture is lacking. Spiral sculpture consists of four major cords on the body and two on the canal. The uppermost spine, that at the shoulder margin, is the most prominent. Minor cords alternate with majors on the body. Where the cords intersect the varices, short to moderately long, sharp, open spines are developed, these covered with fine threads. In addition, the entire shell is scabrously laminate.

Shell color and degree of spininess vary with locality and/or population. Specimens from Panamá (Pl. 27, fig. 13) are robust, quite long-spined, and generally chocolate-brown to umber-brown, with paler whitish zones between the varices and on portions of the spines. Specimens from west central Mexico (Manzanillo) (Pl. 27, fig. 14) are less robust and shorter-spined; the varices, except for the spines, are black, and the spines are white, grading to yellow-brown on their slopes. Specimens from the Gulf of California (Pl. 27, fig. 15) are as large and as robust as the Panamá forms, but lack almost totally the typical spines and are purple-black, grading to dark brown in the intervarical spaces; the aperture is white to deep blue-white.

Northern Gulf of California to Panamá and the Galápagos Islands.

See Pl. 27, figs. 12–14.

Genus SUBPTERYNOTUS
Olsson & Harbison, 1953

TYPE SPECIES: *Murex textilis* Gabb, 1873 (fossil), by original designation.

The shell in this genus is of moderate size (25–50 mm long) and roughly trigonal. The spire is moderately produced and includes only four or five postnuclear whorls. The suture is weakly impressed and marked by an excavated channel. The body whorl, large and more or less tapering anteriorly, bears three or more well-developed winged varices, these heavily fimbriate on their leading edges and strongly dorsally reflected marginally. The aperture is small and ovate to subovate, with a weak anal sulcus and a limited outlet to the long, exceedingly narrowly open siphonal canal. Microscopic axial-growth lamellae are rippled, the rippling imparting a finely filigreed surface texture to the shell.

?Subpterynotus tatei (Verco, 1895)
Murex tatei Verco, 1895: 84

The shell is of moderate size (maximum length 25 mm) and roughly trigonal. The spire is moderately high and acute, consisting of about two somewhat swollen, brown nuclear whorls and four or more weakly shouldered postnuclear whorls. The suture is slightly impressed. The body whorl is large (three-fourths or more of total shell length) and fusoid. The aperture is moderately small and ovate, with a very weak anal sulcus. The outer apertural lip is erect and finely, marginally serrate; its inner surface is weakly crenulate. The columellar lip is detached and erect. The siphonal canal is moderately long and broad, narrowly open, and sharply, dorsally bent at its distal end.

The body whorl bears five varices, four of these fimbriate, low, and distinct. The final varix is moderately broadly flangelike and densely fimbriate on its leading edge; the margin of the final varix is thrown into a series of short, sharp, reflected points corresponding to the major spiral sculptural elements of the outer shell surface. Spiral sculpture consists of major and minor cords, the majors distributed two on the shoulder, five on the body, and four on the canal, the minors alternating with the majors over the entire shell. Fine axial-growth lamellae covering the entire shell are developed into fine scales over the cords, the scales imparting a scabrous or imbricate appearance to the shell.

Shell color is off-white, with a chestnut-brown shoulder, interrupted by the whitish varices that cross the shoulder in a strongly oblique orientation; at the base of the body, immediately after each varix, there is a weak, nebulous blotch of red-brown. The aperture is porcelaneous white.

Known only from South Australia (type locality, Backstairs Passage; our studied specimen from Smoky Bay).

See Pl. 29, fig. 5.

Genus VITULARIA Swainson, 1840

TYPE SPECIES: *Vitularia tuberculata* Swainson, 1840 (=*Murex miliaris* Gmelin, 1791), by monotypy.

One of the two valid species in the genus, *V. miliaris*, exhibits a great deal of shell variation. This has led to the introduction of numerous superfluous names for this Indo-Pacific form, these based primarily on variability in number, form, and degree of development of the varices, and on other apparently superficial features. The shell of *V. miliaris* has a closed canal, and its operculum is *Ocenebra*-like. Its radular features, however, appear to contradict these other characters, for they are not notably *Ocenebra*-like. *V. salebrosa*, the other species, differs in having an open canal.

Vitularia miliaris (Gmelin, 1791)

Murex miliaris Gmelin, 1791: 3536; *M. vitulinus* Lamarck, 1816: pl. 419, figs. 1, 7, Liste p. 5; *Vitularia tuberculata* Swainson, 1840: 297; *M. crenifer* Montrouzier, 1861: 279; *M. sandwichensis* Pease, 1861: 397; *Transtrafer longmani* Iredale, 1929: 290

The shell is of moderate length (maximum length 50 mm) and pyriform. Its spire is broad, low to moderately high, and consists of one and one-half nuclear whorls and four or five postnuclear whorls. The suture is strongly defined, undulate, and impressed. The body whorl is large, moderately shouldered, and slightly longer than broad. The aperture is large and broadly lenticular, with a negligible anal sulcus and a broadly open entrance into the siphonal canal. The outer apertural lip flares, its posterior end reaching the shoulder of the body whorl; the inner surface of the outer lip bears ten or 11 denticles. The columellar lip is adherent or slightly detached. The siphonal canal is short, slightly recurved, and sealed along the upper one-half to two-thirds of its length; to the left of the canal is a ridge composed of the vestiges of former canals.

Axial sculpture varies in strength and character, consisting of seven to nine oblique, more or less lamellose varices, these ascending the shoulder and appressed to the preceding whorl. Immediately below the shoulder-edge is a broad spiral depression or furrow, followed by a broad spiral ridge that encircles the body whorl at its midpoint. A second, lower spiral furrow is followed by a less pronounced spiral ridge above the canal. The portion of each spiral furrow following each varix may be more strongly depressed. In addition, the shells of most specimens have a finely malleated surface, this strongest on the varices.

Shell color is white to fleshy or, exceptionally, orange or brown; in some specimens there are spiral rows of brown spots on the shoulder-edge and on each of the two spiral ridges. The interior of the aperture is white, with an apricot-colored margin, or the entire aperture may be pale apricot in color. In some populations, particularly those from Australia, the generally low, rounded varices are replaced by short, suberect lamellae.

Generally throughout the Indo-West Pacific. See Pl. 7, figs. 7, 12–13.

Vitularia salebrosa (King & Broderip, 1832)

Murex salebrosa King & Broderip, 1832: 347

The shell is moderately large (maximum length 85 mm) and pyriform. Its spire is moderately high, with three nuclear whorls and five to seven sharply shouldered postnuclear whorls. The suture is deeply impressed and somewhat undulate. The body whorl is large (two-thirds of total shell length) and massive, about half as broad as long. The aperture is subovate, with a weakly to moderately well-developed anal sulcus posteriorly and a broad opening anteriorly into the siphonal canal. The outer apertural lip is somewhat thickened by the development of two to five thin,

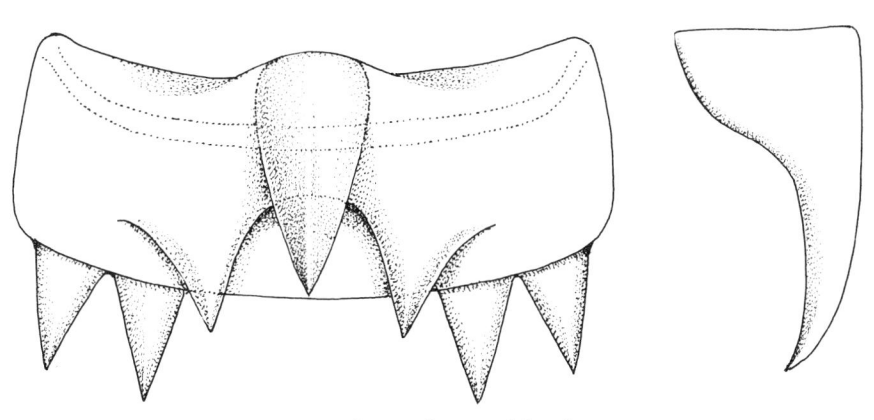

113. *Vitularia miliaris*, radular dentition

densely packed lamellae; the inner surface of the lip bears 12 to 16 strong, closely spaced denticles, and from this line of denticles to the edge of the lip it is slightly undulate and flares outward. The columellar lip is entirely adherent. The short siphonal canal is broadly open; to the left of the canal is a ridge bearing the vestiges of former canals.

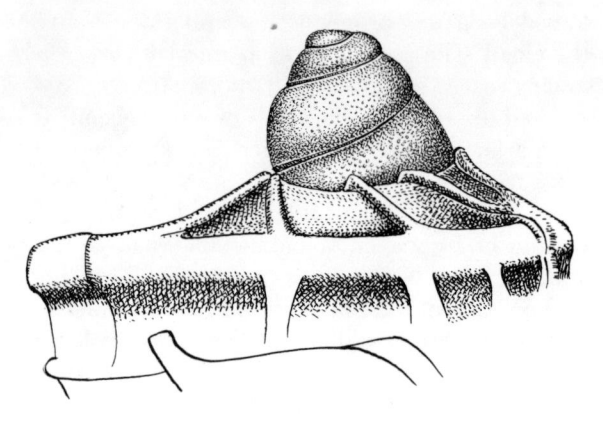

114. *Vitularia salebrosa*, protoconch

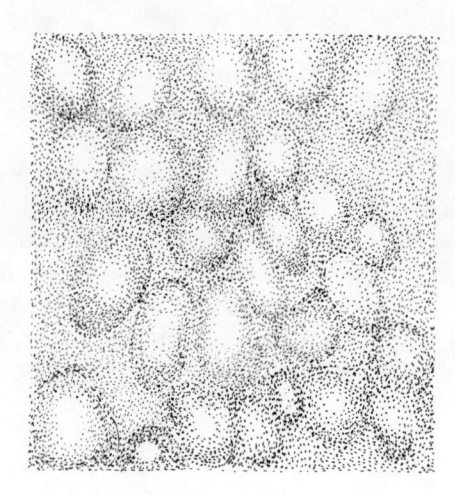

115. *Vitularia salebrosa*, enlarged microsculpture

The body whorl bears six or seven sharp, lamellose varices, flaring posteriorly to touch the preceding whorl at about its midpoint. Intervarical spaces are generally devoid of prominent axial sculpture. Spiral sculpture generally consists solely of a prominent shoulder keel. In addition, a microsculpture, most strongly developed over the varices, imparts to the entire surface of the shell a finely malleated appearance. In some specimens there is a diffuse or discontinuous spiral band of stronger microsculpture a short distance below the shoulder keel.

Shell color is light to dark brown, with four or five darker spiral bands: two on the shoulder, one on the shoulder margin, and two broader ones below the shoulder. The interior of the aperture is white, and the rim is burnt orange.

Isla Cedros, Mexico, and the southern Gulf of California to Panamá and the Galápagos Islands.

See Pl. 7, fig. 14.

Subfamily Trophoninae

COSSMANN, 1903

The following subfamilial definition is based primarily on the boreal and tropical genera, as well as on the austral nominate genus. For an explanation see discussion below.

The shell is small for the family (16–60 mm in length), is generally fusiform or stoutly fusiform in shape, and bears a generally white ground color, occasionally with bands of brown or pink. The aperture is simple and ovate and both lips are generally nondenticulate. The siphonal canal is short to long and narrowly open. Most species have more or less strongly developed lamellose sculptural elements, these perhaps corresponding to varices; spiral sculpture is weak or lacking in most cases. Virtually all of the northern genera, and many austral species, have a more or less well-developed, simple intritacalx over a smooth shell surface.

Trophonine protoconchs are uniformly short, with few, simple, convex whorls. The operculum is generally of the muricine type.

The radular dentition resembles that of the Muricinae, but the five independent cusps of the rachidian tooth are crowded toward the center of the tooth, leaving a gap between each lateral cusp and its corresponding tooth-base endpoint.

Distribution: worldwide in deeper and cooler waters, in depths of 0 to 500 m, most in 100 to 300 m.

The subfamily has been the site of assignment of many dissimilar forms that seem, on the basis of the shell and radular morphology of the type species of *Trophon* (*T. geversianus*), unlikely to belong there. Several problems complicate a full understanding and treatment of this group. First, the cold-water habitat of many northern species assigned here (primarily the genus *Boreotrophon*) seems to favor the development of great variability in shell form, as is the case in most boreal faunas. This has led to great difficulty in determining species limits, which in turn has led to the introduction of numerous names for boreal forms, many undoubtedly superfluous. Species determination is further hindered by the paucity of collections from deep water in these severe northern climates; work can progress usefully only with the accumulation of specimen-series of adequate size and geographical distribution. We have listed below several of the best known and most readily circumscribed of these northern species, but we have made no extensive attempt to unravel the tangle of names and species represented by the remainder.

In austral waters a different problem prevails. Of 26 trophonine genera listed herein, 20 are austral. Three of these are the South American *Trophon s.s.*, and two probable synonyms. The remaining 17 genera are from Australia, New Zealand, and South Africa, and most represent very small forms, the type species of which, in many cases, is known from only a few specimens. An examination of original illustrations and a few actual specimens suggests to us that although these may be all muricid in nature (and this is by no means certain, as several resemble members of the Turridae, Pyramidellidae, etc.), there is certainly no reason to assume a trophonine placement for them all. In some cases several nominal genera have been synonymized; Ponder (1972) has "lumped" *Axymene, Lenitrophon, Xymenella,* and *Zeatrophon* under *Xymene*.

We have determined that present information is not adequate to deal authoritatively with this group, and we have decided instead simply to offer such information as we have for the use of future workers. In addition, the heterogeneity of these austral forms and their doubtful placement here have caused us to base our subfamilial definition on those forms about whose placement we felt most confident (i.e. the boreal forms).

We have eliminated from consideration several genera generally classed with the trophons, including *Austrotrophon* Dall, 1902 (type species: *Trophon cerrosensis* Dall, 1891); *Forreria* Jousseaume, 1880 (type species: *Murex belcheri* Hinds, 1844); and *Zacatrophon* Hertlein & Strong, 1951 (type species: *Trophon beebei* Hertlein & Strong, 1951). These omissions are based on the finding that all had radulae characteristic of the family Thaididae, and thus were beyond the taxonomic scope of this book.

The type species of such non-austral genera as *Boreotrophon* (*clathratus*), *Trophonopsis* (*muricatus*), *Nodulotrophon* (*dalli*), *Actinotrophon* (*actinophorus*), *Pagodula* (*vaginata*), and *Pascula* (*citrica*) are treated fully herein. The following list includes some other of the better known nominal species,* exclusive of austral forms.

alaskanus Dall, 1902: 545
avalonensis Dall, 1902: 546
banffius Donovan, 1804: pl. 169, fig. 1
barvicensis Johnston, 1825: 221
bentleyi Dall, 1908: 249
beringi Dall, 1902: 544
candelabrum Reeve, 1848: sp. 79
cymatus Dall, 1902: 548
eucymatus Dall, 1902: 547
multicostatus Eschscholtz, 1829: pl. 9, fig. 4
orpheus Gould, 1849: 142
pacificus Dall, 1902: 544
paucicostatus Habe & Ito, 1965: 18, 32
peregrinus Dall, 1902: 543
smithi Dall, 1902: 542
stuarti E. A. Smith, 1880: 481
triangulatus Carpenter, 1864: 224
truncatus Gmelin, 1791: 3547

Genus ACTINOTROPHON Dall, 1902

TYPE SPECIES: *Trophon (Boreotrophon) actinophorus* Dall, 1889, by original designation.

The following is taken, with modifications, from the original description:

"Resembling *Boreotrophon*, with long coronating spines, but also possessing successive canals that are so curved that their projecting portions, recurving from the siphonal fasciole, form a whorl of hollow, split spines, diverging from a deep umbilical [pseudoumbilical] pit, as in some murices."

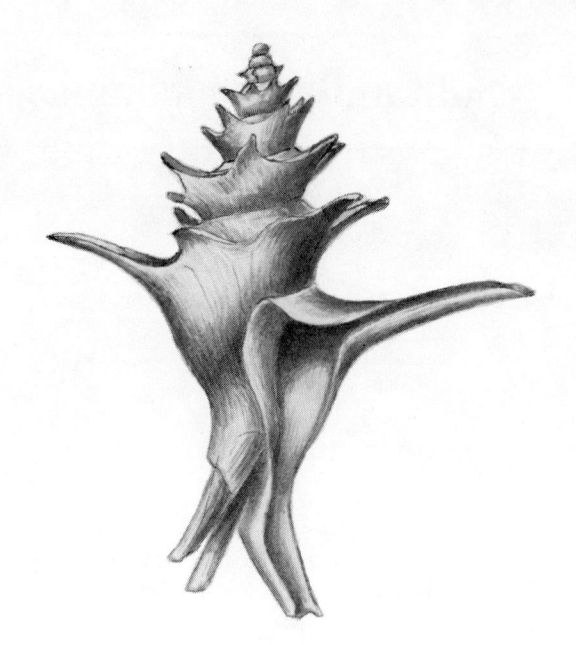

* Some references in this list do not appear in the bibliography.

116. *Actinotrophon actinophorus*

Actinotrophon actinophorus (Dall, 1889)
Trophon (Boreotrophon) actinophorus Dall, 1889: 206

We have not seen a specimen of this species; the following is taken from the original description:

"Shell translucent white, very thin, glassy, seven-whorled; nucleus white, smooth, two-whorled; spiral sculpture of very fine, faint, irregular spiral lines; transverse sculpture [consists] of the incremental lines and a keel or angulation at the shoulder of the whorl, which is produced into long, nearly horizontally extended triangular spines, [these] deeply guttered out, and having the upper or posterior side shorter in the direction of rotation than the other, so that looked at from the apex the spines recall the paper whirligigs or wind-wheels used as children's toys. There are six of these spines on the last whorl and 31 on the whole shell figured. Spire elevated; suture distinct, not channelled; aperture narrow, long, angulated at the spine, continuous with the open canal, which is curved to the right; at the left of the canal projects a whorl of three or more tips of antecedent canals (often broken away). Interior of aperture simple, not thickened. Maximum length of shell 17.5 mm; of last whorl 12.3 mm; of aperture and canal 10.0 mm; maximum width of aperture 3.0 mm; of the shell exclusive of spines 6.0 mm; of the whole shell 14.0 mm.

"Habitat: ['Blake'] Station 134, off Santa Cruz [U.S. Virgin Islands], in 248 fathoms [500 m], sand; ['Blake'] Station 206, off Martinique, in 170 fathoms [340 m], sand; and ['Blake'] Station 299, near Barbados, in 140 fathoms [280 m], coral; temperatures from 49° to 56.5° F."

Genus **AFRITROPHON** Tomlin, 1947

TYPE SPECIES: *Trophon kowieensis* Sowerby, 1901, by original designation.

The following is taken, in modified form, from the original description:

"Shell small, somewhat the appearance of an *Ocenebra*, canal very short, suture deep, whorls with one or more strong spiral ribs, the space between these ribs crossed by small riblets so as to produce a latticed effect."

Afritrophon kowieensis (Sowerby, 1901)

Trophon kowieensis Sowerby, 1901: 213

The shell is tiny (ca. 6 mm in length) and roughly fusiform. The spire is high and acute, consisting of one and one-half or two nuclear whorls and three or four shouldered postnuclear whorls. The suture is impressed. The body whorl is of moderate size and fusoid. The aperture is of moderate size and ovate, with no perceptible anal sulcus. The outer apertural lip is not markedly thickened and is fluted, the high points reflecting the spiral sculptural cords. The columellar lip is smooth and adherent. The siphonal canal is short, open, and bent to the left.

The shell is nonvaricate. The body whorl bears seven moderately strong spiral cords: three on the shoulder, three on the body, and one on the canal. Numerous fine axial ribs are apparent between the cords, each causing a swelling as it traverses a cord; the effect is latticelike, with a predominant spiral sculpture.

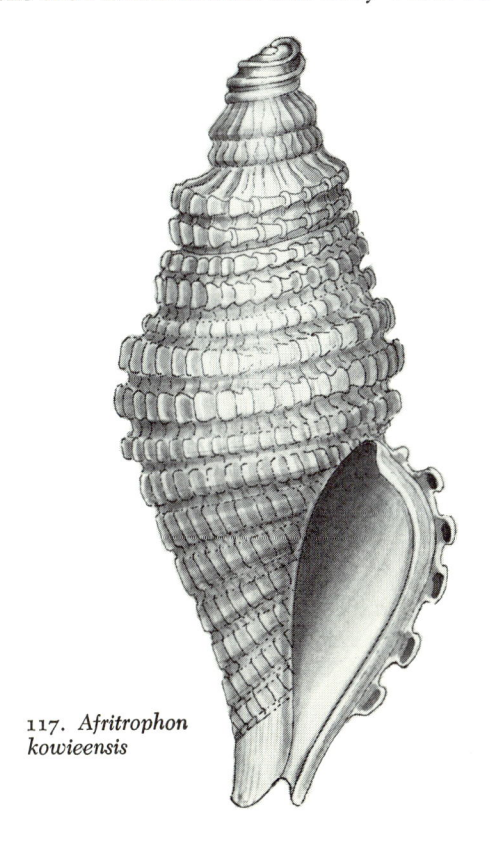

Shell color is uniform waxy yellow or orange, with a white aperture and protoconch.

Known to us from various South African localities ("the Kowie" [= Port Alfred], Jeffreys Bay, Agulhas Bank, St. Francis Bay, and Algoa Bay).

Genus **ANATROPHON** Iredale, 1929

TYPE SPECIES: *Trophon sarmentosus* Hedley & May, 1908, by original designation.

No generic diagnosis was ever given; the type-species designation is the sole indication of the generic limits. See the treatment of *A. sarmentosus* for an understanding of the genus.

Anatrophon sarmentosus (Hedley & May, 1908)

Trophon sarmentosus Hedley & May, 1908: 121

On the basis of the type species, a species assignable to *Anatrophon* could be characterized as follows: The shell is small (ca. 6 mm in length) and fusiform. The spire is high, consisting of four convex postnuclear whorls and a protoconch of undetermined nature. The suture is distinct, if not impressed. The aperture is of moderate size and ovate, with a V-shaped anal sulcus. The outer apertural lip is nonerect and slightly reflected at its margin. The columellar lip is entirely adherent. The siphonal canal is very short, open, and bent.

The shell is nonvaricate, and the dominant sculpture consists of nine strong axial costae; these are high and rounded, with little apparent interspace between. Spiral sculpture consists of extremely weak lines, numbering about seven or eight on the body whorl. At the intersections of the axial costae and spiral striae the costae develop small bumps.

Shell color is apparently lustrous white.

Known only from the type locality (11 km east of Cape Pillar, Tasmania, in 200 m).

See Pl. 29, fig. 13.

Genus **APIXYSTUS** Iredale, 1929

TYPE SPECIES: *Trophon stimuleus* Hedley, 1907, by original designation.

No generic diagnosis was ever given; the type-species designation is the sole indication of the generic limits. See the treatment of *A. stimuleus* for an understanding of the genus.

117. *Afritrophon kowieensis*

Apixystus stimuleus (Hedley, 1907)

Trophon stimuleus Hedley, 1907: 293

We have not seen a specimen of this species; the following is taken from the original description:

"Shell minute, thin, prickly, ovately fusiform, angled at the shoulder. Whorls five, two of which compose the glossy, conical protoconch. Color white. Sculpture: thin, close, laminate varices, about 12 to a whorl, ascend the spire obliquely, produced on the shoulder in a claw projecting to the suture, crumpled into folds by a ridge on the shoulder and two lesser ones below the periphery, the shoulder folds rise in hollow thorns. On the base the varices cease. Aperture round, the outer lip projecting in a broad, squamose varix. The inner lip expanding over the axis. Canal short, broad, and open. Length 3.5 × 2.1 mm."

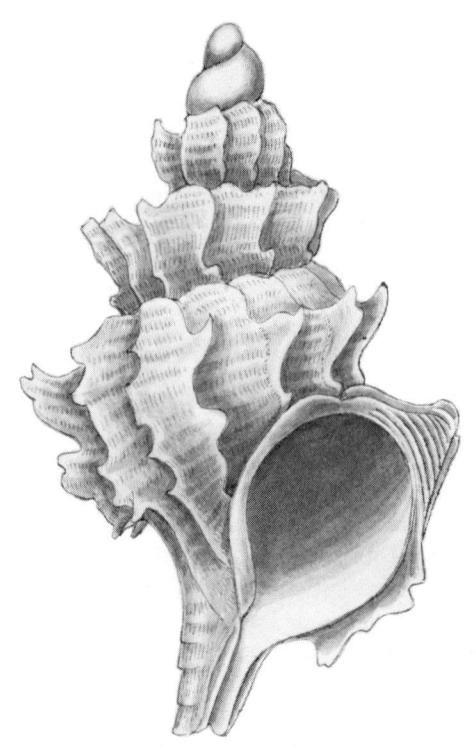

118. *Apixystus stimuleus*

Known only from off Narrabeen (New South Wales), Australia, in 160 m.

Genus AXYMENE Finlay, 1927

TYPE SPECIES: *Trophon turbator* Finlay, 1927, by original designation.

No generic diagnosis was ever given; the type-species designation is the sole indication of the generic limits. See the treatment of *A. turbator* for an understanding of the genus.

Axymene turbator (Finlay, 1927)

Trophon turbator Finlay, 1927: 424

We have not seen a specimen of this species; the following is taken from the original description:

"Shell small, dark-colored. Apex small, papillate, of one and one-half smooth whorls, the nucleus globose and asymmetric. 14–16 axial ribs per whorl, faint and thin on shoulder, thence prominent to lower suture (interstices narrow at bottom, subequal to ribs at top of ribs), rapidly vanishing on base. Four spirals on penultimate whorl below shoulder (which is smooth), nine on body whorl, cords thickish (with subequal interstices), undulated and faintly thickened by axials, the ninth on neck of canal, very prominent. Faintly lamellose growth lines over the whole surface. Spire subequal to aperture with canal, outlines stepped but straight. Whorls strongly shouldered at upper third, shoulder lightly concave, straight below. Suture inconspicuous, margined below by a pronounced swelling, above by the lowest cord. Aperture trapezoidal, widely angled above, produced below into a moderately long narrow canal, flexed a little to left, not notched at base. Outer [apertural] lip thin and sharp, vertical in middle, straight and oblique in opposite directions at shoulder base. [Columellar] lip defined as a narrow glaze. Pillar subvertical, twisted near inception of canal and thence

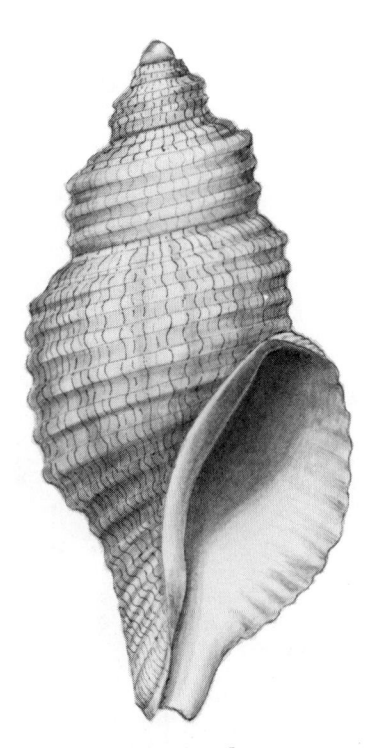

119. *Axymene turbator*

narrowing to a long fine point. Fasciole weak, smooth except for growth lines. Color sienna-chocolate, outside with grayish tints, inside chocolate, pillar touched with white.

"Height 12.5 mm; diameter 6 mm.

"Locality: Dunedin Harbour, New Zealand (type locality) [only record]."

Genus BENTHOXYSTUS Iredale, 1929

TYPE SPECIES: *Trophon columnarius* Hedley & May, 1908, by original designation.

No generic diagnosis was ever given; the type-species designation is the sole indication of the generic limits. See the treatment of *B. columnarius* for an understanding of the genus.

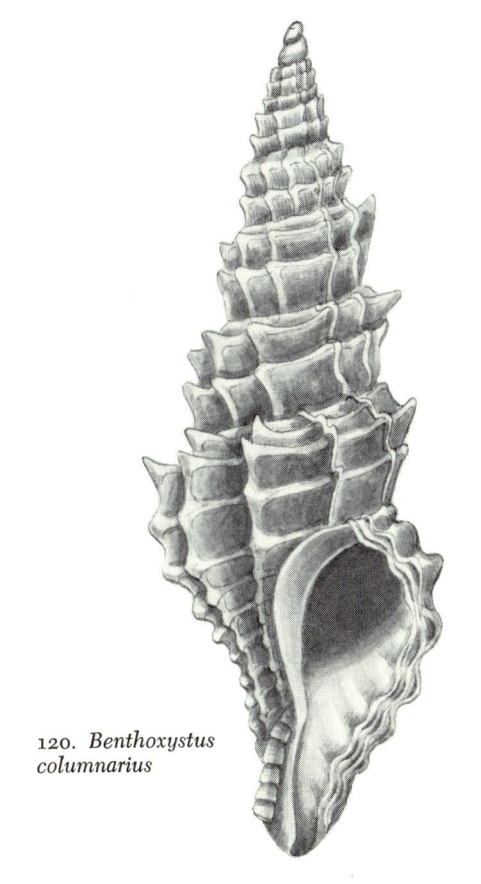

120. *Benthoxystus columnarius*

Benthoxystus columnarius (Hedley & May, 1908)

Trophon columnarius Hedley & May, 1908: 121

We have not seen a specimen of this species; the following is taken from the original description:

"Shell of medium size, elongate, roughened by the profuse decoration. Color pale yellow, with brown on the apex, a basal and a sutural band. Whorls nine, including a smooth conical protoconch of two and one-half whorls. Sculpture: thin projecting varices, nine to a whorl on the larger whorls, ascend obliquely and continuously from whorl to whorl. These varices are scalloped by the passage of the spirals, and develop sharp points on the shoulder; on the base they degenerate to mere scales. The spirals amount to 12 on the body whorl, and to three or four on the upper whorls; they are crowded on the base, but separated on the shoulder by flat interstices of equal or greater breadth. A secondary microscopic sculpture of faint radial threads, and still fainter spiral scratches, appears between the varices. Aperture oval, shielded by the youngest varix; columella excavate. Length 20 mm; breadth 8 mm."

Dredged in 80 fathoms (160 m) 22 miles (ca. 31 km) east of Narrabeen (New South Wales), Australia, as well as from the type locality (100 fathoms [200 m] 7 miles [ca. 10 km] east of Cape Pillar, Tasmania).

Genus BOREOTROPHON Fischer, 1884

TYPE SPECIES: *Murex clathratus* Linné, 1767, by monotypy.

The following is taken, with modifications, from Grant & Gale (1931: 721):

"Shell somewhat fusiform, with long, slender anterior canal, axial ribs moderately or weakly developed into thin lamellae with no substantial spines on the shoulder of the whorls; spiral sculpture absent or faint. Color white, with few exceptions."

Neptunea Röding, 1798, was used by Dall (1919b) for some members of this group because he was apparently unaware of an earlier type-species designation for *Neptunea* by Monterosato (1872), *Murex antiquus* Linné, 1758, a buccinid species.

Boreotrophon clathratus (Linné, 1767)

Murex clathratus Linné, 1767: 1223

The shell is of moderate size for the genus (ca. 22 mm in length). The spire is high and acute, consisting of five or six shouldered postnuclear whorls and a protoconch of undetermined nature. The suture is impressed. The body whorl is of moderate size and fusiform. The aperture is moderately large and ovate, with a very weak, inconspicuous anal sulcus. The outer apertural lip is erect and marginally nonserrate; its inner surface is smooth. The columellar lip is arcuate and entirely adherent. The siphonal canal is moderately long, slender, narrowly open, and bent to the left above, then straight distally.

The body whorl bears ten to 15 simple, lamellose varices and is completely lacking in spiral ornamentation.

Shell color is pale, translucent yellow-tan, covered by a simple, flat-white intritacalx and a thin, light-brown periostracum.

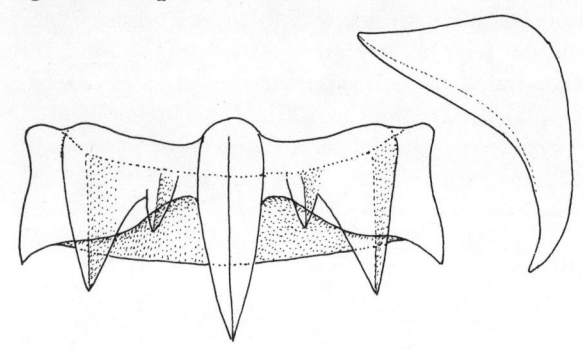

121. *Boreotrophon clathratus*, radular dentition

Circumarctic and the boreal coasts of most northern continents (south to Norway, Labrador, and Alaska).

See Pl. 28, fig. 9.

Genus COMPTELLA Finlay, 1927

TYPE SPECIES: *Trophon curtus* Murdoch, 1905, by original designation.

No generic diagnosis was ever given; the type-species designation is the sole indication of the generic limits. See the treatment of *C. curta* for an understanding of the genus.

Comptella curta (Murdoch, 1905)

Trophon (Kalydon) curtus Murdoch, 1905: 228

We have not seen a specimen of this species; the following is taken from the original description:

"Shell small, ovate, rather solid, spirally and longitudinally ribbed, the latter strongest and forming prominent nodules on the lines of intersection. Color whitish, occasionally a brown band on the base, rarely a few ill-defined scattered spots on the periphery. Whorls six, lightly shouldered. Protoconch of two whorls, smooth except the last half-turn, upon which two small spirals arise. The sculpture consists of ten or 11, rarely 12, longitudinal ribs, narrower than the interspaces, except where the latter number occurs, then equal or rather wider. Of the spirals there are two on the spire whorls and six or seven on the last—occasionally three on the penultimate and eight on the last; the anterior spiral not infrequently prominent and the nodules sometimes obsolete. Aperture ovate. Outer [apertural] lip slightly expanded, the margin occasionally feebly dentate; anterior canal short and somewhat curved. Length 5.7 mm; breadth 2.59 mm.

"Type in the Colonial Museum [= Dominion Museum].

"Whangaroa Harbour (Mr. A. Hamilton)."

122. *Comptella curta*

Genus ENATIMENE Iredale, 1929

TYPE SPECIES: *Trophon simplex* Hedley, 1903, by original designation.

No generic diagnosis was ever given; the type-species designation is the sole indication of the generic limits. See the treatment of *E. simplex* for an understanding of the genus.

Enatimene simplex (Hedley, 1903)

Trophon simplex Hedley, 1903: 380

The shell is small (ca. 11 mm in length) and fusiform. The spire is high, consisting of one and three-fourths convex, horn-colored, granulose nuclear whorls and four rather strongly convex postnuclear whorls. The suture is distinct. The body whorl is of moderate size and fusoid. The aperture is of moderate size and ovate, with a weakly defined anal sulcus. The outer apertural lip is simple and weakly undulate, reflecting the spiral sculpture. The columellar lip is adherent with a distinctly thickened edge. The siphonal canal is moderately long, bent to the left, open, and weakly recurved at its tip.

Axial sculpture in the nonvaricate shell consists, on the body whorl, of 12 costae, each of which is aligned with one on the preceding whorl. Each costa is approximately as broad as an interspace. Spiral sculpture consists, on the body whorl, of three primary cords on the body and six secondary cords, each becoming weaker anteriorly. These cords rise above the costae. There are also strong spiral growth lines.

The shell is pale horn color (brownish to pale yellow-ochre).

Known from off the coast of New South Wales, Australia (Port Kembla, Cape Three Points, Botany Bay, Wata Mooli, off Crookhaven River, and Port Hacking) in depths of 40–200 m.

Genus ENIXOTROPHON Iredale, 1929

TYPE SPECIES: *Trophon carduelis* Watson, 1883, by original designation.

No generic diagnosis was ever given; the type-species designation is the sole indication of the generic limits. See the treatment of *E. carduelis* for an understanding of the genus.

Enixotrophon carduelis (Watson, 1883)

Trophon carduelis Watson, 1883: 387

The shell is small (about 10 mm in length) and fusiform. The spire is high and acute, consisting of one and three-fourths nuclear whorls and four tabulate postnuclear whorls. The suture is distinct. The body whorl is fusoid. The aperture is of moderate size and ovate; the anal sulcus is extremely shallow and broad. The outer apertural lip is simple, the columellar lip adherent. The siphonal canal is of moderate length and open.

The body whorl bears ten strong axial costae, these more elevated near and on the shoulder, where the trailing side of each costa is thin and lamellate and rises above the shoulder to form a "crown." Spiral sculpture is lacking.

Shell color is white.

Off New South Wales (Australia), in deep water.

Genus FUEGOTROPHON Powell, 1951

TYPE SPECIES: *Fusus crispus* Gould, 1849, by original designation.

No generic diagnosis was ever given; the type-species designation is the sole indication of the generic limits. See the treatment of *F. crispus* for an understanding of the genus.

Fuegotrophon crispus (Gould, 1849)

Fusus crispus Gould, 1849: 141

We have not seen a specimen of this species; the following is taken, with modifications, from the original description:

"Shell small, subrhomboidal, elongate, coarse, gray; eight lamellate varices and numerous incremental growth lines comprise the axial sculpture, and spiral sculpture consists of several weak cords. The spire is conical and acute, consisting of about seven or eight convex whorls, the earlier ones more angulate than the later ones. The last whorl constitutes about two-thirds of the entire shell length. The siphonal canal is slender and moderately long, and is bent to the right. The aperture is round to ovate; the lip is semicircular and crenulate on its inner surface. Length 7/8 inch [22 mm], diameter ca. 3/8 inch [9.3 mm], columella straight."

Orange Harbor, Tierra del Fuego.

123. *Fuegotrophon crispus*

Genus GEMIXYSTUS Iredale, 1929

TYPE SPECIES: *Trophon laminatus* Petterd, 1884, by original designation.

No generic definition was ever given; the type-species designation is the sole indication of the generic limits. See the treatment of *G. laminatus* for an understanding of the genus.

Gemixystus laminatus (Petterd, 1884)

Trophon laminatus Petterd, 1884: 136

The shell is fusiform and small (about 5 mm in length), but the studied specimen is probably immature, for its shell has only three convex postnuclear whorls. The protoconch consists of one and three-fourths lustrous, semitranslucent nuclear whorls, of which the first three-fourths of a whorl is flattened above, with a soft shoulder angle. The suture is distinct. The body whorl is of moderate size. The aperture is moderately large and subovate, with an inconspicuous anal sulcus. The margin of the outer apertural lip is undulate, reflecting the spiral sculpture of the shell. The columellar lip is adherent. The siphonal canal is short, open, and somewhat recurved.

The last whorl bears nine spiral cords, a weak one on the shoulder and eight distributed evenly from just below the shoulder margin to the tip of the canal. Axial sculpture consists of about 18 low, bladelike laminae, these distorted to the left on the shoulder and undulate over the spiral cords.

Shell color is a warm, semilustrous white.

Tasmania.

See Pl. 29, fig. 12.

Genus LENITROPHON Finlay, 1927

TYPE SPECIES: *Trophon convexus* Suter, 1909, by original designation.

No generic diagnosis was ever given; the type-species designation is the sole indication of the generic limits. See the treatment of *L. convexus* for an understanding of the genus.

Lenitrophon convexus (Suter, 1909)

Trophon convexus Suter, 1909: 126

We have not seen a specimen of this species; the following is taken verbatim from the original description:

"Shell very small, fusiform, thin, axially costate and spirally lirate. Sculpture consisting of strong, broadly rounded axial costae, about ten on a whorl, extending from suture to suture, but absent on the base, crossed by distant and prominent spiral cords, with a few intercalated fine threads upon the neck of the canal, produced into oval nodules upon the axial ribs; the spire whorls with a fine thread below the suture, margining it, and three distant strong spirals below it; body whorl with 14–15 cinguli, those upon the base not nodulose. Fasciole hardly discernible. Color yellowish-brown, neck of canal and inner lip whitish, interior of aperture light brown. Spire acuminate, conic, of the same height as the aperture with canal. Protoconch papillate, of one and one-half smooth and convex whorls, the globular nucleus slightly lateral. Whorls five, regularly increasing, convex; base contracted toward the canal. Suture but little impressed, undulating, margined below.

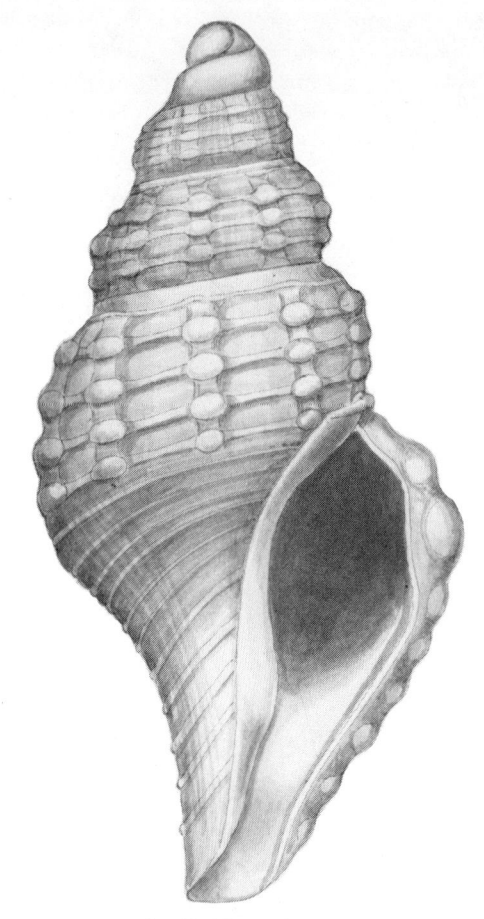

124. *Lenitrophon convexus*

Aperture subvertical, ovate, angled above, produced below into a moderately long, oblique and slightly recurved, widely open canal. Outer [apertural] lip thin and sharp, convex, crenulated by the spiral sculpture, smooth inside. Columella vertical, straight, twisted and narrowed below; inner [columellar] lip thin and narrow, extending over the excavated parietal wall, drawn out to a narrow ridge toward the inner margin of the canal. Operculum unknown.

"Diameter 3.5 mm; height 7 mm.

"Type in the Canterbury Museum, Christchurch (N.Z.)."

Southeast of Cape Saunders, New Zealand, in 100 fathoms [200 m].

Genus **LITOZAMIA** Iredale, 1929

TYPE SPECIES: *Peristernia rudolphi* Brazier, 1894, by original designation.

No generic diagnosis was ever given; the type-species designation is the sole indication of the generic limits. See the treatment of *L. rudolphi* for an understanding of the genus.

Litozamia rudolphi (Brazier, 1894)

Peristernia rudolphi Brazier, 1894: 166

We have not seen a specimen of this species; the following is taken from the original description:

"Shell small, fusiform, turreted, yellowish-brown, dotted with dark reddish-brown spots, larger below the sutures; apex smooth, mammillate; whorls six, slightly convex, longitudinally ribbed, crossed with spiral lirae, very conspicuous on the edge of the ribs, finer between and at the sides; aperture ovate, outer [apertural] lip rather thick, slightly variced behind; interior of aperture with three or four small nodules; columella straight, the canal short, curved.

"Length 6.5 mm, greatest breadth 4 mm, least 3.5 mm. Five specimens.

"This pretty little shell may be known by the large dark reddish-brown spots below the suture, and nearly on the angle of the whorls."

Known only from southern Tasmania.

Genus **MINORTROPHON** Finlay, 1927

TYPE SPECIES: *Daphnella crassilirata* Suter, 1908, by original designation.

No generic diagnosis was ever given; the type-species designation is the sole indication of the generic limits. See the treatment of *M. crassiliratus* for an understanding of the genus.

126. *Minortrophon crassiliratus*

Minortrophon crassiliratus (Suter, 1908)

Daphnella crassilirata Suter, 1908: 190

We have not seen a specimen of this species; the following is taken from the original description:

"Shell very small, elongate-fusiform, white with stout spiral cords, turriculate. Sculpture: the protoconch, the shoulders on the following whorls, and the base are smooth, the lower spire whorls have four strong spiral cords, separated by very narrow interstices, the uppermost forming the angle of the narrow and but little sloping shoulder; body whorl with six or seven spiral cords, the greater part of the base in front of the aperture smooth; growth lines fine. Colour white. Spire elevated, conic, turriculate, one and three-fourths the height of the aperture. Protoconch papillate, of one and one-half smooth and convex whorls.

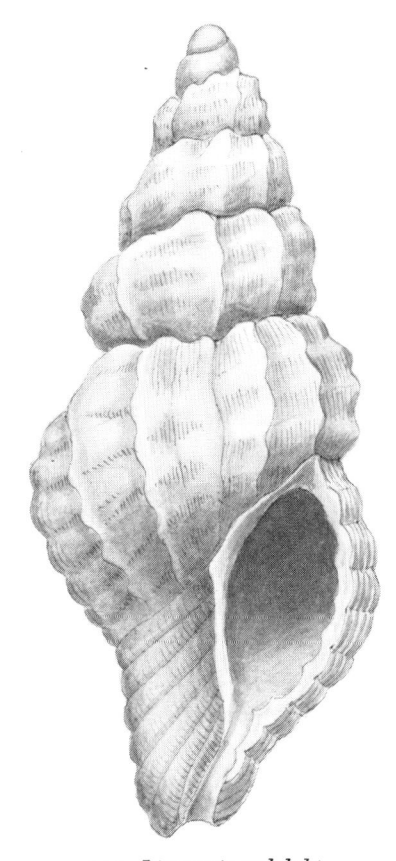

125. *Litozamia rudolphi*

Whorls four and one-half, rather rapidly increasing, narrowly and flatly shouldered, convex below; base slightly contracted. Suture linear. Aperture broadly oval, angularly rounded above, with a broad short canal, which often is wanting, faintly emarginate at the base. Outer lip slightly angled above, straightened at the middle, rounded or contracted below, smooth inside. Columella vertical, excavated toward the lightly concave parietal wall, somewhat bent to the left below. Inner lip thin and narrow.

"Diameter 1.5 mm; height 3.2 mm.

"Animal unknown.

"Habitat: near the Snares, in 50 fathoms [100 m]; Stewart Island in 50–54 fathoms [100–108 m] (all New Zealand)."

Genus NODULOTROPHON Habe & Ito, 1965

TYPE SPECIES: *Trophon dalli* Kobelt, 1878, by original designation.

The following is taken from the original description:

"The shell is roundly ovate in shape, with a very long siphonal canal. The spire is conically elevated and consists of five whorls, the surface of which is sculptured with many lamellate costae and crowded with a series of triangular nodules on the shoulders. This genus is also well recognized by [its] particularly long siphonal canal."

Nodulotrophon dalli (Kobelt, 1878)

Trophon dalli Kobelt, 1878: 289

The shell is moderately large (ca. 60 mm in length) and club-shaped. The spire is moderately high and acute, consisting of five subangulate, slope-shouldered postnuclear whorls and a protoconch of undetermined nature. The suture is distinct. The body whorl is proportionately small. The aperture is moderately large and ovate, with a distinct anal sulcus delimited by a parietal bulge. The outer apertural lip is simple. The columellar lip is adherent. The siphonal canal is very long, curved to the left, and open.

The body whorl bears numerous close-set lamellae, these traversing the whorl diagonally, with the upper portion in advance of the lower. Where these lamellae cross the shoulder margin, pronounced nodules or nodose spines are formed.

Shell color is white, overlaid by a thick, white intritacalx and a periostracum.

Bering Strait, northern Pacific Ocean.
See Pl. 28, fig. 12.

Genus PAGODULA Monterosato, 1884

TYPE SPECIES: *Murex vaginatus* Cristofori & Jan, 1832, by original designation.

The following is translated from the original description:

"A section of trophoniform species, but with a long and perpendicular canal, canal open, whorls carinate, lamellose, spiny with lamellae compressed and spiny, forming a corona."

Pagodula vaginata (Cristofori & Jan, 1832)

Murex vaginatus Cristofori & Jan, 1832: 11

The shell is of moderate size (approximate length 22 mm) and narrowly fusiform. The spire is high and acute, consisting of one and three-fourths nuclear whorls and seven angulate postnuclear whorls. The suture is well-impressed. The body whorl is of moderate size and fusoid. The aperture is ovate for the most part, with the outer margin drawn out above and emptying into the shoulder lamella. The margin of the outer apertural lip is very thin and smooth, as is its inner surface. The columellar lip is essentially adherent, but barely detached anteriorly. The siphonal canal is long, curved, broadly open, and with a well-developed laminate siphonal fasciole.

Axial sculpture consists of six laminae or laminate varices, weakly elevated except at the shoulder, where they rise into long, open spinelike projections, at slightly more than a 90° angle to the long axis of the shell. Spiral sculpture is limited to a single rounded, cordlike structure, this forming the shoulder angle.

Shell color is entirely pale brown or tan.
The Mediterranean, mainly around Italy.
See Pl. 28, fig. 8.

Genus PARATROPHON Finlay, 1927

TYPE SPECIES: *Polytropa cheesemani* Hutton, 1882, by original designation.

No generic diagnosis was ever given; the type-species designation is the sole indication of the generic limits. See the treatment of *P. cheesemani* for an understanding of the genus.

Paratrophon cheesemani (Hutton, 1882)

Polytropa cheesemani Hutton, 1882: 69

The shell is moderately small (ca. 15 mm) and broadly fusiform. The spire is high and sharp, consisting of one and three-fourths nuclear whorls and five convex postnuclear whorls. The suture is well defined. The body whorl is roughly fusoid. The aperture is ovate, with a broad, V-shaped anal sulcus. The outer apertural lip is strongly undulate, reflecting the spiral shell sculpture; the interior of the outer lip bears six strong denticles. The columellar lip is adherent. The siphonal canal is comparatively broad, short, and open.

The body whorl bears four primary cords on the body and two others on the siphonal canal. Earlier whorls bear numerous fairly close-set axial lamellae, these diagonally oriented. These are generally subobsolete on the body whorl but may be more apparent on the canal.

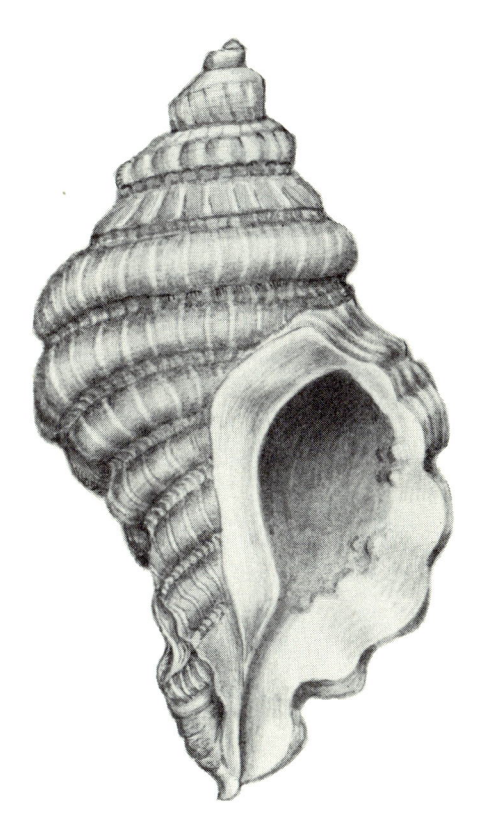

Shell color is dirty white. The interior of the aperture is orange-brown.

New Zealand.

Genus PASCULA Dall, 1908

TYPE SPECIES: *Trophon (Pascula) citricus* Dall, 1908, by original designation.

The following is taken from the original description:

"Shell small with nodular surface: the aperture with a projecting margin, feebly lirate within the outer lip when adult, constricted in front at the beginning of the canal: dentition like *Boreotrophon*; operculum purpuroid, lozenge-shaped, with a raised border on the inside face; mouth provided with an arcuate chitinous jaw."

Pascula citrica (Dall, 1908)

Trophon (Pascula) citricus Dall, 1908: 311

We have not seen a specimen of this species; the following is taken, with modifications, from the original description:

"Shell small, fusiform, acute, the spire longer than the aperture, the shell livid flesh color with orange knobs and aperture; whorls about six; apex rather acute, but in all the specimens overgrown with nullipore, etc., or eroded so as to be inassessable; whorls moderately rounded, suture appressed; axial sculpture of, on the last whorl, about ten inconspicuous vertical ribs, these bearing, near the suture, a feeble spiral row, at the shoulder a very conspicuous row, and on the body whorl three less conspicuous rows of smooth, more or less orange-tinted, rounded, prominent nodules; between the spiral rows of nodules there are four or five equal and equidistant fine spiral striae; the surface of the shell is semitranslucent, recalling that of *Purpura lapillus* L. Aperture ovate, in the adult minutely channelled behind,

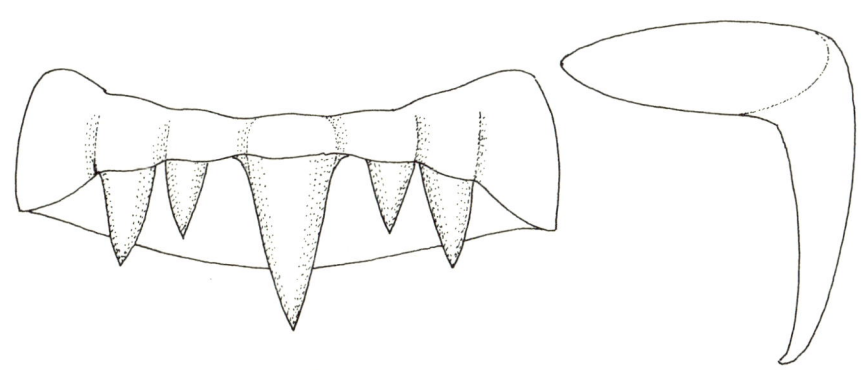

127. *Paratrophon cheesemani*

128. *Paratrophon cheesemani*, radular dentition

glazed with rich orange enamel, contracted sharply at the beginning of the canal; outer lip not reflected, thin-edged with an internal thickening, which is faintly lirate; body with a broad layer of callus, of which the left hand or outer border is a little raised; a small subsutural nodule in the adult and one on each side of the entrance to the canal; pillar short, canal very short, deep, and strongly recurved, siphonal fasciole prominent, with a constriction behind it and a deep umbilical chink.

"15.5 × 6.5 mm."

Endemic at Easter Island.

129. *Pascula citrica*

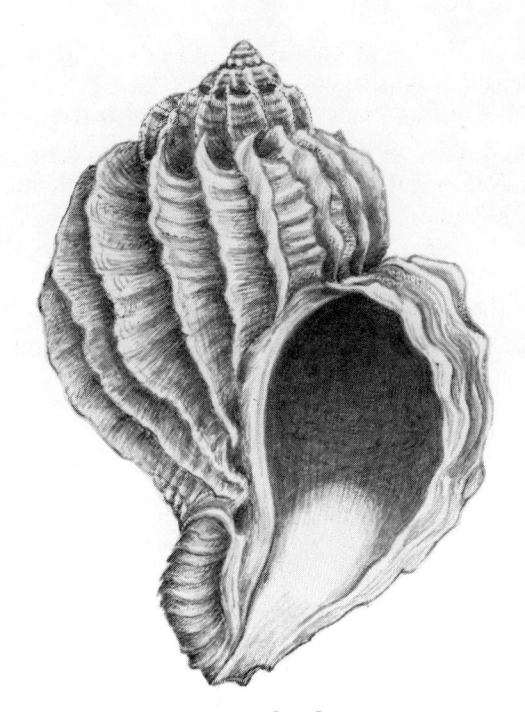

130. *Stramonitrophon laciniatus*

whorls and five weakly angulate postnuclear whorls. The suture is strongly impressed. The body whorl is heavy and broad. The aperture is broad, capacious, and ovate to subcircular, and the anal sulcus is not clearly defined. The outer apertural lip is simple and reflected. The columellar lip is entirely adherent. The siphonal canal is comparatively short, open, and distally recurved.

The body whorl bears nine strongly raised axial laminae. At the shoulder margin the laminae are curved to form broadly open incipient spines. Spiral sculpture is lacking.

Shell color is entirely white.

Straits of Magellan and generally from the entire Magellanic region.

Genus STRAMONITROPHON Powell, 1951

TYPE SPECIES: *Buccinum laciniatum* Martyn, 1788 (non-binominal) (=*Buccinum laciniatum* Dillwyn, 1817), by original designation.

No generic diagnosis was ever given; the type-species designation is the sole indication of the generic limits. See the treatment of *S. laciniatus* for an understanding of the genus.

Stramonitrophon laciniatus (Dillwyn, 1817)

Buccinum laciniatum Dillwyn, 1817: 730

The shell is very broad at its widest point and rather large (maximum length 50 mm). The spire is moderately high and subacute, consisting of one and three-fourths regular, convex nuclear

Genus TEREFUNDUS Finlay, 1927

TYPE SPECIES: *Trophon crispulatus* Suter, 1908, by original designation.

No generic diagnosis was ever given; the type-species designation is the sole indication of the generic limits. See the treatment of *T. crispulatus* for an understanding of the genus.

Terefundus crispulatus (Suter, 1908)

Trophon crispulatus Suter, 1908: 178

We have not seen a specimen of this species; the following is taken from the original description:

"Shell very small, fusiform, turreted, very thin, white, translucent, reticulated by numerous axial crispate varices and a few spiral lirae. Sculpture consisting of close, fine, and sharp varices, usually 20 to 25 on a whorl, but occasionally their number reduced to about 15; they are either straight or strongly crispate lamellae, [and] retractive on the shoulder, but vertical below it; on the base they extend as fine striae upon the neck of the canal; they are reticulated by distinct spiral threads, [these, however, sometimes] inconspicuous, the points of crossing raised into sharp, short spines; the spire whorls with three spirals, the first carinating the shoulder, the body whorl with five cingula, the lower part of the base without spirals, the interstice between the first and second spiral always broader than the succeeding ones. Fasciole minute, transversely striated. Color white. Spire conical, turreted, higher than the aperture with canal. Protoconch small, papillate, of one and one-half smooth and convex whorls, the globose nucleus slightly lateral. Whorls five, regularly increasing, shouldered and keeled; base contracted above the canal. Suture well-impressed, the varices passing across it. Aperture somewhat oblique,

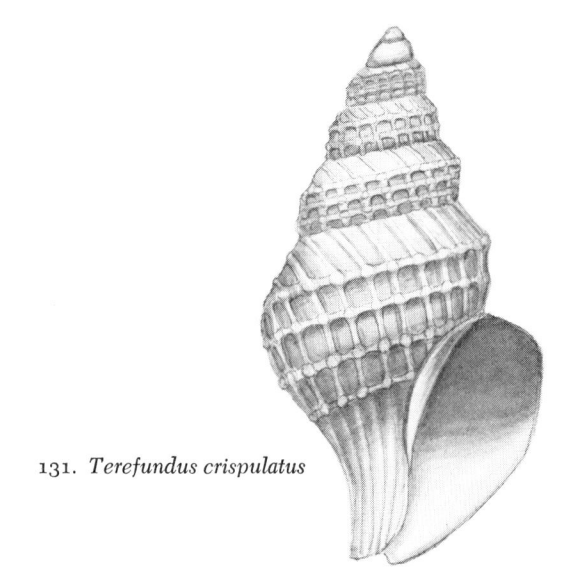

131. *Terefundus crispulatus*

oval, biangulate above, with a short, slightly oblique, and recurved open canal. Outer [apertural] lip sharp, prominently angled above, a little strengthened by the last varix, smooth inside. Columella subvertical, straight, twisted and tapering below; columellar lip very thin and narrow, polished, spreading over the lightly excavated parietal wall, narrowed below to a fine point. Operculum unknown. Diameter: 1.9 mm; height: 4 mm."

Known to us from New Zealand (Snares Island in 100 m, off Wreck Reef in 100–108 m, and off Long Point in 240 m).

Genus **TROMINA** Dall, 1918

TYPE SPECIES: *Fusus unicarinatus* Philippi, 1868, by original designation.

No generic diagnosis was ever given; the type-species designation is the sole indication of the generic limits. See treatment of *T. unicarinata* for an understanding of the genus.

Tromina unicarinata (Philippi, 1868)
Fusus unicarinatus Philippi, 1868: 223

We have not seen a specimen of this species; the following is translated, with modifications, from the original description:

"Shell minute, violet-hued, oblong-fusiform, smooth, the upper whorls medially keeled and angulate, sharply incut above, subcylindrical below, the canal well distinguished, moderately open, the aperture open and confluent with the canal.

"One specimen seen. Whorls six, the first two very smooth embryonic whorls. The remaining whorls are distinctly carinate, the carina prominent but quite obtuse. The striae are of irregular growth, broadly spaced. The aperture, with canal, makes up four-sevenths of the total, and the canal is scarcely distinct from the remainder of the aperture.

"Color violet as in chalcedony, the keel white."
Known to us only from the Magellanic region.

Genus **TROPHON** Montfort, 1810

TYPE SPECIES: *Murex magellanicus* Gmelin, 1791 (=*Buccinum geversianum* Pallas, 1774), by original designation.

The following is translated from the original description:

"Shell elongately globular; spire high, the body whorl larger than the remainder of the shell; aperture subcircular, broad; columella straight, without plaits; shell exteriorly sculptured with elevated axial lamellae; base umbilicate [pseudo-umbilicate], the canal short and open."

Trophon geversianus (Pallas, 1774)
Buccinum geversianum Pallas, 1774: 33; *Murex magellanicus* Gmelin, 1791: 3548

The shell is large for the Trophoninae (maximum length 60 mm) and obesely fusiform. The spire is high, consisting of four to six shouldered postnuclear whorls and a protoconch of undetermined nature. The suture is not impressed. The body whorl is large, broad, and fusoid. The aperture is large and subovate, flattened posteriorly under the shoulder, and attenuated where it enters the siphonal canal; the anal sulcus is imperceptible. The outer apertural lip is feebly, broadly, marginally crenulate, and weakly lirate within. The columellar lip is entirely adherent. The siphonal canal is short, broadly open, and bent to the left.

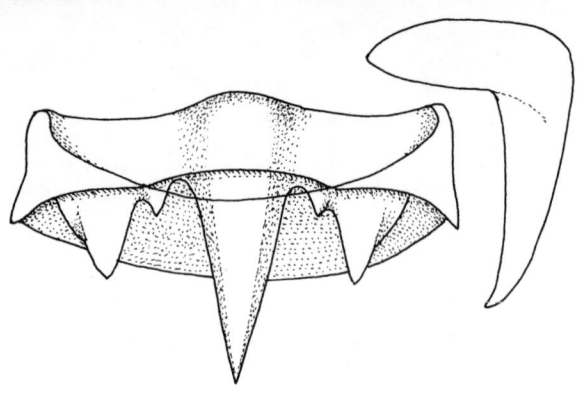

132. *Trophon geversianus*, radular dentition

The body whorl bears numerous (16–20) more or less developed lamellate axial ridges or blades, some or all of which may represent true varices. Spiral sculpture consists of six or more major cords on the body and three or four more on the siphonal canal; between these cords are, generally, three minor cords, the central somewhat stronger.

Shell color is dirty white or yellow-white, with a pinkish tinge. The interior of the aperture is red-brown, except for a white marginal band.

Magellanic region (particularly the Falkland Islands).

See Pl. 28, figs. 10–11; Pl. 29, fig. 2.

Genus **TROPHONOPSIS** Bucquoy & Dautzenberg, 1882

TYPE SPECIES: *Murex muricatus* Montagu, 1803, by original designation.

The following is taken verbatim from Grant & Gale (1931):

"Shell like that of *Boreotrophon* but with prominent spiral sculpture and secondary axial sculpture."

Trophonopsis muricatus (Montagu, 1803)

Murex muricatus Montagu, 1803: 262

The shell is of moderate size for the Trophoninae (maximum length 16 mm) and typically fusiform. The spire is high, consisting of one and one-half smooth, convex nuclear whorls and six convex to weakly subangulate postnuclear whorls. The suture is moderately impressed. The body whorl is of moderate size, long, and fusoid. The aperture is moderately small and ovate, with a narrow, shallow anal sulcus. The outer apertural lip is very finely serrate marginally, reflecting the spiral shell sculpture, briefly, finely lirate within, and strongly indented at the origin of the siphonal canal. The columellar lip is smooth and entirely adherent. The siphonal canal is long, open, and bent to the left.

The body whorl bears nine to 12 low axial ridges, some of which may represent varices. Spiral sculpture consists of up to 16 cords, 12 on the body and four on the canal, all essentially of the same size; where these cords intersect the axial ridges they are slightly uplifted, imparting a scabrous texture to the shell.

Shell color is orange-brown, red-brown, or purple-brown, covered in uneroded specimens by a thin, white intritacalx and a fuzzy, yellow or orange-brown periostracum.

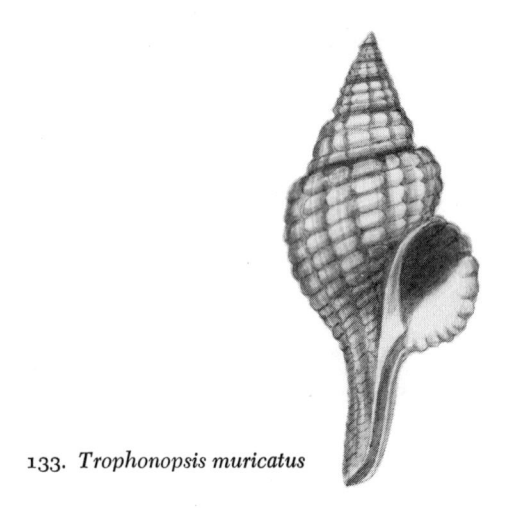

133. *Trophonopsis muricatus*

Reported to occur from the western Mediterranean to the northern British Isles, in moderately deep subtidal depths (our specimens are from Roscoff, France).

Genus **XENOTROPHON** Iredale, 1929

TYPE SPECIES: *Trophon euschema* Iredale, 1929, by original designation.

No generic diagnosis was ever given; the type-species designation is the sole indication of the generic limits. See the treatment of *X. euschema* for an understanding of the genus.

Xenotrophon euschema (Iredale, 1929)

Trophon euschema Iredale, 1929: 184

The following is taken, with some modification, from the original description:

"Shell small, tumid, fusiform, spire a little shorter than aperture, mouth rounded, free, canal long, straight and narrow. Color creamy white.

"Protoconch of one and one-half smooth whorls, apex incurved, flattened, the succeeding four adult whorls separated by an obsolete varix.

"Adult sculpture begins with two concentric ridges, the upper one forming a shoulder, the lower a peripheral ridge; these two persist; a minor ridge appears above the shoulder and six to eight below, all weaker than the primary ones. Where longitudinal growth lines develop into wrinkled laminae, erect frills appear, about one dozen on the first adult whorl; this sculpture continues irregularly, the frills becoming much stronger, as if representing growth periods.

"The mouth is rounded, the outer lip thickened but not varicose; the columellar lip developed and freed from the body whorl, an umbilical chink present.

"17.5 mm × 10 mm.

"Type trawled off Montague Island, New South Wales, 50–60 fathoms (100–120 m)."

See Pl. 29, fig. 3.

Genus XYMENE Iredale, 1915

TYPE SPECIES: *Fusus plebeius* Hutton, 1873, by original designation.

No generic diagnosis was ever given; the type-species designation is the sole indication of the generic limits. See the treatment of *X. plebeius* for an understanding of the genus.

Xymene plebeius (Hutton, 1873)

Fusus plebeius Hutton, 1873: 9

The shell is small (about 15 mm in length) and fusiform. The spire is high and acute, consisting of almost two swollen, convex nuclear whorls and four angulate postnuclear whorls. The suture is moderately impressed. The body whorl is of moderate size and fusoid. The aperture is of moderate size and ovate, with a well-defined, inverted, broadly V-shaped anal sulcus. The outer apertural lip is simple, but with some reflection of the spiral sculptural elements. The columellar lip is entirely adherent, over a sinuous columella. The siphonal canal is moderately short, broad, open, weakly bent, and distally recurved.

The body whorl bears numerous axial ridges (?varices). Spiral sculpture on the body whorl consists of eight cords, these of equal size and equally spaced. Where the spiral and axial elements intersect, nodules are formed, and the sculpture may impart a fenestrate or reticulate appearance to the shell.

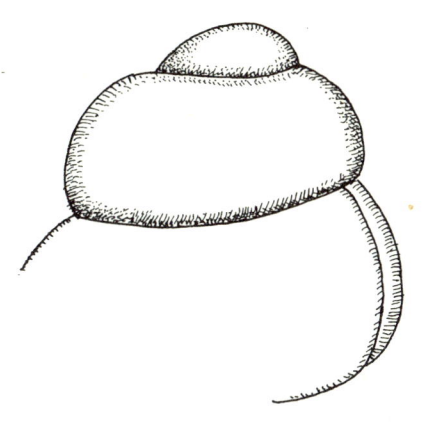

134. *Xymene plebeius*, protoconch

The shell is flesh-colored, with brown cords and a yellow-brown shoulder region, these colors showing through to color the apertural interior similarly. In fresh specimens a substantial intritacalx is apparent.

New Zealand (our specimen from Kaiteriteri, Motuoka Is.).

See Pl. 29, fig. 14.

Genus XYMENELLA Finlay, 1927

TYPE SPECIES: *Trophon pusillus* Suter, 1907, by original designation.

No generic diagnosis was ever given; the type-species designation is the sole indication of the generic limits. See the treatment of *X. pusilla* for an understanding of the genus.

Xymenella pusilla (Suter, 1907)

Trophon pusillus Suter, 1907: 253

We have not seen a specimen of this species; the following is taken from the original description:

"Shell small, fusiform, fairly solid, imperforate, with nodulous varices. Sculpture formed by spiral ribs and varices, produced into oval nodules at the points of intersection; there are 11 varices on the last whorl, reticulating the spiral sculpture; two spirals on the upper whorls succeeding the protoconch, three on the penultimate, and ten on the last whorl; from the base of the fourth whorl minute and close radiate striae are beginning to ornament the whole surface, most of the nodules, however, remaining partly smooth. Colour yellowish-white. Spire conical, a little shorter than the aperture with canal. Protoconch mammillate, smooth, consisting of three strongly convex whorls. Whorls six, lightly shouldered, the base concave. Suture impressed, undulate. Aperture elongately pyriform, produced into a comparatively long canal which is subtruncate and slightly deflexed to the right. Outer [apertural] lip thin and sharp, crenulated by the spiral sculpture. Columella vertical, straight, obliquely truncate below, terminating in a sharp point on reaching the left margin of the canal. [Columellar] lip forming a rather narrow callosity, with a longitudinal furrow parallel to the margin on the outer side.

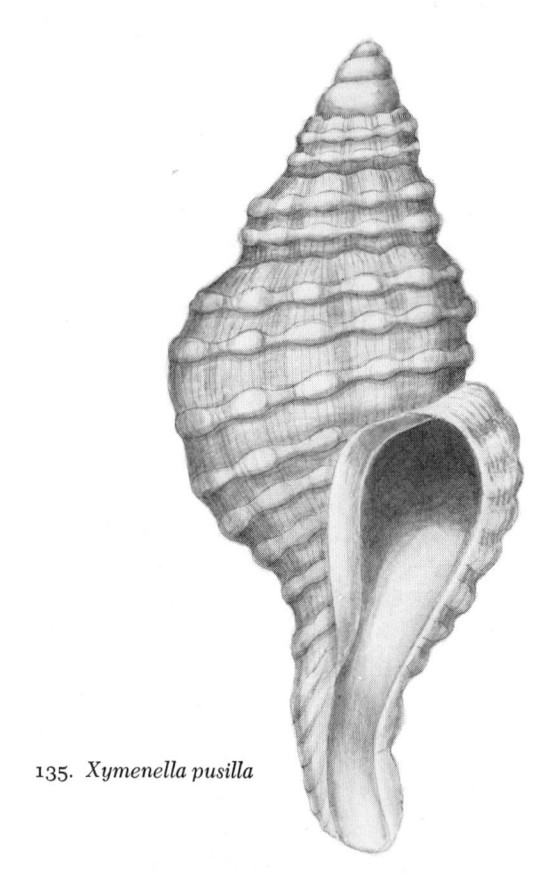

135. *Xymenella pusilla*

"Operculum unknown.
"Diameter 3.5 mm; height 6 mm.
"Animal unknown.
"Type in the Dominion Museum, Wellington [New Zealand].
"Near Channel Island, Hauraki Gulf, in 25 fathoms [50 m] (type); near Cuvier Island in 38 fathoms [76 m] (Captain Bollons); Lyttelton Harbour (Iredale)."

Genus XYMENOPSIS Powell, 1951

TYPE SPECIES: *Fusus liratus* Gould, 1849, by original designation.

Shell moderately small and fusiform, the spire high, the suture deeply impressed; aperture moderately large and ovate, the siphonal canal broadly open and long and sinuous; sculpture consisting of numerous more or less rounded axial ridges cut by very numerous, deep spiral lines. Shell color brownish-white, grayish-white, or pale yellowish-white.

136. *Xymenopsis liratus*

Xymenopsis liratus (Gould, 1849)

Fusus liratus Gould, 1849: 141

The shell is of moderate size (maximum length 23 mm) and fusiform. The spire is high, consisting of one and one-half nuclear whorls and five or six convex to barely shouldered postnuclear whorls. The suture is strongly impressed. The body whorl is of moderate size and fusoid. The aperture is moderately large and ovate, with a small anal sulcus that is angled in the direction of growth. The outer apertural lip is thin and minutely crenulate, reflecting the spiral sculptural elements at the lip-edge. The columellar lip is entirely adherent, over a sinuous columella. The siphonal canal is long, open, and strongly sinuous.

The body whorl bears 13 closely spaced axial ridges (?varices), these crossed by 19 deeply in-

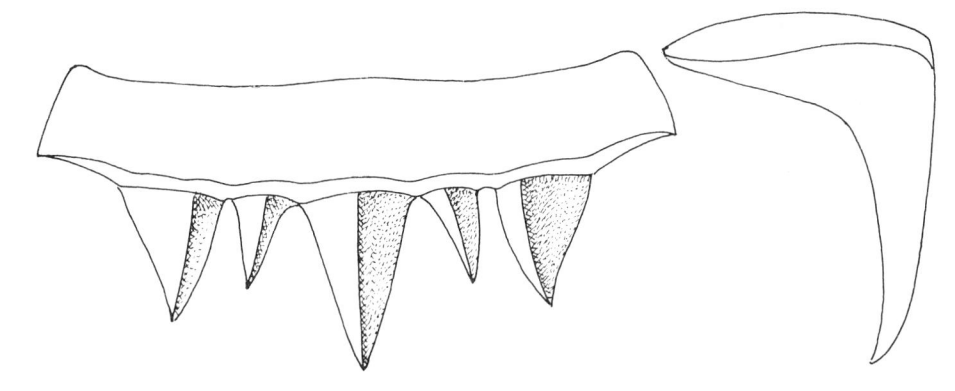

137. *Xymenopsis liratus*, radular dentition

cised and erratically spaced spiral lines, 15 on the shoulder and body and four on the canal.

The shell is flesh-colored to yellowish- or brownish-white.

Orange Bay (type locality, Tierra del Fuego) to Peru.

Genus ZEATROPHON Finlay, 1927

TYPE SPECIES: *Fusus ambiguus* Philippi, 1844, by original designation.

No generic diagnosis was ever given; the type-species designation is the sole indication of the generic limits. See the treatment of Z. *ambiguus* for an understanding of the genus.

Zeatrophon ambiguus (Philippi, 1844)

Fusus ambiguus Philippi, 1844: 107

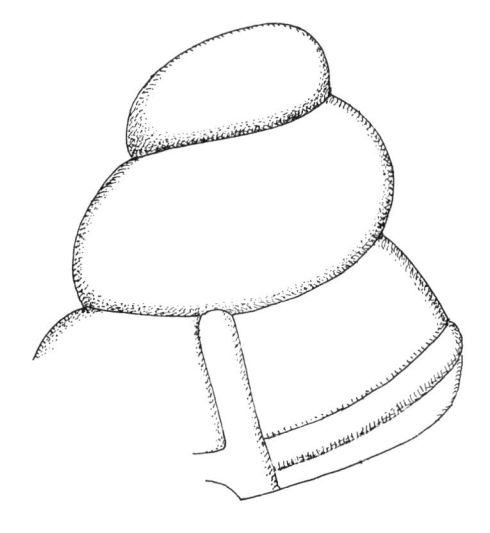

The shell is large for the subfamily (maximum length 80 mm) and fusiform or ovate-fusiform. The spire is high, consisting of two and one-half convex nuclear whorls and six shouldered postnuclear whorls. The suture is impressed. The body whorl is moderately large and fusoid. The aperture is large and ovate, with a poorly marked anal sulcus. The outer apertural lip is thin and smooth, or finely lirate on its inner surface. The columellar lip is entirely adherent, with a twist as it enters the canal. The siphonal canal is moderately long, bent strongly to the right, and open.

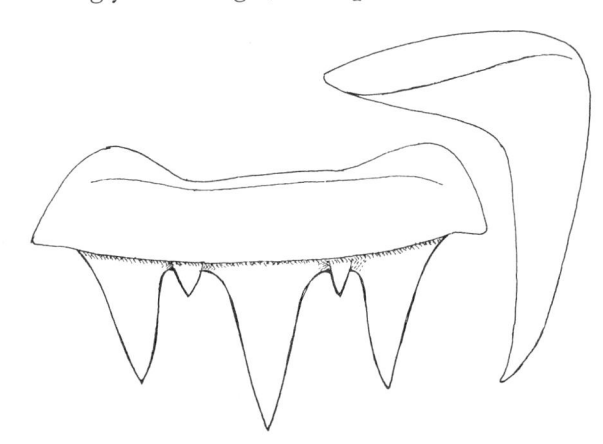

139. *Zeatrophon ambiguus*, radular dentition

The body whorl bears numerous narrow axial costae or lamellae, their degree of development variable. Spiral sculpture consists of numerous more or less close-set cords of unequal strength.

Shell color is white or off-white.

Coasts of New Zealand.

See Pl. 29, figs. 9–10.

138. *Zeatrophon ambiguus*, protoconch

Subfamily Typhinae

COSSMANN, 1903

The shell is small for the family (5–40 mm in length) and roughly fusiform in shape, and bears a color pattern consisting generally of a pale-tan or white ground suffused with translucent fleshy brown, purple, or pink. The aperture forms an entire, generally projecting peristome, with a flaring margin and no apparent anal sulcus. The siphonal canal is sealed by an overlap of the left side over the right. Most forms have three or four varices per whorl, these either winglike or forming heavy axial swellings. In the trivaricate group (*Tripterotyphis* et al.) each varix bears a shoulder spine that is more or less coalescent with an anal siphonal tube; in the group with four varices per whorl (most typhine genera), the varices bear spines marginally and the anal tubes lie between the varices at the shoulder margin (exceptions are the genus *Siphonochelus*, in which the four or five varices are represented by low axial ridges, and the genus *Trubatsa*, with four varices, each with a shoulder spine that is coalescent with an anal siphonal tube). Only the current anal tube is functional; older tubes are generally plugged. In several groups a shelly "partition" connects the varix with the preceding whorl. Spiral sculpture is mostly lacking. The surface texture is almost always smooth; the intritacalx of most species is simple, but that of the trivaricate group is complex.

Typhine protoconchs are uniformly simple and short, with convex whorls. The operculum is essentially of the muricine type.

The radula is similar, in general, to that of the Muricinae; there are several aberrant modes, with the appearance of supernumerary and not consistently symmetrical cusps on the rachidian tooth, in scattered species of several genera. The trivaricate group has consistent, muricinelike radular features; *Typhisopsis* is aberrant in its excessively broad, shallow, multicuspate rachidian. Denticles, where present, are erratic in position and size.

Distribution: worldwide (tropical and subtropical), in depths of 0–1900 m, most in 15–600 m.

Genus CINCLIDOTYPHIS DuShane, 1969

TYPE SPECIES: *Cinclidotyphis myrae* DuShane, 1969, by original designation.

The shell reaches a moderately large size for the subfamily and is broadly fusiform. The high spire consists of an unexceptional protoconch and a teloconch of an unusually small number of whorls (about four). The large, roughly ovate aperture has a thin, erect, nondenticulate outer lip with weak crenulation or none at all, and an adherent, smooth columellar lip. A short anal siphonal tube is located approximately midway in each intervarical space. The siphonal canal is short and open (this being unique in the Typhinae). The body whorl, as also in *Pterotyphis* and *Tripterotyphis*, bears three varices, the varices in *Cinclidotyphis* much less well-developed and lacking posterior points on the rounded shoulder-margin site. A finely scabrous surface is produced by the development of fine scales at the intersections of the multitude of fine spiral threads and the equally numerous fine axial-growth lamellae.

Cinclidotyphis myrae DuShane, 1969

Cinclidotyphis myrae DuShane, 1969: 343

The shell is of moderate size (maximum length 19 mm) and broadly fusiform. The spire is high, consisting of one and one-half convex nuclear whorls and four convex postnuclear whorls. The suture is well-impressed. The body whorl is moderately large and ventricosely fusoid. The aperture is large and ovate-lenticular, and formed into an erect peristome, its outer margin crenulate, the columellar lip smooth and adherent, except at its anterior end. In the shoulder region, midway between each two consecutive varices, a short, open, dorsally facing anal siphonal tube is formed. The siphonal canal is short, broad, narrowly open, and distally recurved.

The body whorl bears three varices, represented by barely discernible former outer apertural margins posteriorly and thin, bladelike varical flanges anteriorly. Each varix is comparatively simple and is composed of a thin, flattened vane, showing the outer shell sculpture on both its inner and outer surfaces, in the form of closely spaced corrugations. Major axial sculpture is otherwise lacking. Spiral sculpture consists of numerous fine cords or threads of equal strength on most of the body of the shell, changing to alternating major and minor cords near the base of the body, and back to cords of equal strength on the canal. Very fine axial growth lamellae are crossed by the cords, and where these two types of sculptural elements intersect, low, laterally expanded scales are formed.

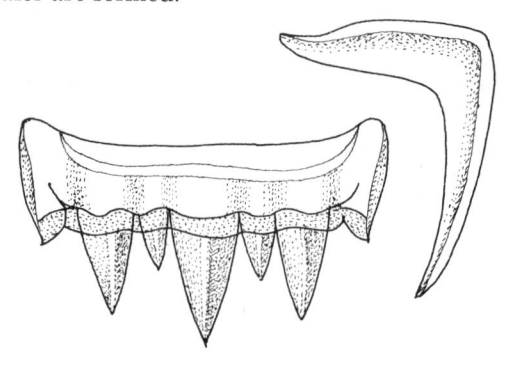

140. *Cinclidotyphis myrae*, radular dentition

Shell color is white or yellow-white. There are indications that a thin intritacalx layer covers the entire shell, imparting to it a flat-white color.

San Blas, Nayarit, to Bahía Tenacatita, Jalisco, Mexico.

See Pl. 30, figs. 3–4.

Genus **DISTICHOTYPHIS** Keen & Campbell, 1964

TYPE SPECIES: *Distichotyphis vemae* Keen & Campbell, 1964, by original designation.

The shell is small and roughly fusiform. The short, unexceptional protoconch is followed by three postnuclear whorls. The small aperture forms an entire, erect peristome. The siphonal canal is tubular and fused, the left side overlapping the right. The two varical sites on each whorl appear as weakly marked former outer-apertural margins; the anal siphonal tubes, large for the shell, are oriented at 90° to the anteroposterior axis of the shell, their bases occupying the whole whorl. Spiral cords number two.

Distichotyphis vemae Keen & Campbell, 1964
Distichotyphis vemae Keen & Campbell, 1964: 56

The shell is very small (size of holotype 8 mm in length) and roughly fusiform. The spire is high, consisting of about one and one-half nuclear whorls and three compressed postnuclear whorls. The suture is deeply impressed. The body whorl is small and roughly fusoid. The aperture, small and ovate, forms an erect, tubular peristome. The large anal siphonal tubes, two per whorl, lie at 90° to the long axis of the shell, each constituting at its base the entire height of the whorl; each tapers to about one-fifth of its basal diameter away from its origin, and is about equal to the diameter of the whorl, except for the last tube formed, which is much longer. The siphonal canal is of moderate length, tubular, bent slightly to the right, distally recurved, and closed, with the line of fusion apparent where the left side overlaps the right.

The body whorl bears two varices, these represented by two barely raised former outer-apertural margins. Axial sculpture is otherwise lacking. Spiral sculpture consists of two cords: a strong, midwhorl, carina-like swelling and a slightly less strong one at the base of the body. Where the medial cord terminates on the outer apertural margin a small notch is formed.

Shell color is shiny white, and no growth lines are apparent on the holotype.

The unique holotype was dredged off the Panamá-Costa Rica coast at a depth of 1,892 m.

See Pl. 31, fig. 10.

Genus **HAUSTELLOTYPHIS** Jousseaume, 1880

TYPE SPECIES: *Typhis cumingii* Broderip, 1833, by original designation.

The shell is of moderate length for the subfamily and fusiform to roughly club-shaped. The high spire consists of a short, unexceptional protoconch and a teloconch of moderate size. A long, straight, slender siphonal canal is exceptional for the family. The body whorl bears four varices, terminating at the shoulder margin in straight to slightly curved spines pointing posteriorly; an anal siphonal tube is located at the shoulder margin midway in each intervarical space. The small aperture forms a raised peristome.

Haustellotyphis cumingii (Broderip, 1833)

Typhis cumingii Broderip, 1833: 177

The shell is moderately long (ca. 32 mm in length) but not large, and roughly club-shaped, with a short body and a long siphonal canal. The spire is high and acute, consisting of one and three-fourths rounded, polished nuclear whorls and six weakly subangulate postnuclear whorls. The suture is well-impressed. The body whorl is moderately small, but broad and roughly fusoid. The aperture is small and ovate, with an entire peristome, this erect, except at its posterior end. The outer apertural lip is thickened and fimbriate, reflected and finely dentate marginally. A narrow partition connects the outer lip to the preceding whorl. Midway between each two consecutive varices at the shoulder margin of each whorl is a posteriorly and slightly dorsally bent anal siphonal tube. The siphonal canal is long, straight, slender, and closed, obliquely overlapping from left to right.

The body whorl bears four distinct varices of moderate strength, these slanting away from the direction of growth posteriorly, and each extended posteriorly (as well as, in the case of the last varix, dorsally) into a moderately long, tapering, hollow spine. Immediately below each anal tube is a small, prominent tubercle and a short, weak, axial ridge. Spiral sculpture is faint to entirely obsolete between varices, and where visible is erratic in strength and spacing; it is more apparent on the broad, reflected surface of the outer lip. On the varices, seven moderately weak cords are apparent on the body from the shoulder margin to the base of the body; on the last varix these cords are extended at the margin of the varical flange into short, sharp, dorsally reflected points.

141. *Haustellotyphis cumingii*, radular dentition

Shell color is porcelaneous violet-white, with bands of nebulous purple-brown at the shoulder and at the base of the body, and chocolate-brown markings on the varices at the base of the body, the anal tubes, the shoulder-margin varical spines, and the tip of the canal.

Known to us from Manzanillo, Mexico, to Guayaquil, Ecuador.

See Pl. 31, fig. 4.

Genus LAEVITYPHIS Cossmann, 1903

TYPE SPECIES: *Typhis coronarius* Deshayes, 1865 (=*T. muticus* J. Sowerby, 1834) (fossil), by original designation.

Each whorl bears four varices and four anal siphonal tubes. The varices are smooth to slightly crenulate and thickened; each varix generally bears a spine at the shoulder margin. The tubes, similar to those in *Siphonochelus* but not incorporated into the varices, point outward or upward, never forward, and are generally equidistant from both varices or nearer to the succeeding varix.

Laevityphis bullisi (Gertman, 1969)

Siphonochelus (*Laevityphis*) *bullisi* Gertman, 1969: 178

The shell is of moderate size (ca. 25 mm in length) and biconic. The spire is high and very acute, consisting of one and one-half tiny, convex nuclear whorls and six squarely angled postnuclear whorls. The suture is weakly impressed. The body whorl is moderately large (more than one-half entire shell length) and roughly trigonal. The aperture forms a moderately small, ovate peristome, its outer apertural lip erect and smooth within, its inner lip detached and erect. In each intervarical space, roughly equidistant from both varices, is a hollow anal siphonal tube, bent dorsally and anteriorly. The siphonal canal is moderately long, sealed, and bent to the right and dorsally.

The body whorl bears four moderately thickened varices, each of which bears a moderately long, slightly ventrally bent spine at the shoulder margin. Intervarical costae originate at or near the base of the body, each leading directly into an anal tube. Spiral sculpture consists of two cords, a sharp, narrow cord at the shoulder margin between a spine and the preceding tube (but not between a tube and its preceding varix), and a broader, ephemeral cord at the base of the body, apparent only on the crests of the axial elements.

Shell color is white, with a series of narrow, oblique spiral bands of pale yellow-brown; the fused portion of the canal and the tubes are flat-white. The aperture is porcelaneous white within.

Known from the Gulf of Darién, Panamá (type locality), and from off Surinam (figured specimen).

See Pl. 30, fig. 12.

Laevityphis transcurrens (von Martens, 1902)

Typhis transcurrens von Martens, 1902: 240

We have not seen a specimen of this species; the following is translated, without change, from von Martens (1902):

"Shell biconic, four-varixed, otherwise smooth, white; varices very thick, smooth, and dorsally reflected. Tubes projecting obliquely, broadly open distally and fused along their entire length; whorls six, shouldered, the body whorl barely so; aperture small, ovate, the peristome barely connected to the body of the shell by a thin keel; canal moderately elongate, bent near the end; tip open, continuous with the previous varix; other canals present as the ends of varices.

"Length 13 mm, diameter exclusive of tubes 6 mm, aperture length 3 mm, width 2.3 mm, length of last tube 4 mm."

Laevityphis tubuliger (Thiele, 1925)

Typhis tubuliger Thiele, 1925: 171

We have not seen a specimen of this species; the following is translated from Thiele (1925):

"[Von] Martens has described a new species as *Typhis transcurrens* from station 245 (Deutschen Tiefsee-Expedition), where I found a pair of immature shells that I doubt are different from this species. Besides this species there is another, seemingly new species that is smaller, the spire higher, and the protoconch clearly smaller. The spirally arranged tubes are farther away from the body, with no connection to the varices. Heavy axial ridges are located roughly medially between the tubes and the growth stoppages (corresponding to varices) and protrude squarely at the shoulder margin. The siphonal canal is rather slender, slightly bent, and clearly distinct from the remainder of the shell. The figured specimen is 5.5 mm in length and 2.5 mm wide, exclusive of the tubes."

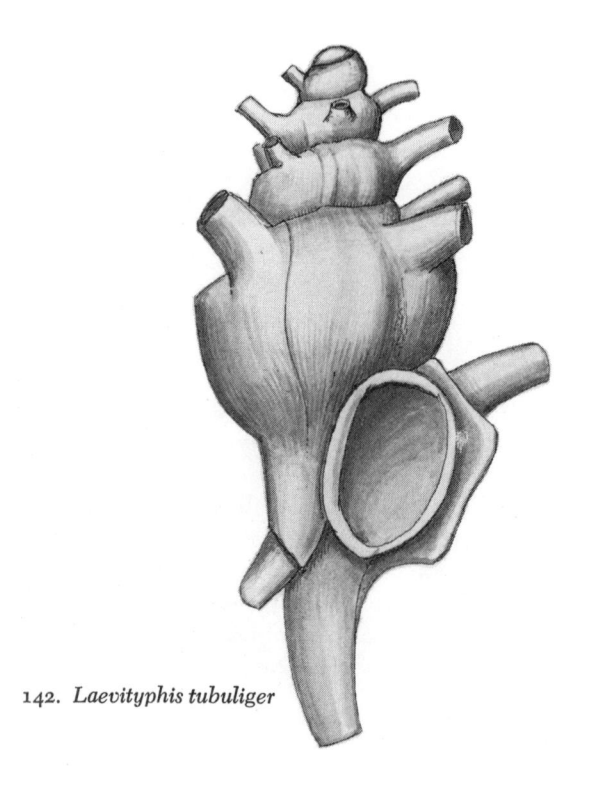

Genus MONSTROTYPHIS Habe, 1961

TYPE SPECIES: *Typhis (Typhinellus) tosaensis* Azuma, 1960, by original designation.

The shell is comparatively large and attenuated, with sharply angulate whorls widely separated from one another (as in a form of *Homalocantha scorpio*). The apertural margin forms an entire, broadly flaring peristome. No partition is apparent. The body whorl bears four varices, each of which bears several (four in the type species) hollow, dorsally recurved spines. An additional hollow spine is borne medially on the siphonal canal; the canal is sealed, the left side overlapping the right. Each anal siphonal tube (particularly the last one) is very long, arising at or near the shoulder margin and a short distance behind the varical costa.

Monstrotyphis tosaensis (Azuma, 1960)

Typhis (Typhinellus) tosaensis Azuma, 1960: 99

The shell is moderately large for the subfamily (ca. 22 mm in length) and narrowly fusiform. The spire is high, consisting of five angulate postnuclear whorls and a protoconch of undetermined nature. The suture is strongly impressed. The body whorl is moderately large or long and narrowly fusoid. The aperture is small and subcircular, with an entire, erect, tubular, marginally flaring peristome. Four anal siphonal tubes are formed on the periphery of each whorl, midway between varices or slightly closer to the older of the two adjacent varices. The siphonal canal is long and weakly recurved at its distal end and sealed, the left side overlapping the right.

The body whorl bears four oblique varices, each bearing four hollow, strongly dorsally recurved spines, the upper and lower ones longest and deflected respectively posteriorly and anteriorly. The leading surface of the varical flange bears several scalloped lamellae, these imparting collectively the appearance of gathered drapes. A fifth varical spine appears medially on the canal

142. *Laevityphis tubuliger*

after a substantial gap in spination. Spiral sculpture is not apparent in the specimens we have examined.

Shell color is translucent or dirty white, with some evidence of the existence of a flat-white intritacalx in unworn specimens.

Known from Kii and the Tosa Bay region of southeastern Japan and from Taiwan (South China Sea).

See Pl. 31, fig. 2.

Genus PTEROTYPHIS Jousseaume, 1880

TYPE SPECIES: *Typhis pinnatus* Broderip, 1833, by original designation.

The shell has three varices and tubes per whorl, the tubes nearer to the succeeding than to the preceding varix, and pointing dorsally and posteriorly. The siphonal canal is not closed, but is barely open by a narrow slit. Strong spiral sculpture is present.

Pterotyphis fimbriatus (A. Adams, 1854)

Typhis fimbriatus A. Adams, 1854: 70

The shell is moderately large for the Typhinae (maximum length 23 mm) and roughly, broadly fusiform. The spire is high and acute, consisting of five convex or weakly subangulate postnuclear whorls and a protoconch of undetermined nature. The suture is strongly impressed. The body whorl is roughly fusoid but is given a broad, stocky appearance by the presence of a broad, simple varical flange. The aperture is ovate, and the peristome is weakly erect in the center of a depression formed by the presence of two surrounding varical flanges. The outer apertural lip is thickly erect and crenulate and reflects on its outer surface several diverse kinds of sculpture; the inner lip is thickened, adherent above, and detached and erect below. The anal siphonal tubes are not prominent, each sitting on the shoulder margin immediately behind the receding side of a varix; the opening of each tube is spoutlike, with the spout turned obliquely backward and upward. The siphonal canal is closed, deeply excavated at the base of the varix, and then abruptly bent backward and tapering into a short tube, this (in the specimen examined) open in this area; the closure is formed by the meeting and fusing of the two sides of the canal, as in the members of the Ocenebrinae.

The body whorl bears three prominent, winglike or bladelike varices. The advancing side of the varix is comparatively low, but the receding side extends outward tangentially to the normal growth direction of the shell, and the outer margin curls ventrally (in the direction of growth) and is supported by several strutlike cords on the ventral side of the varical flange. A high, narrow partition connects the varix region above the aperture with the posterior end of the last varical flange. Other axial sculpture consists solely of fine, raised growth lines. Spiral sculpture consists of cords and threads: there are four prominent cords on the shoulder and upper portion of the body, these apparent only on the varical flange; the body and canal bear about 50 fine, deeply divided spiral threads, these varying in prominence and grouped into paired stronger ones and lesser intercalary ones. The intersection of these threads and the fine axial-growth lines imparts a scabrous texture to the surface of the shell, a feature seen throughout the Muricidae but uncommon in the Typhinae. Between the receding edge of the varical flange and the bulge of the body, the shell is depressed and shows a surface of large, deep pits; these are found inconsistently over the remainder of the shell and appear to be arranged roughly spirally.

Shell color is pale brown or tan, with off-white varical flanges and darker purple-brown blotches on the body just before and after each varix. The tubes are also dark purple-brown. A row of small dark-brown spots follows the outer apertural lip from just within it.

Central Mexican coast; known to us from Barra de Navidad and Bahía Coastocomate (Jalisco) and Sayulita (Nayarit), Mexico.

See Pl. 30, fig. 1.

Pterotyphis pinnatus (Broderip, 1833)

Typhis pinnatus Broderip, 1833: 178

The shell is of moderate size (about 20 mm in length) and roughly fusiform. The spire is high and acute, consisting of four convex or weakly subangulate postnuclear whorls and a protoconch of undetermined nature. The suture is strongly impressed. The body whorl is moderately large and fusoid. The aperture is moderately large and ovate, the posterior end somewhat lopsided to the right. The peristome is erect, except for the parietal portion, where it is adherent. Each anal siphonal tube is situated at the periphery of its whorl intervarically, slightly closer to the later varix. The few specimens we have seen have not enabled us to determine whether the siphonal canal is closed or open; the canal is otherwise of moderate length, sinuous, and distally recurved.

The body whorl bears three moderately briefly winglike varices. Except for the anal tubes, axial sculpture is not apparent. Spiral sculpture consists of 25 raised, sharply demarcated cords, these distributed from the base of each anal tube to the canal termination, the cords narrower than the interspaces. Finer intercalary threads are interspersed among the stronger cords. Above the periphery of the whorl there are about 12 finer cords extending to the suture. The body cords impart an undulate leading surface to the varical flange.

The entire shell has an intritacalx forming the greater part of the close axial growth lamellae, which are strongest between the cords and roll over the cords as fine, scabrous elements. Some of this axial lamellate structure, especially over the receding side of each varix, is bent downward, becoming adherent to the following lamellae, with the result, in some areas, that only oblique pits are apparent.

Color is uniformly white in the specimens we have seen.

Known to us only from the Bahamas and Panamá (Gertman, 1969).

See Pl. 30, fig. 2.

Genus SIPHONOCHELUS Jousseaume, 1880

TYPE SPECIES: *Typhis avenatus* [sic] Hinds, 1844 (=*T. arcuatus* Hinds, 1843), by original designation.

The shell bears four (rarely five) varices per whorl. Each short anal siphonal tube originates just behind a varix and is bent dorsally and posteriorly; the tube is flanked on one side by the varix and on the other by a strong rounded axial ridge, this terminating at the shoulder margin in a knoblike swelling. There are no true varical flanges, the varices represented only by the slightly flaring former outer-apertural margins.

Siphonochelus arcuatus (Hinds, 1843)

Typhis arcuatus Hinds, 1843: 19

We have not seen a specimen of this species; the following is taken, with modifications, from Barnard (1959):

"Protoconch one and one-half whorls, height 1.3 mm, diameter 1 mm, smooth, glistening. Postnatal whorls five; four tubes and four varices on each whorl; tubes subcircular on early whorls, becoming oval and carinate in front on later whorls, sometimes on last whorl narrowly oval (complanate); varices curving forward, carinate, connected with the tubes, but each with a shallow notch on base of tube defined by a feeble angulation. Size 20 × 10–11 mm (excluding tubes).

"Operculum broadly oval, fitting the continuous peristome, the nucleus apical, the growth lines well marked.

"Surface dull or chalky-white, except the glistening protoconch."

South Africa (Cape Point to East London).

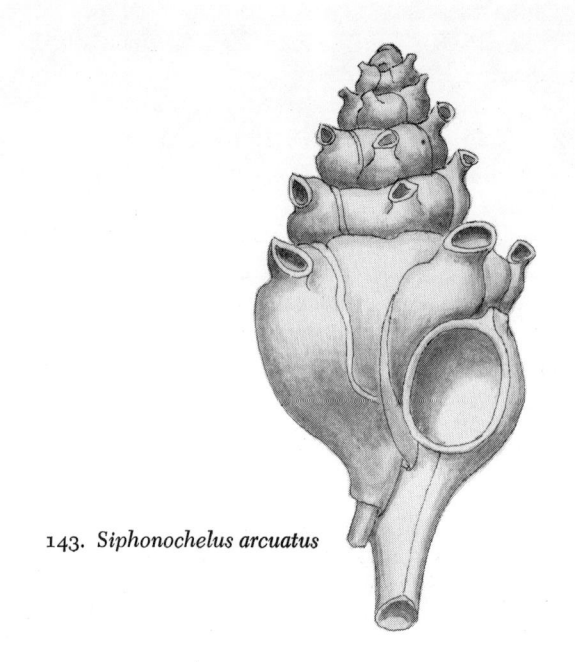

143. *Siphonochelus arcuatus*

Siphonochelus japonicus (A. Adams, 1863)

Typhis japonicus A. Adams, 1863: 374

The shell is small (maximum length 11 mm) and fusiform. The spire is high and acute, consisting of one and one-half nuclear whorls and four postnuclear whorls. The suture is well-impressed and undulate, owing to the presence of intervarical costae. The body whorl is of moderate size and fusoid. The aperture is moderately small and ovate, with a peristome consisting of a weakly erect outer lip and a more or less adherent inner lip. Anal siphonal tubes as below. The siphonal canal is of moderate length, sealed, and straight.

The body whorl bears four varices, represented by the former outer-apertural margins. Between each two consecutive varices there is a massive, rounded ridge, deeply excavated centrally, thus appearing as two more slender ridges joined above and below; at the posterior end of this ridge, at about its midpoint on the shoulder margin, is a short, broad anal tube. Spiral sculpture is lacking.

Shell color is waxy yellow-white, with two spiral bands of diffuse red-brown, one on the shoulder and one at the base of the body. The entire shell is covered with a thin dusting of intritacalx.

This species closely resembles both *S. nipponensis* and *S. syringianus*. It differs from the latter species in its shorter, broader siphonal canal, its heavier intervarical ridge, and its color banding, and from the former species in its more bulbous protoconch, its larger size, its heavier intervarical ridge, and its banded color pattern.

Known to us only from central and southeastern Japan.

See Pl. 32, fig. 1.

Siphonochelus nipponensis Keen & Campbell, 1964

Siphonochelus (S.) *nipponensis* Keen & Campbell, 1964: 50

The shell is small (the specimen we have seen is an apparently immature paratype, length 7 mm) and fusiform. The spire is high and acute, consisting, in the studied paratype, of one and one-fourth swollen nuclear whorls and three weakly shouldered postnuclear whorls. The suture is moderately impressed. The body whorl is of moderate size and fusoid. The aperture is moderately small and ovate, with an entire and weakly erect peristome. Each anal siphonal tube, originating about midway between two moderately weak varices, is short and broad and projects posteriorly at 45° to the long axis of the shell. The siphonal canal is moderately short, sealed, and weakly bent to the right.

Each whorl bears four moderately weak varices, these represented by the weakly erect former outer-apertural margins. The three species of *Siphonochelus* that we have been able to study from specimens in hand, *S. japonicus*, *S. nipponensis*, and *S. syringianus*, the first two of these with overlapping Japanese ranges, may be distinguished from each other most readily by the form of the intervarical costae; in *S. nipponensis* these are unequal, the leading one stronger, the intervening groove very weak, the anal tube apparently arising from, or at the posterior end of, the weak, receding costa. Spiral sculpture is lacking.

Shell color is pale yellow-white, under a thin white intritacalx. The tubes, canal, and apertural region are white.

Kuroda and Habe (1971) have suggested that this species is identical to *S. japonicus*, but differences in protoconch, color pattern, and other features indicate the distinctness of the two species.

Known to us only from off Tosa, Shikoku, Japan.

See Pl. 32, fig. 9.

Siphonochelus pentaphasios (Barnard, 1959)

Typhis pentaphasios Barnard, 1959: 211

We have not seen a specimen of this species; the following is taken, with modifications, from Barnard (1959):

"Protoconch corroded. Postnatal whorls four; five tubes and five varices on each whorl; tubes oval-subcircular, with a broadly rounded rib below extending to the suture; varices broadly rounded midway between tubes and growth lines, the profile evenly curved, not shouldered; peristome not quite continuous where the varix from the tube impinges upon it. Size 11 (including the corroded protoconch) by 5.5 mm. White."

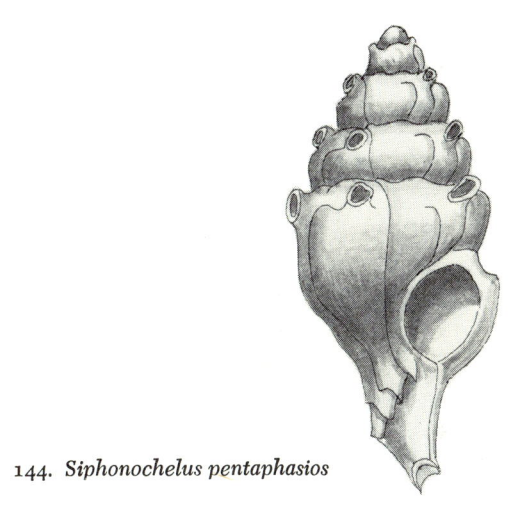

144. *Siphonochelus pentaphasios*

From the comparison made by Barnard it appears that he felt that the possession by this species of an extra varix (five in all) and an extra anal tube (five in all) warrants its nomenclatural distinction from *S. arcuatus*. With five varices and tubes, *S. pentaphasios* would indeed appear to be unique within the subfamily.

Known only from the type locality (off Cape Point, South Africa).

Siphonochelus solus Vella, 1961

Siphonochelus solus Vella, 1961: 388

We have not seen a specimen of this species; the following is taken verbatim from Vella (1961):

"Shell small, elongate, fusiform, solid, apex worn, final two growth steps mostly broken off, four and one-half whorls intact; peripheral angle high, shoulder narrow and deeply channeled behind tubes and varices; spire whorls contracting slightly below periphery; base gently convex, contracting gradually to the anterior canal; varices rounded, oblique folds raised above the shoulder and curved back to join the preceding tubes; in front of each varix a deep sulcus about one-third of a growth stage in width, containing apertural scars slightly in front of the middle; sulcus followed by a broad rounded fold initiating the next growth step, decreasing downward and dying before reaching the anterior canal; tubes all worn down to stumps, directed steeply upwards and obliquely backwards, flattened, broadened in the spiral direction extending from the initial fold to somewhat behind the varix to which it is united; below the tube, between the initial fold and varix, a broad, shallow concavity about two-thirds the width of the total growth step, surface of shell smooth except for growth lines; aperture not seen.

"Dimensions. Height 8 mm; maximum diameter 4 mm.

145. *Siphonochelus solus*

"Repository. Holotype (the only specimen) (*M. 11067*), Dominion Museum, Wellington (N.Z.).

"Locality. 113–130 fathoms [226–260 m] off Mayor Island, Bay of Plenty (N.Z).

"Age. Recent.

"Remarks. *Siphonochelus solus* seems close to the South African species *S. arcuatus*, judged by the figures of Tryon (1880, pl. 30, fig. 293) and Keen (1944, p. 54, fig. 11). *S. solus* is distinguished by its broad, flattened intervarical tubes.

"The holotype of *S. solus* and a specimen of *Typhina pauperis* were dredged from the same locality. Both are chalky, broken shells, and these species may not be living there now."

Siphonochelus syringianus (Hedley, 1903)
Typhis syringianus Hedley, 1903: 381

The shell is small (maximum length 10 mm) and fusiform. The spire is high, consisting of one and one-half swollen nuclear whorls and four weakly shouldered postnuclear whorls. The suture is impressed. The body whorl is of moderate size. The aperture is moderately small and ovate, with a slight posterior callus. The peristome is thickened marginally, detached, and erect, except posteriorly, in the parietal region. Each anal siphonal tube originates at the shoulder margin, just behind a varix, and is bent dorsally and anteriorly to open midway between varices; immediately behind each tube a single massive, rounded axial ridge almost entirely fills the intervarical space. The siphonal canal is sealed, moderately short, and straight.

The body whorl bears four heavy, rounded varices, these curving dorsally at the shoulder margin to merge with the anal tube. Spiral sculpture is lacking.

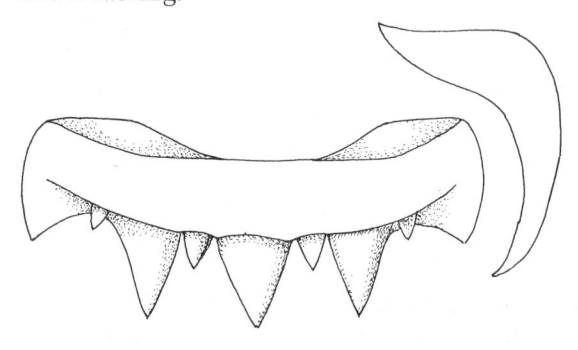

146. *Siphonochelus syringianus*, radular dentition

Shell color is pale, fleshy, pinkish-tan, covered with a more or less thick, white, axially striate intritacalx and a relatively thick tan periostracum. The interior of the aperture is a rich orange-brown.

Known to us only from South Australia and Tasmania.

See Pl. 32, fig. 2.

Genus TALITYPHIS Jousseaume, 1882

TYPE SPECIES: *Typhis expansus* Sowerby, 1874, by original designation.

Members of this group have four varices and tubes per whorl. The origin of each tube is situated closer to the older of each two consecutive varices, and the tube is bent dorsally and slightly posteriorly. The varix at the growing edge is greatly expanded, broad throughout its length, with a partition posterior to the aperture. Weak spiral sculpture may be present.

(For new species of *Talityphis*, see the Appendix.)

Talityphis expansus (Sowerby, 1874)

Typhis expansus Sowerby, 1874: 719; *Typhis (Talityphis) puertoricensis* Warmke, 1964: 1

The shell is moderately small for the genus (maximum length 22 mm) and more or less broadly fusiform. The spire is high, consisting of one and one-fourth convex nuclear whorls and five or six angulate postnuclear whorls. The suture is obscured by subsequent whorls. The body whorl is moderately large and trigonal. The aperture is small and ovate. The peristome is entire and slightly erect, except posteriorly, where it is adherent. Each anal siphonal tube is moderately long, originates at the shoulder margin, near the midpoint of an intervarical space, and is directed dorsally and posteriorly; the base of each tube is aligned with a varix on the preceding whorl, and where these two structures touch, the shoulder is bisected. The siphonal canal is moderately broad, short, sealed, and weakly bent to the right and dorsally.

The body whorl bears four heavy, ropelike varices; the most recent one forms a moderately broadly expanded wing, drawn into a dorsally and posteriorly extended point at the shoulder margin, and dorsally reflected at its free margin. The ends of the spiral cords form small, dorsally curved points. The varical point at the shoulder margin is partially resorbed in older varices, leaving only a small, posteriorly in-hooked spine. Spiral sculpture consists of seven moderately strong body cords and two cords on the canal, these most prominent on the crests of older varices and on the leading edge of the most recent varix. The cords are discontinuous and nonaligned from one varix to the next.

Shell color is fleshy pink-orange, with purple-brown suffusions on parts of the spire, the anal tubes, and the tip of the canal. The ventral surface of the last varix and the interior of the aperture are white. A thin, flat-white, minutely axially striate intritacalx covers the shell where not abraded.

The Bahamas (Nassau) and Puerto Rico (west coast) to the southern Caribbean (Trinidad and off Surinam).

See Pl. 31, fig. 3.

Talityphis latipennis (Dall, 1919)

Typhis latipennis Dall, 1919: 339

The shell is large (maximum length 39 mm) and broadly biconical. The spire is moderately high, consisting of six or seven angulate postnuclear whorls and a protoconch of undetermined nature. The suture is impressed and obscured by the succeeding whorl. The body whorl is large and broadly, unequally trigonal. The aperture is moderately small and ovate, with a raised peristome. Each very long, hollow anal siphonal tube originates nearer the older of its two adjacent varices and projects dorsally and slightly posteriorly. The siphonal canal is long, bent to the right, broad for the upper third of its length, slender and tubular for the remaining two-thirds, and entirely sealed.

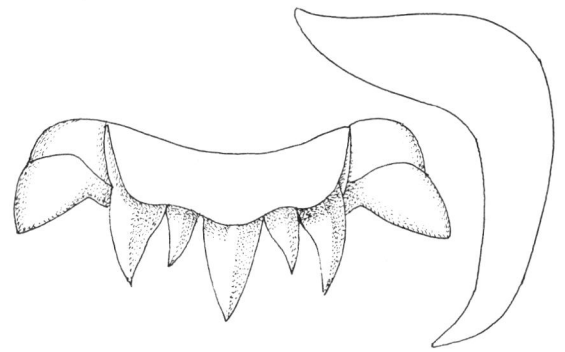

147. *Talityphis latipennis*, radular dentition

The body whorl bears four sharp varices, each composed of two appressed laminae; the lamina on the receding side extends further outward than the one on the leading side, and on the last varix is moderately strongly dorsally reflected, extending for a considerable distance and forming a broadly winglike structure, strongly dorsally reflected at its free edge and extending anteriorly to the upper end of the canal. At the shoulder margin the last varix is drawn into a dorsally and posteriorly curved spine. In all but the last varix only a posteriorly hooked portion is retained, the remainder having been resorbed. A thickened callus pad at the posterior end of the aperture is backed by an extended perpendicular partition; the anal tube is bent so far dorsally that part of it is appressed to and perhaps buttressed by the partition. Spiral sculpture consists of six faint cords, these visible only on the receding and leading sides of the varices; between varices, they are obsolete.

Shell color is fleshy orange-pink to orange-brown, with paler orange on the leading side of the last varix. The siphonal and anal canals are suffused with purple-brown. The entire shell is covered with a moderately thick, axially striate intritacalx.

Gulf of California (off Guaymas) to Panamá Bay.

See Pl. 30, figs. 13–14.

Genus TRIPTEROTYPHIS
Pilsbry & Lowe, 1932

TYPE SPECIES: *Typhis lowei* Pilsbry, 1931, by original designation.

The shells are small to moderately large. Each whorl bears three broadly winglike varices, each varix coalescent with an anal siphonal tube. The shell is white, white with brown bands, or entirely light brown. Most species are covered with a thick, white, minutely frilled intritacalx. The typically muricine radula also serves to distinguish this group from most other typhine groups, these having aberrant muricine features.

Tripterotyphis arcana (DuShane, 1969)

Pterotyphis (Tripterotyphis) arcana DuShane, 1969: 344

The shell is of moderate size for the genus (maximum length 22 mm) and roughly fusiform. The spire is high and acute, consisting of one and three-fourths nuclear whorls and seven weakly subangulate postnuclear whorls. The suture is obscured. The body whorl is of moderate size and narrowly trigonal. The aperture is small and subovate, the posterior margin flattened. The peristome is barely erect, except parietally, where it is adherent. Each short, stout anal siphonal tube originates at the shoulder margin as an integral part of a varical shoulder spine, which originates immediately after the preceding varix and sweeps ventrally and posteriorly. The siphonal canal is of moderate length, comparatively narrow, sealed except for its distal one-third, and weakly, dorsally recurved.

The body whorl bears three weakly developed varices, each with a coarsely serrate margin and a single broad-based, dorsally and posteriorly projecting spine, this housing the anal tube. A series of amorphous, confluent, obliquely aligned nodes extends from the base of the varical spine of the previous varix to a point about medial on the current varix. Spiral sculpture, ephemeral except at the varical margin, consists of seven weak cords on the canal and three bifid cords on the body and on the shoulder-margin spine.

Shell color is dark red-brown to dark purple-brown intervarically, with pale red-brown on the varices; the leading edge of the last varix, the siphonal canal, and the peristome are white. The interior of the aperture is white mottled with red-brown. A thin, white frosting of intritacalx covers the entire shell.

Known to us only from Mazatlán, Mexico (type locality), and La Cruz, Nayarit, Mexico.

See Pl. 30, figs. 8–9.

Tripterotyphis fayae (Keen & Campbell, 1964)

Pterotyphis (Tripterotyphis) fayae Keen & Campbell, 1964: 54

The shell is moderately large (maximum length 28 mm) and broadly trigonal. The spire is high and acute, consisting of one and three-fourths nuclear whorls and five or six generally convex postnuclear whorls. The suture is obscured. The body whorl is large and broadly trigonal. The aperture is of moderate size and ovate, and forms a weakly erect peristome. Each short, stout anal siphonal tube originates at the shoulder margin within a varical spine that seems to arise immediately after the preceding varix, and sweeps forward and posteriorly. The siphonal canal is broad and sealed for most of its length, barely open, and dorsally recurved near its tip.

The body whorl bears three broadly alate varices, each with a finely serrate margin and a single broad-based, dorsally projecting spine with a triangular cross section, the spine housing the anal tube. Other axial sculpture consists of two or three obliquely aligned nodes, the upper one at the shoulder margin and the lower one or two below it. Spiral sculpture consists of 20 low cords over the whole shell: seven are on the canal; of 13 on the body, six are below the shoulder margin, seven above.

Shell color is white, with dark red-brown between the spiral cords; between the varices a dark blue-gray suffusion is apparent. The anal tubes, inner-apertural and siphonal margins, and intervarical nodes are white. The interior of the aperture is dark brown.

A distinctive form from the southern end of Baja California is entirely white, except for a few slender spiral bands of light brown. A thin, white, often ephemeral intritacalx may be in evidence as thin lamellae between the spiral cords.

Cabo Pulmo, Baja California, to Manzanillo, Colima, Mexico.

See Pl. 30, figs. 10–11.

Tripterotyphis lowei (Pilsbry, 1931)

Typhis lowei Pilsbry, 1931: 72

The shell is small to moderately large (maximum length 18 mm) and broadly trigonal. The spire is high and acute, consisting of one and one-fourth nuclear whorls and six convex postnuclear whorls. The suture is obscured. The body whorl is large and broadly trigonal. The aperture is of moderate size and ovate, and forms an almost entirely erect peristome, the parietal margin being adherent. Each anal siphonal tube is coalescent with a broad shoulder-margin spine of triangular cross section; although the tube originates within the varical plane, the dorsal side of the varical spine originates immediately after the preceding varix, afterwards sweeping ventrally and sharply posteriorly, to end with the distal end of the tube. The siphonal canal is broad and sealed, except for a short, barely open portion near its dorsally recurved anterior end.

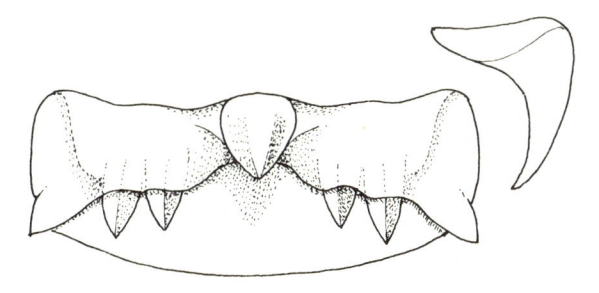

148. *Tripterotyphis lowei*, radular dentition

The body whorl bears three broadly alate varices. A series of two or three obliquely aligned nodules extends in each interspace from above the shoulder margin, in the direction of growth, to below the shoulder margin, just before the next varix. In addition, the shell bears 13 weak spiral cords, the seven on the canal barely discernible, the six on the body slightly heavier; the 13 cords are more apparent as serrations on the varical margin and on the interior of the outer apertural lip.

Shell color is white, overlaid by a flat-white, minutely frilled intritacalx. The interior of the aperture is white to cream-colored.

A larger (to 23 mm), more coarsely sculptured form is known only from the Galápagos Islands.

Escondido Bay, Baja California, to Panamá and the Galápagos Islands.

See Pl. 30, figs. 5–6.

Tripterotyphis norfolkensis (C. A. Fleming, 1962)

Pterynotus (Nothotyphis) norfolkensis C. A. Fleming, 1962: 117

The shell is the smallest in the genus (maximum length 10 mm) and generally biconic. The spire is high, consisting of five weakly subangulate postnuclear whorls and a protoconch of undetermined nature. The suture is obscured. The body whorl is moderately large and trigonal. The aperture is small and ovate, with an erect peristome. The outer apertural margin is strongly, coarsely serrate, the serrations reflecting the spiral cords as they traverse the leading edge of the last varix. Each anal siphonal tube is confluent with a long, broad, posteriorly bent varical spine at the shoulder margin, the spine originating almost midway between varices but terminating slightly closer to the succeeding varix; the cross-sectionally triangular spine then sweeps briefly ventrally and strongly posteriorly, where it meets and encloses the tube. The siphonal canal is broad and closed, except briefly, near its anterior end, where it is sharply dorsally bent.

The body whorl bears three broad, winglike varices. Spiral sculpture consists of nine spiral cords, four on the canal and five on the body, these ephemeral between varices and more prominent on them, throwing the varical margin into fine crenulations. A low, oblique ridge extends from each varix, ventrally and anteriorly, to a point just before the next varix.

Shell color is translucent off-white to fleshy yellow-brown. The entire shell is covered by a moderately thick, minutely ruffled, flat-white intritacalx.

This species was originally assigned to *Pterynotus (Nothotyphis)* on the basis of a misconception of its author concerning its manner of varix formation; it is clearly a *Tripterotyphis*. Recently, Ponder (1972) has reduced this species to a subspecies of *T. lowei*, an eastern Pacific species. The idea of two forms separated by the entire Pacific Ocean for presumably a considerable period of time and differing (also presumably) only subspecifically is incompatible with our concept of subspecies.

Known to us from Norfolk Island, the Solomon Islands, and the Philippines.

See Pl. 28, fig. 2.

Tripterotyphis robustus (Verco, 1895)

Murex (Poropteron Jousseaume 1880) *robustus* Verco, 1895: 85

The shell is moderately small for the genus (length ca. 12 mm) and trigonal. The spire is high and acute, consisting of five convex postnuclear whorls and a protoconch of undetermined nature. The suture is well defined. The body whorl is moderately large and broadly trigonal. The aperture is moderately small and ovate, with an erect peristome. Anal siphonal tubes are typical in form and location for the genus. The siphonal canal is short, broad, and closed, except at the dorsally recurved distal end, where it is briefly open.

The body whorl bears three moderately broad, winglike varices, each projecting posteriorly at the shoulder margin to enclose the anal siphonal tube. Spiral sculpture consists of a single strong, diffuse cord at the periphery, this imparting an angulate appearance to the whorl, and numerous finer cords, these very diffuse. There are also numerous close-set, incised lines over the entire shell and numerous small, "chiseled" pits arranged in a somewhat irregular pattern. The leading edge of the varix bears five strongly raised cords; a weaker cord leads into and is confluent with the canal-closure seam just below the aperture.

Shell color is pale yellow-white, covered with a moderately thick, intricately sculptured intritacalx (typical for the genus) of a flat-white color.

South Australia (our description based on a specimen from Smoky Bay).

See Pl. 29, fig. 11.

Tripterotyphis triangularis (A. Adams, 1855)

Typhis triangularis A. Adams, 1855: 124

The shell is large for the genus (maximum length 29 mm), triangular in cross section, and broadly biconic. The spire is high and acute, consisting of five or six essentially convex postnuclear whorls and a protoconch of undetermined nature. The suture is weakly impressed where not obscured. The body whorl is large and broadly trigonal. The aperture is moderately small and ovate, and the peristome is erect, except parietally, where it is adherent, and serrate at the outer apertural margin. Each anal siphonal tube is coalescent with a shoulder-margin spine, the spine originating midway between varices and swinging ventrally and posteriorly to its tubular apex. The siphonal canal is broad, of moderate length, and sealed, except for a short distance as it turns sharply dorsally.

The body whorl bears three broadly winglike varices; other axial sculpture is lacking. Spiral sculpture, in addition to the threads on the dorsal surface of the shoulder-margin spine, consists of 12 cords, three on the canal and nine on the body; the cords are ephemeral intervarically but terminate as more or less strongly developed ruffles at the varical margin, the uppermost three crowded on the anterior flank of the shoulder spine. A strong, oblique ridge extends from just below the shoulder margin in front of the preceding varix to a point medial on the current varix, to form the two strongest ruffles. Portions of the dorsal surface of the varix, between the shoulder spine and the ridge and anterior to the ridge, appear sunken by contrast with the raised features. The cords are also apparent on the leading edge of the varix, and the cord interspaces on the outer surface of the outer apertural lip are comparatively depressed; on each preceding varix these depressions appear as a single axial row of deep pits.

Shell color is translucent blue-white or white, with a lustrous white aperture. The entire shell is covered by a flat-white, minutely axially frilled intritacalx.

Known to us from the Bahamas and reported in the literature (Gertman, 1969) from off the Yucatán Peninsula and the Caribbean coast of Panamá.

See Pl. 30, fig. 7.

Genus TRUBATSA Dall, 1889

TYPE SPECIES: *Typhis (Trubatsa) longicornis* Dall, 1888, by original designation.

The shell is essentially similar to that in *Siphonochelus*, though each anal siphonal tube in *Trubatsa* originates within a varix. The tube and that entire portion of the varix are swept sharply dorsally, each such portion aligned with corresponding portions on former whorls; in *Siphonochelus* the tube is not integrally associated with the varix and does not impart this swept appearance to the upper portion of each whorl.

Trubatsa erythrostigma (Keen & Campbell, 1964)

Siphonochelus (S.) erythrostigma Keen & Campbell, 1964: 51

The shell is small for the genus (length 14 mm) and roughly fusiform. The spire is high, consisting of one and one-half translucent-white nuclear whorls and five angulate postnuclear whorls; the first whorl of the protoconch is notably angulate. The suture is largely obscured by the extensive swelling at the base of each tube. The body whorl is fusoid. The aperture is small and subcircular, with an erect peristome. The outer apertural lip is somewhat erect; its inner surface is smooth. The anal siphonal tubes as below. The siphonal canal is of moderate length, sealed, and straight.

The body whorl bears four more or less heavy, ropelike varices. The upper half of each varix is swept posteriorly and dorsally and includes the typical anal tube of typhine species. Spiral sculpture consists of six faint cords on the varices, these completely obsolete in the narrow intervarical spaces.

Shell color is white. As in most muricid forms the tips of former canals are retained and form a spiral ridge from the lower-left corner of the aperture to the tip of the most recent canal; the tip of each canal in the present species is stained red-brown, and this series of former canal-tips forms a spiral line of red-brown spots, hence the name "*erythrostigma*."

Known only from the type locality (Moreton Bay, Queensland, Australia—27° 20′ S lat., 153° 15′ E long.).

See Pl. 31, fig. 8.

Trubatsa longicornis (Dall, 1888)

Typhis (Trubatsa) longicornis Dall, 1888: 70

The shell is of moderate size (maximum length 24 mm) and fusiform. The spire is high, consisting of one and one-half bulbous, translucent nuclear whorls and six convex postnuclear whorls. The suture is impressed. The body whorl is moderately large and fusoid. The aperture is small and subcircular, with an erect peristome. The upper corner of each varix and adjoining partition is swept dorsally, forming a moderately long, hollow, dorsally swept anal siphonal tube connecting the varix to the preceding whorl. The siphonal canal is long and barely angled dorsally, consisting of a moderately broad upper one-third and a lower, slender, tubular two-thirds.

The body whorl bears four sharp varices, these (as noted above) swept dorsally at their upper (i.e. posterior) ends. The crest of each varix is weakly dorsally reflected. Immediately below each anal tube there is a single inconspicuous cusp or weak point on the varical margin. Spiral sculpture is essentially lacking.

Shell color is waxy white, with suffusions of fleshy to rosy brown between varices. The leading edge of the varix and the interior of the aperture are invariably white, and the siphonal canal is translucent.

Straits of Florida and off Cuba in deep water (350–600 m).

See Pl. 31, fig. 9.

Trubatsa pavlova (Iredale, 1936)

Typhina pavlova Iredale, 1936: 324

The shell is small (maximum length 16 mm) and fusiform. The spire is moderately high, consisting of five convex postnuclear whorls and a protoconch of undetermined nature. The suture is not much impressed. The body whorl is of moderate size and generally fusoid. The aperture is small and circular, with an entirely erect peristome. The upper corner of each varix is swept dorsally and, together with a diminutive partition, gives rise to a long, dorsally and posteriorly oriented anal siphonal tube. The siphonal canal is moderately long, its proximal quarter moderately broad, and its distal three-quarters long, slender, tubular, and bent slightly to the left and dorsally.

The body whorl bears four heavily thickened varices, these trigonal in cross section. The upper

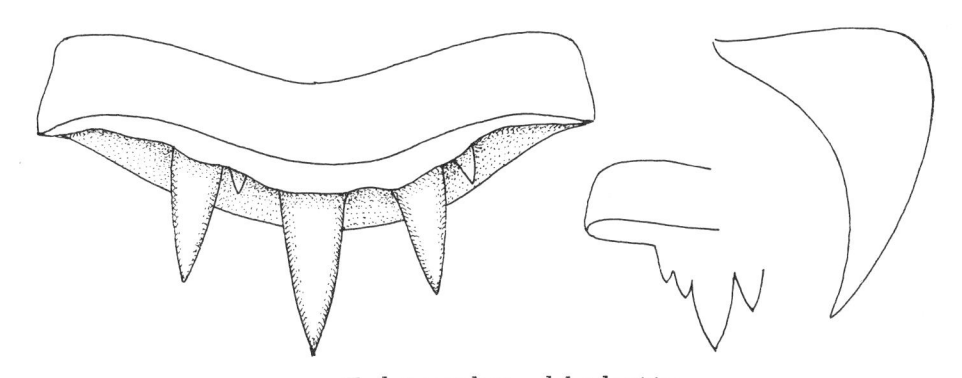

149. *Trubatsa pavlova*, radular dentition (number and placement of denticles erratic)

half of each varix is dorsally swept, and includes the origin of an anal tube. The breadth of each varix at its base obliterates the intervarical spaces and most of the horizontally oriented shoulder region. Spiral sculpture is lacking.

Shell color is white, with random red-brown maculations; the bases of the canal and the anal tube are suffused with red-brown; and the remainder of both tubes is fleshy pink, grading to translucent white. The aperture is porcelaneous white.

This species is the type of *Choreotyphis* Iredale, 1936, a subjective synonym of *Trubatsa*.

Known to us only from the coast of New South Wales, Australia.

See Pl. 31, fig. 6.

Genus **TYPHINA** Jousseaume, 1880

TYPE SPECIES: *Typhis belcheri* Broderip, 1833, by original designation.

The following is taken, with modifications, from Gertman (1969):

"Shell with four varices terminating in spines at the shoulder margin; four tubes midway between varices pointing dorsally and somewhat posteriorly; spiral sculpture often present, varical flange short, recurved, variously spiny."

The holotype of the type species is apparently lost, and no specimens definitely identified as *T. belcheri* have been found subsequently. The limits of the genus are thus dependent on two moderately clear figures in the *Conchological Illustrations*. We can verify only *T. belcheri* (whatever that may prove to be) as truly *Typhina*. Several other species, however, have been assigned to that taxon by subsequent authors and, until we have a clearer concept of *Typhina*, rather than erecting a possibly unnecessary generic taxon we shall treat these species as belonging to *Typhina*, for which the reader may read "*Typhina* of authors."

Typhina belcheri (Broderip, 1833)

Typhis belcheri Broderip, 1833: 178

We have not seen a specimen of this species; the following is translated, without change, from Broderip (1833):

"Shell subovate, white, transversely substriate, the tubes recurved, five-varicate, the varices laminate, sublaciniate with branched fronds. Canal elongate, subrecurved, gracefully curved: length 9/12 [inches, or 18 mm]; width 1/2 [inch, or 12 mm], counted total."

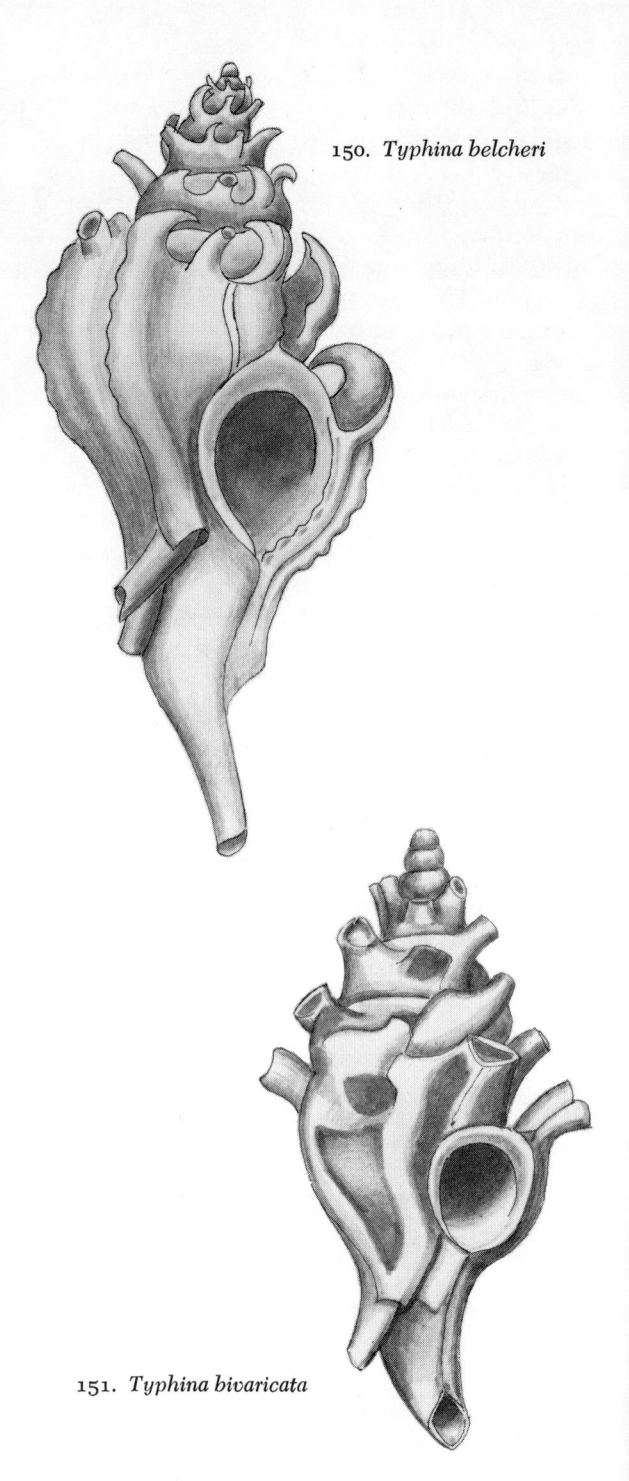

150. *Typhina belcheri*

151. *Typhina bivaricata*

Typhina bivaricata (Verco, 1909)

Typhis bivaricata Verco, 1909: 272

We have not seen a specimen of this species; the following is taken verbatim from Vella (1961):

"Shell very small, biconic, compact, with moderately elevated spire, peripheral angle high on the whorls; base moderately convex; secondary varices nearly as large as the primary varices, extending from top to bottom of the outer edge of the aperture; primary varices decreasing downward, not reaching the anterior canals.

"Dimensions. Hypotype height 4.8 [mm]; maximum diameter 3.0 mm.

"Repository. Hypotype (cotype), New Zealand Geological Survey.

"Locality. 104 fathoms [208 m], 35 miles southwest of Neptune Islands, South Australia.

"Age. Recent.

"Remarks. *T. bivaricata* is distinguished from all other species by the extraordinary development of its secondary varices."

Typhina cleryi (Petit de la Saussaye, 1840)
Murex (Typhis) cleryi Petit de la Saussaye, 1840: 327

The shell is large for the group (maximum length 24 mm) and broadly fusoid. The spire is high, consisting of one and one-half nuclear whorls and five angulate postnuclear whorls. The suture is weakly impressed, where visible. The body whorl is large and trigonal. The aperture is of moderate size and subcircular to ovate. The peristome is moderately erect, except posteriorly, where it is adherent. Each anal siphonal tube is stout and moderately long; it arises at the shoulder margin, midway between varices, and is bent almost dorsally and somewhat anteriorly at its tip. The siphonal canal is of moderate length, broad proximally, slender, and tubular, bent to the right distally, and completely fused.

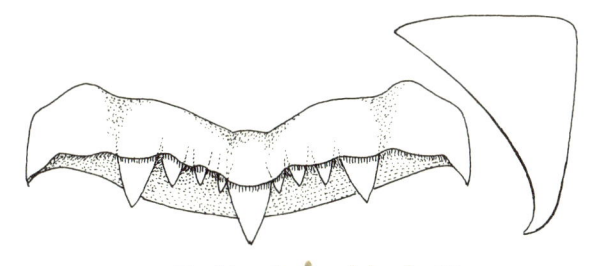

152. *Typhina cleryi*, radular dentition

The body whorl bears four moderately prominent varices. The most recent varix forms an expanded varical wing, this strongly pointed and hooked posteriorly and dorsally at the shoulder margin; the free edge of the varix is thrown into a series of five additional frill-like, dorsally curved points. The other varices lack most of these details, each consisting primarily of a sharp axial ridge and part of the shoulder margin hook. A moderately thickened axial ridge extends anteriorly from the receding side of the origin of the anal tube and may represent the outer edge of the former peristome. Spiral sculpture consists of a few weak, erratic lines between varices.

Shell color is purple to fleshy pink. A series of more or less faint, spiral, red-brown lines encircle the body and are not aligned from one varix to the next. The aperture is white, with a few red-brown spots, these representing the ends of the encircling color lines, at the outer edge of the peristome. The tips of the siphonal canal and anal tubes are stained purple-brown.

South-central Brazil (Rio de Janeiro, Joatínga) and western Africa (Canary Islands).

See Pl. 32, fig. 6.

Typhina imperialis (Keen & Campbell, 1964)
Typhis (Typhina) imperialis Keen & Campbell, 1964: 46

The shell is of moderate size (paratype length 16 mm) and roughly fusiform. The spire is high, consisting of one full nuclear whorl and four or five angulate postnuclear whorls. The suture is impressed. The body whorl is moderately large and roughly fusoid. The aperture is subcircular and forms an entirely detached and erect peristome. Each anal siphonal tube originates about midway between the adjacent varices and projects directly toward the dorsal surface of the shell. The siphonal canal is moderately long, slender, closed, and barely bent dorsally.

The body whorl bears four weakly developed, oblique varices. The spine at the upper end of each varix is situated some distance dorsal to the apertural margin, slanting toward the aperture anteriorly, almost touching the apertural margin. Small, frill-like ornamentations are apparent on the leading edge of the varix. The right margin of the canal bears an almost closed, spinelike fold. Below the body the varix is sharply indented and almost fuses with the canal. Coherent spiral sculpture is lacking.

Shell color is waxy white, with a yellow-brown band at the suture and another marking the base of the body.

Known to us only from off southeastern Japan (off Tosa) in deep water (200 m).

See Pl. 32, fig. 8.

Typhina montforti (A. Adams, 1863)
Typhis montforti A. Adams, 1863: 374; *Typhis (Typhina) teramachii* Keen & Campbell, 1964: 48

The shell is small (maximum length 14 mm) and fusiform. The spire is high and acute, consisting of one and three-fourths nuclear whorls and four or five strongly angulate postnuclear whorls. The suture is strongly impressed. The body whorl is long (but not broad) and fusoid. The aperture is small, entire, and subcircular, with a strongly erect and distally flaring peristome.

Each anal siphonal tube originates nearer the earlier of its adjacent varices and sweeps anteriorly, dorsally, and counter to the direction of growth. The siphonal canal is moderately long, slender, closed, bent first to the left and then to the right, and weakly dorsally recurved.

The body whorl bears four sharp, relatively undeveloped varices. The leading edge of the upper portion of each varix bears a series of crescentic ruffles; at the base of the body the varix cuts sharply inward to merge with the right margin of the siphonal canal. Spiral sculpture is not apparent.

Shell color is purple-brown, under a thin, flat-white, axially striate intritacalx. The aperture is pale yellow-brown.

Central to southeastern Japan (Kii to Sagami Bay).

See Pl. 32, fig. 5.

?Typhina nitens (Hinds, 1843)

Typhis nitens Hinds, 1843: 19

The shell is small (length 6.0 mm) and roughly biconic. The spire is moderately high and acute, consisting of about one and three-fourths nuclear whorls and four flat-sided postnuclear whorls. The body whorl is roughly fusoid and quadrangular, as seen apically. The suture is strongly impressed. The aperture is ovate and erect on its left side; on its right side the varix closely approaches the margin. The anal siphonal tubes are short, situated very near the preceding varix, and bent dorsally and posteriorly. The siphonal canal is short, broad, and closed, with the closure seam strongly bent to the left in an arc from the base of the aperture; the distal end of the canal is open and dorsally bent.

Axial sculpture is limited to the four varices. No varical costae are present; the intervarical areas are entirely smooth and flat. Each varical margin is composed of two elements; the leading element is weakly defined, appressed to one side of the tube, and turned inward below, disappearing at the base of the body beneath the preceding, stronger varix; the other element is stronger, somewhat raised above the shell, its edge curved forward in areas, and at its shoulder, where it becomes folded, it forms an incipient, broadly open spine. The tubes, arising from the shoulder margin, are low; they project at 45° to the long axis of the shell and are bent slightly dorsally. The apertural varix exhibits a single incipient spine, and the remainder of the varix forms a short flange, tangential to the shell, this bearing five projecting, scalloplike folds, each made up of several fimbriate layers.

Shell color is white, but no live-collected specimens have been seen by us.

Southeastern Japan (Kii, Tosa Bay region).

See Pl. 29, fig. 8.

Typhina pauperis (Mestayer, 1916)

Typhis pauperis Mestayer, 1916: 127

We have not seen a specimen of this species; the following is taken verbatim from Vella (1961):

"Shell very small, moderately elongate, pagodiform, thin and fragile, three and three-quarter post-nuclear whorls with carinate periphery high on spire whorls; base tapering from the periphery, lightly convex; no secondary varices; primary varices not extending on to the anterior canal, crenulated by three deep radial folds, each bearing a prominent trough-shaped spine curving gently inward toward the spire and backward; tubes straight, pointing slightly backward and upward; anterior canal narrow, slightly flattened, bent gently to the right.

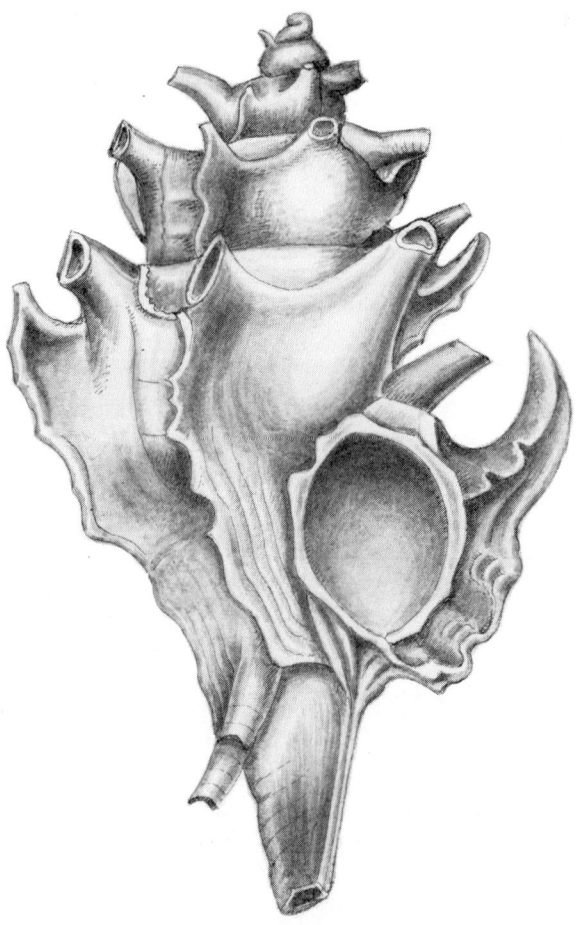

153. *Typhina pauperis*

"Dimensions. Holotype: [length] 8 [mm]; [width] 5 [mm]; [depth] 3.2 [mm].

"Repository. Holotype (*M. 1749*) and paratype (*M. 779*), Dominion Museum, Wellington, New Zealand.

"Localities. Holotype 58–60 fathoms [116–120 m] off Poor Knight's Island. Paratype 25–30 fathoms [50–60 m] off Hen and Chickens Islands, Hauraki Gulf, New Zealand. One specimen (*M. 11067*) 113–120 fathoms [226–240 m] off Mayor Island, Bay of Plenty, New Zealand (same locality as *Siphonochelus solus*).

"Age. Recent.

"Remarks: *Typhina pauperis* is distinguished from other species mainly by its small size, regularly tapering body whorl, and lack of secondary varices."

Typhina philippensis (Watson, 1883)
Typhis philippensis Watson, 1883: 605

The shell is of moderate size (maximum length 17 mm) and broadly fusiform. The spire is high, consisting of one and three-fourths nuclear whorls and five angulate postnuclear whorls. The suture is weakly impressed. The body whorl is moderately large and fusoid. The aperture is ovate and entire, and bears an erect peristome. Each anal siphonal tube originates at the shoulder margin, about midway between varices; the distal end of the tube projects dorsally and is bent slightly posteriorly and counter to the direction of growth. The siphonal canal is of moderate length and width, sealed, and bent slightly to the right.

The body whorl bears four moderately prominent, dorsally reflected varices. Each varix bears five dorsally reflected points and a posteriorly swept spine at the shoulder margin. Spiral sculpture consists of five faint cords associated with the varical points, the cords most apparent on the leading edge of the varix. A partition between shoulder margin and suture is lacking.

Shell color is pale fleshy orange-pink, except at the suture and at the base of the anal tubes, where the shell is suffused with dark rust-brown. The peristome and the siphonal canal are white. A very thin, white intritacalx may be present on the freshest shells.

Known to us only from off Queensland, Australia.

See Pl. 32, fig. 7.

Typhina ramosa (Habe & Kosuge, 1971)
Typhis ramosus Habe & Kosuge, 1971: 82

The shell is moderately large for the genus (maximum length 20 mm) and roughly fusiform. The spire is high and acute, consisting of almost two full nuclear whorls and about five moderately angulate postnuclear whorls. The suture is moderately impressed. The body whorl is moderately large and fusoid. The aperture is small and ovate, with a completely erect peristome. The anal siphonal tubes are very long; each originates midway between varices and projects dorsally and slightly posteriorly. The siphonal canal is long, sealed, tapering anteriorly, and bent to the right and dorsally.

The body whorl bears four moderately prominent, dorsally reflected varices. The margin of each varix bears five spinelike points, four of these dorsally curved and one swept posteriorly at the shoulder margin. Spiral sculpture consists of faint threads associated with the four varical points.

Shell color is primarily fleshy orange-pink, with thin rust-colored bands following the crests of the cords. The aperture and canal are white, and the tip of the canal is stained rust-color. The entire shell is covered with a thin frosting of flat-white intritacalx.

Known only from the South China Sea.

See Pl. 32, fig. 4.

Typhina yatesi (Crosse & Fischer, 1865)
Typhis yatesi Crosse & Fischer, 1865: 54

The shell is moderately large for the genus (maximum length 20 mm) and roughly fusiform. The spire is high, consisting of six angulate postnuclear whorls and a protoconch of undetermined nature. The suture is strongly impressed. The body whorl is moderately large and fusoid. The aperture is moderately large for the genus and ovate, with an erect peristome. The anal siphonal tubes are moderately long; each originates slightly closer to the earlier of the two bracketing varices and projects slightly posteriorly and dorsally. The siphonal canal is moderately long, closed, slightly bent to the right, and barely dorsally recurved.

The body whorl bears four low, oblique, marginally scalloped varices. The free edge of each varix bears four rounded, scalloplike lobes, these diminishing in size posteriorly, and a strongly anteriorly hooked spine at the shoulder margin. The shoulder of the shell in advance of this spine rises to form a brief partition above the aperture. The margin of the canal bears a single short, blunt projection medially. Spiral sculpture consists of weak, rounded swellings on the receding edge of the varix, these associated with the varical lobes.

Shell color is pinkish-white, with brown suffusions at the tips of the anal tubes and the siphonal canal and an ephemeral brown line following the base of the body from whorl to whorl; an interrupted, rusty-brown band follows the shoulder. A thin, flat-white intritacalx covers the shell.

Known to us only from South Australia.

See Pl. 31, fig. 1.

Genus TYPHINELLUS Jousseaume, 1880

TYPE SPECIES: *Typhis sowerbiyi* [sic] Broderip, 1833 (=*Typhis sowerbii* Broderip, 1833), by original designation.

Members of this group have shells with four varices and tubes per whorl, the tubes situated slightly closer to the older of two consecutive varices. Each tube is bent posteriorly and dorsally. The varix at the growing edge is constricted above the aperture and flaring at its anterior end. Faint spiral sculpture is not uncommon.

Typhinellus occlusus (Garrard, 1963)

Typhisopsis occlusum Garrard, 1963: 46

The shell is large (maximum length 32 mm) and coarsely biconic. The spire is high and acute, consisting of six or seven angulate postnuclear whorls and a protoconch of undetermined nature. The suture is impressed and somewhat obscured. The body whorl is moderately large and roughly trigonal. The aperture is small and subcircular, with an almost entirely erect peristome, the posterior end being adherent. Each anal siphonal tube is moderately long, hollow, dorsally and posteriorly oriented, and buttressed by a vertical flange, the partition, that arises from the shoulder margin at the site of the preceding varix. The siphonal canal is sealed, and broad for most of its length; the distal portion is slender, tubular, and sharply dorsally bent.

The body whorl bears four thin, sharp varices, these all, except for the most recent varix, low to obsolete. The most recent varix, broadly alate and barely dorsally reflected at its free edge, extends from the shoulder margin to near the distal end of the canal. At the shoulder margin each varical wing is extended posteriorly and slightly dorsally to form a weak shoulder spine. Spiral sculpture appears to be lacking, except for five faint lines on the leading edge of the last varix.

Shell color is white, with random suffusions of fleshy purple-brown. A single narrow brown line encircles the body medially, and the tip of the canal is dark purple-brown; six axially aligned red-brown spots are evident on the outer apertural lip. A thick, flat-white, finely axially striate intritacalx is evident.

Known only from Queensland, Australia (Whitsunday Passage, type locality; off Langford Island, figured specimen).

See Pl. 32, fig. 3.

Typhinellus sowerbii (Broderip, 1833)

Typhis sowerbiyi Broderip, 1833: 178

The shell is of moderate size (maximum length 22 mm) and broadly fusiform. The spire is high, consisting of five or six angulate postnuclear whorls and a protoconch of undetermined nature. The suture is generally hidden by material making up the shoulder. The body whorl is large and broadly fusoid. The aperture is small and ovate, forming a raised peristome that flares out over the columella and posteriorly, where it forms a thin, vertical flange; behind this a portion of the body arises at right angles to the remainder to form a thin flange, the partition. A long, hollow tube, arising medially in the last intervarical space and reflected outward and toward the preceding varix, houses the anal siphon; earlier tubes are sealed and are generally broken off, leaving stumps. The siphonal canal is moderately long, broad above, slender and tubular below, and sealed for its entire length.

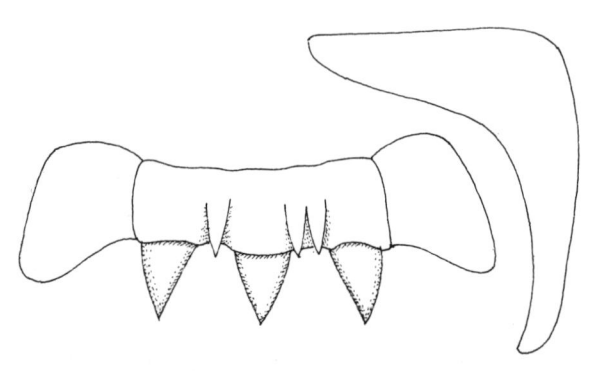

154. *Typhinellus sowerbii*, radular dentition

The body whorl bears four thin, sharp varices, each made up of two shell laminae. The lamina on the receding side of each varix projects above the lamina on the leading side, forming a webbed portion of the varix at the base of the body and the upper canal. Where the varix crosses the shoulder margin a flat, moderately long, dorsally and inhooked spine is formed. Additional axial sculpture consists of a low, ephemeral ridge, extending from the base of the anal tube to the base of the body; the base of the anal tube corresponds in position to a portion of a varix on the preceding whorl, and the juxtaposition of these two features bisects the shoulder. Spiral sculpture consists of five subobsolete cords on the body and two additional cords on the upper portion of the canal. The shell of this species, as of other typhine species, appears to be composed of a patchwork of various portions of shell, these portions delimited by distinct microscopic suture lines.

Shell color is pale purple-white to mauve, with faint red-brown spiral lines alternating with the spiral cords; the newest portions of the shell, as well as the webbing on each varix and the distal ends of full-length tubes, are white. A red-brown suffusion colors the tubular distal end of the siphonal canal. The interior of the aperture is porcelaneous white, with pale red-brown markings on the margin of the outer apertural lip.

Mediterranean Sea and the Atlantic coast of northern Africa. Gertman (1969) figured a specimen that he identified as this species from off Nevis, Leeward Islands, and several others have been reported from the Gulf of Mexico, as far west as Texas.

See Pl. 31, fig. 7.

Genus TYPHISALA Jousseaume, 1881

TYPE SPECIES: *Typhis grandis* A. Adams, 1855, by original designation.

This genus was erected, according to the practice at the time, by simply designating a type species. This practice typically, in tending to exclude all but the type species, led to an overly narrow definition of the genus. In spite of this failing, it appears that *Typhisala* is both distinct and not monotypic.

Typhisala includes those large, broad typhine forms with broadly expanded varical "wings" that are fimbriate on their leading surface. The anal siphonal tubes originate midway between varices and are bent severely dorsally. This definition would include *Typhisopsis*, a superficially similar group; species in *Typhisala*, however, differ in having the thin, sharp lamina that forms the receding slope of each varix extend well beyond the one forming the leading edge, in having a comparatively simple, axially striate intritacalx, instead of the regularly pitted intritacalx of *Typhisopsis coronatus* (the type species), and in having a greatly differing radular dentition with a much more typically typhine rachidian tooth.

Typhisala clarki (Keen & Campbell, 1964)

Typhis (*Typhisopsis*) *clarki* Keen & Campbell, 1964: 48

The shell is moderately large for the Typhinae (maximum length 27 mm) and broadly fusiform. The spire is high, consisting of two nuclear whorls and five or six angulate postnuclear whorls. The suture is largely obscured by material extending from the last whorl onto the preceding one. The body whorl is moderately large and broadly fusoid. The aperture is small and ovate, and bears a partially erect peristome, this including the outer apertural lip and the anterior portion of the inner lip. Each long, hollow anal siphonal tube originates at the shoulder margin roughly midway in an intervarical space, and is strongly bent dorsally; generally only the most recent tube is complete and open (i.e. functional). The siphonal canal is moderately long, broad for two-thirds of its length, slender and tubular for the distal one-third, and sealed for its entire length.

The body whorl bears four thin, sharp varices, each composed of two appressed laminae, the lamina on the receding edge extending further out from the body than the lamina on the leading edge. Each varix ends in an inwardly hooked spine at the shoulder margin. The spine on the last varix is broader and is hooked dorsally rather than inwardly. The last varix is more broadly flangelike, with a serrate, dorsally reflected, and fimbriate edge. It is assumed that the numerous tiny, reflected points of the last varix are resorbed in the preceding varices. Spiral sculpture is lacking, except for traces of numerous fine spiral cords on the receding side of some varices and the fine rippling of the shell just behind the reflected, serrated edge of the last varix. Each tube is buttressed by a thin partition that bisects the shoulder.

Shell color varies from white to fleshy pink-yellow to dark purple-brown; in paler-colored specimens the tubes, the distal tip of the siphonal canal, and the shoulder region are suffused with dark purple-brown. The newly formed ventral face of the shell is white, and the interior of the aperture is porcelaneous white.

San Felipe, Baja California, to Panamá.

See Pl. 31, fig. 5.

Typhisala grandis (A. Adams, 1855)

Typhis grandis A. Adams, 1855: 42

The shell is large (maximum length 36 mm) and massive. The spire is moderately high, consisting of one and three-fourths nuclear whorls and five shouldered postnuclear whorls. The suture, where not obscured, is deeply impressed. The body whorl is large and broadly fusoid. The aperture is of moderate size and ovate, with an almost completely erect peristome, the posterior and posteroparietal regions being adherent. The broad-based, quickly tapering anal siphonal tube originates further dorsally than that of many typhine species and from its origin swings sharply dorsally; it is buttressed by the partition of the preceding varix. The siphonal canal is very broad and sealed, the left margin overlapping the right; it tapers abruptly and is bent sharply dorsally at its distal end.

The body whorl bears four heavy, ropelike varices, each of which is overridden by a thin, sharp lamina that covers the receding edge of the varix. The leading edge of the last varix is densely fimbriate on its outer portion and abruptly constricted just above the canal; the varix bears a broad, finely lamellate upper section that extends across the shoulder to adhere to the preceding whorl, this partition and the whole shoulder section presumably the last part of the shell to be formed. Spiral sculpture consists of numerous fine, sharp spiral cords. The upper angle of the varix is marked by a moderately weak, dorsally hooked spine. Immediately in front of all spines but the most recent one on the last whorl there is a deep, sharp anterior indentation. Below this, three brief cords climb the base of the anal tube, six more traverse the body, ending in dorsally reflected points at the varical margin, and ten others have varying degrees of completeness; these 19 cords tend to be obsolete intervarically, and are more apparent just before and on the varix. The fimbriations on the leading edge of the last varix are arranged in rows of furbelows, the rows associated with the cord interspaces, and the inner portion of the leading edge showing numerous fine cords in the body region. Other sculpture on the ventral surface of the last varix is obscured posteriorly by the partition and anteriorly by the overlapping of the siphonal canal.

Shell color is pale fleshy yellow-white or tan-white, with purple-brown suffusions on the anal tubes and the tip of the siphonal canal; the spire has a diffuse pale-purple cast. The entire shell is covered by a thin, finely axially striate, flat-white intritacalx.

Although there has been a great deal of confusion in the literature concerning the identity of this species and its distinctness from *Typhisopsis coronatus*, examination of the original illustration (A. Adams, 1855, pl. 27, fig. 4), combined with the presence of a type lot including representatives of the two species, indicates the correctness of the present identification.

Guaymas, Mexico, to Isla Venado, Panamá.

See Pl. 29, fig. 1.

Genus TYPHISOPSIS Jousseaume, 1880

TYPE SPECIES: *Typhis coronatus* Broderip, 1833, by original designation.

The shell is large for the Typhinae and coarsely biconic. The body whorl bears four heavy, rounded, ropelike varices. Each anal siphonal tube is close to the preceding varix (actually appressed to it) and is buttressed by a partition (a posterior lamina of the former outer apertural lip). The partition bridges the shoulder region and is appressed to a varix on the preceding whorl. The upper angle of the varical flange forms a spine that, on all but the last varix, is compressed and tapers rapidly to a sharp, incurved point.

Typhisopsis coronatus (Broderip, 1833)

Typhis coronatus Broderip, 1833: 178; *Typhis quadratus* Hinds, 1843: 18; *Typhis martyria* Dall, 1902: 550

The shell is large for the subfamily (maximum length 38 mm) and coarsely biconic. The spire is high and acute, consisting of two and one-fourth convex nuclear whorls and six or seven angulate

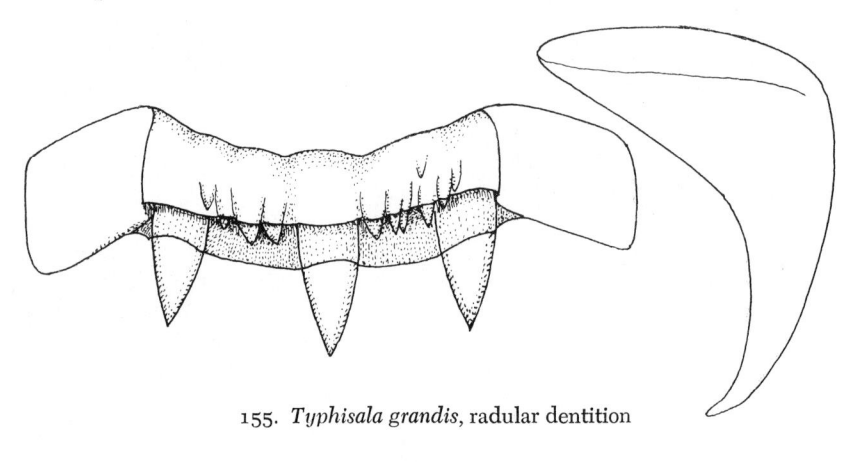

155. *Typhisala grandis*, radular dentition

156. *Typhisopsis coronatus*, radular dentition

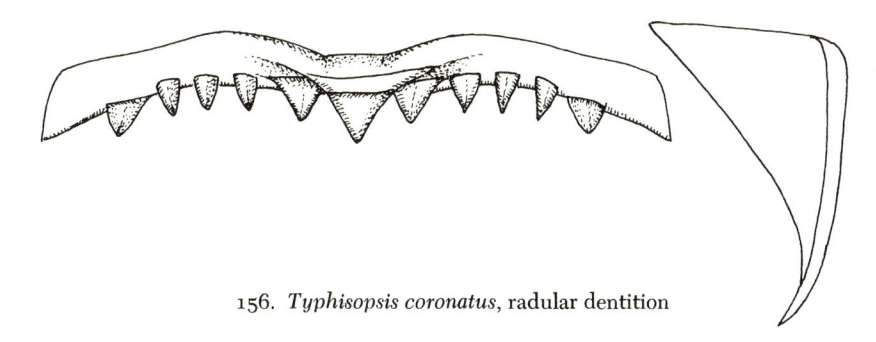

postnuclear whorls. The suture is moderately impressed and obscured. The body whorl is moderately large and roughly trigonal. The aperture is subcircular, moderately small, and entire at the weakly erect peristome. Each anal siphon empties through a moderately long, dorsally directed, hollow tube that arises somewhat nearer the preceding varix; the tube is appressed to, and apparently buttressed by, a flangelike portion of the preceding varix, the partition, this connecting the whorl with the preceding one. The completely sealed siphonal canal is broad for the upper three-fourths of its length; the distal one-fourth of the canal is slender, tubular, and dorsally bent.

The body whorl bears four varices; the three earliest of the four are heavy, rounded, and ropelike; the last is alate, with a moderately broad flange extending from the preceding whorl to below the middle of the canal, and is reflected dorsally at its free edge. The varix is drawn into a moderately long, sharp, dorsally incurved spine at the shoulder margin. Spiral sculpture consists of five cords on the body and seven on the canal; although prominent on the varices, these cords vary from strong to obsolete in the intervarical spaces.

Shell color is white, with orange-brown suffusions on the varices, purple-brown on the tubes and on the tip of the siphonal canal, and porcelaneous white in the aperture; four or five red-brown spots on the last outer apertural lip margin also persist just in front of each of the former outer lips.

The winglike varical flange is apparently the last part of each growth increment to be formed, since a slender form, found in many collections and lacking a varical flange, is otherwise apparently mature.

According to the figure of the "holotype" of *Typhis grandis* in Keen (1971), that species is synonymous with *"Typhis" coronatus*. As it happens the figure is of one specimen of a syntypic lot of three in the British Museum (Natural History) that was indicated as a lectotype by markings on the label. Such a lectotype designation without publication is invalid, and in fact the original illustration of *"Typhis" grandis* (q.v.) shows it to be a distinct species, based on another specimen from the same lot.

Puerto Peñasco, Sonora, Mexico, to Santa Elena, Ecuador.

See Pl. 32, figs. 10–12.

Incertae Sedis

We have not been able to determine the generic affinities of the following three species, owing in part to the ambiguity of their shell characters, or to their possessing characters that seem to relate them equally to several different groups. Moreover, radular evidence did not, in one case (*M. pleurotomoides*), seem to align the species to any of the better-known generic groupings.

Placing these species in Incertae Sedis has allowed us to include them in this book, without attempting to force them into one or another unlikely generic niche, and thereby to make available both a description and an illustration adequate for purposes of identification.

"Murex" alfredensis Bartsch, 1915

Murex alfredensis Bartsch, 1915: 59

The shell is very small (length of holotype 6 mm) and broadly fusiform. The spire is high and acute, consisting of three or more weakly convex postnuclear whorls and a protoconch of undetermined nature. The suture is impressed. The body whorl is moderately large and broadly fusoid. The aperture is subovate, and thrust out in the direction of the shoulder; the anal sulcus is imperceptible. The outer apertural lip is erect and smooth, as is the columellar lip. The siphonal canal is moderately long, narrowly open, and bent to the left.

The body whorl bears six sharp, bladelike varices, five closely spaced and the last separated from the penultimate by a comparatively broad interspace. Earlier whorls bear seven varices; each varix becomes a horizontal plate as it crosses the shoulder and is appressed to the preceding varix at least one intervarical space offset from its original position. The last varix is extended posteriorly and dorsally to form a spinelike projection. Spiral sculpture consists of 24 prominent cords extending from the shoulder margin to the tip of the canal, the cords also quite prominent on the leading edge of each varix.

Shell color is white, with a broad band of yellow-brown medial on the body.

Known to us only from the type locality, Port Alfred, South Africa.

See Pl. 29, fig. 15.

"Murex" exquisitus Sowerby, 1904

Murex (Pteronotus) exquisitus Sowerby, 1904: 176

We have not seen a specimen of this species; the following is freely translated from the original Latin of Sowerby:

"Shell elongate-trigonal, white with a transverse brown band; spire acutely conical, the whorls seven, including two oblique, papillate, smooth nuclear whorls and two convex postnuclear whorls (juvenile?). Eight to ten exceptionally squamose costae. Additional axial sculpture consists of three varices covered with very undulate minute imbrications running along the spiral sculptural elements. The body whorl is angulate above, attenuate below, and rostrate. The siphonal canal is slender and slightly reflected dorsally at its tip. The canal is moderately long and straight and bears four short spines. The aperture is small and ovate to subcircular. The oper-

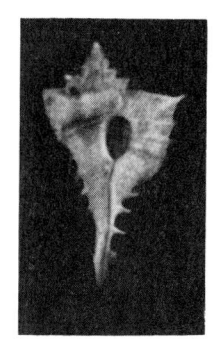

157. *"Murex" exquisitus*

culum is corneous and laminate. Length 26 mm, major diameter 9.5 mm."

Range not known; other species in the same collection are from the coast of western Africa.

"Murex" pleurotomoides Reeve, 1845

Murex pleurotomoides Reeve, 1845: sp. 173

The shell is small (maximum length 20 mm) and roughly fusiform. The spire is high, consisting of two and three-fourths convex, gradually tapering nuclear whorls and five or six weakly shouldered postnuclear whorls. The suture is moderately impressed. The body whorl is of moderate size and roughly trigonal. The aperture is small and ovate, with a deep, narrow, turridlike anal sulcus. The outer apertural lip is erect and minutely serrate; its inner surface is strongly lirate. The columellar lip is entirely adherent and bears five strong, elongate-oblique, plica-like ridges at its anterior end. The siphonal canal is of moderate length, open, and dorsally recurved at its tip.

The body whorl bears seven low varices. Spiral sculpture consists of numerous cords, perhaps five of which, all on the body, could be called major. Innumerable fine axial lamellae are thrown into scalelike projections at their intersections with the spiral cords. In very fresh specimens the major cord at the shoulder margin may give rise to very short, sharp, straight, open spines.

Shell color is uniform light yellow-brown to red-brown. The aperture is white.

The Philippines to western Australia, in moderately deep water (40–130 m).

See Pl. 25, fig. 7.

Species of Uncertain Identity

In the course of the research on which this volume is based, many names have been located which, for one of several reasons, we have not been able to associate with living forms known to us. The various circumstances leading to this result are, in order of importance:

1. No type specimen extant
2. No adequate published figure
3. Ambiguous or otherwise inadequate description given
4. No collection locality given
5. Publication in extremely obscure and essentially unobtainable source.

Generally, a combination of two or more of these conditions has contributed to our relegating a name to the following list. The most damaging of all are the first two items, for nowhere is it so true that "one picture is worth a thousand words" as in a descriptive area such as identification of species. However, even photos or other illustrations do not always give an accurate idea of the actual shape and/or texture of a particular shell.

The inclusion of a name in this list should in no way imply to the reader that the name is of no value or has no validity. Rather, its inclusion indicates that we are not in possession of sufficient evidence to come to a satisfactory decision regarding the status of the name. All the following names should be read as if prefixed by "*Murex*":

alabastrum A. Adams, 1864
baeticus Reeve, 1845
bandana Schepman, 1911
bituberculatus F. C. Baker, 1891
briskasi A. H. Verrill, 1953
castus A. Adams, 1854
clenchi Carcelles, 1953
dearmatus Odhner, 1922
dentifer Watson, 1883
duthiersi Vélain, 1877
exiguus Broderip, 1833
falcatiformis Thiele, 1925
flexirostris Melvill, 1898
fusiformis A. Adams, 1853
hermanni Vélain, 1877
interserratus Sowerby, 1879
jenksi F. C. Baker, 1889
kopua Dell, 1956
maculatus Reeve, 1845
medicago Watson, 1897
natalensis E. A. Smith, 1906
nitens A. Adams, 1854
niveus A. Adams, 1853
nucleus Broderip, 1833
oligocanthus Euthyme, 1889
pallidus Broderip, 1833
percoides Löbbecke, 1879
pettardi Brazier, 1870
pudicus Reeve, 1845
puniceus Oliver, 1915
puteola A. Adams, 1863
pyrrhias Watson, 1882
rusticus Reeve, 1845
singaporensis A. Adams, 1853
solidus A. Adams, 1853
strigatus Reeve, 1849
sykesi Preston, 1904
tumida Petterd, 1884

Appendix: New Species

As might be expected, in compiling the present guide we have encountered several unidentifiable forms that differ sufficiently from all known species to encourage us to describe them as new. The following are, to our knowledge, the first published descriptions of these entities as species.

Aspella castor sp. nov.
(Muricinae; for genus, see p. 21)

Distribution: known only from Puerto Rico and St. Thomas, Virgin Islands.

The shell is of moderate size for the genus (maximum length 13.4 mm) and lanceolate. The spire is high and markedly acute, and consists of one and one-third nuclear whorls and six or seven broad, flattened postnuclear whorls. The suture is impressed and obscured at intervals by narrow varical buttresses. The body whorl is of moderate size, broad, and flattened. The aperture is small and ovate, with a barely perceptible trace of an anal sulcus. The outer apertural lip is weakly erect and bears five very weak denticles on its inner surface. The columellar lip is smooth, detached, and erect. The siphonal canal is moderately long for the genus, moderately open, bent to the left, and moderately dorsally recurved.

The body whorl bears four moderately broad lateral varices, the right ventral and left dorsal ones most prominent. Two moderately strong costae, representing the single ventral and dorsal varices seen on the first two or three postnuclear whorls, are apparent on the body whorl. Spiral sculpture is present only in the intritacalx. Six broad cords with equal interspaces are apparent on the varices and become more apparent between the varices as the intritacalx is eroded. The microsculpture of the intritacalx (see Fig. 159) is similar to that of *A. pollux* and *A. senex* in consisting of axial striae and numerous transverse tubes (see D'Attilio & Radwin, 1971, under *Aspella* cf. *A. pyramidalis*).

The shell is translucent white, covered by a flat-white intritacalx and a yellow-brown periostracum. The aperture is porcelaneous yellow-white.

The radular dentition is muricine and is very similar to that of *A. pollux* (following). The rachidian tooth bears five cusps; the relative lengths of the central, lateral, and intermediate cusps are in the ratio of 5:3:2.

Measurements: holotype, length 13 mm, width 5.9 mm; largest paratype, length 13.4 mm, width

158. *Aspella castor*

5.0 mm; smallest paratype, length 9.4 mm, width 4.3 mm.

Type locality: Puerto Rico, Coll. J. A. Weber, August 30, 1956.

Material studied: holotype, USNM 663525; 1 paratype, USNM 708414, type locality; 1 paratype, SDSNH 62682, type locality; 5 paratypes, ANSP 36935, St. Thomas, Virgin Islands, R. Swift; 2 paratypes, USNM 702779, St. Thomas, Virgin Islands, R. Brody, 1958.

Mörch (1877) was probably referring to this species when, in describing *Aspella* for the first time, he cited one species (as *A. anceps* Lamarck) from the Danish West Indies (now the Virgin Islands).

This species resembles *A. senex* and *A. pollux* but differs from these species in several ways. It differs from *A. senex* in its relatively more slender shell, its more rounded (almost circular) aperture, its detached and erect columellar lip, its weaker denticulation of the inner surface of the outer apertural lip, and its more flattened body whorl. *A. castor* differs from *A. pollux* in its coarser axial intritacalx sculpture, its more slender and more gradually tapering spire, its weaker, unstained denticles on the inner surface of the outer apertural lip, the occurrence of two (rather than two and one-half) buttresses between varices, and the fact that the varical flange on the body whorl meets the flange on the preceding whorl directly (rather than passing behind the earlier flange, as in *A. pollux*).

This species and *A. pollux*, another new species described herein, are named respectively for the gemini of Greek mythology. The close similarity of the shells of these two species would seem to indicate that they are Atlantic-Pacific cognates ("twin species"). The two names are also meant to honor Clifton and Clifford Martin of Oceanside, California, two amateur malacologist-twins whose cooperation and helpfulness have been of consistent benefit to local malacological research.

See Pl. 28, fig. 1.

Aspella cryptica sp. nov.
(Muricinae; for genus, see p. 21)

Distribution: northeastern Brazil (known only from the type locality).

The shell is small (maximum length 6.5 mm) and lanceolate. The spire is high and acute, consisting of one and one-half convex nuclear whorls and five dorsoventrally flattened postnuclear whorls. The suture is impressed but is largely obscured by varical buttresses. The body whorl is comparatively long for the genus. The aperture is small and ovate, with no apparent anal sulcus. The outer apertural lip is barely erect. The columellar lip is smooth and entirely adherent. The siphonal canal is short, narrowly open, and weakly dorsally recurved.

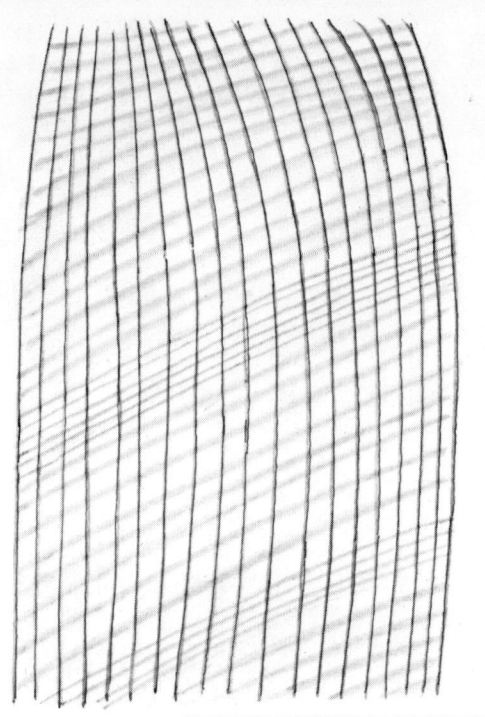

159. *Aspella castor*, intritacalx

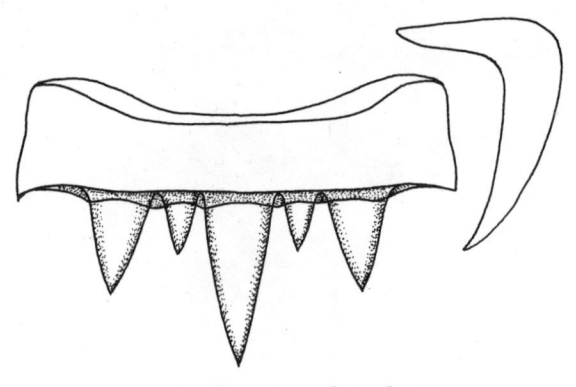

160. *Aspella castor*, radular dentition

The body whorl bears two poorly developed major lateral varices. A single minor varix ventral to the left major varix may be present as a low axial costa. In the holotype, however, only the two major varices are discernible. Early whorls preceding the penultimate bear the typical six varices of aspelloids. Spiral sculpture consists of four or five barely perceptible threads on the body.

The shell is waxy yellow-white, with a covering of flat-white, finely axially striate, and incompletely spirally lined intritacalx and a translucent brown periostracum. The interior of the aperture is suffused with pale apricot.

The radular dentition and the operculum of this species are unknown; both specimens were empty when collected.

Measurements: holotype, length 6.2 mm, width 2.8 mm; paratype, length 6.5 mm, width 3.0 mm.

Type locality: Itapoán (Bahía), Brazil, under coral heads at 2 m, B. Tursch.

Material studied: holotype, SDSNH 62608; paratype, AMNH 129091, type locality.

The present species has remained undiscovered, or hidden (whence comes its name), to the present almost certainly because of its small size and the brown periostracum covering its intritacalx.

In spite of its small size *A. cryptica* appears to represent a mature biological entity that seems to most closely resemble *A. pyramidalis* of the tropical eastern Pacific. It differs from that species in its minute size at maturity and in its intritacalx, which has, in addition to axial striations, interrupted spiral lines of punctations.

See Pl. 1, fig. 10.

Aspella mauritiana sp. nov.
(Muricinae; for genus, see p. 21)

Distribution: apparently limited to Mauritius.

The shell is moderately small for the genus (maximum length 9 mm) and lanceolate. The spire is high, consisting of one and one-half tilted nuclear whorls and five moderately narrow, flattened postnuclear whorls. The suture is impressed but is largely obscured by varical buttresses. The body whorl is of moderate size, slender, and flattened. The aperture is moderately small and ovate, with no perceptible anal sulcus. The outer apertural lip is moderately thickened, barely erect, and bears six or seven barely perceptible denticles on its inner surface. The columellar lip is entirely adherent. The siphonal canal is moderately short, narrowly open, bent to the left, and dorsally recurved.

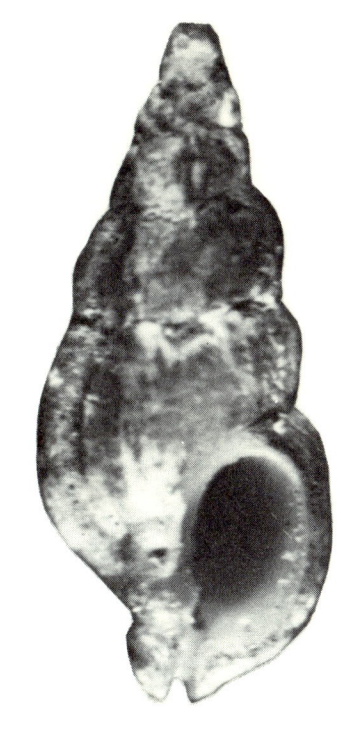

161. *Aspella cryptica*

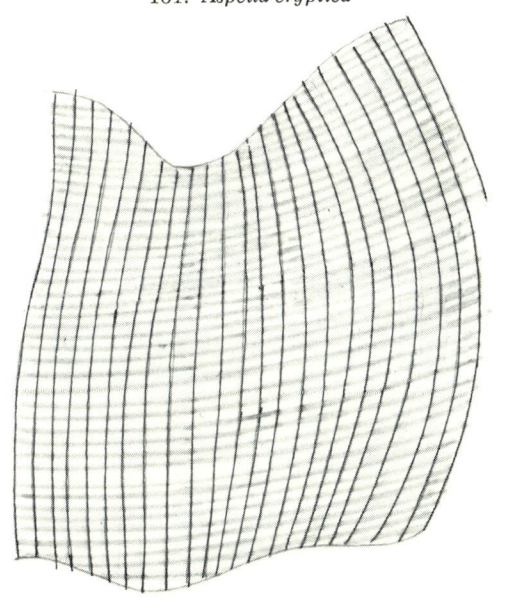

162. *Aspella cryptica*, intritacalx

163. *Aspella mauritiana*

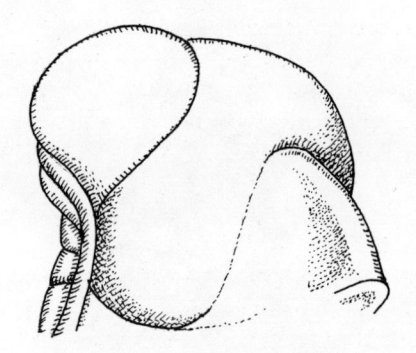

164. *Aspella mauritiana*, protoconch

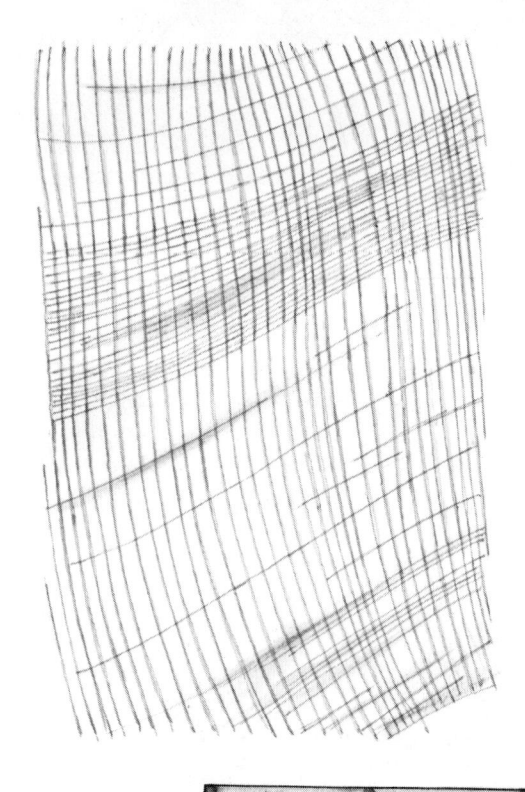

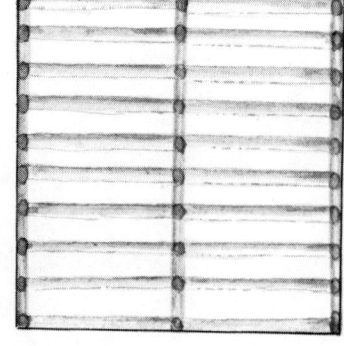

The body whorl bears two major lateral varices. The first postnuclear whorl bears six varices. The first two or three postnuclear whorls mark the disappearance of the dorsal and the ventral varices. The two minor lateral varices are reduced to axial costae, except at their anterior ends, where they are moderately prominent. Spiral sculpture in the form of seven broad, weak cords is apparent only on the leading edges of the varices.

The shell is waxy translucent white, covered by a flat-white intritacalx. The moderately strong axial striae of the intritacalx are interrupted by regularly incised pits that are deeper opposite the direction of growth. These pits or furrows are transversely aligned but are not continuous.

No live-collected specimens have been seen and, thus, nothing is known about the radula or operculum.

Measurements: holotype, length 8.8 mm, width 3.7 mm; largest paratype, length 8.3 mm, width 3.6 mm; smallest paratype (juvenile), length 3.9 mm, width 2.9 mm.

Type locality: Flic en Flacq, West Mauritius, R. Ostheimer, V. Orr, Sta. M203, November 2, 7, 23, 1960.

Material studied: holotype, ANSP 273236; 1 paratype, ANSP 273368, 1 km northwest of Black River, West Mauritius, R. Ostheimer, M. Baissac, V. Orr, Sta. M208, November 5, 1960; 1 paratype,

165. *Aspella mauritiana*, intritacalx

ANSP 273084, Pt. Pimente, north side of Arsenal Bay, West Mauritius, R. Ostheimer, V. Orr, Sta. M212, November 9, 1960.

This species most resembles *A. ponderi*, but differs in its peculiarly tilted protoconch, its coarser, axially striate intritacalx, and the presence in the intritacalx of open or partly closed transverse tubes. The shell of *A. mauritiana* is also more compressed and lacks the pale periostracum of *A. ponderi*.

See Pl. 28, fig. 4.

Aspella morchi sp. nov.
(Muricinae; for genus, see p. 21)

Distribution: northeastern Brazil (known only from the type locality and Fortaleza).

The shell is small (maximum length 6.6 mm) and lanceolate. The spire is high and acute, consisting of five or six dorsoventrally flattened postnuclear whorls. The suture is impressed but is obscured by varical buttresses. The body whorl is comparatively large for the genus and broadly fusoid. The aperture is moderately small and ovate, with a weakly developed anal sulcus. The outer apertural lip is moderately thickened and nonerect; its inner surface bears six very weak denticles. The columellar lip is entirely adherent. The siphonal canal is short, narrowly open, and dorsally recurved.

The body whorl bears two major lateral varices and, in some cases, a weaker third one ventral to the left lateral. Additional axial sculpture consists of four moderately weak costae in each intervarical space. Spiral sculpture consists of four moderately weak cords on the body and two or three on the canal. Where each body cord intersects a costa, a single pustule is developed. Earlier whorls show the typical six varices of the genus.

The shell is translucent milk-white, covered with a flat-white, minutely cancellate intritacalx in which the spiral elements appear to be continuous but are really discontinuous transverse tubes within the chalky layer.

The radular dentition and the operculum of this species are unknown; all specimens were empty when collected.

Measurements: holotype, length 6.6 mm, width 3.3 mm; largest paratype, length 6.2 mm, width 2.8 mm; smallest mature paratype, length 6.0 mm, width 2.8 mm.

Type locality: Natal Bay, Brazil, F. Baker.

Material studied: holotype, SDSNH 62609; 1 paratype, SDSNH 62610, type locality; 3 para-

166. *Aspella morchi*

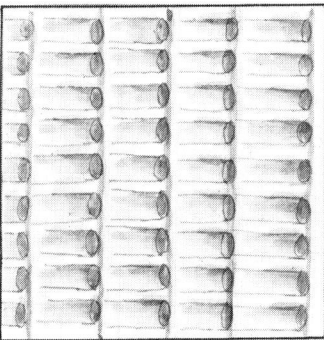

167. *Aspella morchi*, intritacalx

224 APPENDIX: NEW SPECIES

types, SDSNH 42854, Ceára (Fortaleza), Brazil.

A. morchi resembles the robust Galapagan form of *A. pyramidalis* but differs from it in its small size at maturity and its minutely cancellate intritacalx. The small size of *A. morchi* may cause it to be confused with the other Brazilian species, *A. cryptica*, described herein; *A. morchi* differs from *A. cryptica* in its more robust, less flattened shell, its much more strongly cancellate intritacalx sculpture, and in its sculpture of spiral rows of distinct pustules.

The name *morchi* honors O. A. L. Mörch, the prominent nineteenth-century conchologist who established the genus *Aspella*.

See Pl. 1, fig. 9.

Aspella platylaevis sp. nov.
(Muricinae; for genus, see p. 21)

Distribution: Western Australia (Cockburn Sound) to the Palau Islands, western Caroline Islands.

The shell is of moderate size (maximum length 14 mm) and lanceolate. The spire is high and acute, consisting of one and one-fourth nuclear whorls and five or six canted postnuclear whorls. The suture is moderately impressed and partially obscured by varical buttresses. The body whorl is moderately broad and much flattened. The aperture is small and ovate. The outer apertural lip is slightly erect and bears a series of five more

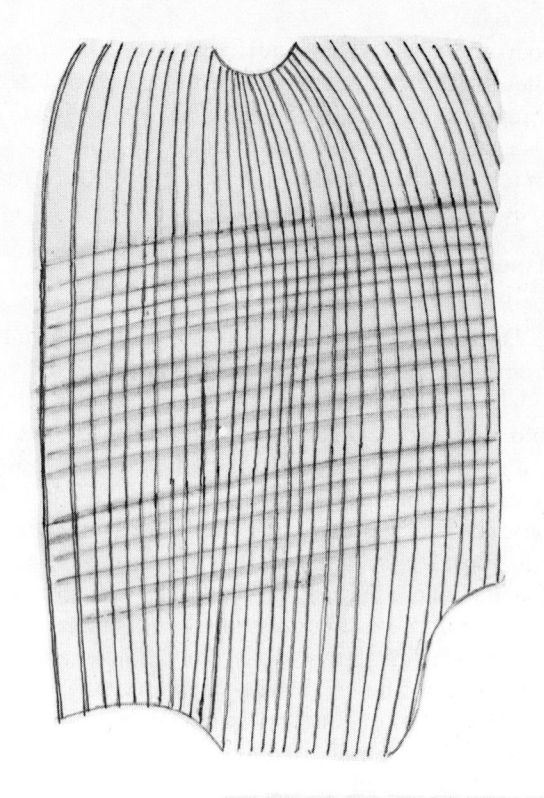

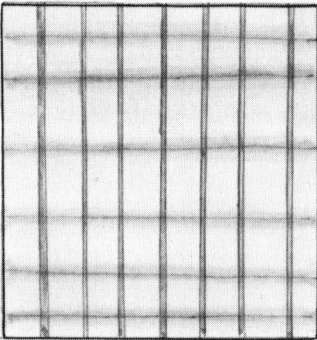

169. *Aspella platylaevis*, intritacalx

or less prominent denticles on its inner surface. The columellar lip is smooth and adherent. The siphonal canal is moderately short, narrowly open, bent to the left, and dorsally recurved.

The body whorl bears four lateral varices, two of them more prominent. The earlier whorls each bear six varices, but the ventral and dorsal ones are reduced to buttresses in all but the first two postnuclear whorls. Spiral sculpture appears to be limited to the intritacalx, and consists of several broadly spaced grooves, these visible on the leading edge of each varix, and many faint spiral striae. The intritacalx also shows numerous axial striae that are much stronger than the spiral lines, thus never producing the truly cancellate appearance of *A. producta*.

The shell is milk-white under the flat-white intritacalx and an almost transparent pale-brown periostracum.

168. *Aspella platylaevis*

The radular dentition is composed of two typically muricine, sickle-shaped lateral teeth flanking a single five-cusped rachidian tooth, which in turn bears a central cusp, two laterals, and two intermediates, the lengths of which are in the ratio of 4:3:2. The two denticles at each extremity of the rachidian tooth, i.e. between the lateral cusp and the end of the tooth, are unique in the genus.

The operculum is typically muricine in its unguiculate shape, its thickened inner margin, and its centrally depressed, concentrically lined center.

Measurements: holotype, length 13.6 mm, width 5.7 mm; paratype, length 11.8 mm, width 5.2 mm.

Type locality: Woodman's Point, Cockburn Sound, Western Australia, B. Wilson, V. Orr, March 9, 1963.

Material studied: holotype, ANSP 285147; 1 paratype, SDSNH 63167, type locality; 1 paratype, ANSP 201642, southwestern Rattakadokorn Island (Palau Islands), western Caroline Islands, A. J. Ostheimer, August 21, 1955.

This species resembles *A. producta* to some degree but differs from it in its more flattened shell, its more gradually tapering spire, its lack of strongly cancellate intritacalx microsculpture, and its lack of spiral rows of pustules on the shell. *A. platylaevis* also resembles, somewhat, *A. pollux* and *A. castor* from the New World; it differs from these in its less rounded aperture, its adherent columellar lip, its much less prominent minor varices, its blunter angles at the periphery, and its finer axial intritacalx sculpture, in addition to substantial radular differences.

The present name is derived from the Greek and Latin combining forms for flat (Greek) and smooth (Latin), two of the more outstanding characteristics of this species.

See Pl. 28, fig. 3.

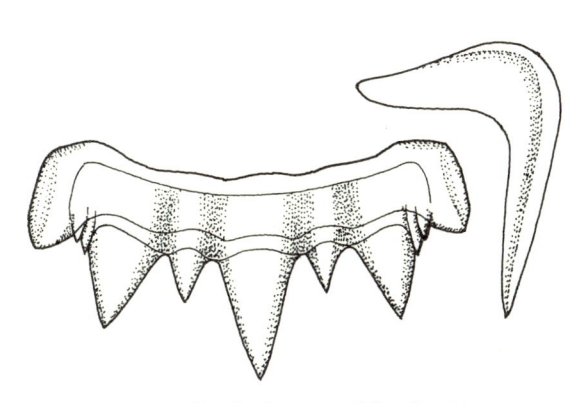

171. *Aspella pollux*

Aspella pollux sp. nov.
(Muricinae; for genus, see p. 21)

Distribution: southern end of the Gulf of California to Costa Rica.

The shell is large for the genus (maximum length 25 mm) and broadly lanceolate. The spire is high and acute, consisting of one and one-half narrow, convex nuclear whorls and eight or nine broad, strongly dorsoventrally flattened postnuclear whorls. The suture is deeply impressed but is largely obscured by varical buttresses. The body whorl is very broadly fusoid. The aperture is small and ovate, with a barely perceptible anal sulcus. The outer apertural lip is weakly erect; immediately behind it is a more or less broadly expanded varical wing. The inner surface of the outer lip bears five or six rather weak denticles corresponding roughly to the spiral cords on the shell's exterior. The columellar lip is smooth, detached, and weakly erect anteriorly. The siphonal canal is moderately long, narrowly open, and dorsally recurved.

The body whorl bears two expanded, lateral varical flanges and two minor, costate varices. Two additional varices, seen in the first three or four whorls, recede with later growth and eventually are represented solely by buttresses at the suture. The spiral sculpture consists of five broad weak cords.

170. *Aspella platylaevis*, radular dentition

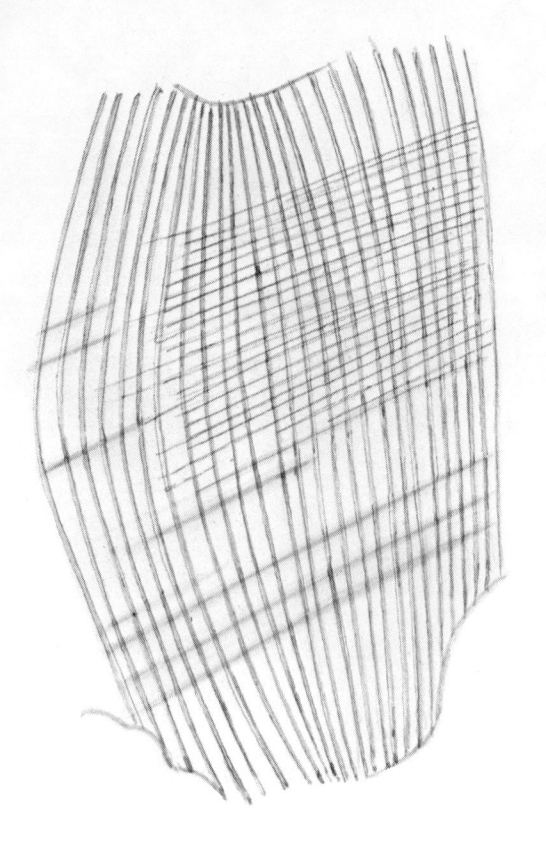

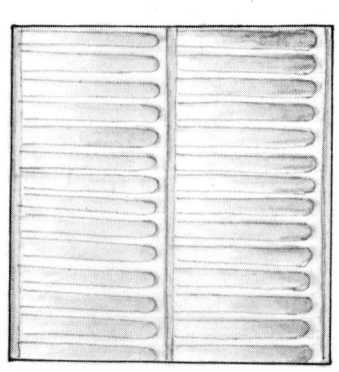

The shell is translucent gray-white, with a nebulous brown spiral band on the upper portion of each whorl, grading into white below. The whole is covered by a thick, flat-white, axially striate, and spirally incised intritacalx. The aperture is porcelaneous white.

The muricine radular dentition shows a five-cusped rachidian tooth with the lengths of the central, lateral, and intermediate cusps in the ratio of 4:3:1.

The operculum is typically muricine.

Measurements: holotype, length 12.4 mm, width 6.3 mm; largest paratype, length 25 mm, width 13.3 mm; smallest mature paratype, length 7.7 mm, width 4.3 mm.

Type locality: Bahía Coastocomate (Jalisco), Mexico, in 2–32 m, G. E. Radwin, October 13–20, 1968.

Material studied: holotype, SDSNH 62607; 2 paratypes, SDSNH 51838, type locality; 3 paratypes, LACM 68-41, type locality; 3 paratypes, D. R. Shasky Coll., type locality; 1 paratype (largest), J. Bailey Coll., in 33 m depth, off Pta. Pulmo (Baja California), Mexico, October 1969; 1 paratype, LACM-AHF-MS 276, in 16 m depth, off Isla San Esteban (Baja California), Mexico (28° 38′ N, 112° 36′ W), March 9, 1936; 1 paratype, D. R. Shasky Coll., in 13–26 m, off Isla Montserrate, Gulf of California (*Ariel* Expedition), September 1, 1960; 1 paratype, LACM (uncatalogued), in 13 mm, near La Peñita (Nayarit), Mexico, February 1971; 1 paratype, LACM 69-13, between Pta. Mita and Puerto Vallarta (Nayarit), Mexico, January 1969; 1 paratype, W. L. Woods Coll., in 7–8 m, Bahía Coastocomate (Jalisco), Mexico (19° 15′ N, 104° 49′ W), December 17–20, 1970; 2 paratypes, A. D'Attilio Coll., Barra de Navidad (Jalisco), Mexico; 2 paratypes, SDSNH 34671, in 7 m, Acapulco (Guerrero), Mexico,

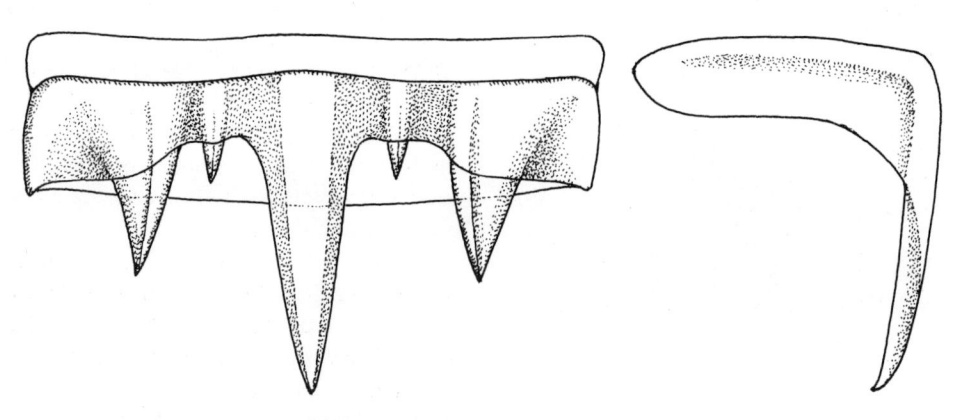

172. *Aspella pollux*, intritacalx

173. *Aspella pollux*, radular dentition

April 1930; 2 paratypes, ANSP 246457, Islas Tortugas, Golfo de Nicoya, Costa Rica, 1952; 1 paratype, LACM-AHF 772-38, in 10–17 m, off Isla Nuez (Isla Cocos), Costa Rica (5° 34′ N, 86° 59′ 20″ W), January 13, 1938.

This species has been known for some time but has been assumed by many workers to be *A. pyramidalis* (see Keen, 1958; Radwin and D'Attilio, 1971). It may be distinguished from *A. pyramidalis* in the broadness and flatness of the whorls, the degree of expansion and dorsal reflection of the varical flanges, and the intritacalx, with its spiral, as well as axial, sculpture. For distinctions between this species and its cognate in the Caribbean, *A. castor*, see p. 219.

For the etymology of the name *A. pollux*, see under *A. castor*, above.

See Pl. 1, figs. 3, 29.

Aspella ponderi sp. nov.
(Muricinae; for genus, see p. 21)

Distribution: northwestern Australia (Cockburn Sound, Broome) to southeastern Australia (Woolgoolga, New South Wales).

The shell is moderately small (maximum length 12 mm) and lanceolate. The spire is high, consisting of one and one-half nuclear whorls and six or seven dorsoventrally flattened postnuclear whorls. The suture is moderately impressed and partially obscured by varical buttresses. The body whorl is flattened and rather narrow. The aperture is moderately large and ovate, with an almost imperceptible anal sulcus. The outer apertural lip is barely erect and faintly denticulate on its inner surface. The columellar lip is entirely adherent. The siphonal canal is relatively short, narrowly open, slightly bent to the left, and dorsally recurved.

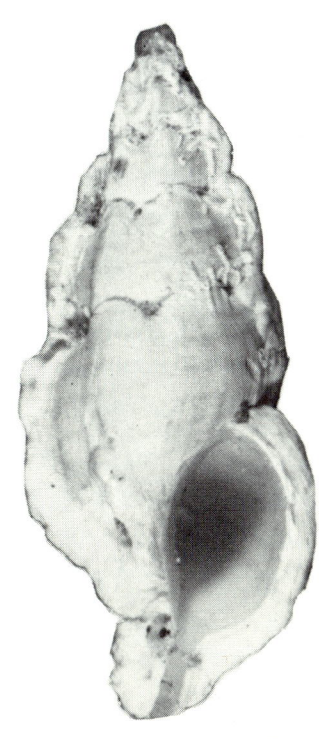

The body whorl bears two relatively weak lateral varices and two minor varices reduced to very weak costae. The fifth and sixth varices seen in the first two or three postnuclear whorls are represented only by varical buttresses on the later whorls. Axial intritacalx sculpture consists of numerous fine striae. Minute transverse tubes may appear aligned and may thus impart a spirally threaded appearance to the shell under high magnification. Other spiral sculpture consists of eight

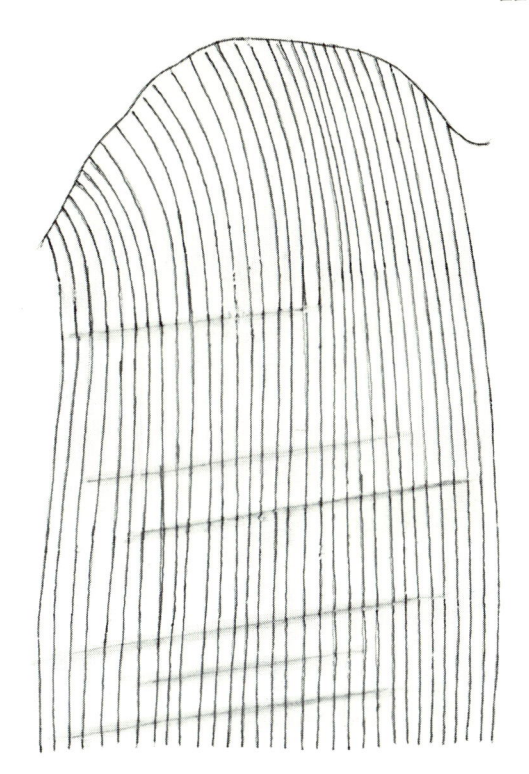

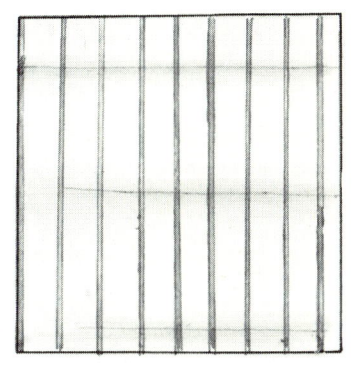

175. *Aspella ponderi*, intritacalx

174. *Aspella ponderi*

broad cords, visible on the leading edge of each varix.

The shell is translucent yellow-white under a flat-white intritacalx and a pale, yellowish periostracum.

The radular dentition of *A. ponderi*, cited and figured as *A. anceps* in Ponder (1972: text fig. 12), shows a rachidian tooth of muricine form in which the central cusp is broad and long, the lateral cusps are shorter but also broad, and the intermediate cusps are shortest and slender.

We have seen no live-collected specimens and thus have not seen the operculum.

Measurements: holotype, length 9.9 mm, width 4.2 mm; largest paratype, length 9.6 mm, width 4.3 mm; smallest paratype, length 7 mm, width 3.5 mm.

Type locality: 3 km southwest of Broome, Australia, on reefs and flats, V. Orr, September 20, 1958.

Material studied: holotype, ANSP 233056; 1 paratype, SDSNH 63168, type locality; 1 paratype ANSP 329056, type locality; 1 paratype, ANSP 285080, Peron Point, Cockburn Sound, Western Australia, in 0–3 m, March 9, 1963.

The name honors Dr. Winston F. Ponder, The Australian Museum, Sydney.

See Pl. 28, fig. 6.

Chicoreus akritos sp. nov.
(Muricinae; for genus, see p. 32)

Distribution: Australia (Broome to the Keppel Bay region of southern Queensland and to northern New South Wales).

The shell is moderately small (maximum length 50 mm) and fusiform. Its spire is high, comprising three polished nuclear whorls and eight or nine convex postnuclear whorls. The suture is impressed. The body whorl is moderately small and fusoid. The aperture is ovate, with an anal sulcus strongly reinforced on both sides by a spiral ridge. The outer apertural lip is barely erect beyond the last varix, with small, sharp denticles briefly extending into the aperture as lirae. The columellar lip is adherent. The siphonal canal is about one-half the spire height, broad above, tapering below, and distally recurved.

The body whorl bears three rounded varices with open foliaceous spines. Additional axial sculpture consists of two or three moderately developed intervarical costae extending from the suture to the anterior portion of the body, or to the canal. Spiral sculpture consists of major and minor cords and numerous finely imbricate threads. Where the cords intersect the varices, short, foliated spines are developed. On the upper portion of the varix the spines are quite reduced, the spine length increasing moderately toward the anterior. Small intercalating spinelets are developed on the body portion of the varix. The spines on the body are ventrally bent; the two spines on the canal are straight.

Shell color is pink, in some cases suffused with pale orange or pale orange-brown. The color is more intense in intervarical areas. The spiral cords are darker brown, the early whorls uniformly pink, and the margin of the aperture pale orange.

We have not been able to obtain the soft parts and thus have not examined the radular dentition. We have, however, examined M. Azuma's unpublished drawings of *Chicoreus damicornis* and *C. territus*, two close relatives of *C. akritos*, and they show characteristics that are typical for *Chicoreus*.

The operculum is typical for this genus and subfamily in its unguiculate shape, its thickened, corneous margins, and its depressed, annulate central region.

Measurements: holotype, length 50.1 mm, width 24.2 mm; largest paratype, length 43.3 mm, width 21.1 mm; smallest "mature" paratype, length 34.5 mm, width 19.5 mm.

Type locality: off Keppel Isles, Keppel Bay (Queensland), Australia, M. Bowman, 1963.

Material studied: holotype, SDSNH 53173, under dead coral at low tide; 3 paratypes, A. D'Attilio Coll., Middle Islands, Keppel Isles, Keppel Bay (Queensland), Australia, M. Bowman, 1963; 2 paratypes, A. D'Attilio Coll., off Keppel Isles [Keppel Bay] (Queensland), Australia, October 31, 1966; 2 paratypes, A. D'Attilio Coll., off Keppel Isles [Keppel Bay] (Queensland), Australia, A. R. Bowman, 1960; 1 paratype, A. D'Attilio Coll., New South Wales, Australia; 1 paratype, A. D'Attilio Coll., Broome, Western Australia.

Chicoreus akritos (*C. penchinati* of authors, not Crosse, 1861) apparently belongs to the group of *C. territus*, *C. denudatus*, and *C. damicornis*, though it differs from all of these in its uniform soft pink-violet color and its short, open, frondose spines. Its spines are shorter and less palmate distally than those of *C. damicornis*; it lacks the extensive varical webbing of *C. territus*; and it has a higher, more slender spire and a different color and softer texture than *C. denudatus*, which is mottled pale yellow-brown and white.

The epithet is the Greek word for "confused," in reference to the confusion as a result of which this species—which has been confused with *C. denudatus* and *C. penchinati* and has also been called *C. palmiferus* (a junior synonym of *C. denudatus*)—had gone undescribed.

See Pl. 4, fig. 1.

Marchia bibbeyi sp. nov.
(Muricinae; for genus, see p. 57)

Distribution: known to us only from the southeastern coast of Japan (in precious coral beds).

The shell is of moderate size for the genus (maximum length 42 mm) and broadly fusiform. The spire is high and acute, consisting of six convex postnuclear whorls and a protoconch of undetermined nature. The suture is weakly impressed, if at all. The body whorl is moderately large and fusoid. The aperture is roughly ovate but is flattened on the left (columellar) side. The outer apertural lip is erect and marginally crenulate. More deeply within the aperture, six elongate denticles are apparent; the denticle in the shoulder region is separated from the others and delimits the anal sulcus on its right side. The columellar lip is attached above; below, in most specimens, the lip is erect and laterally extended into a flange. Three or more moderately prominent denticles are apparent at the anterior end of the columella. The siphonal canal is narrowly open, broad, and distally recurved.

The body whorl bears four varices, extended into moderately high, fluted flanges; the varical margin is somewhat erect. There is generally a strong ridge just behind the varix. In addition, closely spaced, scabrous lamellae cover the shell, except on the leading side of the varix and flange, where the lamellae are fewer and more pronounced. Spiral sculpture consists of 11 primary cords on the body whorl, each cord flanked on both sides by a single secondary cord.

The shell is yellow-orange, the area around all old varical margins more whitish. The apertural interior is pinkish-white.

We have been unable to obtain a live-collected specimen of this species, but Azuma (1973) has figured its radular dentition (as *Pterynotus barclayanus*), and it appears to be rather typical for the genus.

The operculum of the holotype is corneous and unguiculate. The outer surface shows numerous fine concentric lines; on the inner surface is a thickened, calluslike portion that encompasses the pointed end. The callused area is raised; the remaining area of the operculum is depressed, and within this depressed area may be discerned 5–7

176. *Marchia bibbeyi*

flat-topped concentric ridges that do not correspond to those on the outer surface.

Measurements: holotype, length 37 mm, width 19 mm; largest paratype, length 42 mm, width 20.1 mm; smallest paratype, length 34.5 mm, width 17.7 mm.

Type locality: off Kii Channel, Japan, in 300 m, coral fishermen.

Material studied: holotype, SDSNH 56074; 3 paratypes, A. D'Attilio Coll., type locality, in 40 m; 1 paratype, ANSP 241471, A. R. Cahn Coll., Wakayama Prefecture, Japan; 1 paratype, ANSP 300503, A. R. Cahn Coll., Wakayama Prefecture, Japan.

The only species with which this species may be compared is *Marchia barclayana* (H. Adams, 1873). Azuma (1973) and Shikama (1963) have confused this species with *M. barclayana*. The latter with a smaller, dark brown to violet shell, has a much wider Indo-West Pacific distribution.

The patronym honors Loyal J. ("Joe") Bibbey, friend, shell collector, and dealer, who supplied the holotype as well as other specimens and much observational data.

Murex purdyae sp. nov.
(Muricinae; for genus, see p. 60)

Distribution: known to us only from off Tugela River mouth, Natal, South Africa.

The shell is moderate in size for the genus (maximum length 58.5 mm) and club-shaped. The spire is high, consisting of one and one-half bulbous nuclear whorls and four weakly shouldered postnuclear whorls. The suture is distinct to impressed. The body whorl is moderately small and roughly fusoid. The aperture is broadly ovate, with a weakly indicated anal sulcus. The outer apertural lip is erect. The columellar lip is almost entirely adherent, the edge slightly detached over the columella. The siphonal canal is long, narrow, and weakly recurved at its lower (anterior) end.

The body whorl bears three varices, with one or two very weak axial costae between each two. Brief, sharp varical spines are formed by the varical margin, which is folded at the shoulder margin. A short, weakly undulate flange proceeding from the direction of growth projects beyond the varix. On the final varix the flange is fluted and crenulate, and extends over the entire length of the varix. More or less strong growth lines are apparent on the shell and especially on the leading edges of the intervarical costae. The spiral sculpture of low primary and secondary threads in the intervarical areas is most prominent on both sides of each varix: about three or four may be seen on the shoulder; seven or eight stronger ones are apparent on the body, these consistently intercalated with secondaries. The canal bears numerous close-set spiral cords, these strongest intervarically.

Shell color is pale fleshy pink-orange. The varices are pale waxy yellow-white with three pale brown marks, at the shoulder margin, at the middle of the body, and at the base of the body. A thin, evanescent intritacalx covers those parts of the shell that are not eroded. The interior of the aperture is porcelaneous white.

The radular dentition is muricine, consisting of a single five-cusped rachidian tooth and a single sickle-shaped lateral tooth flanking it on each side.

The operculum is essentially indistinguishable from that of other *Murex* species. It is ovate and

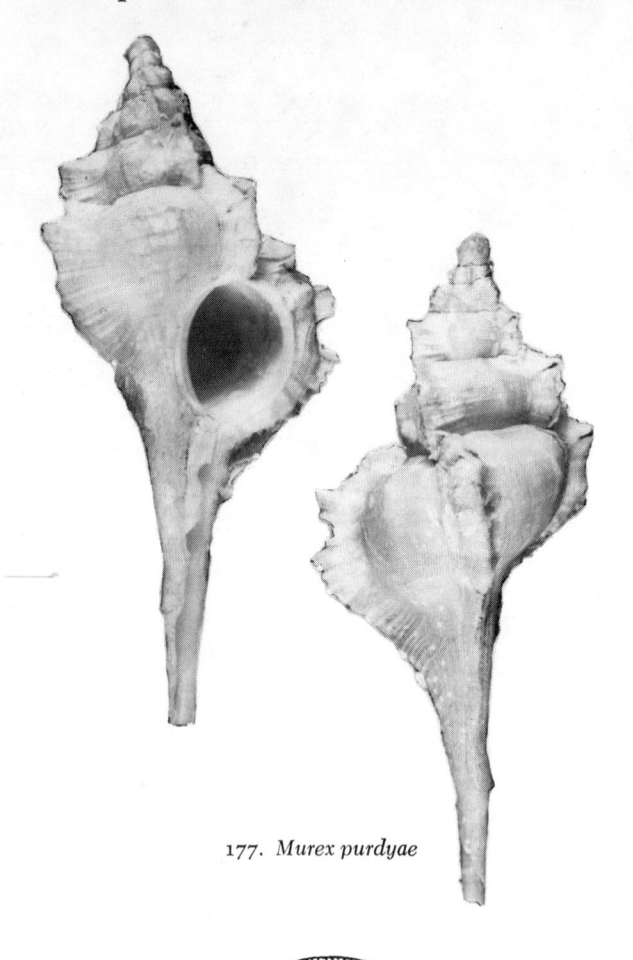

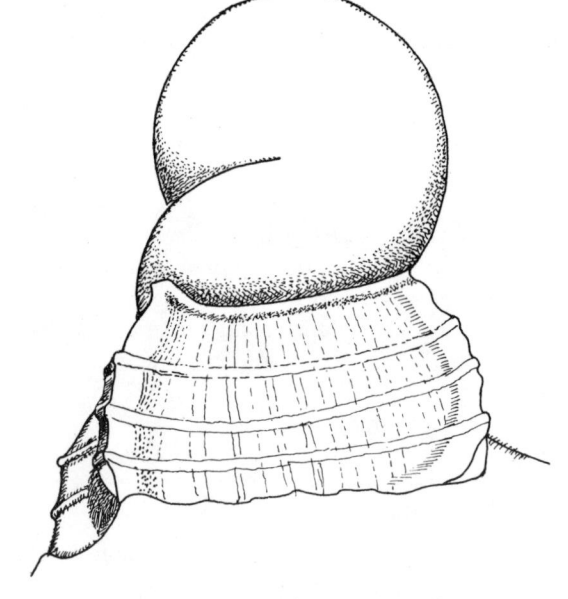

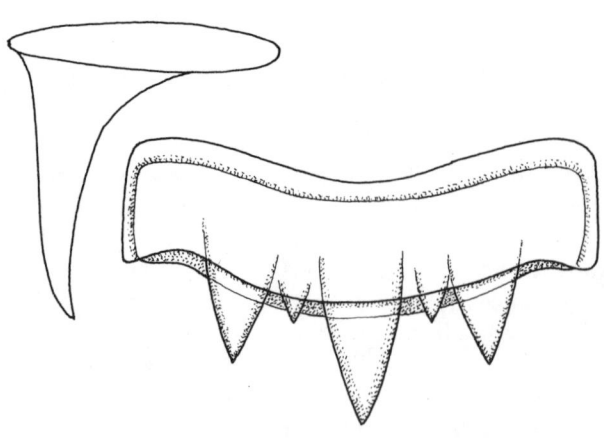

177. *Murex purdyae*

178. *Murex purdyae*, protoconch

179. *Murex purdyae*, radular dentition

finely striate on its outer surface. The inner surface has a broad callused area surrounding an eccentrically placed depressed area that bears a small number of broad, flat-topped annuli.

Measurements: holotype, length 57.9 mm, width 24.1 mm; largest paratype, length 58.5 mm, width indeterminable (outer lip badly broken); smallest paratype, length 43.9 mm (canal apparently broken), width 20.2 mm.

Type locality: off Tugela River mouth, Natal, South Africa, in 160 m depth, November 1971.

Material studied: holotype, SDSNH 63024; 1 paratype, A. D'Attilio Coll., Natal, South Africa; 1 paratype, SDSNH 55261, Natal, South Africa, February 1967; 1 paratype, C. & C. Martin Coll., off the coast of Natal, South Africa, in 360 m, April 1967; 1 paratype, C. & C. Martin Coll., off Natal, South Africa, July 1970.

Comparison with *Murex serratospinosus* and *M. mindanaoensis*, the only other species that resemble it, shows that the shell of *M. purdyae* has a larger, more mammillate protoconch, much more modest spiral sculpture, and a shorter, less bent siphonal canal. The varical webbing is sparser than that of *M. serratospinosus*, and the overall color pattern is much less strongly marked than in either of the other two species.

This patronym honors Ruth Purdy of San Diego, California, through whom we first became aware of this species.

Favartia poormani sp. nov.
(Muricopsinae; for genus, see p. 144)

Distribution: known to us only from off San Carlos Bay (Sonora), Mexico; Manzanillo (Colima), Mexico; and from Islas Perlas, Panamá; reported in Keen (1971) as distributed in the "Gulf of California from La Paz to coast of Sonora" under the name *F. peasei* (Tryon, 1880).

The shell is of moderate size for the genus (maximum length 20 mm) and stoutly fusiform. The spire is high, consisting of five or six weakly angulate postnuclear whorls and a protoconch of undetermined nature. The body whorl is moderately large and broadly fusoid. The aperture is moderately small and ovate, with a shallow, moderately broad anal sulcus. The outer apertural lip is weakly erect and crenulate; its inner surface bears eight moderately strong denticles, all of equal size except for the uppermost one—the denticle delimiting the anal sulcus is about twice the size of the others. The columellar lip is entirely adherent, with two or three weak denticles apparent at its anterior end. The siphonal canal is of

180. *Favartia poormani*

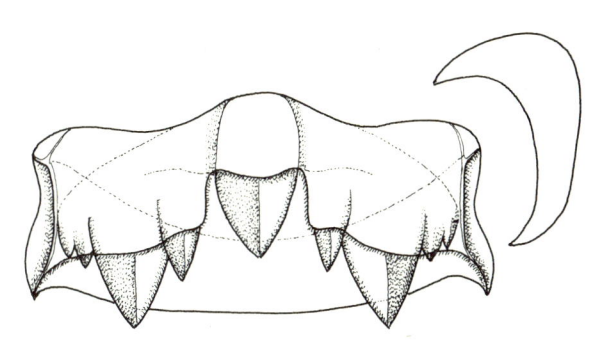

181. *Favartia poormani*, radular dentition

moderate length, moderately narrowly open, and weakly dorsally recurved.

The body whorl bears six briefly winglike varices. Intervarical axial sculpture is lacking. Spiral sculpture consists of eight closely spaced, rounded major cords on the body and five on the canal, these finely spirally striate and extending to the varical margin, thus rendering it serrate. An extension of the varix connects the shoulder margin to the spire. The entire shell surface is microscopically scabrously laminate, and the leading edge of the varix is densely fimbriate.

The shell is white, with three interrupted, transverse, chestnut-brown bands, one subsutural, one medial on the body, and one at the base of the body, the brown strongest just before and on the varices and lacking immediately beyond each varix.

The radula is typical for the genus. Beyond its generally muricopsine appearance, the rachidian tooth is very compact and is limited in its major dimension (width). The central cusp, while typically fanglike, is short and strongly downwardly bent, as in a parrot's beak. Nothing in the radular dentition would suggest discrepancy with an assignment to *Favartia*.

The operculum is unguiculate, also typical for *Favartia*; it is thickened and reddish-brown, and has a more or less central depression surrounded by a marginal thickening.

Measurements: holotype, length 19.2 mm, width 11.5 mm; largest paratype, length 17.0 mm, width 9.5 mm; smallest paratype, length 14.4 mm, width 9.0 mm.

Type locality: off Bahía San Carlos, Guaymas (Sonora), Mexico, dredged in ca. 34 m, L. & F. Poorman, March 1964 to May 1970.

Material studied: holotype, SDSNH 63080; 1 paratype, LACM, type locality; 1 paratype, USNM, type locality; 3 paratypes, L. & F. Poorman Coll., type locality; 2 paratypes, USNM 46795, Islas Perlas, Panamá, R. Stearns.

The shell of this species, in its combination of size, color pattern, and the thin, delicate structure of its varices, differs from all other New World species of *Favartia* and from all other *Favartia* known to us.

The species was first figured as *Tritonalia margaritensis* Dall ?Mss by M. Smith (1939), on the basis of the Stearns specimens from the Islas Perlas. Keen (1958) suggested that Smith's figure "may represent the species" (i.e. *peasei* Tryon, 1880, a replacement name for *Murex foveolatus* Pease, 1869, not Hinds, 1844). Discovery of the holotype of *M. foveolatus* Pease at the Academy of Natural Sciences, Philadelphia, has allowed us to determine that the true *M. foveolatus* Pease (i.e. *M. peasei*) is a western Pacific species for which Pease gave an erroneous locality. See *Favartia peasei* in the body of the book.

This name honors L. Poorman, who collected most of the specimens of this species extant in collections.

See Pl. 24, fig. 9.

Muricopsis huberti sp. nov.
(Muricopsinae; for genus, see p. 165)

Distribution: known to us only from Grenada and St. Vincent, West Indies.

The shell is small for the genus (maximum

182. *Muricopsis huberti*

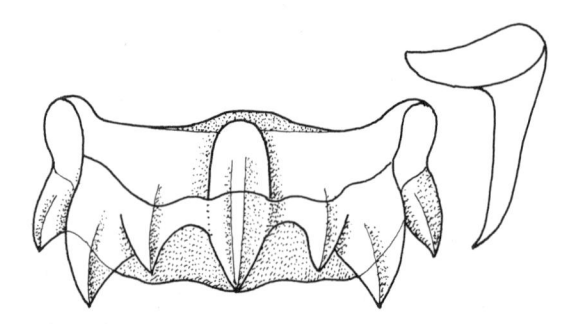

183. *Muricopsis huberti*, radular dentition

length 14.8 mm) and stoutly fusiform. The spire is high and acute, consisting of five weakly shouldered postnuclear whorls and a protoconch of undetermined nature. The suture is distinct where the shell is not eroded. The body whorl is comparatively short and broadly fusoid. The aperture is moderately small and ovate, with a narrow, shallow anal sulcus. The outer apertural lip is briefly erect and finely serrate, reflecting the outer shell sculpture; its inner surface bears five equal-sized, moderately prominent denticles, the posteriormost slightly set off from the others. The columellar lip is adherent, except at its extreme anterior end, where it bears two low, small, oblique pustules. The siphonal canal is very broad and short, and tends to be more or less bent to the left.

The body whorl bears five or six low, sharp-crested varices, these aligned obliquely up the spire. All but the last-formed varix are comparatively featureless, and the last one or two are developed into weak flanges with three or four very short, sharp spines at the margin. Spiral sculpture consists of five major cords: a slightly weaker one on the shoulder, three on the body, and one on the canal. In addition there are one or two minor threads between each two major cords. The varices are very broad-based, the intervarical spaces very narrow.

Shell color is white. The aperture is porcelaneous white.

The radula is typical of the subfamily and genus, with small lateral teeth and a rachidian tooth with a large, broad, strongly curved central cusp, large, long lateral cusps, and moderately large, semi-independent intermediate cusps.

The operculum is typical for the genus and subfamily.

Measurements: holotype, length 14.2 mm, width 7.4 mm; largest paratype, length 14.8 mm, width 8.5 mm.

Type locality: west side of Grenada, West Indies, in 4.5 m, R. Hubert, September 1970.

Material studied: holotype, SDSNH 63078; 1 paratype, A. D'Attilio Coll., Westerhall Bay, Grenada, West Indies, in 5.5 m, R. Hubert, September 1970; 4 paratypes, ANSP 296490, west side of Mt. Hardman Bay, southwestern Grenada, West Indies, in 0–1.5 m, R. Ostheimer, M. Buerk, January–February 1964; 4 paratypes, ANSP 332226, 1 km south of Calliagua, St. Vincent, West Indies, in 0.3 m, V. O. Maes, February 1972; 5 paratypes, ANSP 297051, Little Bacaye Harbor, southern Grenada, West Indies, in 0–1.2 m, R. Ostheimer, M. Buerk, January 23, 1964; 1 paratype, Southwest Point, Calliagua Bay, St. Vincent, West Indies, intertidal, V. O. Maes, February 1972; 7 paratypes, ANSP 297035, cove west of True Blue, southwestern Grenada, West Indies, in 0–1.4 m, R. Ostheimer, M. Buerk, January 1964.

This species has no apparent close relatives among the New World species of *Muricopsis* living today. The only species to which it bears substantial resemblance is *Muricopsis praepauxillus* (Maury, 1917) from the Miocene of "Santo Domingo," which was originally described as *Murex (Phyllonotus) praepauxillus*. Examination of the holotype of that species shows that it differs from *Muricopsis huberti* in its less truncate siphonal canal, proportionately higher spire, more impressed suture, and larger aperture.

The name honors Royce Hubert, through whose generosity we first received specimens of *M. huberti*.

Muricopsis tulensis sp. nov.
(Muricopsinae; for genus, see p. 165)

Distribution: known only from the southern tip of Baja California, Mexico (Rancho el Tule, El Pulmo Reef, Cabo San Lucas).

The shell is tiny for the genus (maximum length 7.8 mm) and fusiform. The spire is high and acute, consisting of one and one-half convex nuclear whorls and five weakly shouldered postnuclear whorls. The suture is somewhat impressed. The body whorl is of moderate size and fusoid. The aperture is of moderate size and ovate, with a

184. *Muricopsis tulensis*

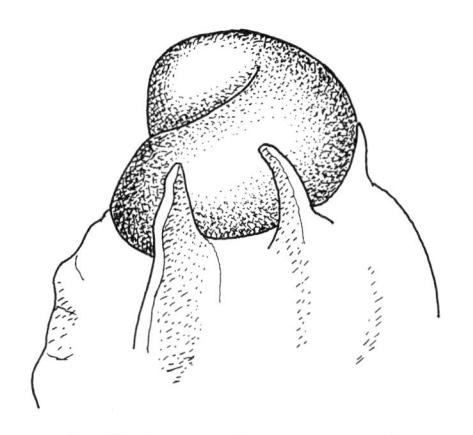

185. *Muricopsis tulensis*, protoconch

broad, rather shallow anal sulcus. The outer apertural lip is briefly erect and gently undulate, corresponding to the sculpture of the outer shell surface; its inner surface bears four subprominent denticles, the anteriormost slightly larger than the others and the posteriormost slightly set off from the others. The columellar lip is smooth and adherent; at its posterior end there is a spirally oriented ridge that delimits the left side of the anal sulcus. The siphonal canal is of moderate length, narrowly open, slightly bent to the left and barely dorsally recurved.

The body whorl bears eight sharp, moderately prominent varices, the last of these the most fully developed. Spiral sculpture consists of four major cords, a slightly weaker one on the shoulder and three on the body. Of these three the upper one at the shoulder margin is slightly farther from the other two than they are from each other. Additional sculpture consists of three or four minor cords on the canal. Between the body and canal there is a more or less broad band devoid of spiral sculpture. Where the major cords on the shoulder and body intersect the varices, more or less sharp points are formed. Numerous fine axial lamellae are apparent in areas of the shell that are completely unworn. The leading edge of the last-formed varix shows numerous axial lamellae and radial lines corresponding to the spiral cords on the body.

Shell color is white, with two moderately broad, dark chestnut-brown bands, one on the shoulder and one at the base of the body. The aperture is porcelaneous white.

All specimens studied were collected empty; thus the radular dentition and the operculum are not known.

Measurements: holotype, length 7.0 mm, width 3.5 mm; largest paratype, length 7.8 mm, width 3.5 mm; smallest mature paratype, length 5.7 mm, width 3.1 mm.

Type locality: Rancho el Tule (Baja California), Mexico, Faye Howard, February 9–14, 1964.

Material studied: holotype, SDSNH 61232; 4 paratypes, SDSNH 63161, type locality; 1 paratype, D. R. Shasky Coll., Cabo San Lucas (Baja California), Mexico, in 13 m, January 15, 1967; 3 paratypes, D. R. Shasky Coll., El Pulmo Reef (Baja California), Mexico, in 1.5 m, February 3, 1966; 5 paratypes, H. DuShane Coll., El Pulmo Reef (Baja California), Mexico, intertidal, January 19–27, 1967.

Among *Muricopsis* species only the long known Panamic species *M. pauxillus* (A. Adams, 1854) is similar. *M. tulensis* may be distinguished by its smaller size at maturity (about one-half the size of *M. pauxillus*, with the same number of whorls), its brown spiral bands lying between spiral sculptural elements rather than covering some of them, and the low protoconch of convex whorls, in contrast to the prominent protoconch of strongly tabulate to carinate whorls in *M. pauxillus*.

Talityphis bengalensis sp. nov.
(Typhinae; for genus, see p. 201)

Distribution: The Philippines and the Bay of Bengal.

The shell is tiny (holotype length 9.5 mm) and broadly biconic. The spire is moderately high, consisting of one and three-quarters shining, off-white, convex nuclear whorls and four or more shouldered postnuclear whorls. The suture is well-impressed. The body whorl is large (three-fourths shell length) and broadly trigonal. The aperture is small and ovate to subcircular, with an entire and erect peristome and no trace of an anal sulcus. Only at the posterior, parietal corner of the aperture is the peristome adherent. A more or less long anal siphonal tube originates approximately medially between each two varices and is oriented for the most part laterally and, to a smaller extent, dorsally and posteriorly. The siphonal canal is short and broad and is sealed, the left side overlapping the right.

The body whorl bears four varices; three of these are brief, sharp, and vanelike. The last-formed varix is moderately broadly winglike, extending from a moderately developed spine at the shoulder margin to the upper third of the siphonal canal. Between the shoulder-margin spine and the periphery of the preceding whorl a flat, vertical expanse of shell—the partition—is apparent, touching the preceding whorl just below the shoulder margin and the shoulder-margin spine about one-fourth of the way down from the point. Immediately below the base of each anal siphonal tube a low axial swelling extends to the shell's periphery. Spiral sculpture appears to be lacking.

The radula and operculum are unknown.

The shell specimens we have seen are shining pinkish-gray, except for the protoconch. The postnuclear whorls are covered by a thin, flat-white intritacalx with a gray veneer.

Measurements: holotype, length 9.5 mm, width 5.75 mm; smallest mature paratype, length 7.6 mm, width indeterminable (shell fragmentary).

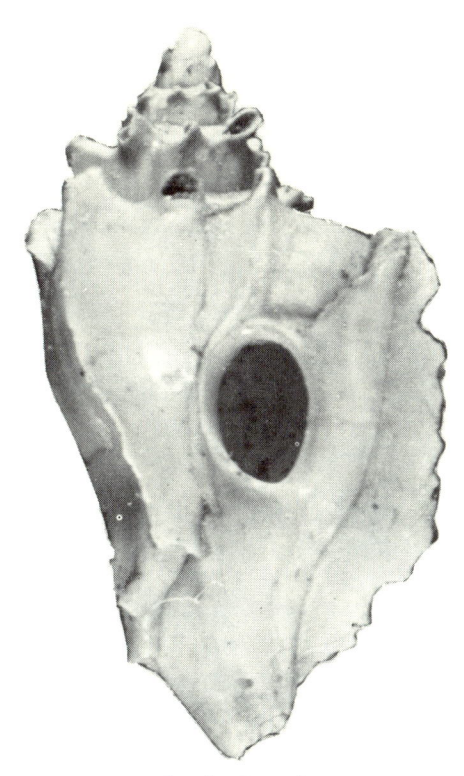

186. *Talityphis bengalensis*

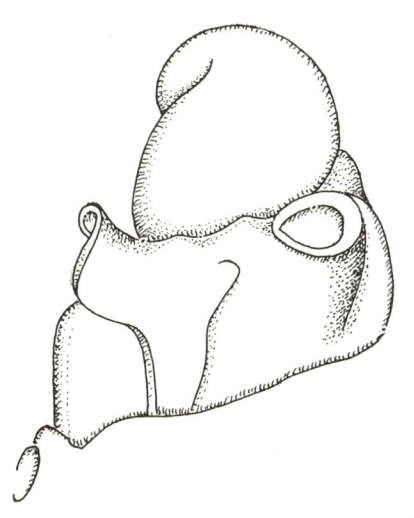

187. *Talityphis bengalensis*, protoconch

Type locality: Bay of Bengal, 25 km southeast of Vizagapatnam, India (17° 35′ N, 83° 25′ E), *Anton Bruun* Indian Ocean Expedition sta. 90, April 28, 1963, in 79 m, on sand, shell bottom.

Material studied: holotype, ANSP 294561; 1 paratype (fragmentary), ANSP 334492, type locality; 7 paratypes, USNM 276147, off Marinduque Island, Philippines.

The shell of this species could be compared with *Talityphis perchardei* and *T. latipennis*. It is, of course, much smaller than these species, has a shorter spire and siphonal canal, a proportionately broader body whorl, a thicker intritacalx, and a less highly colored shell under the intritacalx.

The description of this species and of *T. campbelli* (following) extends the Recent distribution of the typhine genus *Talityphis* to encompass the Indo-West Pacific.

Talityphis campbelli sp. nov.
(Typhinae; for genus, see p. 201)

Distribution: known to us only from the type locality (8.4 km south of Corregidor (Luzon), Philippines).

The shell is moderately small for the genus (holotype length 18 mm) and stoutly biconic. The spire is moderately high, consisting of one and one-half slender nuclear whorls and five or six sharply angulate postnuclear whorls. The suture is distinct but not strongly impressed. The body whorl is large (about two-thirds of the total shell length) and broadly trigonal. The aperture is small and ovate, forming an entire peristome, this briefly erect, except at the extreme posterior end. No true anal sulcus is present, but an anal siphonal tube originates at the shoulder margin medially between each two varices; from its point of origin each tube swings dorsally and slightly posteriorly, tapering distally. The siphonal canal is of moderate length, broad above, tapering to a slender tube below, fused (with the left side overlapping the right), and bent strongly to the right and weakly, dorsally recurved.

The body whorl bears four varices, the three older ones represented by brief, sharp keels, the final or newest one by a broadly expanded, dorsoventrally flattened, winglike flange extending from a prominent spine at the shoulder margin to just below midway on the canal. Between the shoulder-margin spine and the periphery of the preceding whorl, but not reaching beyond the midpoint of the shoulder-margin spine, is a moderately well-developed partition. Below each anal siphonal tube a slightly raised axial swelling extends anteriorly to a low node at the periphery. Spiral sculpture consists of five almost completely obsolete fine cords, two on the canal and three on the body, each ending in a minute point on the margin of the varical flange.

Shell color is pale purple-brown, with numerous slender, discontinuous, pale-red-brown color bands, and with off-white coloration with erratic pale-yellow-brown markings on the shoulder margin, siphonal canal, the last varix, and the peristome.

The unique holotype of this species is an empty shell, although in quite fresh condition; no information on the radular dentition or opercular morphology is available.

Measurements: holotype, length 18 mm, width 11.2 mm.

Type locality: 8.4 km south of Corregidor (Luzon), Philippines, in 170 m.

188. *Talityphis campbelli*

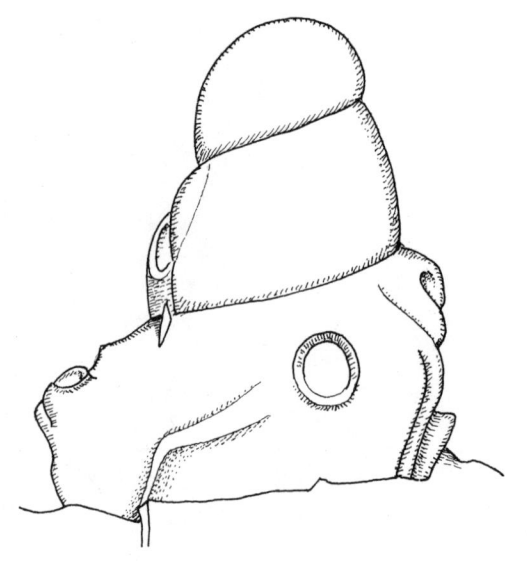

189. *Talityphis campbelli*, protoconch

Material studied: holotype, SDSNH 63077.

Although clearly assignable to *Talityphis*, this species combines the high color and light to negligible intritacalx of the New World species (*T. perchardei* and *T. latipennis*) with the proportional breadth of *T. bengalensis*. It is smaller than the New World species but twice the size of *T. bengalensis* and has a more angulate shoulder than any of the known species of *Talityphis*.

This species and one other newly described (*T. bengalensis*, above) are the only two Recent *Talityphis* ever to have been described from outside the New World.

The species is named for Dr. G. Bruce Campbell, a well-known student of the Typhinae, whose untimely death in 1973 is much regretted and whose efforts in the present group will be missed.

Talityphis perchardei sp. nov.
(Typhinae; for genus, see p. 201)

Distribution: the southern Caribbean (Trinidad and Surinam).

The shell is large for the genus (maximum length 28.8 mm) and broadly fusiform. The spire is high and acute, consisting of one and one-half polished convex nuclear whorls and six sharply angulate postnuclear whorls. The suture is moderately well defined but is not impressed. The body whorl is large (about three-fourths of the total shell length) and broadly trigonal. The aperture is small and ovate, forming an entire peristome, this erect except for the upper parietal corner. No anal sulcus is apparent, but a single more or less long, hollow tube originates at or near the midpoint of each intervarical space on the shoulder margin; these tubes are long, when unbroken, tapering distally, and bent slightly dorsally and posteriorly. The siphonal canal is moderately long, broad above but tapering to a very slender tube below, fused, the left side strongly overlapping the right, and bent more or less to the right.

The body whorl bears four varices, the three older ones represented by moderately brief, sharp keels, the final or newest one by a broadly expanded, dorsoventrally flattened, winglike flange extending from a prominent spine at the shoulder margin to just below midway on the canal. Between the shoulder-margin spine and the periphery of the preceding whorl a moderately well-developed partition reaches just beyond the midpoint of the shoulder-margin spine. Below each anal siphonal tube there is a faintly raised ridge extending anteriorly to the periphery of the shell, where there is a faint drop-off in the shell surface

APPENDIX: NEW SPECIES 237

190. Talityphis perchardei

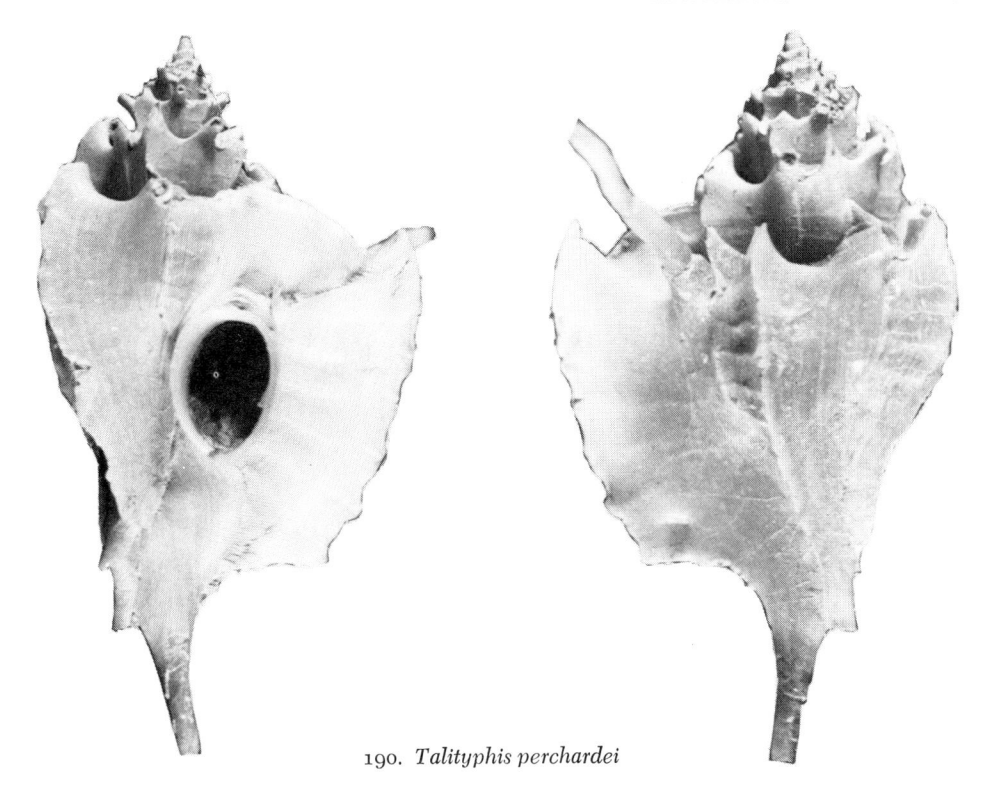

level. Spiral sculpture consists of seven faint, narrow cords on the body, these ending at the margin of the varical flange in minute, slightly dorsally reflected points; the cords are barely perceptible between varices, but are somewhat more prominent toward the next varix, on the trailing edge of the varical flange, and on its leading edge.

Shell color is fleshy purple-pink to fleshy orange-brown, with the margin of the varical flange, the leading edge of the last varix, and the aperture white. The siphonal canal is off-white, the tip stained with purple-brown. The entire shell is covered with a thin frosting of flat-white intritacalx.

The radula consists of multiple three-across rows of teeth, each row consisting of a single

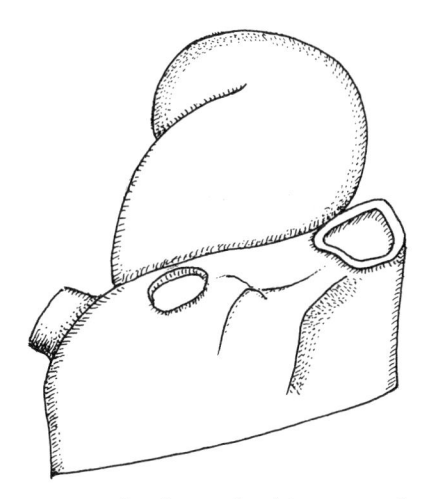

191. Talityphis perchardei, protoconch

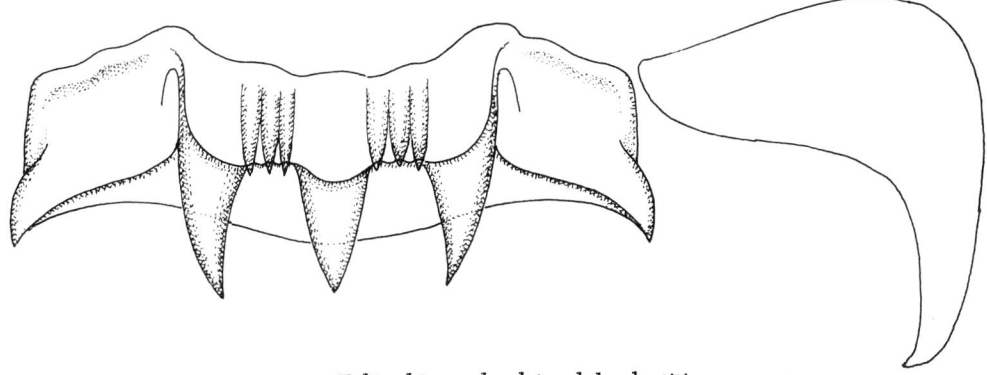

192. Talityphis perchardei, radular dentition

five-cusped rachidian tooth flanked on each side by a single heavily sickle-shaped lateral tooth. The rachidian tooth has an arrangement of cusps and, in some cases, denticles that is variable within a single radular ribbon. Typically, the lengths of the central, lateral, and intermediate cusps are in the ratio of 4:3:1. In some rachidian teeth the two small intermediate cusps are replaced by two or three smaller denticles. This variability notwithstanding, the morphology of the radular dentition clearly allies this species to the species *T. latipennis*, as does the morphology of the shell.

Measurements: holotype, length 28.5 mm, width 16.2 mm; largest paratype, length 27.9 mm, width 17.1 mm; smallest mature paratype, length 18.2 mm, width 11.0 mm.

Type locality: Bocas, Trinidad, West Indies, P. Percharde, August 1972, in 47–55 m.

Material studied: holotype, SDSNH 63079; 1 paratype, SDSNH 63169, type locality; 1 paratype, A. D'Attilio Coll., south of Isla Gaspar Grande, Golfo de Pária, Trinidad, West Indies, in 60 m, in very fine silt, P. Percharde, 1971; 1 paratype, SDSNH 61972, off Surinam (6° 21.2′ N, 55° 17′ W), Snellius Expedition, in 34 m, on sandy clay bottom, April 25, 1966; 1 paratype, SDSNH 61973, off Surinam (6° 44.3′ N, 55° 13.5′ W), Snellius Expedition, in 40–47 m, on sandy mud with clay bottom, April 28, 1966.

Most closely resembling the fossil species *Talityphis alatus* and *T. obesus*, this species must be considered a Caribbean cognate of the Panamic *T. latipennis* (Dall, 1919). (See also Gertman, 1969.)

The name honors Peter Percharde, Port Fortin, Trinidad.

See Pl. 30, fig. 15.

Glossary, Sources, and Index

Glossary

Nearly all of the technical terms employed in the text are included in this Glossary. Where useful, terms are also illustrated in the accompanying drawings. If a term has several valid meanings in the literature, as often happens, the definition given is that most often applied in describing the Muricidae.

ABUTTING. Touching; contiguous; adjacent.

ACUMINATE. Tapering to a slender point.

ACUTE. Sharply angled.

ADHERENT. Closely attached.

ADULT WHORLS. All whorls beyond those of the nucleus, or protoconch. *See also* Nuclear whorls.

ALATE. Winged; having alae.

ANAL SIPHON. A tube exiting at the posterior end of the gastropod aperture, through which solid waste matter is voided; in the Typhinae the anal siphon is housed in a shelly tube.

ANAL SULCUS. A groove in the posterior portion of the aperture that accommodates the anal siphon.

ANGULATE. Tabulate, as distinct from convex; said of the whorl profile. Formed with corners; angled.

ANGULATION. *See* Angulate.

ANNULATE. Bearing more or less concentric rings, as on the inner surface of a gastropod operculum.

ANNULUS (pl. ANNULI). One of several concentric rings.

ANTERIOR. At or toward the front or head end of an object.

APERTURAL. Pertaining to the aperture.

APERTURAL LIP. The most recently formed margin of the aperture.

APERTURE. The major opening of a gastropod shell.

APEX (pl. APICES). The first-formed end of a gastropod shell, generally more or less pointed; the tip of the protoconch or nuclear whorls. *See also* Base.

APICAL. Pertaining to the apex.

APPRESSED. Pressed against or lying flat against another surface; having the whorls overlapping. *See also* Adherent.

ARCUATE. Arched or curved.

AUSTRAL. Pertaining to the south (i.e. the Southern Hemisphere); southern.

AXIAL. Pertaining to or more or less parallel to the axis of coiling in a gastropod shell. *See also* Spiral.

AXIAL SCULPTURE. Sculpture running parallel to the axis of the gastropod shell.

BASAL. Pertaining to the base.

BASAL FOLD. A fold (plica) near the anterior end of the columella and above the siphonal canal. *See also* Columellar fold.

BASE. In coiled gastropods, the area below the periphery of the body whorl, excluding the aperture.

BEADED. Sculptured in such a way as to resemble beads or strings of beads.

BIANGULATE. Having two angles.

BICONIC. Composed of two conical shapes, base to base; diamond-shaped and having the spire about the same size and shape as the body whorl.

BIFID. Having two parts.

BIFURCATE. Forked; divided into two parts by a groove or cleft (= Bifid, Bisected).

BIPECTINATE. Having two comblike margins; branched like a feather.

BISECTED. Divided into two parts.

BLADE. An erect, flattened sculptural element perpendicular to the shell surface.

BODY. In a gastropod shell, the body whorl exclusive of the shoulder and the siphonal canal.

BODY WHORL. The most recently formed whorl of a gastropod shell, enclosing most of the animal's body.

BOREAL. Pertaining to the north (i.e. the Northern Hemisphere); northern.

BUCCAL. Pertaining to the organs of the mouth area; in a gastropod, pertaining especially to the bulging, flexible tissue mass that supports the radula.

BULBOUS. Bulging or globular.

BUTTRESS. A shell-strengthening structure; e.g. a complete or partial supporting ridge. *See also* Varical buttress.

CALCAREOUS. Composed mostly of, or impregnated with, calcium carbonate (lime).

CALLUS. A thickened portion of a gastropod shell, especially over the columella or around the aperture.

CANAL. In gastropods, a narrow notch or semitubular extension of the aperture, usually enclosing a siphon. *See also* Siphonal canal.

CANCELLATE. Having sculptural lines that intersect at right angles; reticulate; decussate.

CANTED. Slanted or sloped in relation to an adjoining structure; nonperpendicular.

CAPACIOUS. Large, roomy, spacious; said of the aperture or shell body.

CARINA (pl. CARINAE). A keel-like part; a prominent knife-edged ridge.

CARINATE. Having a carina, especially at the periphery of a whorl; keeled.

242 GLOSSARY

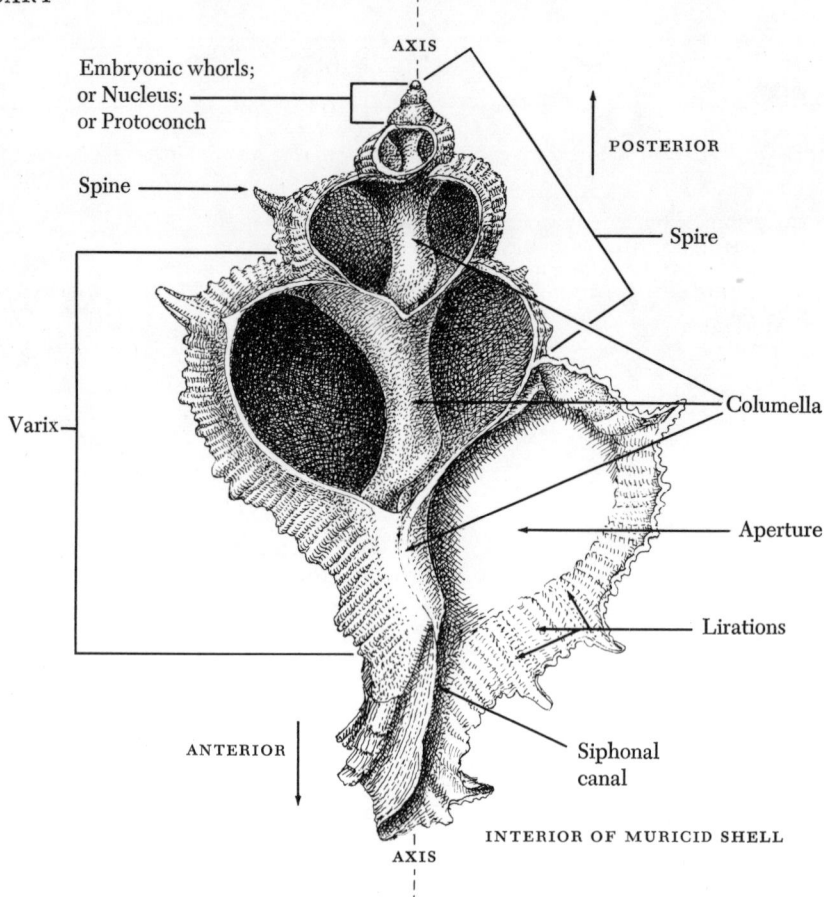

Interior of Muricid Shell — labeled: Axis, Embryonic whorls; or Nucleus; or Protoconch, Spine, Posterior, Spire, Varix, Columella, Aperture, Lirations, Anterior, Siphonal canal, Axis.

CERATUS. A hornlike structure; a large spur. *See also* Labial tooth.

CHANNEL. A deep groove.

CHANNELED. Sculptured with grooves; having a groove. *See also* Fluted, Striate.

CHINK. A long, narrow cleft, especially in the umbilical area.

CHITIN. The general name for a group of horny, proteinaceous substances, one of which, conchiolin, is found in protoconchs, radulae, etc.

CHITINOUS. Chitinlike; composed of chitin.

CINGULUM (pl. CINGULA). A band or girdle, e.g. a band of color or raised sculpture.

CLOSURE SEAM. A line of junction; a line, groove, or ridge formed by or between abutting edges.

CLUB-SHAPED. In a gastropod shell, having a compact, rounded body and a long siphonal canal.

COALESCED. Fused or merged together.

COGNATE. Of, or proceeding from, the same stock; allied; of the same or similar nature, as in the case of closely related forms or mollusks on both sides of the Central American isthmus.

COLUMELLA. A pillar surrounding the axis around which the shell is coiled, formed by the inner surface of the whorls; the wall opposite the outer apertural lip.

COLUMELLAR. Pertaining to the columella.

COLUMELLAR FOLD. A raised ridge on the columella that follows the helical growth pattern of a gastropod shell.

COLUMELLAR WALL. Surface of the columella.

COMPLANATE. Flattened; level; unsculptured.

COMPRESSED. Laterally flattened; having reduced thickness.

CONCAVE. Hollowed and curved or rounded; opposite of convex.

CONCAVITY. The quality or state of being concave; a concave point.

CONCENTRIC. Having a common center, as circles. In gastropod shells, said of structures roughly parallel to the growth lines.

CONCHIOLIN. A horny, proteinaceous material that makes up the periostracum of a shell and also forms the organic matrix for calcareous parts of the shell. Often termed chitin.

CONCHOLOGIST. A specialist in the study of molluscan shells. *See also* Malacologist.

CONFLUENT. Coming together; merging. *See also* Coalesced.

CONGENER. A species belonging to the same genus as the species used as a point of reference.

CONICAL. Cone-shaped; tapering.

CONSPECIFIC. Of the same species as an organism used as a point of reference.

CONSTRICTED. Marked by a more or less abrupt narrowing; waistlike; pinched.

CONSTRICTION. The state of being constricted; a constricted point.

CONTRACTED. Drawn together; reduced in extent; shrunken.

CONVEX. Curved or rounded; bulging outward. Opposite of concave.

CORD. A thickened round-topped transverse (i.e. spiral) or axial sculptural element.

CORDED. Sculptured with cords.
CORNEOUS. Horny in texture and composition.
CORONA. A crownlike structure.
CORONATE. Crownlike; having a corona.
CORRUGATE. Folded or ridged on the surface; broadly or heavily sculptured with folds.
COSTA (pl. COSTAE). An axial rib or ridge.
COSTATE. Having riblike axial sculptural elements.
COSTULATION. A pattern of sculpture in small ridges.
COTYPE. One of a series of specimens composing original type material of a species for which no holotype has ever been selected (= syntype).
COWL. A hood; a foldlike structure extending over the front or outward like a hood.
CRENATE. Having a regularly notched or scalloped edge.
CRENULATE. Same as crenate, but implying smaller or finer divisions.
CREST. The apex of a peak or ridge; the top of a sculptural element.
CRISPATE. Irregularly curled; roughened into small frets, waves, or folds.
CRUMPLED. Creased or pressed into wrinkles or folds.
CUSP. A prominence or point, especially on a radular tooth.
DECUSSATE. Having intersecting sculptural elements, not necessarily at right angles; reticulate. See also Cancellate.
DEFLEXED. Bent sharply backward or downward.
DELIMITING. Bounding; fixing a limit.
DENTATE. Toothed; having a toothed margin. See also Denticulate.
DENTICLE. A small, toothlike projection.
DETICULATE. Having small, toothlike projections. See also Dentate.
DENTICULATION. The overall pattern of denticles in a given shell specimen.
DENTITION. The number, kind, and arrangement of teeth, especially on a radula.
DEPAUPERATE. Poorly developed.
DEPRESSED. Pressed down; low in proportion to diameter.
DEPRESSION. A hollowed area; a concavity.
DETACHED. Separated; marked off.
DIAGNOSTIC. Central to identification; especially characteristic; reflecting critical comparative scrutiny.
DIGITATE. In a fingerlike fashion; having fingerlike processes.
DIGITATION. A fingerlike part; a pattern of such parts.
DIMORPHISM. Having two forms: e.g. differing forms for different sexes.
DISTAL. Situated away from the base or point of attachment, e.g. the distal end of a spine; opposite of proximal.
DORSAL. Of, pertaining to, or situated on the back or upper surface; in a gastropod shell, opposite the aperture. See also Ventral.
DORSUM. The dorsal surface of the shell.
DWARF. Of less than usual or normal size for a given stage of development.
DWARF. Of less than usual or normal size.
ECCENTRIC. Not having the same center; not concentric; deviating from the center, as in an elliptical orbit. In the gastropod shell, not following the growth lines.

EDENTATE. Toothless.
EDENTULATE. Toothless.
ELEVATED. Erect; raised; said of prolonged sculptural elements and other structures. See also Depressed.
ELONGATE. Lengthened; extended in one dimension.
EMARGINATE. Notched at the margin.
EMBAYMENT. An indentation; a bay.
EMBRYONIC WHORL. A single whorl of the nucleus or protoconch; a portion of the larval shell.
ENCRUSTED. Covered with foreign matter derived from living organisms.
ENDEMIC. Confined to a particular area; native. See also Indigenous.
ENTIRE. Continuous; having no breaks; said of the margin (peristome) of the shell aperture.
EPHEMERAL. Short-lived; appearing and disappearing.
ERECT. Upthrust or upright. See also Elevated.
ERODED. Worn away.
EVANESCENT. Transient; ephemeral; barely discernible.
EXCAVATED. Strongly depressed; hollowed out.
EXPANDED. Enlarged; swollen; distended. See also Compressed.
FASCIOLE. See Siphonal fasciole.
FENESTRATE. Having depressed, rectangular, pitlike "windows."
FIDE. Trusting to; on the word of.
FIMBRIA (pl. FIMBRIAE). A border; a fringe.
FIMBRIATE. Fringed; bordered by fine, frilly sculptural elements.
FLANGE. A rib lending strength and reinforcing the juncture of two shell structures.
FLARING. Opening or spreading outward; said especially of the outer apertural lip.
FLATTENED. Level; even.
FLUTED. Grooved; decorated with flutes or channels.
FOLD. A spirally wound ridge on the columellar wall.
FOLIACEOUS. Leaflike; resembling foliage. See also Frond.
FOLIATE. Bearing leaflike structures.
FOOT. The muscular organ of locomotion in most mollusks, projecting anteriorly through the aperture of gastropods.
FREE EDGE. The outer margin or outer apertural lip of a gastropod shell.
FRILLED, FRILLY. Having a wrinkled, fluted, or crumpled edging of laminae, flanges, or bladelike varices. See also Fimbriate.
FRINGED. Having an edging or trimming of projecting ends of sculptural elements; twisted or plaited at the margin.
FROND. A foliaceous, leaflike extension of a sculptural element, as on a varical spine.
FRONDOSE. Resembling a much divided leaf; like a palm leaf.
FURROW. A narrow channel, groove, or wrinkle.
FUSED. United or bound together; merged into a single structure or surface.
FUSIFORM. Spindle-shaped; biconic.
FUSION. Something formed by merging; the process of merging.
GERONTIC. Showing the characteristics of old age.
GLAND. A body organ producing one or more specific chemical substances.
GLOBOSE. Roughly spherical in form; rounded.

CLUB-SHAPED SHELL

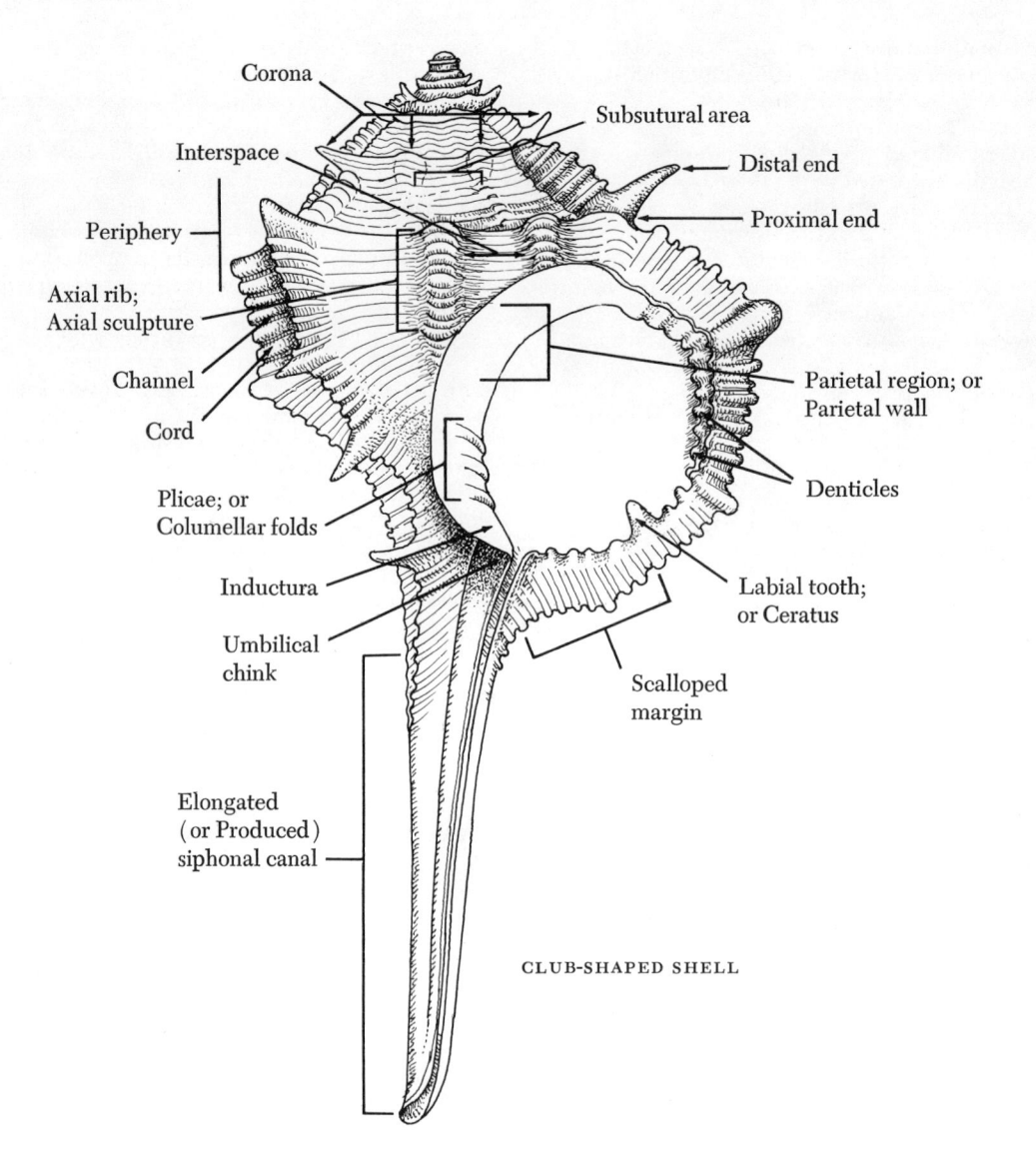

Labels: Corona, Subsutural area, Interspace, Distal end, Proximal end, Periphery, Axial rib; Axial sculpture, Channel, Cord, Parietal region; or Parietal wall, Denticles, Plicae; or Columellar folds, Inductura, Labial tooth; or Ceratus, Umbilical chink, Scalloped margin, Elongated (or Produced) siphonal canal

GRANULOSE. Grainy or finely pustulose; covered with granules.
GROOVE. An elongate and fairly uniform depression; a channel or furrow.
GROWING EDGE. The outermost edge of the outer apertural lip of a gastropod shell.
GROWTH LINE. A line on the shell surface indicating the position of the shell margin at an earlier stage of growth.
GUTTERED. Marked with wide, shallow grooves.
HALF WHORL. Half of a full turn in the shell spiral; 180° of shell growth.
HOLLOW SPINE. A stiff, sharp, sculptural structure, the interior of which is not filled with shell matter.
HOLOTYPE. A single specimen upon which a species is based; the only specimen unquestionably identifiable as a given species; the name-bearer. *See also* Lectotype, Type specimen.
HOMONYMY. A nomenclatural situation in which two or more different species bear the same name.
HOOK. A spine tip that is bent or strongly recurved.

HYPOBRANCHIAL. Situated below the gills.
HYPOTYPE. A specimen not in the original type series of a species but known from a published illustration or description.
ICONOGRAPHY. An illustrated systematic treatment.
IMBRICATE. Having overlapping scales or laminae.
IMMATURE. Not fully developed; said of shell characters that are partly or completely different from those of maturity.
IMPERFORATE. Not open or perforated; often said of a closed umbilicus.
IMPRESSED. Indented, as in the case of a line pressed into an otherwise unscored surface; said of a shell suture.
INCIPIENT. About to develop or appear; beginning to appear.
INCISED. Sculptured with sharply cut grooves.
INCREMENTAL LINE. *See* Growth line.
INCURVED. Curved inwardly toward the shell or upward and inward toward the spire.
INCUT. *See* Incised.

INDENTATION. A notch or recess in the margin of an apertural lip, varical margin, or other structure.

INDENTED. Pressed in or having dents.

INDIGENOUS. Occurring naturally in a particular region; not introduced. *See also* Endemic.

INDUCTURA. An unusually large and erect expansion of the inner apertural lip of a gastropod shell; a smooth, shelly layer extending from the inner side of the aperture.

INFLATED. Swollen.

INNER LIP. The portion of the apertural margin of a gastropod shell opposite the outer lip and abutting the earliest portion of the body whorl.

INTERCALATE. Interposed; interspersed.

INTERGRADE. To possess characters (as in a series of specimens) that bridge the morphological gap between one entity and another.

INTERSPACE. Space between regular sculptural features; in particular, channels between sculptural ribs.

INTERSTICE. A space between structures.

INTERSTITIAL. Pertaining to or occurring in interstices.

INTERTIDAL. Located on the shore between low-tide and high-tide levels.

INTERVAL. A space or gap, in many cases between sculptural or color elements.

INTERVARICAL. Lying between two varices.

INTERVARICAL SPACE. The area between one varix and another; a shell area indicative of active growth.

INTRITACALX. A chalky, white surface layer in the shells of many marine molluscan groups. Prominent in the Muricidae, where its patterns of microsculpture are often useful in identification.

INVALID. Not to be used; incorrect; said of a name in taxonomy.

JUNIOR SYNONYM. A later name for a species with an acceptable prior name.

JUVENILE. Demonstrating the characteristics of immaturity, as in shell growth.

KEEL. A prominent, sharply raised sculptural element, most frequently spiral in orientation. *See also* Carina.

KEELED. Having a prominent sharp ridge. *See also* Carinate.

KNOBBY. Bumpy or nodulous.

LABIAL. Pertaining to the outer apertural lip margin (by common usage; properly labral).

LABIAL TOOTH. A ceratus; a relatively long, spurlike or hornlike extension of the outer lip margin of a gastropod shell.

LABIUM (pl. LABIA). The inner lip of the aperture.

LABRUM (pl. LABRA). *Same as* labium.

LAMELLA (pl. LAMELLAE). A thin plate or scale, generally more or less erect. *See also* Lamina.

LAMELLAR. Platelike.

LAMELLOSE. Having numerous plates or scales on the surface.

LAMINA (pl. LAMINAE). A plate or scale, generally parallel to the shell surface.

LAMINATE. Formed of thin, overlapping plates or scales.

LAMINOSE. Having many laminae.

LANCEOLATE. Shaped like a lance; extended to a point at both ends.

LATERAL. Situated at the side of or arising from the side of a structure (in reference to a shell, radular tooth, etc.).

LATERAL TOOTH. A radular projection lying between the central and marginal elements in a row of dentition.

LATTICED. Having crossed sculptural elements. *See also* Decussate.

LEADING EDGE. The side or surface of a sculptural structure nearest the line of active growth.

LECTOTYPE. A specimen selected from primary type material to serve in place of a holotype where one either was never selected by the original author or has definitely been lost or destroyed.

LENTICULAR. Shaped like a lentil or lens; having a narrowly doubly convex form, as in the aperture of certain gastropod shells.

LIP. One side of the apertural margin or peristome; an inner or an outer lip.

LIRA (pl. LIRAE). A fine, spirally oriented ridge, often on the inner surface of the outer lip of the aperture.

LIRATE. Sculptured with spirally oriented ridges, as in the aperture of a shell.

LIRATION. A fine, threadlike spiral sculptural element. *See also* Lira.

LOBATE. Having prominent projecting and rounded divisions.

LUMEN. The hollow center of a tube or cylinder.

LUMPING. In taxonomy, recognizing fewer names than some other workers and grouping under these names forms differing from each other in minor details. *See also* Splitting.

MACROSCULPTURE. Large, obvious sculpture; opposite of microsculpture.

MACULATION. An arrangement of regular or irregular spots or markings.

MALACOLOGIST. A specialist in the study of mollusks, especially one who deals with soft parts as well as shells. *See also* Conchologist.

MALLEATE. Having a minutely hammered or beaten appearance.

MAMMILLATE. Having nipplelike structures.

MANTLE. The fleshy outer layer of a molluscan body that secretes the shell. The mantle edge may be folded or otherwise modified to form a siphon or other structure.

MANTLE CAVITY. In mollusks, a space or chamber formed where the mantle edge overlaps the visceral mass, housing the gills (or lung) and the outlets of most body systems.

MANTLE EDGE. The portion of the mantle that contains the shell-secreting cells.

MANTLE SKIRT. *See* Mantle edge.

MARGIN. The free edge, generally of a sculptural element; also, the edge of the aperture.

MARGINAL. Located on the margin.

MEDIAL. Occurring in the middle.

MEDIAN. Central; a central line or axis.

MICROSCULPTURE. Minute sculpture; opposite of macrosculpture.

MONOTYPE. The type species of a genus so designated by virtue of being the only species originally associated with the genus.

MORPHOLOGY. Structure or form; the study of physical structure.

MOUTH. The aperture of the shell.

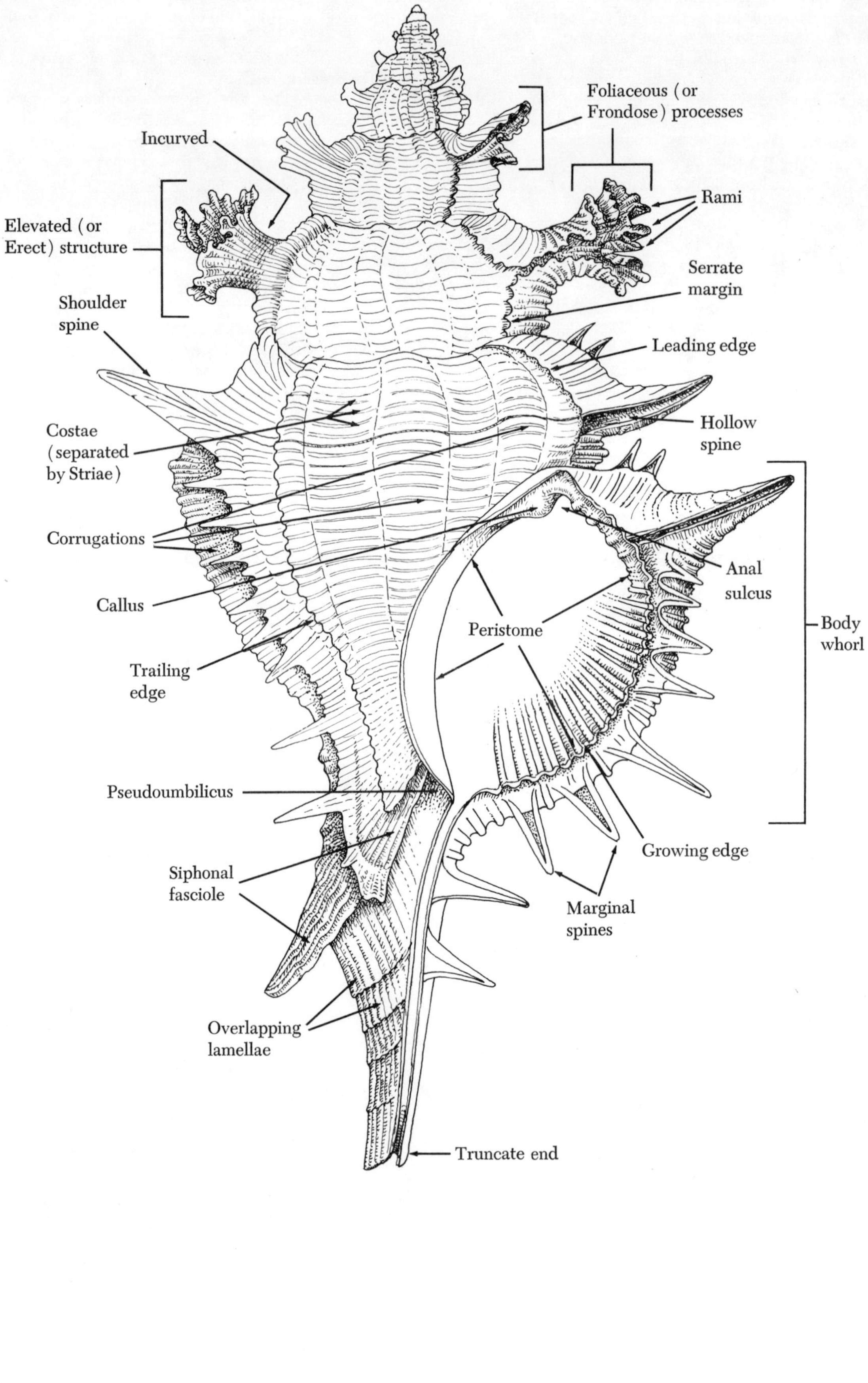
Foliaceous (or
Frondose) processes
Incurved
Rami
Elevated (or
Erect) structure
Serrate
margin
Shoulder
spine
Leading edge
Hollow
spine
Costae
(separated
by Striae)
Corrugations
Anal
sulcus
Callus
Body
whorl
Peristome
Trailing
edge
Pseudoumbilicus
Growing edge
Siphonal
fasciole
Marginal
spines
Overlapping
lamellae
Truncate end

FUSIFORM SHELL

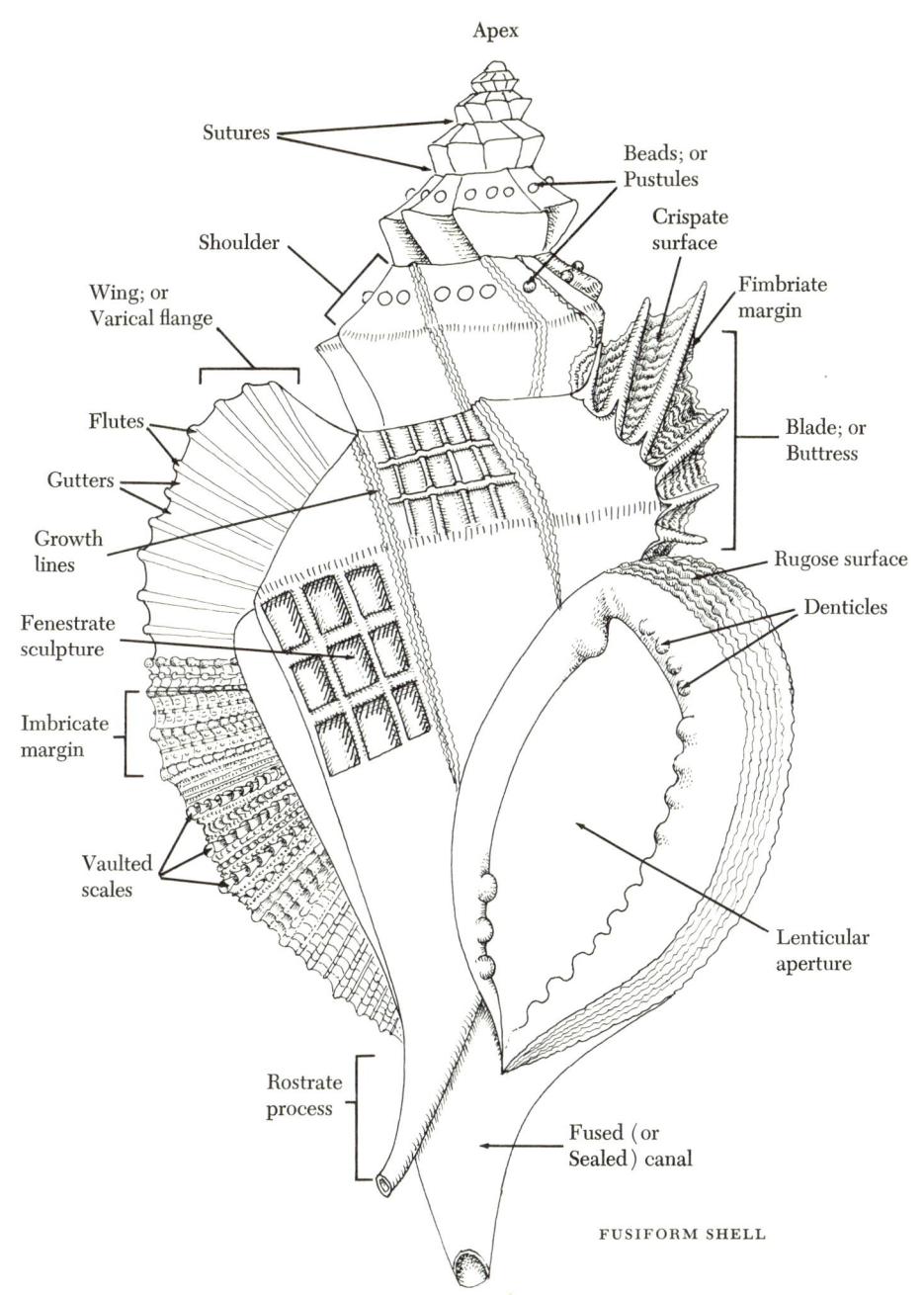

Labels on diagram: Apex; Sutures; Beads; or Pustules; Crispate surface; Fimbriate margin; Shoulder; Wing; or Varical flange; Blade; or Buttress; Flutes; Gutters; Growth lines; Rugose surface; Denticles; Fenestrate sculpture; Imbricate margin; Vaulted scales; Lenticular aperture; Rostrate process; Fused (or Sealed) canal.

NEBULOUS. Vague; not clearly defined.

NEW NAME. A replacement name for a species having a preoccupied previous name or one that is otherwise invalid (Latin *nomen novum*).

NEW SPECIES. A previously undescribed species.

NODE. A knot, protuberance, or knob.

NODOSE. Having numerous protuberances; pustulose.

NODULOSE. Having small, rounded protuberances (i.e. nodules).

NOMENCLATURAL. Pertaining to naming in classification.

NOMEN DUBIUM. A name of doubtful validity for nomenclatural purposes.

NOMEN NOVUM. A new name.

NOMINAL SPECIES. Any named species, irrespective of its validity.

NOMINATE. The subspecies that bears the species name.

NOTCH. An indentation on the margin of a structure.

NUCLEAR. Pertaining to the protoconch, or to the larval shell.

NUCLEAR WHORL. The larval shell; the protoconch. *See also* Adult whorls.

NUCLEUS. *See* Nuclear whorls.

OBESE. Fat; corpulent; swollen.

OBLIQUE. Slanting; inclined from the horizontal or vertical.

OBLITERATED. Eroded; worn away by attrition; rendered imperceptible.

OBSCURED. Not readily seen; not observable.

OBSOLETE. Weakly marked; indistinct; weak to the point of absence.

THE MURICID RADULA

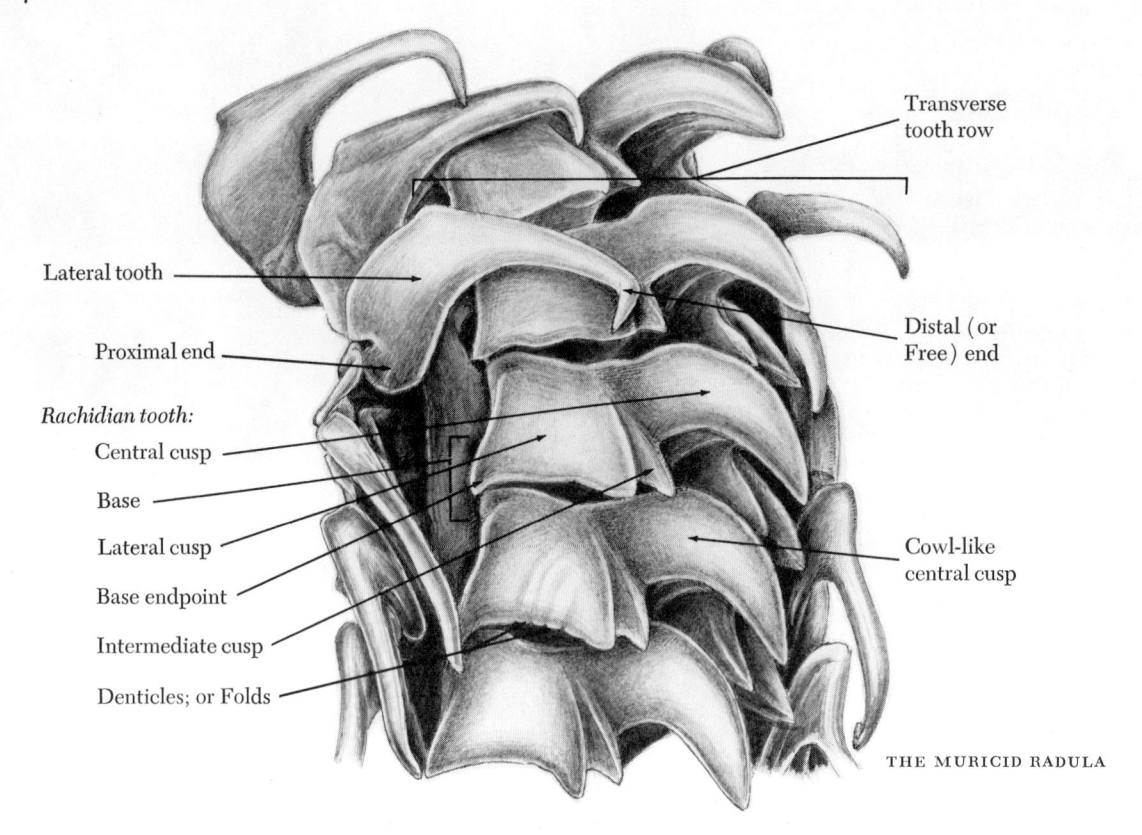

Labels on figure:
- Transverse tooth row
- Lateral tooth
- Distal (or Free) end
- Proximal end
- Rachidian tooth:
  - Central cusp
  - Base
  - Lateral cusp
  - Base endpoint
  - Intermediate cusp
  - Denticles; or Folds
- Cowl-like central cusp

OBTUSE. Not pointed or acute; blunt; having an internal angle of between 90° and 180°

OPERCULAR. Pertaining to the operculum.

OPERCULUM. A generally oval, lidlike structure, situated on the posterior end of the foot of many gastropods, that closes off the aperture when the animal withdraws into its shell.

ORNAMENTATION. Sculptural elements that form part of the shell morphology.

ORNAMENTED. Sculpturally embellished.

OSPHRADIUM. A sense organ, near the gills.

OUTER APERTURAL LIP. The last-formed portion of the apertural margin.

OUTER LIP. See Outer apertural lip.

OVATE. Egg-shaped.

OVERLAPPING. Lying at least partially one over another, as with sculptural elements such as laminae, scales, or plates.

PALLIAL. Pertaining to the mantle; also, pertaining to the region of the gills.

PALMATE. Shaped like an open palm; like a hand with the fingers extended.

PAPILLA (pl. PAPILLAE). Any small bump or small projection.

PAPILLATE. Nipple-shaped.

PARATYPE. A specimen from the original type material of a species, designated as such to serve as an auxiliary specimen to the holotype; one of a series from primary type material, exclusive of the holotype.

PARIETAL. Pertaining to the region of a gastropod shell that extends from the columella posteriorly and around the curve of the shell.

PARIETAL WALL. The region just above the columellar region, partly outside and partly inside the aperture. See also Parietal.

PARTITION. The erect plate of shell matter deposited in some typhine species between the shoulder spine of each varix and the previous whorl, and against which the next spine often rests.

PATRONYM. A species name honoring a specific person. (Also, Patronymic).

PEDAL GLAND. A gland on the gastropod foot that secretes a lubricant aiding in locomotion.

PELAGIC. Living in the open sea; free-swimming, especially near the surface.

PELLUCID. Transparent; limpid.

PENULTIMATE. Last but one; next to last.

PERIOSTRACUM. The outermost molluscan shell layer; composed of conchiolin.

PERIPHERY. The part of a gastropod shell that is farthest from the axis of coiling.

PERISTOME. The margin of the aperture; generally said of a margin that is either continuous or interrupted only by the parietal region of the body whorl.

PERSISTENT. Lasting; not lost; generally present throughout the development of a shell. See also Ephemeral.

PHARYNX. The throat; the section of the alimentary canal just behind the mouth.

PILLAR. The columella.

PIT. A small cavity or hole; a pinpoint depression.

PLAIT. A shelflike fold, generally on the columella of a gastropod shell. See also Plica.

PLATE. A lamina or scalelike structure.

PLICA (pl. PLICAE). A columellar fold.

PLICATE. Folded or twisted; having plicae.

PLICATION. A fold or plica.
POLYMORPHISM. A circumstance in a group of molluscan specimens in which both the close affinities of a species and other, divergent details of morphology are present.
PORCELANEOUS. Polished; similar in color and texture to porcelain ceramic.
POSTERIOR. The tail end; in a gastropod shell, toward the apex.
POSTNUCLEAR. Succeeding the nucleus or protoconch in the growth of a gastropod shell.
POSTNUCLEAR WHORL. Any turn of a gastropod shell formed after the formation of the nucleus.
PRECEDING WHORL. The turn of a gastropod shell just previous to the one being described.
PREOCCUPIED NAME. A name that has been used by a previous author for a different species in the same genus and is therefore unavailable for the present species.
PRICKLE. A small, pointed protuberance.
PRIMARY. Of the first order; most dominant or conspicuous.
PROBOCIS. In gastropods, a tubelike anterior organ bearing the mouthparts at its tip.
PROCESS. A sculptural structure projecting from the main body of a shell.
PRODUCED. Drawn out; elongate.
PROSOBRANCH. Having the gills in a position anterior to the heart.
PROTOCONCH. The larval shell, formed by all the nuclear whorls.
PROXIMAL. Nearest to the base or point of attachment; opposite of distal.
PSEUDOUMBILICUS. An opening formed by the distal portions of the canals of previous varices that are arranged obliquely but adjacent to one another to form an umbilicuslike pit.
PUNCTATION. A pattern of many minute pits.
PUSTULE. A pimplelike or blisterlike swelling.
PUSTULATE. Having a knobby texture, the knobs generally smaller than tubercles; pustulose.
PUSTULOSE. Full of pustules; pustulate.
PYRAMIDAL. Having the form of a solid triangle, i.e. formed like a pyramid.
PYRIFORM. Pear-shaped.
QUADRANGULAR. Having four sides and four angles.
QUADRATE. Square.
QUATERNARY. Of the fourth order; generally indicating little prominence or strength, as in sculptural elements.
RACHIDIAN. *See* Rachidian tooth.
RACHIDIAN TOOTH. The larger, middle tooth of a row of three in the typical stenoglossan radular dentition.
RACHIGLOSSATE. Having radular teeth arranged like or resembling the vertebrae in a backbone.
RADIAL. Arranged in a raylike pattern; characterized by divergence from a center.
RADULA (pl. RADULAE). The main feeding organ of snails and other mollusks, composed of a series of chitinous teeth arranged on a flexible ribbon and housed in the mouth cavity.
RADULAR. Pertaining to the radula.
RADULAR RIBBON. The flexible, rasplike feeding organ of mollusks. *See also* Radula.

RAMUS (pl. RAMI). A branching, leaflike process, generally borne distally on a spine.
RECESSED. Situated within a cavity, as within the aperture.
RECURVED. Curved or bent backward. *See also* Deflexed.
REMOTE. Distant from the point of reference.
RESORBED. Dissolved and removed from a solid structure, as in the removal of a portion of the shell's surface in order to permit the further growth of the shell after a resting stage (marked in the Muricidae by a varix).
RESTING STAGE. A stage between periods of active growth, marked in the shell by the formation of a varix.
RETICULATE. Netted; covered with a network. *See also* Cancellate.
RHOMBOID. Roughly diamond-shaped.
RIB. A raised, elongate structural element, generally axially oriented.
RIBBED. Having ribs.
RIBBON. The flexible structure in which the radular teeth are embedded. *See also* Radula.
RIBLET. A minor rib.
RIPPLED. Finely and indistinctly ribbed.
ROBUST. Strong in structure; prominently formed.
ROSTRATE. Having a beaklike projection (as in a long, straight siphonal canal).
ROTUND. Approximately circular or globular.
RUFFLED. Having many erect lamellae; like a ruff.
RUGOSE. Full of wrinkles or ripples.
SCABROUS. Rough; covered with minute points, denticles, or scales.
SCABROUS LAMELLAE. Thin axial lamellae having scalelike projections at their intersections with spiral cords.
SCALE. Thin, erect, platelike structures.
SCALLOPED. Edged with rounded projections.
SCULPTURE. The morphological elements of shell structure and ornamentation.
SEALED. Closed; said of the siphonal canal, anal tubes, or spines. *See also* Coalesced.
SEAM. A closure line, along which two surfaces are fused.
SECONDARY. Less than primary in strength; second-order.
SERRATE. Finely notched or sawlike at the edge.
SERRATION. A single tooth in a notched edge.
SHELF. A flattened surface, as on the upper portion of a plait or carina.
SHELL. The calcareous structure secreted by the molluscan mantle.

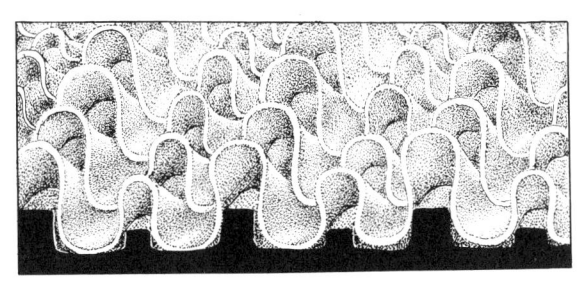

SCABROUS SHELL SURFACE

SHELLY. Composed of calcium carbonate; calcareous.
SHOULDER. The portion of each whorl of a gastropod shell lying between the suture and the angle, periphery, or shoulder margin.
SHOULDERED. Having an angulation of the whorl at its periphery or outermost edge, even if this is indefinite, as in the case of a convex profile.
SHOULDER MARGIN. The periphery or outermost edge of a whorl.
SHOULDER SPINE. A spine borne at or above the shoulder margin.
SICKLE-SHAPED. Strongly curved in a single arc.
SINUOUS. Winding.
SIPHON. A tubelike structure in gastropods; a tubular fold of mantle tissue.
SIPHONAL CANAL. A complete or incomplete tubular shell extension through which the anterior siphon is extended.
SIPHONAL FASCIOLE. A ridge formed on the columellar side of the siphonal canal, sometimes bearing remnants of previous canals.
SPINATION. The total complement of spines; the spine pattern.
SPINDLE-SHAPED. Round; tapering toward each end; fusiform.
SPINE. A more or less slender and elongate projection of a shell, either tapering to a point or spreading out distally into fronds or foliations.
SPINELET. A minor spine.
SPINE-TUBE. A tapering spine having a hollow interior.
SPINIFEROUS. Bearing many spines.
SPINOSE. See Spiniferous.
SPIRAL SCULPTURE. Sculpture following the helical growth of the gastropod shell.
SPIRE. The cone formed by all shell whorls exclusive of the body whorl.
SPIRE WHORL. One turn (360°) of the spire (exclusive of the body whorl).
SPLIT SPINE. A spine with incurled but not fused margins.
SPLITTING. Opposite of lumping; i.e. the perception of a multiplicity of forms and the acceptance of them as discrete entities.
SPOUT. An elongated, tubelike canal structure.
SQUAMOSE. Scaly; with the appearance of being scaly.
STENOGLOSSATE. "Close-toothed" or "narrow-tongued"; pertaining to the Stenoglossa, in which the Muricidae are included.
STOUT. Sturdy; solid; bulky.
STRIA (pl. STRIAE). A fine incised or raised line, especially one of a series of parallel lines.
STRIATE. Marked with fine parallel grooves or scratches.
STRIATION. A single line or scratch; a stria; a pattern of stria.
STRUT. A sculptural element lending strength or stiffness to the whole structure.
STUMP. A stub; a small remnant of structure.
SUB-. Prefix indicating less than, below, almost.
SUBACUTE. Only moderately acute.
SUBANGULATE. Weakly angled; obtuse.
SUBJECTIVE SYNONYM. A name representing, in the author's opinion, the same entity as that represented by another name.

SUBMICROSCOPIC. Not clearly visible under a light microscope.
SUBSEQUENT DESIGNATION. The designation of the type species of a genus subsequent to the description of the genus.
SUBSTRATUM. The surface on which a gastropod lives, generally under water.
SUBSUTURAL. Below the suture; at the upper margin of the younger (newer) of two successive whorls.
SUBTIDAL. Below the lowest tide line and extending generally to the edge of the continental shelf.
SUCCEEDING WHORL. A whorl later in the growth sequence and usually larger than the whorl in question.
SUFFUSED. Covered over or flushed with a tint of color.
SULCATE. Having a deep slit, fissure, or furrow.
SULCUS. A deep slit, fissure, or furrow. See also Anal sulcus.
SUPERFLUOUS NAME. An unnecessary name, in most cases one applied to an entity that already has a valid name.
SUPRASUTURAL. Above the suture.
SURFACE SCULPTURE. The ornamentation of the exterior of a molluscan shell.
SUTURAL. Referring to or associated with the suture.
SUTURE. A continuous spiral line following the junction of consecutive whorls in a gastropod shell.
SWELLING. An enlargement, generally globose.
SWOLLEN. Enlarged; inflated.
SYNONYMIZE. To state that two or more names represent the same biological entity.
SYNONYM. One of two or more names given to a species. See also Junior synonym.
SYNONYMY. A list of the various different scientific names, regardless of validity or correctness, that have been used to designate a single biological entity.
SYNTYPE. One of a number of specimens studied by the author of a species name, of which group no specimen was designated as a holotype.
SYNTYPIC. Pertaining to a syntype or syntypes.
SYSTEMATICS. The discipline of biological classification.
SYSTEMATIST. One who forms, revises, or adheres to a system of classification of biological categories.
TABULATE. Tablelike; sharply angulate (approaching 90°); said especially of the shoulder or periphery of each whorl.
TABULATION. A tablelike angulation.
TANGENTIAL. Divergent, digressive; of the nature of a tangent; touching briefly and then divergent.
TAPERING. Decreasing gradually in circumference; generally said of a cylindrical form or structure.
TAUTONYMY. A situation in which the type species of a genus is designated as such by virtue of having a specific name identical to that of the newly erected generic name.
TAXON (pl. TAXA). A grouping of organisms under a common name; a unit of classification at any level, implying biological relationship.
TAXONOMY. The classification of animals or plants according to relationship. See also Systematic.
TELOCONCH, TELEOCONCH. The gastropod shell, apart from the nucleus; complement of protoconch. See also Adult whorls.

TERTIARY. Of the third order; generally said of minor sculpture.

THREAD. A very fine spiral sculptural element of a shell. *See also* Lira.

THREADED. Sculptured with many very fine spiral lines.

TILTED. Slanted away from the long axis of the shell. *See also* Canted.

TOOTH. A spurlike projection on the margin of a shell structure; more especially, an element of radular dentition.

TRAILING EDGE. The hind portion of a structure, behind the leading edge.

TRANSVERSE. Crossing the shell horizontally (i.e. spirally). *See also* Axial, Spiral.

TRIAD. A group of three (as in spiral cords).

TRIANGULATE. Having the shape of a triangle.

TRIGONAL. Having three sides and angles; triangular in outline.

TRIPARTITE. Having three parts.

TRIPTEROUS. Three-winged; generally meaning trivaricate with alate varices.

TRIVARICATE. Having three varices for each full turn of a whorl (360°).

TRUNCATE. Terminating bluntly.

TUBE. A long, slender, hollow structure.

TUBERCLE. A small, rounded projection.

TUBERCULATE. Having tubercles.

TUMID. Swollen, enlarged, or distended. *See also* Inflated, Swollen.

TUNNEL. A tube; generally said of subsurface structures in the intritacalx of aspelloid species.

TURRETED. Having a tall and generally tabulate spire.

TURRICULATE. Having the form of a tower.

TYPE DEPOSITORY. The scientific collection in which a type specimen is deposited.

TYPE LOCALITY. The geographical area from which type material was originally collected and which was cited as such by the author.

TYPE SPECIES. A species chosen as representative of an entire genus.

TYPE SPECIMEN. The single specimen upon which a name is based; the name-bearer. *See also* Holotype.

ULTIMATE. Final; apical; distal.

UMBILICAL. Pertaining to the umbilicus.

UMBILICAL CHINK. A long, narrow cleft in the umbilicus.

UMBILICAL PIT. An opening or depression in the umbilicus.

UMBILICUS. The open axis of coiling in a loosely spiral gastropod shell; in the Muricidae, actually a pseudoumbilicus.

UNDULATE. Wavy; having a wavy margin or surface.

UNGUICULATE. Claw-shaped; said of an operculum.

VARICAL. Pertaining to a varix.

VARICAL BUTTRESS. A reinforcing structure attached to a varix and to the shell surface.

VARICAL FLANGE. A winglike, elevated lamina growing from the top of the varix. *See also* Varical wing.

VARICAL FRINGE. The usually brief terminal edge of a varix, slightly raised from the shell surface or otherwise distinct.

VARICAL MARGIN. The free, often sculptured, generally serrate or crenulate edge of a varix.

VARICAL PLANE. The orientation of the varix with reference to the shell surface.

VARICAL SPINE. A sharp projection arising from a varix.

VARICAL WEBBING. A finely undulate flange that is reinforced by laminae or scalelike elements.

VARICAL WING. An expanded, thin, bladelike or flangelike projection or extension of the varix.

VARICED. Having varices.

VARICOSE. See Variced.

VARIX (pl. VARICES). A thickened or extensive axial ridge indicative of a resting stage in the growth of the mollusk, as reflected in the shell; in some cases including all structures associated with interruption of growth.

VAULTED SCALE. A curved, erect scale tilted in the direction of shell growth.

VELIGER. A larval stage of most mollusks; possessing a shell and enclosed within the egg capsule, or released and free-swimming for a variable period of time.

VELUM (pl. VELA). The locomotory organ of a veliger; a membranous structure composed of two or more lobes fringed with minute, hairlike structures.

VENTRAL. Of, pertaining to, or situated on the lower side in a dorsiventral organism; on the apertural surface of a gastropod shell. *See also* Dorsal.

VENTRICOSE. Swelling out on one side; inflated.

WEAKLY. Poorly; not strongly; generally said of the development or strength of a sculpture.

WEBBING. Lamellate sculptural elements crossed by other reinforcing sculpture.

WHORL. A single complete turn of 360° in the spiral growth of the gastropod shell.

WING. *See* Varical wing.

WINGED. Having a wing or wings.

WRINKLED. Corrugated; furrowed; ridged.

Supplementary Data on Figures

The data that follow furnish supplementary information of various types for many of the illustrations in text and for all of the color plates. Usually, what is supplied is the source for the original illustration (where figures have been redrawn) and/or the identification of the specimens figured.

Unless otherwise specified below, all drawings and halftones used in the text are our own, the drawings prepared by the junior author from published figures or from material in hand. Where the data below are of the form "after Viader, 1938," the text illustration in question is a redrawing (again, by the junior author) of an illustration originally reproduced elsewhere. Where the data are of the form "holotype, BM(NH), Antofagasta, Chile," the text halftone in question is a photograph of a type specimen, in this case a holotype collected in Chile and deposited in the British Museum (Natural History).

The data for the color plates are of a more consistent form, and all specimens figured in color are listed. "Species" is the species name as given in the text and in the legends for the color plates. "Locality" is the collection locality, as originally cited for the specimen figured. "Repository" is the museum or collection where the specimen figured is permanently deposited: those indicated as "Coll." are private collections; those as "SDSNH" are museums and the like (their abbreviations are identified in the list at the front of the book, on p. x); and the catalog numerals ("51685") identify the particular museum specimen figured.

Text Figures

Fig. 2. *Acanthotrophon sorenseni*, after Hertlein & Strong, 1951.
Fig. 22. *Dermomurex abyssicola*, after Crosse, 1865.
Fig. 33. *Murex antelmei*, after Viader, 1938, pl. 1, figs. 8, 9.
Fig. 34. *Murex blakeanus*, after E. H. Vokes, 1967, pl. 3, figs. 1, 2.
Fig. 47. *Nipponotrophon elegantulus* (Dall, 1907); holotype, USNM 110501, off Attu I., Aleutian Is.
Fig. 49. *Nipponotrophon pagodus*, after Hayashi & Habe, 1965, pl. 1, figs. 1, 2.
Fig. 51. *Pazinotus smithi*, after Schepman, 1911, pl. 21, fig. 3.
Fig. 59. *Pterochelus ariomus*, after Clench & Pérez Farfante, 1945, pl. 20, figs. 5, 6.
Fig. 62. *Pterochelus phillipsi*, after E. H. Vokes, 1966, pl. 25, figs. 1–3.
Fig. 63. *Pterynotus leucas* (Locard, 1897); holotype, MNHN.
Fig. 80. *Poropteron sanctaehelenae* (E. A. Smith, 1891); holotype, BM(NH).
Fig. 87. *Xanthochorus buxeus* (Broderip, 1833); holotype, LACM AE.70-28, Antofagasta, Chile.
Fig. 91. *Favartia confusa*, after Brazier, 1877, fig. 1.
Fig. 93. *Favartia funafutiensis*, after Hedley, 1899, fig. 35.
Fig. 94. *Favartia kurodai*, after Nakamigawa & Habe, 1964, pl. 2, fig. 2.
Fig. 95. *Favartia marjoriae* (Melvill & Standen, 1903); holotype, BM(NH).
Fig. 96. *Favartia tetragona* (Broderip, 1833); ANSP 230819.
Fig. 98. *Murexiella bojadorensis* (Locard, 1897); holotype, MNHN.
Fig. 101. *Murexiella phantom*, after Ponder, 1972, pl. 21, fig. 8.
Fig. 105. *Murexsul zonatus*, after Hayashi & Habe, 1965, pl. 1, fig. 3.
Fig. 116. *Actinotrophon actinophorus*, after Dall, 1889.
Fig. 117. *Afritrophon kowieensis*, after Sowerby, 1901.
Fig. 118. *Apixystus stimuleus*, after Hedley, 1907.
Fig. 119. *Axymene turbator*, after Finlay, 1927.
Fig. 120. *Benthoxystus columnarius*, after Hedley & May, 1908.
Fig. 122. *Comptella curta*, after Murdoch, 1905.
Fig. 123. *Fuegotrophon crispus*, after Gould, 1852.

Fig. 124. *Lenitrophon convexus*, after Suter, 1909.
Fig. 125. *Litozamia rudolphi*, after Brazier, 1894.
Fig. 126. *Minortrophon crassiliratus*, after Suter, 1908.
Fig. 127. *Paratrophon cheesemani* (Hutton, 1882); SDSNH 24078, "New Zealand."
Fig. 129. *Pascula citrica*, after Dall, 1908.
Fig. 130. *Stramonitrophon laciniatus*, after Carcelles, 1944, pl. 2, fig. 25.
Fig. 131. *Terefundus crispulatus*, after Suter, 1908.
Fig. 133. *Trophonopsis muricatus*, after Montagu, 1803.
Fig. 134. *Xymene plebeius*, after Ponder, 1971.
Fig. 135. *Xymenella pusilla*, after Suter, 1907.
Fig. 136. *Xymenopsis liratus*, after Powell, 1951.
Fig. 138. *Zeatrophon ambiguus*, after Ponder, 1972, fig. 2:9.
Fig. 139. *Zeatrophon ambiguus*, after Ponder, 1972.
Fig. 142. *Laevityphis tubuliger*, after Thiele, 1925.
Fig. 143. *Siphonochelus arcuatus*, after Barnard, 1959.
Fig. 144. *Siphonochelus pentaphasios*, after Barnard, 1959.
Fig. 145. *Siphonochelus solus*, after Vella, 1961.
Fig. 150. *Typhina belcheri*, after Hinds, 1844.
Fig. 151. *Typhina bivaricata*, after Verco, 1907.
Fig. 153. *Typhina pauperis* (Mestayer, 1916); holotype, after Vella, 1961, pl. 47, fig. 24.
Fig. 157. "*Murex*" *exquisitus* (Sowerby, 1904); holotype, BM(NH).

Fig. 158. *Aspella castor* sp. nov.; holotype, USNM 663525.
Fig. 161. *Aspella cryptica* sp. nov.; holotype, SDSNH 62608.
Fig. 163. *Aspella mauritiana* sp. nov.; holotype, ANSP 273236.
Fig. 166. *Aspella morchi* sp. nov.; holotype, SDSNH 62609.
Fig. 168. *Aspella platylaevis* sp. nov.; holotype, ANSP 285147.
Fig. 171. *Aspella pollux* sp. nov.; holotype, SDSNH 62607.
Fig. 174. *Aspella ponderi* sp. nov.; holotype, ANSP 233056.
Fig. 176. *Marchia bibbeyi* sp. nov.; holotype, SDSNH 56074.
Fig. 177. *Murex purdyae* sp. nov.; holotype, SDSNH 63024.
Fig. 180. *Favartia poormani* sp. nov.; holotype, SDSNH 63080.
Fig. 182. *Muricopsis huberti* sp. nov.; holotype, SDSNH 63078.
Fig. 184. *Muricopsis tulensis* sp. nov.; holotype, SDSNH 61232.
Fig. 186. *Talityphis bengalensis* sp. nov.; holotype, ANSP 294561.
Fig. 188. *Talityphis campbelli* sp. nov.; holotype, SDSNH 63077.
Fig. 190. *Talityphis perchardei* sp. nov.; holotype, SDSNH 63079.

Color Figures

Figure	Species	Locality	Repository
PLATE 1			
1	*Aspella senex* Dall	Off western Florida	Fla. State Board Fish.
2	*A. senex* Dall	Off Cape Lookout, North Carolina	Inst. Mar. Sci., N. Car.
3	*A. pollux* sp. nov.	Bahía Coastocomate, Jalisco, Mexico	Holotype, SDSNH 62607
4	*A. pyramidalis* (Broderip)	Sayulita, Nayarit, Mexico	LACM 70-4
5	*A. pyramidalis* (Broderip)	Mazatlán, Mexico	SDSNH 34670
6	*A. pyramidalis* (Broderip)	Bahía Bacochibampo, Guaymas, Mexico	Coll. Shasky
7	*A. pyramidalis* (Broderip)	I. Santa Cruz, Galápagos Is.	Coll. Shasky
8	*A. pyramidalis* (Broderip)	I. Santa Cruz, Galápagos Is.	Coll. Shasky
9	*A. morchi* sp. nov.	Natal Bay, Brazil	Holotype, SDSNH 62609
10	*A. cryptica* sp. nov.	Itapoán, Bahía, Brazil	Holotype, SDSNH 62608
11	*A. acuticostata* (Turton)	False Bay, South Africa	Coll. D'Attilio
12	*A. producta* (Pease)	Hilo, Hawaii	USNM 337902
13	*A. producta* (Pease)	Lambay, Formosa	SDSNH 6578
14	*A. producta* (Pease)	Lambay, Formosa	SDSNH 6578
15	*Dermomurex elizabethae* (McGinty)	Off Sand Key, Florida	Fla. State Board Fish.
16	*D. elizabethae* (McGinty)	Middle Sambo Shoal, Florida	Holotype, ANSP 76449
17	*D. indentatus* (Carpenter)	I. Venado, Canal Zone	LACM 72-94
18	*D. bakeri* (Hertlein & Strong)	Bahía Escondido, Baja Calif.	SDSNH 56394
19	*D. bakeri* (Hertlein & Strong)	I. Cerralbo, Gulf of California	Coll. D'Attilio
20	*D. cunninghamae* (Berry)	Puerto San Carlos, Sonora, Mexico	Paratype, Coll. S. S. Berry

SUPPLEMENTARY DATA ON FIGURES

Figure	Species	Locality	Repository
21	*D. obeliscus* (A. Adams)	Western Nicaragua	Coll. D'Attilio
22	*D. obeliscus* (A. Adams)	Puntarénas, Costa Rica	SDSNH 23356
23	*D. obeliscus* (A. Adams)	Bahía Coastocomate, Jalisco, Mexico	Coll. Shasky
24	*D. obeliscus* (A. Adams)	Bahía Coastocomate, Jalisco, Mexico	Coll. Shasky
25	*D. pauperculus* (C. B. Adams)	Key West, Florida	SDSNH 42852
26	*D. pauperculus* (C. B. Adams)	Miami Beach, Florida	SDSNH 38754
27	*D. scalaroides* (Blainville)	Palermo, Sicily	SDSNH 24037
28	*D. myrakeenae* (Emerson & D'Attilio)	Is. Tres Marias, Mexico	SDSNH 23358
29	*Aspella pollux* sp. nov.	Pta. Pulmo, Baja Calif.	Paratype, Coll. J. Bailey
30	*Takia infrons* (E. H. Vokes)	Kii, Shikoku, Japan	Coll. D'Attilio
31	*T. infrons* (E. H. Vokes)	Tosa, Shikoku, Japan	Coll. D'Attilio

PLATE 2

1	*Muricopsis schrammi* (Crosse)	Devil's Beach, Canal Zone	USNM 620639
2	*Bedeva paivae* (Crosse)	Pt. Adelaide River, S. Australia	SDSNH 24031
3	*Muricopsis muricoides* (C. B. Adams)	Barbados, B.W.I.	USNM 19526
4	*Bedeva livida* (Reeve)	Malabuyoc, Cebu, Philippines	SDSNH 50964
5	*Muricopsis roseus* (Reeve)	Off Falmouth, Antigua	USNM 459608
6	*Bedeva birileffi* (Lischke)	Wakayama, Honshu, Japan	Coll. D'Attilio
7	*Murexsul umbilicatus* (Tenison-Woods)	Semaphore, S. Australia	SDSNH 23978
8	*Bedeva blosvillei* (Deshayes)	Clair View, Queensland, Australia	Coll. Hertz
9	*B. paivae* (Crosse)	Yeppoon, Queensland, Australia	Coll. D'Attilio
10	*Ergalatax contracta* (Reeve)	Zanzibar, East Africa	SDSNH 51209
11	*E. contracta* (Reeve)	Kii Channel, southeastern Japan	Coll. D'Attilio
12	*E. contracta* (Reeve)	Kagamiru, Honshu, Japan (Japan Sea)	Coll. D'Attilio

PLATE 3

1	*Attiliosa incompta* (Berry)	Fishermen docking at Guaymas, Mexico	AMNH 138277
2	*Nipponotrophon echinus* (Dall)	Kii Channel, southeastern Japan, in 200 m	Coll. D'Attilio
3	*Muricopsis infans* (E. A. Smith)	South of Andaman Is.	Coll. E. Wright
4	*Calotrophon ostrearum* (Conrad)	Boca Ciega Bay, Florida	SDSNH 24088
5	*Evokesia ferruginosa* (Reeve)	Bahía San Luis Gonzaga, Baja Calif.	SDSNH 52727
6	*Nipponotrophon galapaganus* (Emerson & D'Attilio)	Academy Bay, Santa Cruz I., Galápagos Is.	Paratype, Coll. Shasky
7	*Trachypollia lugubris* (C. B. Adams)	Bahía Magdalena, Baja Calif.	SDSNH 50255
8	*T. didyma* (Schwengel)	Off Palm Beach, Florida	Coll. D'Attilio
9	*T. nodulosa* (C. B. Adams)	Key West, Florida	SDSNH 24207
10	*Attiliosa philippiana* (Dall)	Off Cabo Catoche, Yucatán, Mexico	Syntype, USNM 93337
11	*Evokesia rufonotata* (Carpenter)	Bahía Coastocomate, Jalisco, Mexico	SDSNH 45221
12	*Calotrophon turritus* (Dall)	I. Asuncion, Baja Calif.	LACM 67-66
13	*C. turritus* (Dall)	Gorda Bank, Gulf of Calif., Mexico	Paratype (of *C. bristolae*) SDSNH 12297
14	*Nipponotrophon gorgon* (Dall)	Tosa Bay, Shikoku, Japan	Coll. D'Attilio

SUPPLEMENTARY DATA ON FIGURES

Figure	Species	Locality	Repository
PLATE 4			
1	*Chicoreus akritos* sp. nov.	Southern Queensland, Australia	Coll. D'Attilio
2	*C. axicornis* (Lamarck)	*Ex* Calvert Coll. (no data)	Coll. D'Attilio
3	*C. damicornis* (Hedley)	Off Woolongong, New South Wales, Australia	Coll. D'Attilio
4	*C. artemis*, new name	Tosa Bay, southeastern Japan	Coll. D'Attilio
5	*C. denudatus* (Perry)	Off Sydney Hbr., New South Wales, Australia	Coll. D'Attilio
6	*C. rossiteri* (Crosse)	Kii Channel, southeastern Japan	Coll. D'Attilio
7	*C. microphyllus* (Lamarck)	Zamboanga, Philippines	Coll. D'Attilio
8	*C. ramosus* (Linné)	Kenya, East Africa	Coll. D'Attilio
9	*C. brunneus* (Link)	Sisiman Bay, Bataan, Philippines	Coll. D'Attilio
10	*C. brevifrons* (Lamarck)	Bahía Cabo Rojo, Puerto Rico	Coll. D'Attilio
11	*C. cornucervi* (Röding)	Broome, W. Australia	Coll. D'Attilio
12	*C. banksii* (Sowerby)	Mozambique, East Africa	Coll. D'Attilio
PLATE 5			
1	*Chicoreus spectrum* (Reeve)	Off Piranji, Rio Grande do Sul, Brazil	Coll. Richmond
2	*C. palmarosae* (Lamarck)	Ceylon	Coll. D'Attilio
3	*C. cnissodus* (Euthyme)	Kii, Tosa, southeastern Japan	Coll. Ames
4	*C. insularum* (Pilsbry)	Off Kauapali, Lahaina, Maui, Hawaiian Is.	Coll. Richmond
5	*C. maurus* (Broderip)	Marquesas Is., South Pacific	Coll. Purdy
6	*Phyllonotus trunculus* (Linné)	Grand Hbr., Valetta, Malta	SDSNH 24174
7	*Chicoreus microphyllus* (Lamarck)	Subic Bay, Luzon, Philippines	Coll. Ames
8	*C. saulii* (Sowerby)	Okinawa, Japan	Coll. Purdy
PLATE 6			
1	*Phyllonotus superbus* (Sowerby)	Kii Channel, southeastern Japan	Coll. D'Attilio
2	*P. superbus* (Sowerby)	Southwestern Kochi Prefecture, Shikoku, Japan	Coll. D'Attilio
3	*P. laciniatus* (Sowerby)	Magellan Bay, off Mactan I., Philippines	Coll. D'Attilio
4	*Chicoreus penchinati* (Crosse)	Ryukyu Is., Japan	SDSNH 24121
5	*C. rubescens* (Broderip)	"Hawaii"	AMNH 93746
6	*C. florifer* (Reeve)	(No data)	Coll. D'Attilio
7	*C. florifer* (Reeve)	West coast of Florida	Coll. D'Attilio
8	*C. asianus* Kuroda	Kii Channel, southeastern Japan	Coll. D'Attilio
9	*C. territus* (Reeve)	Off Townsville, Queensland, Australia	Coll. D'Attilio
10	*C. rubiginosus* (Reeve)	Broome, W. Australia	Coll. D'Attilio
11	*C. gubbi* (Reeve)	"West Africa"	AMNH 48185
12	*C. trivialis* (A. Adams)	Radell Beach, northwestern Australia	Coll. D'Attilio
PLATE 7			
1	*Hexaplex stainforthi* (Reeve)	Port Hedland, W. Australia	Coll. D'Attilio
2	*H. stainforthi* (Reeve)	Northwestern Australia	SDSNH 24140
3	*Phyllonotus trunculus* (Linné)	Canary Is.	SDSNH 12046
4	*Xanthochorus xanthostoma* (Broderip)	Valparaiso, Chile	SDSNH 44106
5	*X. xanthostoma* (Broderip)	Middle Chincha I., Peru	AHF-LACM 387-35

Figure	Species	Locality	Repository
6	*Murex olssoni* E. H. Vokes	San Blas, Panamá	Paratype, SDSNH 63045
7	*Vitularia miliaris* (Gmelin)	Coron, Philippines	Coll. D'Attilio
8	*Pterynotus phyllopterus* (Lamarck)	Off Ste. Anne, Martinique, French West Indies	Coll. Janowsky
9	*Murexsul mariae* Finlay	Waiwera, Auckland, New Zealand	Coll. Richmond
10	*Muricanthus saharicus* (Locard)	Mauritania, West Africa	Coll. D'Attilio
11	*Murex gallinago* Sowerby	Ogasawara, Japan (Bonin Is.)	CAS 14590
12	*Vitularia miliaris* (Gmelin)	Howick I., Queensland, Australia	Coll. D'Attilio
13	*V. miliaris* (Gmelin)	New Caledonia	SDSNH 55807
14	*V. salebrosa* (King & Broderip)	La Paz, Baja Calif.	Coll. D'Attilio
15	*Murex anniae* M. Smith	Campeche Bank, off Yucatán, Mexico	Coll. D'Attilio
16	*Hexaplex cichoreum* (Gmelin)	Marintoque Bay, Masbate, Philippines	Coll. D'Attilio
17	*H. cichoreum* (Gmelin)	Cebu, Philippines	Coll. D'Attilio
18	*Murex tryoni* Hidalgo	Off Egmont Key, Florida	Tulane Univ. Museum

PLATE 8

1	*Homalocantha secunda* (Lamarck)	(No data)	Coll. D'Attilio
2	*H. secunda* (Lamarck)	Port Hedland, W. Australia	Coll. D'Attilio
3	*H. zamboi* (Burch & Burch)	Cebu, Philippines	Paratype, SDSNH 16816
4	*H. melanamathos* (Gmelin)	Lobito, Angola	Coll. D'Attilio
5	*H. secunda* (Lamarck)	New Caledonia	AMNH 92464
6	*H. anatomica* (Perry)	Kii Channel, southeastern Japan	Coll. D'Attilio
7	*H. anatomica* (Perry)	Zanzibar, East Africa	Coll. D'Attilio
8	*H. anatomica* (Perry)	Kii Channel, southeastern Japan	Coll. D'Attilio
9	*H. anatomica* (Perry)	Eilat, Gulf of Aqaba, Israel	Coll. D'Attilio
10	*H. anatomica* (Perry)	Kii Channel, southeastern Japan	Coll. D'Attilio
11	*H. scorpio* (Linné)	(No data)	Coll. D'Attilio
12	*H. scorpio* (Linné)	Coron, Palawan I., Philippines	Coll. D'Attilio
13	*H. scorpio* (Linné)	(No data)	Coll. D'Attilio
14	*H. oxyacantha* (Broderip)	?Costa Rica	Coll. D'Attilio
15	*H. oxyacantha* (Broderip)	Manzanillo, Colima, Mexico	Coll. Martin
16	*H. tortua* (Sowerby)	(No data)	Coll. D'Attilio

PLATE 9

1	*Marchia martinetana* (Röding)	Off Tarawa Is., Ryukyus, Japan	Coll. Richmond
2	*Pterynotus vespertilio* (Kira)	Tosa Bay, southeastern Japan	Coll. D'Attilio
3	*P. phaneus* (Dall)	Off Fernandina, Florida	USNM 108012
4	*P. bednalli* (Brazier)	Darwin, N. Australia	Coll. Richmond
5	*Marchia laqueata* (Sowerby)	Facpi Pt., Guam	Coll. Richmond
6	*Pterynotus alatus* (Röding)	Kii Channel, southeastern Japan	Coll. Ames
7	*Marchia pellucida* (Reeve)	Kii Channel, southeastern Japan	Coll. D'Attilio
8	*Pterynotus bednalli* (Brazier)	Darwin, N. Australia	Coll. D'Attilio
9	*Marchia barclayana* (H. Adams)	Gasan, Marinduque I., Philippines	Coll. D'Attilio
10	*M. elongata* (Lightfoot)	Cebu I., Philippines	Coll. Richmond
11	*M. bipinnata* (Reeve)	Maquinit I., Palawan Is., Philippines	Coll. D'Attilio
12	*M. triptera* (Born)	Cavit, Boac, Marinduque Is., Philippines	Coll. D'Attilio

Figure	Species	Locality	Repository
13	*Pterynotus patagiatus* (Hedley)	North of Townsville, Queensland, Australia	Coll. D'Attilio
14	*P. loebbeckei* (Kobelt)	Off Tosa Bay, southeastern Japan	Coll. Richmond

PLATE 10

Figure	Species	Locality	Repository
1	*Murex pecten* Lightfoot	Zamboanga, Philippines	Coll. D'Attilio
2	*M. serratospinosus* Dunker	Bushehr, Iran	Coll. D'Attilio
3	*M. donmoorei* Bullis	Gulf of Paria, Trinidad	Coll. D'Attilio
4	*M. mindanaoensis* Sowerby	Tayabas Bay, Quezon I., Philippines	Coll. D'Attilio
5	*M. troscheli* Lischke	Kii Channel, southeastern Japan	Coll. D'Attilio
6	*M. scolopax* Dillwyn	*Ex* Calvert Coll. (no data)	Coll. D'Attilio
7	*M. scolopax* Dillwyn	Nicobar Is., Indian Ocean	SDSNH 24170
8	*M. tribulus* Linné	*Ex* Calvert Coll. (no data)	Coll. D'Attilio
9	*M. tribulus* Linné	Off Keppel Bay, Queensland, Australia	Coll. D'Attilio
10	*M. chrysostoma* Sowerby	Buccoo Bay, Tobago, B.W.I.	Coll. D'Attilio
11	*M. chrysostoma* Sowerby	Off Awa Blancoe, Curaçao	Coll. D'Attilio
12	*M. cabritii* Bernardi	Off Florida Keys	Coll. I. & H. Thompson
13	*M. tweedianus* Macpherson	Tin Can Bay, Queensland, Australia	Coll. D'Attilio
14	*M. trapa* Röding	Taiwan	SDSNH 11074

PLATE 11

Figure	Species	Locality	Repository
1	*Murex coppingeri* E. A. Smith	Off Darwin, N. Australia	Coll. D'Attilio
2	*M. brevispinus* Lamarck	Zanzibar, East Africa	Coll. D'Attilio
3	*M. rectirostris* Sowerby	"China" *ex* Constable Coll.	AMNH 47199
4	*M. longicornis* Dunker	Off Cape Moreton, Queensland, Australia	Coll. D'Attilio
5	*M. cervicornis* Lamarck	Northeastern Australia	Coll. D'Attilio
6	*M. anniae* M. Smith	Sombrero Key Light, Florida Keys	Coll. D'Attilio
7	*M. messorius* Sowerby	*Ex* Calvert Coll. (no data)	Coll. D'Attilio
8	*Bolinus brandaris* (Linné)	*Ex* Calvert Coll. (no data)	Coll. D'Attilio
9	*B. cornutus* (Linné)	Luanda, Angola	Coll. Purdy
10	*Haustellum haustellum* (Linné)	Subic Bay, Philippines	Coll. Bibbey
11	*Murex recurvirostris* Broderip	Pacific coast of southern Baja Calif.	SDSNH 51685
12	*M. hirasei* "Dautzenberg" Hirase	Kii Channel, southeastern Japan	Coll. D'Attilio
13	*M. elenensis* Dall	Off Guaymas, Mexico	Coll. D'Attilio
14	*M. kiiensis* Kira	Subic Bay, Philippines	Coll. Bibbey
15	*M. rubidus* (F. C. Baker)	Sanibel I., Florida	Coll. D'Attilio
16	*M. multiplicatus* Sowerby	Broome, W. Australia	Coll. D'Attilio

PLATE 12

Figure	Species	Locality	Repository
1	*Muricanthus radix* (Gmelin)	(No data)	Coll. Purdy
2	*M. radix* (Gmelin)	"Gulf of California"	Coll. Purdy
3	*M. fulvescens* Sowerby	Off mouth of St. John's River, northeastern Florida	SDSNH 39655
4	*M. angularis* (Lamarck)	*Ex* Calvert Coll. (no data)	Coll. D'Attilio
5	*M. varius* (Sowerby)	"Atlantide" Sta. 101, Bight of Benin, West Africa	AMNH 118199

Figure	Species	Locality	Repository
6	*M. varius* (Sowerby)	*Ex* Calvert Coll. (no data)	Coll. D'Attilio
7	*M. kusterianus* (Tapparone-Canefri)	Gulf of Oman, Indian Ocean	Coll. D'Attilio
8	*M. megacerus* (Sowerby)	*Ex* Calvert Coll. (no data)	Coll. D'Attilio
9	*M. radix* (Gmelin)	"Panamá"	Coll. Purdy
10	*M. princeps* (Broderip)	Manzanillo, Colima, Mexico	Coll. Martin

PLATE 13

1	*Murex elenensis* Dall	Off Los Frailes, Baja Calif.	Coll. J. Bailey
2	*Murex rectirostris* Sowerby	Kii Channel, southeastern Japan	Coll. D'Attilio
3	*Muricanthus angularis* (Lamarck)	(No data)	Coll. D'Attilio
4	*Murexiella bojadorensis* (Locard)	Somune, Senegal, West Africa	Coll. P. Clover
5	*Murex kiiensis* Kira	Kii Channel, southeastern Japan	Coll. D'Attilio
6	*Nipponotrophon lasius* (Dall)	San Juan I., Puget Sound, Wash.	SDSNH 22941
7	*N. lasius* (Dall)	Port Simpson, Br. Columbia	SDSNH 22938
8	*N. lasius* (Dall)	San Juan I., Puget Sound, Wash.	SDSNH 22941

PLATE 14

1	*Acanthotrophon carduus* (Broderip)	N. Jervis I., Galápagos I.	Coll. Shasky
2	?*Ocenebra hamata* (Hinds)	Off Peru	Inst. Del Mar, Peru
3	*Favartia tetragona* (Broderip)	Wading I., Fiji Is.	Coll. D'Attilio
4	*Ergalatax tokugawai* Kuroda & Habe	Enshu-Nada, Honshu, Japan	NSMT 42227
5	?*Murexsul auratus* Kuroda & Habe	Sagami Bay, Japan	Holotype, Biol. Lab. Imperial Household
6	*Favartia planilirata* (Reeve)	Cockburn Sound, south of Fremantle, W. Australia	Coll. D'Attilio
7	*Nipponotrophon pagodus* (Hayashi & Habe)	Enshu-Nada, Honshu, Japan	NSMT 38587
8	*Murex olssoni* E. H. Vokes	Agua Largana, Hollandes Cay, Is. San Blas, Panamá	SIO Invert. Coll. M. 656
9	*Bedeva paivae* (Crosse)	S. Australia	SDSNH 24016
10	*Nipponotrophon scitulus* (Dall)	Bowers Bank, Bering Sea	CAS 36923
11	*N. scitulus* (Dall)	"West Coast" [of the U.S.]	SDSNH 14318
12	*Favartia kurodai* Nakamigawa & Habe	Minato, Izu Peninsula, Honshu, Japan	NSMT 37264

PLATE 15

1	*Pterochelus acanthopterus* (Lamarck)	Broome, W. Australia	Coll. D'Attilio
2	*Pterochelus acanthopterus* (Lamarck)	Broome, W. Australia	Coll. D'Attilio
3	*Pterochelus acanthopterus* (Lamarck)	Cape Preston, W. Australia	Coll. D'Attilio
4	*Prototyphis angasi* (Crosse)	Sydney Hbr., New South Wales, Australia	Coll. D'Attilio
5	*Pterochelus duffusi* Iredale	Cape Moreton, Queensland, Australia	Coll. D'Attilio
6	*Pterochelus triformis* (Reeve)	Port Philip Bay, Victoria, S. Australia	SDSNH 24297
7	*Pterochelus triformis* (Reeve)	Albany, southwestern Australia	Coll. D'Attilio
8	*Naquetia barclayi* (Reeve)	Taiwan	Coll. Bibbey
9	*N. annandalei* (Preston)	Gulf of Akaba, Israel	Coll. D'Attilio
10	*N. annandalei* (Preston)	Gulf of Akaba, Israel	Coll. D'Attilio
11	*N. triquetra* (Born)	Zanzibar, East Africa	Coll. D'Attilio
12	*N. trigonula* (Lamarck)	Sulu Sea, Philippines	Coll. D'Attilio
13	*N. capucina* (Lamarck)	Sulu Sea, Zamboanga, Philippines	Coll. D'Attilio

SUPPLEMENTARY DATA ON FIGURES

Figure	Species	Locality	Repository
PLATE 16			
1	*Phyllonotus duplex* (Röding)	"West Africa"	SDSNH 18891
2	*P. regius* (Swainson)	Palo Seco, Canal Zone	SDSNH 46272
3	*P. peratus* Keen	Off Salina Cruz, Oaxaca, Mexico	Coll. Shasky
4	*P. erythrostomus* (Swainson)	Santa Inez, Baja Calif.	SDSNH 51186
5	*P. brassica* (Lamarck)	Mazatlán, Mexico	SDSNH 23010
6	*P. margaritensis* (Abbott)	Porlomar, Venezuela	SDSNH 9716
7	*P. duplex* (Röding)	*Ex* Calvert Coll. (no data)	Coll. D'Attilio
8	*P. pomum* (Gmelin)	Bahamas	SDSNH 38835
PLATE 17			
1	*Siratus senegalensis* (Gmelin)	Off mouth of Amazon River, Brazil	Paratype (of *S. springeri* Bullis), AMNH 111200
2	*S. articulatus* (Reeve)	(No data)	Coll. D'Attilio
3	*S. articulatus* (Reeve)	Port-au-Prince Bay, Haiti	Coll. D'Attilio
4	*S. cailleti* (Petit de la Saussaye)	Off Priory, Jamaica, B.W.I.	Coll. D'Attilio
5	*S. cailleti* (Petit de la Saussaye)	"West Indies"	SDSNH 23983
6	*S. cailleti* (Petit de la Saussaye)	Barbados, B.W.I.	Coll. D'Attilio
7	*S. senegalensis* (Gmelin)	Bahía Guanabara, Rio de Janeiro, Brazil	Coll. D'Attilio
8	*S. beauii* (Fischer & Bernardi)	Gulf of Mexico, off mouth of Mississippi River	Coll. Richmond
9	*S. formosus* (Sowerby)	Off Pta. Maisi, Oriente, Cuba	Coll. D'Attilio
10	*S. alabaster* (Reeve)	Taiwan Channel, Taichung, Taiwan	Coll. Richmond
11	*S. perelegans* (E. H. Vokes)	Off Bridgetown, Barbados, B.W.I.	Coll. Richmond
12	*S. ciboney* (Clench & Pérez Farfante)	Jamaica, B.W.I.	Coll. D'Attilio
13	*S. consuela* (A. H. Verrill)	Dominica, B.W.I.	Coll. D'Attilio
14	*S. motacilla* (Gmelin)	Dominica, B.W.I.	Coll. D'Attilio
15	?*S. virgineus* (Röding)	(No data)	Coll. D'Attilio
16	*S. tenuivaricosus* (Dautzenberg)	Litoral fluminense, Brazil	Coll. D'Attilio
17	*S. pliciferoides* (Kuroda)	Enoshima, Honshu, Japan	SDSNH 2492
PLATE 18			
1	*Ceratostoma foliatum* (Gmelin)	Puget Sound, Washington	SDSNH 50929
2	*C. foliatum* (Gmelin)	San Pedro, Calif.	SDSNH 22989
3	*Ocenebra erinaceoides* (Valenciennes)	Guaymas, Mexico	Coll. D'Attilio
4	*O. erinacea* (Linné)	(No data)	Coll. D'Attilio
5	*O. erinacea* (Linné)	Melilla, Spanish Morocco	Coll. D'Attilio
6	*Ceratostoma burnetti* (Adams & Reeve)	Wando I., South Korea	Coll. Martin
7	*C. burnetti* (Adams & Reeve)	Rikuzen, Honshu, Japan	SDSNH 24133
8	*C. fournieri* (Crosse)	Tokyo Bay, Japan	Coll. Ames
9	*Ocenebra vokesae* (Emerson)	San Pedro, Calif.	SDSNH 23028
10	*Ceratostoma inornatum* (Récluz)	(No data)	SDSNH 55706
11	*C. inornatum* (Récluz)	Puget Sound, Washington (introduced)	SDSNH 44428
12	*C. inornatum* (Récluz)	Matsushima, Honshu, Japan	SDSNH 47692
13	*C. rorifluum* (Adams & Reeve)	Hirado, Kyushu, Japan	SDSNH 24284
14	*C. nuttalli* (Conrad)	Baja Calif.	SDSNH 22979
15	*C. nuttalli* (Conrad)	Off San Pedro, Calif.	SDSNH 22985

Figure	Species	Locality	Repository
PLATE 19			
1	*Eupleura triquetra* (Reeve)	La Paz, Baja Calif.	SDSNH 23194
2	*Eupleura sulcidentata* (Dall)	Lake Worth, Florida	SDSNH 12594
3	*Eupleura caudata* (Say)	Falmouth, Massachusetts	SDSNH 50068
4	*Eupleura caudata* (Say)	Beaufort, North Carolina	SDSNH 15626
5	*Eupleura muriciformis* (Broderip)	Guaymas, Mexico	SDSNH 51738
6	*Eupleura nitida* (Hinds)	Palo Seco, Canal Zone	SDSNH 52564
7	*Eupleura pectinata* (Hinds)	*Ex* Calvert Coll. (no data)	Coll. D'Attilio
8	*Roperia poulsoni* (Carpenter)	San Diego, Calif.	SDSNH 22918
9	*R. poulsoni* (Carpenter)	San Diego, Calif.	SDSNH 42372
10	*Lataxiena fimbriata* (Hinds)	Kii Channel, southeastern Japan	Coll. D'Attilio
11	*L. fimbriata* (Hinds)	Near Dawson Reef, Cooktown, Queensland, Australia	Coll. D'Attilio
12	*Acanthotrophon carduus* (Broderip)	Mazatlán, Mexico	SDSNH 22904
13	*Ergalatax contracta* (Reeve)	Kii Channel, southeastern Japan	Coll. D'Attilio
14	*Maxwellia angermeyerae* (Emerson & D'Attilio)	Academy Bay, Santa Cruz I., Galápagos Is.	Coll. D'Attilio
15	?*M. santarosana* (Dall)	Catalina I., Calif.	SDSNH 40001
16	?*M. santarosana* (Dall)	Off Newport Beach, Calif.	Coll. D'Attilio
17	*M. gemma* (Sowerby)	San Diego, Calif.	SDSNH 51245
18	*Ergalatax contracta* (Reeve)	Japan Sea, Japan	Coll. D'Attilio
PLATE 20			
1	*Ocenebra inermicosta* (E. H. Vokes)	Cape St. Mary, Gambia, West Africa	Coll. D'Attilio
2	*O. grippi* (Dall)	Off Pt. Conception, Calif.	Coll. Richmond
3	*O. circumtexta* (Stearns)	Off Pismo Beach, Calif.	SDSNH 23320
4	*O. lurida* (Middendorff)	Off Monterey, Calif.	SDSNH 23351
5	*O. lurida* (Middendorff)	Off Br. Columbia	SDSNH 22353
6	*O. interfossa* Carpenter	Brandon I., Br. Columbia	SDSNH 23363
7	*O. seftoni* Chace	Off Is. Guadalupe, Mexico	Holotype, SDSNH 12995
8	?*O. painei* (Dall)	Off Catalina I., Calif.	SDSNH 23363
9	*O. foveolata* (Hinds)	Off Catalina I., Calif.	SDSNH 23317
10	*O. gracillima* (Stearns)	La Jolla, Calif.	SDSNH 15662
11	*O. interfossa* Carpenter	San Diego, Calif.	SDSNH 6739
12	*O. interfossa* Carpenter	San Pedro, Calif.	SDSNH 23345
13	*O. interfossa* Carpenter	Cayucos, Calif.	SDSNH 23344
14	*O. foveolata* (Hinds)	San Clemente I., Calif.	Coll. D'Attilio
15	*O. foveolata* (Hinds)	San Pedro, Calif.	SDSNH 23334
16	*O. foveolata* (Hinds)	La Jolla, Calif.	SDSNH 23333
17	*O. foveolata* (Hinds)	San Pedro, Calif.	SDSNH 23334
PLATE 21			
1	?*Urosalpinx purpuroides* (Reeve)	Table Bay, South Africa	Coll. D'Attilio
2	?*U. scrobiculata* (Philippi)	East London, South Africa	Coll. D'Attilio
3	*U. cala* (Pilsbry)	La Paloma, Rocha, Uruguay	Coll. D'Attilio
4	*U. cinerea* (Say)	Cape Cod, Massachusetts	SDSNH 43420
5	*U. cinerea* (Say)	Wachapreague, Virginia	SDSNH 14536
6	*U. haneti* (Petit de la Saussaye)	Guanabára Bay, Brazil	SDSNH 54630
7	*Ocinebrina edwardsi* (Payraudeau)	Valencia, Spain	SDSNH 24055
8	*O. aciculata* (Lamarck)	England	SDSNH 17936
9	?*O. emipowlusi* (Abbott)	Eastern Gulf of Mexico	SDSNH 50968

Figure	Species	Locality	Repository
10	*O. hybrida* (Aradas & Benoit)	Sicily	SDSNH 24071
11	?*Urosalpinx puncturata* (Sowerby)	False Bay, South Africa	Coll. D'Attilio
12	*U. tampaensis* (Conrad)	Wall Springs, Florida	SDSNH 24150
13	?*U. subangulata* (Stearns)	Pt. Cayucos, Calif.	SDSNH 2821
14	*U. perrugata* (Conrad)	Pta. Gorda Beach, Florida	SDSNH 16200

PLATE 22

1	*Pteropurpura bequaerti* (Clench & Pérez Farfante)	Off Egmont Key, Florida	Coll. D'Attilio
2	*Poropteron uncinarius* (Lamarck)	Natal, South Africa	SDSNH 24153
3	*Poropteron incurvispina* (Kilburn)	East London, South Africa	Coll. D'Attilio
4	*Pteropurpura modesta* (Fulton)	Tosa Bay, southeastern Japan	Coll. D'Attilio
5	*Pteropurpura esycha* (Dall)	Tosa Bay, southeastern Japan	Coll. D'Attilio
6	*Pteropurpura trialata* (Sowerby)	Off San Pedro, Calif.	SDSNH 23029
7	*Pteropurpura leeana* (Dall)	East of I. Cedros, Baja Calif.	Coll. D'Attilio
8	*Pteropurpura plorator* (Adams & Reeve)	Kii Channel, southeastern Japan	Coll. D'Attilio
9	*Pteropurpura festiva* (Hinds)	San Diego Bay, Calif.	SDSNH 53916
10	*Pteropurpura adunca* (Sowerby)	Tokyo Bay, Japan	SDSNH 47942
11	*Pteropurpura centrifuga* (Hinds)	Fishermen docking at Guaymas, Mexico	SDSNH 9826
12	*Jaton decussatus* (Gmelin)	Baie de Gorée, Senegal	Coll. D'Attilio
13	*Pteropurpura macroptera* (Deshayes)	Off San Pedro, Calif.	SDSNH 23026

PLATE 23

1	*Bizetiella shaskyi* Radwin & D'Attilio	I. Maria Madre, Is. Tres Marias, Mexico	Holotype, SDSNH 56119
2	*Murexsul kieneri* (Reeve)	East London, South Africa	Coll. D'Attilio
3	*Pazinotus stimpsonii* (Dall)	Off Palm Beach, Florida	Coll. D'Attilio
4	*Evokesia grayi* (Dall)	Off Barbados, B.W.I.	Syntype, USNM 94778
5	*Calotrophon velero* (E. H. Vokes)	Off Guajira Peninsula, Venezuela	Paratype, SDSNH 61579
6	*Bizetiella micaela* Radwin & D'Attilio	Bahía Coastocomate, Jalisco, Mexico	Holotype, SDSNH 56118
7	*B. carmen* (Lowe)	Off I. Angel de la Guarda, Gulf of Calif., Mexico	Paratype, SDSNH 44717
8	*Ceratostoma lugubre* (Broderip)	Bayovar, Peru	CAS 36658
9	*Ceratostoma lugubre* (Broderip)	Bayovar, Peru	CAS 36660
10	*Chicoreus benedictinus* Löbbecke	Eilat, Gulf of Aqaba, Israel	Coll. D'Attilio
11	*Favartia brevicula* (Sowerby)	Ata'a, Malaita, Br. Solomon Is.	Coll. D'Attilio
12	*Muricopsis nicocheanus* (Pilsbry)	Nicochea, Argentina	Coll. D'Attilio
13	*Pteropurpura macroptera* (Deshayes)	Off La Jolla, Calif.	Coll. Mulliner
14	*Muricopsis blainvillei* (Payraudeau)	*Ex* Calvert Coll. (no data)	Coll. D'Attilio
15	*Haustellum wilsoni* D'Attilio & Old	Jurien Bay, W. Australia	Paratype, AMNH 154655

PLATE 24

1	*Favartia brevicula* (Sowerby)	Kii Channel, southeastern Japan	Coll. D'Attilio
2	*F. brevicula* (Sowerby)	Ata'a, Malaita, Br. Solomon Is.	Coll. D'Attilio
3	*F. minatauros*, new name	*Ex* Calvert Coll. (no data)	Coll. D'Attilio
4	*F. cellulosa* (Conrad)	Off Carrabelle, Franklin Co., Florida	SDSNH 51701
5	*F. cellulosa* (Conrad)	Off Gulfport, Florida	SDSNH 23985
6	*F. cellulosa* (Conrad)	San Juan, Puerto Rico	Coll. D'Attilio
7	*F. emersoni*, new name	Luanda Hbr., Angola	Coll. D'Attilio

SUPPLEMENTARY DATA ON FIGURES 263

Figure	Species	Locality	Repository
8	*F. incisa* (Broderip)	Balboa, Canal Zone	Coll. D'Attilio
9	*F. poormani* sp. nov.	Bahía San Carlos, Sonora, Mexico	Coll. Poorman
10	*F. garretti* (Pease)	Hilo, Hawaii	SDSNH 3461
11	*F. cyclostoma* (Sowerby)	Zanzibar, East Africa	Coll. D'Attilio
12	*F. rosea* Habe	Kii Channel, southeastern Japan	Coll. Richmond
13	*Muricopsis brazieri* (Angas)	Coff's Hbr., New South Wales, Australia	Coll. D'Attilio
14	*Favartia munda* (Reeve)	Kii Channel, southeastern Japan	Coll. D'Attilio
15	*F. salmonea* (Melvill & Standen)	Zanzibar, East Africa	Coll. D'Attilio
16	*F. alveata* (Kiener)	Natal Bay, Brazil	SDSNH 52012
17	?*F. crossei* (Liénard)	*Ex* Calvert Coll. (no data)	Coll. D'Attilio
18	?*F. crossei* (Liénard)	*Ex* Calvert Coll. (no data)	Coll. D'Attilio
19	*F. balteata* (Sowerby)	New Guinea	Coll. D'Attilio
20	*F. erosa* (Broderip)	Mazatlán, Mexico	SDSNH 23327
21	*F. erosa* (Broderip)	San Juan del Sur, Nicaragua	SDSNH 51618

PLATE 25

1	*Murexiella diomedaea* (Dall)	Off Pta. Gorda, Baja Calif.	AHF-LACM 1729-49
2	?*Murexsul tokubeii* Nakamigawa & Habe	Off Tosa Bay, southeastern Japan	Coll. D'Attilio
3	*Murexiella humilis* (Broderip)	Off White Friars, Mexico	AHF-LACM 264-34
4	*Murexiella humilis* (Broderip)	Off Guaymas, Mexico	Coll. Ames
5	*Murexiella humilis* (Broderip)	Cameron, Vera Cruz, Panamá	Coll. D'Attilio
6	?*Murexsul multispinosus* (Sowerby)	Off Kii Channel, southeastern Japan	Coll. D'Attilio
7	"*Murex*" *pleurotomoides* Reeve	Off Onslow Bay, W. Australia	WAM 3391-67
8	*Murexiella hidalgoi* (Crosse)	West of Ft. Myers, Florida	Coll. Richmond
9	*Murexiella radwini* Emerson & D'Attilio	Tagus Cove, Isabella I., Galápagos Is.	Holotype, AMNH 155903
10	*Murexiella macgintyi* (M. Smith)	West of Tampa, Florida	SDSNH 48506
11	*Murexiella macgintyi* (M. Smith)	La Belle, Lake Okeechobee, Florida (Pleistocene fossil)	Coll. D'Attilio
12	*Paziella hystricina* (Dall)	Northwest of Puerto Rico	USNM 430708
13	*Murexiella cirrosa* (Hinds)	(No data)	Coll. D'Attilio

PLATE 26

1	*Paziella pazi* (Crosse)	Southwest of Key West, Florida	Coll. Richmond
2	*Paziella pazi* (Crosse)	Off Surinam (Dutch Guiana)	Paratype (of *P. oregonia* Bullis), AMNH 111202
3	*Paziella pazi* (Crosse)	Off Sarasota, Florida	Coll. Richmond
4	*Murexiella vittata* (Broderip)	I. Venado, Canal Zone	Coll. Purdy
5	*Murexiella lappa* (Broderip)	I. Taboga, Panamá	Coll. Shasky
6	*Murexsul octogonus* (Quoy & Gaimard)	Hauraki Gulf, New Zealand	Coll. D'Attilio
7	*Murexsul octogonus* (Quoy & Gaimard)	"New Zealand"	Coll. D'Attilio
8	*Murexiella perita* (Hinds)	Gulf of Tehuántepec, Central America	Coll. Shasky
9	*Poirieria zelandica* (Quoy & Gaimard)	Hauraki Gulf, New Zealand	Coll. D'Attilio
10	*Murexiella levicula* (Dall)	West of Sanibel I., Florida	Coll. D'Attilio
11	*Murexiella jacquelinae* (Emerson & D'Attilio)	Off Jarvis I., Galápagos Is.	Paratype, Coll. D'Attilio
12	*Murexiella jacquelinae* (Emerson & D'Attilio)	North of Barrington I., Galápagos Is.	Coll. Richmond

Figure	Species	Locality	Repository
13	*Purpurellus macleani* (Emerson & D'Attilio)	Loreto Channel, Baja Calif.	Holotype, LACM 1230
14	*Purpurellus pinniger* (Broderip)	Fishermen docking at Guaymas, Mexico	Coll. Purdy
15	*Purpurellus gambiensis* (Reeve)	Senegal, West Africa	Coll. D'Attilio

PLATE 27

1	*Muricopsis armatus* (A. Adams)	La Paz, Baja Calif.	SDSNH 11691
2	*Marchia nodulifera* (Sowerby)	Coron I., Calaman Group, Philippines	Coll. Ames
3	*Muricopsis armatus* (A. Adams)	Bahía de Los Angeles, Baja Calif.	SDSNH 54426
4	*Muricopsis jaliscoensis* Radwin & D'Attilio	Bahía Coastocomate, Jalisco, Mexico	Holotype, SDSNH 51251
5	*Muricopsis oxytatus* (M. Smith)	Guantánamo Bay, Cuba	Coll. D'Attilio
6	*Muricopsis bombayanus* (Melvill)	Bombay Hbr., Bombay, India	Coll. Richmond
7	*Muricopsis pauxillus* (A. Adams)	Tamarindo Cove, Bahía Tenacatita, Jalisco, Mexico	SDSNH 51592
8	*Muricopsis pauxillus* (A. Adams)	Tamarindo Cove, Bahía Tenacatita, Jalisco, Mexico	SDSNH 51592
9	*Muricopsis cuspidatus* (Sowerby)	New Caledonia	Coll. D'Attilio
10	*Muricopsis cristatus* (Brocchi)	Gulf of Salerno, Italy	Coll. Richmond
11	*Muricopsis angolensis* (Odhner)	Pt. Formosa, Fernando Poo I., West Africa	Coll. D'Attilio
12	*Muricopsis zeteki* Hertlein & Strong	Bahía Coastocomate, Jalisco; Mexico	SDSNH 50821
13	*Muricopsis zeteki* Hertlein & Strong	*Ex* Calvert Coll. (no data)	Coll. D'Attilio
14	*Muricopsis zeteki* Hertlein & Strong	San Felipe, Baja Calif.	SDSNH 20486
15	*Muricopsis blainvillei* (Payraudeau)	Catania, Sicily	Coll. D'Attilio

PLATE 28

1	*Aspella castor* sp. nov.	Puerto Rico	USNM 663525
2	*Tripterotyphis norfolkensis* (C. A. Fleming)	Ata'a, Malaita, Br. Solomon Is.	ANSP 301974
3	*Aspella platylaevis* sp. nov.	Woodman's Point, Cockburn Sound, W. Australia	Holotype, ANSP 285147
4	*Aspella mauritiana* sp. nov.	Flic en Flac, western Mauritius	Holotype, ANSP 273236
5	*Attiliosa aldridgei* (Nowell-Usticke)	Rat I., Antigua, B.W.I.	Paratype, AMNH 168901
6	*Attiliosa ponderi* sp. nov.	Broome, W. Australia	Holotype, ANSP 233056
7	*Murexsul zonatus* Hayashi & Habe	Enshu-Nada, off Honshu, Japan	NSMT 38585
8	*Pagodula vaginata* (Cristofori & Jan)	Off Elba I., near Naples, Italy	Coll. Richmond
9	*Boreotrophon clathratus* (Linné)	Greenland	SDSNH 10923
10	*Trophon geversianus* (Pallas)	Falkland Is., South Atlantic	SDSNH 24020
11	*Trophon geversianus* (Pallas)	Falkland Is., South Atlantic	SDSNH 24020
12	*Nodulotrophon dalli* (Kobelt)	North of Unimak I., Bering Sea	NSMT 38655

PLATE 29

1	*Typhisala grandis* (A. Adams)	I. Venado, Canal Zone	Coll. A. Marti
2	*Trophon geversianus* (Pallas)	Off Argentina	SDSNH 63052
3	*Xenotrophon euschema* (Iredale)	Cape Moreton, Australia	Coll. Richmond
4	*Hadriania craticuloides* (E. H. Vokes)	Valencia, Spain	SDSNH 9518
5	?*Subpterynotus tatei* (Verco)	Smoky Bay, S. Australia	Coll. E. Wright

Figure	Species	Locality	Repository
6	*Favartia peasei* (Tryon)	(No data)	Holotype (of *Murex foveolatus*), ANSP 36144
7	*F. peasei* (Tryon)	Ata'a, Malaita, Br. Solomon Is.	Coll. D'Attilio
8	?*Typhina nitens* (Hinds)	Amami-Oshima, south of Kyushu, Japan	SDSNH 62590
9	*Zeatrophon ambiguus* (Philippi)	Waupii, New Zealand	SDSNH 37869
10	*Z. ambiguus* (Philippi)	Off Mt. Maunganui, Bay of Plenty, New Zealand	SDSNH 24029
11	*Tripterotyphis robustus* (Verco)	Smoky Bay, S. Australia	Coll. J. Phillips
12	*Gemixystus laminatus* (Petterd)	Off Cape Kembla, New South Wales, Australia	SDSNH 57047
13	*Anatrophon sarmentosus* (Hedley & May)	Off Cape Pillar, S. Australia	Paratype, SDSNH 57046
14	*Xymene plebeius* (Hutton)	Beachlands Beach, Hauraki Gulf, New Zealand	Coll. Richmond
15	"*Murex*" *alfredensis* Bartsch	Port Alfred, South Africa	Holotype, USNM 227763
16	*Favartia minirosea* (Abbott)	Southwest of Egmont Key, Gulf of Mexico	SDSNH 61673

PLATE 30

1	*Pterotyphis fimbriatus* (A. Adams)	Bahía Coastocomate, Jalisco, Mexico	LACM 68-41
2	*P. pinnatus* (Broderip)	Nassau, Bahamas	Paratype (of *P. fordi*), ANSP 179712
3	*Cinclidotyphis myrae* DuShane	Sayulita, Nayarit, Mexico	LACM 70-4
4	*C. myrae* DuShane	Bahía de Los Angeles, Jalisco, Mexico	Coll. C. Skoglund
5	*Tripterotyphis lowei* (Pilsbry)	Is. Tres Marias, Mexico	Paratype, SDSNH 23178
6	*Tripterotyphis lowei* (Pilsbry)	Academy Bay, Santa Cruz I., Galápagos Is.	Coll. Shasky
7	*Tripterotyphis triangularis* (A. Adams)	South Bimini I., Bahamas	Coll. Pisor
8	*Tripterotyphis arcana* (DuShane)	La Cruz, Nayarit, Mexico	Coll. Skoglund
9	*Tripterotyphis arcana* (DuShane)	Marmol, Sinaloa, Mexico	Coll. Hanselman
10	*Tripterotyphis fayae* (Keen & Campbell)	Bahía Coastocomate, Jalisco, Mexico	Coll. Shasky
11	*Tripterotyphis fayae* (Keen & Campbell)	El Pulmo Reef, Baja Calif.	Coll. Shasky
12	*Laevityphis bullisi* (Gertman)	Off Surinam	Coll. Richmond (LACM)
13	*Talityphis latipennis* (Dall)	Bahía de la Paz, Baja Calif.	SIO Invert. Coll. M. 313
14	*Talityphis latipennis* (Dall)	Off Pta. Penasco, Sonora, Mexico	Coll. Michel
15	*Talityphis perchardei* sp. nov.	Gulf of Paria, Trinidad	Coll. D'Attilio

PLATE 31

1	*Typhina yatesi* (Crosse & Fischer)	St. Vincent Gulf, S. Australia	Coll. S. S. Berry
2	*Monstrotyphis tosaensis* (Azuma)	Cape Ashizuri, Kochi Pref., Shikoku, Japan	NSMT 42226
3	*Talityphis expansus* (Sowerby)	Pta. Cadena, north of Mayaguez, Puerto Rico	Holotype (of *T. puertoricensis*), SUPTC 9722
4	*Haustellotyphis cumingii* (Broderip)	Puerto Madero, Chiapas, Mexico	Coll. D'Attilio
5	*Typhisala clarki* (Keen & Campbell)	Pta. San Felipe, Baja Calif.	SDSNH 53452
6	*Trubatsa pavlova* (Iredale)	Cape Moreton, Queensland, Australia	Coll. D'Attilio
7	*Typhinellus sowerbii* (Broderip)	Cape Verde, West Africa	Coll. D'Attilio

Figure	Species	Locality	Repository
8	*Trubatsa erythrostigma* (Keen & Campbell)	Moreton Bay, Queensland, Australia	Holotype, SUPTC 9732
9	*Trubatsa longicornis* (Dall)	Off Havana, Cuba	Holotype, USNM 94780
10	*Distichotyphis vemae* Keen & Campbell	Off Panamá and Costa Rica	AMNH 110459

PLATE 32

Figure	Species	Locality	Repository
1	*Siphonochelus japonicus* (A. Adams)	Sagami Bay, Japan	AMNH 123508
2	*S. syringianus* (Hedley)	Tasmania, Australia	SDSNH 24083
3	*Typhinellus occlusus* (Garrard)	Off Langford I., Queensland, Australia	Coll. Richmond (LACM)
4	*Typhina ramosa* (Habe & Kosuge)	South China Sea	Paratype, NSMT 39016
5	*Typhina montforti* (A. Adams)	Gorombane, Sagami Bay, Japan	NSMT 42228
6	*Typhina cleryi* (Petit de la Saussaye)	Off Rio de Janeiro, Brazil	Coll. D'Attilio
7	*Typhina philippensis* (Watson)	Cape Moreton, Queensland, Australia	Coll. D'Attilio
8	*Typhina imperialis* (Keen & Campbell)	Tosa, Shikoku, Japan	Paratype, SUPTC 9727
9	*Siphonochelus nipponensis* Keen & Campbell	Tosa, Shikoku, Japan	SUPTC 9730
10	*Typhisopsis coronatus* (Broderip)	Fishermen docking at Guaymas, Mexico	Coll. Purdy
11	*Typhisopsis coronatus* (Broderip)	Bahía de Los Angeles, Baja Calif.	SDSNH 23214
12	*Typhisopsis coronatus* (Broderip)	Fishermen docking at Guaymas, Mexico	Coll. Purdy

Literature Cited

Abbott, R. T. 1954a. New Gulf of Mexico gastropods (*Terebra* and *Ocenebra*). Nautilus 68(1): 37–44, pl. 2.
— 1954b. American seashells. Van Nostrand, New York, xiv + 541 pp., 40 pls.
— 1958. The marine mollusks of Grand Cayman Island, B.W.I. Acad. Nat. Sci., Phila., monogr. 11, 138 pp., pls. 1–5.

Adams, A. 1850. Descriptions of new species of shells from the Cumingian collection. Proc. Zool. Soc. London (1849) 17: 169–70.
— 1853. Descriptions of several new species of *Murex, Rissoina, Planaxis* & *Eulima* from the Cumingian collection. Proc. Zool. Soc. London (1851) 19: 267–72.
— 1854. Descriptions of new shells from the collection of H. Cuming Esq. Proc. Zool. Soc. London (1853) 21: 69–74.
— 1855a. Description of a new genus and of several new species of gasteropodous Mollusca, from the Cumingian collection. Proc. Zool. Soc. London (1854) 22: 41–42.
— 1855b. Descriptions of two new genera and several new species of Mollusca from the collection of H. Cuming, Esq. Proc. Zool. Soc. London (1855) 23: 119–24.
— 1863. On the species of Muricinae found in Japan. Proc. Zool. Soc. London (1863) 31: 370–76.
— 1864. Description of a new genus and of twelve new species of Mollusca. Proc. Zool. Soc. London (1864) 34: 506–9.

Adams, A., and L. A. Reeve. 1848–50. Mollusca. *In* A. Adams, ed., The zoology of the voyage of "H.M.S. Samarang...," Reeve, Benham and Reeve, London, x + 87 pp., pls. 1–24.
— 1849. *In* L. A. Reeve, Conchologia iconica. London, Reeve, vol. 3, *Murex*, suppl. pl. 1.

Adams, C. B. 1845. Specierum novarum conchyliorum Jamaica repertorum synopsis. Proc. Boston Soc. Nat. Hist. 2: 3–17.
— 1850. Descriptions of supposed new species of marine shells which inhabit Jamaica. Contributions to Conchology 1(4): 56–68; 1(5): 69–75.
— 1852. Catalogue of shells collected at Panamá, with notes on their synonymy, station, and geographical distribution. Ann. Lyc. Nat. Hist. N.Y. 5: 229–527.

Adams, H. 1873. Descriptions of seventeen new species of land and marine shells. Proc. Zool. Soc. London (1873) 41: 205–9, pl. 33.

Adams, H., and A. Adams. 1853. The genera of Recent Mollusca. Van Voorst, London, vol. 1, xl + 484 pp.

Adanson, M. 1757. Histoire naturelle du Sénégal. Paris, 269 pp. + 6 pp. index, 1 map, pls. 1–19.

Anderson, D. T. 1966. Further observations on the life histories of littoral gastropods in New South Wales. Proc. Linn. Soc. New South Wales 90: 242–51.

Angas, G. F. 1867. Descriptions of thirty-two new species of marine shells from the coast of New South Wales. Proc. Zool. Soc. London (1867) 35: 110–17, pl. 13.
— 1878. Descriptions of one genus and twenty-five species of marine shells from New South Wales. Proc. Zool. Soc. London (1877) 45: 171–77, pl. 26.

Aradas, A., and L. Benoit. 1870. Conchigliologia vivente marina della Sicilia e della isole che la circondano. Atti Accad. Gioenia Sci. Nat. Ser. III 6: 1–324, pls. 1–5.

Arakawa, K. Y. 1958. On the remarkable sexual dimorphism of the radula of *Drupella*. Venus 19: 206–14.
— 1964. A study on the radulae of the Japanese Muricidae (2), The genera *Vexilla, Nassa, Rapana, Murex, Chicoreus* and *Homalocantha*. Venus 22(4): 355–64.

Azuma, M. 1960. A catalogue of the shell-bearing Mollusca of Okinoshima, Kashiwajima and the adjacent area (Tosa Province), Shikoku, Japan. Osaka, 102 pp., pls. 1–5, 17 pp. index.
— 1961. Descriptions of six new species of Japanese marine Gastropoda. Venus 21(3): 296–303, 1 pl.
— 1973. On the radulae of some remarkable gastropods from off Kirimezaki, Kii Peninsula, Japan, with the description of a new cone shell. Venus 32(1): 9–16, pl. 1.

Baily, J. L., Jr. 1950. *Maxwellia*, genus novum of Muricidae. Nautilus 64(1): 9–14.

Baird, W. 1863. Descriptions of new species of shells collected at Vancouver Island and in British Columbia by J. K. Lord Esq., Naturalist to the

British North American Boundary Commission, in the years 1858–1862. Proc. Zool. Soc. London (1863) 31: 66–70.

Baker, B. B. 1951. Interesting shells from the Delmarva Peninsula. Nautilus 64(3): 73–77.

Baker, F. C. 1889. Description of a new species of *Ocinebra*. Nautilus 3(7): 80–81.

—— 1890. On the modification of the apex in *Murex*. Proc. Acad. Nat. Sci. Phila. 42: 66–72.

—— 1891. Remarks on the Muricidae with descriptions of new species of shells. Proc. Acad. Nat. Sci. Phila. 43: 56–61.

—— 1894. Further notes on the embryonic whorls of the Muricidae. Proc. Acad. Nat. Sci. Phila. 46: 223–24.

—— 1895. Preliminary outline of a new classification of the family Muricidae. Bull. Chicago Acad. Sci. 2(2): 169–89.

—— 1897. Critical notes on the Muricidae. Trans. Acad. Sci. St. Louis 7(16): 372–91.

Barnard, K. H. 1959. Contributions to the knowledge of the South African marine Mollusca, pt. 2, Gastropoda, Prosobranchia, Rachiglossa. Ann. S. Afr. Mus. 45: 1–256.

Bartsch, P. 1915. Report on the Turton collection of South African marine mollusks, with additional notes on other South African shells contained in the U.S. National Museum. Bull. U.S. Nat. Mus. 91: i–xiii + 1–305, pls. 1–54.

Bartsch, P., and H. A. Rehder. 1939. Mollusks collected on the Presidential Cruise of 1938. Smithsonian Misc. Coll. 98(3535): 1–18, pls. 1–5.

Bellardi, L. 1872–1904. I Molluschi dei terreni Terziarii del Piemonte e della Liguria. Torino, 30 pts.

Bernardi, A. 1858. Descriptions d'espèces nouvelles. J. de Conchyl. 7: 301–3.

—— 1860. Descriptions d'espèces nouvelles. J. de Conchyl. 8: 211–12.

Berner, L. 1942. La croissance de la coquille chez les gastéropodes. Bull. Inst. Oceanogr. Monaco 816: 1–16.

Berry, S. S. 1953. Notices of new West American marine Mollusca. Trans. San Diego Soc. Nat. Hist. 11(16): 405–28.

—— 1958. Notices of new eastern Pacific Mollusca II. Leaflets in Malac. 1(15): 83–90.

—— 1959. Comments on some of the trivaricate muricines. Leaflets in Malac. 1(17): 106; 1(18): 113–14.

—— 1960. Notices of new eastern Pacific Mollusca IV. Leaflets in Malac. 1(19): 115–22.

—— 1964. Notices of new eastern Pacific Mollusca VI. Leaflets in Malac. 1(24): 147–54.

—— 1968. Notices of new eastern Pacific Mollusca VII. Leaflets in Malac. 1(25): 155–58.

—— 1969. Notices of new eastern Pacific Mollusca VIII. Leaflets in Malac. 1(26): 159–66.

Beyrich, H. E. 1854. Die Conchylien des Norddeutschen Tertiärgebirges. Zeit. d. deutsch geol. gesell., Berlin, 336 pp., pls. 1–30.

Bivona-Bernardi, A. 1832. Caratteri di alcune specie de conchiglie, estratti come sopra. Effem. Sci. Lett. Sicilia 2: 16–24.

Blainville, H. M. D. de. 1829. Faune française ou histoire naturelle, générale, et particulière des animaux qui retrouve en France. Mollusques. Levraux, Paris, 320 pp., pls. 1–41.

Blake, J. W. 1958. A biotic factor influencing the gastropod *Urosalpinx cinerea* in its choice of prey. A.S.B. Bull. 5: 3.

—— 1960. Oxygen consumption of bivalves and their attractiveness to the gastropod *Urosalpinx cinerea*. Limn. & Ocean. 5(3): 273–80.

Bonnet, A., and A. Joullien. 1951. Toxicité comparée des extraits de la glande à pourpre chez *Murex trunculus* et *Murex brandaris*. C.R. Soc. Biol. Paris 135: 958–60.

Bormann, M. 1946. A survey of some West American Ocenebras, with description of a new species. Nautilus 60(2): 37–43.

Born, I. 1778. Index rerum naturalium Musei Caesarei Vindobonensis. Pt. 1, Testacea. Vienna, xiii + 458 pp., 1 pl.

—— 1780. Testacea Musei Caesarei Vindobonensis. Vienna, xxxvi + 442 pp., pls. 1–18.

Bouchilloux, S., and J. Roche. 1955. Contribution à l'étude biochimique de la pourpre des *Murex*. Bull. Inst. Oceanogr. Monaco 1054: 1–23.

Brazier, J. 1870. Description d'espèces nouvelles de coquilles marines des côtes d'Australie. J. de Conchyl. 18: 300–301.

—— 1877. List of marine shells with descriptions of the new species collected during the "Chevert" expedition. Proc. Linn. Soc. New South Wales 1: 169–81.

—— 1878. Mollusca of the "Chevert" expedition. Proc. Linn. Soc. New South Wales 2: 1–7.

—— 1894. *In* A. U. Henn, List of Mollusca found at Green Point, Watson's Bar, Sydney ... with a few remarks upon some of the most interesting species and descriptions of new species by J. Brazier. Proc. Linn. Soc. New South Wales 9: 165–82.

Brocchi, G. B. 1814. Conchiologia fossile subappenina. Milan, 2 vols., 712 pp., pls. 1–16.

Broderip, W. J. 1825. Some account of two new species of shells from Mauritius. Zool. Jour. 2: 198–204.

—— 1833. Characters of new species of Mollusca and Conchifera collected by Mr. Cuming. Proc. Zool. Soc. London (1833) 1: 4–8.

Broderip, W. J., and G. B. Sowerby. 1829. Observations on new and interesting Mollusca contained, for the most part, in the Museum of the Zoological Society. Zool. Jour. 4: 359–77.

—— 1833. Characters of new species of Mollusca and Conchifera collected by H. Cuming. Proc. Comm. Sci. Corresp. Zool. Soc. London (1832) 2: 173–79, 194–202.

Bronn, H. G. 1827. Verzeichnis der bei dem Heidelberger Mineralien Komploir verkauflichen Konchylien, Pflangenthier—und anderen Versteinerungen. Z. Min., pp. 529–44.

Brown, A., and H. A. Pilsbry. 1911. Fauna of the Gatun Formation, Isthmus of Panama. Proc. Acad. Nat. Sci. Phila. 43: 336–73.

Bucquoy, E., and P. Dautzenberg. 1882. *In* E. Bucquoy, P. Dautzenberg, and G. Dollfus, Mollusques marins du Roussillon. Baillière, Paris, vol. 1, 570 pp.

Bullis, H. 1964. Muricidae (Gastropoda) from the northeast coast of South America, with descriptions of four new species. Tulane Stud. Zool. 11(4): 99–107, 1 pl.

Burch, T. 1940. Addition to the molluscan fauna of California. Nautilus 54(2): 46–47, pl. 2.

Burch, J. Q., and R. Burch. 1960. Notes on the subgenus *Homalocantha* Mörch, 1852, with description of a new subspecies. Hawaiian Shell News 8(5): 2, 7.

Burch, J. Q., and G. B. Campbell. 1963. *Shaskyus*, new genus of Pacific coast Muricidae (Gastropoda). J. de Conchyl. 93: 201–6, pl. 6.

Bush, K. J. 1893. Report on the Mollusca dredged by the "Blake" in 1880, including descriptions of several new species. Bull. Mus. Comp. Zool. Harvard 23: 199–244, pls. 1–2.

Cantraine, F. 1835. Diagnoses ou descriptions succinctes de quelques espèces nouvelles de mollusques qui feront partie de l'ouvrage: Malacologie méditerranéenne et littorale... Bull. Acad. Roy. Sci. Belles Lettres Bruxelles 2: 376–406.

Carcelles, A. R. 1944. Catalogo de los moluscos marinos de Puerto Quequen, Republica Argentina. Rev. Mus. de La Plata (N.S.) Secc. Zool. 3: 233–309, pls. 1–15.

— 1955. Nuevas especies des gastropodos marinos de las republicas oriental del Uruguay y Argentina. Commun. Zool. Mus. Montevideo 4(70): 1–16.

Carpenter, P. P. 1857a. Monograph of the shells collected by Mr. Nuttall on the California coast in the years 1834–35. Proc. Zool. Soc. London (1856) 24: 209–29.

— 1857b. Catalogue of the collection of Mazatlán shells.... London, i–iv + ix–xvi + 552 pp.

— 1864a. Supplementary report on the present state of our knowledge with regard to the Mollusca of the west coast of North America. Rep. Brit. Assoc. Adv. Sci. 33 (1863): 517–686.

— 1864b. Diagnoses of new forms of mollusks collected at Cape San Lucas, Lower California, by Mr. J. Xantus. Ann. Mag. Nat. Hist., Ser. 3, 13: 311–15, 474–79; 14: 45–49.

— 1865a. Diagnoses de mollusques nouveaux provenant de Californie et faisant partie du musée de l'institution Smithsonienne. J. de Conchyl. 13: 129–49.

— 1865b. Diagnoses specierum et varietatum novarum molluscorum, propre sinum Pugetianum a Kennerlio Doctore nuper decesso, collectorum. Proc. Acad. Nat. Sci. Phila. 17: 54–64.

— 1866a. Descriptions of new marine shells from the coast of California, pt. 3, Proc. Cal. Acad. Sci. 3: 207–24.

— 1866b. Diagnoses of new species of mollusks from the west tropical region of North America, principally collected by the Rev. J. Rowell of San Francisco. Proc. Zool. Soc. London (1865) 33: 278–82.

— 1869. *In* W. Gabb, Paleontology (of California). Vol. 2, Cretaceous and Tertiary fossils. Calif. State Geol. Survey, pp. xiv + 1–299, 29 pls.

Carriker, M. R. 1955. Critical review of the biology and control of oyster drills *Urosalpinx* and *Eupleura*. U.S. Fish and Wildlife Svc., Spec. Sci. Rep. Fish. 148: 1–150.

— 1957. Preliminary study of behavior of newly hatched drills *Urosalpinx cinerea* (Say). J. Elisha Mitchell Sci. Soc. 73(2): 328–51.

— 1959. Comparative functional morphology of the drilling mechanism in *Urosalpinx* and *Eupleura* (muricid gastropods). Proc. Int. Cong. Zool. 15: 373–76.

— 1961. Comparative functional morphology of boring mechanisms in gastropods. Amer. Zool. 1(2): 263–66.

Carriker, M. R., and E. H. Smith. 1969. Comparative calcibiocavitology: summary and conclusions. Amer. Zool. 9(3): 1011–20, 1 table.

Cernohorsky, W. O. 1966. The radula, egg-capsules and young of *Murex torrefactus* Sowerby (Mollusca: Gastropoda). Veliger 8(4): 231–33.

— 1967. The Muricidae of Fiji (Mollusca: Gastropoda), pt. 1, subfamilies Muricinae and Tritonaliinae, plus an addendum. Veliger 10(2): 111–32.

— 1971. Contribution to the taxonomy of the Muricidae. Veliger 14(2): 187–91.

Chace, E. P. 1958. The marine molluscan fauna of Guadelupe Island, Mexico. Trans. San Diego Soc. Nat. Hist. 12: 319–32.

Chew, K. K. 1960. Study of food preferences and rate of feeding of the Japanese oyster drill *Ocenebra japonica*. U.S. Fish and Wildlife Svc., Spec. Sci. Rep. Fish. 365, 27 pp.

Clench, W. J. 1947. The genera *Purpura* and *Thais* in the western Atlantic. Johnsonia 2(23): 61–91, pls. 32–40.

— 1953. The genus *Murex* in the western Atlantic. Johnsonia 2: 360–61, pl. 179.

— 1955. A new *Murex* from Matanzas, Cuba. Breviora 44: 1–2, 3 figs.

— 1959. The genus *Murex* in the western Atlantic. Johnsonia 3: 331–34, pls. 174–75.

Clench, W. J., and I. Pérez Farfante. 1945. The genus *Murex* in the western Atlantic. Johnsonia 1(17): 1–56, pls. 1–28.

Comfort, A. 1951. The pigmentation of molluscan shells. Biol. Rev. 26: 285–301.

Conrad, T. A. 1837. Descriptions of new marine shells from Upper California collected by Thomas Nuttall Esq. J. Acad. Nat. Sci. Phila. 7: 227–68, pls. 17–20.

— 1846a. Descriptions of new species of fossil and Recent shells and corals. Proc. Acad. Nat. Sci. Phila. 3: 19–27.

— 1846b. Catalogue of shells inhabiting Tampa Bay and other parts of the Florida coast. Amer. J. Sci., Ser. 2, 2: 393–98.

— 1869. Notes on Recent Mollusca. Amer. J. Conch. 5: 104–8.

Cossmann, M. 1903. Essais de Paléoconchologie Comparée, vol. 5, 215 pp., pls. 1–9.

— 1921. Rectifications de nomenclature. Rev. Crit. de Paléozool. 25: 79–80.

Couturier, M. 1907. Etude sur les mollusques gastropodes... J. de Conchyl. 55: 123–78.

Cristofori, J., and G. Jan. 1832. Catalogus in IV sectiones divisus rerum naturalium in museo extantium Josephi de Cristofor et Georgyii Jan. Milan. Sectio II, pars i, Conchyliologia, 16 pp.

Crosse, H. 1861. Description de deux *Murex* nouveaux. J. de Conchyl. 9: 351–54, pl. 16.

———. 1862. Description d'espèces marines recueillies par M. H. Cuming dans le nord de la Chine. J. de Conchyl. 10: 51–57, pl. 1.

———. 1863. Description d'une espèce nouvelle de la Guadeloupe. J. de Conchyl. 11: 82–84, pl. 1.

———. 1864. Description d'espèces nouvelles de l'Australie méridionale. J. de Conchyl. 12: 275–79, pl. 11.

———. 1865a. Description d'espèces nouvelles de la Guadeloupe. J. de Conchyl. 13: 27–38, pl. 1.

———. 1865b. Description d'espèces nouvelles. J. de Conchyl. 13: 213–15.

———. 1869a. Diagnoses molluscorum novorum. J. de Conchyl. 17: 183–88.

———. 1869b. Diagnoses molluscorum novorum. J. de Conchyl. 17: 408–10.

———. 1872a. Diagnoses molluscorum Novae Calendoniae. J. de Conchyl. 20: 69–75, pl. 13.

———. 1872b. Diagnoses molluscorum novorum. J. de Conchyl. 20: 211–14.

———. 1873a. Descriptions d'espèces nouvelles. J. de Conchyl. 21: 248–54, pl. 11.

———. 1873b. Diagnoses molluscorum novorum. J. de Conchyl. 21: 284–85.

Crosse, H., and P. Fischer. 1865. Descriptions d'espèces nouvelles de l'Australie méridionale. J. de Conchyl. 13: 38–55, pls. 1, 2.

Dall, W. H. 1888. (*In* L. Agassiz.) The three cruises of the "Blake," pt. 18 (mollusks). Bull. Mus. Comp. Zool. Harvard 15(2): 58–75, figs. 282–312.

———. 1889. Report on the Mollusca. II, Gastropods, Report on dredgings ... by U.S. Coast Survey steamer "Blake." Bull. Mus. Comp. Zool. Harvard 18: 1–492, pls. 10–40.

———. 1890a. Scientific results of explorations by the U.S. Fish Commission steamer "Albatross." VII, Preliminary report on the collection of Mollusca and Brachiopoda obtained in 1887–1888. Proc. U.S. Nat. Mus. 12(773): 219–362, pls. 5–14.

———. 1890b. Contributions to the Tertiary fauna of Florida. Trans. Wagner Free Inst. Sci. 3(1): 1–200, pls. 1–12.

———. 1891. Scientific results of explorations by the U.S. Fish Commission steamer "Albatross." XX, On some new or interesting West American shells obtained from the dredgings of the U.S. Fish Commission steamer "Albatross" in 1888 and from other sources. Proc. U.S. Nat. Mus. 14 (849): 173–91, pls. 5–7.

———. 1895. Diagnoses of new species of mollusks from the west coast of America. Proc. U.S. Nat. Mus. 18: 7–20.

———. 1896. The mollusks and brachiopods of the Bahama Expedition of the State Univ. of Iowa. Bull. Lab. Nat. Hist. State Univ. Iowa 4(1): 12–17, pl. 1.

———. 1898. On a new species of *Fusus* from California. Nautilus 12(1): 4–5.

———. 1899. A new *Pteronotus* from California. Nautilus 12(12): 138.

———. 1900. A new *Murex* from California. Nautilus 14 (4): 37.

———. 1902. Illustrations and descriptions of new, unfigured or imperfectly known shells, chiefly American, in the U.S. National Museum. Proc. U.S. Nat. Mus. 24(1264): 499–566, pls. 27–40.

———. 1903a. Diagnoses of new species of mollusks from the Santa Barbara Channel, Calif. Proc. Biol. Soc. Wash. 16: 171–76.

———. 1903b. Contributions to the Tertiary fauna of Florida. Trans. Wagner Free Inst. Sci. 3(6): 1219–1647, pls. 48–60.

———. 1905. Two undescribed California shells. Nautilus 19(2): 14–15.

———. 1907. Descriptions of new species of shells, chiefly Buccinidae, from the dredgings of the U.S.S. "Albatross" during 1906 in the northwestern Pacific, Bering, Okhotsk and Japan Seas. Smithsonian Misc. Coll. 50: 139–73.

———. 1908. Reports on the dredging operations off the west coast of Central America ... Galápagos ... west coast of Mexico ... by the U.S. Fish Commission steamer "Albatross" ... XIV, the Mollusca and Brachiopoda. Bull. Mus. Comp. Zool. Harvard 43(6): 205–487, pls. 1–22.

———. 1909. Report on a collection of shells from Peru, with a summary of the littoral marine Mollusca of the Peruvian zoological province. Proc. U.S. Nat. Mus. 37(1704): 147–294, pls. 20–28.

———. 1911. A new California *Eupleura*. Nautilus 25(8): 87.

———. 1913. Diagnoses of new shells from the Pacific. Proc. U.S. Nat. Mus. 45(2002): 587–97.

———. 1918a. Notes on *Chrysodomus* and other mollusks from the North Pacific Ocean. Proc. U.S. Nat. Mus. 54(2234): 207–34.

———. 1918b. Pleistocene fossils of Magdalena Bay, Lower California, collected by Charles Russell Orcutt. Nautilus 32(1): 23–26.

———. 1919a. New shells from the northwest coast. Proc. Biol. Soc. Wash. 32: 249–52.

———. 1919b. Descriptions of new species of mollusks from the North Pacific Ocean in the collection of the U.S.N.M. Proc. U.S. Nat. Mus. 56(2295): 293–371.

———. 1921. Summary of the marine shell-bearing mollusks of the northwest coast of America ... U.S. Nat. Mus. Bull. 112: 1–217, pls. 1–22.

———. 1925. Illustrations of unfigured types of shells in the collection of the United States National Museum. Proc. U.S. Nat. Mus. 66(2554): 1–41, pls. 1–36.

D'Attilio, A., and G. E. Radwin. 1971a. The intritacalx, an undescribed shell layer in mollusks. Veliger 13(4): 344–47, figs. 1–8.

D'Attilio, A., and W. Old, Jr. 1971b. A new muricid gastropod from Western Australia. Veliger 13(4): 316–18.

Dautzenberg, P. 1927. Résultats des campagnes scientifiques du Prince de Monaco ... Monte Carlo, Fasc. 72, 400 pp., pls. 1–9.

DeFrance, J. L. M. 1827. Dictionnaire de sciences naturelles ..., v. 45. Paris, 547 pp.

Dell, D. 1956. The archibenthal Mollusca of New Zealand. Dominion Museum Bull., Wellington, 18: 1–235, pls. 1–27.

Deshayes, G. P. 1832. *In* J. G. Bruguière, J. P. B. A. Lamarck, and G. P. Deshayes, Encyclopédie méthodique... Histoire naturelle des vers et mollusques, 1789–1832. Paris, vol. 2, pp. v–vii, 1–594.

— 1839. Nouvelles espèces de mollusques, provenant des côtes de la Californie, du Mexique, du Kamtschatka et de la Nouvelle Zélande, décrites par M. Deshayes. Rev. Zool. Soc. Cuvierienne 2: 356–61.

— 1865. Descriptions des animaux sans vertèbres découvertes dans le Bassin de Paris.... 3 vols. + 2 vols. Atlas, Paris.

Dillwyn, L. W. 1817. Descriptive catalogue of Recent shells, arranged according to the Linnaean method, with particular attention to synonymy. 2 vols., 1,092 pp.

Dohrn, H. 1862. Descriptions of new shells. Proc. Zool. Soc. London (1862), 30: 202–3.

Donovan, E. 1802–3. The natural history of British shells. London, vol. 4, pls. 109–44, text, index.

Dubois, R. 1909. Recherche sur la pourpre et sur quelques autres pigments animaux. Arch. Zool. Exp. et Gen. 42: 471–590.

Dujardin, E. 1837. Mémoire sur les couches du sol en Touraine, et description de coquilles de la craie et des faluns. Mém. Soc. Géol. France 2(2): 211–311.

Dunker, W. 1846. *In* R. A. Philippi, Abbildungen und Beschreibungen neuer oder wenig gekannter Conchylien, Cassel, vol. 2, pp. 1–232, pls. 1–43.

— 1860. Neue Japanische Mollusken. Malak. Blätt. 6: 221–40.

— 1864. Funf neue Mollusken. Malak. Blätt. 11: 99–102.

— 1868–69. Novitates Conchologicae, 2d series. Meeres-Conchylien. Fischer, Cassel, pp. 1–144, pls. 1–45.

— 1879. Mollusca quaedam nova. J. de Conchyl. 27: 212–17, pls. 8–9.

— 1883. Zwei neue murices. Malak. Blätt. (neue folge) 6: 35–36, pl. 1.

Durham, J. W. 1950. 1940 E. W. Scripps cruise to the Gulf of Calif.; pt. 2, Megascopic paleontology and marine stratigraphy. Geol. Soc. Amer., Memoir 43, pp. 1–216, pls. 1–48.

DuShane, H. 1969. A new genus and two new species of Typhinae from the Panamic. Veliger 11(4): 343–44, pl. 54.

Duval, ?. 1853. Description d'une nouvelle espèce de *Murex*. J. de Conchyl. 4: 203–4, pl. 5.

Emerson, W. K. 1964. A new name for *Murex rhyssus* Dall, 1919 (Mollusca: Gastropoda). Veliger 7(1): 5–7.

— 1968. Taxonomic placement of *Coralliophila incompta* Berry, 1960, with the proposal of a new genus, *Attiliosa* (Gastropoda: Muricacea). Veliger 10(4): 379–81, pl. 53.

Emerson, W. K., and A. D'Attilio. 1965. *Aspella (Favartia) angermeyerae*, n. sp. Nautilus 79(1): 1–4, pl. 1.

— 1969a. A new species of *Murexsul* (Gastropoda: Muricidae) from the Galápagos Islands. Veliger 11(4): 324–25, pl. 50.

— 1969b. Remarks on the taxonomic placement of *Purpurellus* Jousseaume, 1880, with the description of a new species. Veliger 12(2): 145–48, pls. 26–27.

— 1970. *Aspella myrakeenae*, new species from western Mexico. Nautilus 83(3): 88–94.

Eschscholtz, J. F. von. 1829. Zoologischer atlas... pt. 2. Berlin, pp. 1–13, pls. 6–10.

Euthyme (le frère). 1889. Description de quelques espèces nouvelles de la faune marine exotique. Bull. Soc. Malac. France 6: 259–82, pl. 6.

Finlay, H. J. 1927a. A further commentary on New Zealand molluscan systematics. Trans. Proc. N.Z. Inst. 57: 320–485.

— 1927b. Additions to the Recent molluscan fauna of New Zealand, no. 2. Trans. Proc. N.Z. Inst. 57: 485–87, pl. 24.

— 1930. Addition to the Recent molluscan fauna of New Zealand, no. 3. Trans. Proc. N.Z. Inst. 61: 222–47.

Fischer de Waldheim, G. 1806–7. Muséum Démidoff, ou catalogue systematique et raissoné des curiosités de la nature et de l'art. Moscou, vols. 1–2, 1806; vol. 3, 1807.

Fischer, P. 1870. Description des espèces nouvelles. J. de Conchyl. 18: 176–79.

— 1876. Descriptions d'espèces nouvelles de l'Afrique occidentale. J. de Conchyl. 24: 236–40, pl. 8.

— 1884. Manuel de Conchyliologie. Paris, 1,369 pp., pls. 1–23.

Fischer, P., and A. Bernardi. 1856. Descriptions d'espèces nouvelles. J. de Conchyl. 5: 292–300.

Fleming, C. A. 1962. The genus *Pterynotus* Swainson (Gastropoda: Muricidae) in New Zealand and Norfolk Island. Trans. Roy. Soc. New South Wales 2(14): 109–19, pl. 1.

Fleming, J. 1828. A history of British animals. Edinburgh, pp. i–xxiii, 1–565, index, corrigenda.

Ford, J. 1888. Description of a new species of *Ocinebra*. Proc. Acad. Nat. Sci. Phila. 40: 188.

Franc, A. 1940. Recherches sur le développement d'*Ocinebra aciculata* Lamarck. Biol. Bull. France-Belg. 74: 327–45.

— 1952. Notes écologiques et anatomiques sur *Tritonalia (Ocinebrina) aciculata* (Lam.) (Mollusques Prosobranche). Bull. Lab. Marit. Dinars. 36: 31–34.

François, P. 1891. Choses de Nouméa. III. Moeurs d'un *Murex*. Arch. Zool. Exp. 9: 240–42.

Fretter, V. 1941. The genital ducts of some British stenoglossan prosobranchs. J. Mar. Biol. Assoc. U.K. 25(1): 173–211.

Fretter, V., and A. Graham. 1962. British prosobranch Mollusca. Ray Society Publ. 144, i–ix + 1–754 pp.

Fulton, H. 1936. Descriptions of five new species and varieties. Proc. Malac. Soc. London 22: 9–10, pl. 2.

Gabb, W. 1865. Description of new species of marine shells from the coast of California. Proc. Calif. Acad. Sci. 3: 182–90.

— 1873. On the topography and geology of Santo Domingo. Trans. Amer. Philos. Soc. (N.S.) 15: 49–259.

Galtsoff, P. S., H. F. Prytherch, and J. B. Engle. 1937. Natural history and methods of controlling the common oyster drills (*Urosalpinx cinerea* Say and *Eupleura caudata* Say). Circ. U.S. Bur. Fish. 25: 1–24.

Garrard, T. A. 1961. Mollusca collected by M.V. "Challenge" off the east coast of Australia. J. Malac. Soc. Aust. 5: 3–38, pls. 1–2.

——— 1963. New species of Mollusca from eastern Australia. J. Malac. Aust. 7: 42–46, pl. 10.

Garrett, A. 1857. New species of marine shells of the Sandwich Islands. Proc. Calif. Acad. Sci. 1: 114–15.

Gertman, R. 1969. Cenozoic Typhinae (Mollusca: Gastropoda) of the western Atlantic region. Tulane Stud. Geol. Paleo. 7(4): 143–91, pls. 1–8.

Gmelin, J. F. 1791. Linnaeus systema naturae . . . ed. 13. Aucta reformata. Lipsiae, vol. 1, 4,120 pp.

Gould, A. A. 1848–49. Shells collected by the U.S. Exploring Expedition under the command of Chas. Wilkes. Proc. Bost. Soc. Nat. Hist. 3: 83–85; 89–92; 106–9; 118–21; 140–44.

Grant, U. S., IV, and H. R. Gale. 1931. Pliocene and Pleistocene Mollusca of California. Mem. San Diego Soc. Nat. Hist. no. 1, 1,036 pp., pls. 1–32.

Gray, J. E. 1847. A list of the genera of Recent Mollusca, their synonyma and types. Proc. Zool. Soc. London (1847), 15: 129–219.

De Gregorio, A. 1885. Continuazione degli studi su talune conchiglie mediterranee viventi e fossile. Bull. Soc. Malac. Ital. 11: 27–203.

Griffith, G. W., and M. Castagna. 1962. Sexual dimorphism in oyster drills of Chincoteague Bay, Maryland. Chesapeake Sci. 3: 215–17.

Habe, T. 1945. On the radulae of Japanese marine Gastropoda (3). Japanese Jour. Malac. 14(5–8): 190–99, figs. 1–23.

——— 1961. Coloured illustrations of the shells of Japan (II). Hoikusha, Osaka, 183 pp., pls. 1–66.

——— 1964. Shells of the western Pacific in color, vol. 2. Hoikusha, Osaka, 233 pp., pls. 1–66.

Habe, T., and K. Ito. 1965. New genera and species of shells chiefly collected from the North Pacific. Venus 24(1): 16–45.

Habe, T., and S. Kosuge. 1971. New typhid species from the South China Sea. Nautilus 84(3): 82–83.

Hancock, D. 1954. The destruction of oyster spat by *U. cinerea* on Essex oysterbeds. Jour. Conseil Instit. Explor. Mer. 20: 186–96.

——— 1956. The structure of the capsule and the hatching process in *Urosalpinx cinerea* (Say). Proc. Zool. Soc. London (1956), 127: 565–71.

Hargis, W. J., and C. L. MacKenzie. 1961. Sexual behavior of the oyster drills *Eupleura caudata* and *Urosalpinx cinerea*. Nautilus 75: 7–16.

Haskin, H. H. 1940. The role of chemotropism in food selection by the oyster drill *Urosalpinx cinerea* Say. Anat. Rec. 78: 95.

——— 1950. The selection of food by the common oyster drill *Urosalpinx cinerea* Say. Proc. Nat. Shellfish Assoc. 40: 62–68.

Hayashi, S., and T. Habe. 1965. Descriptions of four new gastropods from Enshu-Nada. Venus 24: 10–15, pl. 1.

Hedley, C. 1899. The Mollusca of Funafuti. Pt. 1, Gastropoda. Mem. Aust. Mus. 3: 397–488.

——— 1903. Scientific results of the trawling expedition of H.M.C.S. "Thetis" off the coast of New South Wales in Feb. and Mar., 1898, pt. 6. Mem. Aust. Mus. 4(1): 326–402, figs. 61–113, pls. 36–38.

——— 1907. The results of deep sea investigations in the Tasman Sea. 3. Mollusca from eight fathoms off Narrabeen, Sydney, N.S.W. Rec. Aust. Mus. 6(4): 283–304, pls. 54–56.

——— 1912. Descriptions of some new or noteworthy shells in the Australian Museum. Rec. Aust. Mus. 8: 131–60, pls. 1–6.

——— 1915. Studies on Australian Mollusca, pt. 12. Proc. Linn. Soc. New South Wales 39: 695–755, pls. 1–7.

Hedley, C., and W. L. May. 1908. Mollusca from one hundred fathoms, seven miles east of Cape Pillar, Tasmania. Rec. Aust. Mus. 7: 108–25.

Herrmannsen, A. N. 1846–47. Indicis generum Malacozoorum. Cassel, vol. 1, 637 pp.

Hertlein, L. G., and A. M. Strong. 1951a. Descriptions of three new species of marine gastropods from West Mexico and Guatemala. Bull. S. Cal. Acad. Sci. 50(2): 76–80, pl. 26.

——— 1951b. Eastern Pacific expeditions of the N.Y. Zool. Soc. 43. Mollusks from the west coast of Mexico and Central America. Zoologica 36(2): 67–120, pls. 1–11.

Hidalgo, J. G. 1880. *In* G. W. Tryon, Jr., Manual of Conchology. Vol. 2, Muricinae Purpurinae, Philadelphia, p. 134, pl. 70, fig. 427.

Higgins, H. H., and F. P. Marrat. 1878. Mollusca of the "Argo" Expedition to the West Indies. Publ. Lib., Mus. and Gallery of Art of the Borough Liverpool. Mus. Report 1, pp. 1–20, pl. 1.

Hinds, R. B. 1843. On new species of shells collected by Sir Edward Belcher, C.B. Proc. Zool. Soc. London (1843), 11: 17–19.

——— 1844. Descriptions of new species of *Scalaria* and *Murex* from the collection of Sir Edward Belcher, C.B. Proc. Zool. Soc. London (1843), 12: 124–29.

——— 1844–45. The zoology of the voyage of H.M.S. Sulphur . . . . London, Mollusca, pt. 1, pp. 1–24, pls. 1–7, 1844; pt. 2, pp. 25–28, pls. 8–14, 1844; pt. 3, pp. 49–72, pls. 15–21, 1845.

Hirase, Y. 1914–15. Illustrations of a thousand shells, pts. 1–4 (not paginated). Kyoto.

Hutton, F. W. 1873. Catalogue of the marine Mollusca of New Zealand with diagnoses of the species. New Zealand Colonial Museum and Geological Survey Dept., Wellington, i–xx + 116 pp., 1 pl.

——— 1882. Additions to the molluscan fauna of New Zealand. New Zealand Jour. Sci. 1: 69.

——— 1884. Revision of the Recent rachiglossate Mollusca of New Zealand. Proc. N.Z. Inst. 16: 216–33.

——— 1886. New species of Tertiary shells. Trans. Proc. N.Z. Inst. 18: 333–35.

Hyman, L. H. 1967. The Invertebrates. Vol. 6, Mollusca 1, Aplacophora, Polyplacophora, Mono-

placophora, Gastropoda. McGraw-Hill, New York, i–vii + 1–792 pp.
Iredale, T. 1915. A commentary on Suter's "Manual of New Zealand Mollusca." Trans. New Zealand Inst. 47: 417–97.
———. 1924. Results from Roy Bell's molluscan collections. Proc. Linn. Soc. New South Wales 49: 179–278, pls. 31–36.
———. 1929a. Queensland molluscan notes #1. Mem. Queensland Mus. 9(3): 261–97.
———. 1929b. Mollusca from the continental shelf of eastern Australia, no. 2. Rec. Aust. Mus. 17: 157–89.
———. 1931. Australian molluscan notes #1. Mem. Aust. Mus. 18: 201–35, pls. 22–25.
———. 1936. Australian molluscan notes #2. Rec. Aust. Mus. 19: 267–340, pls. 20–24.
Jousseaume, F. 1880. Division méthodique de la famille des Purpuridés. Le Naturaliste, 42: 335–36.
———. 1881. Diagnoses de mollusques nouveaux. Le Naturaliste 44: 349–50.
———. 1882. Etude des Purpuridae et description d'espèces nouvelles. Rev. Mag. Zool. 3(7): 314–48.
———. 1883. Description d'espèces et genre nouveaux de mollusques. Bull. Soc. Zool. 8: 186–204, pl. 10.
———. 1888. Description des mollusques recueillis par M. le Dr. Faurot dans la Mer Rouge et le Golfe d'Aden. Mem. Soc. Zool. Franc. 1: 165–223.
———. 1894. Diagnose de coquilles de nouveaux mollusques. Bull. Soc. Philomat. Paris 78: 67–71.
Keen, A. M. 1944. Catalogue and revision of the gastropod subfamily Typhinae. Jour. Paleo. 18(1): 50–72.
———. 1958. New mollusks from tropical West America. Bull. Amer. Paleont. 38: 235–55, pls. 1–2.
———. 1960. New *Phyllonotus* from the eastern Pacific. Nautilus 73(3): 103–9, pl. 9.
———. 1969. *Purpura* Bruguière and *Muricanthus* Swainson (Gastropoda): designations of type-species under the plenary powers with grant of precedence to Thaididae over Purpuridae. Bull. Zool. Nomen. 26(3/4): 128–32.
———. 1971. Sea Shells of Tropical West America, 2d ed. Stanford Univ. Press, Stanford, Calif., i–xiv + 1–1,064 pp., pls. 1–22.
Keen, A. M., and G. B. Campbell. 1964. Ten new species of Typhinae (Gastropoda: Muricidae). Veliger 7: 46–57, pls. 8–11.
Kiener, L. C. 1842–43. Spécies général et iconographie des coquilles vivantes.... Vol. 7, Rocher (*Murex*), pp. 1–130 (text); 1843, pls. 1–47.
Kilburn, R. N. 1970. Taxonomic notes on South African marine Mollusca, I. Ann. Cape Prov. Mus. (Nat. Hist.) 8(4): 39–48.
King, P. P., and W. J. Broderip. 1832. Description of Cirrhipeda, Conchifera and Mollusca... the southern coasts of South America. Zool. Jour. 5(19): 332–49.
Kira, T. 1959. Coloured illustrations of the shells of Japan. Hoikusha, Osaka, Japan, 239 pp., pls. 1–71.
Knudsen, J. 1950. The eggs and larvae of some marine prosobranchs from tropical West Africa. Atlantide Report 1: 85–130.
———. 1956. Marine prosobranchs of West Africa. Atlantide Report 4: 7–110, pls. 1–4.

Kobelt, W. 1878. *Triton, Trophon,* und *Hindsia. In* W. Kobelt and H. C. Küster, Systematisches Conchylien-Cabinet von Martini und Chemnitz. Von Bauer & Raspe, Nuremberg. Pts. 272 and 275, pp. 239–326, pls. 68–77.
Krauss, C. F. F. 1848. Die Sudafrikanischen Mollusken. Stuttgart, 140 pp., pls. 1–6 (not seen).
Kuroda, T. 1929. Notes and descriptions of some new and noteworthy species from Tateyama Bay in the report of M. T. Fujita. Venus 1(3): 91–97, pl. 3.
———. 1942. Two Japanese murices whose names have been preoccupied. Venus 12(1–2): 80–81.
———. 1953. New genera and species of Japanese gastropods (1). Venus 17(4): 179–85.
———. 1964a. *In* T. Habe, Shells of the western Pacific in color. Hoikusha, Osaka, 233 pp., pls. 1–65.
———. 1964b. A new muricid species from Japan. Venus 23: 129–30.
Kuroda, T., and T. Habe. 1952. Check list and bibliography of the Recent marine Mollusca of Japan. Stach, Tokyo, 210 pp.
Kuroda, T., and T. Habe. 1971. *In* T. Kuroda, T. Habe, and K. Oyama. The sea shells of Sagami Bay. Maruzen, Tokyo, xix + 741 pp. (Japanese), and 489 pp. (English); indexes, pp. 1–28 (Japanese), pp. 1–51 (Latin), pls. 1–121.
Küster, H. C., and W. Kobelt. 1843–78. Die Geschwantzen und bewehrten purpurschnecken (*Murex, Ranella, Tritonium, Trophon, Hindsia*). *In* W. Kobelt and H. C. Küster, Systematisches Conchylien-Cabinet von Martini und Chemnitz. Von Bauer & Raspe, Nuremberg. III–2: 1–8, 1843; 9–12, 1844; 13–52, 1856; 53–60, 1868; 61–118, 1869; 119–34, 1870; 135–90, 1871; 191–206, 1872; 207–38, 1876; 239–336, 1878.
Lamarck, J. B. P. A. 1802–6. Mémoires sur les fossiles des environs de Paris. Ann. Mus. Hist. Nat. Paris 2: 57–64, 163–69, 217–27, 315–21, 385–91.
———. 1816. Mollusques et polypes divers. *In* J. G. Bruguière, J. P. B. A. Lamarck, and G. P. Deshayes, Encyclopédie méthodique. Paris, pt. 23, pls. 391–488, Liste pp. 1–16.
———. 1822. Histoire naturelle des animaux sans vertèbres. Paris, vol. 7, 232 pp.
Liénard, E. 1873. Description d'un *Murex* nouveau, provenant de l'île Maurice. J. de Conchyl. 21: 285–86.
Lightfoot, J. 1786. A Catalogue of the Portland Museum... London, i–vii + 1–194 pp.
Link, H. F. 1807. Beschreibung der Naturalien-Sammlung der Universität zu Rostock, Rostock, pp. 1–160.
Linné, C. von. 1758. Systema naturae... Stockholm, 10th ed., vol. 1, pp. 1–824.
———. 1767. Systema naturae, 12th ed., vol. 1, pt. 2, 1,327 pp. + 32 pp. addenda.
Lischke, C. E. 1868. Diagnosen neuer Meeres-Conchylien von Japan. Malak. Blätt. 15: 218–22.
———. 1871. Diagnosen neuer Meeres-Conchylien von Japan. Malak. Blätt. 18: 39–45.
Löbbecke, T., and W. Kobelt. 1879. Diagnosen neuer Murices. Jahr. Deutsch. Mal. Gesell. 6: 78–79.
Locard, A. 1886. Prodrome de malacologie française.

Catalogue général des mollusques vivants de France (Mollusques marins). Lyon, Paris, x + 779 pp.

— 1897. Expedition scientifique de *Travailleur* et du *Talisman*, Paris, vol. 1, 515 pp., pls. 1–22.

— 1899. Notices conchyliologiques LIII. Sur les *Ocenebra* des côtes de France. Echange 15: 19–72, 75, 76.

Lowe, H. N. 1935. New marine Mollusca from West Mexico, together with a list of shells collected at Punta Penasco, Sonora, Mexico. Trans. San Diego Soc. Nat. Hist. 8(6): 15–34, pls. 1–4.

McGinty, T. 1940. New marine shells dredged off Palm Beach, Florida. Nautilus 54(2): 63.

MacKenzie, C. L., Jr. 1960. Interpretation of varices and growth ridges on shells of *Eupleura caudata*. Ecology 41: 783–84.

— 1961. Growth and reproduction of the oyster drill *Eupleura caudata* in the York River, Virginia. Ecology 42: 317–38.

McMichael, D. 1964. A new *Murex* from the Great Australian Bight (Gastropoda: Muricidae). J. Malac. Soc. Austr. 8: 31–32, 1 pl.

Macpherson, J. H. 1959. New gasteropods from North Australia. Mem. Nat. Mus. Victoria 24: 51–57.

— 1962. New name for *Murex espinosus*. Mem. Nat. Mus. Victoria 25: 176.

Maes, V. O. 1966. Sexual dimorphism in the radula of the muricid genus *Nassa*. Nautilus 79(3): 73–80.

Martens, E. von. 1880. *In* T. Löbbecke and W. Kobelt, Museum Loebbeckeanum. Jahr. Deutsch. Malak. Gesell. 7: 81–82.

— 1902. Einige neue Arten von Meer-Conchylien aus den Sammlungen der Deutschen Tiefsee-Expedition. Gesell. Naturf. Freunde Berlin Sitzungsber. 9: 237–44.

Martins, A. 1967. Pequeño contributo para o estudo da malacologia dos Açores. Atlantida 10: 101–18.

Martyn, T. 1788. The universal conchologist. London, vol. 2 (no pagination).

Maury, C. J. 1917. Santo Domingo type sections and fossils, pt. 1. Bull. Amer. Paleo. 5(29): 1–251, pls. 1–39.

Mawe, J. 1823. The Linnaean System of Conchology. Longman et al., London, 207 pp., pls. 1–36.

Melvill, J. C. 1893. Description of twenty-five new species of marine shells from Bombay. Mem. Manchester Soc. 7: 52–67, pl. 1.

— 1898. Further investigations into the molluscan fauna of the Arabian Sea, Gulf of Oman, and Persian Gulf, with descriptions of forty new species . . . Mem. Manchester Soc. 42(4): 1–40, pls. 1–2.

Melvill, J. C., and R. Standen. 1899. Report on the marine Mollusca obtained during the first expedition of Prof. A. C. Haddon to the Torres Straits in 1888–89. Jour. Linn. Soc. Lond. 27: 150–206, pls. 1–2.

— 1903. Descriptions of 68 new Gastropoda from the Persian Gulf, G. of Oman and N. Arabian Sea dredged by Mr. F. W. Townsend of the Indo-European Telegraph Svc., 1901–1903. Ann. Mag. Nat. Hist. 12: 289–324, pls. 20–23.

Melville, R. V. 1970. ICZN Opinion 911, Six misidentified type species in the superfamily Muricacea (Gastropoda). Bull. Zool. Nomenclat. 27(1): 20–27.

Menzel, R. W., and F. E. Nichy. 1958. Studies on the distribution and feeding habits of some oyster predators in Alligator Harbor, Florida. Bull. Mar. Sci. Gulf Carib. 8(2): 125–45.

Mestayer, M. K. 1916. Preliminary list of Mollusca from dredgings taken off the northern coasts of New Zealand. Trans. Proc. N.Z. Inst. 48: 122–28, pl. 12.

Michelotti, G. 1841. Monografia de genre *Murex*. Ann. Sci. Reg. Lomb. Veneto 11: 1–27, pls. 1–4.

Middendorff, A. T. von. 1848. Vorläufige anzige einiger neuer Konchylien aus dem Geschlechtern: *Littorina, Tritonium, Bullia, Natica*, und *Margarita*. Bull. Phys. Math. Acad. Imp. Sci. St. Petersburg 7(16): 241–46.

— 1851. Reise in den Aussersten und Osten Sibiriens. Buchdruckerei der Kaiserlichen Akademie der Wissenschaften, St. Petersburg, vol. 2 (Zoologie), pt. 1 (Wirbellose Thiere), 516 pp.

Molina, G. I. 1782. Saggio sulla storia naturale del Chile. Bologna, 367 pp.

Montagu, G. 1803. Testacea Britannica, or natural history of British shells, marine, land, and fresh water. London, 2 vols. & supplement, 606 pp. + 183 pp. (suppl.), pls. 1–16 + 17–30 (suppl.).

Monterosato, T. A. di. 1872. Notizie intorno alle Conchiglie Mediterranee. Palermo, 61 pp.

— 1875. Nuova rivista Conchiglie Mediterranee. Atti Reale Academia de Scienze, Lettere e Belle Arti, n.s. 5: 1–50, 1 pl.

— 1884. Nomenclatura Generica e Specifica di alcune Conchiglie Mediterranee. Palermo, 152 pp.

— 1890. Conchiglie della profundita del mare di Palermo. Nat. Sicil. 9: 140, 151, 157–66, 181–91.

— 1917. Molluschi viventi e quaternari raccolti lungo le coste della Tripolitana dall'ing Camillo Crema. Boll. Soc. Zool. Ital. 4: 1–28.

Montfort, P. D. de. 1810. Conchyliologie systematique. Paris, vol. 2, 676 pp.

Montrouzier, R. P. 1861. *In* M. Souverbie, Description d'espèces nouvelles de l'Archipel Calédonien. J. de Conchyl. 9: 271–84, pl. 11.

Moore, H. B. 1936. The biology of *Purpura lapillus*. 1. Shell variation in relation to environment. J. Mar. Biol. Ass. U.K. 21: 61–89.

Mörch, O. A. L. 1850. Catalogus Conchyliorum quae reliquit C. P. Kierulf. Hafniae, 33 pp., 2 pls.

— 1852. Catalogus Conchyliorum quae reliquit . . . Comes de Yoldi. Klein, Hafniae, pt. 1, 170 pp.

— 1877. Synopsis molluscorum marinorum Indiarum occidentalium imprimis insularum danicarum. Malak. Blätt. 24: 14–66.

Morton, J. E. 1958. Molluscs. Hutchinson, London, 232 pp.

Murdoch, R. 1905. Additions to the marine Mollusca of New Zealand. Trans. N.Z. Inst. 37: 217–32, pls. 7, 8.

Murray, F. V., and M. H. Goldsmith. 1963. Some observations on the egg-capsules and embryos of *Torvamurex territus* (Reeve, 1845). J. Malac. Soc. Aust. 7: 21–25, pls. 1–3.

Nakamigawa, K., and T. Habe. 1964. Descriptions of two new muricid species dedicated to Dr. Kuroda's 77th birthday. Venus 23(1): 25–29, pl. 1.

Nicklés, M. 1950. Mollusques testaces marins de la côte occidentale d'Afrique. Manuels Ouest-Africains. Vol. ii de l'Institut Français d'Afrique Noire, Lechevalier, Paris, 269 pp.

Nicolay, K. 1972. A new *Murex* from the coast of Senegal. La Conchiglia 4(9–10): 43–44.

Nowell-Usticke, G. W. 1968. A supplementary listing of new shells (illustrated), St. Croix, U.S.A., 31 pp.

Odhner, N. H. 1922. Contributions to the Marine molluscan fauna of South and West Africa. Medd. fran Göteborgs Musei Zoologiska Avdelning 26: 1–39, pl. 3.

Oldroyd, I. S. 1927. The marine shells of the west coast of North America. Stanford Univ. Publ., Univ. series, Geol. Sci., vol. 2, Gastropoda, Scaphopoda, and Amphineura, pt. 2, pp. 1–304, pls. 20–72.

Oliver, W. R. B. 1915. The Mollusca of the Kermadec Islands. Trans. Proc. N.Z. Inst. 47: 509–68.

Olsson, A. A., A. Harbison, et al. 1953. Pliocene Mollusca of southern Florida. Acad. Nat. Sci. Phila. Monogr. 8: 1–457.

Olsson, A. A., and T. McGinty. 1958. Recent marine mollusks from the Caribbean coast of Panamá with the description of some new genera and species. Bull. Amer. Paleo. 39(177): 1–58, pls. 1–5.

Orbigny, A. d'. 1839–45. Voyage dans l'Amérique Méridionale, 1826–33. Bertrand, Paris, vol. 5, pt. 3 (mollusques), 801 pp., pls. 1–85.

Orton, J. H. 1929. Habitats and feeding habits of *Ocinebra erinacea*. Nature, 124: 370–71.

Paine, R. T. 1963. Trophic relationships of eight sympatric predatory gastropods. Ecology 44: 63–73.

——— 1966. Function of labial spines, composition of diet and size of certain marine gastropods. Veliger 9: 17–24.

Pallary, P. 1906. Addition à la faune malacologique du Golfe de Gabes. J. de Conchyl. 54: 77–124.

Pallas, P. S. 1774–80. Spicilegia Zoologica... Berolini, ? pp. (not seen).

Payraudeau, B. C. 1826. Catalogue descriptif et méthodique des Annélides et des Mollusques de l'île de Corse. Paris, pp. 1–218, pls. 1–8.

Pease, W. H. 1861. Descriptions of seventeen new species of marine shells from the Sandwich Islands in the collection of Hugh Cuming. Proc. Zool. Soc. London (1860), 28: 397–400.

——— 1868. Synonymy of marine gasteropodae inhabiting Polynesia. Amer. J. Conch. 4: 103–32.

——— 1869. Remarks on marine gasteropodae, inhabiting the west coast of America; with descriptions of two new species. Amer. J. Conch. 5: 80–84.

Pelseneer, P. 1914. L'influence des courants dans la dispersion des organismes marins. Ann. Soc. Zool. Malacol. Belgique 48: 11–22.

Perrilliat Montoya, C. 1972. Monographia de los moluscos del Mioceno medio de Santa Rosa, Vera Cruz, Mexico. Pt. I (Gasteropodos: Fissurellidae a Olividae). Paleontologia Mexicana, numero 32. Mexico City, pp. 1–130, pls. 2–51.

Perry, G. 1810. Arcana, or the museum of natural history; containing the most recent discovered objects... London (not seen).

——— 1811. Conchology, or the natural history of snails... Miller, London, 4 pp., pls. 1–61.

Petit de la Saussaye, S. 1840. Description de deux espèces de coquilles nouvelles, appartenant aux genres *Rostellaria* et *Murex*. Revue Mag. Zool. 3: 326–27.

——— 1852. Description de coquilles nouvelles. J. de Conchyl. 3: 51–59.

——— 1856. Description de coquilles nouvelles. J. de Conchyl. 5: 87–92, pl. 2.

Petitjean, M. 1960. Sur la structure du test des gastéropodes muricides. Comptes Rendus Acad. Sci. Paris 251: 2,245–47.

Petterd, W. F. 1884. Description of New Tasmanian shells. J. Conch. 4: 135–45.

Philippi, R. A. 1836, 1844. Enumeratio Molluscorum Siciliae cum viventium tum tellure tertiara fossilum... Berolini, Simonis Schroppii et Soc., vol. 1, xiv + 267 pp., 12 pls., 1836; Halis Saxonum, vol. 2, iv + 303 pp., pls. 13–18, 1844.

——— 1842–50. Abbildungen und Beschreibungen neuer oder wenig gekannter Conchylien. Kassel. I: 1–20, 1842; 21–76, 1843; 77–186, 1844; 187–204, 1845. II: 1–64, 1845; 65–152, 1846; 153–231, 1847. III: 1–10, 1847; 11–82, 1848; 83–88, 1849; 89–138, 1850. Pls. 1–144.

——— 1868. Conchylia nove postissimum magellanica. Malak. Blätt. 15: 222–26.

Piéron, H. 1933. Notes éthologiques sur les gastropodes perceurs et leur comportement. Arch. Zool. Exp. et Gen. 2: 75.

Pilsbry, H. A. 1897. New species of mollusks from Uruguay. Proc. Acad. Nat. Sci. Phila. 49: 290–98.

——— 1900. A new species of *Sistrum*. Nautilus 14: 3–4.

——— 1904. New Japanese marine Mollusca: Gastropoda. Proc. Acad. Nat. Sci. Phila. 56: 3–37, pls. 1–6.

——— 1921. Marine mollusks of Hawaii. Proc. Acad. Nat. Sci. Phila. 72: 296–328.

——— 1931. *Typhis lowei* n.sp. Nautilus 45(2): 72.

Pilsbry, H. A., and E. L. Bryan. 1918. Notes on some Hawaiian species of *Drupa* and other shells. Nautilus 21(3): 99–102, pl. 9.

Pilsbry, H. A., and H. N. Lowe. 1932. West Mexican and Central American mollusks collected by H. N. Lowe, 1929–31. Proc. Acad. Nat. Sci. Phila. 84: 33–144.

Poirier, J. 1883. Revision des *Murex* du Muséum. Nouvelles Archives du Muséum d'Histoire Naturelle, ser. 2, 5: 13–128, pls. 4–6.

Poisson, H. 1952. Quelques notes sur la biologie de *Murex tenuispina*. Bull. Acad. Malgache, N.S., 29: 97–98.

Ponder, W. F. 1972. Notes on some Australian genera and species of the family Muricidae (Neogastropoda). Jour. Malac. Soc. Aust. 2(3): 215–48.

Powell, A. W. B. 1951. Antarctic and subantarctic Mollusca: Pelecypoda and Gastropoda. Discovery Reports 26: 47–196, pls. 5–10.

Preston, H. B. 1904. Descriptions of some new species of Cingalese and Indian Ocean marine shells. J. Malac. 11: 76–77, pl. 6.

1910. Descriptions of five new species of marine shells from the Bay of Bengal. Rec. Indian Mus. 5: 117–21.

Purchon, R. D. 1968. The biology of the Mollusca. Pergamon, London, xxv + 560 pp.

Pusch, G. G. 1837. Polens Paläontologie... Stuttgart, 218 pp., pls. 1–16.

Quoy, J. R. C., and J. P. Gaimard. 1832–35. Voyage de découvertes de l'Astrolabe... Paris, Zoologie, Mollusca. II: 1–320, 1832; 321–686, 1833. III: 1–366, 1834; 367–954, 1835. Atlas, pls. 1–107.

Radwin, G. E. 1964. Morphological and ecological differentiation in muricid gastropods of the northeastern Gulf of Mexico. Unpublished master's thesis, Florida State University, 73 pp., pls. 1–14.

———. 1972. A systematic note on *Ocenebra poulsoni* Carpenter, 1865. Veliger 15(1): 35–37.

Radwin, G. E., and J. L. Chamberlin. 1973. Patterns of larval development in stenoglossan gastropods. Trans. San Diego Soc. Nat. Hist. 17(9): 107–17.

Radwin, G. E., and A. D'Attilio. 1970. A new species of *Muricopsis* from West Mexico. Veliger 12(3): 351–56, pl. 52.

———. 1971. Muricacean supraspecific taxonomy based on the shell and radula. Echo, 4: 55–67.

———. 1972. The systematics of some New World muricid species (Mollusca: Gastropoda), with description of two new genera and two new species. Proc. Biol. Soc. Wash. 85(28): 323–52.

Radwin, G. E., and H. W. Wells. 1968. Comparative radular morphology and feeding habits of muricid gastropods from the Gulf of Mexico. Bull. Mar. Sci. 18(1): 72–85.

Raeihle, D. 1966. An observation of captive *Murex cellulosus* Conrad. Amer. Malac. Union Annual Report for 1966, p. 28.

———. 1967. Notes on the feeding habits of captive *Murex brevifrons* and *Voluta musica*. N.Y. Shell Club Notes 134: 5–6.

Rafinesque, C. S. 1815. Analyse de la nature ou tableau du univers et des corps organisés. Barravecchia, Palermo, pp. 5–6, 136–49, 218–23.

Récluz, M. C. 1851. Description de quelques coquilles nouvelles. J. de Conchyl. 2: 194–216.

Reeve, L. A. 1843. On a new species of the genus *Murex*. Proc. Zool. Soc. London (1842) 10: 104.

———. 1844a. Conchologia iconica, or illustrations of the shells of molluscous animals. London, Reeve, vol. 2, *Ranella*, pls. 1–8.

———. 1844b. Descriptions of new species of *Ranella*. Proc. Zool. Soc. London (1843) 12: 136–40.

———. 1845–46. Conchologia iconica, or illustrations of the shells of molluscous animals. London, Reeve, vol. 3, *Murex*, pls. 1–36.

———. 1846a. Conchologia iconica, or illustrations of the shells of molluscous animals. London, Reeve, vol. 3, *Ricinula*, pls. 1–6.

———. 1846b. Conchologia iconica, or illustrations of the shells of molluscous animals. London, Reeve, vol. 3, *Buccinum*, pls. 1–14.

———. 1849. Conchologia iconica, or illustrations of the shells of molluscous animals. London, Reeve, *Murex*, suppl. pl. 1.

———. 1858. Descriptions of seven new shells from the collection of the Hon. Sir David Barclay of Pt. Louis, Mauritius. Proc. Zool. Soc. London (1857) 25: 209–10, pls. 37–38.

Rehder, H. A. 1946. Notes on some groups in the Muricidae of the West Atlantic with description of a new subgenus. Nautilus 59(4): 142–43.

Rehder, H. A., and R. T. Abbott. 1951. Some new and interesting mollusks from the deeper waters of the Gulf of Mexico. Revista de la Soc. Malac. (Carlos de la Torre) 8(2): 53–66, pls. 8–9.

Risbec, J. 1932. Notes sur la ponte et la développement de mollusques gastéropodes de Nouvelle-Calédonie. Bull. Soc. Zool. France 57: 358–74.

Risso, A. 1826. Histoire naturelle des principales productions de l'Europe méridionale et principalement de celles des environs de Nice et des Alpes maritimes. Paris and Strasbourg, vol. 4, 439 pp., pls. 1–12.

Röding, J. F. 1798. Museum Boltenianum... Hamburg, 199 pp.

Say, T. 1822. An account of some of the marine shells of the United States. J. Acad. Nat. Sci. Phila. 2: 221–48.

Scacchi, A. 1836. Catalogus Conchyliorum Regni Neapolitani quae usque adhuc Reperit... Fitiatre-Sebetii, Naples, 18 pp., pl. 1.

Schepman, M. M. 1911. The prosobranchia of the Siboga Expedition. Pt. 4, Rachiglossa. Livr. 58, Leiden. Monog. 49d, 116 pp., pls. 1–7.

Schumacher, H. C. F. 1817. Essais d'un nouveau Système des vers testaces. Schultze, Copenhagen, 287 pp., pls. 1–22.

Schwengel, J. 1943. New marine shells from Florida. Nautilus 56(3): 76–77, pl. 7.

Shikama, T. 1963. Selected shells of the world illustrated in colours (II). Hokuryu-Kan, 212 pp., pls. 1–70.

———. 1964. Description of new species of *Murex* and *Conus* from the Arafura Sea. Venus 23(1): 33–37, pl. 3.

Smith, E. A. 1875. A list of the Gastropoda collected in the Japanese seas by Commander H. S. St. John, R.N. Ann. Mag. Nat. Hist., ser. 4, 15: 414–27; 16: 103–15.

———. 1876. A list of marine shells principally from the Solomon Islands with descriptions of new species. Jour. Linn. Soc. 12: 535–62.

———. 1879. On a collection of Mollusca from Japan. Proc. Zool. Soc. London, 47: 181–218.

———. 1880. Description of twelve new species of shells. Proc. Zool. Soc. London (1880): 478–85.

———. 1884. Report of the zoological collections made in the Indian Ocean during the voyage of H.M.S. *Alert*, 1881–1882. Trustees of the British Museum, 684 pp., pls. 1–54.

———. 1891. Report on the marine molluscan fauna of the island of St. Helena. Proc. Zool. Soc. London (1890) 58: 247–317, pls. 21–24.

———. 1894. Natural history notes from H.M. Indian Marine Survey Steamer *Investigator*... Ser. II, #10, Report upon some Mollusca dredged in the Bay of Bengal and the Arabian Sea. Ann. Mag. Nat. Hist., ser. 6, 14: 157–74, pls. 3–5.

———. 1901. On South African marine shells with description of a new species. J. Conch. 10: 104–16, pl. 1.

1906. On South African marine Mollusca with descriptions of new species. Ann. Natal Govt. Mus. 1: 19–71, pls. 7, 8.

Smith, M. 1938. Further notes upon Tertiary and Recent mollusks from Florida, with descriptions of new species. Nautilus 51(3): 88–89, pl. 6.

1939. An illustrated Catalog of the Recent Species of the Rock Shells. Tropical Laboratory, Lantana, Florida, pp. v–ix + 39 pp., pls. 1–21.

1940a. Two new marine molluscs from Japan. Nautilus 54(2): 43.

1940b. New Recent and fossil mollusks from Florida. Nautilus 54(2): 44–46, pl. 2.

Sowerby, G. B. 1825. A catalogue of the shells contained in the collection of the late Earl of Tankerville ... together with an appendix containing descriptions of many new species. London, 92 pp. + 34 pp. (Appendix), pls. 1–9.

Sowerby, G. B. (second of name). 1834–41. The conchological illustrations, *Murex*. Sowerby, London, pls. 58–67, 1834; pls. 187–99 and catalogue, pp. 1–9, 1841.

1860. Descriptions of new shells in the collection of H. Cuming. Proc. Zool. Soc. London (1859) 27: 428–29, pl. 49.

1874. Descriptions of twelve new species of shells. Proc. Zool. Soc. London (1874) 42: 718–22, pl. 59.

1879. Thesaurus conchyliorum. London, vol. 4, pts. 33–34, 55 pp., pls. 380–402.

Sowerby, G. B. (third of name). 1886. Marine shells of South Africa, collected at Port Elizabeth, with descriptions of some new species. J. Conch. 5(1): 1–13.

1889. Descriptions of fourteen new species of shells from China, Japan and the Andaman Islands ... Proc. Zool. Soc. London (1888) 56: 565–70, pl. 28.

1892. Marine shells of South Africa. Sowerby, London, iv + 89 pp., pls. 1–5.

1894. Descriptions of twelve new species, chiefly from Mauritius. Proc. Malac. Soc. London 1(2): 41–44, pl. 1.

1901. On seven new species of marine Mollusca collected by Dr. H. Becker at "the Kowie," South Africa. Proc. Malac. Soc. London 4: 213–15.

1903. Descriptions of fourteen new species of marine Mollusca from Japan. Ann. Mag. Nat. Hist. 12: 496–501.

1904a. Descriptions of *Dolium magnificum* n.sp. and *Murex multispinosus* n.sp. Proc. Malac. Soc. London 6(1): 7–8.

1904b. Descriptions of six new species of marine Mollusca from the collection of the late Admiral Keppel. Proc. Malac. Soc. London 6: 174–77.

Sowerby, J. 1823. The mineral conchology of Great Britain ... London, vol. 6.

Stearns, R. E. C. 1871. Descriptions of new California shells. Amer. J. Conch. 7: 172–73.

1873. Descriptions of new marine mollusks from the west coast of North America. Proc. Calif. Acad. Sci. 5: 78–82, pl. 1.

Stimpson, W. 1865. On certain genera of zoophagous gasteropods. Amer. J. Conch. 1: 55–64, pls. 8–9.

Suter, H. 1907. Results of dredging in Hauraki (New Zealand); with descriptions of seven new species. Trans. N.Z. Inst. 39: 252–64.

1908. Descriptions of new species of New Zealand marine shells. Proc. Malac. Soc. London 8(3): 178–91.

1909. Scientific results of the New Zealand Govt. trawling expedition, 1907. Mollusca. Records of the Canterbury (N.Z.) Mus. 1(2): 117–30, 1 pl.

Swainson, W. 1820–33. The zoological illustrations ... London, series 1, pls. 1–18, 1820; 19–83, 1821; 84–134, 1822; 135–82, 1823; series 2, pls. 1–30, 1829; 31–45, 1830; 46–85, 1831; 86–96, 1832; 97–136, 1833.

1821. Exotic conchology.... London, 39 pp., pls. 1–48.

1822. A catalogue of the ... shells which formed the collection of Mrs. Bligh, with an appendix containing ... descriptions of many new species. London, 58 pp., pls. 1–2.

1840. A treatise on malacology ... Longman et al., London, 419 pp.

Tapparone-Canefri, C. M. 1875. Viaggio dei ... O. Antinori, O. Beccari ed. A. Issel nel Mar Rosso ... 1870–71. Studio monografico sopra il Muricidi etc. Ann. Mus. Civ. Stor. Nat. Genova 7: 560–640, pl. 1.

Tate, R. 1888. The gastropods of the older Tertiary of Australia. Trans. Roy. Soc. South Australia 10: 91–176.

Tenison-Woods, J. E. 1877. On some new species of Tasmanian marine shells. Proc. Roy. Soc. Tasmania, pp. 132–63.

Thiele, J. 1925. Gastropoda der Deutschen Tiefsee-Expedition. II teil, Wissenschaftenliche Ergebnisse der Deutschen Tiefsee-Expedition aus dem dampfer Valdivia 1898–1899, 17(2): 38–382, pls. 13–46.

Thorson, G. 1950. Reproductive and larval ecology of marine bottom invertebrates. Biological Reviews 25: 1–45.

Tomlin, J. R. LeB. 1947. New South African genus of Muricidae. J. Conch. 22: 271.

Tournouër, R. 1875. Etude sur quelques espèces de *Murex* fossiles du falun de Pont Levoy en Touraine. J. de Conchyl. 23: 144–67, pl. 5.

Tryon, G. W., Jr. 1880. Manual of Conchology. Vol. 2, Muricidae, Purpuridae. Philadelphia, 289 pp., pls. 1–70.

Turton, W. H. 1932. Marine shells of Port Alfred, South Africa. Oxford Univ. Press, 331 pp., pls. 1–70.

Valenciennes, A. 1832. Coquilles univalves marines de l'Amérique équinoxiale. *In* F. H. A. von Humboldt and A. J. A. Bonpland, Voyage aux régions équinoxiales du nouveau continent. Paris, pt. 2, Recueil d'observations de zoologie et d'anatomie comparée 2: 262–339, pls. 53–57.

1846. *In* A. A. Du Petit-Thouars, Voyage autour du monde sur la frégate *La Vénus* pendant 1836–1839. Paris, Atlas de zoologie, Mollusques, pls. 1–24.

Vélain, C. 1877. Passage de Vénus sur le Soleil. Exped. Franc. aux Iles Saint-Paul et Amsterdam. Zoologie. Observations générales sur la faune des deux. Arch. Zool. Exp. 6: 1–144.

Vella, P. 1961. Australasian Typhinae (Gastropoda), with notes on the subfamily. Paleontology 4(3): 362–91, pls. 1–2.

Verco, J. C. 1895. Descriptions of new species of marine Mollusca of S. Australia. Trans. Roy. Soc. S. Aust. 19: 84–94, pls. 1–3.

—— 1909. Notes on South Australian marine Mollusca with descriptions of new species, pt. 10. Proc. Roy. Soc. S. Aust. 33: 270–76.

Verrill, A. E. 1884. Second catalogue of Mollusca recently added to the fauna of the New England coast... Trans. Conn. Acad. Sci. 6: 139–294, pls. 28–32.

Verrill, A. H. 1950. A new subspecies from the West Indies. Min. Conch. Club S. Calif., 101: 7.

—— 1953. A new *Murex* from the West Indies. Min. Conch. Club Calif. 128: 2.

Viader, R. 1938. Descriptions of nine marine shells from Mauritius and its dependencies. Mauritius Inst. Bull. 1(3): 3–8, pls. 1–2.

Vokes, E. H. 1963. Cenozoic Muricidae of the western Atlantic region. Pt. 1, *Murex* sensu stricto. Tulane Stud. Geol. Paleo. 1(3): 95–123.

—— 1964. Supraspecific groups in the subfamilies Muricinae and Tritonaliinae (Gastropoda: Muricidae). Malacologia 2(1): 1–41, pls. 1–3.

—— 1965. Cenozoic Muricidae of the western Atlantic region. Tulane Stud. Geol. Paleo. 3(4): 181–204, pls. 1–3.

—— 1966. A new species of *Pterochelus* (Muricidae) from Santa Barbara, California. Veliger 8(3): 165–66, pl. 25.

—— 1967. Observations on *Murex messorius* and *M. tryoni*, with the description of two new species of *Murex*. Tulane Stud. Geol. Paleo. 5(2): 81–90, pls. 1–4.

—— 1968a. *Chicoreus (Siratus) carioca*, new name for *Murex calcar* Kiener. Tulane Stud. Geol. Paleo. 6(1): 39–40.

—— 1968b. Cenozoic Muricidae of the western Atlantic region. Pt. 4, *Hexaplex* and *Murexiella*. Tulane Stud. Geol. Paleo. 6(3): 85–123.

—— 1969. *Murex tenuivaricosus* Dautzenberg, an older name for *Chicoreus (Siratus) carioca* Vokes (*Murex calcar* Kiener, non Sowerby). Tulane Stud. Geol. Paleo. 7(2): 84.

—— 1970a. The west American species of *Murexiella* (Gastropoda: Muricidae). Veliger 12(3): 325–29, pl. 50.

—— 1970b. Cenozoic Muricidae of the western Atlantic region. Pt. 5, *Pterynotus* and *Poirieria* 8(1): 1–50, pls. 1–7.

—— 1970c. Some comments on Cernohorsky's "Muricidae of Fiji." Veliger 13(2): 182–87.

—— 1971a. The geologic history of the Muricinae and Ocenebrinae. Echo 4: 37–54.

—— 1971b. Catalogue of the genus *Murex* Linné (Mollusca: Gastropoda): Muricinae, Ocenebrinae. Bull. Amer. Paleo. 61(268): 1–141.

—— 1974. A new species and subgenus of Australian *Dermomurex* (Gastropoda: Muricidae). Jour. Malac. Soc. Australia 3(1): 1–5.

Warmke, G. 1964. A new Caribbean muricid mollusk, *Typhis puertoricensis*. Nautilus 78(1): 1–3, pl. 1.

Watson, R. B. 1883. Mollusca of H.M.S. Challenger expedition. J. Linn. Soc. London 16: 494–611.

—— 1897. On the marine Mollusca of Madeira; with descriptions of thirty-five new species, and an index-list of all the known sea-dwelling species of that island. J. Linn. Soc. 26: 233–329.

Webb, W. F. 1942. United States Mollusca. Bookcraft, New York, 220 pp.

Wells, H. W. 1958. Feeding habits of *Murex fulvescens*. Ecology 39: 556–58.

Wolfson, F. H. 1968. Spawning notes. I, *Hexaplex erythrostomus*. Veliger 10(3): 292.

Wood, W. 1828. Supplement to the Index testaceologicus, or a catalogue of shells, British and foreign... London, i–vi + 59 pp., pls. 1–8.

Woodring, W. P. 1925–28. Miocene Mollusks from Bowden, Jamaica. Pt. 2, Gastropoda and discussion of results. Carnegie Inst. Washington, Pub. No. 385, 460 pp., 40 pls.

Woodring, W. 1959. Geology and paleontology of Canal Zone and adjoining parts of Panamá. Descriptions of Tertiary Mollusks (gastropods: Vermetidae to Thaididae). U.S. Geol. Surv. Prof. Pap. 306-B: 1–329, pls. 24–38.

Woolacott, L. 1957. Notes on Australian shells, no. 2. Proc. Roy. Soc. New South Wales (1955–56), pp. 112–17, figs. 1–10.

Wright, B. 1878. *Murex huttoniae*, sp. nov. Ann. Soc. Malac. Belg. 13: 85–86, pl. 9.

Yokoyama, M. 1926. Fossil shells from Sado. Jour. Fac. Sci. Imp. Univ. Tokyo, ser. 2, 1(8): 249–312, pls. 32–37.

Index

Boldface type indicates valid living taxa as proposed here. Species are followed by their generic names in italics. Other names here, in all-italic type, include synonyms, fossils, taxa removed from the Muricidae, etc. Subfamilies and other higher-order taxa are given in small capitals. Numerals in roman type indicate major discussions and color-plate numbers; italic numerals give pages where taxa are also mentioned. The original generic assignments of species since (and in our treatment) assigned elsewhere are not given here, except where they are designated in text as type species. Other synonyms *are* listed here.

abyssicola, *Dermomurex*, 16, 44
acanthodes, Murex, 62
acanthophorus, *Phyllonotus*, 129
acanthopterus, Murex, 95
acanthopterus, *Pterochelus*, 16, 95, 97; pl. 15
Acanthotrophon, 15, 19
aciculata, *Ocinebrina*, 16, 125; pl. 21
aciculatus, Murex, 125
actinophorus, *Actinotrophon*, 17, 176
actinophorus, Trophon (Boreotrophon), 176
Actinotrophon, 17, 176
aculeatus, Murex, 32, 171
acuticostata, *Aspella*, 15, 21; pl. 1
adamsi, Murex, 76
adunca, *Pteropurpura*, 10, 17, 129; pl. 22
aduncospinosus, Murex, 72
adustus, Murex, 35
Afritrophon, 17, 177
aguayoi, Murex, 106
akritos, *Chicoreus*, 16, 228; pl. 4
alabaster, *Siratus*, 16, 103; pl. 17
alabastrum, "Murex," 217
alaskanus, Trophon, 176
alata, Purpura, 98
alatus, *Pterynotus*, 16, 98; pl. 9
alatus, Talityphis, 238
aldridgei, *Attiliosa*, 15, 25; pl. 28
alfredensis, *"Murex,"* 18, 215; pl. 29
alveata, *Favartia*, 17, 144; pl. 24
ambiguus, Fusus, 191
ambiguus, Murex, 77
ambiguus, Muricanthus, 78
ambiguus, *Zeatrophon*, 17, 191; pl. 29
ananas, Murex, 88
anatomica, *Homalocantha*, 16, 52, 56; pl. 8
anatomica var. zamboi, Murex, 55
Anatrophon, 17, 177
anceps, *Aspella*, 15, 21, 25, 220, 228
anceps, Ranella, 21
angasi, *Prototyphis*, 16, 95, 127; pl. 15
angasi, Typhis, 94
angermeyerae, *Maxwellia*, 17, 154; pl. 19
angolensis, *Muricopsis*, 17, 165; pl. 27
angularis, *Muricanthus*, 16, 75, 76; pls. 12, 13
anguliferus, Murex, 108
annandalei, *Naquetia*, 16, 80; pl. 15

anniae, Murex, 16, 61; pls. 7, 11
anniae bellegladensis, Murex, 61
antelmei, Murex, 16, 61
antillarum, Murex, 106
antiquus, Murex, 179
Apixystus, 17, 177
arcana, *Tripterotyphis*, 17, 202; pl. 30
arcuatus, *Siphonochelus*, 17, 198, 199, 200
arcuatus, Typhis, 198
argo, Murex, 43
ariomus, *Pterochelus*, 16, 96
armatus, *Muricopsis*, 17, 165; pl. 27
artemis, *Chicoreus*, 16, 32; pl. 4
articulatus, *Siratus*, 16, 104; pl. 17
asianus, *Chicoreus*, 16, 32; pl. 6
Aspella, 4, 15, 19, 21, 25, 220, 224
asper, Vitularia, 123
asperrimus, Murex, 91
assisi, Trophon, 28
asteriae, Murex, 156
atlantis, Murex, 86
atropurpurea, Ocenebra, 123
Attiliosa, 15, 19, 25
auratus, *Murexsul*, 17, 161; pl. 14
australiensis, Murex, 36
Austrotrophon, 176
avalonensis, Trophon, 176
avenatus, Typhis, 198
axicornis, *Chicoreus*, 16, 33; pl. 4
Axymene, 17, 175, 178
azami, Poirieria, 162

babingtoni, Murex, 138
badius, Murex, 125
baeticus, "Murex," 217
bakeri, *Dermomurex*, 16, 45; pl. 1
balteata, *Favartia*, 17, 145; pl. 24
bandana, "Murex," 217
banffius, Trophon, 176
banksii, *Chicoreus*, 16, 33; pl. 4
barbarensis, Murex, 120
barclayana, *Marchia*, 16, 57, 229; pl. 9
barclayi, *Naquetia*, 16, 80; pl. 15
barvicensis, Trophon, 176
Bathymurex, 86
beauii, *Siratus*, 16, 104; pl. 17
beckii, Murex, 88
Bedeva, 15, 19, 27
Bedevina, 27, 48
bednalli, *Pterynotus*, 16, 98; pl. 9
beebei, Trophon, 176

belcheri, Murex, 176
belcheri, *Typhina*, 17, 206
belcheri, Typhis, 206
bellus, Murex, 64
benedictinus, *Chicoreus*, 16, 34; pl. 23
bengalensis, *Talityphis*, 17, 234, 236
Benthoxystus, 17, 179
bentleyi, Trophon, 176
bequaerti, *Pteropurpura*, 17, 129; pl. 22
beringi, Trophon, 176
beta, Tritonalia, 120
bibbeyi, Marchia, 16, 229
bicolor, Murex, 89
bifasciata, Murex, 88
bipinnata, *Marchia*, 16, 57; pl. 9
birileffi, *Bedeva*, 15, 27; pl. 2
bituberculatus, "Murex," 217
bivaricata, *Typhina*, 17, 206
Bizetiella, 17, 141
blainvillei, Murex, 165
blainvillei, *Muricopsis*, 17, 165; pls. 23, 27
blakeanus, Murex, 16, 62
blosvillei, Bedeva, 15, 27; pl. 2
boivini, Murex, 140
bojadorensis, *Murexiella*, 17, 156; pl. 13
Bolinus, 15, 16, 28, 49
bombayanus, *Muricopsis*, 17, 166; pl. 27
Boreotrophon, 17, 175, 176, 179, 185, 188
bourguignati, Murex, 33
branchi, Murex, 104
brandaris, *Bolinus*, 12, 16, 28; pl. 11
brandaris, Murex, 28
brassica, *Phyllonotus*, 16, 88; pl. 16
brazieri, *Muricopsis*, 17, 166; pl. 24
brevicula, *Favartia*, 17, 145; pls. 23, 24
breviculus, Murex, 144
brevifrons, *Chicoreus*, 7, 16, 34; pl. 4
brevispinus, Murex, 16, 62; pl. 11
briskasi, "Murex," 217
bristolae, *Calotrophon*, 16, 30, 31
brocchii, Murex, 118
brunneus, *Chicoreus*, 10, 13, 16, 35, 38, 43, 44; pl. 4
BUCCINIDAE, 4
bullisi, *Laevityphis*, 17, 195; pl. 30
burnetti, *Ceratostoma*, 16, 111; pl. 18
bushae, Pterynotus, 100

INDEX

buxeus, *Xanthochorus, 17,* 139

cabritii, *Murex, 16,* 63; pl. 10
cailleti, *Siratus, 16,* 105; pl. 17
cailleti var. *kugleri, Murex,* 105
cala, *Urosalpinx, 17,* 136; pl. 21
calcar, *Murex,* 108
calcareus, *Ergalatax,* 48
calcitrapa, Murex, 34
Calcitrapessa, 131
caledonica, Muricidea, 59
californicus, Murex, 120
callidinus, *Murex,* 77
callidinus, *Muricanthus,* 78
Calotrophon, *16, 19, 27, 30, 31, 32*
campbelli, *Talityphis, 17,* 235
candelabrum, Trophon, 176
capensis, Murex, 128
capucina, *Naquetia, 16,* 80; pl. 15
carbonnieri, Acupurpura, 27
carduelis, *Enixotrophon, 17,* 181
carduelis, Trophon, 181
carduus, *Acanthotrophon, 15,* 19; pls. 14, 19
carduus, Murex, 19
caribbaea, Tritonalia, 168
carioca, Chicoreus, 108
carmen, *Bizetiella, 17,* 141; pl. 23
carmen, Tritonalia, 141
carnicolor, Panamurex, 31
carpenteri, Pteronotus, 131
castor, *Aspella, 15,* 219, 225; pl. 28
castus, *"Murex,"* 217
cataphractus, Murex, 167
caudata, *Eupleura, 6, 7, 8, 10, 11, 16,* 115; pl. 19
    var. *etterae,* 115
    var. *sulcidentata,* 117
caudata, Ranella, 115
cellulosa, *Favartia, 7, 8, 17,* 146; pl. 24
centrifuga, *Pteropurpura, 17,* 130; pl. 22
Ceratostoma, *16,* 111
cerrosensis, Trophon, 176
cervicornis, *Murex, 16,* 63; pl. 11
cheesemani, *Paratrophon, 17,* 184
cheesemani, Polytropa, 184
Chicomurex, 87
Chicoreus, *15, 16, 32, 50, 75, 76, 79*
Choreotyphis, 206
chrysostoma, *Murex, 16,* 64; pl. 10
ciboney, *Siratus, 16,* 105; pl. 17
cichoreum, *Hexaplex, 16,* 50; pl. 7
cichoreum, Murex, 50
Cinclidotyphis, *5, 17,* 193
cinerea, *Urosalpinx, 6, 7, 8, 10, 11, 13, 17,* 136; pl. 21
    var. *follyensis,* 136
cinereus, Fusus, 136
circumtexta, *Ocenebra, 16,* 119; pl. 20
cirrosa, *Murexiella, 17,* 156; pl. 25
citrica, *Pascula, 17, 176,* 185
citricus, Trophon (Pascula), 185
clarki, *Typhisala, 18,* 211; pl. 31
clathratus, *Boreotrophon, 17, 176,* 179; pl. 28
clathratus, Murex, 179
clausi, Murex, 79
clavus, Marchia, 16
clavus, Murex, 57, 58
clenchi, *"Murex,"* 217
cleryi, *Typhina, 18,* 207; pl. 32

cnissodus, *Chicoreus, 16,* 35; pl. 5
COLUMBARIIDAE, *3*
COLUMBELLIDAE, *144*
columnarius, *Benthoxystus, 17,* 179
columnarius, Trophon, 179
Comptella, *17,* 180
conatus, Murexsul, 163
confusa, *Favartia, 17,* 146
consuela, *Siratus, 16,* 80, 106; pl. 17
contracta, *Ergalatax, 16,* 48; pls. 2, 19
contractum, Buccinum, 48
convexus, *Lenitrophon, 17,* 182
convexus, Trophon, 182
coppingeri, *Murex, 16,* 64; pl. 11
corallina, *Ocinebrina,* 16
corallinus, Fusus, 125
corallinus, Murex, 125
CORALLIOPHILIDAE, *3*
coreanicus, Murex, 111
cornucervi, *Chicoreus, 16,* 36; pl. 4
cornutus, *Bolinus, 16,* 28, 29; pl. 11
coronarius, Laevityphis, 17
coronarius, Typhis, 195
coronatus, Typhis, 212
coronatus, *Typhisopsis, 18, 211,* 212; pl. 32
corrugatus, Murex, 36
crassilirata, *Daphnella,* 183
crassiliratus, *Minortrophon, 17,* 183
crassus, Murex, 113
craticulata, Hadriania, 16
craticulatus, Murex, 117, 118
craticuloides, *Hadriania, 16,* 118; pl. 29
craticuloides, Tritonalia (Hadriania), 117
crawfordi, Murex, 138
crenifer, Murex, 173
crispatissima, Ocenebra, 120
crispulatus, *Terefundus, 17,* 186
crispulatus, Trophon, 186
crispus, *Fuegotrophon, 17,* 181
crispus, Fusus, 181
crispus, Murex, 55
cristatus, *Muricopsis, 17,* 167; pl. 27
crossei, *Favartia, 17,* 146; pl. 24
cryptica, *Aspella, 15,* 220, 224; pl. 1
cumingii, *Haustellotyphis, 17,* 195; pl. 31
cumingii, Typhis, 194
cunninghamae, *Dermomurex, 16,* 44, 45; pl. 1
curta, *Comptella, 17,* 180
curtus, Trophon, 180
cuspidatus, *Muricopsis, 17,* 167; pl. 27
cuvierensis, Murexsul, 163
cyacantha, Murex, 108
cyclostoma, *Favartia, 17,* 147; pl. 24
cymatus, Trophon, 176
Cytharomorula, 48

dalli, *Nodulotrophon, 17, 176,* 184; pl. 28
dalli, Trophon, 184
Dallimurex, 31, 86
damicornis, *Chicoreus, 16,* 36, 228; pl. 4
dearmatus, *"Murex,"* 217
decussatus, *Jaton, 16,* 118; pl. 22
decussatus, "Murex," 118
densus, Murex, 76
dentifer, *"Murex,"* 217

denudatus, *Chicoreus, 16,* 36, 228, 229; pl. 4
Dermomurex, *4, 16, 19, 21,* 44
deroyana, Pteropurpura, 130
despectus, Murex, 35
didyma, *Trachypollia, 17,* 134; pl. 3
digitatus, Murex, 54
dilectus, Murex, 37
diomedaea, *Murexiella, 17,* 157; pl. 25
dipsacus, Murex, 158
Distichotyphis, *17,* 194
distinctus, Murex, 47
donmoorei, *Murex, 16,* 65; pl. 10
DRUPINAE, *134*
dubius, Murex, 171
ducalis, Murex, 88
duffusi, *Pterochelus, 16,* 96, 97; pl. 15
dunkeri, Murex, 138
duplex, *Phyllonotus, 16,* 88; pl. 16
duthiersi, *"Murex,"* 217

echinus, *Boreotrophon,* 82
echinus, *Nipponotrophon, 16,* 82; pl. 3
ednae, Murex, 163
edwardsi, *Ocinebrina, 16,* 125; pl. 21
elegans, *Aspella,* 144
elegans, Lataxiena, 56
elegans, Murex, 107
elegantulus, *Nipponotrophon, 16,* 83
elenensis, *Murex, 16,* 66; pls. 11, 13
elizabethae, *Dermomurex, 16,* 45; pl. 1
elongata, *Marchia, 13, 16, 57, 60, 128;* pl. 9
elongatus, Murex, 32, 57
emarginatus, Murex, 112
emersoni, *Favartia, 17,* 147; pl. 24
emipowlusi, *Ocinebrina, 16,* 126; pl. 21
Enatimene, *17,* 180
endermonis, Murex, 113
endivia, Murex, 50
Enixotrophon, *17,* 181
eos, Murex, 95
epiphanea, Tritonalia, 120
Ergalatax, *16, 19,* 48
ERGALATAXINAE, *48*
erinaceoides, *Ocenebra, 16, 120, 124, 125;* pl. 18
erinaceoides var. *indentata, Murex,* 46
erinaceus, Murex, 119
erinaceus, *Ocenebra, 7, 8, 10, 16,* 119; pl. 18
erosa, *Favartia, 17, 21,* 148; pl. 24
erythraeus, Murex, 108
erythrostigma, *Trubatsa, 17,* 204; pl. 31
erythrostomus, *Phyllonotus, 7, 10, 16,* 89; pl. 16
espinosus, Murex, 75
esycha, *Pteropurpura, 17,* 130; pl. 22
etterae, Eupleura, 115
eucymatus, Trophon, 176
Eupleura, *16,* 115
eurypteron, Murex, 129
euschema, Trophon, 188
euschema, *Xenotrophon, 17, 188,* 189; pl. 29
Evokesia, *15, 17,* 143
exiguus, Murex, 149, 151, 162
exiguus, *"Murex,"* 217
expansus, Murex, 129
expansus, *Talityphis, 17,* 201; pl. 31
expansus, Typhis, 201

INDEX

exquisitus, *"Murex,"* 18, 215
extraneus, Torvamurex, 36

falcatiformis, *"Murex,"* 217
falcatus, Murex, 129
fallax, Haustellum, 50
fallax, Murex, 49
fasciatus, Murex, 10, 122
fauroti, Homalocantha, 54
Favartia, 15, 17, 21, 144, 156, 161, 232
fayae, Tripterotyphis, 17, 202; pl. 30
fenestratus, Murex, 59
ferrugineum rubidum, Sistrum, 171
ferruginosa, Evokesia, 17, 143; pl. 3
festiva, Pteropurpura, 17, 130; pl. 22
festivus, "Murex," 118
fimbriata, *Lataxiena*, 16, 56; pl. 19
fimbriatus, Murex, 155
fimbriatus, Pterotyphis, 17, 197; pl. 30
fimbriatus, Trophon, 56
finlayi, Murex, 106
flexirostris, "Murex," 217
floridana, Urosalpinx, 30
florifer, Chicoreus, 8, 16, 37; pl. 6
florifer arenarius, Murex, 37
foliacea, Hexaplex, 50
foliatum, Ceratostoma, 16, 111, 112; pl. 18
fontainei, Murex, 113
formosus, Siratus, 16, 106; pl. 17
Forreria, 176
fortispina, Murex, 7
fournieri, *Ceratostoma*, 10, 16, 111, 112; pl. 18
foveolata, *Ocenebra*, 16, 120; pl. 20
foveolatus, Murex, 151, 152, 232
fraseri, Tritonalia, 122
Fuegotrophon, 17, 181
fulvescens, Muricanthus, 7, 8, 9, 16, 76; pl. 12
funafutiensis, *Favartia*, 17, 148
funiculus, Lowenstamia, 13
fuscofrondosa, Ocenebra, 145
fusconatata, Tritonalia, 120
fusiformis, "Murex," 217
fusinoides, Panamurex, 32

galapaganus, *Nipponotrophon*, 16, 83; pl. 3
gallinago, *Murex*, 16, 66; pl. 7
gambiensis, Murex, 101
gambiensis, *Purpurellus*, 16, 102; pl. 26
garrettii, Favartia, 17, 149; pl. 24
gatunensis, Murex, 31
gatunensis, Panamurex, 32
gemma, Maxwellia, 17, 154; pl. 19
gemma, Murex, 154
Gemixystus, 17, 181
geversianum, Buccinum, 187
geversianus, Trophon, 17, 123, 175, 187; pls. 28, 29
gibbosus, Murex, 118
glyptus, Murex, 159
goniophorus, Murex, 76
gorgon, Nipponotrophon, 16, 83; pl. 3
gracillima, Ocenebra, 16, 121; pl. 20
grandis, Typhis, 211, 213
grandis, Typhisala, 18, 211; pl. 29
gravidus, Murex, 147
grayi, Evokesia, 17, 143; pl. 23
grippi, Ocenebra, 16, 121; pl. 20

gubbi, *Chicoreus*, 16, 38; pl. 6

Hadriania, 16, 117
hamata, *Ocenebra*, 16, 121; pl. 14
haneti, Urosalpinx, 17, 137; pl. 21
Hanetia, 137
hanleyi, Bedeva, 10, 16
hanleyi, Trophon, 27, 28
hastula, Aspella, 21, 24
Haustellotyphis, 17, 194
Haustellum, 15, 16, 49
haustellum, Haustellum, 7, 16, 49; pl. 11
haustellum, Murex, 49
havanensis, Pterynotus, 100
hemitripterus, Murex, 118
hermanni, *"Murex,"* 217
heros, Murex, 74
hexagonus, Murex, 169
Hexaplex, 13, 16, 50, 75
hidalgoi, Murex, 155
hidalgoi, Murexiella, 17, 157; pl. 25
hippocastanum, Murex, 89
hirasei, Murex, 16, 66; pl. 11
hirsutus, Murex, 76
Homalocantha, 4, 15, 16, 19, 52
hoplites, Murex, 88
horridus, Murex, 140
huberti, Muricopsis, 17, 232
humilis, Murexiella, 17, 157; pl. 25
huttoniae, Murex, 35
hybrida, *Ocinebrina*, 16, 126; pl. 21
hystricina, Paziella, 16, 85; pl. 25

imbricatus, Fusus, 56
imbricatus, Murex, 43
immunitus, Torvamurex, 36
imperialis, Murex, 87, 90
imperialis, Phyllonotus, 16
imperialis, Typhina, 18, 207; pl. 32
incarnata, Purpura, 40
incisa, Favartia, 17, 146, 149; pl. 24
incompta, Attiliosa, 15, 26; pl. 3
incompta, Coralliophila, 25
incurvispina, *Poropteron*, 16, 127; pl. 22
indentatus, *Dermomurex*, 16, 46; pl. 1
inermicosta, Ocenebra, 10, 16, 122; pl. 20
inermis, Murex, 109, 167
inermis, Takia, 16
infans, *Muricopsis*, 17, 168; pl. 3
infrons, *Takia*, 16, 109; pl. 1
inglorius, Murex, 125
innotabilis, Urosalpinx, 48
inornatum, Ceratostoma, 8, 16, 111, 113; pl. 18
inornatus, Murex, 76
insularum, Chicoreus, 16, 38; pl. 5
interfossa, *Ocenebra*, 16, 122; pl. 20
  var. *atropurpurea*, 122
interfossa fraseri, Ocenebra, 123
intermedius, Murex, 144
interserratus, "Murex," 217

jacquelinae, Murexiella, 17, 158; pl. 26
jaliscoensis, Muricopsis, 17, 168; pl. 27
jamaicensis, Murex, 146
japonica, Ocenebra, 8
japonicus, Murex, 113
japonicus, Siphonochelus, 17, 198, 199; pl. 32

Jaton, 16, 118
jatonus, Murex, 118
jenksi, "Murex," 217
jickelii, Murex, 89
jousseaumei, Murex, 39

kawamurai, Murex, 33
keenae, Murexiella, 157
keenae, Ocenebra, 120
kieneri, Murexsul, 17, 162; pl. 23
kiiensis, Murex, 16, 67; pls. 11, 13
kopua, "Murex," 217
kowieensis, Afritrophon, 17, 177
kowieensis, Trophon, 177
kurodai, Favartia, 17, 149; pl. 14
kurodai, Haustellum, 50
kurodai, Murex, 49
kurranulla, Poirieria, 67
kusterianus, Muricanthus, 16, 76; pl. 12

laciniatum, Buccinum, 186
laciniatus, Murex, 87–88
laciniatus, Phyllonotus, 16, 89, 93; pl. 6
laciniatus, Stramonitrophon, 17, 186
Laevityphis, 17, 195
lamberti, Murex, 55
laminatus, Gemixystus, 17, 181, 182; pl. 29
laminatus, Trophon, 181
lapillus, Purpura, 185
lappa, Murexiella, 17, 158; pl. 26
laqueata, Marchia, 16, 58; pl. 9
lasius, Nipponotrophon, 16, 84; pl. 13
Lataxiena, 16, 19, 56
lataxiena, Lataxiena, 16, 56
latipennis, Talityphis, 17, 201, 235, 236, 238; pl. 30
laurae, Murexiella, 157
leeana, Pteropurpura, 17, 131; pl. 22
Lenitrophon, 17, 175, 182
lepidus, Murex, 161
leucas, Pterynotus, 16, 99
leucoderma, Murex, 47
leucostephes, Hertleinella, 30
levicula, Murexiella, 17, 159; pl. 26
lienardi, Murex, 57
lingua, Murex, 118
linguavervecina, Murex, 118
liratus, Fusus, 190
liratus, Xymenopsis, 17, 190
Litozamia, 17, 183
LITTORINIDAE, 4
livida, Bedeva, 15, 28; pl. 2
loebbeckei, Pterynotus, 16, 99; pl. 9
longicaudus, Haustellum, 50
longicaudus, Murex, 49
longicornis, Murex, 16, 67; pl. 11
longicornis, Trubatsa, 17, 205; pl. 31
longicornis, Typhis (Trubatsa), 204
longmani, Transtrafer, 173
lowei, Tripterotyphis, 17, 203; pl. 30
lowei, Typhis, 202
luculentus, Murex, 56
lugubre, Ceratostoma, 16, 113; pl. 23
lugubris, Murex, 114
lugubris, Trachypollia, 17, 134; pl .3
lumaria, Ocenebra, 113
lurida, Ocenebra, 16, 123; pl. 20
lurida var. *munda, Ocenebra, 123*
lychnia, Panamurex, 32
lyratus, Murex, 76

macgillivrayi, Murex, 62
macgintyi, *Murexiella,* 17, 159; pl. 25
macleani, *Purpurellus,* 16, 102; pl. 26
macra, *Urosalpinx,* 17, 137
macroptera, *Pteropurpura,* 17, 131; pls. 22, 23
macropterus, Murex, 129
maculatus, *"Murex,"* 217
magellanicus, Murex, 187
malabaricus, Murex, 72
Marchia, 16, 57, 98
margaritensis, Murex, 87
margaritensis, *Phyllonotus,* 16, 90; pl. 16
margaritensis, Tritonalia, 152, 232
mariae, *Murexsul,* 17, 162; pl. 7
marjoriae, *Favartia,* 17, 150
martinetana, *Marchia,* 16, 59; pl. 9
martinianus, Murex, 72
martyria, Typhis, 212
mauritiana, *Aspella,* 15, 221; pl. 28
maurus, *Chicoreus,* 16, 39; pl. 5
mauryae, Panamurex, 31, 32
Maxwellia, 17, 154
medicago, *"Murex,"* 217
megacerus, *Muricanthus,* 10, 16, 75, 77, 79; pl. 12
melanamathos, *Homalocantha,* 16, 53; pl. 8
melonulus, Murex, 88
messorius, *Murex,* 16, 68; pl. 11
    var. *rubidum,* 71
mexicanus, Murex, 91
micaela, *Bizetiella,* 17, 142; pl. 23
michaeli, Ocinebra, 138
microphyllus, *Chicoreus,* 10, 16, 39; pls. 4, 5
miliaris, Murex, 173
miliaris, *Vitularia,* 17, 173; pl. 7
minatauros, *Favartia,* 17, 150; pl. 24
mindanaoensis, *Murex,* 16, 68, 231; pl. 10
minirosea, *Favartia,* 17, 151; pl. 29
minor, Ocenebra, 123
Minortrophon, 17, 183
mitraeformis, Murex, 127, 128
mitriformis, Murex, 127, 128
modesta, *Pteropurpura,* 17, 132; pl. 22
monachus, Murex, 114
monoceros, Murex, 113, 114
monodon, Murex, 36
monoptera, Ocinebra, 113
Monstrotyphis, 17, 196
montforti, *Typhina,* 18, 207; pl. 32
moquinianus, Murex, 77
morchi, *Aspella,* 15, 223; pl. 1
Morula, 134
motacilla, Murex, 104
motacilla, *Siratus,* 16, 106; pl. 17
multicostatus, Trophon, 176
multicrispatus, Murex, 55
multiplicatus, *Murex,* 16, 68; pl. 11
multispinosus, *Murexsul,* 17, 162; pl. 25
munda, *Favartia,* 17, 151; pl. 24
Murex, 2, 4, 12, 15, 16, 19, 60, 103, 230
"Murex," 2, 11, 18, 217
Murexiella, 13, 15, 17, 155, *161*
Murexsul, 13, 17, 161
Muricanthus, 16, 75
muricatus, Murex, 188

muricatus, Trophonopsis, 17, *176,* 188
muriciformis, *Eupleura,* 16, 115; pl. 19
MURICINAE, 2, 3, 4, 5, 13, 15, 19, *141, 175, 193*
muricoides, *Muricopsis,* 17, 168; pl. 2
MURICOPSINAE, 3, 5, 13, 15, 17, 21, 141
Muricopsis, 17, 165
muticus, Typhis, 195
myrae, *Cinclidotyphis,* 17, 193; pl. 30
myrakeenae, *Dermomurex,* 16, 44, 45, 46; pl. 1

Naquetia, 15, 16, 79
natalensis, *"Murex,"* 217
Neptunea, 179
nicocheanus, *Muricopsis,* 17, 169; pl. 23
nigrescens, Murex, 70
nigrispinosus, Murex, 72
nigritus, Murex, 77
nigritus, Muricanthus, 78
nipponensis, *Siphonochelus,* 17, 199; pl. 32
Nipponotrophon, 16, 19, 82
nitens, *"Murex,"* 217
nitens, *Typhina,* 18, 208; pl. 29
nitida, *Eupleura,* 16, 116; pl. 19
nitidus, Murex, 77
nitidus, Muricanthus, 78
niveus, *"Murex,"* 217
nodatus, Murex, 104
nodulifera, *Marchia,* 16, 59; pl. 27
nodulosa, *Trachypollia,* 17, 135; pl. 3
Nodulotrophon, 17, 184
norfolkensis, *Tripterotyphis,* 17, 203; pl. 28
norrisii, Murex, 157
nuceus, Murex, 146
nucleus, *"Murex,"* 217
nucula, Murex, 147
nuttalli, *Ceratostoma,* 16, 111, 114; pl. 18
nuttalli, Murex, 111
nuttingi, Murex, 31, 86

obeliscus, *Dermomurex,* 16, 46; pl. 1
obesus, Talityphis, 238
obtusus, Murex, 150, 157
occa, Murex, 71
occlusus, *Typhinellus,* 18, 210; pl. 32
Ocenebra, 16, 119, 125, 129, 177
OCENEBRINAE, 2, 3, 4, 13, 15, 16, 111, 141, 197
Ocinebrellus, 129
Ocinebrina, 15, 16, 125
octogonus, Murex, 157, 161
octogonus, *Murexsul,* 17, 163; pl. 26
oculatus, Murex, 91
oligocanthus, *"Murex,"* 217
olssoni, *Murex,* 16, 69; pls. 7, 14
oregonia, Murex, 86
orpheus, Trophon, 176
osseus, Murex, 102
ostrearum, *Calotrophon,* 7, 8, 9, 10, 16, 30, *31*; pl. 3
oxyacantha, *Homalocantha,* 16, 52, 53; pl. 8
oxytata, *Muricopsis,* 17, 179; pl. 27

pacificus, Trophon, 176
Pagodula, 17, 184

pagodus, *Nipponotrophon,* 16, 84; pl. 14
painei, *Ocenebra,* 16, 123; pl. 20
paivae, *Bedeva,* 10, 16, 28; pls. 2, 14
paivae, Trophon, 27
pallidus, *"Murex,"* 217
palmarosae, *Chicoreus,* 11, 16, 40; pl. 5
palmiferus, Chicoreus, 229
palmiferus, Murex, 36
Panamurex, 31, 32
Paratrophon, 17, 184
Pascula, 17, 185
patagiatus, *Pterynotus,* 16, 100; pl. 9
paucicostatus, Trophon, 176
pauperculus, *Dermomurex,* 16, 44, 45, 46, 47; pl. 1
pauperis, *Typhina,* 18, 200, 208
pauxillus, *Muricopsis,* 17, 169, 234; pl. 27
pavlova, *Trubatsa,* 17, 205; pl. 31
pazi, Murex, 31, 85
pazi, *Paziella,* 16, 86; pl. 26
Paziella, 13, 16, 19, 27, 31, 32, 85
Pazinotus, 16, 19, 86
peasei, *Favartia,* 17, 151, 231, 232; pl. 29
pecten, *Murex,* 11, 16, 60, 69, 71; pl. 10
pecten, Murex, 16
pectinata, *Eupleura,* 16, 116; pl. 19
pele, Murex, 52, 53
pellucida, *Marchia,* 16, 60; pl. 9
penchinati, *Chicoreus,* 16, 40, 228, 229; pl. 6
pentaphasios, *Siphonochelus,* 17, 199
peratus, *Phyllonotus,* 16, 90; pl. 16
peratus decoris, Phyllonotus, 90
perchardei, *Talityphis,* 17, 235, 236; pl. 30
percoides, *"Murex,"* 217
peregrinus, Trophon, 176
perelegans, *Siratus,* 16, 107; pl. 17
perita, *Murexiella,* 17, 159; pl. 26
permaestus, Murex, 80
perplexa, Aspella, 46
perrugata, *Urosalpinx,* 7, 8, 9, 10, 17, 137; pl. 21
peruvianus, Murex, 163
petri, Murex, 131
petri, Murex (Pteropurpura), 124
pettardi, *"Murex,"* 217
phaneus, *Pterynotus,* 16, 100; pl. 9
phantom, Murexiella, 17, 160
philippensis, *Typhina,* 18, 209; pl. 32
philippiana, *Attiliosa,* 15, 26; pl. 3
phillipsi, *Pterochelus,* 16, 97
Phyllonotus, 16, 79, 87
phyllopterus, Murex, 133
phyllopterus, *Pterynotus,* 16, 100; pl. 7
pinnatus, Murex, 98
pinnatus, *Pterotyphis,* 17, 197; pl. 30
pinnatus, Pterynotus, 16
pinnatus, Typhis, 197
pinniger, *Purpurellus,* 16, 102; pl. 26
planilirata, *Favartia,* 17, 152; pl. 14
platylaevis, *Aspella,* 15, 224; pl. 28
plebeius, Fusus, 189
plebeius, *Xymene,* 17, 189; pl. 29
pleurotomoides, *"Murex,"* 18, 215, 216; pl. 25
plicata, Ranella, 117

plicatus, Murex, 66
pliciferoides, *Siratus, 16*, 107; pl. 17
plorator, Pteropurpura, 17, 132; pl. 22
poirieri, Murex, 39
Poirieria, *13, 16, 19*, 93
pollux, *Aspella, 15, 25, 219, 220, 225*; pl. 1
pomiformis, Murex, 91
pomum, *Phyllonotus, 7, 8, 9, 10, 16*, 91; pl. 16
ponderi, *Aspella, 15, 222, 227*; pl. 28
ponderosus, Murex, 108
poormani, *Favartia, 17, 152*, 231; pl. 24
Poropteron, *16*, 58, 95, 126, *128*
poulsoni, Ocinebra, 133
poulsoni, Roperia, 17, 133; pl. 19
praepauxillus, Muricopsis, 233
princeps, *Muricanthus, 16*, 77; pl. 12
producta, *Aspella, 15, 22, 224, 225*; pl. 1
propinquus, Murex (Siratus), 107
Prototyphis, *16*, 94, *127*
Pterochelus, *16*, 95, 98, 203
Pteropurpura, *17, 118*, 129
Pterorytis, 118, 122
Pterotyphis, 5, *17, 193*, 197
Pterynotus, 4, *13, 16, 19*, 57, 95, 98, *129*
pudicus, "Murex," 217
puertoricensis, Typhis (Talityphis), 201
pulcher, Murex, 106
  var. *consuela*, 106
pumilus, Murex, 153
puncturata, *Urosalpinx, 17*, 137; pl. 21
puniceus, "Murex," 217
purdyae, Murex, 16, 229
purpuratus, Murex, 34
Purpurellus, 4, *16, 19*, 101
purpuroides, *Urosalpinx, 17*, 138; pl. 21
pusilla, *Xymenella, 17*, 189
pusillus, Trophon, 189
puteola, "Murex," 217
pygmaeus, Murex, 100
pyramidalis, *Aspella, 15, 21, 23, 221, 224, 227*; pl. 1
pyrrhias, "Murex," 217

quadratus, Typhis, 212
quadrifrons, Murex, 10
quinquelobatus, Murex, 128

radicatus, Murex, 158
radix, Murex, 75
radix, Muricanthus, 7, 16, 77; pl. 12
radwini, *Murexiella, 17*, 160; pl. 25
ramosa, Typhina, 18, 209; pl. 32
ramosus, Chicoreus, 7, 15, 16, 40; pl. 4
ramosus, Murex, 32
Rapanidae, 3
rarispina, Murex, 72
recticornis, Murex, 67
rectirostris, *Murex, 16*, 70; pls. 11, 13
recurrens, *Ergalatax, 16*, 48
recurvirostris, *Murex, 16*, 70; pl. 11
  var. *lividus*, 66
recurvirostris rubidus, Murex, 71
recurvirostris sallasi, Murex, 61
reevei, Chicoreus, 105
regius, *Phyllonotus, 16*, 92; pl. 16
requieni, Murex, 125
rhyssus, Murex (Alipurpura), 124

Risomurex, 165
robustus, *Tripterotyphis, 17*, 204; pl. 29
roperi, Fusus, 133
Roperia, *15, 17*, 133
rorifluum, *Ceratostoma, 16, 111*, 114; pl. 18
rosaria, Triplex, 40
rosarium, Purpura, 88, 89
rosea, *Favartia, 17*, 152; pl. 24
roseotinctus, Murex, 82
roseus, *Muricopsis, 17*, 170; pl. 2
rossiteri, *Chicoreus, 16*, 41; pl. 4
rota, Murex, 52
rubescens, *Chicoreus, 16*, 41; pl. 6
rubidus, *Murex, 16*, 71; pl. 11
rubiginosus, *Chicoreus, 16*, 42; pl. 6
rubridentatus, Murex, 100
rudolphi, *Litozamia, 17*, 183
rudolphi, Peristernia, 183
rufonotata, *Evokesia, 17*, 144; pl. 3
rufonotatum, Sistrum, 143
rufus, Murex, 37
rushi, Urosalpinx, 137
rusticus, "Murex," 217

saharicus, *Muricanthus, 16*, 75, 78; pl. 7
salebrosa, *Vitularia, 17*, 173; pl. 7
salleanus, Murex, 37
salmonea, *Favartia, 17*, 153; pl. 24
saltatrix, Chicoreus, 41
sanctaehelenae, Poropteron, 16, 128
sandwichensis, Murex, 173
santarosana, *Maxwellia, 17*, 155; pl. 19
sarmentosus, *Anatrophon, 17*, 177; pl. 29
sarmentosus, Trophon, 177
saulii, *Chicoreus, 16*, 42; pl. 5
saxatilis, Murex, 89
saxicola, Murex, 50
scabrosus, Murex, 89
scalariformis, Murex, 47
scalarinus, Dermomurex, 16
scalarinus, Murex, 21, 44, 47
scalaroides, *Dermomurex, 16*, 44, 47; pl. 1
scalaroides, Murex, 21, 44
schrammi, *Muricopsis, 17*, 171; pl. 2
scitulus, *Nipponotrophon, 16*, 85; pl. 14
sclera, Trachypollia, 17, 134
sclera, Tritonalia, 123
scolopax, *Murex, 16*, 71; pl. 10
scorpio, *Homalocantha, 16*, 54, *196*; pl. 8
scorpio, Murex, 52
scrobiculata, *Urosalpinx, 17*, 138; pl. 21
secunda, *Homalocantha, 16*, 55; pl. 8
seftoni, *Ocenebra, 16*, 124; pl. 20
semiclausus, Murex, 125
senegalensis, Murex, 79, 103
senegalensis, *Siratus, 16*, 107, 108; pl. 17
senex, *Aspella, 15, 25, 219, 220*; pl. 1
sentus, Acanthotrophon, 19
serratospinosus, *Murex, 16*, 72, 231; pl. 10
shaskyi, *Bizetiella, 17*, 142; pl. 23
Shaskyus, 118, 131
similis, Murex, 105
simplex, Enatimene, 17, 180

simplex, Trophon, 180
sinensis, Murex, 32
singaporensis, *"Murex,"* 217
Siphonochelus, 5, *17, 193, 195*, 198, *199*, 204
"sirat, Purpura," 103
Siratus, *16*, 79, 103
smithi, *Pazinotus, 16*, 86
smithi, Trophon, 176
smithi, Urosalpinx, 48
sobrinus, Murex, 70
solidus, "Murex," 217
solus, Siphonochelus, 17, 199, 209
sorenseni, Acanthotrophon, 15, 20
sorenseni, Trophon (Acanthotrophon), 19
sowerbii, *Typhinellus, 18*, 210; pl. 31
sowerbii, Typhis, 210
sowerbiyi, Typhis, 210
sowerbyi, Murex, 157
speciosus, Murex, 129
spectrum, *Chicoreus, 16*, 43; pl. 5
spinicosta, Murex, 76
spinosus, Murex, 76
springeri, Murex, 107, 108
squamulata, Muricidea, 165
squamulifer, Trophon, 120
stainforthi, *Hexaplex, 16*, 51; pl. 7
stearnsii, Murex (Phyllonotus), 53
steeriae, Murex, 39
stimpsonii, Eupleura, 86
stimpsonii, *Pazinotus, 16*, 87; pl. 23
stimuleus, Apixystus, 17, 178
stimuleus, Trophon, 177
Stramonitrophon, *17*, 186
strigatus, "Murex," 217
stuarti, Trophon, 176
subangulata, *Urosalpinx, 17*, 138; pl. 21
Subpterynotus, *17*, 172
sulcidentata, *Eupleura, 16*, 117; pl. 19
superbus, Murex, 87
superbus, *Phyllonotus, 16*, 92; pl. 6
swansoni, Pterynotus, 130
sykesi, "Murex," 217
syringianus, *Siphonochelus, 17, 199*, 200; pl. 32

taeniatus, Murex, 161
Takia, *16*, 109
talienwhanensis, Murex, 113
Talityphis, *17, 201*, 236
tampaensis, *Urosalpinx, 7, 8, 9, 17*, 139; pl. 21
tarentinus, Murex, 119
tatei, *Subpterynotus, 17*, 172; pl. 29
tenuispina, Murex, 69
tenuivaricosus, *Siratus, 16*, 108; pl. 17
teramachii, Typhis (Typhina), 207
Terefundus, *17*, 186
ternispina, Murex, 72
territus, *Chicoreus, 10, 16*, 43, *228*; pl. 6
tetragona, *Favartia, 17*, 153; pl. 14
textilis, Murex, 172
textilis, Subpterynotus, 17
Thaididae, 3, *13*
thomasi, Murex, 39
tokubeii, *Murexsul, 17*, 163; pl. 25
tokugawai, *Ergalatax, 16*, 48; pl. 14
torosus, Murex, 119
torrefactus, Chicoreus, 10

torrefactus, Murex, 39
    var. *insularum,* 38
tortua, *Homalocantha, 16,* 55; pl. 8
tortuus, Murex, 55
tosaensis, *Monstrotyphis, 17,* 196; pl. 31
tosaensis, Typhis (Typhinellus), 196
Trachypollia, *15, 17,* 134, *143*
transcurrens, *Laevityphis, 17,* 196
trapa, *Murex, 16,* 72; pl. 10
trialata, *Pteropurpura, 17,* 132; pl. 22
Trialatella, 45
triangularis, *Tripterotyphis, 17,* 204; pl. 30
triangulatus, Trophon, 176
tribulus, *Murex, 7, 16, 60,* 72; pl. 10
tricoronis, Murex, 66
triformis, *Pterochelus, 16,* 97; pl. 15
trigonula, *Naquetia, 16,* 81; pl. 15
trilineatus, Murex, 105
triptera, *Marchia, 16,* 60; pl. 9
Tripterotyphis, *5, 17, 193,* 202
triqueter, Murex, 79
    var. *amanuensis,* 81
triquetra, *Eupleura, 16, 116,* 117; pl. 19
triquetra, *Naquetia, 16, 81,* 82; pl. 15
triremis, Aranea, 69
tristichus, Murex, 100
tristichus, Pterynotus, 100
trivialis, *Chicoreus, 16,* 43; pl. 6
Tromina, *17,* 187
Trophon, *13, 17, 175,* 187
Trophoninae, *2, 3, 5, 13, 15, 17,* 175
Trophonopsis, *17,* 188
troscheli, *Murex, 16,* 74; pl. 10
Trubatsa, *17, 193,* 204, *206*

truncatus, Trophon, 176
Trunculariopsis, 93
trunculus, *Phyllonotus, 12, 16,* 93; pls. 5, 7
tryoni, *Murex, 16, 62,* 74; pl. 7
tuberculata, Vitularia, 173
tubuliger, *Laevityphis, 17,* 196
tulensis, *Muricopsis, 17,* 233
tumida, *"Murex,"* 217
turbator, *Axymene, 17,* 178
turbator, Trophon, 178
turbinatus, Murex, 93
turrita, Tritonalia, 30
turritus, *Calotrophon, 16,* 30; pl. 3
tweedianus, *Murex, 16,* 75; pl. 10
Typhina, *17,* 206
Typhinae, *3, 5, 13, 15, 17,* 193
Typhinellus, *18,* 210
Typhis, 95
Typhisala, *18,* 211
Typhisopsis, *5, 18, 193, 211,* 212

umbilicatus, *Murexsul, 17,* 164; pl. 2
uncinarius, Murex, 58, 126
uncinarius, *Poropteron, 16, 127,* 128; pl. 22
unicarinata, *Tromina, 17,* 187
unicarinatus, Fusus, 187
Urosalpinx, *17,* 136
uva, Purpura, 134

vaginata, *Pagodula, 17, 176,* 184; pl. 28
vaginatus, Murex, 184
varicosus, Murex, 54
varius, *Muricanthus, 16, 75, 79,* 108; pl. 12

velero, *Calotrophon, 16,* 31; pl. 23
vemae, *Distichotyphis, 17,* 194; pl. 31
vespertilio, *Pterynotus, 16, 100,* 101; pl. 9
virgineus, *Siratus, 15, 16,* 108; pl. 17
vittata, *Murexiella, 17,* 161; pl. 26
Vitularia, *17,* 173
vitulinus, Murex, 173
vokesae, *Ocenebra, 16,* 124; pl. 18

wilsoni, *Haustellum, 16,* 50; pl. 23
woodringi, Murex, 68

Xanthochorus, *17,* 139
xanthostoma, Purpura, 139
xanthostoma, *Xanthochorus, 17, 139,* 140; pl. 7
Xenotrophon, *17,* 188
Xymene, *17, 175,* 189
Xymenella, *17, 175,* 189
Xymenopsis, *17,* 190

yatesi, *Typhina, 18,* 209; pl. 31
yoldii, Murex, 93

Zacatrophon, 176
zamboi, *Homalocantha, 16,* 55; pl. 8
zealandica, Typhis, 95
zealandicus iredalei, Pterynotus (Pterochelus), 95
Zeatrophon, *17, 175,* 191
zelandica, *Poirieria, 16,* 94; pl. 26
zelandicus, Murex, 93
zeteki, *Muricopsis, 6, 17,* 171; pl. 27
zonatus, Murex, 95
zonatus, *Murexsul, 17,* 164; pl. 28